MODERN IRISH COMPANY LAW

MODERN IRISH COMPANY LAW

Henry Ellis LLM, PhD, PGC Ed, FCII
Professor of Corporate, Commercial and Economic Law
University of Limerick

JORDANS

2001

Published by
Jordan Publishing Limited
21 St Thomas Street
Bristol BS1 6JS

British Library Cataloguing-in-Publication Data
A catalogue record for this book is available from the British Library.

ISBN 0 85308 705 9

Typeset by Mendip Communications Ltd, Frome, Somerset
Printed by MPG Books Ltd, Bodmin, Cornwall

PREFACE

The Irish legal system is based on the common law. As a result, much of the substantive law is generated by judicial decisions and the doctrine of precedent. Examples of traditional common law would include contract and the law of torts.

Even statutory-based laws, such as those contained in the Sale of Goods Act 1893, whilst set out in codified form, are essentially 'old' case-law in new format. But company law is different.

THE COMPANY LAW CODE

Both UK and Irish company law originated in codes with particular legislative economic aims and objectives. These laws are examples of political, rather than judge-made law. Company law therefore, as a type, seems to have more in common with European civil-based (Roman law) codes, than with traditional common-law branches such as contract law. However, the company law code, whilst based on statute, is quite different to a civil law code such as the Treaty of Rome. The reason, as we shall see, is that company law itself is essentially a law of corporate contracts.

The company law code currently in force is contained in the Companies Act 1963–2001. Because of the underlying economic nature of this code, it is appropriate, first, to examine the public policy underlying it.

Policy underlying the company law code

The Joint Stock Companies Act of 1844 laid the foundations of English and Irish company law. The policy underlying this piece of legislation was the desire of government to encourage enterprise by facilitating the incorporation of companies.

The Act of 1844, and its successors, have achieved their objectives in stimulating trade and business. For example, in the foreword to the Companies Report 1997,[1] the Minister for Science, Technology and Commerce, Mr Noel Treacy, TD, wrote:

---

1 Department of Enterprise, Trade and Employment, Dublin (Stationery Office, 1998).

'A comprehensive and effective company law code is fundamental to the commercial life of a State ...

Over the last 60 years, there has been a veritable explosion in the use of limited liability companies. In 1937, there were 2,731 companies on the Register and last year this had increased to just under 165,000 companies. This increase reflects the changing face of our commercial environment.'

Even a brief examination of the combined Companies Acts will reveal a bewildering mass of detailed rules. To make sense of this bulk, and to unravel the intricacies of company law, one must, in the writer's opinion, break down the company law code into its constituent legal parts.

CONSTITUENT PARTS OF COMPANY LAW

The constituent parts of the company law code may be categorised into the following main elements:

(1) legislative aims;
(2) conceptual aspects;
(3) contractual elements;
(4) tortious aspects; and
(5) compliance and enforcement matters.

Let us briefly consider these distinctive constituent parts.

Legislative aims

While the economic objective of the company law code is to encourage enterprise, there are two fundamental legal aims underlying company law. These are the protection of investors in, and creditors of, companies.

Investor protection

The Companies Acts grant shareholders the privilege of limited liability and additional contractual rights and remedies. For example, s 205 of the 1963 Act offers an alternative remedy to members in cases of oppression by the majority.

Creditor protection

Creditors enjoy many protections in company law, but perhaps the most important are the facility to register charges securing company loans and creditors' legal rights to avail of receivership and winding up procedures where a company defaults on its contractual obligations to them.

To give a company a modicum of protection against the use by creditors of their potent remedies, the concept of *examinership* was introduced in 1990 – see below.

Chapter 2 elaborates on these two fundamental legal aims of company law.

Conceptual aspects

The core concepts underlying company law include:

(1) incorporation;
(2) separate legal personality;
(3) limited liability;
(4) the 'veil of incorporation'; and
(5) corporate governance.

We shall now consider these concepts individually.

Incorporation

The idea involved in incorporation is one of merging individuals together to form a whole. In the context of company law, this idea means permitting an association of persons to incorporate their activities by registering a company. As s 18(2) of the 1963 Act provides 'from the date of incorporation ... the subscribers to the memorandum ... shall be a body corporate with the [company] name'.

The law recognises such a company as a distinct legal person in its own right. The company, for example, can sue and be sued in its own name.

Separate legal personality

Once registered, a company is legally entirely separate from its shareholders. This idea of separate legal personality is developed further in the Introduction and explained in Chapter 3.

Because a company has no mind of its own, problems arose in criminal law in relation to corporate crimes and 'mens rea'. Chapter 5 illustrates how the judiciary have ascribed criminal liability to companies.

The main consequence of separate corporate personality is the divergence of company ownership and management. A company is owned by its shareholders, but managed by directors on their behalf. This aspect of incorporation is also dealt with in Chapter 3. Other consequences of incorporation are detailed in Chapter 4.

Limited liability

The privilege of limited liability means that a shareholder can lose only the amount of his investment in a company, if it fails. This concept is outlined further in the Introduction and Chapter 1, and analysed in detail in Chapters 2 and 4.

The 'veil of incorporation' metaphor

As the company is a separate legal person distinct from its members, there is said to be a 'veil' drawn between the company and its shareholders. Courts will not usually 'lift' this veil to identify the shareholders/owners of the company.

In exceptional circumstances, a court may look behind the corporate form to see who actually owns a company. This action is known as 'lifting the veil'. The veil may also be lifted by statute.

The 'veil of incorporation' metaphor is developed further in the Introduction and Chapter 1 and explained in Chapter 6.

Corporate governance

Because of the importance of financial markets, and relations between company shareholders and directors, the idea of corporate governance is emerging in the context of listed companies. This idea is defined in Chapter 1. Chapter 54 looks at the extent of corporate governance for Irish listed companies, and the potential for future influence in this sphere by the Company Law Review Group.

Contractual elements

The bulk of company law relates to contractual matters and revolves around three key legal relationships. These core relationships involve the company itself, its shareholders and its creditors, and will be outlined in the law of corporate contracts below.

Pre-incorporation contracts

Even before a company is incorporated under the registration procedure, a number of contractual matters arise. For example, chapter 6 deals with promoters and pre-incorporation contracts.

The actual incorporation of a company normally gives rise to a number of contractual relationships between investors, the company itself, its directors, officers and creditors.

The law of corporate contracts

The main classes of contracts which a registered company enters into are:

(1) contracts for investment capital;
(2) contracts for the sale of goods and/or the supply of services; and
(3) contracts for loan capital.

Companies may also employ executives and staff, and usually enter into contractual arrangements with an auditor.

Company contracts for investment capital

Many private companies are formed with little capital, eg the well known £2 company. Some private companies may indeed have substantial capital funding contributed by a few investors. However, where a company wishes to raise money from the public, the Companies Acts ensure that investors are protected by compelling the company's directors and/or promoters to publish a prospectus or, more usually, Stock Exchange listing particulars.

The law relating to public offers of shares is set out in Chapters 10 and 11, including the effects of the Investment Intermediaries Act 1995 and the Investor Compensation Act 1998.

The extent to which a share price can be supported by stabilisation measures is also noted in Chapter 10.

A contract for the purchase of shares in a company is completed when the investors' offers are accepted by the directors allotting them shares on the company's behalf. The articles of association constitute the express terms of such contracts – a fact not universally appreciated. Because of the importance of contract terms, parts IVA to IVE (Chapters 12 to 24) are devoted to an analysis of the articles of association.

Express contract terms embrace matters which often arise between the company and its investors. These matters are indicated by the following chapter titles:

♦ The nature of investors' legal interests and their statutory contract (Chapter 13).
♦ Appointment of directors and company meetings (Chapter 15).
♦ Majority control and the protection of minority investors (Chapter 16).
♦ Members' remedies for infringements of their rights (Chapter 17).
♦ Capital, shares and class rights (Chapter 18).
♦ The members' section 25 contract (Chapter 20).
♦ Dividends and calls on shares (Chapter 21).
♦ Disclosure and transfers of shareholders' interests (Chapter 22).
♦ Limitations on directors' powers of management (Chapter 24).

An unusual feature of the shareholders' contract is that, in addition to their common-law contractual rights, shareholders also enjoy what this writer has labelled 'top-up' statutory rights – see Chapter 13.

Company contracts with external persons

The purpose of registering a company is usually to enable it to trade, ie to enter into commercial contracts with external persons or outsiders. By outsiders we mean persons other than a company's own shareholders.

Commercial contracts include those for borrowing money (or obtaining loan capital) and the buying and selling of goods and services generally.

Contractual capacity of a company

The distinctions between a company's articles of association and its memorandum of association are outlined in the Introduction and Chapter 1 and explained in Chapter 12.

Any company contract for a purpose outside the objects clause in its memorandum of association, was void at common law. Chapter 36 deals with a company's contractual capacity and statutory reform of the ultra vires doctrine.

Because a company is a non-human legal person, it cannot act on its own behalf. A company can only operate through human agents. Accordingly, Chapter 37 looks at company contracts and the authority in agency law of its various human agents. Chapter 38 focuses on trends in judicial protection for creditors against ultra vires actions by directors.

Company contracts for the sale of goods and/or services

A company, acting through its agents, ie its directors, officers or employees, can enter into contracts with outsiders for the sale or purchase of goods and services.

Any outsider who enters into such a contract with a company, and is unpaid for the goods and services supplied, would be classified as a creditor of the company.

Most providers of goods and services to companies would, if unpaid, tend to be unsecured creditors. However, the suppliers of goods to a company may have a 'retention of title' clause in the contract which would give them some security over the goods (see Chapter 41).

Company contracts for loan capital

As well as obtaining capital from investors, a company is usually empowered to borrow money and to pledge its assets as security for any such loan.

A contract for the loan of money to a company is known as a debenture; the interest given on the company's assets by way of security for a loan is labelled a charge.

Registration of charges and receivership

Part VIII deals with a secured creditor's rights against the company and its officers arising out of a failure of the company to honour its contractual obligations under a debenture. The chapters in this part deal with:

♦ Company creditors and charges (Chapter 39).
♦ Ineffective charges and dispositions of company assets (Chapter 40).
♦ Debentures, registration and priority of charges (Chapter 41).
♦ Creditors' remedies against the company – consequences of receivership (Chapter 42).
♦ The receiver's rights and duties (Chapter 43).
♦ Unsatisfied creditors' remedies against an insolvent company's members and officers (Chapter 44).

Chapter 19 shows how the Companies Acts protect a company's capital fund for the benefit of creditors generally, by controlling any reductions in it.

Examinership

Both unsecured and secured creditors enjoy the right to petition for the winding up of a company. Because of this powerful statutory-based contractual remedy which creditors possess over companies, the concept of examinership was introduced in 1990. This concept seeks to give companies some measure of protection against creditors exercising their powerful contractual rights. Chapters 45 and 46 deal with court protection for a company against its creditors, by the appointment of an examiner.

The court appoints an examiner in order to put together a financial rescue package (or compromise) between the company, its creditors and share-holders. Other possible financial arrangements affecting the company and its creditors and members are detailed in Chapters 47 and 48.

Liquidation

If there has been no successful compromise or financial arrangement, creditors can petition for the liquidation of the company. Chapters 49 to 52 focus on the procedures for winding up companies.

The winding up of an insolvent company is usually initiated by a secured creditor exercising his contractual right to have a liquidator appointed. Chapter 50 deals with the role of the Official Liquidator.

Other company contracts

While company directors are office holders rather than employees, executive directors are also employees of the company. Their rights as executives are governed generally by employment law.

Companies may also appoint auditors. The relationship between an auditor and a company is one of independent contractor and principal, rather than that of employee/employer.

In addition to their contractual obligations to the company, auditors may incur considerable tortious liabilities (see below).

The quasi-contractual status and role of directors

Directors are a company's human managing agents. They stand in a quasi-contractual relationship to it.

A director is a quasi-trustee in relation to the company's money and assets. He is an agent when negotiating contracts on behalf of the company.

The management powers and duties of directors are introduced in Chapter 1 and explained in the following chapters:

◆ The roles of directors as managing agents (Chapter 23).
◆ Limitations on directors' powers of management (Chapter 24).
◆ Directors' specific fiduciary duties (Chapter 25).

♦ Directors' duties of care and skill (Chapter 26).
♦ Statutory strengthening of directors' duties (Chapter 27).

Chapters 32 and 33 deal with directors' statutory obligations to maintain books and registers, and to prepare and submit accounts and an annual return.

As the Minister for Science, Technology and Commerce stated in the Foreword to the *Companies Report 1997*:

> 'the privileges of company incorporation and limited liability impose responsibilities on those who avail of them. The public is entitled to expect that such responsibilities are met by companies and their directors.'

Tortious aspects of company law

Directors can incur tortious liability at common law or, more likely, for breach of statutory duty or obligation.

The more important statutory 'company law' torts, imposing unlimited liability on directors to pay damages, include a failure to maintain proper books of account and reckless and fraudulent trading.

Chapters 28 to 30 deal with directors' tortious liability and their restriction and disqualification. The potential criminal liability of directors is outlined in Chapter 31.

Chapter 34 explains the auditors' role in monitoring the directors' stewardship of the company on behalf of its shareholders. Potential shareholders who rely on incorrectly audited accounts may have a claim in negligence against that company's auditors. Chapter 34 also includes comment on post-*Caparo* case liability in Irish law.

Use of a misleading company name can also give rise to an action for the tort of passing off, as shown in Chapter 7.

Other legal aspects

Elements of equity, trusts, land law, employment and commercial, competition and constitutional law also impinge on corporate transactions and company law.

Because of the similarities in legal systems and legislative provisions, many leading post-1922 judicial decisions on the interpretation of UK company law are also included in the text for consideration as persuasive precedents, should the occasion arise.

Compliance and enforcement matters

Unease about the low levels of compliance and problems with enforcing company law led to the passing of the Company Law Enforcement Act 2001.

During the second stage of the Company Law Enforcement Bill, the Tánaiste, Ms Mary Harney, stated that the Bill represented:

> 'the most radical action taken by any Irish Government to reform the enforcement regime ... in respect of the Companies Acts.

> The establishment of the office of Director of Corporate Enforcement, signals a clear intention on the part of government to seriously address corporate crime and malpractice in Ireland ... Never before have such resources been applied to the task.'

Compliance and enforcement matters are outlined in Chapter 1 and explained in Part XI, which deals with:

♦ Striking off; dissolution and restoration of companies (Chapter 53).
♦ Corporate governance and the company law review group (Chapter 54).
♦ The Director of Corporate Enforcement (Chapter 55).

FUTURE REFORMS

Further reforms are likely to be made to company law in the short term, following on from the recommendations of the Audit Review Group.[1]

Plans for company law review, consolidation and simplification are summarised in the *Companies Report 2000.*[2]

ACKNOWLEDGEMENTS

I would like to express my thanks to the following people.

I had some illuminating discussions on the implications of criminal, tort and competition law for the subject matter of this text, with colleagues Ray Friel, Paul McCutcheon, Eoin Quill and Siun O'Keeffe.

The present state of corporate governance in Ireland was clarified for me by Mr Daryl Byrne and Ms Deirdre Sumners of the Irish Stock Exchange. Mr Ian Jenkins, of Barlow, Lyde and Gilbert, Solicitors, London, helped me ascertain the status of the Turnbull Report in the UK.

Mr Paul Appleby was most helpful in responding to my queries regarding progress of the Company Law Enforcement Bill.

The manuscript was patiently typed by Ms Suzanne Nicholas.

---

1 See **34.40** et seq.
2 Department of Enterprise, Trade and Employment (The Stationery Office, September 2001), at pp 10–17.

As usual, Mr Richard Hudson and the staff at Jordans were most efficient in dealing with the publishing of this book. In it, I have attempted to state the law as at 1 August 2001.

Henry Ellis,
School of Law
University of Limerick
September 2001

CONTENTS

TABLE OF CASES

References are to paragraph numbers, except for roman numerals, which are references to page numbers of the Preface.

TABLE OF STATUTES

References are to paragraph numbers, except for roman numerals which are
references to pages of the Preface or Introduction.

TABLE OF FOREIGN STATUTES

References are to paragraph numbers.

TABLE OF STATUTORY INSTRUMENTS

References are to paragraph numbers, except for roman numerals, which are references to page numbers of the Preface.

TABLE OF EU LEGISLATION

References are to paragraph numbers, except for roman numerals, which are references to page numbers of the Preface.

1979 Admission Directive
Directive 79/279/EEC; Council Directive of 5 March 1979 coordinating the
   conditions for the admission of securities to official stock exchange
   listing (1979 OJ L66/21)   10.3, 10.4, 10.6

1980 Listing Particulars Directive
Directive 80/390/EEC; Council Directive of 17 March 1980 coordinating the
   requirements for the drawing-up, scrutiny and distribution of the listing
   particulars to be published for the admission of securities to official stock
   exchange listing (1980 OJ L100/1) 10.3, 10.5, 10.6

1982 Interim Reports Directive
Directive 82/121/EEC; Council Directive of 15 February 1982 on information
   to be published on a regular basis by companies the shares of which have
   been admitted to official stock exchange listing (1982 OJ L48/26)   10.3, 10.6

1982 Sixth Company Law Directive
Directive 82/891/EEC; Sixth Council Directive of 17 December 1982 based
   on Article 54(3)(g) of the Treaty, concerning the division of public
   limited liability companies (1982 OJ L378/47) 48.16

1983 Seventh Company Law Directive
Directive 83/349/EEC; Seventh Council Directive of 13 June 1983 based on
   the Article 54(3)(g) of the Treaty on consolidated accounts (1983
   OJ L193/1)   32.18

1988 Directive on Disclosure of Significant Shareholdings
Directive 88/627/EEC; Council Directive of 12 December 1988 on the
   information to be published when a major holding in a listed company is
   acquired or disposed of (1988 OJ L348/62)   22.7

1989 Prospectus Directive/Public Offers Directive
Directive 89/298/EEC; Council Directive of 17 April 1989 coordinating the
   requirements for the drawing-up, scrutiny and distribution of the
   prospectus to be published when transferable securities are offered to
   the public (1989 OJ L124/8) 10.22

1989 Twelfth EC Company Law Directive
Directive 89/667/EEC; Twelfth Council Company Law Directive of 21
   December 1989 on single-member private limited-liability companies
   (1989 OJ L395/40)   8.7

1989 Mergers Control Regulation
Council Regulation (EEC) 4064/89 of 20 December 1989 on the control of
   concentrations between undertakings (1989 OJ L395/1)   48.32, 48.35

TABLE OF OTHER MATERIALS

References are to paragraph numbers.

TABLE OF ABBREVIATIONS

To avoid unnecessary repetition, the following abbreviations are frequently used in the text when indicating principal statutory sources:

Statute	Abbreviations
Companies Act 1963	The 1963 Act *or* CA 1963
Companies Act 1963, Sch 1, Table A, Part I	Table A
Companies Act 1990	The 1990 Act
Companies (Amendment) Act 1977	The 1977 Amendment Act
Companies (Amendment) Act 1982	The 1982 Amendment Act
Companies (Amendment) Act 1983	The 1983 Amendment Act
Companies (Amendment) Act 1986	The 1986 Amendment Act
Companies (Amendment) Act 1990	The 1990 Amendment Act
Companies (Amendment) Act 1999	The 1999 Act
Companies (Amendment) (No 2) Act 1999	The 1999 (No 2) Act
Company Law Enforcement Act 2001	The 2001 Act

INTRODUCTION

The origin of company law was nineteenth-century legislation enacted to stimulate the growth of trade and enterprise. This legislation sought to achieve its aims by introducing a facility whereby investors and entrepreneurs were permitted to create corporate bodies (companies) through which they could carry on business. Investors could also, if they wished, have their liability for the losses of their companies limited.

LEGISLATIVE AIMS

Company law has developed within the broad statutory aims of:

(1) permitting the use of companies as business associations in order to stimulate the growth of trade and enterprise; and

(2) protecting investors in, and creditors of, companies.

These legislative aims are explained in Part I.

Company law is both lengthy and complex. For example, the Companies Act 1963 consists of 399 sections (and 13 Schedules). The Companies Act 1990 contains a further 262 sections. Much of this law is very detailed. Accordingly, one can easily lose sight of its underlying principles.

To assist readers to keep the fundamental aims of company law in mind as they become immersed in its detailed provisions, I have used transparent chapter titles such as:

> Protection for Investors in Public Companies (Chapter 10);
> Protection of Company's Capital Base for Creditors (and Investors) (Chapter 19);
> The Member's Section 25 Contract (Chapter 20);
> Creditors' Remedies against the Company (Chapter 42);
> Unsatisfied Creditors' Remedies against Insolvent Company's Members and Officers (Chapter 44); and
> Examinership and its Effects on Creditors' Rights (Chapter 45).

CORE IDEAS IN COMPANY LAW

Before delving into the detailed laws affecting the various parties to corporate contracts, it is necessary to understand core concepts underlying company law. Part II, therefore, is devoted to explaining the meaning and relevance of:

(1) a company's separate legal personality;

(2) the 'veil' of incorporation; and

(3) the concept of limitation of liability.

Separate legal personality

A House of Lords' ruling in 1897 is probably the most significant court decision in company law.

In *Salomon v Salomon & Co*, the court made it clear that a company would be recognised judicially as an entirely separate person from its principal share-holders. Thus, the House of Lords gave precedence to *form* over *substance*; in effect accepting that once the form of a company was within the letter of the law, the court would not look behind the company form to identify the beneficial owners of its shares. Chapters 3 and 4 deal with separate corporate personality.

The veil of incorporation

Generally, the courts consider themselves bound by the principle in the *Salomon* case that the company is a separate person distinct from its members. As a result, there is said to be a 'veil' drawn between the company and its members. The courts will not normally 'lift' this veil to look at the economic reality of who owns the company.

There are exceptional circumstances where the courts will look behind the corporate form to see who actually owns and controls a company. This action is known as 'lifting the veil of incorporation'.

The veil may be lifted by statutory provision to require group accounts from holding companies and to identify specific inter-group transactions. Again, under taxation law, the shareholders of a 'close' company may incur personal taxation liabilities for its profits. However, legislation generally does not render investors liable for the debts of the company.[1]

So long as a shareholder acts in good faith, because of the privilege of limitation of liability, he is unlikely to incur liability for company debts. Where, however, a shareholder moves outside his expected passive role and becomes involved in fraudulent trading by the company, he may be held personally liable by statute[2] for company debts.

The process of lifting the veil always overrules the separate legal personality of the company. Usually, this is necessary to give effect to statutory provisions designed to bring greater transparency into transactions involving connected companies.

---

1 Under s 36 of the 1963 Act, a reduction in the number of members below the legal minimum may lead to the remaining member(s) being held liable for the debts of the company. This statutory exception is not of great practical value to company creditors – particularly since the introduction of the single member company.
2 Under s 297A of the 1963 Act.

The judiciary may also lift the veil at common law, eg to prevent the use of corporate form for an inequitable purpose.[1] Generally, though, the courts will only lift the veil to make the members liable for company debts, where the company has been used as a 'cloak' for fraud or other criminal activities. Accordingly, notwithstanding any lifting of the veil, investors will normally retain the privilege of limited liability, providing they do not become involved in corporate transactions nor attempt to influence the directors and officers in the management of the company. This could happen by investors acting as 'shadow' directors or by corporate members interfering in their capacity as a 'related' company.

This book attempts to rationalise the 'jungle of judgments' relating to lifting the veil in Chapter 6. The extent to which a liquidator can utilise the related company relationship to increase an insolvent company's assets is dealt with in Chapter 50.

Limitation of liability

In company law, limitation of liability essentially means that a shareholder can only lose the amount of his investment in a company if it fails. He is not liable to the creditors of an insolvent company for company debts.

The limited liability company or corporation was invented as a means of attracting the large aggregations of capital required for construction and other major business projects during the Industrial Revolution of the 19th century. Such projects required capital contributions from a wide range of passive investors not actually involved in running the businesses.

The original intention of the legislature seemed to envisage granting limited liability to investors in substantial companies. The real significance of the House of Lords' decision in the *Salomon* case is that it confirmed that the privilege of forming a limited liability company was also available to the owners of small businesses which had been operating as sole traders. A result of the *Salomon* decision was to generate an explosion in the growth of private companies which today form the vast majority of companies registered in Ireland.

TYPES OF COMPANY PERMITTED

The companies legislation permitted the formation of several types of company.

Persons seeking to promote companies under the Companies Acts were permitted to form companies which were either limited by shares or by guarantee. Promoters could also, if they so desired, choose to forego the

---

1 For example by a person attempting to escape his liability to pay royalties under a licence agreement by transferring the licence to a company formed for that purpose. This happened in *Cummins v Stewart* [1911] 1 IR 236.

benefits of limited liability and form unlimited companies. Chapter 8 mentions the factors to be considered by company promoters before deciding on the type of corporate form most appropriate to their needs.

All companies can be classified as either private or public (plc), generally according to the numbers of their shareholders or members. Private companies need a minimum of one member and are subject to a maximum limit of 50 members. Public companies must have at least seven members but are subject to no upper limit on membership numbers.

In Ireland, over 90 per cent of all companies are private.

FORMATION OF A COMPANY

Promoters can form a company by following a statutory procedure known as registration. The documentation to be submitted to the registrar of companies when forming a new company includes its 'constitutional' documents: its memorandum and articles of association.

The *memorandum of association* is the more fundamental document. It sets out the company's name, objects and nominal capital. It also records (if applicable) the fact that the liability of the members is to be limited.

The *articles of association* consist of the rules governing the internal management of the company. These deal with such matters as the appointment and powers of directors, shareholders' rights and liabilities, and proceedings at company meetings. Table A is a model set of articles for the management of public and private companies limited by shares, set out in the First Schedule to the Companies Act 1963. Many companies adopt all, or part, of Table A for their articles.

When the registrar of companies is satisfied that the registration application is in order, he issues a certificate of incorporation. This certificate is essentially the company's 'birth' certificate.

From the date of incorporation mentioned in the certificate of incorporation, the subscribers to the memorandum, together with such other persons who may from time to time become members of the company, become a body corporate with the name contained in the memorandum of association. From this moment, the company has a separate legal existence from its members.

HOW A COMPANY CARRIES ON BUSINESS

Although a company is recognised as a separate legal person by the law, it has no 'mind or body' like a human being. As a result, it can only carry on its business by using human agents.

Members of the company cannot act as agents for it; this restriction is part of the 'price' paid by members for the privilege of incorporating companies. The members do, however, elect a board of directors who will act as the company's managing agents.

Directors must act in a fiduciary or trustworthy manner in relation to the property and assets of the company. Such property and assets are owned by the company, however, and not by the directors.

The directors also act as agents for the company when negotiating contracts for it with 'outsiders', eg when borrowing money for the company from banks, or buying goods and services for it generally. 'Outsiders' owed money by the company are usually styled 'creditors'.

FINANCIAL DIFFICULTIES

If the company encounters financial difficulties, secured creditors may appoint a receiver and manager over the company's property. Ultimately, unpaid creditors may petition the court to terminate the 'life' of the company.

TERMINATING THE 'LIFE' OF A COMPANY

A company is brought into existence by utilising a legal procedure known as registration. A company's existence may be terminated by following another procedure. The usual procedure for ending the 'life' of a company is known as 'winding up' or 'liquidation'.

Even unsecured creditors, if they are owed at least £1,000, can petition the court to appoint a liquidator to wind up a company.

CONTRACTUAL RELATIONSHIPS IN COMPANY LAW

The business relationships affecting registered companies may involve:

(1) the company itself;
(2) its promoters;
(3) its directors and officers;
(4) its members (or investors);
(5) its creditors; and
(6) if the company encounters financial or other difficulties, office-holders such as:
    (a) inspectors;
    (b) receivers (and managers);
    (c) examiners; and/or
    (d) liquidators.

Company law provides a framework of rules and procedures which underpin these contractual relationships.

THE CORE CONTRACTUAL RELATIONSHIPS

As already mentioned, the purpose of company law is to encourage trade and enterprise. In carrying out this aim, three core contracting parties emerge. These parties are:

(1) investors in the company;
(2) the company itself; and
(3) creditors of the company.

These core relationships are explored in Parts II, III, IV A to E, VIII, IX, X A and X B.

PART I

THE CONTRACTUAL RELATIONSHIPS IN COMPANY LAW

Chapter 1

COMPANY LAW ORIGINS AND OVERVIEW

THE STATUTORY FRAMEWORK

1.1 Incorporated business associations, which in Ireland are styled as 'companies', are active in any Western European (and, indeed, world) market economy involving the selling and buying of goods, products and services.

In Ireland, company law provides the legal framework within which investors, entrepreneurs and labour organise themselves into corporations which become recognised as separate and independent persons in the eyes of the law.

1.2 The political pressure to permit associations of individuals to trade as companies culminated in the 1840s. Government felt that economic activity would be stimulated if entrepreneurs were permitted to register companies – a much faster and more efficient process than that of obtaining a Royal Charter. As a result of this political/economic pressure, the Joint Stock Companies Act was passed in 1844. The Act provided for the registration of companies without the need to obtain a Royal Charter. It did not, however, include provisions limiting the liability of shareholders.

Shortly after the 1844 Act, political lobbying on behalf of investors commenced to add the protection of limited liability to the benefits of company registration.

The principle of limited liability was introduced by the Limited Liability Act 1855. This Act was quickly repealed by the Joint Stock Companies Act 1856 which retained the principle of limited liability but also introduced the constitutional documents of the modern registered company, requiring a memorandum of association and a set of articles of association.

The first 'modern' Companies Act was enacted in 1862. It contained over 200 sections and consolidated all the previous statutes. The current legislation regulating companies is contained largely in the Companies Acts 1963 to 2001, which contain almost 1,000 sections and 23 Schedules.

1.3 It is worth noting, at this stage, that the current framework of Irish company law reflects many ideas introduced over 150 years ago which may not be entirely appropriate for business enterprises entering the third millennium. In particular, the emphasis given to public companies in the legislation does not reflect the present structure of Irish business associations, where private companies make up an overwhelming majority. Notwithstanding this, a major revision of company law seems unlikely in the foreseeable future. Accordingly, corporate business transactions in Ireland will continue to take place within the legal framework of a large and complex body of company law, originating in England in 1844, and consisting of thousands of individual rules.

The significance of the 1844 and 1856 legislation was that these Acts introduced the methods of registering a company with separate legal personality and limited liability for its investors.

SEPARATE LEGAL PERSONALITY OF COMPANY

1.4   A registered company is treated, in law, as a separate and distinct person from its shareholders.

In *Salomon v Salomon & Co Ltd*,[1] Salomon held 20,001 of the company's 20,007 shares, the other shares not owned by him being held by his wife and five children.

The liquidator claimed that the company was entitled to be indemnified by Salomon against the whole of the company's unsecured liabilities, contending that the company was a 'mere nominee and agent' of Salomon. Vaughan Williams J made a declaration accordingly and this was affirmed by the Court of Appeal. Salomon appealed to the House of Lords.

The decision of the Court of Appeal was reversed by the House of Lords, Lord Halsbury LC stating:

> 'It seems to me impossible to dispute that once a company is legally incorporated it *must be treated like any other independent person* with its rights and liabilities appropriate to itself, and *that the motives[2] of those who took part in the promotion of the company are absolutely irrelevant* in discussing what those rights and liabilities are.'

Thus it is clear that even a so-called 'one man' company could not, at common law, necessarily be identified with its controlling shareholder.

The concept of a company's separate legal personality is explained further in Chapter 3 of this book.

The veil of incorporation

1.5   The corporate personality of a registered company is also often likened to a veil, protecting the shareholders of a company against legal actions against them for the debts of the company. There are, however, exceptional occasions when the courts will 'lift this protective veil' and allow a company's creditors to pursue actions against its shareholders. In Chapter 6, an attempt is made to unravel the confusing miscellany of case-law on this subject. The legislature has also made provision, in some circumstances, for the veil of incorporation to be lifted. Examples are also included in Chapter 6 of the *exceptional statutory* cases where the veil of incorporation offers *no protection* to shareholders.

---

1   [1897] AC 22 (HL) – see **3.2**.
2   The motivation of the promoters may, in fact, be relevant to a lifting of the veil of incorporation by a court – see **3.12** and Chapter 6.

LIMITED LIABILITY OF INVESTORS

1.6   The liability of a registered company which fails financially is limited to the assets of the company remaining at the time of the liquidation. Because the company's liability is limited, so too is that of its investors. This is because, generally, a company's creditors cannot make its shareholders liable for the debts of the company, which is a separate person and quite distinct from them at law. It is only in the exceptional cases where the court or statute penetrates the veil of incorporation (or separate personality of the company), that the shareholders may be rendered liable for the debts (or other activities) of the company. As indicated in the Introduction, this is usually only likely to happen when a shareholder acts improperly or becomes involved with the management or affairs of the company. For example, if it is proved that the company was formed for some fraudulent or illegal purpose, a court may 'lift the veil' and make the shareholders liable for the company's debts.

The concept of limited liability is explained in **2.6**.

THE ARTIFICIAL NATURE OF A COMPANY

1.7   A company is, obviously, very different to a human legal person. A company has 'neither body, mind nor soul'. If the law recognises a person with neither body, mind nor soul as a full legal person, the question arises as to how such a company can exercise its legal rights: in particular, how does a company operate and trade? The short answer is by a series of agency contracts with humans. Companies can therefore only operate by using human agents.

The company's human agents

1.8   Before any company is registered, some person (or persons) must have the idea and energy to start the incorporation procedure. Such a person is styled a *promoter.*

A promoter enters into contracts both with the company and on its behalf, even before it is registered. There were some problems at common law relating to the validity of pre-incorporation contracts made by promoters, but this situation was remedied in 1963. In Part III of this book, the rights and liabilities of promoters are explained. This part also outlines the formal procedure to be taken to register and incorporate a private company and explains the importance of the memorandum and articles of association.

1.9   Once the registrar of companies issues a certificate of incorporation, the company is legally 'born'. What this means is that the law now recognises the *company* as an artificial but legal person which is entitled to trade in its own right. A company, therefore, has the legal power to enter into contracts with investors, trading contracts and contracts, to borrow money and to give security for its borrowings.

Company capital and initial finance

1.10   A private company is entitled to commence trading once it receives its certificate of incorporation from the registrar of companies. Public companies, on the other hand, have to raise their capital from the public before the registrar licenses them to commence business by means of a Trading Certificate. Chapters 10 and 11 illustrate how investors in public companies are protected before such a company is allowed to trade. The composition of a company's capital base, and the statutory restrictions on any reduction of it, are dealt with in Chapters 18 and 19.

COMPANY ORGANISATION BY MEANS OF ITS HUMAN AGENTS

1.11   When a company is being formed, the human agents most directly connected with it will be its investors or shareholders. However, shareholders cannot negotiate contracts and act as agents for the company. Their input is limited to electing the board of directors. It is this body of human agents which has the authority to manage the company. They constitute the 'mind'[1] of the company. All company decisions emanate from the board of directors. The board may, however, delegate powers to a *Managing Director* or indeed, to senior employees (executives). Provided directors' decisions are lawful and within their powers ('intra vires'), they cannot be overruled by the members.

Parts IV A, B, D and E deal with the respective roles of investors and directors in operating the company.

Corporate governance

1.12   The term 'corporate governance' broadly refers to the interaction between members and directors in operating the company.

Having explained the importance of the memorandum and articles of association in Part IV A, Part IV B focuses on the articles of association and corporate governance; in particular, the role of shareholders in appointing directors and voting at company meetings. The potential for the improvement of corporate governance, in the post-Eircom plc AGM scenario, is discussed in Chapter 54.

Chapter 16 shows how the concept of protection of minority investors has been developed, despite the general rule of majority control in company decision making.

Members' remedies for infringement of their collective or corporate (as distinct from their individual) rights, are identified in Chapter 17.

---

1 But not its body and soul! A company's business premises and staff employed also give it a physical presence.

Company capital and shareholders' class rights

1.13 The main function of shareholders is to provide the company's capital.

In Chapter 18, the concept of a company's capital is explained, including the different types of capital and shares, and their class rights.

Company law makes provision to protect the company's capital fund, in the general interest of its creditors. Chapter 19 explains how this is done by preventing unauthorised reductions of capital and imposing 'capital maintenance' rules.

Shareholders' individual rights and responsibilities

1.14 In Part IV D, the terms of the shareholders' statutory contract are further examined in the context of identifying members' individual (as distinct from collective) rights and responsibilities.

Shareholders' individual rights to vote having been dealt with in Parts IV A to C, Part IV D focuses on shareholders' rights to be paid dividends, and members' responsibilities to respond to calls for payment of monies due on their (partly paid) shares.

Disclosure of interests

1.15 The statutory duties on members to disclose their interests in shares are outlined in Chapter 22, which also deals with the process of transferring the ownership of shares when they are being sold.

Transfer of interests

1.16 The transfer process involves two stages. The first is an assignment by the seller of his interest in the shares to the purchaser. The second stage involves the registration of the purchaser as a member in place of the seller.

Company directors have rights to refuse the registration of a purchaser of shares. If the directors exercise these rights, then the purchaser concerned will hold only an equitable, rather than a legal, interest in the shares purchased.

The consequences of non-registration of a share transfer are also dealt with in Chapter 22.

Compulsory purchase

1.17 Following a successful *takeover bid*, the purchasing company may be entitled compulsorily to acquire the shares of the dissenting minority – see **1.39**.

Directors and officers – the company's managing agents

1.18 While the investors may own the company, they are not entitled to manage it or to negotiate contracts on its behalf. This function is given to the directors. It is they who control the day-to-day trading activities of the shareholders' company.

The directors are elected by the members. A director elected by the members is an office holder rather than an employee of the company, ie he is typically a non-executive director.

Directors may also enter into service contracts (of employment) with the company. For example, the managing director or, indeed, any other executive director, has a dual role. He is an office holder; he is also an employee of the company of which he is a director. These distinctions are explained in **15.24** et seq.

In view of the critical role of directors under company law, Parts IV E, V A and B, VI and VII B are devoted to looking at their powers, duties and legal responsibilities in discharging their obligations to the company.

Directors' powers of company management

1.19 Part IV E looks at the provisions in the articles of association for company management, with Chapter 23 explaining the role of directors as human managing agents for the non-human company, and Chapter 24 delineating the scope of their powers.

Directors' duties

1.20 Part V A distinguishes between directors' common-law and statutory duties.

Chapters 25 and 26 deal with directors' fiduciary duties and duties of care and skill respectively, whilst Chapter 27 shows how these common-law duties have been strengthened by statute.

Traditionally, the judicial attitude to directors' duties was to emphasise the need for honesty towards company assets. The common law did not expect too much by way of commercial skills from directors. However, the Companies Act 1990 significantly extends the common law duties of directors (and officers). For example, s 204 renders any officer personally liable for the debts of the company, if proper books of account have not been kept. Again, the creditors' statutory remedy of rendering directors (and others) liable for fraudulent trading, which had not proved very satisfactory in practice, was extended by the 1990 Act to make officers liable also for reckless trading. In addition, the Act regulates specific company transactions involving directors, such as service contracts, loans, share and property deals.

Liabilities of directors

1.21 The Companies Act 1990 has changed the modern attitude towards directors' duties, responsibilities and liabilities. This statute recognises the fact that directors constitute the controlling 'mind and will' of a company and it is generally they, rather than its owners, who should be accountable for any corporate wrongdoings.

Part V B explains the extent of the civil and criminal liabilities of directors and officers, dealing with:

(1) the tortious liability of company directors – Chapter 28;
(2) civil remedies against directors – Chapter 29;
(3) restriction and disqualification of directors – Chapter 30; and
(4) criminal liabilities of directors and officers – Chapter 31.

The company secretary

1.22 Every company must appoint an officer known as the company secretary. His role is essentially to ensure that the company complies with the provisions of the Companies Acts – see **23.15** et seq.

The authority of the company secretary to bind the company in contracts with 'outsiders' is also considered.

Monitoring the directors' management of the company

1.23 The law prescribes the keeping of statutory registers, books, records and accounts in which the business transactions of the company must be recorded. Certain of these documents must be open to inspection by the investors.

The directors must prepare annual accounts and lay them before the members in general meetings. The company's independent auditors will report to the members on the accounts. Approval of the annual accounts by the members is, essentially, a vote approving the directors' management of their company.

The directors must also submit an annual return to the registrar of companies.

Chapters 32 to 34 detail the statutory requirements for monitoring the directors' stewardship of the company. These include the role and responsibilities of the independent auditor.

If directors are unhelpful and refuse to provide information to members or creditors, the latter may apply to the court seeking the appointment of an Inspector to investigate the conduct of the company's affairs. The Director of Corporate Enforcement can also have an Inspector appointed to investigate company ownership – see Chapter 35.

Company employees

1.24 In practice, when managing the company, the directors will employ staff on the company's behalf, and delegate its day-to-day operational tasks to them. Nevertheless, company law does not encompass the rights and duties of company employees. This is the province of labour/employment law. As far as company law is concerned, the relevant fact is that a company can act as an employer in much the same way as a human person.

Notwithstanding, some ambiguities have arisen in connection with the duties of directors who are also employees, eg managing and other executive directors. Therefore, discussion of the blurring of the distinction between the role (or roles) of directors as office holders and employees is included in Chapter 25.

CONTRACTUAL CAPACITY OF THE COMPANY AND ITS AGENTS

1.25   A company, as a recognised legal person, can enter into contracts (by using its directors and employees as human agents). Generally, however, a company can only enter into contracts within the powers contained in the objects clause of its memorandum of association. If it enters into a contract outside its objects, that contract is 'ultra vires' and void at common law. In Part VII A, we show how the legislature has intervened to protect creditors against ultra vires contracts.

The agency law principles underlying the authority of directors, officers and employees to act on the company's behalf are explained in Part VII B.

Chapter 38 isolates trends in judicial protection for creditors against ultra vires actions by directors.

COMPANY CONTROL AND OWNERSHIP

1.26   A feature of company law is that it separates control of a company from its ownership. As mentioned above, a company is controlled by its board of directors. It is, however, owned by its *shareholders or members*. The members of a company are simply *investors* who contribute to the company's *capital.*

In practice, the same person may be both a shareholder and a director. In fact, in many small private companies, including the recently introduced *single-member company*, the majority shareholder may also be the managing director. Nevertheless, in company law, these roles are seen as distinct: the person involved 'wearing two hats' – one when acting as member, the other when acting as director.

In company law, legal relationships between the company, its directors and members (shareholders) can be classified as matters *internal to the company.* However, the company also enters into legal relationships with persons external to it. Such relationships usually arise out of trading or borrowing transactions.

EXTERNAL OR THIRD PARTY RELATIONSHIPS

1.27   When a company enters into a trading transaction and that trader remains unpaid for the goods or services supplied to the company, the 'third party' or external trader becomes a creditor of the company.

Similarly, if the company borrows money,[1] the lender will be a creditor for the monies remaining unpaid on the loan. If, as would usually be the case, the lender insists on the company furnishing security before granting it the loan, the lender will be classified as a 'secured creditor'.

Creditors' rights against the company

1.28   The different types of company creditors and the nature of their security on the company's assets are noted in Chapters 39 to 41.

Secured creditors are generally known as debenture-holders; their contract with the company being evidenced by a debenture deed.

The usual terms of a debenture are outlined in the deed. Charges on the company's assets as security for the debenture must be registered with the registrar of companies. The company must also maintain a register of debenture holders.

Debentures can be transferred (sold and bought) in much the same way as shares.

The remedies of unpaid creditors, both unsecured and secured, are detailed in Chapters 42 to 44.

1.29   Secured creditors can appoint a receiver over the company's property for its failure to repay monies borrowed. The consequences of receivership for the company, and the rights, powers and duties of the receiver are explained in Chapter 43.

Because of the privilege of limited liability which investors enjoy, if a company is insolvent on winding up, the creditors have little chance of recovering company debts from them. Recent statutory developments have made the company's managing agents, ie its directors and officers, a much better target – see **1.32**. Chapter 44 focuses on unsatisfied creditors' remedies against an insolvent company's investors and officers.

Rights against insolvent company's assets

1.30   The most frequent reason for liquidating a company is because it has become insolvent, ie unable to pay its debts to creditors.

---

1 Sometimes classified as 'loan' capital as distinct from capital supplied by shareholders (investment capital).

As the liability of investors is limited to the fully paid up value of their shares, if there is a lack of company funds to meet all the claims of creditors, what does the law prescribe?

Suppose, for example, that Alpha Ltd, a private company, is to be wound up with assets totalling £800,000 and liabilities of £2.4 million. Which creditors (if any) will be paid, and, assuming some are, how much of their debts will they receive? To answer this question, one has to classify the various company creditors.

1.31   The general rule regarding ranking of payments is that secured creditors are entitled to be paid in preference to unsecured creditors. As most companies being wound up will have insufficient assets to pay all their creditors, the likely losers in this scenario will be the unsecured creditors.

Again, if there are insufficient assets to pay the unsecured creditors, the shareholders, who rank below them, will also lose their total investments in the company.

The full ranking of creditors' debts and creditors' rights generally is outlined in Chapter 2 and in Parts VIII and X B. These parts also explain the distinctions between a company liquidation and receivership, and the differing roles of a liquidator and a receiver.

Creditors' rights against directors and others

1.32   At this stage, it is clear that the principle of limited liability protects investors if the company in which they are members is wound up. The creditors only have rights against company assets, and these rights depend on their legal ranking as creditors. In practice, such rights may only be useful to secured creditors.

This situation is unsatisfactory, from a creditor's point of view. As a result, unsatisfied creditors have looked for sources of redress, other than the company assets.

The obvious target for creditors were the company's directors, who, in certain circumstances, can be held *personally* liable (without limitation) for the unpaid debts of the company. For example, under s 297A of the Companies Act 1963,[1] an officer of the company, such as a director or manager, can be held by a court to be personally responsible for all the debts of the company, where it appears that he was knowingly a party to the carrying on of the business in a reckless manner.

During 1990, two important Companies Acts were passed. The first[2] introduced the office of Examiner into Ireland – see **1.34**. The second[3] greatly increased the responsibilities and liabilities of company directors.

---

1 Inserted by s 138 of the Companies Act 1990.
2 Companies (Amendment) Act 1990.
3 Companies Act 1990 – see Chapter 2 and Parts V A and B.

Creditors' rights to terminate the life of a company

1.33 Under s 214 of the Companies Act 1963,[1] a creditor (secured or unsecured) who is owed a sum exceeding £1,000 may, if the company, after due written notice, fails to pay the amount, petition or apply to the court to wind up that company. In fact, the majority of petitions to the court to wind up companies are presented by creditors.

From a company's perspective, therefore, creditors are given real powers under company law. They possess the ultimate sanction of bringing the life of the company to an end, without seeking the consent, or even against the express wishes, of that company's directors and shareholders.

It was the possibility of the use by creditors of that ultimate sanction against Mr Larry Goodman's companies, in 1990, which led to a special sitting of the Dail in August, and the passing of the Companies (Amendment) Act 1990. This Act introduced the office of Examiner in Ireland.

The idea of protecting a company from action taken against it by its creditors was explained by McCarthy J in *Re Atlantic Magnetics Ltd*[2] thus:

> 'It is, I believe, of great importance to bear in mind in the application of the Act, that its purpose is protection – *protection of the company and consequently of its shareholders, workforce, and [unsecured] creditors.* It is clear that Parliament intended that the fate of the company, and of those who depend upon it, should not lie solely in the hands of one or more large creditors who can, by appointing a receiver pursuant to a debenture, effectively terminate its operation and secure, as best they may, the discharge of monies due to them to the inevitable disadvantage of those less protected. *The Act is to provide a breathing space, albeit at the expense of some creditor or creditors.*'

Protecting the company against its creditors

1.34 The policy underlying the appointment of an Examiner is that companies in financial difficulties might be given time to place their finances on a firmer footing, thereby avoiding a winding up with all its negative consequences for company, directors, shareholders, employees and creditors alike. Accordingly, under the 1990 Amendment Act, an application for the appointment of an Examiner by the court may be presented by any or all of the following persons:

(1) the company;
(2) the directors;
(3) a creditor (including an employee); and
(4) a member holding at least 10 per cent of the voting shares.

1.35 If, on hearing the petition, the court appoints an Examiner, the company is deemed to be *under the protection* of the court for a period of three

---

1 Amended by s 123 of the Companies Act 1990.
2 [1993] 2 IR 561 (SC).

months. During this three-month period, no receiver may be appointed over any part of the company's property; no proceedings for the winding up of the company may be commenced, nor resolution for its winding up passed.

This three-month 'breathing space' from its creditors, for a debtor company, was intended to enable the Examiner to work out a financial arrangement to save the company – hence the term 'debtor protection', in company law.

The protection of a company against its creditors and the role of the Examiner are explained further in Part IX.

1.36 Major reforms were made to the examinership process by the Companies (Amendment) (No 2) Act 1999. The three-month protection period was shortened and court petitions had to be supported by a report from an independent accountant. The 1999 reforms are included in the text of Chapters 45 and 46.

Compromising company debts and corporate restructuring

1.37 In a successful examinership, the company may be 'saved' by the Examiner coming to an arrangement or compromise with the company's creditors. It is not, however, necessary for the company to be placed in examinership in order simply to compromise its debts. This can be done by entering into a scheme of arrangement or compromise under s 201 of the Companies Act 1963.

Chapter 47 outlines the procedures for a s 201 compromise between a company and its investors or creditors. Such an arrangement needs the approval of a majority of the investors and creditors.

1.38 Where a scheme provides for the transfer of company assets to a new company, this is often referred to as a *reconstruction*.

An *amalgamation* is a joining together of two or more companies to form a single new company.

Both reconstructions and amalgamations may be carried out under ss 201 to 203 of the 1963 Act in connection with schemes of arrangements with creditors, or under s 260 of the 1963 Act in the course of a voluntary winding up.

Changes in company ownership by takeover and merger

1.39 The term *takeover* is often used to describe a bid by a company to purchase the majority or all of the shares in a 'target' company. If the bid is not contested, the transaction will be described as a *merger*. It is the prior agreement (or the lack of it) to an amalgamation of companies that distinguishes the process of merger from that of takeover. Mergers are usually the result of an agreed takeover bid.

Chapter 48 outlines the statutory takeover procedures, including the power of the bidding company compulsorily to acquire the shares of a minority of investors in the target company and the rights of the dissident investors. As takeovers and mergers afford an opportunity for directors and shareholders to make sizeable profits, the legal and other controls designed to prevent excessive profit-taking are discussed: as is the government interest in ensuring that the takeover or merger does not result in a monopoly situation which could reduce competition and lead to product (or services) price increases for consumers.

Winding up a company

1.40 The procedure for terminating the 'life' of a company is known as winding up.

Part X B shows how the winding-up procedure can be initiated by creditors, members and others. Irrespective of who initiates the liquidation, the task of realising the company's assets and paying its creditors falls upon the liquidator. The role and responsibility of an official liquidator appointed by the court is examined in Chapter 50, whilst the duties of liquidators appointed by investors and creditors in 'voluntary' liquidations are compared in Chapters 51 and 52.

Dissolving the company

1.41 When the liquidator has completely wound up the affairs of the company, the final procedure is for the company to be dissolved. For example, in a creditors' voluntary winding up, three months after the registrar of companies has received the liquidator's final account, the company will be deemed to be dissolved.

A company ceases to exist as a separate legal entity only when it has been dissolved.

IMPROVING COMPANY LAW COMPLIANCE AND ENFORCEMENT

1.42 Whilst the most usual procedure for systematically dissolving a company was to wind it up, nevertheless most companies were actually dissolved because they had been struck off the register.

Striking off

1.43 The Companies Registration Office (CRO) has sought to improve compliance with company law obligations, eg the filing of annual returns, by initiating the striking off process. Details of this CRO compliance campaign and the consequences for the company and its directors of being struck off are outlined in Chapter 53.

Striking off also leads to the dissolution of a company.

Restoration to the register

1.44 Whatever may be the truth about the idea of life after death for humans, it is possible for dissolved (deceased) companies. Companies which have been dissolved either following their liquidation, or their striking off, can be brought back to 'life' by a process known as restoration to the register. This process is also explained in Chapter 53.

THE DIRECTOR OF CORPORATE ENFORCEMENT

1.45 A Working Group on Company Law Compliance and Enforcement made recommendations which led to the passing of the Company Law Enforcement Act 2001.

The main changes brought about by the 2001 Act include:

(1) the establishment of the office of Director of Corporate Enforcement, who also has a supervisory role over the activities of liquidators and receivers in the discharge of their functions under the Companies Acts. The 2001 Act also transfers to the Director the functions of the Minister for Enterprise, Trade and Employment relating to the investigation and enforcement of the Companies Acts; and

(2) the establishment, on a statutory basis, of a Company Law Review Group.

These developments are detailed in Chapters 54 and 55.

Chapter 2

COMPANY LAW OBJECTIVES – PROTECTION OF INVESTORS AND CREDITORS

INTERNAL AND EXTERNAL INTERESTS

2.1 The many and various contractual interests affected by corporate transactions are outlined in Chapter 1. Some of these interests are internal to the company; others are external.

Internal interests

2.2 Shareholders (or members), as investors, supply a company's capital. However, they take no part in the day-to-day management of the company. Nevertheless, investors have contracts with the company and enjoy both corporate and individual rights[1] against the company on the basis of these contracts.

Companies are managed by the directors, who may be non-executive or executive. The board of directors will employ persons to carry out the work of the company.

In the normal course of business, therefore, one might encounter a range of contractual relationships which concern largely the internal affairs of the company.

2.3 Examples of such *internal* relationships include the following contracts between:

(1) a company and its *members*, involving both (a) collective and (b) individual aspects of membership rights;
(2) a company and its *directors* as office holders and, perhaps, also as employees;
(3) a company and its *promoter* (or *promoters*);
(4) a company and its *employees*;
(5) an investor and another investor (or investors);
(6) an investor may also have dealings with *directors* and *employees*, acting on behalf of the company.

External (or third party) interests

2.4 When a company engages in business and borrows money, it enters into contracts with traders and banks. Neither of these interests are involved with the internal affairs of running the company. Such interests are classified, therefore, as *external*, or *third party interests*.

---

1 See Parts IV A, B and D.

External (or third party) corporate transactions include the following between:

(1) a *company* and a third party, eg the company buys a lorry from a garage.
     The garage is a third party creditor of the company until paid;
(2) a *promoter* (on behalf of the company) and a third party;
(3) a *director* (or *directors*) (on behalf of the company) and a third party;
(4) an *employee* (on behalf of the company) and a third party;
(5) a *promoter* and a third party;
(6) an *investor* and a third party (buying his shares).

2.5   When a company finds itself in financial difficulties, it may have to enter into special arrangements with its creditors, have a receiver appointed over its property by secured creditors, or be wound up by a liquidator appointed by either the court, its investors or creditors.

The body of company law contains a framework underpinning each of these internal and external legal relationships. The core policy objectives underlying company law seek, essentially, to protect two broad categories of interests, ie those of investors (internal) and creditors (external). One can, therefore, state succinctly the twin core aims of company law as being Investor Protection and Creditor Protection.

INVESTOR PROTECTION

2.6   In the 1850s, entrepreneurs were not satisfied solely with the introduction of a simpler procedure to register a company. They also sought, successfully, to have losses arising out of their investments (shares) in companies capped.

Limitation of liability

2.7   The most fundamental form of investor protection is the privilege of trading with limited liability. Investors (or shareholders) in companies registered under the Companies Acts were protected by having their liability for losses sustained in the event of the company collapsing limited to the amount (if any) unpaid on their shares. Thus, the most the shareholder would lose was the amount which he had invested in a company which failed. The advantage of this privilege has been underlined recently by the huge losses incurred by investors in Lloyd's Syndicates. These investors, called 'Names', invested without the privilege of limited liability. When the syndicates made very heavy trading losses, they were able to pass them on to their 'Names'.

The limitation of liability available to investors in registered companies, since 1855, has been most successful in protecting them against the type of Lloyd's Names scenario. As a general immunity for shareholders against claims made by company creditors, this fundamental form of investor protection has withstood the test of time. The concept of limited liability for investors in companies complying with certain conditions (eg that the company's name end with the word 'Limited' or 'Ltd') was introduced by the Limited Liability Act 1855.

In moving the Second Reading of the Limited Liability Bill in the House of Commons on 29 June 1855, a member (Mr Bouverie) said[1] in regard to the principle of limited liability for companies:

> 'All men must desire, on embarking in a Joint-stock Company, *that their liability for the acts of the directors should be limited to the amount they staked in the concern.* Joint-stock Companies ... differed from [partnerships] in as much as there did not exist in the one as in the other the same mutual knowledge and confidence among the partners, and in a Joint-stock Company although at a given time a shareholder might have the fullest confidence in the directors, yet the next day a new set might be put in, of whom the shareholder, who would be bound to the extent of his whole fortune by their acts, knew nothing.
>
> The proposal which the [member] had laid before the House was simply that such companies as chose to carry on concerns on that basis, *and to give notice to the public that they did so,* should be allowed to trade under limited liability.
>
> Many objections had been raised to the proposed plan. It was alleged that it would encourage fraud, and an hon. Friend had told him that the present Bill was a bill for promoting swindling. He thought that a great deal of misapprehension existed in the public mind with reference to fraud.
>
> One of the great objects of the law was to prevent fraud in the dealings between man and man; but it was the duty of the Legislature to prevent fraud, not by prohibiting a class of transactions, many of which were honest and advantageous to the public and the parties concerned, but by taking care that fraud, wherever it existed, should be detected and punished.
>
> Another objection raised against Joint-stock Companies was that they encouraged speculation. Now the word speculation had two very different meanings, according to the sense in which it was used. *In one sense it meant that spirit of enterprise and progress which had made the people of this country what they now were: but in its bad sense it meant rash and imprudent undertakings,* which ought never to have been commenced, or which had been improperly carried out. He did not think it was his duty as a legislator to prevent imprudence in commercial undertakings. The real preventive against imprudence was the loss which it entailed on the imprudent man; no security against it was so great as the punishment which the imprudent man brought on himself by committing it.' (author's emphasis)

From this speech during the Second Reading, it was obvious that the legislature did not consider it had a duty to prevent imprudence in commercial or business dealings.

Following the coming into force of the Limited Liability Act 1855, the intention of the legislature was also clearly expressed by the judiciary. In *Oakes v Turquand and Harding,*[2] Lord Cranworth reiterated that investors/members enjoyed immunity for the debts of their company, saying:

---

1 (1855) 139 *Hansard* 310 et seq.
2 (1876) LR 2 HL 325 (HL).

'There is no doubt that the direct remedy of a creditor is solely against the incorporated company. He has no dealing with any individual shareholder, and if he is driven to bring an action to enforce any right he may have acquired, he must sue the company, and not any of the members of whom it is composed.'

Similarly, Cotton LJ said in *Guinness v Land Corporation of Ireland*:[1]

'[Legislation] provides that in the case of a company limited by shares being wound up, no contribution shall be required from any member exceeding the [nominal] amount on the shares in respect of which he is liable as a present or past member ...'

Again, in the Commission of *Inland Revenue v Governor and Company of the Bank of Ireland*,[2] Murnaghan J stated:

'[In the absence of fraud or criminal activity] There is at common law no liability upon the members of a body corporate in respect of the debts and liability of the body corporate, and such liability in respect of the corporate *acts must be created by statute* ...' (author's addition).

The only erosion of the privilege of limited liability has been where the 'veil of incorporation' has been lifted. In these quite exceptional cases,[3] a court may be able to effectively ignore the investors' fundamental immunity and render them liable to the company creditors for contract debts or other personal obligations. For example, in *Re Aluminium Fabricators Ltd*,[4] O'Hanlon J stated:

'The privilege of limitation of liability which is afforded ... in relation to companies incorporated under the [1963] Act with limited liability, cannot be afforded to those who use a limited company as a cloak or shield beneath which they seek to operate a fraudulent system of carrying on business for their own personal enrichment and advantage.'

Price paid for limitation of liability

2.8   The price paid by investors for having their liability limited includes that of being debarred from taking any part in the day-to-day management of the company.

Whilst investors own the company, they are nonetheless, prohibited from managing it (as members) or negotiating contracts with third parties on the company's behalf. Thus, in company law, ownership and management diverge. These principles of company law are reflected in public companies where ownership is separate from management. However, for the over 95 per cent of all Irish companies which are private, the larger shareholders will also be directors. These member directors embrace two different relationships within the one person. For company law purposes, one has to distinguish and classify the actions of a member director into those exercised by him as a shareholder and those exercised as a director. Again, the formation of a registered company

---

1   (1882) 22 Ch D 349.
2   (1925) 2 IR 90.
3   See Chapter 6.
4   [1984] ILRM 399 (HC). See also Chapter 6 and the case of *Re Kelly's Carpetdrome Ltd*.

involves a formal registration procedure before the registrar issues the Certificate of Incorporation. Once registered, the company (acting through its directors) must comply with the provisions of the Companies Acts relating to publicity, maintenance of registers, submissions of returns and accounts, etc.

Other protections for investors

2.9 The whole idea of limited liability is clearly a fundamental protection for investors. However, the detailed provisions of the Companies Acts 1963 to 2001 give investors many more protections. These include protection against certain actions taken by fellow (majority) shareholders and by company directors.

In relation to resolutions at meetings, the basic rule in company law is majority control. A simple majority (51 per cent) of ordinary shareholders is normally sufficient to control most decisions taken at company general meetings. Nevertheless, even in such situations there are statutory protections for minority investors. These minority protections range from s 205[1] remedies in cases of oppression to s 10(3) rights of objecting to a change in the memorandum of association.

2.10 Indeed, the majority of shareholders may need protection more from the actions of the directors than from the other shareholders. Accordingly, there are many rules of company law which attempt to protect investors from the actions of directors in abusing their positions of power and of trust. For example, under s 298,[2] the court may compel any director who has misapplied or retained any property[3] of the company, or who has been guilty of any misfeasance or breach of trust, to repay or restore the property.

Again, directors may be liable to compensate investors who were induced to purchase shares in a public company by incorrect information in a prospectus.[4]

CREDITOR PROTECTION

2.11 Persons entering into trading contracts with, or lending[5] money to, the company are generally referred to as creditors.

In reality, a company is akin to a legally recognised 'front' permitting investors to become involved in the financing of trade. As a result, the policy underlying company law also builds into the legislation elements of protection for the creditors of registered companies.

There are, broadly, three aspects to creditor protection in company law. The first relates to the public nature of the memorandum and articles of association of registered companies. The second aspect is the protection company law

---

1 Of the 1963 Act. See Chapter 16.
2 Of the 1963 Act.
3 *Guinness v Land Corporation of Ireland* (1882) 22 Ch D 349.
4 See Chapter 10.
5 With or without security – see Part VIII.

gives to maintaining the integrity of a company's share capital fund, and the third is the power given to creditors to interfere in the management of a company which places their interests in jeopardy.

Let us now look briefly at the type of actual protection within these broad categories of creditor protection.

Public nature of constitutional documents

2.12   The constitutional documents of a company are its memorandum and articles of association. These are available for inspection by any persons trading with or lending money to the company. Reference to them would enable potential creditors to check basic information such as authorised capital and the company's objects before granting it credit.

Often, trade creditors do not avail themselves of the opportunity of checking a company's memorandum of association. Notwithstanding, s 8[1] and reg 6 of the European Communities (Companies) Regulations 1973[2] may protect them.

Maintenance of company's capital

2.13   The registrar will not issue a trading certificate to a public company until satisfied that its minimum capital requirements have been raised from the public.[3]

Company law aims to protect and maintain[4] the capital fund of the company so that it is available to meet the company's contractual obligations. The law does this by stipulating that capital may only be reduced if proper safeguards are in place.

Again, a company is only permitted to buy its own shares in a few exceptional cases. It is also restricted in the circumstances in which it can lend money to a third party to buy the (lending) company's shares.

2.14   The Companies (Amendment) Act 1983 introduced a minimum share capital for a public limited company. The amount of the minimum paid-up capital, effectively £7,500, is quite modest.

Under s 40 of the 1983 Amendment Act, where the net assets of the company are half, or less, of the amount of the company's called-up share capital, the directors must convene an extraordinary general meeting for the purpose of considering what measures, if any, should be taken to deal with the situation.

Laudable capital maintenance rules such as those outlined above lose much of their effectiveness when one realises that their impact, if any, on private companies, is minimal.

---

1 Of the Companies Act 1963.
2 SI 1973/163 – see Chapter 36.
3 See Chapters 10 and 11.
4 See Chapters 18 and 19.

Creditors' powers to intervene

2.15 The rights of creditors to liquidate the company are outlined in Chapter 1. Secured creditors have the power to appoint a receiver over the company's property.

Whilst creditors are not members of the company, and take no active part in the management of it, if the company is placed in receivership or is being wound up, *creditors are given more authority in controlling the company's affairs.* Examples include the power of the creditors to decide who becomes liquidator in a creditors' voluntary winding-up.[1]

Creditors' rights of recovery[2] against the company

2.16 If the company fails to pay any monies owing to a third party creditor, the latter's rights depend on whether his debt is secured or unsecured. The contract document under which a company acknowledges its indebtedness under a loan is called a *debenture*.[3]

Secured creditors

2.17 Debentures usually give a fixed and/or floating charge over the company's assets as security.

When a loan is made to a company, the debenture trust deed involved normally gives the lender the power to appoint a receiver (and, perhaps, manager) in the event of the company defaulting on its repayments. The power bestowed on a receiver and manager would include the right to sell the company's assets. Thus, a creditor secured by a fixed charge can realise his security and effectively remain outside of the company liquidation procedure.

Unsecured creditors

2.18 When an unsecured creditor is owed money by the company, he can petition for its winding up and seek to recover his debt from the company's liquidated assets. The problem such a creditor faces, however, is that there may not be monies realisable to pay his debts. This unsatisfactory situation arises because of the ranking of creditors' claims in a winding-up situation.

Ranking of creditors' claims

2.19 A *fixed* charge is a mortgage of land or fixed plant and machinery. The property must be identified and any necessary formalities for the creation of the charge must be observed. The company cannot sell the assets covered by a fixed charge without the consent of the debenture holder. However, the company can sell assets which are the subject of a *floating charge*. The latter

---

1 See Parts VIII and X B.
2 See Part VIII for a more detailed treatment.
3 The term 'debenture' may also be used to describe the loan itself.

charge is an equitable mortgage of a type of the company's assets, without specifying any particular items, eg stock in trade.

Priorities in a distribution

2.20 Holders of fixed charges are entitled to realise their security. If the realised security is insufficient to repay them, then they can prove for the shortfall as unsecured creditors in the liquidation.

After the holders of fixed charges have realised their security, the liquidator will pay the remaining company creditors in the following order:

(1) *preferential* creditors, eg arrears of rates, income tax, wages and salaries of employees, redundancy payments, etc;[1]
(2) creditors secured by *floating* charges;
(3) *unsecured* creditors.

If a surplus remains after paying the preferential creditors, those secured by floating charges would be paid. The unsecured creditors are only paid if monies remain after paying category (2) above. In many liquidations, it would be unlikely that assets existed to pay the unsecured creditors, who constitute the most vulnerable group of external interests.

Creditors' other rights of recovery

2.21 If one can use the phrase 'typical' liquidation, it might be said that, in such a case, not only would the unsecured creditors not be paid, but some or all of those holding floating charges, and even preferential creditors,[2] might also lose out. Because of these creditor losses, it would not be unusual to find creditors seeking avenues of redress other than the company's own assets.

The company investors are protected by the separate personality of the company and the veil of incorporation. Much of the case-law dealing with *lifting the veil* relates to company creditors seeking to overturn the investors' immunity for company debts. However, this is a rather limited 'window of opportunity'.

A more fertile source of legal redress, particularly since 1990, is an action against the company's managing agents, ie its directors and officers.

Significance of the two 1990 Acts

2.22 The Companies Act 1990 increased the scope of remedies available to creditors by extending significantly the legal liability of company officers. For example, the s 297[3] remedy of rendering directors liable for fraudulent trading, which had not proved very satisfactory in practice, was extended to make officers (and others) liable also for reckless trading.

---

1 See s 285 of the 1963 Act.
2 For example, the Revenue Commissioners are often cited as unpaid creditors when a company is liquidated.
3 Of the 1963 Act.

Again, s 204[1] renders any company officer liable for the debts of the company if proper books of account have not been kept.

2.23   Part VII of the 1990 Act introduces new preventative measures to protect potential company creditors, by providing for the making of Disqualification and Restriction Orders against directors.

Part V B focuses on the civil (and criminal) liabilities of company directors and officers.

Creditors' rights are dealt with in detail in Part VIII.

The Companies (Amendment) Act 1990, as amended, which preceded the 1990 Act, actually takes some rights away from creditors. It does this by allowing the appointment of an Examiner to delay the creditors (particularly secured creditors) from exercising their remedies against the company for a period of time.[2]

1 Of the 1990 Act.
2 See Part IX.

PART II

FUNDAMENTAL PRINCIPLES OF COMPANY LAW

Chapter 3

THE CONCEPT OF CORPORATE PERSONALITY

THE EFFECT OF INCORPORATION

3.1 When a company is formed, the effect of its incorporation is to create a distinct legal entity with rights and obligations quite separate from those possessed by its members (shareholders). One therefore has to consider the company as a separate person in its own right.

Separate legal personality of the company and the *Salomon* case

3.2 Whilst introduced in the early 19th century, the concept of corporate legal personality was not fully appreciated until the landmark case of *Salomon v Salomon & Co*,[1] in 1897.

Salomon developed a thriving business as a sole trader. He then converted it into a limited liability company, the shareholders being himself, his wife and their five children.[2] Salomon placed a value of £39,000 (approximately £1.4 million at 2000 values) on his business and received from the company as consideration for the sale of his business to it, cash, a debenture or secured loan of £10,000 and 20,001 £1 shares out of the issued capital of £20,007. Salomon's wife and children each held one of the remaining six £1 shares.[3]

An economic depression occurred in the boot and shoe trade in which Salomon & Co traded. To assist the company, Salomon borrowed money on the security of the debentures and lent it to the company. Despite this financial assistance, the company failed and was forced into liquidation.

Liquidator's contention

3.3 The liquidator of Salomon & Co claimed that the company was entitled to be indemnified by Salomon against all its unsecured liabilities because, he contended, the company was '*a mere nominee* and agent' of Salomon.

The liquidator was successful as far as the Court of Appeal. In *Broderip v Salomon*,[4] it was held that the company was the agent of Salomon, and therefore Salomon, as principal, was liable for the debts of his agent, the company.

---

1 [1897] AC 22.
2 At that time, a minimum of seven members was required.
3 Probably as Salomon's nominees.
4 [1895] 2 Ch 323.

The case on appeal

3.4 On appeal, the Court of Appeal upheld the decision against Salomon, suggesting that the company was a trustee holding the business in trust for Salomon. However, when Salomon appealed to the House of Lords, he won the case: their Lordships reversing unanimously the Court of Appeal decision.

In the House of Lords' judgment, Lord Macnaghten stated:

> 'The *Company is at law a different person altogether* from the [members] ... and, though it may be that after incorporation the business is precisely the same as it was before, and the same persons are managers, and the same hands receive the profits, the company is not in law the agent of the [members] or for them. *Nor are the [members] liable*, in any shape or form, except to the extent and in the manner provided by the Act.' (author's emphasis)

Essence of judgment

3.5 The House of Lords held, essentially, that Salomon & Co had been properly formed and was a separate legal person in its own right, despite the dominant position of Salomon within it.

As Salomon had paid for his shares in full by selling his business to the company, his liability to company creditors was discharged because the full nominal value of the company shares had been paid.

One-man companies

3.6 The company was not an 'alias' (or alter ego – other self) for Aaron Salomon, nor his agent or trustee. It was, in fact, a 'one-man' company. To quote from Lord Macnaghton's judgment again:

> 'It has become the fashion to call companies of this class "one man companies". This is taking a nickname, but it does not help one much in the way of argument. If it is intended to convey the meaning that a company which is under the absolute control of one person is not a company legally incorporated, although the requirements of the Act ... may have been complied with, it is inaccurate and misleading: if it merely means that there is a predominant partner possessing an overwhelming influence and entitled practically to the whole of the profits, there is nothing in that that I can see contrary to the true intention of the Act ... or against public policy, or detrimental to the interests of creditors. If the shares are fully paid up, it cannot matter whether they are in the hands of one or many. If the shares are not fully paid, it is as easy to gauge the solvency of an individual as to estimate the financial ability of a crowd ...'

Salomon's case established that corporate legal personality would be recognised even when one shareholder effectively controlled the company and had himself decided on the value of assets used to pay for his shares.

Lord Halsbury LC stated:

> 'It seems to me impossible to dispute that once a company is legally incorporated it *must be treated like any other independent person* with its rights and liabilities

appropriate to itself, and that *the motives of those who took part in the promotion of the company are absolutely irrelevant* in discussing what those rights and liabilities are.' (author's emphasis)

The motivation of the company promoters became an issue in *Roundabout Ltd v Beirne*. Again, the courts will not allow corporate form to be used to evade a person's contractual liabilities – see **3.12** and Chapter 6.

Subsequent case-law

3.7 The principle *that a company is a legal person separate and distinct from its members*, emanating from the *Salomon* case, was applied by the Privy Council, in 1960.

In *Lee v Lee's Air Farming Ltd*,[1] Lee held 2,999 shares in the company: his wife held the remaining share. Lee was killed in an air crash whilst working for the company. Mrs Lee claimed statutory[2] workman's compensation for injuries to her husband whilst an employee of the company. It was disputed on the grounds that Lee and Lee's Air Farming Ltd were the same person.

The Privy Council applied the *Salomon* case and held that Lee was a separate person from the company he formed. Accordingly, Mrs Lee was entitled to compensation.

3.8 In *Battle v Irish Art Promotion Centre Ltd*,[3] the managing director, a major shareholder in the company, sought to represent the company in legal proceedings. The Supreme Court held that he had no authority to represent the company in legal proceedings, O'Dalaigh CJ stating:

'One sympathises with the purpose which the [managing director] has in mind, ... to safeguard his business reputation; but, as the law stands, he cannot as major shareholder and Managing Director now substitute his persona for that of the company.'

3.9 More recently, in the case of *Irish Permanent Building Society v Registrar of Building Societies and Irish Life Building Society*,[4] the fundamental principle of separate corporate personality was again applied by Barrington J. The principle has clearly received judicial recognition in the Irish jurisdiction.[5]

3.10 Despite the clarification of a company's separate legal personality in the *Salomon* case, up to 1980 the better legal opinion was that a registered company could not be granted a liquor licence: such a licence having to be held by a (human) nominee.

---

1 [1960] 3 All ER 420.
2 Under the New Zealand Workman's Compensation Act 1922.
3 [1968] IR 252. A decision repeated by the Supreme Court in *DBP Construction Ltd & Ors v I.C.C.* (Unreported) 21 May 1998.
4 [1981] ILRM 242. See also *Gresham's Industries Ltd (In Liquidation) v Cannon* (Unreported) 2 July 1980.
5 See the article by G. McCormack 'Judicial Application of Salomon's Case in Ireland', *Law Society Gazette*, May 1984, at pp 97–100.

In *McMahon v Murtagh Properties Ltd*,[1] Barrington J found that the practice of companies holding their licences through nominees had no basis in sound logic. Accordingly, he concluded:

> 'First, a limited liability company is entitled itself to hold its licence without resorting to the device of having a nominee. Secondly, it is not incorrect to refer to the nominee as being the "holder" of the licence as long as it is remembered that the company is the beneficial and as previously indicated, the real holder of the licence. The nominee must comply with all legal instructions of the company in relation to the licence and he is, in effect, no more than a peg on which the company finds it convenient to hang its licence. This being so, if the company, through its agents, breaks the law in the running of the business, it is at all times liable as the holder of the licence. The nominee, provided he does no more than hold the licence, commits no offence, but if the nominee is also the manager of the business or if he assists in the commission of the offence, then he may be liable for aiding and abetting the company as a holder of the licence, notwithstanding that he is a nominal "holder" himself.'[2]

Importance of the Salomon *decision*

3.11   The *Salomon* case was very significant in that it finally established the legality of the 'one-man' company and showed that incorporation was available to small businesses as well as to large enterprises. Nevertheless, the decision causes some concern because it demonstrated how it was possible to limit, not merely money invested in the company, but also how to reduce the speculative risk by loaning money to the company (by debenture) rather than investing in more shares.

The main consequence of incorporation for a registered company is that it becomes a legal person distinct from its members. A registered company is therefore a legalised 'front' through which the company owners (its investors) can trade. Because the separate legal personality of the company acts as a bar to outsiders (eg company creditors) taking action against its investors, commentators have likened this personality to a 'veil'.

THE VEIL OF INCORPORATION

3.12   The corporate personality is often likened to a veil; the idea being that investors are shielded from legal actions behind this 'veil of incorporation'. The case of *The Roundabout Ltd v Beirne*[3] illustrates the protection given to members by the veil of incorporation.

Marian Park Inn Ltd was a public house trading in Dublin using non-union staff. During May 1958, all the staff joined a union. As a result of this action, the company's three directors closed the premises and dismissed the staff. The union then picketed the premises.

---

1   [1982] ILRM 342.
2   The criminal liability of companies is dealt with in Chapter 5.
3   [1959] IR 423 at p 426.

One month later, a new company re-opened the bar premises. This new company was The Roundabout Ltd. Its directors included the three former directors of the Marian Park Inn Ltd. The new company sought an injunction against the union to prevent them picketing the premises whilst used by The Roundabout Ltd. It was argued in favour of the injunction that the business was being conducted by a new legal person and the union had no trade dispute with The Roundabout Ltd. Dixon J agreed and granted the injunction against the union picketing, commenting:

> 'Each company is what is known as a legal person. I have to regard the two companies as distinct in the same way as I would regard two distinct [human] individuals.

McCormack[1] criticises this decision as being a case where legal technicalities were allowed to prevail over industrial relations and common sense, pointing out that Lord Denning had viewed with suspicion the notion that statutory provisions governing industrial disputes could be eroded in this fashion.

Lord Denning was prepared to consider lifting the veil of incorporation in such circumstances – see Chapter 6.[2]

Company ownership and management

3.13 An important implication of separate corporate personality and the veil of incorporation is that company law draws a clear distinction between ownership and management. The shareholders or investors own the company. In doing so, they are protected against the company's creditors by the veil of incorporation. However, because of this protection, shareholders are not entitled (as investors) to take part in the management of their company, nor to enter into contracts on its behalf.

Investors elect directors to manage their company. In practice, a large shareholder may also be a director and take part in the management of the company. In such instances, however, the management tasks are undertaken by virtue of that person's role as director, not because he is (also) an investor.

This divergence of ownership and management reinforces the principle of limited liability for company investors by restricting their roles essentially to the passive one of contributing capital and the election of company officers to manage the enterprise.[3]

---

1 G. McCormack 'Judicial Application of Salomon's Case in Ireland', *Law Society Gazette*, May 1984, at p 98. See also **6.35**.
2 Since the European Communities (Safeguarding of Employees' Rights on Transfer of Undertakings) Regulations 1980, SI 1980/306; incorporation may not now be used to evade responsibility under collective agreements in a takeover situation – see **48.21**.
3 See Parts IV A–D.

Company ownership and management

Chapter 4

LIMITED LIABILITY AND THE CONSEQUENCES OF INCORPORATION

INTRODUCTION

4.1 Section 18(2) of the Companies Act 1963 provides that:

'from the date of incorporation mentioned in the certificate of incorporation, the subscribers of the memorandum, together with such other persons as may from time to time become members of the company, shall be a body corporate with the name contained in the memorandum, capable forthwith of exercising all the functions of an incorporated company, and having perpetual succession and a common seal, *but with such liability on the part of the members* to contribute to the assets of the company in the event of it being wound up as is mentioned in [ss 5 and 6 of] this Act ...' (author's emphasis)

Section 18(2) of the Companies Act 1963 therefore encapsulates the two fundamental principles of company law, ie separate legal personality of the company and limitation of liability for its members.

Having already explained the meaning of the separate/legal personality of the company in Chapter 3, and the concept of limited liability in Chapter 2, this section will now focus more precisely on the meaning of limitation of liability and the main consequences of incorporation.

Meaning of limited liability

4.2 A shareholder's fundamental protection is contained in the memorandum of association. For example, clause 3 of the model memorandum in Table B provides that the liability of the members is limited.

The meaning of limited liability for members of a company limited by shares[1] is defined in s 5(2) of the 1963 Act as being 'the amount, if any, unpaid on the shares held by them'.

Under s 381 of the 1963 Act, as amended by s 98 of the 2001 Act, any person who trades under a name or title of which 'Ltd' or 'Teo' is the last word shall, unless duly incorporated with limited liability, be guilty of a criminal offence.

4.3 The previous chapter illustrates how the investors in a company are immune from liability for the debts of a company which they own. However, complete immunity from liability is not permitted. Each investor is liable to be called upon to contribute the full nominal value of his shares if they are not already fully paid up. If a shareholder has agreed to pay more than the nominal value, then his liability is limited to the amount he has agreed to pay.

---

1 See s 6(3) for the extent of the liability of a member in a company limited by guarantee.

For example, suppose Alpha Ltd issues 100p shares and X invests in them. If X pays 100p for each share, then that is the limit of his liability. Again, suppose Alpha issued the shares below par value, say at 50p paid per share. If Y bought 5,000 of these shares – an investment of £2,500 – then in the event of Alpha Ltd's liquidation, Y could be called upon to contribute a further £2,500 to the liquidated company's assets – but no more.

The liability of an investor may be limited either by share or by guarantee.

Memorandum of association and limitation of liability

4.4   Section 6(2) of the Companies Act 1963 provides that the memorandum of association of a company limited by shares or by guarantee must also state that the liability of its members is limited.

In addition, the memorandum of a company limited by guarantee must state that each member undertakes to contribute to the assets of the company, in the event of its being wound up while he is a member, for payment of the debts and liabilities of the company contracted before he ceases to be a member,[1] such amount as may be required, not exceeding a specified amount.

In the case of a company having a share capital, the memorandum of association is also required, unless the company is an unlimited company, to state the amount of share capital with which the company proposes to be registered, and its division into shares of a fixed amount.

Effect of registration of a company

4.5   On the registration of the memorandum of a company, the registrar will certify that the company is incorporated and, in the case of a limited company, that the company is limited.

Since this liability is limited to the amount unpaid on any shares, and as most shares are issued fully paid, shareholders generally incur no liability for the debts of the company.

OTHER CONSEQUENCES OF INCORPORATION

4.6   The other effects of separate corporate personality are set out below.

A company can sue and be sued in its own name

4.7   A company[2] can enter into trading and other *contracts* and be liable under them. (See Chapters 36 to 38.)

---

1 Or within one year after he ceases to be a member.
2 It is the company which is entitled to sue, not its shareholders – see *McSweeney v Burke* (Unreported) 24 November 1980.

A company can also sue for any *torts* committed against it.[1] It is also responsible for torts committed by it. Because of the non-human or artificial nature of a company, responsibility in tort will usually devolve through vicarious liability. Vicarious liability arises when one person is held liable in law for the actions of another. Vicarious liability in tort usually arises where an employer is held responsible for negligent acts committed by his employees in the course of their employment. A principal may also be liable for torts committed by his agents.

There are limits to the degree to which companies can incur vicarious liability under criminal law. As Viscount Reading CJ stated in *Mousell Bros Ltd v London & North Western Rly Co*,[2] 'it may be the intention of Parliament ... to impose [such] a liability upon a principal [company]. Many statutes are passed with this object'.

At common law, the (tortious) doctrine of vicarious liability does not generally[3] apply to criminal actions by company employees.

The criminal liabilities of companies and their employees are dealt with in Chapter 5; while the criminal liabilities of directors are considered in Chapter 31.

A company can own property

4.8 One major advantage of incorporation is that the property of the company can be distinguished from that of its members. Company property is owned by the company. Members have no proprietary interests in it.

4.9 In *Macaura v Northern Assurance*,[4] a majority shareholder was owed money by the Irish Canadian Sawmill Co Ltd, Skibbereen, County Cork. As a precaution, he insured a company stock of timber against loss. A fire occurred and the member claimed from the insurance company involved. They refused to pay him, on the grounds that he had no insurable interest.[5]

The House of Lords held that the insurers were entitled to repudiate the claim, Lord Sumner commenting:

> 'It is clear that the applicant had no insurable interest in the timber provided. It was not his. It belonged to the [company] ... [The appellant] owned almost all the shares in the company, and the company owed him a good deal of money, but, neither as creditor or shareholder, could he insure the company's assets ... His relation was to the company, not to its goods, and after the fire he was directly prejudiced by the paucity of the company's assets, not by the fire.'

---

1 It is the company itself which is entitled to sue, not its shareholders – see *McSweeney v Burke* (Unreported) 24 November 1980.

2 [1917] 2 KB 836.

3 But a company may be vicariously liable for the crime of public nuisance at common law – see *R v Great North of England Railway Co* [1843] 3 QB 315.

4 [1925] AC 619, [1925] All ER Rep 51, 59 ILTR 45.

5 A financial involvement necessary to acquire legal rights under an insurance contract.

4.10   A more recent case where the insurance of company property by a shareholder was raised as a defence by an insurance company is *P.J. Carrigan Ltd and P.J. Carrigan v Norwich Union Fire Insurance Society Ltd and Scottish Union and National Insurance Company Ltd (No 2).*[1] These insurers contended that the premises insured by them were owned by the first plaintiff, P.J. Carrigan Ltd (the company), whilst the insured person was the second plaintiff, P.J. Carrigan, who had no insurable interest in the property.

The facts in this case were complex and detailed. However, the result was a finding against the insurers, Lynch J stating:

> '... my findings that the second plaintiff is the insured and has an insurable interest ... involves a rejection of the plaintiff's case and of the second plaintiff's evidence that the Company is the insured and was also the sole owner of the Glebe [the insured property].'

Even though the decision went against the insurance company, it did so on evidential grounds. Accordingly, because of Lynch J's comments it would seem that the principle of separate company ownership of property, reinforced by the *Macaura* decision, is still good law in Ireland. However, it may need refining in the light of a Canadian judgment.

4.11   In *Constitution Insurance Co of Canada et al v Kosmopoulos et al,*[2] the respondent (K), on the advice of his solicitor, incorporated his business in order to protect his financial assets.

Even though the business was then carried on through the company, K always thought he owned the business and its assets. Almost all the documentation required in running the business, including bank accounts, sales tax payments and telephone accounts, made no reference to the company. Instead the business was referred to as 'Kosmopoulos carrying on business as Spring Leather goods'.

The lease of the premises occupied by the company was in the name of Kosmopoulos and not the company. The premises were damaged by fire. K claimed from his insurers. The appellant insurers refused to indemnify K under his fire insurance policy, because K did not have an insurable interest in the company's property.

The person named as the insured in the fire policy was 'Kosmopoulos o/a Spring Leather Goods'. When the policy was being effected, the insurance agent was aware that K was transacting his business by means of an incorporated company.

In 1983, Ontario's Court of Appeal had summarised the issue thus:[3]

> '... the Supreme Court of Canada had accepted the rule in *Macaura* only to the extent that it needed to do to decide the case of *Guarantee Co of North America v Aqua –Land Exploration Ltd* (SCC 1966), ie that one shareholder in three had no

---

1 (Unreported) 11 December 1987 (HC).
2 (1987) 22 CCCL 1 296.
3 (1983) 1 CCCL 1 83.

insurable interest in the assets of the corporation. Therefore, the issue of whether a sole shareholder had an insurable interest ... remained open in (that) Province.'

The court then granted the insurers leave to appeal to the Supreme Court, K already having won his case in the state courts below.

The Supreme Court examined the three public policies underlying the requirement of an insurable interest in insurance contracts.[1] These policies were:

(1) **The policy against wagering**. The court concluded that the *Macaura* principle was an imperfect tool to further public policy against wagering;
(2) **Indemification for loss**. The Court felt that the *Macaura* case actually illustrated how the indemnity principle was poorly implemented by the current definition of the insurable (financial) interest requirement in insurance contract law; and
(3) **Destruction of the insured property**. Under this policy, the Court took the view that the objective of minimising an insured's incentive to (fraudulently) destroy the insured property could not be seriously advanced as an argument in support of the *Macaura* principle. Consequently, the Supreme Court held that K, as *sole shareholder* in the company, had an insurable interest in its property capable of supporting the fire insurance policy. Accordingly, Kosmopoulos was entitled to be indemnifed under the insurance policy for the fire loss.

Company assets

4.12 It is indisputable that all assets of the company are the property of the company and a shareholder, even a controlling one, cannot simply help himself to the company's cash. As a result, a managing director, even though he may own 99 per cent of the company's shares, cannot lawfully:

(1) lodge cheques payable to the company into his own bank account; nor
(2) draw cheques to meet his own personal expenditure on the company's bank account.

In *A L Underwood Ltd v Bank of Liverpool & Martins Ltd*,[2] A.L. Underwood was the controlling shareholder of A L Underwood Ltd. On occasions Mr Underwood indorsed cheques payable to the company to himself and lodged them into his personal bank account.

The Court found the bank involved was liable for conversion to A L Underwood Ltd, because it was put on enquiry and failed to distinguish between Mr Underwood, in his personal capacity, and the company.

The suspicious circumstances in this case meant that the defendant bank was not entitled to rely on the rule in *Royal British Bank v Turquand* (see Chapter 37).

---

1 For a full review of this case see M.G. Baer and J.A. Rendell (eds) *Cases on the Canadian Law of Insurance* (Carswell, Thompson Professional Publishing, 5th edn, 1995), at Chapter 3.
2 [1924] 1 KB 775 (CA).

4.13 A further extension of company ownership is the idea that controlling shareholders can be guilty of stealing from their company. In *R v Philippou*,[1] the facts were as follows.

The two directors and shareholders of Sunny Tours Ltd had withdrawn £369,000 from the company's account to buy themselves a property in Spain. The company later went into liquidation, owing creditors £11.5 million.

In defence against a charge of stealing from the company, the accused shareholders pleaded that, since they were the sole owners of the company and, through their shareholdings, the sole owners of all its property, they could not be guilty of, in effect, stealing from themselves. When they gave instructions to the bank to transfer money to Spain, the instructions were those of the company, so the company had consented to the transfer in the sense that such a transfer could not be said to be adverse to any right of the company.

The court disagreed with these arguments put forward by the accused, pointing out that:

> 'The order to the bank is only one part of a composite transaction. The other component is the fact that the money was being used to put the block of flats into the pockets of the appellant and Panayides through the Spanish company. That component was the fact from which the jury could infer not only that the transaction was dishonest, but was intended to deprive Sunny Tours permanently of its money. There was no "consent" by the company on which the appellant (one of the defendants had fallen ill and the appellant was the remaining shareholder/director) can rely. His position is not improved by substituting "authority" for consent. Once the two components are put together, the drawing of the money from the bank is shown to be adverse to the rights of the company and there was an appropriation.'

Thus, the separate personality of a company may be recognised in criminal law to the extent that a controlling shareholder can be convicted of stealing from his own company (see Chapter 5 for the extent to which companies can themselves commit criminal offences).

A company can employ people

4.14 A company can not only employ human agents, it can also employ its controlling shareholders as its managing director – see *Lee v Lee's Air Farming Limited* in **3.7**.

4.15 In *Sweeney v Duggan*,[2] it has been suggested[3] that because a controlling shareholder and manager of a one-man company could be regarded as having an insurable interest in the company's own assets, he may have a financial duty to effect employer's liability insurance for the company's unskilled and

---

1 (1989) 89 Cr App R 290 (CA).
2 (1997) 2 IR 531.
3 By M. Forde in *Cases and Materials on Irish Company Law* (Round Hall, Sweet and Maxwell, 2nd edn, 1988), at p 98 – the case of *Constitution Insurance Co of Canada* is cited as authority – see **4.11**.

non-union employees, when the company's finances are in a perilous state at the time of an accident.

The writer considers this suggestion a step too far.

The traditional purpose in seeking to give a controlling shareholder an insurable interest in the company's assets was essentially to enable that person to benefit from insurances effected by them on the company's property (mistakenly) in their own name, rather than in the name of the company itself. Insurable interest as a concept has no place in tort law.

In a case such as *Sweeney v Duggan*, the question of a duty to insure employees on behalf of the company should be considered on the basis of the company owner's position as its (managing agent) director; not *qua* his position as controlling shareholder(owner).[1]

References to the principle of insurable interest should be confined to insurance contract law matters only.

A company has perpetual succession

4.16 A company, being an artificial person, does not die when its human members expire. What happens, in these circumstances, is that the deceased member's shares pass, as part of his estate, to the beneficiaries named in his will. If the member leaves no will, the shares pass as part of his property according to the rules of intestate succession.

Because a company exists until it is wound up, property, once transferred to the company, remains the property of the company.

Again, because the company never dies, no question of death duties on real property will arise. Furthermore, any change in company investors will have no effect on company property as it is owned by the company, and not its shareholders.

Formation of a company may increase potential borrowing opportunities

4.17 A company, by owning property, also has the power to borrow money by mortgaging that property. In particular, a company can give, as security, a floating charge[2] over its stock-in-trade. This is a facility not available to sole traders and partnerships.

A floating charge is one that is linked to any or all of the company's assets of a certain type, but not to any specific item.

---

1 Thus preserving the distinction between company management and ownership – see **3.13**.
2 See Chapters 39–41.

Incorporation facilitates the transfer of investors' interests

4.18 Shares are items of property. Where a company has transferable shares, ownership of the company can be changed or divided without affecting the company itself. Similarly, the death of an investor will not affect the company (see **4.16**).

Taxation implications

4.19 Whilst the company is viewed in law like a human legal person, it is treated differently to sole traders, and partnerships, for taxation purposes.

Companies are taxed on the whole of their trading profits (and capital gains) under a single rate of corporation tax.[1] Income tax is payable on the fees and salaries of directors, who can claim refunds of certain Pay Related Social Insurance (PRSI) contributions.[2] Income tax is also payable on profits distributed to shareholders in the form of dividends.

Companies controlled by five or fewer shareholders or participators who are directors, are known as 'close' companies. The provisions in taxation law for the apportionment of certain income of close[3] companies have the effect of lifting the veil of incorporation and rendering their shareholders subject to extra personal taxation.

The detailed provisions of corporate taxation law are outside the scope of this work.[4] Promoters should, therefore, avail themselves of professional taxation advice before proceeding to form a company. However, as a general rule, the larger the scale of the business enterprise to be started, the greater the probability that taxation advantages will favour trading by means of a company. Once a certain scale of operational size has been reached, use of the corporate form becomes almost a practical necessity. In fact, in the case of a large group of companies, the trading losses of group members may be offset against the profits of others – thereby reducing the overall taxation liability of the group as a whole. This taxation treatment of companies within a group is yet another example of the veil of incorporation being lifted – this time clearly for the benefit of the shareholders of the holding company.

The question of company residence is critical for taxation purposes.[5] In *De Beers Consolidated Mines Ltd v Howe*,[6] Lord Loreburn stated:

---

1 Certain manufacturing companies may be entitled to a reduced rate of corporation tax under s 38 of the Finance Act 1980, as amended.
2 As a result, they are entitled to reduced social security benefits.
3 See Chapter 6.
4 See G. Saunders *Tolley's Taxation in the Republic of Ireland 1996/97* (Tolley Publishing Co Ltd, 1996); A. Moore (ed) *Tax Acts, 1996–97* (Butterworth (Ireland) Ltd), and B. Giblin and S. Keegan (eds) *Irish Tax Reports (1922–1996)* (Butterworth (Ireland) Ltd, 1997).
5 See S. Nolan 'Dual Resident Companies' (1988) 121 (3148), *Taxation Journal* 120, at pp 120–124.
6 [1906] AC 455.

'A company resides, for the purposes of tax, where its real business is carried on ... and the real business is carried on where central management and control actually resides.'

However, in *John Hood and Co Ltd v Magee*,[1] the court held that a company was controlled, and thus resident, at the place where its AGM took place, rather than at the place where its managing director resided.

---

1 [1918] 2 IR 34.

Chapter 5

ASCRIBING CRIMINAL LIABILITY TO COMPANIES

5.1   One of the consequences of incorporation mentioned in Chapter 4 was that a company can employ human agents. In terms of civil wrongs committed by a company's employees, there has been no particular problem in rendering employer companies vicariously liable for torts committed by employees[1] in the course of their employment. The position is different in criminal law.

5.2   To commit a crime, one must generally have displayed 'mens rea' (guilty intention or mind). Because the company has no mind of its own, difficulties have arisen in ascribing criminal responsibility to companies.

In *Lennard's Carrying Co Ltd v Asiatic Petroleum Co Ltd*,[2] Viscount Haldane LC stated:

> 'A corporation is an abstraction. It has no mind of its own any more than it has a body of its own; its active and directing will must consequently be sought in the person of somebody who for some purposes may be called an agent, *but who is really the directing mind and will of the corporation*, the very ego and centre of the personality of the corporation.' (author's emphasis)

The 'directing mind and will' doctrine was invoked by distinguishing between a person who was 'merely a servant or agent' from someone whose knowledge (and actions) were those of the company itself. Viscount Haldane LC explained that the person representing the directing mind and will of a company may be under the direction of the shareholders in general meeting; or it may be the board of directors itself; or it may be, and in some companies it is so, that the person has an authority co-ordinate with the board of directors given to him under the articles of association, and is appointed by the general meeting of the company, and can only be removed by the general meeting of the company.

Viscount Haldane was essentially suggesting that to find out or determine what a company, a non-human legal person, thinks, knows or intends, one must identify the 'directing mind and will of the company'. This judgment led to the development of an 'identification' theory.

THE IDENTIFICATION THEORY

5.3   Originally, it was considered that a company could not be charged with an offence requiring proof of a criminal state of mind (mens rea).[3] This position changed following the case of *DPP v Kent and Sussex Contractors Ltd*.[4] As a result

---

1 And, indeed, its other agents.
2 [1915] AC 705.
3 See *Pearks, Dunston and Tee Ltd v Ward* [1902] 2 KB 1.
4 [1944] KB 146, [1944] 1 All ER 119.

of the court's decision in this case, it was held that the identification theory could be used to impute criminal intention to a corporate body. Identification theory was also applied in *Moore v I Bressler Ltd*,[1] where the company secretary and a branch sales manager who had made improper purchase tax returns were identified as agents of the company for the purpose of attributing criminal liability to it; the mens rea of the relevant employees being that of the company. As Macnaghten J said in *DPP v Kent and Sussex Contractors Ltd*:

> 'it is true that a corporation can only have knowledge and form an intention through its human agents, but circumstances may be such that the knowledge and intention of the agent must be imputed to the body corporate'.

Generally, the officers are considered to be the company for the purpose of imputing mens rea and corporate criminal liability.

In this case, the agent/employee whose criminal conduct was imputed to the company was its transport manager. He had signed a false statement of the distance that had been travelled by one of the company's vehicles.

In *Tesco Supermarkets Ltd v Nattrass*,[2] Lord Reid said:

> 'A human person has a mind which can have knowledge or intention or be negligent and he has hands to carry out his intentions. A corporation has none of these; it must act through human persons, though not always one or the same person. Then the person who acts is not speaking or acting, for the company ... *He is an embodiment of the company ... and his mind is that of the company.* If it is a guilty mind, then that guilt is the guilt of the company.' (author's emphasis)

5.4 The identification[3] theory or doctrine was based upon the idea that the person and personality of a body corporate could be identified with persons who, to cite Viscount Haldane LC, were its 'directing mind and will'.

In *El Ajou v Dollar Land Holdings plc*,[4] Lord Hoffmann commented on Viscount Haldane's analysis thus:

> 'Viscount Haldane LC ... regarded the identification of the directing mind as primarily a constitutional question, depending in the first instance upon the powers entrusted to a person by the articles of association. A person held out by the company as having plenary authority or in whose exercise of such authority the company acquiesces, may be treated as its directing mind.
>
> It is well known that Viscount Haldane LC derived the concept of the "directing mind" from German law which distinguishes between the agents and organs of the company. A German company with limited liability (GmbH) is required by law to appoint one or more directors (*Geschäftsführer*). They are the company's organs and for legal purposes represent the company. The knowledge of any one director, however obtained, is the knowledge of the company. English law has never taken the view that the knowledge of a director is ipso facto imputed to the company. Unlike the German *Geschäftsführer*, an English director may, as an individual, have no powers whatever. But English law shares the view of German law that whether a

---

1 [1944] KB 551.
2 [1972] AC 153.
3 Also referred to as the 'alter ego' doctrine.
4 [1994] 2 All ER 685 (CA).

person is an organ or not depends upon the extent of the powers which in law he has express of implied authority to exercise on behalf of the company.'

The Supreme Court of Canada in *Canadian Dredge & Dock Co v The Queen*[1] explained that:

> 'the identification theory was inspired in order to find some pragmatic, acceptable middle ground which would see a corporation under the umbrella of the criminal law ... but which would not saddle the corporation with the criminal wrongs of all its employees and agents'.

5.5 Lord Hoffmann also articulated the agency test, whereby the knowledge of an agent can be imputed to his principal (the company). The aspects of agency law relevant to companies are outlined in Chapter 37.

Limits to the identification theory

5.6 The identification theory does not seek to attribute criminal liability to a company for the acts of all its employees. The theory is probably limited to the directing minds and wills of company officers at the apex of the corporate structure. But statutory provisions may provide otherwise,

Viscount Reading CJ stated in *Mousell Bros Ltd v London & North-Western Rly Co:*[2]

> 'Prima facie, a master is not to be made criminally liable for the acts of his servant to which the master is not a party. But it may be the intention of Parliament ... To impose (such) a liability upon a principal (company). Many statutes are passed with the object.'

Staughton LJ summarised this confusing aspect of criminal law in *Tesco Stores Ltd v Brent London Borough Council*[3] thus:

> '*Tesco Supermarkets Ltd v Nattrass* [1972] AC 153 was, as it seems to me, concerned with three topics. The first was the general rule as to criminal liability of a corporate body. In the ordinary way a company is not guilty of a crime unless the criminal conduct and the guilty mind exist not merely in a servant or agent of the company of junior rank but in those who truly manage its affairs. Statutes may and sometimes do provide otherwise. There are offences for which, in derogation of the general rule, a company may incur liability through the behaviour of its servants.

> Secondly, it was evident in *Tesco Supermarkets Ltd v Nattrass* that the offence in question there was one which could be committed by a company through one of its junior employees acting on its behalf. Otherwise there would have been no need to consider whether the company could rely on a defence which the statute provided ... [s 24 of the Trade Descriptions Act 1968] for the vicarious liability of the company for an employee ...

> The third point considered in *Tesco Supermarkets Ltd v Nattrass*, which was critical to the decision, was that s 24 of the 1968 Act was concerned with the conduct of the

---

1 [1985] 1 SCR 662.
2 [1917] 2 KB 836 (see also offences of strict criminal liability in **5.26**).
3 [1993] 2 All ER 718, [1993] 1 WLR 1037.

company itself by those who managed its business. The "person charged" in the section clearly meant the company. The words "he", "himself" and "his" meant the company by its directing mind and will.'

When the board of directors act, this will generally be seen as the act of the company. However, when company powers are delegated to individuals, it is more difficult to classify their actions categorically as being those of the company. It depends on the amount of authority which has been delegated to the company's manager. In *The Lady Gwendolin*[1] it was held that the marine superintendent, to whom the assistant managing director had designated 'all the relevant powers of control' over the operation of the company's ships, was deemed to be its directing mind.

5.7 Generally, in the aftermath of *Tesco Supermarkets v Nattrass*, the directing mind and will limitation on imputing mens rea to bodies corporate seemed to be revitalised. Therefore one would only have expected the criminal conduct of persons at the apex of the corporate hierarchy to be imputed to the company.

In practice, for large corporations, the gap between the directing minds and operational levels within the organisation may be so great that it makes it difficult, if not unjust, to impute mens rea to the company or corporation.

The significance of company size

5.8 The significance of company size to the attribution of criminal liability under the identification theory was illustrated in the case of *R v Alcinder and Ors.*[2] Here, the company and two senior managers were charged with manslaughter arising out of the capsizing of the ferry *Herald of Free Enterprise* off Zeebrugge on 6 March 1987 with the loss of 192 lives. The trial judge directed an acquittal of the company and its senior managers because it had not been proved that the latter (and by imputation, the company) had been reckless in causing the deaths.

5.9 Similarly, in *R v P&O European Ferries (Dover) Ltd,*[3] an indictment against five senior managers, also in respect of the *Herald of Free Enterprise* disaster, was rejected on the grounds that the prosecution were unable to prove that any single one of the managers had the mens rea necessary to be guilty of the crime alleged and accordingly the necessary mens rea could not be attributed to the company. However, the court did hold that it was possible to bring a charge of corporate manslaughter. Manslaughter is not restricted to when one human kills another.

5.10 The first ever conviction in England and Wales of a company for manslaughter suggests that company size is relevant to criminal liability. The

---

1 [1965] 2 All ER 283.
2 (Unreported) 19 October 1990, English Central Criminal Court.
3 (1991) 93 Cr App R 73. But see M. Childs 'Medical manslaughter and corporate liability' (1999) 19 LS 316.

implication of the decision in *R v OLL Ltd*[1] is that it is easier to secure a conviction against a small company because the directing mind is more likely to be involved in the actual management and operation of the company business.

In *R v OLL Ltd*, a group of secondary school students were sent on a canoeing trip with totally inadequate supervision and organisation. Four of them drowned. The company was found guilty of manslaughter; the mens rea of its managing director being attributed to it. The company was fined £60,000[2] and the managing director jailed for three years.

5.11   Following the decision in *Tesco Supermarkets Ltd v Nattrass* in 1972, when a local store manager was considered senior enough to impute mens rea to his employer the company, doubts were raised as to which person in an organisation constituted its 'directing mind and will'.

A refinement and expansion of the identification theory in more recent court decisions has resulted in the growth of the doctrine of attribution.

THE ATTRIBUTION DOCTRINE

5.12   In *Re Supply of Ready Mixed Concrete (No 2)*,[3] the court was not prepared to absolve a company from criminal liability because its senior management had expressly banned a statutory prohibition which was then breached by its employees. The court felt that the purpose of the statutory prohibition would be frustrated if a company were not held liable for (unlawful) agreements entered into by its employees in the course of their employment, which ignored the statutory ban.

5.13   The principle of reaching below the organisational levels of a company's senior management (directing mind), which emerged in the *Ready Mixed Concrete* case, was subsequently confirmed and rationalised in *Meridian Global Funds Management Asia Ltd v Securities Commission*.[4] This decision has significantly widened the circumstances in which the knowledge of a company's officers or agents are imputed, or attributed, to it.

In the *Meridian* case, the company argued that its failure to notify certain transactions to the Securities Commission was caused by a junior executive who was not part of the company's directing mind and will. Consequently, mens rea should not be imputed to the company.

The court rejected this argument, Lord Hoffmann stating that:

> 'the correct approach was to determine how the criminal statute was intended to be applied to corporations which would involve a consideration of the underlying policy grounds of the statute. In this case, the legislation sought rapid notification

---

1   (Unreported) 8 December 1995. The sentence of three years' imprisonment, imposed on the managing director, was reduced, on appeal, to two years – see *R v Kite* (1996) 2 Cr App R (S) 295.
2   Virtually all its assets.
3   [1995] 1 All ER 135, [1995] 1 AC 456 (HL).
4   [1995] 2 AC 500.

of transactions in the fast moving financial markets and a corporation could not therefore wait until senior management became aware of the transaction.'

Accordingly the company was held criminally liable for the failure of its junior management to comply with the statutory notification provisions. For the court to have decided otherwise would act as an incentive for the board and senior management to pay as little attention as possible to the conduct of its junior (investment) managers.

The **Lennard's** *case revisited*

5.14   In delivering its judgment in the *Meridian* case, the court noted that the expression 'directing mind and will' was derived from Viscount Haldane LC's judgment in *Lennard's Carrying Co Ltd v Asiatic Petroleum Co Ltd* [1915]. However, Lord Hoffmann believed there had been some misunderstanding of the true principle on which that case was decided.

5.15   In the *Lennard's* case, the relevant law was a provision in the Merchant Shipping Act 1894 which provided a shipowner with a defence to liability for a claim for loss of cargo on board its ship where the loss occurred 'without his fault or privity'. Viscount Haldane LC held that this rule applied to companies, and sought to identify the person whose functions in the company corresponded to those expected of the individual shipowner. It so happened that the person so identified, Mr Lennard, was also the person who ran the company's business in general. Hence Lord Hoffmann explained that subsequent cases had misinterpreted the *Lennard's* case as requiring attribution of knowledge where the person concerned was the 'directing mind and will' of the entire company, *rather than in relation to the specific transaction to which the substantive statutory rule in question was aimed.*

Applying the attribution doctrine

5.16   Having clarified the 'directing mind and will' doctrine (certainly in respect of breaches of statutory provisions), Lord Hoffmann then proceeded to expound rules by which criminal acts could be attributed to a company.

5.17   Lord Hoffmann distinguished between 'primary' and 'general' rules of attribution.

Primary and general rules of attribution

5.18   Primary rules of attribution are to be found in the company's constitution (such as clauses in the company's articles of association, which provide that for the purpose of appointing members of the board, a majority vote of the shareholders is equated to being a decision of the company) and also provided for by company law though not expressly stated in the articles (such as the rule that a unanimous decision of shareholders of a solvent company is the decision of the company). Because the primary rules of attribution were not sufficiently broad to enable a company to transact business with all the world, they were supplemented by 'general rules of attribution' derived from the law of agency which are equally applicable to natural persons. Hence the company would appoint servants or agents whose acts, by a combination of the principles of agency and the company's primary rules of attribution, would count as acts of the company. Having appointed human agents, the company would be subject to the general rules by which liability for the acts of others can be attributed to natural persons (such as estoppel or ostensible authority in contract and vicarious liability in tort).

5.19 Usually the combination of primary rules of attribution and general principles of agency, vicarious liability, etc would be sufficient to determine the rights and obligations of the company. In exceptional cases, however, they will not provide an answer. For example, the substantive legal rule sought to be applied may exclude attribution on the basis of agency principles because it may be framed in language primarily applicable to a natural person or require a state of mind by the person 'himself' as opposed to his or her servants or agents. Unless the court concludes that the rule was not intended to apply to companies at all, it must fashion a special rule of attribution for the particular substantive rule. This is always a matter of interpretation.

Exceptional cases

5.20 Where a court concluded that the primary and general rules of attribution do not apparently apply, it might first decide whether the particular substantive rule was intended to apply to the company and if so, how was it intended to apply? Whose act (or knowledge) was for its purpose intended to count as the act, etc of the company? This would depend on the usual canons of interpretation, taking into account the language of the rule (if it was a statute) and its content and policy.

MODERN INTERPRETATION OF IDENTIFICATION THEORY AND DOCTRINE

5.21 Since the *Meridian* judgment, it would appear to be necessary for a court to apply the directing mind principle to the persons responsible for the specific transaction in question, rather than those who are at the apex of the company's organisational structure. As a result, mens rea may now be attributable to a company for the knowledge (and acts) of employees lower down the management structure than previously,[1] particularly where the offence is a regulatory breach concerning the state of mind of the employee(s) responsible who, at the time of the offence, was authorised to act for the company.

5.22 Under the rules of attribution expounded by Lord Hoffmann, in the *Meridian* case, a company may be liable for the fraud or dishonesty of its employees, unless the company itself is the victim of the fraud.[2] Again, as Estey J

---

1 See Yeung 'When does a company acquire knowledge' [1997] CFILR 67.
2 See *Group Josi Re v Walbrook Insurance Co Ltd* [1996] 1 WLR 1152.

stated in the *Canadian Dredge* case, 'when [the directing mind defrauds the company] ... the doctrine of identification [also] ceases to operate'.

CONSTITUTIONAL LIMITS ON IMPOSING VICARIOUS CORPORATE CRIMINAL LIABILITY

5.23   In *Re Employment Equality Bill 1996*,[1] the Supreme Court, while confirming that vicarious liability is part of Irish criminal law because it was 'a part of the established legal order at the birth of the State as well as on the coming into operation of the present constitution', set out a number of criteria for such offences to ensure their constitutional validity.

Conditions necessary to ensure constitutionality

5.24   The Supreme Court, in the *Employment Equality Bill* case, held that such offences should:

> 'essentially be regulatory in character; apply where a person has a particular privilege (such as a licence) or a duty to make sure that public standards as regards health or safety or the environment or the protection of the consumer, and such like, are upheld and where it might be difficult, invidious or redundant to seek to make the employee liable.'

STATUTORY DUTIES IMPOSED ON COMPANIES AS EMPLOYERS

5.25   While the general rule in criminal law is that a person cannot be convicted of an offence without proof of mens rea, there are several examples of offences created by statute where the legislature decrees that no proof of mens rea is necessary. Such exceptional cases are known as offences of 'strict liability'.

OFFENCES OF STRICT LIABILITY

5.26   In a case of strict criminal liability under statute, the duty of compliance may be imposed directly upon the corporate employer, rather than indirectly (vicariously) through responsibility for the actions of its employees.

5.27   In *R v British Steel plc*,[2] the accused company was held liable for a breach of s 3 of the UK's Health and Safety at Work Act 1974 where the misconduct was carried out by junior employees. The court concluded that the duty imposed by the 1974 Act was 'absolute' and applied directly to the company, as an employer. It imposed a personal duty on an employer.

---

1 [1997] 2 IR 321.
2 [1995] 1 WLR 1356.

5.28 In *R v Associated Octel Co Ltd*,[1] the House of Lords make it clear that the nature of the contractual relationship by which the (corporate) employer chooses to satisfy its statutory obligation is immaterial. Liability for breach will attach to the employer whether he uses employees or independent contractors to perform his obligations. In effect, the House of Lords fashioned a special rule of attribution for the particular 'substantive rule'[2] which permitted the attribution of the criminal liability for the acts of an independent company to the accused company.

Future trends

5.29 In the *Canadian Dredge & Dock Co* case, the Canadian Supreme Court considered that 'the corporate vehicle now occupies such a large portion of the industrial and commercial sectors that it is as essential to make corporations as amenable to . . . criminal law as is the case for natural persons'.

In the UK on 9 May 2000, the DPP called for a new offence of 'corporate killing' after his office ruled out manslaughter charges over the Paddington rail crash. Thirty-one people died when two trains collided outside Paddington Station in October 1999.

It is likely, therefore, that the prosecution of companies may increase,[3] opening up the prospects[4] of recovering larger fines, causing shareholders in turn to demand better standards from their company's officers.

Company directors and corporate crimes

5.30 Companies, being artificial persons, can only act through human agents. Companies' managing agents[5] can also incur personal criminal liability arising out of corporate crimes.

5.31 Directors may commit crimes when they act as the controlling mind of the company. Generally, though, they must possess actual 'mens rea'; criminal intent for corporate crimes will not normally be attributed or imputed to them – see Chapter 31.

5.32 A good example of this conceptual thinking (when imputing criminal liability to directors and officers) occurs in reg 12(4) of the European Communities (Supplementary Supervision of Insurance Undertakings in an Insurance Group) Regulations 1999.[6] Regulation 12(4) provides as follows:

> 'Where an offence under these Regulations is committed by a body corporate and is proved to have been so committed with the consent, connivance or approval of a

---

1 [1996] 1 WLR 1543.
2 See **5.20**.
3 See McDermott 'Defences to corporate criminal liability' *Bar Review*, Vol 5, Issue 4, Jan/Feb 2000, and Gardiner 'Corporate Manslaughter' (2000) 7 CLP 218.
4 See F. McAuley and J.P. McCutcheon *Criminal Liability* (Round Hall, Sweet & Maxwell, 2000), at pp 391–399.
5 Ie their directors and officers.
6 SI 1999/399.

person being a director, manager, secretary or other officer or to be attributable to any neglect on the part of a person who is acting or purporting to act in any such capacity, that person, as well as the body corporate, shall be guilty of an offence and shall be liable to be proceeded against and punished as if he or she were guilty of the first mentioned offence.'

Chapter 6

LIFTING THE VEIL OF INCORPORATION WHICH PROTECTS INVESTORS

The separate corporate personality of a registered company is also often likened to a veil, protecting the shareholders of a company from legal actions against them for the debts of the company.

THE NATURE OF THE 'VEIL' METAPHOR

6.1   Corporate personality is viewed as a veil which prevents outsiders taking legal action against company members, even though the outsiders can ascertain the identities of members and the number of shares which they hold. However, this blocking of action against members by the 'veil of incorporation' metaphor is a general rule. There are instances where judges have allowed outsiders to take action against the members of companies. In these exceptional cases, it has been said that the veil of incorporation has been 'lifted'.

Traditionally, one would look at instances of the veil being lifted either by the legislature or by the courts.

THE STATUTORY LIFTING OF THE VEIL

6.2   The more important examples of lifting of the veil of incorporation by the legislature include:

(1) imposing liability for fraudulent trading;
(2) seeking greater transparency in intra-group company dealings; and
(3) introducing the related company concept.

Persons liable for fraudulent trading

6.3   *Any persons* who were knowingly parties to the carrying on of the business of a company with intent to defraud creditors may be made liable to contribute to the insolvent company's assets under s 297A(I)(b) of the Companies Act 1963.

In *Re Aluminium Fabricators Ltd,*[1] on an application from the liquidator, a company's former directors were held liable for fraudulent trading, O'Hanlon J stating:

'The privilege of limitation of liability which is afforded by the Companies Act 1963 in relation to companies incorporated under the Act with limited liability, cannot

---

1 [1984] ILRM 399 (HC).

be afforded to those who use a limited company as a cloak or shield beneath which they seek to operate a fraudulent system of carrying on business for their own personal enrichment and advantage.'

6.4   A wide range of persons could incur liability under s 297A(I)(b). It would obviously include shareholders, and may even apply to creditors. For example, it was held in *Re Gerald Cooper Chemicals Ltd,*[1] that it was possible for a creditor of the company to be a party to the carrying on of the business of the company for the purpose of the equivalent UK statutory liability, ie s 213 of the Insolvency Act 1986. In this case, the creditor received a part payment of his debt out of money which was paid in advance to the company in fraudulent circumstances where there was no intention ever to supply the goods ordered.

6.5   However, for liability to be incurred under s 297A(I)(b), the *persons must be party to the carrying on of the company's business in a fraudulent manner.* Therefore a member who confines his activities to contributing capital and electing company directors will not incur a liability for subsequent fraudulent trading by the company which was carried on by its directors (and indeed, other members).

In *Re Hunting Lodges Ltd,*[2] it was decided that the 'carrying on a business' can include a single transaction.

The company owed substantial sums in revenue, and proceedings were brought to recover these. Negotiations began for the sale of the company's main asset (Durty Nelly's Public House) and a sale was agreed. A lesser figure than the true price was inserted in the documentation and the remainder of £160,000 was to be paid to the directors 'on the side'. The purchaser of the company's property made this 'under the table' payment partly in cash and partly in bank drafts made out in fictitious names, which were deposited by one director in a building society. The Revenue Commissioners successfully applied for the company's liquidation and the liquidator applied to have the directors and the purchaser declared personally responsible for the company's debts. The court found that each of the parties to the transaction had acted for a fraudulent purpose, Carroll J stating:

> 'I am satisfied that carrying on business is not synonymous with trading. In my opinion it is not necessary that all the company's business should be carried on with fraudulent intent nor is it necessary that there should be a course of dealing or series of transactions before the section can be called into operation.
>
> The section refers to "any business". In the course of the conduct of its affairs, a company will have many different aspects of its business. One single transaction can properly be described as "business of the company" and so also can constituent parts of a transaction. One single act committed with the fraudulent intent specified by the section can, in my opinion, suffice to ground a declaration under the section. The fact that the piece of business is a transaction which involves the sale of the entire assets of the company does not alter the position in any way.

1 [1978] Ch 262.
2 [1985] ILRM 75.

In this case, while the sale of the premises with a payment on the side can be viewed as one transaction, it also breaks down into different elements. There are the negotiations culminating in the signing of the contract, the closing of the sale and the disposition of the purchase money. Each of these elements can be designated together or separately as "business of the company."

In particular, I include the disposition of the purchase money as part of the business of the company. Unlikely though it was, Mr P [a director] could have deposited the £160,000 to the credit of the company, which would have negatived an intent on his part to defraud creditors in respect of that money. Instead he concealed the money under false names in the building society accounts, thus completing the transaction which was part of the business of the company.'

Other cases dealing with what actions constitute fraudulent trading are detailed in Chapter 28.

6.6 It was held in *O'Keeffe v Ferris, Ireland and the Attorney General*,[1] that statutory imposed liability for fraudulent trading, notwithstanding its punitive and compensatory nature, is not unconstitutional.

The plaintiff sought a declaration that s 297(1) of the 1963 Act was unconstitutional because it created a criminal offence which was not minor in nature and, accordingly should only be tried before a jury. She also argued that the section was punitive in its effect and not merely compensatory.

The High Court held that s 297(1) of the 1963 Act (which was replaced by s 297A(1) following the enactment of the 1990 Companies Act) neither created a criminal offence nor infringed the constitution.

In 1997, the Supreme Court dismissed an appeal against Murphy J's decision in the High Court (see Part V).

Liabilities of directors and members compared

6.7 If it can be shown that a director or officer was knowingly a party to the carrying on of business in a reckless manner, or if any person is knowingly a party to the carrying on of any business of the company with intent to defraud creditors of the company, then by virtue of s 297A(1)(a) and (b) a court may hold them personally liable for the debts of the company, without any limitation of liability.

There are several other examples of directors and managers, rather than members, being rendered liable for company debts.[2] The question now arises as to whether these instances of potential unlimited liability for company directors (and others) involve a lifting of the veil.

If one limits the protection of the veil of incorporation simply to company shareholders, then clearly directors and managers may incur legal liabilities without a lifting of the veil. These onerous statutory liabilities on directors and

---

1 [1993] 3 IR 165.
2 See Part V B.

officers essentially render them liable for company debts as a company's human managing agents. In practice, these potential liabilities of companies' managing agents will probably offer a much more fertile source of funding to unpaid company creditors that the older methods of attempting to recover from investors by seeking to pierce the veil. While investors still enjoy substantial immunity against actions brought by company creditors by virtue of the limitation of their liability as members, creditors now enjoy significant new statutory avenues and sources of recovery for company debts from directors and officers.

Liability of shadow and de facto directors

6.8   A shadow director is defined in s 27 of the Companies Act, 1990 as a 'person in accordance with whose directions or instructions the directors of the company are accustomed to act'. However, a person is not deemed to be a shadow director by reason only that the directors act on advice by him in a professional capacity (see also **27.5**).

In *Re Hydrodam (Corby) Ltd*,[1] it was held in the UK that liability for wrongful trading[2] may extend to a 'de facto' director.

In the same case, Millet J described a 'de facto' director as:

> '... a person who assumes to act as a director. He is held out as a director by the company, and claims and purports to be a director, although never actually or validly appointed as such. To establish that a person was de facto director of a company, it is necessary to plead and prove that he undertook functions in relation to the company which could properly be discharged only by a director.'

UNRAVELLING INTRA-GROUP COMPANY DEALINGS

6.9   From this outline of instances which are sometimes cited as statutory examples of lifting the veil, it is clear that:

(1) the imposition of personal liability on directors and officers does not involving a lifting of the veil; so
(2) *the number of occasions when statutory provisions lift the veil to make an investor liable for the debts of a company are quite rare and exceptional.*

In fact, most instances of statutory lifting of the veil incorporation relate to rendering more transparent transactions and/or dealings between connected companies within a group. For example, statutory provisions require group accounts (see ss 150 to 152 of 1963 Act) and prohibit or impose safeguards on specific intra-group transactions – see s 32(1) of the 1963 Act, which contained a general rule prohibiting a subsidiary from becoming a member of its holding company, as amended by s 224 of the CA 1990, which now allows such relationships, subject to specific safeguards.

---

1 [1994] 2 BCLC 180.
2 Under s 214 of the Insolvency Act 1986.

Related companies

6.10 Section 140 of the Companies Act 1990 introduced the new concept of a 'related company', ie one which may be required to contribute to the assets of a company in liquidation. Section 140 constitutes a clear case of statutory lifting of the veil of incorporation. As the veil lifting only occurs if the company is being wound up, the related company concept will be dealt with in **6.23** and in **50.37**.

LIFTING OF THE VEIL AT COMMON LAW

6.11 Lord Denning said:[1]

> 'The doctrine [of separate personality] has to be watched very carefully. It has often been supposed to cast a veil over the personality of a limited company through which the courts cannot see. But that is not true. The courts can and often do, pull off the mask. They look to see what really lies behind. The legislature has shown the way with group accounts and the rest. And the courts should follow suit. I think we should look at the [Fork] company and see it as it really is – the wholly owned subsidiary of the tax payers. It is the *creature*, the *puppet* of the tax payers in point of fact, and it should be so regarded in point of law.'

6.12 Schmitthoff[2] classifies the instances where the judiciary have lifted the veil into two categories. The first is where a principal and agent reasoning has been applied. The second is where the courts have found a clear abuse of corporate form had occurred.

6.13 Ottolenghi[3] points out that the courts use lifting the veil as a metaphor in various circumstances. For example, they can, in the same case:

> 'both ignore the veil completely and issue injunctions against the company as a separate legal entity. Again, two incompatible terms for the company may be used side by side in a judgment – a "puppet" and "an agent",[4] the first totally negating the possibility of an independent legal entity, the latter recognising its existence as a separate legal body and attributing to it the power to negotiate and finalise a contract on behalf of its principal. Which of these two should prevail?'

This article will be considered further in **6.19**.

6.14 Friedman[5] has reasoned that judges would lift the veil:

> 'In the frustration of tax evasion, the consideration of the real purpose of a transaction as against its legal form, the disguise of the controlling hand through subsidiary companies.'

---

1 In *Littlewoods Mail Order Stores v Inland Revenue Commissioners* [1969] 3 All ER 442, [1969] 1 WLR 1241 (CA).
2 C. Schmitthoff 'Salomon in the Shadows' [1976] JBL 305, at p 307.
3 S. Ottolenghi 'From Peeping Behind the Corporate Veil to Ignoring it Completely' (1990) 53 MLR 338, at pp 338–353.
4 By Lord Denning MR in *Wallersteiner v Moir (No 1)* [1974] 3 All ER 217 (CA).
5 W. Friedman *Legal Theory* (Stevens, 1967).

As noted above, the veil may be lifted by statutory provision to require group accounts from holding companies and to identify specific inter group transactions. Again, under taxation law, the shareholders of a 'close' company may incur personal taxation liabilities for its profits (see **6.28**). Notwithstanding this, legislation generally does not render investors liable for the debts of the company.[1]

6.15   The courts may also penetrate the veil at common law to make the members liable for company debts. Generally, though, the courts will only take this action where the company has been used as a 'cloak' for fraud or other criminal activities. For example, in *Re a Company Ltd*,[2] the defendant, knowing that the plaintiff companies were insolvent, disposed of his personal assets[3] so that his true beneficial interests were concealed. He took this action to prevent the liquidator of the plaintiff company recovering those assets from him on grounds of alleged fraud. The defendant was restrained by injunction; the court piercing the veil in order to achieve justice.

The Court of Appeal, upholding the injunction, limited such relief to companies and trusts over which the defendant exercised 'substantial' or effective control.

6.16   Again, in *Re H (restraint order: realisable property)*,[4] where the company was used as a façade to conceal criminal activities, the veil was pierced to treat the assets of the company as reachable property of the shareholders under s 77 of the Criminal Justice Act 1988.

6.17   Whilst the courts will pierce the veil to make controlling or dominant shareholders liable for company debts in cases of fraud and criminal activities, such instances are quite exceptional. As Sealy wrote:[5]

> '... one will search the reports in vain for a single English case where the principle of limited liability, as distinct from that of corporate personality, has not been respected – statute apart. This is true of cases brought against directors and dominant shareholders alike. Those cases where the corporate veil has been pierced on the basis that the company was a façade or sham, or was the agent of its controllers, turn out on examination to have been concerned with the evasion of a statutory provision or a contractual obligation, or some similar issue, and not with imposing personal liability on the (directors or) shareholders for the company's debts.'

6.18   These comments would appear to apply equally to Ireland. More often, therefore, the veil is lifted not to make controlling shareholders liable for

---

1 Under s 36 of the 1963 Act, a reduction in the number of members below the legal minimum may lead to the remaining member(s) being liable for the debts of the company.
2 [1985] BCLC 333 (CA).
3 Transferring them to a network of interlocking foreign and UK companies and trusts.
4 [1996] 2 All ER 391 – see also *Creasey v Breachwood Motors Ltd* [1993] BCLC 480.
5 See the article 'Personal liability of directors and officers for debts of an insolvent company' in Ziegler (ed), *Current Developments in International and Comparative Corporate and Insolvency Law* (1994), at p 485.

company debts, but (i) to impose responsibility on them for the improper use of corporate form, or (ii) to establish their economic interest in the company assets. This latter reason may underly court decisions affecting connected companies within a group – such instances of veil lifting being based on statutory authority.

Rationalising the 'jungle of judgments'

6.19   There are many examples of lifting the veil. The problem is how to rationalise the circumstances in which a judge is likely to deviate from the strict rule of the separate legal entity of the company (the rule in the *Salomon* case), and lift the veil of incorporation. As McCormack[1] comments:

> 'The doctrine of separate corporate personality is relaxed in certain exceptional instances where it tends towards an inequitable conclusion. It is not easy to discern any unifying set of guidelines among this wilderness of single instances. Cases are decided on a fairly ad hoc basis with little regard for satisfactory concepts that admit of more generalised application. This approach breeds uncertainty. Judges need to intellectualise their decisions to a greater extent. Until this task is achieved, the subjective judgment is likely to hold sway.'

The need to rationalise the 'jungle of judgments' relating to the veil metaphor was the subject of an interesting article by Ottolenghi, which suggests that before asking *when* the veil is lifted, one should ascertain what is actually done by the courts and the legislature. The practice of lifting the veil is not always detrimental to a company or its shareholders. Sometimes this action may benefit them as well as the (outsider) company creditors. Accordingly, he suggests that in lifting the veil, four different attitudes towards the company can be detected.[2] These attitudes may be classified as:

(1)   peeping behind the veil;
(2)   penetrating the veil;
(3)   extending the veil; and
(4)   ignoring the veil.

Peeping behind the veil

6.20   'Peeping' may consist of the court lifting the veil to identify ownership of the company, and then 'dropping' the veil again. The statutory definition of holding company,[3] is an example of a statutory peeping behind the veil. Once the court has obtained the relevant information, the veil is then 'pulled down' once more and the company may be treated as a separate legal entity.

The courts may also peep behind the veil as a preliminary information seeking exercise before making a decision on whether or not to lift it.

---

1   G. McCormack 'Judicial application of Salomon's case in Ireland' *Law Society Gazette*, May 1984, at p 100.
2   Each of these attitudes may be used in different circumstances and for different reasons.
3   Section 115 of the Companies Act 1963. A holding company must normally prepare group accounts – see Chapter 32.

6.21   In *The State (Thomas McInerney & Co Ltd) v Dublin County Council*,[1] the
company argued that because it and the landowner, another company, were
subsidiaries of the holding company, the veil should be lifted and the plaintiff
company deemed to be the owner of the land in question.

Carroll J refused to lift the veil, stating:

> 'This is not a case where justice demands that the corporate veil be lifted ... It is
> not for a corporate group to claim that the veil should be lifted to illuminate one
> aspect of its business while it (the veil) should be left *in situ* to isolate the individual
> actions of its subsidiaries in other respects ...'

In short, Carroll J was saying that the veil of incorporation could not be lifted, or
left in place, at the plaintiff company's whim.

6.22   In *Rex Pet Foods Ltd v Lamb Bros (Ireland) Ltd*,[2] 'peeping' by the court
elicited that a change of management, occurring in March 1982, was a perfectly
normal commercial transaction and did not affect the separate corporate entity
of the plaintiff company, which had become a subsidiary of the defendant
company.

A declaration was sought when Rex Pet Foods Ltd went into receivership,
seeking to treat both companies as one legal entity, thereby aggregating their
joint assets. The High Court refused to lift the veil in the absence of evidence to
suggest that any funds of the plaintiff company were wrongfully siphoned off
into the defendant company.

Related companies

6.23   Since the *Rex Pet Foods Ltd* decision, there has been legislative action
aimed at giving creditors access to funds of related companies.

A related company is defined in s 140(5) of the Companies Act 1990. On the
application of the liquidator or any creditor of a company which is being wound
up, the court, if it is satisfied that it is just and equitable to do so, may order that
any company that is or has been related to the company being wound up shall
pay an amount equivalent to the whole or part of the debts provable in that
winding up.

Where two or more related companies are being wound up, the court may
order the aggregation of assets and that the companies be wound up together
as one company. In deciding whether or not to make such an order, the court
will consider the following factors:[3]

(1)   the extent to which any of the companies took part in the management of
      any of the other companies;
(2)   the conduct of any of the companies towards the creditors of any of the
      other companies;

---

1 [1985] ILRM 513.
2 (Unreported) 5 December 1985 (HC).
3 See s 141 of Companies Act 1990. See also s 16 of the Companies (Amendment) Act 1986 for
definition of new term 'associated' company introduced by that Act.

(3) the extent to which the circumstances that gave rise to the winding up of any of the companies are attributable to the actions or omissions of any of the other companies;

(4) the extent to which the businesses of the companies have been intermingled.

Clearly, the related company concept introduced by the Companies Act 1990 is another example of the legislature lifting the veil of incorporation. It is designed to give a liquidator the opportunity of maximising company assets – see Chapter 50.

Veil lifted by the court

6.24 There are examples where the court, after 'peeping' behind the veil, then proceeds to lift it.

In *Power Supermarkets Ltd v Crumlin Investments Ltd,*[1] the plaintiff company held part of a shopping centre under a lease. *This lease had a clause which prohibited the granting of further leases to traders in the grocery business.* This clause was designed to protect Power Supermarkets from competition.

Dunnes Stores Group, which operated a chain of supermarkets in competition with Power Supermarkets, purchased[2] Crumlin Investments Ltd, the defendant company. Following the purchase, Crumlin Investments Ltd were prepared to let a unit in the shopping centre to Dunnes Stores (Crumlin) Ltd, another subsidiary company in the Dunnes Stores Group, which intended to engage in the grocery business there. Power Supermarkets sought an injunction to restrain Crumlin Investments Ltd from infringing the terms of their lease. Costello J granted the injunction, stating:

> 'It seems to me to be well established ... that a court may, if the justice of the case so requires, treat two or more related companies as a single entity so that the business notionally carried on by one will be regarded as the business of the group, or another member of that group, if it conforms to the economic and commercial realities of the situation. It would ... be very hard to find a clearer case than the present one for the application of this principle.'

Costello J concluded that if he did not treat the two defendant companies as a single economic entity, it could involve a considerable injustice to the plaintiff company, whose legal rights under their lease might be defeated:

> 'by the mere technical devise of the creation of a company with a £2 issued capital which had no real independent life of its own.'

6.25 When giving his judgment in the *Power Supermarkets Ltd* case, Costello J approved the decisions in *Smith, Stone and Knight Ltd v Birmingham Corporation* and *D.H.N. Food Distributors Ltd v Tower Hamlets London Borough Council.*[3] In the

---

1 (Unreported) 22 June 1981 (HC).
2 The purchasing company was, in fact, Cornelscourt Shopping Centre Ltd, a wholly owned subsidiary of Dunnes Stores Ltd, which, in turn, was a wholly owned subsidiary of Dunnes Holding Co.
3 [1939] 4 All ER 116 and [1976] 1 WLR 852, respectively.

D.H.N. case, three group companies were regarded as a single legal entity because they constituted, in reality, a single economic entity.

Doubts had been expressed by the House of Lords as to the correctness of the decision to lift the veil in the *D.H.N.* case. These doubts were expressed in *Woolfson v Strathclyde Regional Council.*[1] Notwithstanding, in *Re Bray Travel Ltd and Bray Travel (Holdings) Ltd,*[2] the principles enunciated by Costello J in the *Power Supermarkets Ltd* case were approved and followed by the Supreme Court.

Directors and officers

6.26 From these illustrations, it is clear that 'peeping' behind the veil takes place only when the courts or the legislature desire to identify those who really govern companies or give controlling instructions to their directors.

A court does not have to 'peep behind the veil' when recourse is made to a company's directors. The directors are a company's human managing agents. They stand in front of the veil so there is no need to look behind the company's separate corporate personality to identify them. Thus, the fact that s 138 of the Companies Act 1990 imposes personal liability on officers or others in respect of fraudulent and reckless trading[3] does not entail a lifting of the veil. These liabilities:[4]

> 'are better regarded as "punitive" measures, a sort of statutory *caveat* directed at those who purport to act in the name of the company, knowing that the company would not honour their acts.'

The purpose of peeping

6.27 Peeping behind the veil is not, in itself, a step necessarily leading to personal responsibility of shareholders for company debts or actions. Rather, it is the preliminary investigative act of examining certain features relating to the company which can only be achieved by 'peeping' behind the veil. These features would include the company's type (holding, subsidiary, related, etc), character (alien[5]), residence (for tax purposes), control, etc. Having carried out its preliminary examination of the issues which necessitated peeping behind the veil of incorporation, the court must then decide what to do with the information it has elicited. This will entail a positive decision by the court either:

(1) that the veil should not be lifted and the separate corporate personality remains intact; or

---

1 1978 SLT 159, 38 P & CR 521 (HL).
2 (Unreported) 13 July 1981.
3 See Part VB.
4 To quote from Ottolenghi's article.
5 In determining the ownership of agricultural land, the Land Commission will look at the nationality of an owner company's shareholders rather than the place of registration of the company. See also *Daimler v Continental Tyre and Rubber Co* [1916] 2 AC 307 (HL).

(2) that the circumstances are such that the court must penetrate the veil. The instances when the court might take this action, already illustrated by the *Power Supermarkets* case in **6.24**, are outlined below.

Penetrating the veil

6.28   As mentioned above, in the case of *Woolfson v Strathclyde Regional Council*, the House of Lords expressed doubts on whether the lower court decision in the *D.H.N.* case properly applied the *principle that it is appropriate to pierce the corporate veil only where special circumstances exist indicating that it is a mere facade* concealing the true facts. This seems to imply that the veil, generally, should only be lifted to permit legal actions be taken *against* shareholders, and *not by* them. This is reflected also in the exceptional instances where the legislature pierces the veil.

The purpose of penetrating the veil of incorporation is sometimes to make (controlling) shareholders personally responsible for the debts of the company.[1] For example, in *Re Kelly's Carpetdrome*,[2] Costello J imposed personal liability for company debts, not only on the directors but also on the persons who beneficially owned the company.

The pooling of the assets of a related company under ss 140 and 141 of the Companies Act 1990 (see **6.23**) is another example of statutory penetration of the veil; as is the classification of 'close company' for the purposes of taxation.

Close companies are those controlled by five or fewer shareholders. Taxation law provisions for the apportionment of certain income of a close company amongst its investors have the effect of treating the investors as if they each own portions of the company property; thereby rendering them liable to extra personal taxation.

The Landlord and Tenant (Amendment) Act 1980[3] is another example of statutory penetration of the veil – this time, exceptionally, for the benefit of the company's controlling shareholder.

In practice, the veil is usually penetrated to impose responsibility upon shareholders for the improper use of corporate form (as happened in the *Power Supermarkets* case) or to establish their economic interest in the company assets.

Extending the veil

6.29   When a court peeps behind the veil to find that the company in question is one of a group of companies, it may, instead of treating each company as a separate corporate entity, treat the whole group as one single corporate entity.

---

1 Effectively depriving them of the privilege of limited liability.
2 (Unreported) 1 July 1983 (HC).
3 By virtue of the Landlord and Tenant (Amendment) Act 1980, a tenant's statutory right to renewal of his tenancy is not lost because he has converted his business to a private company.

This technique has the effect of extending, rather than piercing, the veil by treating all group companies as a single business entity, perhaps reflecting the economic or commercial reality of the situation.

The legislative requirement[1] for a group of companies to provide group accounts also illustrates this extension of the veil.

The decision in *Power Supermarkets Ltd v Crumlin Investments Ltd* (see **6.24**) would be classified (by this writer) as piercing the veil on grounds of an improper use of corporate form.

Ignoring the veil

6.30   There are circumstances when it is said that the courts will *ignore* the separate personality of a company. This situation can arise where the company was formed for some fraudulent, illegal or improper purpose or for the evasion of legal obligations. Names used by the courts to describe such companies are 'puppet', 'sham', 'scheme', 'cloak' (for fraud) and 'bubble company', to mention a few. In the case of *Jones v Lipman*,[2] X contracted to sell his house to Jones. He then decided to avoid the sale. In order to frustrate a court order of specific performance[3] being made against him, X formed a company and then sold his house to it.

The court held that Jones was entitled to a decree of specific performance against the defendant and his company, Russell J stating that the company was:

> 'the creation of the defendant, a devise and a sham, a mask which he holds before his face in an attempt to avoid recognition (by the law).'

6.31   Again, in *Re Bugle Press Ltd*,[4] members holding 90 per cent of the shares in a company, Y Ltd, formed a new company, X Ltd. X Ltd then made an offer to buy the shares of Y Ltd. The investors holding 90 per cent of Y Ltd's shares accepted X Ltd's offer. X Ltd then served notice on the 10 per cent minority shareholder of Y Ltd, stating that they wished to compulsorily acquire his shares under the equivalent of s 204 of the 1963 Act – see Chapter 48. He opposed the scheme on the basis that it amounted, in effect, to an expropriation of his shares by the majority shareholders of Y Ltd.

The minority shareholder's claim succeeded. The court lifted the veil and identified the actual identity of the majority shareholders involved.

6.32   Where the controllers of a company have committed nothing worse than mismanagement, the court will not lift the veil – see *Dublin County Council v Elton Homes Ltd*.[5]

---

1 Section 152 of the Companies Act 1963.
2 [1962] 1 All ER 442.
3 Compelling X to complete the transaction.
4 [1960] 3 All ER 791 (CA).
5 [1984] ILRM 297 (HC). See also *Dun Laoghaire Corporation v Parkhill Development* [1989] IR 477.

COMMENTS ON OTTOLENGHI'S ANALYSIS

6.33 Ottolenghi considered 'lifting' the veil was a term used to describe four different actions taken by a court, ie peeping behind, penetrating or piercing, extending and ignoring the veil.

This author considers it preferable to consider only three of these actions when discussing a lifting of the veil; in effect to treat ignoring the veil as a 'negative' form of 'piercing' it.

Peeping behind the veil

6.34 In *The State (Thomas Mc Inerney & Co Ltd) v Dublin County Council* (see **6.21**), the court peeped behind the veil, and having done so, decided that it should not be lifted at the plaintiff company's behest. Similarly in the *Rex Pet Foods* case, peeping behind the veil elicited that a change of management was a normal commercial transaction which meant that the court had to take no further action.

If a company is being wound up and the liquidator asks the court to aggregate the assets of a related company under s 140 of the 1990 act, the court must 'peep' behind the veil to ascertain:

(1) whether the connected company relationships exist; and, inter alia,
(2) the extent to which an alleged related company took part in, or influenced the management of the company being liquidated (see **6.23**).

After peeping behind the veil (or veils) of incorporation, the court will only order the aggregation of assets if satisfied that the related company actively interfered in the running of the liquidated company's business.

Penetrating or piercing the veil

6.35 In the *Power Supermarkets* case (see **6.24**), having again peeped behind the veil to establish a group company relationship, the court then proceeded to penetrate the veil in order to stop the defendant using the veil as an excuse to avoid their contractual obligations. In short, this writer considers Costello J correctly pierced the veil in this case to prevent an improper use of corporate form. Other cases where the courts have penetrated the veil to prevent an improper use of corporate form include *Jones v Lipman* (see **6.30**), *Cummins v Stewart*[1] and *Cockburn v Newbridge Sanitary Steam Laundry Co Ltd.*[2]

In *Cummins v Stewart*, Cummins entered into a licence agreement with Stewart. Stewart attempted to escape his liability to pay royalties under this licence by transferring the licence to a company formed for that purpose.

The formation of the new company was to evade the defendant's liability under the original licence agreement. Accordingly, the court lifted the veil so that the defendant was made personally liable for all arrears of royalty payments.

1 [1911] 1 IR 236 (ChD).
2 [1915] 1 IR 237 (CA).

6.36   In *Cockburn v Newbridge Sanitary Steam Laundry Co Ltd*, it was decided that the court would lift the veil of incorporation when the company was used for fraudulent, illegal or improper purposes.

The facts in this case were that Llewellyn, a large shareholder in the company and its managing director, entered into contracts in his own name on the company's behalf. When the company did the work, he paid the company only a portion of the monies received, on foot of an arrangement with his co-directors that he was not to account for profits. The managing director claimed that some of the monies were expended in paying bribes.

The court held that the transactions were illegal and, therefore, ultra vires. A company could not be used as a vehicle for fraudulent or illegal activities. O'Brien said:

> 'It has been argued most ingeniously by counsel for the company that there was a contract with Llewellyn, which it is suggested would be perfectly lawful, that he was to give the company whatever he thought right out of what he received. There is no evidence of such a contract having been made, even if it could lawfully be made; and the only question is whether, on the facts as we have now got them, it would be within the powers of the company to take up the attitude "we will not inquire." If this company had entered into a contract with Llewellyn, giving him authority to commit a crime on behalf of himself and the company, such a contract would, of course, be absolutely illegal, and it requires no argument to see that it would be equally illegal to adopt such a contract either affirmatively or indirectly.
>
> Illegality and ultra vires are not interchangeable terms, but it is difficult, if not impossible, to conceive a case in which a company can do an illegal act [one arising from policy], and act within its powers ... How much stronger is the position when the whole matter is tainted with criminality.'

However, where the primary reason for forming the company is legal; the court will be slow to lift the veil, notwithstanding the fact that the new company may give legal advantages to the promoters.

6.37   In *Roundabout Ltd v Beirne*,[1] the court held that whilst the formation of the new company was an element in dealing with the existing trade dispute, *it was not the whole end and object of the arrangement. The promoters also wanted to introduce new blood into the business.* Accordingly, Dixon J refused to lift the veil and granted Roundabout Ltd the injunction against the picketers which it sought:

> 'The trade dispute still exists with what I may call the old company, and the question is whether the union can avail itself of that dispute for the purpose of picketing the premises which are now occupied, and in which business is now carried on, by the new company.
>
> The new company is, in law, a distinct entity, as is the old company. I must therefore proceed on the basis that a new and different person is now in occupation of the premises and carrying on business there.

---

1   [1959] IR 423 (HC) – the facts are set out in **3.12**.

It has been suggested – and there is some basis for the suggestion – that the new company was formed for the purpose of getting rid of the trade dispute and also of enabling the employment of union staff to be dispensed with. There is considerable substance in that suggestion. I think that it is quite permissible to describe and enable the business to be carried on without the inconvenience of being subject to the picket. To this description there are two qualifications: first, that even though the formation of the new company may be a subterfuge, the question I have to decide is not ruled by that; the question which I must determine is whether it is a successful subterfuge, capable of effectually achieving its purpose. The *second qualification is that I do not think that the sole, or possibly even the primary, purpose of the formation of the new company was to get rid of the trade dispute. I think that there was a genuine idea of getting new blood into the business* ...

While this new arrangement contains a considerable element of subterfuge, as a scheme designed to get rid, if legally possible, of the existing trade dispute, *that is not the whole end and object of the arrangement.* I must regard the new company as what it is, a distinct legal entity, and approach the position from the same point of view as if some individual or company totally unconnected with the old company had taken a lease of these premises similar to the lease taken here ...' (author's emphasis)

6.38 This writer has difficulty with accepting the fact that the primary purpose of registering the new company in this case was not to prevent the old company's employees exercising their statutory right to picket. Accordingly, because Dixon J failed to lift the veil, he at the very least, allowed the directors of the Marian Park Inn an opportunity of using corporate form for an improper purpose.

Purpose of piercing the veil

6.39 It is clear from **6.3** et seq, that a court will, on statutory authority, hold members personally liable for the debts of a company in quite exceptional circumstances when they actually interfere in the running of the company.

When a court lifts the veil at common law, it normally does so to compel the defendant to honour his legal obligations – usually under contract.[1] An analysis of the various cases mentioned above seems to reinforce Murnaghan J's comment in *Commissioners of Inland Revenue v The Governor and Company of the Bank of Ireland*[2] that:

'[In the absence of fraud or criminal activities] there is, at common law, no liability upon the members of a body corporate in respect of the debts and liabilities [of the company], and such liability in respect of the corporate acts must be created by statute.'

Extending the veil

6.40 In order to implement the policy of the legislature in requiring group accounts, a court may, as a preliminary fact finding exercise, have to peep

---

1 The court may also identify individual shareholders in order to determine the company's character, status and residence, for tax purposes.
2 See **2.7** and **4.2**.

behind the veils of separate companies to establish whether or not a 'group' of companies exists. If such a group does exist, it must prepare 'group accounts' as required by s 158 of the 1963 Act to reflect the economic reality of their corporate relationships. However whilst the legislature may extend the veil on grounds of economic reality, the better legal opinion now is that a judge should not do so without statutory authority – see the Supreme Court decision in the *Allied Irish Coal Suppliers* case in **6.41**.

The veil of incorporation is also extended by statute to render more transparent transactions and/or dealings between connected companies within a group – see **6.9**.

Despite these exceptional instances where the veil is extended, holding companies and subsidiaries remain separate legal persons at common law.

In the UK, Robert Goff LJ in *Bank of Tokyo Ltd v Karoun*[1] repudiated the notion of the 'single economic entity' by saying that while economically, parent and subsidiary were one, 'we are concerned with law, not with economics. The distinction between the two is, in law, fundamental and cannot here be bridged'.

The Court of Appeal took a similar view in *Ord v Belhaven Pubs Ltd*,[2] when it refused to lift the veil of incorporation following the restructuring of a corporate group.

GROUPS OF COMPANIES AT COMMON LAW

6.41 It should be noted, therefore, that whilst company law may make special provision for holding companies and subsidiaries,[3] their position at common law is one of separate legal entities. The subsidiary is not necessarily to be treated as the implied agent of the holding company. This situation was considered by Laffoy J in *Allied Irish Coal Suppliers Ltd v Powell Duffryn International Fuels Ltd.*[4]

In this case, the plaintiff alleged that the defendant and its parent company constituted a single economic entity, and asked the court to exercise its discretion to regard them as such on the basis of the decision in *Power Supermarkets Ltd v Crumlin Investments Ltd*.

Laffoy J commented:

'... the situation here ... is that the plaintiff traded with the defendant during 1983 and 1984 in the knowledge that the latter was a subsidiary of the [parent] plc.

---

1 [1987] AC 45n.
2 [1998] BCC 607.
3 See Companies Act 1963, s 32 (as amended) dealing with membership and ss 150–158 prescribing group accounts.
4 [1997] 1 ILRM 306. See also *Adams v Cape Industries plc* [1990] Ch 433, *Kleinwort Benson Ltd v Malaysian Mining Corporation* [1989] 1 All ER 785 – a case dealing with a 'letter of comfort' issued by the holding company – and *Re Polly Peck International plc (in administration) (No 3)* [1996] 2 All ER 433.

The plaintiff does not allege that there was privity of contract between it and the plc, nor does it assert that the statements which it alleges were fraudulent or negligent or were made by or on behalf of the plc. In essence, what the plaintiff seeks by joinder of the plc *is to render the assets of the plc available to meet the liabilities of its subsidiary.*

The issue I have to address is whether the principle enunciated in the *Power Supermarkets* case, can be applied to achieve this end.' (author's emphasis)

The judge then decided that the principle whereby a court, when the justice of the case so requires, treats two or more related companies as a single business entity (so that the business notionally carried on by one will be regarded as the business of the group, if this conforms to the economic and commercial realities of the situation) could not be utilised to render the assets of a parent company available to meet the liabilities of its trading subsidiary to a party with which it had traded. For her to have done so appeared to Laffoy J:

'... to be fundamentally at variance with the principle of separate corporate legal personality laid down in *Salomon v Salomon* and the concept of limited liability.'

This common-law position that a holding company is generally not liable for the trading debts of its subsidiary, may be subject to the provisions of the Companies Act 1990 on the pooling of assets of related companies, which are outlined above. These statutory provisions, however, only come into operation where a company is being wound up.

THE STATUS OF THE SINGLE ECONOMIC UNIT PRINCIPLE IN IRISH LAW

6.42   The single economic unit principle was introduced into Irish law in the *Power Supermarkets* case. In this case, Costello J held that a court may, 'if the justice of the case so requires, treat related companies as a single entity ... if this conforms to the economic and commercial realities of the situation'. However, the same judge, in *Rex Petfoods Ltd v Lamb Bros Ltd* (see **6.23**) refused to lift the veil of incorporation and make an order aggregating the assets of individual group companies, in the absence of misbehaviour, such as the siphoning off of assets.

6.43   Any doubts about the applicability[1] of the single economic unit principle were dispelled by the Supreme Court decision in *Allied Irish Coal Suppliers Ltd v Powell Duffryn International Fuels Ltd.*[2] The High Court judgment of Laffoy J had been appealed. In the Supreme Court judgment, Murphy J stated:

'As considerable debate took place before Laffoy J and in this Court with regard to the relationship between the defendant and the plc, I feel that I should comment on it.

---

1 In England, Slade J had said in *Adams v Cape Industries plc* [1990] Ch 433: 'There is no general principle that all companies in a group are to be regarded as one. [Quite] the contrary ... Each [group] company is a separate legal entity [at common law]'.

2 [1997] 1 ILRM 306, [1998] 2 IR 519 (HC), [1998] 2 IR 529 (SC).

The corner stone of company law was put in place just one hundred years ago by the decision of the House of Lords in *Salomon v Salomon & Co*. Not merely did that case decide that a company incorporated under the companies acts is a legal entity separate from its promoters and members, but it was recognised that this was so, even though the company was incorporated for that purpose and with the result that the distinction operated to the manifest detriment of these dealing with the company in the ordinary course of its business. It is sometimes helpful to recall (as Barrington J did in *IPBS v Cauldwell* [1981] ILRM 242) that in laying down this principle, the House of Lords unanimously reversed the decision of the Court of Appeal, likewise unanimous, which had utterly condemned the conduct of Mr Salomon and his friends for the way in which they had incorporated and operated the family enterprise ...

These are some decisions, particularly in other jurisdictions and much academic writing which would seem to advocate a restriction of the principles so clearly established by the House of Lords in *Salomon v Salomon & Co*. However, I am in complete agreement with the comments made by [Laffoy J] in the present case' (see above).

On the question of applying the principle in the *Power Supermarkets* case, Murphy J stated:

'the crucial feature of [the *Power Supermarkets* case] is that Costello J did not propose to question the authority of *Salomon v Salomon & Co*. Indeed, no reference was made to that case in the course of his judgment nor, as far as I am aware, the argument on which it was based. Again, it is clear from the judgement in *Rex Pet Foods Ltd v Lamb Brothers (Ireland) Ltd* that Costello J had not intended [in the *Power Supermarkets* case] to lay down any revolutionary principles of law.

The fact that the activities of subsidiaries may be reflected in the accounts of the group, show the extent to which the legislature recognised how companies trading in this way may require to be viewed as an economic entity, but there is no question of the legislature making the assets of one company within the group, liable for the debts of another. Such a consequence could operate very unjustly to persons dealing, as they would be entitled to do, with any member of the group as a separate legal entity:'

After citing the above reasons, Murphy J confirmed the decision of Laffoy J in the High Court.

Statutory qualification

6.44   The common-law position that a holding company is generally not liable for the trading debts of its subsidiary may be subject to the provisions of ss 140 and 141 of the Companies Act 1990 on the pooling assets of related companies (see **6.10** and **6.22**).

The single economic unit principle in EU law

6.45   The single economic unit principle may be received more favourably by the European Court of Justice (ECJ) than by domestic Irish (and English) courts.

In *VHO Europe BV v Commission of the European Communities (supported by Parker Pen Ltd, intervener)*,[1] the ECJ held that a company and its subsidiaries were to be regarded as a single economic entity for the purposes of Article 85(1) of the Treaty of Rome which prohibits anti-competitive agreements.

A divergence of approach therefore exists between the ECJ and the courts of the EU's common-law jurisdictions. This is not altogether surprising because of the underlying economic objectives in the EEC Treaty.

The ECJ will not only settle disputes between litigating parties; it will do so on the basis of its view or interpretation of what the economic objectives of the Treaty of Rome are attempting to achieve.

The ECJ sees the Treaty of Rome as a framework, and its own function to fill in any gaps left in the Community legal system.

As Professor Hartley explained[2]

> 'the court prefers to interpret texts on the basis of what it thinks they should be trying to achieve; it moulds the law according to what it regards as the needs of the Community. This is sometimes called the "Teleological method of interpretation" but it really goes beyond interpretation properly so-called: it is decision making on the basis of policy.'

Because of the underlying economic objectives in the Treaty of Rome, it would be almost absurd if the ECJ did not recognise the competitive power of a number of companies within a group which constituted a single economic entity. In doing so, the court is not in fundamental disagreement with the common-law approach to the single economic unit principle. It is simply a case of different courts exercising their function according to different criteria.

---

1 [1997] All ER (EC) 163.
2 T.C. Hartley *The Foundations of European Community Law* (OUP, 1988), at Chapters 3 and 4.

PART III

COMPANY REGISTRATION AND EARLY CORPORATE TRANSACTIONS

Chapter 7

THE COMPANY NAME

7.1 As the company is an artificial person created under the law, it must be given a name.

Requirement in memorandum

The memorandum of every company must state:[1]

(1) in the case of a public limited company, the name of the company, with 'public limited company' or 'cuideachta phoibli teoranta' as the last words of the name;

(2) in the case of a company (other than a public limited company) which is limited by shares or by guarantee, the name of the company, with 'limited' or 'teoranta' as the last word of the name.

Power to dispense with the word 'limited'

7.2 Section 24[2] gives the Registrar the power to dispense with 'limited' or 'teoranta' in the name of a company formed for promoting commerce, art, science, religion or any other useful object, which will not apply its profits (if any) to pay dividends to its members.

During 1997, the Minister authorised 17 companies to omit 'Limited' from their names. Authorised companies included 'Action Aid Ireland', 'Parentline' and 'St Brigid's Family Law and Community Centre'.

Change of name

7.3 A company may, by special resolution, change its name.[3] A change of name will not affect company contracts in existence prior to the name change.

Publication of name

7.4 Section 114(1) of the 1963 Act provides that every company must:

(1) paint or affix, and keep painted or affixed, its name on the outside of every office or place in which its business is carried on, in a conspicuous position, in letters easily legible;

(2) have its name engraved in legible characters on its seal;

---

1 Section 6(1) of the 1963 Act. Section 114(5) permits the use of the abbreviations 'Ltd' or 'Teo' and 'plc' or 'cpt'.
2 Of the 1963 Act, as inserted by s 88 of the 2001 Act.
3 See s 23 of the 1963 Act, as amended by s 87 of the 2001 Act.

(3) have its name mentioned in legible characters in all *business letters* of the company and in all notices and other official publications of the company, and in all bills of exchange, promissory notes, endorsements, cheques and orders for money or goods purporting to be signed by or on behalf of the company and in all invoices, receipts and letters of credit of the company.

Fines are imposed on the company and its officers for non-compliance with s 114(1).

Officers' liability for use of name incorrectly

7.5   If an officer issues a business letter, cheque, order or invoice showing the name of the company incorrectly, that officer or any other person acting for the company, will be subject to a fine not exceeding £250, and be personally liable for the debts of the company in the transaction involved, if the company were to default.

In *Penrose v Martyr*,[1] the secretary, who had accepted as agent of the company, a bill drawn on the company in which the word 'limited' as part of its name was omitted, was held personally liable on the bill when it was not paid by the company. In that case, Compton J stated:

> 'The intention of the enactment (a similarly worded clause in the Act of 1856) plainly was to prevent persons from being deceived into the belief that they had a security with the unlimited liability of common law, when they had but the security of a limited company.'

This decision was reinforced by that in *Atkin v Wardle*,[2] where the directors were held personally liable for a bill which they accepted on behalf of 'South Shields Salt Water Baths Co' rather than 'The South Shields Salt Water Baths Company Ltd'.

In *Durham Fancy Goods Ltd v Michael Jackson (Fancy Goods) Ltd*,[3] the defendant company was referred to in the bill of exchange drawn up by the plaintiff as M Jackson (Fancy Goods) Ltd. When the company went into liquidation, the plaintiff sought to make its officer, Michael Jackson, who had accepted the bill on behalf of the company, liable. Mr Jackson had not corrected the error in the company name when signing on its behalf.

Mr Jackson was personally liable. However, because the plaintiff who drew up the bill was responsible for the misdescription in the company name, he was estopped from enforcing the (equivalent of) s 114(4) liability against Mr Jackson.

The officer is only liable as security for the company's debt under s 114(4). It is considered irrelevant to the question of liability whether or not the recipient of

---

1   [1858] 28 LJ (QB) 28.
2   [1889] 5 TLR 734.
3   [1968] 2 All ER 987 (QBD).

a company's cheque was actually misled by the incorrect use of the company name – *Scottish and Newcastle Breweries Ltd v Blair*.[1]

A recent softening of judicial attitude?

7.6 In *Jenice v Dan*,[2] the misspelling of the company's name as Primakeen Ltd rather than Primkeen Ltd did not lead to the director involved being held personally liable. This recent decision illustrates an uncharacteristic judicial approach to a less strictly semantic interpretation of the provisions of the UK's equivalent to s 114(4).[3] It should be remembered, though, that in this case, the misspelling consisted merely of the addition of one letter, 'a', and the plaintiff was in no doubt as to the identity of the company with whom he was dealing. The Court of Appeal took a strict liability approach in *Blum v OCP Repartition SA*,[4] holding a director personally liable when the word 'Ltd' was missing from the company name on one of its cheques – see May LJ's comments advocating strict statutory interpretation.

SIGNIFICANCE OF COMPANY NAME

7.7 Suppose J. Mannion and R. Whyte decide to form a company for the purpose of canning peas and selling these products through the usual wholesale and retail outlets.

If the company is named, as one might expect, Mannion and Whyte Ltd, it is clear that the company will have had no trade record in the vegetable canning business. If, however, the company name was to be, for example, Crosse and Blackwell Ltd, it is likely that this name would make it easier for Mannion and Whyte's company to succeed in business, because customers would confuse it with the well-established Crosse & Blackwell Ltd.

There are statutory controls in place to prevent promoters such as Mannion and Whyte using names for their companies which could take unfair advantage of the reputation of other established businesses. These controls largely take the form of compulsory regulation of business names for new companies under the Registration of Business Names Act 1963 ('RBNA 1963').

Before registering a name under the RBNA 1963, the registrar will take care to see that the name is not likely to mislead the public or affect the reputation of an existing business. However, s 14(3) of the RBNA 1963 does point out that even if a business name is registered under the Act, registration 'shall not be construed as authorising the use of that name, if apart from such registration, the use thereof could be prohibited'. Section 14(3), therefore, makes it clear that even if a business name is registered, if the name is likely to mislead the public into believing that the company is linked to another established

---

1 1967 SLT 72.
2 [1993] BCLC 134, [1994] BCC 333.
3 Section 349(4) of the Companies Act 1985.
4 (1988) 4 BCC 771.

company so as to take advantage of its reputation, the latter company may take action to protect its business reputation in tort: in particular by relying on the tort of passing off.

Let us now focus on these two broad categories of third party protection against misleading business names, ie statutory protection under the RBNA 1963 and the tort of passing off.[1]

Registration of Business Names Act 1963

7.8 There are few legal restrictions on either sole traders or partners using their own names for the purposes of their trading enterprises. However, if either type of 'trader' uses a business name, other than their own true surname, this business name must be registered under the RBNA 1963. So, too, must 'every body corporate having a place of business in the State and carrying on business under a business name which does not consist of its corporate name without any addition'.[2]

The information to be registered under the Act includes:[3]

(1) the business[4] name;
(2) the general nature of the business and principal place where it is carried on;
(3) the company's corporate name and particulars of its principal office;
(4) the date of the adoption of the business name by that company.

The Register is maintained by the Companies Registration Office. The registrar keeps an index of business names registered under the RBNA 1963. The certificate of registration must be displayed prominently at the principal place of business. Any changes of name must also be registered[5] – see s 23 of the 1963 Act as amended by s 87 of the 2001 Act. Section 9(3) of the District Court Rules 1997[6] provides for a person using a trade name to be sued under that name.

Refusal to register a name

7.9 Under s 14(1) of the RBNA 1963, the Minister may refuse to permit the registration of a name which, in his opinion, is undesirable. Section 21 of the Companies Act 1963 contains a similar provision. Registrations refused under ss 14(1) or 21 are subject to appeal to the courts.

Section 21 was amended by s 86 of the 2001 Act so that the Registrar was substituted for the Minister.

---

1 Company officials may also incur a legal liability if they use an incorrect name for the company – see **7.5**.
2 Section 3(d) of the RBNA 1963, reinforced by s 22 of the Companies Act 1963.
3 See s 4 of the RBNA.
4 The use of the abbreviations 'Ltd', 'Teo', 'plc' or 'cpt' alone need not give rise to registration under the RBNA – see s 22(2) of the Companies Act 1963.
5 See s 7 of the RBNA 1963.
6 SI 1997/93.

Penalties

7.10   The penalties for non-observance of the RBNA 1963 are set out in ss 10 and 11. These include a maximum fine of £100 and/or, on summary conviction, imprisonment for up to six months.

Publication of registered business name

7.11   Every company must affix or print its name legibly on the outside of every office in which its business is carried on. Each company must also engrave its name on the company seal and print or write it in all business letters and cheques – see s 114(1) of the Companies Act 1963.

Directors' particulars on letterheadings

7.12   Generally, under s 196 of the Companies Act 1963, in all business letters which are sent by a company to any person, the following particulars relating to a director must be included:

(1) his present Christian name, or initials, and present surname;
(2) any former Christian names and surnames; and
(3) his nationality, if not Irish.

Mistaken registration

7.13   If, through inadvertence or otherwise, a company is registered with a name which, in the opinion of the Registrar, is too similar to the name of a company in existence which is already registered, the newer company may change its name voluntarily with the approval of the Registrar, or if the Registrar so directs within six months of registration, must change its name within six weeks of being ordered to do so.[1]

During 1997, 1,901 name changes were approved by the Minister. He also directed 18 companies to change their names because of some or all of the following factors: the degree of similarity between the two names either phonetically or in spelling; similarities in the objects of the two companies; or the proximity to each other of the registered offices of the companies.

THE TORT OF PASSING OFF

7.14   As mentioned above, registration of a company name under the RBNA 1963 will be no bar to proceedings taken against the company if the registered name too closely resembles that of an existing company or business. The company with the offending name may be liable for the tort of 'passing off'.

---

1 See s 23(1), (2), (3) and (4), as amended by s 87 of the 2001 Act.

A tort is a civil wrong. The tort of passing off, essentially, encompasses the civil wrong of representing a business which is being carried on by another as being carried on by oneself.

7.15 The purpose of this tort is to protect a plaintiff company's proprietary interest in the goodwill of its business. In *Ewing v Buttercup Margarine Co Ltd*,[1] the plaintiff, who carried on business under the trade name of Buttercup Dairy Co, was successful in restraining a company from being registered under the business name of the Buttercup Margarine Co Ltd.

At common law, if a company carries on, or proposes to carry on business under a name which is *likely to deceive the public* into thinking that the company's business is that of the complaining party, an injunction may be granted to protect the complainant against a form of unfair competition.

Essentially, the tort of passing off seeks to prevent a different company from reaping the benefit of the goodwill attached to the plaintiff's business. In *CIR v Muller & Co Margarine Ltd*,[2] Lord Macnaghten stated, 'Goodwill is the benefit and advantage of the good name, reputation and connection of a business. It is the attractive force which brings in custom'. Again, in *Spalding A G Bros v Gamage Ltd*,[3] Lord Parker confirmed that the property right protected in a passing off action 'is not property in the mark, name or get-up improperly used by the defendant, but property in the business or goodwill likely to be injured by the misrepresentation'.

In *Dockrell (Thomas) Sons & Co Ltd v Dockrell (William H) and Co Ltd*,[4] the plaintiff company were builders' merchants who had carried on business in Dublin for many years. The defendant company was incorporated to carry on the business of moneylending although there was no promoter connected with it having the name of Dockrell.

The court held that in the absence of any other reasonable explanation, it must be presumed that the Dockrell name was being utilised by the defendant company to benefit from the reputation of the plaintiff company. Accordingly, the court granted an injunction to prevent its use.

However, if a company has a word in ordinary common use as part of its name, it may not be able to prevent another company from using the same word. For example, in *Aerators Ltd v Tollitt*,[5] the plaintiffs sought, unsuccessfully, to prevent the use of the name 'Automatic Aerators Patents Ltd'. The court held that the word 'aerator' was a word in common use in the English language, and therefore the plaintiff company enjoyed no monopoly on its use.

---

1 [1917] 2 Ch 1 (CA).
2 [1901] AC 217.
3 (1915) 32 RPC 273 (HL).
4 [1941] 75 ILTR 222.
5 [1902] 2 Ch 319.

Proof of actual deception may not be necessary

7.16 Passing off can occur where it is established that persons are likely to be deceived. It may not be necessary for a plaintiff to adduce proof of an actual instance of deception.

7.17 In *Muckross Park Hotel Ltd v K. Randles and Dromhall Hotel Co Ltd,*[1] the plaintiff owned the 'Muckross Hotel' in Muckross, Co Kerry. The defendant started building a new hotel on the road from Killarney to Muckross. The new hotel was to be named 'The Muckross Court Hotel'. The plaintiff claimed that the defendant had copied, not only his hotel's name, but also its hotel sign, its note paper and certain aspects of its furnishings. There had been a number of incidents showing great confusion between the two hotels.

Barron J granted the plaintiff an injunction restraining the defendant from using the word 'Muckross' in the title or name of their hotel premises.

The name 'Muckross' had a considerable value, which was the number of people who knew it and knew what it stood for; which was of a similar nature to goodwill. Barron J stated:

> ' "Goodwill" is a term used in some of the reported cases. However, it seems to me that "reputation" is a more correct word in the context of passing off. "Goodwill" is essentially a balance sheet term. It is an intangible asset. It is, in my view, inter alia, the additional sum which would be paid for premises to carry on a business there which has either now or in the past been carried on and which will, accordingly, have a fund of customers already in existence. The value in the name is in the same position. Its importance lies in the number of people who knew it and what it stands for.'

Barron J then decided that the name 'The Muckross', when applied to hotels in this area, had acquired a secondary meaning, and meant the plaintiff's hotel. And even if there were no secondary meaning attached to the name 'The Muckross', all the facts in this instance combined together made it likely that people would be deceived into thinking that the defendant's hotel was that of the plaintiff.

7.18 In *An Post National Treasury Management Agency and the Minister for Finance v Irish Permanent plc,*[2] Kinlen J applied the ratio of the Muckross Park Hotel case, holding that with regard to the alleged confusion of the defendant's product (saving certificates) with that of the plaintiff, the matter which had to be established was whether, in the opinion of the court, persons were likely to be deceived. It was not necessary for the plaintiffs to establish an actual instance of deception.

The nature of the passing off action had evolved so that it was no longer restricted to a trader representing the goods of another party as his own. It is

---

1 [1995] 1 IR 130. See also *Dockrell v Dockrell & Co* in **7.15** where an injunction was granted to avoid confusion caused by the use of similar surnames in the company names.
2 [1995] 1 IR 140.

now extended to the descriptive use of a descriptive term, in order to protect the goodwill in the descriptive term enjoyed by those entitled to use it.

7.19   Further, in considering whether to grant relief, the court should bear in mind that the purpose of the passing off action is to prevent unfair competition likely to be caused by a person seeking to gain commercial advantage from creating confusion in the public mind between its own trading activities and those of another party, as applied in *C & A Modes Ltd v C & A (Waterford) Ltd* case (see **7.23**). This confusion in the public mind was also calculated to operate to the detriment of the goodwill possessed in his goods or products by that other party.

Kinlen J, after reasoning as above, granted the plaintiffs an interlocutory injunction. In doing so, he reinforced the comments of Budd J in *Polycell Products Ltd v O'Carroll and Ors,*[1] who said, 'a person who passes off the goods of another acquires to some extent the benefit of the business reputation of the rival trader and gets the advantages of his advertising'.

Mere registration of the company name may constitute the tort

7.20   In *Guinness Ireland Group and Ors v Kilkenny Brewery Co Ltd,*[2] the plaintiff had launched a new beer in 1987, which it labelled 'Kilkenny Irish Beer'. The defendant company was started in 1995 to develop a microbrewery in Kilkenny. 'Kilkenny Irish Beer' was sold in Europe and in Ireland when the Kilkenny Brewery Co Ltd was formed. The plaintiff claimed, inter alia, that the name of the defendant company was likely to mislead people into believing that there was a link between it, the Guinness Ireland Group and its product 'Kilkenny Irish Beer'.

The court accepted the plaintiff's argument, ordering the defendant company to change its name. It did so, notwithstanding that the defendant company had never actually traded; pointing out that a company still has statutory obligations in relation to the publication of its name (eg on letterheads) where that name could mislead the public.

7.21   Thus, as in this case, the mere registration of a similar company name may constitute sufficient grounds for a passing off action. It is irrelevant that no use was being made of the name, or that the company was dormant.

Occasionally, the appropriate remedy may be damages rather than injunction

7.22   In exceptional circumstances, the court may find the awarding of damages a preferable remedy to the granting of an injunction. For example, in *Falcon Leisure Group v Owners Abroad plc T/A Falcon Leisure Group,*[3] the plaintiff

---

1 [1959] IR Jur Rep 34.
2 [1999] 1 ILRM 531.
3 [1991] 1 IR 175.

company had operated a travel business in Dublin and Wicklow since 1970. The defendants' had carried on business as a major tour operator in the UK.

The defendants opened an Irish office in 1988. They were aware of the plaintiff company, but did not anticipate any confusion between the two different businesses using the 'Falcon' name.

The court held that the plaintiff was entitled to succeed with its passing off action, because its goodwill had been appropriated wrongfully even if innocently, by the defendants. However, because of the enormous expense entailed in granting an injunction, the court decided that it was preferable in this instance to grant the plaintiff company damages, in lieu of an injunction.

The primary purpose of awarding damages was to fund the mounting of an advertising campaign by the plaintiff, to explain to the public and persons engaged in the travel agency business the differences between the two companies.

A passing off action is available to non-Irish based companies

7.23   The protection available to companies in a passing off action is not limited by State boundaries, as the case of *C & A Modes v C & A (Waterford) Ltd*[1] illustrates.

C & A Modes was registered in England and, in 1972, had no branches in the Republic of Ireland. It did, however, advertise there. The defendant company, C & A (Waterford) Ltd, was registered in 1972. It was also, like C & A Modes, involved in the retail clothing business. In the Supreme Court judgment, Henchy J stated:

> 'Goodwill does not necessarily stop at a frontier ... What has to be established for the success of the plaintiff's claim ... is that by his business activities ... he has generated within the State a property right in a goodwill which will be violated by the passing off.'

The Court held that C & A (Waterford) Ltd's name involved a passing off which violated the English company's property right to goodwill. Accordingly, the Court granted an injunction to prevent the continued use of the offending business name.

---

1   [1976] IR 198.

Chapter 8

CHOICE OF COMPANY TYPE AND REGISTRATION PROCEDURES

INTRODUCTION

8.1 When a number of people decide to go into business together, they can elect to trade either as an *unincorporated association* such as a partnership, or as a company incorporated under the registration procedure available by virtue of the Companies Acts 1963 to 1990.[1] This registration procedure is, as we shall see later, also now available to permit the formation of 'one-man' or single member companies.

Registered companies may be formed with either limited or unlimited liability for their investors. Investors' liability may be limited either by shares or by guarantee.

Companies limited by shares

8.2 A company limited by shares is one where the legal liability of each investor for the debts of the company in the event of its winding up, is limited to the amount (if any) unpaid on his shares. For example, suppose the issued share capital of Alpha Ltd is:

Issued and fully paid

10,000 ordinary shares of IR £1 each

£10,000

Issued and partly paid

20,000 ordinary shares of IR £1 each
IR £0.40 per share paid

£8,000

£18,000

In the event of Alpha Ltd becoming insolvent and being wound up, its creditors would have no recourse against the holders of the 10,000 fully paid ordinary shareholders.

---

1 Other corporations also exist which were formed by royal charter or by special act of the Oireachtas, eg what are popularly called the semi-State companies, such as An Post, Aer Rianta Teoranta, Air Lingus Teoranta, etc. These semi-State companies would have been formed by the government using the powers conferred on it by a special Act.

There are also some semi-State corporate bodies which are not companies. These corporations do not have members or share capital; their funding is provided by the government or by borrowings guaranteed by it. Examples of 'non-company' semi-States – usually styled 'board' or 'authority' – include Board Failte and others commonly known by their initials only, such as E.S.B. and R.T.E.

The partly paid shareholders have only paid 40p for each of their £1 shares. They are, therefore, liable to contribute the unpaid balance of 60p per share when requested to do so by the liquidator of the company. Their liability is, however, limited to 100p per share.

Companies limited by shares are the most usual form of company registered.

Companies limited by guarantee

8.3   In this type of registered company, each member undertakes to contribute a certain amount, say £1,000, in the event of the company's liquidation.

The memorandum of association of a company limited by guarantee would include the following typical clauses:[1]

(1) the liability of the members is limited; and
(2) every member of the company undertakes to contribute to the assets of the company in the event of its being wound up while he is a member, or within one year afterwards, for payment of the debts and liabilities of the company contracted before he ceases to be a member, ... such amount as may be required, not exceeding £1,000.

Companies limited by guarantee are more suited to the needs of professional bodies[2] than entrepreneurs and investors seeking to form business associations to engage in commercial trading. This is reflected in the objects clause contained in the specimen memorandum of association in Table C. This clause is as follows:

'The objects for which the company is established are the promotion of research into matters of a scientific nature ...'

The management of companies limited by guarantee may be carried out by an elected council or committee, instead of a board of directors, if the members so decide.

A company limited by guarantee may also have a share capital.[3]

Unlimited companies

8.4   An unlimited company is one where the members are fully liable for the company's debts in the event of its liquidation, ie the *members voluntarily forego* the benefits of trading with limited liability.

The memorandum of association of an unlimited company simply contains name and objects clauses. It does not include clauses limiting the liability of members in the event of the winding up of the company.

---

1 See Table C of the Companies Act 1963 ('CA 1963') at p 703 of the Act.
2 Also educational and charitable bodies.
3 See Table D of the CA 1963 (at p 734 of the Act).

Unlimited companies are not common or, indeed, suitable for trading purposes. However, they may be formed for tax management purposes, with the intention that the company will not actively transact business.

PUBLIC AND PRIVATE COMPANIES

8.5 All companies, whether limited by shares or guarantee, or unlimited, will be formed as either a public or a private company.

Public companies

8.6 These companies must have a minimum number of seven members.[1] Public companies must be formed with a *minimum share capital*[2] of £30,000, of which at least 25 per cent must be paid up. Their names must end with plc or cpt.[3]

The main advantage of forming a public company is that there are no maximum limits on the number of members, and the shares of members are freely transferable by sale on the Stock Exchange or elsewhere. Accordingly, members are facilitated in realising their investment if they desire to sell their shares.[4]

The largest industrial, financial and trading companies are public companies whose shares are quoted on Stock Exchange lists. Daily newspapers, such as the *Irish Times,* normally publish the previous day's market information for shares of public companies under the heading 'Dublin Closing Prices'. The information published is each company name, market guide price, and date of previous bargain, business done and closing quotation. These prices are based on those prevailing at 4.30 pm the previous day. Footnotes to this information will disclose whether the business done was by a connected party, a bargain in a small amount, or whether the price was ex-dividend.

The list of Dublin Closing Prices published in daily newspapers, by courtesy of the Irish Stock Exchange, contains share prices for listed public companies. These include AIB, Arnotts, Bank of Ireland, CRH, DCC, First Active, Fyffes, Golden Vale, Irish Life and Permanent, Kingspan, Smurfit, United Drug and Waterford Wedgwood.

---

1 Section 5 of the CA 1963.
2 The formation of public companies limited by guarantee, and having a share capital, is prohibited by s 7 of the Companies (Amendment) Act 1983. The authorised minimum share capital is prescribed in s 19 of that Act.
3 Section 4 of the Companies (Amendment) Act 1983.
4 For a profit or at a loss – see also Chapter 10.

Private companies

8.7 Private companies cannot have more than 50 members[1] and are not allowed to sell their shares to the public.[2] Because of this limitation, the company, in turn, restricts the rights of investors to transfer (sell) their shares.

Section 5 of the CA 1963 provided that a private company had to be formed with at least *two* members. This provision is now reformed by the European Communities (Single-Member Private Limited Companies) Regulations 1994 (the 1994 Regulations).[3]

Article 3(1) of the 1994 Regulations stipulates that:

> 'notwithstanding any enactment or rule of law to the contrary, a private company limited by shares or by guarantee *may be formed by one person*, and *may have one member*, to the extent permitted by the Companies Acts and these Regulations.'

FACTORS AFFECTING CHOICE OF CORPORATE FORM

8.8 Any investors and/or entrepreneurs wishing to trade as a business association must initially decide on the type of company to form. The relevant factors to consider might include:

(1) the objectives of the business, ie is the enterprise commercial, as distinct from professional services; are its aims educational, charitable or non-profit-making?
(2) does the proposed enterprise need large amounts of capital? If so, will public investment be necessary?
(3) is the company required by external regulations, eg a professional body or statutory requirement,[4] to adopt a particular form?
(4) whether the promoters wish to maintain a level of confidentiality concerning the company's financial position once it has commenced trading.

Taking these, and other factors into account, the promoters will decide on whether the company is to be limited by shares or by guarantee, or (very rarely) unlimited. They then have to follow the appropriate procedure for registering the company. Registration will be complete upon the issue by the registrar of a certificate of incorporation.[5]

---

1 Excluding employees and former employees – see s 33 of the CA 1963.
2 Section 33 of the 1963 Act, and s 21 of the Companies (Amendment) Act 1983.
3 SI 1994/275, implementing the Twelfth EU Company Law Directive No 89/667/EEC – published in [1989] OJ L395/40.
4 Eg Art 7(1) of the European Communities (Non-Life Insurance) Framework Regulations 1994, SI 1994/359, stipulates that only business associations adopting the form of a company limited by shares, or by guarantee or unlimited will be licensed to transact non-life insurance business in Ireland. These regulations also provide substantial minimum capital requirements for insurance companies.
5 The company's 'birth certificate'.

Procedures for the formation of a company

8.9 As a consideration for the privileges of incorporation and, indeed, limitation of liability,[1] registration of a company requires compliance with a formal statutory procedure.

Section 5 of the CA 1963 provides that any two (now one – see **8.7**) or more persons, by subscribing to a memorandum of association, can form an incorporated company.

Memorandum of association

8.10 This document is central to the constitution of the company. Section 6[2] specifies that the memorandum of every company must state:

(1) the company name;
(2) the objects of the company;
(3) that the liability of its members is limited either by share or by guarantee;
(4) in the case of a company having a share capital, the amount of this capital, and its division into shares of a fixed amount.

The memorandum[3] must be printed, stamped as a deed, and be signed by each subscriber, in the presence of at least one witness.[4]

Articles of association

8.11 These are regulations governing the internal management of the company. Together with the memorandum of association, they form the constitution of a company. The two documents are broadly distinguishable by the fact that the memorandum, generally, governs the *external* actions of a company in relation to its structure and objects, whilst the articles govern the *internal* workings and relationships within a company. This internal perspective of the articles focuses on such matters as appointment and powers of directors, shareholders' rights and liabilities, and procedures at meetings.[5]

The articles must be printed, paragraphed and numbered, stamped as a deed, signed by the subscribers and witnessed.[6] The legislature has provided a model set of articles in Table A of the Companies Act 1963.

Section 13 of the CA 1963 permits companies to adopt all or any of the regulations in Table A. Most new companies would adopt this model with such exclusions, additions and amendments as deemed necessary to meet that particular company's needs. Sections 80 to 83 of the 2001 Act introduced a

---

1 Unlike the formation of an unincorporated association, such as a partnership, which can be created informally.
2 Of the CA 1963. See also Parts IV A and VII A.
3 The contents of the memorandum of association will be examined more closely in Chapters 12 and 36.
4 Section 7 of the CA 1963, as amended by s 81 of the 2001 Act.
5 The articles of association are dealt with more fully in Parts IV A, B, C, D, E and VII B.
6 Section 14 of the CA 1963 as amended by s 80 of the 2001 Act.

user-friendly procedure for the filing of reference documents with the Registrar, so as to facilitate the registration of the Memorandum and Articles of Association.

Approval of proposed company name

8.12   It is advisable to write to the registrar of companies submitting a list of proposed names, asking if he would approve all or any of them. The registrar, as we saw in Chapter 7,[1] may object to a name.

Lodgement of documents

8.13   The following documents must be prepared and lodged with the registrar:

(1) the memorandum of association;
(2) the articles (if Table A not adopted);
(3) a statutory declaration of compliance with the requirements of the Companies Acts in respect of registration signed either by the solicitor[2] involved in the company formation, or by a person named in the articles as a director or secretary of the company;
(4) a statement in prescribed form containing particulars of the directors,[3] the company secretary and the registered office. This statement must be signed by, or on behalf of the subscribers and persons named in it as directors and secretary;[4]
(5) a cheque for the stamp duty.

The Companies (Amendment) (No 2) Act 1999 introduced additional requirements for company formation.

A company cannot now be formed and registered unless the registrar is satisfied that the company will carry on an (economic) activity in that State.

Section 42(2) sets out the details to be contained in a statutory declaration to be sworn by a director or secretary (or solicitor) which will satisfy the registrar of the company's intention to carry on the required activity within the State.

Again, a company must have at least one director who is resident in Ireland, unless the promoters lodge a prescribed bond with the registrar (see below).

The test of residence is the same as in the Taxes Acts – see s 44(8) and (9) for precise details.

---

1 See **7.13**, and s 87 of the 2001 Act.
2 See s 397 of the CA 1963 for competitive restriction in s 58 of the Solicitors Act 1954.
3 Where a person proposed as a director has been disqualified under the law of another State, an additional statement has to be delivered to the Registrar – see s 3A of the 1982 Act, inserted by s 101 of the 2001 Act.
4 See s 3 of the Companies (Amendment) Act 1982.

Exemption from resident director requirement

8.14 A company may be exempted from the resident director requirement if it obtains a bond or certificate.

Section 43(2) to (8) details the bond requirements. The bond must be to the value of £20,000.

A copy of the bond must be attached to the registration papers (or in some circumstances, the annual return – see s 43(8).

If a person ceases to be a director of a company, and at the time, was the only director resident in the State, he must, within 14 days, give notice of cessation to the registrar, in writing.

The company and every officer in default can be guilty of a criminal offence if the company does not have a resident director or a bond – see s 44(ii). In addition, the registrar has the power under s 43(15) to strike off a defaulting company.

Section 44 also makes provision for exemption from the resident director requirement when a company is in possession of a certificate complying with s 44(2) to (9).

The registrar has the power to grant a certificate that the company has a real and continuous link with one or more economic activities that are being carried on in the State. However, he will not issue this certificate unless the company concerned tenders proof that it has such a link. Proof could be a letter from the Revenue Commissioners that they had reasonable grounds to believe such a link existed – see s 44(5).

Summary of 1999 (No 2) Act requirements

8.15 The registrar may accept a statutory declaration in prescribed form that the purpose(s) for which the company is being formed include the carrying on of an activity in the State, as required by the 1999 Amendment Act.

Unless the registrar grants a certificate that the (proposed) company has a real and continuous link with one or more economic activities that are being carried on in the State, every Irish registered company must have one resident director, unless it holds a bond, in prescribed from, to the value of £20,000.

Companies already in existence when this section of the 1999 Amendment Act came into force had 12 months to comply with it – see s 43(2)(b).

If none of a company's directors are resident in Ireland, a copy of the bond must be attached to (a) the registration documentation, and (b) the annual return.

The Act prescribes criminal sanctions if a company does not have a resident director[1] or a bond. In addiction, the registrar is given the power to strike off the company for non compliance with these provisions (see Chapter 53).

Issuing of certificate of incorporation

8.16 If the registrar is satisfied that the requirements of the Companies Acts have been complied with, he will issue a certificate of incorporation. The company comes into existence from that moment, as under s 389 of the CA 1963, a certificate of incorporation is deemed to be 'prima facie' evidence of incorporation.

Off the shelf companies

8.17 What we have illustrated in the above procedure is a 'made to measure' company. But in many instances, people simply wish to change their business from being operated on a sole trader basis into a company. To facilitate this conversion, it is possible to buy a 'shelf company'.

Off the shelf companies are generally formed with standard articles, and the objects clause drafted in such a way as to make it suitable for most commercial purposes. The company name, however, can be made specific.

Off the shelf companies may be purchased from company formation agents, some of whom advertise their services in the daily newspapers. A company formation agent will usually send a client the certificate of incorporation, together with the memorandum and articles of association.

Publication in *Iris Oifigiúil*

8.18 Article 4 of the European Communities (Companies) Regulations 1973[2] (the 1973 Regulations) provides that, within six weeks of the issue of the certificate of incorporation, the company is required to publish in *Iris Oifigiúil* that the certificate has been issued by the registrar, and the memorandum and articles of association, together with notice of the address of the registered office, have been delivered to him.

The company is not required to publish the contents of these documents: merely the fact that they have been issued or delivered.

---

1 Any provision in the articles of association prohibiting an Irish resident from being a director is also void under s 43(12).

2 SI 1973/163, implementing the First EU Company Law Directive No 68/151/EEC. These regulations also specify how a failure to publish the prescribed information may affect third parties dealing with the company (see Art 10).

Single-member private companies, limited by shares or by guarantee

8.19 Regulation 4 of the 1994 Regulations (see **8.7**) stipulates that only one person need subscribe his name to the memorandum of association of a single-member company.

All the provisions of the Companies Acts which apply to private companies apply, mutatis mutandis, to single-member companies. At the end of 1997 there were 7,766 single-member companies registered.

Minimum share capital for new public limited company

8.20 If the new company to be formed is a public one, then the minimum share capital requirement applies. This was introduced by s 19 of the Companies (Amendment) Act 1983 and is £30,000,[1] of which at least 25 per cent must be paid up.

Unlike a private company, a public company cannot commence business immediately after the issuing of the certificate of incorporation – see **9.18** and **11.1**.

Unlimited companies

8.21 If persons wished to form an unlimited company, then the memorandum would omit the capital and limitation of liability clauses. Table E, Part I of the CA 1963 contains the model memorandum of association for this type of company, whilst Table E, Part III sets out the appropriate articles of association for a private unlimited company.

Registration activity

8.22 During 1997, a total of 19,023 new companies were registered. These registrations consisted of the following company types:

Private Limited by shares	17,345	(91.2%)
Public Limited	151	(0.8%)
Unlimited	788	(4.1%)
Guarantee	739	(3.9%)

Make-up of register of companies

8.23 On 31 December 1997, 90.9 per cent of all companies registered were private, 0.5 per cent public, 3.4 per cent unlimited and 3.8 per cent guarantee.

There were also 2,842 (1.72 per cent) external companies – see **11.4**.

---

1 The Minister has the power to increase this amount.

CHANGE OF STATUS

8.24 It is possible for companies, once formed, to subsequently change their status. As a result, a 'two-member' company may convert to a single-member company, and vice versa. Similarly, a private company may change to become a public company.

Change to single-member company

8.25 If the number of investors in a private company is reduced to one and all the shares in that company are registered in that same investor's name, then that company will become a single-member company.

Regulation 5 of the 1994 Regulations also provides that when the company becomes a single-member company due to the reduction in members, that fact and the identity of the sole investor must be notified[1] in prescribed form to the registrar of companies, within 28 days of the reduction in membership.

Change from single-member company

8.26 Regulation 6 sets out a similar procedure to that outlined above, where the number of investors in a single-member company increases. In this event, when membership increases to at least two, but not more than 50, the single-member company becomes a private company. Here again, the company must notify the registrar of the change.

Change from public company into private company

8.27 Section 14 of the Companies (Amendment) Act 1983 sets out the circumstances in which a public company may re-register as a private company, together with the procedures involved.

Essentially, a special[2] resolution has to be passed. This resolution must:

(1) alter the memorandum so that it no longer states that the company is to be a public limited company; and
(2) alter the articles to include the provisions necessary under s 33,[3] eg maximum of 50 members and restrictions on members' rights to sell shares.

Minority protection

8.28 Section 15 of the 1983 Act gives a minority of five per cent, or at least 50 members, or those holding five per cent of the value of the company's issued

---

1 If the company fails to notify the registrar, it and its officers who are to blame will be guilty of a criminal offence, and subject, on summary conviction, to a fine not exceeding £1,000.
2 Ie one requiring a 75 per cent majority.
3 Of the CA 1963.

share capital, the right to apply to the court to cancel the special resolution authorising the change in status of the company.

The powers of the court to deal with the minority's complaint are elaborated in s 15(6) and (7).

Re-registration of private company as public company

8.29 Formation of a new plc is quite rare. Most public limited companies start life as successful private companies which subsequently convert to plcs.

Prior to 1983, a special resolution deleting the restrictive articles of association necessary under s 33 might have sufficed to make the change. Now, however, detailed additional requirements and procedures are prescribed by ss 9 and 10 of the Companies (Amendment) Act 1983. These extra requirements are, essentially, aimed at ensuring that a plc possesses the statutory minimum nominal and paid up share capital, and that its net assets at least equal the total of its called up share capital and undistributable reserves (defined in s 46(2)). Proof of the minimum asset requirement will require a written statement by the company auditors that, in their opinion, its balance sheet[1] net assets were sufficient to cover the prescribed aggregated liabilities.

The directors must also forward a copy of the relevant balance sheet, accompanied by an unqualified report by the company's auditors in relation to that balance sheet and make a statutory declaration.[2]

If, and when, the registrar is satisfied with the application, he will:

(1) retain the application and supporting documentation; and
(2) issue the company with a (new) certificate of incorporation stating that the company is a plc.

Third party rights

8.30 Section 9(10) makes it clear that re-registration will not affect any rights or obligations of the company, or render defective any legal proceedings by or against the company.

Conversion of unlimited company into limited company and vice versa

8.31 Under s 20 of the CA 1963, as amended by s 53 of the 1983 Act, an unlimited company may be converted into a company limited by shares or by guarantee. The procedure is again based on the passing of a special resolution.

Since s 52 of the Companies (Amendment) Act 1983 came into force, a limited company may convert into an unlimited company. However, because of the

---

1 Which must have been prepared not more than seven months before the application for re-registration.
2 See s 9(3).

serious nature of this change, in effect foregoing the investor's fundamental protection of limitation of liability, all members must assent to the re-registration of the company as unlimited.

Chapter 9

PROMOTERS AND PRE-INCORPORATION CONTRACTS

PROMOTERS

9.1 The persons who generate the idea of starting up a company and then taking steps to register it, are known as *promoters.*

Definitions of promoter

9.2 In the case of *Whaley Bridge Calico Printing Co v Green,*[1] Bowen J defined the term promoter as:

> 'a term not of law, but of business, usefully summing up in a single word a number of business operations familiar to the commercial world, by which a company is brought into existence.'

Again, in *Twycross v Grant,*[2] a promoter is described as:

> 'one who undertakes to form a company with reference to a given object, and to set it going, and who takes the necessary steps to accomplish that purpose.'

For example, in *Components Tube Co v Naylor,*[3] MacCabe, knowing he could acquire property for £50,000, conceived the idea of purchasing it, in the event of his being able successfully to float a company to buy it. Thenceforth, to cite Palles CB:

> 'the one governing motive which operated upon the minds of MacCabe ..., [and other promoters] in reference to the acquisition of the property, was that they might form a company to take the property off their hands at a profit ... so that ... he was during the entire of the period which we have review, stamped with the character of a promoter.'

Accordingly, Palles CB held that MacCabe was a promoter of the Components Tube Co. In *Twycross v Grant*, Cockburn CJ also stated:

> 'Of course, if a governing body, in the shape of directors, has been formed and they take ... [over] what remains to be done in the way of forming the company into their own hands, the functions of the promoters is at an end.'

There exists a narrower statutory definition of promoter. For the purposes of civil liability, in respect of mis-statements in a prospectus under s 49 of the CA 1963,[4] a promoter is defined as meaning:

---

1 (1880) 5 QBD 109 – a definition approved in *Re Greendale Ltd* (Unreported) 12 March 1996.
2 (1877) 2 CPD 469.
3 [1900] 2 IR 1 (QBD).
4 See **10.59**.

'a promoter who *was a party* to the *preparation of the prospectus* ... but does not include any person by reason of his acting in a professional capacity for persons engaged in procuring the formation of the company.'[1] (author's emphasis)

This statutory definition should be viewed as restricted to actions under s 49. For the remainder of this chapter, the term 'promoter' is used in the wider legal context embraced within the judicial definitions illustrated above. It should be remembered, though, that even within the wider definition of promoter, a solicitor or accountant who provides professional services in connection with forming the company will not, simply by providing these services, be deemed a promoter.[2] If, however, the professional is more closely involved with the creation of the company, actively desiring that it be registered, he may well be deemed to be one of its promoters.

Relationship between promoter and company

9.3 In *Lydney and Wigpool Iron Ore Co v Bird*,[3] Lindley LJ outlined the legal relationship between a promoter and his company thus:

'although not an agent of the company nor a trustee of it before its formation, the old familiar principles of the law agency and of trusteeship have been extended ... to meet such cases.

It is perfectly well settled that a promoter of a company is accountable to it for all moneys secretly obtained by him from it, just as if the relationship of principal and agent, or of trustee and *cestui qui trust*[4] had really existed between him and the company when the money was so obtained'.

Thus, if a promoter makes a secret profit, he must account to the company for it. He is, however, only bound to account for the profit he has made after deducting all legitimate expenses, such as solicitors' and surveyors' fees and printing costs incurred in forming the company.

Whilst, at times, the tests for identifying a promoter may not be precise, nevertheless, once a person is classified as a promoter his legal position is quite unambiguous. A promoter is not a trustee or agent of the company. He stands in a fiduciary relationship towards the company which he promotes. As a result, he must not make, either directly or indirectly, a profit at the expense of the company, without its knowledge and consent. As Lord Cairns said in *Erlanger v New Sombrero Phosphate Co*:[5]

'It is now necessary that I should state ... in what position I understand the promoters to be placed with reference to the company which they proposed to form. They stand, in my opinion, undoubtedly in a fiduciary position. They have in their hands the creation and moulding of the company; they have the power of

---

1 Section 49(8)(a).

2 In *Re Great Wheel Polgooth Ltd* (1883) 53 LJ Ch 42, it was held that a person who merely acts as the agent or employee of a promoter is not himself a promoter – a decision reinforced by s 49(8)(a) of the 1963 Act in relation to the preparation of a prospectus.

3 (1886) 33 Ch D 85, at p 94.

4 Ie beneficiary under a trust.

5 (1878) 3 App Cas 1218 (HL).

defining how, and when, and in what shape, and under what supervision, it shall start into existence and begin to act as a trading corporation. If they are doing all this in order that the company may ... become, through its managing directors, the purchaser of the property of themselves, (the promoters), it is, in my opinion, incumbent upon the promoters to take care that in forming the company they provide it with ... a board of directors, who shall both be aware that the property which they are asked to buy is the property of the promoters, and who shall be competent and impartial judges as to whether the purchase ought or ought not to be made.'

Promoter's fiduciary relationship

9.4   The promoter's fiduciary relationship means that he is under a legal duty towards the company to *disclose* any potential profit and to *account* for it.

If, therefore, the promoter wishes to sell his own property to the company, he will have to disclose his personal interest and account to the company for profits which he might otherwise have retained. It is not the profit which the law forbids; it is the non-disclosure of it.

Duties of disclosure

9.5   If a promoter wishes to sell his own property to the company, he should disclose his interest to either:

(1) a board of independent directors,[1] or the company in general meeting;[2] or
(2) to the intended investors;[3] or
(3) to the public by means of listing particulars or a prospectus.[4]

A promoter cannot contract out of his fiduciary duties by inserting provisions to that effect in the company's articles of association.[5]

A promoter can therefore sell his property to the company provided he makes a full disclosure of all the facts to it. In *Erlanger v The New Sombrero Phosphate Co*, Lord Cairns also suggested that this should be to an independent board of directors, stating:

> 'I do not say that an owner of property may not promote and form a joint stock company, and then sell his property to it, but I do say that if he does he is bound to take care that he sells it to the company through the medium of *a board of directors who can and do exercise an independent and intelligent judgment on the transaction*.'

In *Lagunas Nitrate Co v Lagunas Syndicate*,[6] the court suggested disclosure could be made to the existing and intended shareholders (who must be independent) by *means of a prospectus*.

---

1 *Hopkins v Shannon Transport Systems Ltd* (unreported) 10 July 1972 (HC).
2 *Gluckstein v Barnes* [1900] AC 240.
3 *Salomon v Salomon & Co* [1890] AC 22. Aaron Salomon had disclosed his interest and potential profit to all other members of the company (his family).
4 See **10.14** and **10.19**.
5 *Omnium Electric Palaces Ltd v Baines* [1941] 1 Ch 332.
6 [1899] 2 Ch 392 (CA).

Again, in *Sean Hopkins v Shannon Transport Systems Ltd*,[1] the court decided that disclosure should be made either to an independent board of directors or to the company in general meeting. In that case, Pringle J stated:

> 'Under article 8 of the company's articles where a contract is being entered into in which the directors have an interest, that interest, in order to make the contract valid, must be disclosed at the meeting of the directors at which the contract is determined on and the interested director must not vote (see also s 194(1) of the Companies Act 1963). Furthermore, it has been held that the disclosure must be to directors who are independent, and not to other directors who are equally interested in the contract in question (see *Lagunas Nitrate Co v Langunas Syndicate; Gluckstein v Barnes* [1900] AC 24; *Erlanger v New Sombrero Phosphate Co*) nor does it avail when two or more directors are interested to split up the resolution and for each director to abstain from voting on the part in which he is interested (see *North Eastern Insurance Co* [1919] 1 Ch 198). Here there is no evidence and there is no minute, as to any meeting of directors having been held in reference to this agreement and in fact no such meeting capable of passing any resolution could have been held, because the quorum of directors was two and when a director is not entitled to vote he cannot be reckoned in estimating a quorum. Nor is there any evidence of any general meeting having been held to approve of the contract ...'

Common-law remedies of the company

9.6 The remedies of the company against promoters were originally developed at common law. However, since 1983, there have been statutory rules introduced to protect the company.

Rescission

9.7 At common law, if any profit is not disclosed, the company's remedy can vary according to when the property in question was acquired by the promoter, ie whether the property was acquired before or after the person became a promoter.

When the promoter was not in a fiduciary relationship to the company when he acquired the property, then the company's remedy for non-disclosure of profits by the promoter is rescission. This means that the company can withdraw from the contract with the promoter, return the property to him and recover the contract price paid for it.[2]

Rescission is an option available to the company whose contract for the sale of the property to the promoter is a voidable one. Consequently, the company have the option of continuing with the contract, if they so desire. As Pringle J stated:[3]

> 'So far as these contracts being reprobated by the company, they were, in fact approbated to a substantial extent. It appears to be clear that failure by a promoter

---

1 (Unreported) 10 July 1972 (HC).
2 *Erlanger v The New Sombrero Phosphate Co* (1878) 3 AC 1218 (HL).
3 In *Sean Hopkins v Shannon Transport Systems Ltd*.

or a director to make full disclosure of his contracts with the company renders the contract voidable by the company, but *not* void.' (author's emphasis)

The right of rescission will generally be lost:

(1) if the parties cannot be restored to their original positions, as in *Lagunas Nitrate Co v Lagunas Syndicate*;[1] or

(2) if innocent third parties have acquired rights for value under the contracts, as in *Re Leeds and Hanley Theatres of Varieties Ltd*[2] and in *Northern Bank Finance Corporation Ltd v Charlton*.[3]

Recovery of profits

9.8   Where the promoter is in a fiduciary position to the company both:

(1) when he acquired the property; and

(2) when he sold it to the company,

the company may not only rescind the contract as above, it may also either:

(1) retain the property, paying no more for it than the promoter. This will have the effect of depriving the promoter of his profit; or

(2) recover the secret profit from the promoter. It was held in *Gluckstein v Barnes* that a secret profit of £20,000 had to be repaid by the promoters to the company.

Damages for misfeasance

9.9   If the remedies in **9.7** and **9.8** are either not available or are inappropriate, the company may sue the promoters for damages for breach of their fiduciary duty. The measure of the damage will be the amount of the secret profit made by the promoter.[4]

Damages in tort

9.10   In *Northern Bank Finance Corporation Ltd v Charlton*, the defendants were induced, by fraudulent misrepresentation, to purchase shares of which the plaintiff bank was not the owner.

In the Supreme Court judgment, Henchy J dealt with, inter alia, the measure of damages to be awarded against a promoter, and rescission of contracts made with them.

Measure of damages. Henchy J stated:

'While it is said that the measure of damages for breach of contract is the amount of money necessary to put the damnified person in the position in which he would

---

1   [1899] 2 Ch 392 (CA). See also *Armstrong v Jackson* [1917] 2 KB 822 where rescission was granted even though that meant the person guilty of fraud lost money as a result of the loss in value of the shares in question, and *Northern Finance Corporation Ltd v Charlton* [1979] IR 149 in **9.10**.

2   [1902] 2 Ch 809 – here property had already been sold.

3   [1979] IR 149 (SC).

4   *Re Leeds and Hanley Theatres of Varieties Ltd* [1902] 2 Ch 809.

have been if the breach had not been committed. As far as the tort of fraud or deceit is concerned, *it is well settled that the measure of damages is based on the actual damage directly flowing from the fraudulent inducement,* and that the award may include, in an appropriate case (of which this may not be an example), consequential damages representing what was reasonably and necessarily expended as a result of acting on the inducement ...

It is well established by judicial authority that the correct measure of damages in such a case is the cost of acquiring the shares, less their actual value at the time of acquisition ... The price paid for the shares is to be regarded only as evidence of their value and not as proof of it (*Twycross v Grant*), so it will be for the court to make a true and fair valuation of the shares as they stood when they were transferred to the defendants or their nominees; that is the crucial time for the assessment of their value. Subsequent fluctuations in their value, from whatever cause, may be taken into reckoning for the purpose only to the extent that such movements in value may throw light on their real value at the time they were transferred to the defendants.' (author's emphasis)

Loss of right to rescind. Henchy J also said:

'In this case the defendants sought and were granted rescission of the contract between the defendants and the bank but, in an effort to restore the status quo ante, the court went further. By requiring the bank to take the place of the defendants in each of the many instances of the purchase of shares, the court purported to rescind and amend executed contracts which had been made between the defendants and third-party vendors of shares who were not before the court. In my opinion, that is something which the court had no jurisdiction to do.

Since the purpose of the rescission of a contract on the ground of misrepresentation is the restoration of the status quo ante on the ground the voidable contract is to be deemed wholly void ab initio, each side must divest itself in favour of the other of what it has received under the contract ...

Now in the present case, the orders of rescission made in the High Court cannot operate in that way.'

The Supreme Court, by a majority, refused rescission on the grounds articulated by Henchy J and ordered that the case be returned to the High Court for assessment of the defendants' damages.

Statutory rights of the company

9.11   The common law remedies of a company against a promoter are available to both private and public companies. In the case of the latter, however, they have become less significant because of ss 26 to 37[1] of the Companies (Amendment) Act 1983, which have regulated aspects of company dealings involving non-cash assets. For example, s 30 would make it necessary for any property being offered by a promoter to the company, as consideration for its shares, to be valued by an *independent expert*. Similarly, s 32 also provides for an independent expert's valuation of assets where a public company, within

---

1 See **10.31**.

two years of commencing business, acquires an asset from a subscriber[1] to its memorandum, and the consideration for that asset amounts to one tenth or more of the nominal value of the company's issued capital. In addition, under s 32, the terms of the sale must have been approved[2] by an ordinary resolution of the company, and a copy of the agreement delivered to the registrar of companies.

Effects of breaching the 1983 Act

9.12 Where there is a breach of s 30, the promoter/allottee will be liable to pay the company an amount equal to the true value of the shares, and will also be liable to pay interest.[3]

In the event of a breach of s 32, the company will be entitled to recover its consideration, or an amount equivalent to it, from the relevant person/ promoter and the agreement, so far as not carried out, shall be void.[4]

Remuneration of promoters

9.13 A promoter has no legal right to recover his expenses. As Cozens-Hardy, MR said:[5]

'There is no foundation for any general proposition (that a promoter is entitled to recover his expenses). Indeed, the contrary is well settled. If A voluntarily pays B's debt, B is under no obligation to repay A ...'

Provision in articles of association

9.14 To overcome the unsatisfactory situation over recovery of promoters' expenses, art 80 of Table A stipulates that:

'The directors ... may pay all expenses incurred in *promoting* and *registering* the company ...' (author's emphasis)

An article, such as art 80, gives the directors the discretion to pay the promoters' expenses. As, in many instances, the promoters will also be the company's first directors, they will, in practice, be reimbursed their expenses.

Information to be included in a prospectus

9.15 Any prospectus issued by the company must include 'any amount or benefit paid or given within the preceding five years to any promoter'[6] and short details of any property transaction in which the vendor is a promoter or director of the company.[7]

---

1 Who need not necessarily be a promoter.
2 See s 32(3).
3 Section 30(10).
4 Section 32(8).
5 In *Re National Motor Mail-Coach Co Ltd, Clinton's Claim* [1908] 2 Ch 515 (CA).
6 See CA 1963, Sch 3, para 13.
7 Ibid, para 9.

Promoters and pre-incorporation contracts

9.16   There are similarities between the positions in law of a promoter and an agent.[1] A promoter can be viewed as an agent of the company in its dealings with third parties.

In agency law, for a principal to adopt contracts entered into on his behalf by his agent, that principal must be in existence at the time the contract was made. Otherwise, the agent, and not the principal, is the person who can enforce that contract. For example, in the case of a contract entered into by a promoter on behalf of the company before the certificate of incorporation is issued (a pre-incorporation contract), the company, as principal, is not yet in existence. As a result, the company could not sue on a pre-incorporation contract.[2] To overcome the agency difficulties over pre-incorporation contracts, the CA 1963 provides as follows:[3]

(1)   any pre-incorporation contract may be *ratified*[4] by the company after its formation; and
(2)   prior to ratification, a promoter shall be personally bound by the contract and entitled to the benefit thereof, unless he has expressly agreed to the contrary.

9.17   Section 37 received judicial analysis in *H K N Invest OY v Incotrade Pvt Ltd (in liquidation)*.[5] In that case, Costello J held, inter alia:

(1)   while a formal meeting of the company was not necessary to ratify a contract under s 37, there was no evidence in this case to suggest that the pre-incorporation contract in question had been ratified by the (first) defendant after its incorporation;
(2)   as the power of ratification under s 37 enabled a company to obtain the benefits of pre-incorporation contracts, it could be regarded as an asset of the company;
(3)   that the powers of a liquidator under s 231(2) included an implied power to ratify pre-incorporation contracts, as by this means additional assets could be obtained for distribution to creditors; and
(4)   that payments made to a promoter under a pre-incorporation contract were held by him as a constructive trustee for the company.

Pre-incorporation and pre-trading contracts

9.18   The distinctions between pre-incorporation and pre-trading contracts, and directors' liabilities in respect of the latter, are explained in Chapter 11.

---

1 *Jacobus Marler Estates Ltd v Marler* (1913) 85 LJPC 167n.
2 *Newborne v Sensolid (Great Britain) Ltd* [1954] 1 QB 45 (CA). The promoter could not enforce such a contract either.
3 Section 37(1) and (2).
4 Ie approved or validated retrospectively.
5 [1993] 3 IR 152.

Chapter 10

PROTECTION FOR INITIAL INVESTORS IN PUBLIC COMPANIES

THE NEED FOR PROTECTION

10.1   We have seen[1] that once the registrar issues a certificate of incorporation to a private company, it can immediately commence trading. In 1997, there were 149,522 private companies registered (90.6 per cent of the total).

The shareholders of a private company buy their shares in the company secure in the knowledge that the basic investors' protection of limitation of liability applies to their investment. Each purchase of such shares is a relatively straightforward transaction: both purchaser and vendor of the shares being aware that the general public are prohibited from subscribing for the shares and debentures of a private company.

Investors buying shares in private companies will almost certainly also possess some personal knowledge of the company and its affairs. By contrast, those buying shares in public companies would not normally have access to relevant information about them. Accordingly, as we shall illustrate in this chapter, the companies legislation includes a large amount of 'investor protection' measures for persons buying shares in public companies. The main reasons underlying these protective measures are:

(1) to facilitate the reasonable assessment by prospective investors of the value and price of the shares offered for public sale; and

(2) to contribute to the effective use by shareholders of voting or other rights which they may possess as company members (or, indeed, debenture holders).

The statutory protection to investors in public companies is based upon compelling the companies to provide minimum information to potential investors by the issuing of prospectuses or listing particulars. Investors are given legal remedies for misrepresentations in these documents. They may also be entitled to on-going notification by the company of any 'price sensitive' information.

On 31 December 1997, out of a total 164,958 companies registered in Ireland, only 749 (0.5 per cent) were public. Because of the low number of public companies, the importance given to them in the Companies Act 1963 has sometimes been questioned. However, it should not be forgotten that whilst the number of public companies is relatively small, each public company may have literally thousands of shareholders. Therefore, the provisions relating to public companies in the companies legislation will affect a disproportionately large number of individual investors. Nevertheless, the dominance of private

---

1 In Chapter 9.

companies as the most favoured business association for trading, seems implicitly to have been recognised by the Companies (Amendment) Act 1983 which defines a public company simply as one 'which is not a private company'.

PUBLIC COMPANY FORMATION PROCEDURES

10.2 The normal pattern in company development would be to register a private company – often a family business. As this business grows and its need for extra capital exceeds the owners' capacity, the owners/directors[1] would decide that they needed to re-register as a public company to gain access[2] to the wider capital base. Such a decision to 'go public' is known as 'floating' a company. This would be the usual method of forming a public company.

The flotation of a company will generally take place when a private company decides to 'go public' and 'converts' to plc status, rather than by forming an entirely new plc.

When a public company wishes to raise money from the public by offering to sell them its shares,[3] the company[4] is expected to comply with the requirements of ss 43 to 48 of the 1963 Act relating to prospectuses, or the listing rules of the Stock Exchange.

The Stock Exchange requirements reflect EU reforms which were implemented in Ireland by the European Communities (Stock Exchange) Regulations 1984[5] (the 1984 Regulations).

The European Communities (Stock Exchange) Regulations 1984

10.3 The 1984 Regulations implemented the following three directives:

The Admissions Directive[6]

10.4 This Directive prescribes the conditions which must be fulfilled before securities may be admitted to official Stock Exchange listing. The term 'securities' includes shares, debentures, options, futures, differences and long-term insurance contracts.

The Listing Particulars Directive[7]

10.5 This Directive seeks to ensure that the admission of securities to official listing is dependent upon the publication of an information sheet styled the Listing Particulars.

---

1 Usually the same persons.
2 And, perhaps, also to liquidate some of their 'paper' assets (shares) in the company.
3 Or debentures.
4 Or its agents.
5 SI 1984/282, as amended by SI 1991/18.
6 Directive 79/279/EEC of 5 March 1979.
7 Directive 80/390/EEC of 17 March 1980.

The Interim Reports Directive[1]

10.6 This Directive prescribes the regular publication of information by companies whose shares have been admitted to official Stock Exchange listing.

The three EU Directives are reproduced in full as the first Schedule to the 1984 Regulations.

The Irish Stock Exchange is established as the competent authority under the Regulations, for deciding on the admission of securities to listing. When application is made to the Irish Stock Exchange for admission to official listing, and the relevant particulars are approved by them, reg 12 of the 1984 Regulations applies. Regulation 12(3) makes it clear that these listing particulars shall be deemed to be a prospectus within the Companies Act 1963.[2]

A copy of the listing particulars must be delivered to the Registrar of companies, on or before their publication – reg 13.

Methods of raising capital

10.7 There are several methods by which a new or converted public company can raise capital from the public. These include:

An offer for sale

10.8 An offer for sale involves the company selling all the new shares to an issuing house, who, in turn, sells them to the public.

An issuing house, such as a merchant bank, would expect to sell the shares to the public at a higher price than they paid for them. In return for this, though, the issuing company is guaranteed against the failure of the issue, which has effectively been underwritten by the bank.

A placing

10.9 This transaction is similar to an offer for sale but the issuing house 'places' the shares with their clients – often large institutional investors. The issuing house may or may not have purchased the shares before placing them with their clients.

A public offer

10.10 Whilst a company uses an intermediary in selling its shares in **10.8** and **10.9**, where it makes a public offer it deals directly with the public.

---

1 Directive 82/121/EEC of 15 February 1982.
2 In such case, ss 43, 44(1), 45, 47, 361(1)(b), 361(2) and 364 of the 1963 Act will not apply. Section 48 of the 1963 Act was repealed in 1983 but s 46 still remains in existence and applicable. Section 46 deals with the furnishing of written evidence by an expert of his consent to the issue of a prospectus containing statements by him. Sections 361 and 364 refer to prospectuses related to companies incorporated outside of Ireland.

A rights issue[1]

10.11 This is a method of raising finance from the present members of the company. Members are offered a new issue of shares in proportion to their existing shareholdings. Such issues are usually made by renounceable letters of allotment (see **22.40**).

When contemplating raising capital from the public, directors will have to consider which is the appropriate national securities market, taking into account the size of their company and its particular business.

NATIONAL INVESTMENT MARKETS

10.12 As we saw, a flotation involves selling[2] shares to the public either directly by a Public Offer or indirectly to the clients of an issuing house. This process only applies to companies formed as plcs or converting to public companies.

A flotation will be much more attractive if those shares, when purchased, can be traded on the Stock Exchange. For all practical purposes, therefore, the directors of a public company will have to seek a listing, or at least a public market, for the company's shares.

There were two major potential public markets for shares within the Irish Stock Exchange. These were the *Listed Market* and *Unlisted Securities Market* (USM). A restricted *Smaller Companies Market* (SCM) had also developed for indigenous companies with a minimum market capitalisation of £200,000.

10.13 During 1997, the budget introduced in January included taxation incentives for investors in the planned *Developing Companies Market* (DCM). The DCM is the Irish equivalent of the Alternative Investment Market in London. It was intended to cater for small and medium-sized developing companies who did not seek a full stock market listing. It has less onerous listing requirements than a full listing, and thus is less costly to enter.

A company choosing to enter the DCM in Dublin could also seek a listing on the Alternative Investment Market in London. However, this dual listing can have significant taxation implications in Ireland.

Prior to introducing the DCM, the Stock Exchange had shut down the DCM's immediate predecessors. These were the SCM and the USM – see **10.12**. The discontinuance of the SCM was attributed to the stock market crash of 1987 and the fact that many of the companies which had availed of it were start-up operations which subsequently failed.

The reduction of the required trading record for Official Listing to three years had minimised the distinction between the Listed and Unlisted Markets.

---

1 This must be distinguished from a 'bonus' issue which is a capitalisation of profits, giving investors additional shares in lieu of dividend payments – see **14.15**.

2 The company may also fix a minimum price for its shares and invite bids for them. This method is known as offering shares by tender, but is rarely used in Ireland.

Accordingly, in 1996, the Exchange decided to effectively merge the successful USM with the Listed Market.

The Listed Market

10.14 Mature companies of substantial market value would generally seek Official Listing. To be admitted, a company must produce *listing particulars* giving as complete a picture of itself as possible to the Exchange and potential investors, ie its trading history, financial record, management, business prospects, etc. The Stock Exchange's detailed listing requirements are set out in the Listing Rules.

The Listing Rules

10.15 The Official Listing requirements are set out in the *Yellow Book* and are a substitute for the statutory requirements relating to prospectuses.[1] The detailed listing particulars[2] *include*:

(1) the names of the issuer, persons responsible for listing particulars, the auditors and other advisors;
(2) the securities concerned and any underwriting arrangements;
(3) general information about the issuer and its capital;
(4) details of the group's activities;
(5) financial information;
(6) management information;
(7) recent development and prospects; and
(8) additional information on debt securities.

In addition, an applicant is expected to disclose all such information as investors and advisers may reasonably require to make an informed assessment of:

(1) the issuer's assets and liabilities, its financial position, profit and loss, and prospects; and
(2) the rights attaching to the securities.

The basic requirement for a company seeking to have its shares listed is that it has a three-year trading record, and 25 per cent of its issued shares are owned by the public[3] (achieving a reasonable spread of shareholders), although an exception from the three-year revenue earning record may be made for certain innovative high-growth companies – see Listing Rules, Chapter 25.

Refusal by the Stock Exchange to grant a listing (or to withdraw one) is subject to review by the court.[4]

During 1996, listing particulars were registered for just one applicant company, pursuant to the 1984 Regulations.

---

1 See **10.19**.
2 See the Listing Particulars Directive in Sch A to the 1984 Regulations.
3 Ie by persons other than the company's owners, directors and close associates.
4 Regulation 10 of the 1984 Regulations.

Once listed, companies are under a continuing duty to provide all information necessary to ensure an orderly market and to protect investors' interests. This would include any information that could materially affect its share price.

The Unlisted Securities Market (USM)

10.16   The USM was formed in 1980. It had been developed to encourage smaller companies, with a three-year business record, to seek additional capital from the public.

Because the 1984 Regulations only apply to listed securities, applicants to the USM were subject to the provisions of the 1963 Act relating to prospectuses. They were also subject to the regulations of the Stock Exchange for operating the USM. As mentioned above, this market was discontinued in 1996.

The Developing Companies Market (DCM)

10.17   The entry requirements for access to the DCM include a minimum trading record of one year, compared with three years for full or official listing.

At least 10 per cent of the company's shares must be issued to the public. In practice, one would expect most companies to exceed this figure and to offer 20 per cent to 30 per cent of their shares to the public . This would allow the founding shareholders to broaden the investor base without reducing their own voting power below 51 per cent levels.

Whilst there is a minimum company valuation requirement of £700,000 stg for full listing, none exists for listing on the DCM.

On-going information for investors

10.18   Both Official List and DCM companies will be under the continuing obligation to disclose 'price sensitive' information. This could include potential or planned takeovers. For example, in the case of listed companies contemplating a takeover in which the target company represented more than 25 per cent of its own size under a number of headings (eg net assets, property, etc), the listed company must issue a detailed circular to shareholders and obtain their approval at an extraordinary general meeting.

For DCM companies, the comparable takeover transaction size threshold is 100 per cent. This increased threshold size will tend to dispense with the requirement of issuing a circular to shareholders by a DCM company seeking to expand its business by acquiring another company. There is also a specialised Exploration Securities Market (ESM).

Further information on share listing matters may be obtained from the Listing Department, Irish Stock Exchange, 28 Anglesea St, Dublin 2.

PROSPECTUSES

10.19 Where shares are being offered to the public, and the European Communities (Stock Exchange) Regulations 1984 do not apply, the Companies Acts provide that potential investors must be furnished with detailed information by the issuer to inform and protect them. The prescribed information must be communicated to the public by the issuing of a prospectus. For example, DCM (and ESM) companies, not being listed within the meaning of the 1984 Regulations, would be required to issue a prospectus under the 1963 Act.

A prospectus is defined in s 2 of the 1963 Act as 'any notice, circular, advertisement or other invitation, offering to the *public* for subscription or purchase, any shares or debentures of a company' (author's emphasis).

Public offers

10.20 Section 61(1) further construes an offer to the public as including an offer:

> 'to any section of the public, whether selected as members or debenture holders[1] of the company, or as clients of the person issuing the prospectus or in any other manner ...'

A public offer may not, however, extend to include an invitation restricted to the company's employees. For example, in *Corporate Affairs Commission v David James Finance Ltd,*[2] an invitation restricted to 12,500 company employees was held not to be made to the public.[3] However, by contrast, in *Re South of England Natural Gas and Petroleum Co,*[4] a promoter issued 3,000 copies of a prospectus marked 'For private circulation only' to shareholders of certain companies in which he had an interest. It was held, in this case, that an invitation was made to the public.

Any document which falls within the definitions of a prospectus must meet the statutory information disclosure requirements stipulating that no form of application for shares in a company which are being offered to the public shall be issued without being accompanied by a prospectus[5] complying with the Act.[6]

Contents of prospectus

10.21 The specific information which must be contained in a prospectus is set out in Part I of Sch 3 to the 1963 Act. This includes details of the company's

---

1 Amended by s 238 of the Companies Act 1990 dealing with debentures to be repaid within five years.

2 [1975] 2 NSWLR 710.

3 See also the limitation in s 61(2) of the 1963 Act.

4 [1911] Ch 575.

5 Section 44(3) of the 1963 Act.

6 For limited exceptional cases where no prospectus need be issued, see s 44(4)(a) and (b) and s 45 of the 1963 Act.

capital, its directors, promoters, auditors and property acquired or to be purchased. The prospectus will also seek to elicit whether or not the promoters and directors have any personal interests in the company and/or its assets.

The minimum subscription

10.22 Fundamental matters dealt with in the prospectus include specifying the *minimum subscription*.[1] This is the minimum amount which, in the opinion of the directors, must be raised to pay the purchase price of any property to be acquired, to pay any preliminary expenses and commissions, to repay borrowings and to provide working capital.

The full details required to be included in a prospectus are set out in paras 1 to 18 of Sch 3, Part I of the 1963 Act, as amended by the European Communities (Transferable Securities and Stock Exchange) Regulations 1992.[2]

Reports to be attached

10.23 Part II of Sch 3 prescribes the reports which must accompany the prospectus. For example, there must be a report by the auditors on the profits and losses of the company and its subsidiaries in each of the previous three years and a statement of their assets and liabilities at the latest date to which accounts were made up. If any business is to be acquired from the proceeds of the new issue, similar reports are required on that business.

Registration

10.24 A copy of the prospectus must be delivered to the registrar before it can be issued.[3] This copy must be signed by every person named in it as director or proposed director.[4]

During 1997, 268 domestic and 131 foreign company prospectuses were registered.[5]

A prospectus will be dated, unless the contrary is proved, as being issued on the date of its publication.[6]

The following documents must be attached to the copy delivered to the registrar:

(1) the consent of every expert required by s 46;
(2) a copy of every material contract; and
(3) if the auditors or accountants have made any adjustments to the accounts, a signed statement specifying these adjustments and giving the reasons for them.

---

1 See Sch 3, para 4.
2 SI 1992/202, which implemented EC 'Prospectus' Directives 89/298/EEC of 17 April 1989 and 90/211/EEC of 23 April 1990.
3 Section 47(1)(b).
4 Or by his agent, if authorised in writing.
5 See *Companies Report 1997*, Department of Enterprise and Employment (The Stationery Office, July 1998), at pp 22–25, for the names of these companies.
6 Section 43.

Documents (1) and (3) are required only in the cases of prospectuses issued generally to the public.

Pre-emption rights

10.25 Section 23 of the Companies Act 1983 introduced the concept of compulsory pre-emption rights to Ireland. Pre-emption rights are, essentially, rights of first refusal. As a consequence, the effect of s 23 is to preclude a company allotting 'equity'[1] or ordinary shares unless it has firstly made an offer to its existing shareholders, to buy on equivalent terms, a number of the new shares in proportion to their existing shareholdings.

Where, however, the directors are authorised by the articles of association or by special resolution of the company in general meeting, they may allot equity securities as if pre-emption rights did not apply to the allotment.[2]

When considering the raising of finance for a public company which has been converted from a private one, the directors must, therefore, also bear in mind any pre-emption rights of the existing members.

CONTRACTUAL ASPECTS OF PUBLIC SUBSCRIPTIONS

10.26 In terms of contract law, when a prospectus is issued to the public, it is deemed an 'invitation to treat', ie the public are invited to make offers to purchase the shares which are for sale. To initiate such a deal, the purchaser completes the application form usually attached to the prospectus and forwards it, with his cheque, to the issuing company, or its agents.

When the directors of the issuing company allot shares and advise the applicant that he has been allotted the shares he applied for, then this constitutes acceptance[3] and a valid[4] contract comes into force.

Protecting public investors at allotment stage

10.27 Prior to 1983, there had been few statutory restrictions on the power of directors to allot shares. However, there is now a great deal of statutory protection for investors in public companies. This protection covers the following points:

(1) directors need to be given authority to allot shares either by the articles or by ordinary resolution at a general meeting (under s 20 of the 1983 Act);

---

1 It does not apply to preference shares nor to shares held under an employees' share scheme. Pre-emption rights and the transfer of shares in private companies are dealt with in **22.30**.

2 See s 24 of the 1983 Act.

3 Although the applicant does not become a member until his name has been included in the register of members – see Chapter 20. However, this requirement does not apply to the original subscribers to the memorandum – see s 31 of the 1963 Act.

4 The manner of acceptance, whether oral, written, posted or even implied by the applicant's conduct, will be subject to the rules of contract law – accordingly, see R. Friel *The Law of Contract* (Round Hall Press, 1995), at pp 52–59.

(2) allotment procedures;

(3) minimum subscription; and

(4) payment for allotted shares (including rules on non-cash consideration for shares in plcs under ss 20 and 26 to 37 of the 1983 (Amendment) Act and ss 53 to 59 of the 1963 Act).

In addition, the common law makes it clear that the directors must exercise their power to allot shares in good faith and in the best interests of the company – see **24.5**.

Directors' authority

10.28 This authority to allot shares may be given to the company directors for a specific issue. Alternatively, it may be a general authority covering all issues for no longer than five years. Both types of authority must state the maximum amount of shares that may be allotted, and the date on which it is to expire.

Such instances of authority to allot can be varied, revoked or renewed by the company in general meeting. In addition, directors authorised by s 20 may also be given the power to restrict or withdraw the statutory pre-emption rights for periods up to five years.

Allotments made by directors without s 20 authority will not be invalid. However, the directors will be liable to a fine.

Allotment procedures

10.29 Sections 53 to 59 of the 1963 Act[1] further protect potential public investors by restricting the directors' powers to allot shares. For example, s 53 provides that no allotment can be made of any share capital of a company offered to the public for subscription unless the sum raised in cash exceeds the amount of the *minimum subscription.*[2]

Minimum subscription

10.30 Section 53 has been extended by s 22 of the 1983 Act so that any offer for shares *must be fully subscribed* before allotment can take place, unless the listing particulars or prospectus expressly states that a part subscription is acceptable.

The requirements of ss 53 and 22 need not cause problems, in practice, when the public money is raised by either an Offer for Sale or a Placing. If a company were to offer its shares for sale directly to the public, the risk of failure could be avoided by an underwriting agreement.

An *underwriting agreement* is a contract whereby, before a company offers shares to the public, the underwriters (eg a merchant bank) agree, in return for a commission, to take all or part of the offered shares which were not subscribed for by the public.

---

1 As amended by the Companies (Amendment) Act 1983 – see Sch 1.
2 See **10.22**.

Payment for allotted shares

10.31   Sections 26 to 37 of the Companies (Amendment) Act 1983 introduced further restrictions on payment for shares. Generally, shares must be paid up in money or money's worth, including goodwill and expertise (shares taken by a subscriber to the memorandum of a plc must be paid up in cash).

Shares cannot be issued at a discount. They may only be allotted if 25 per cent of their nominal value and all of any premium, has been paid up.

Non-cash consideration

10.32   In *Re Wragg Ltd*,[1] the court decided that in the case of shares in a private company, it would not enquire into the adequacy or otherwise of a non-cash consideration, in the absence of fraud or other grounds to impeach the transaction. Lindley LJ stated:

> 'It is not law that persons cannot sell property to a limited company for fully paid-up shares and make a profit by the transaction. We must not allow ourselves to be misled by talking of value. The value paid to the company is measured by the price at which the company agrees to buy what it thinks is worth its while to acquire. Whilst the transaction is unimpeached, this is the only value to be considered.'

By way of comparison, ss 30 to 33 of the 1983 Amendment Act require, inter alia, independent valuation of non-cash assets if they are to be used as consideration for shares in a public company.[2]

A public company may only allot shares in return for non-cash assets if the transfer of the assets is to take effect within five years of the allotment. If acceptable non-cash assets are to be used as consideration for shares, ss 30 to 33 make provision for their independent expert valuation.

The non-cash consideration valuation process may also apply in the case of a purchase by a plc of non-cash assets from its subscribers or members. Generally, the asset must be acquired within two years of the company's receipt of its Certificate of Trading,[3] and the consideration for the asset must be valued by an independent person in accordance with s 32.

Directors' liabilities

10.33   If, after 40 days, insufficient share applications have been received to cover the amount of the minimum subscription, applicants' monies must be refunded to them. Failure to refund these monies within 48 days can render the directors jointly and severally liable to repay that money – see s 53(4) and (6) of the 1963 Act. Directors may also be subject to a fine if they begin to allot shares *before* the fourth day[4] after the date the prospectus is issued, or if permission to trade in the shares has not been applied for or granted.[5]

---

1 [1897] 1 Ch 976 (CA).
2 See **9.11** and **9.12**.
3 See Chapter 11.
4 Section 56 of the 1963 Act.
5 Section 57. The directors may also be legally liable to repay the investors – see s 57(2).

Void and voidable allotments

10.34   Where a prospectus states that application has been or will be made for permission for the shares offered to be dealt with on the Stock Exchange, then, if application has not been made within three days after the first issue of the prospectus, or granted within six weeks from the date of the closing of the subscription lists, any allotment shall be void.[1]

Section 55 also deals with irregular allotments. It provides that any allotment made in contravention of the minimum subscription requirement will be voidable within one month after the date of the allotment.

Returns of allotments

10.35   Section 58 provides that whenever a company makes any allotment of its shares, it must, within one month thereafter, deliver prescribed details to the registrar, including the nominal amount of the total shares in the allotment, the individual allottees' names and addresses, and the amount, if any, paid or due and payable on each share.

Where a company fails to comply with s 58, any officer who is in default may be fined up to £500. Some relief is available: s 57(4) empowers the court, if satisfied that the delay was accidental or inadvertant, to make an order extending the time for the delivery of the returns 'for such period as the court may think proper'.

Controlling price stabilisation practices

10.36   Where a firm supports the price of a new issue of shares, such a price stabilisation activity is potentially manipulative. Accordingly, it is only permitted under certain conditions and for a limited period.

The Companies (Amendment) Act 1999 sets out the conditions under which stabilisation activity may be carried out in Ireland. The Schedule to the Act consists of nine stabilisation rules.

The stabilisation process must be under the control of a 'stabilising manager', ie the person (or persons) 'to be the one to conduct stabilising in the State in relation to the issue of the relevant securities'.

The preliminary steps which must be taken before a stabilising manager can act are set out in rule 5.

Any public announcements relating to the issue concerned, must include a reference to the prospectus or include the word 'stabilisation'.

From the beginning of the introductory period, any preliminary offering circular or prospectus and final offering circular or prospectus relating to the issue of the securities concerned must include the following (or similar) statement.

---

1 Section 57(1) of the 1963 Act.

'In connection with this issue [name of stabilising manager] may over-allot or effect transactions which stabilise or maintain the market price of [description or relevant securities] at a level which might not otherwise prevail. Such stabilising, if commenced, may be discontinued at any time.'

Permitted stabilising action

10.37 Rule 3 authorises the stabilising manager to buy or agree to buy or offer to purchase any of the relevant securities during the stabilising period (see definitions in rule 1), with a view to stabilising or maintaining their market price.

The mechanics of stabilising action

10.38 The nine rules in the Schedule dealing with the mechanics of price stabilising action include:

(1) limits on prices – see rule 7;
(2) restrictions in respect of associated securities – rule 6;
(3) maintenance of a register by the stabilising manager – see rules 1(d) and 9;
(4) notification of termination of stabilising action to Irish Stock Exchange – see rule 8.

Effect of stabilising purchases on insider dealing rules

10.39 The insider dealing rules are set out in **27.28** et seq.

Section 2 of the 1999 Act provides that s 108 of the 1990 Act shall not be regarded as having been contravened by reason of:

'(a) anything done in the State for the purpose of stabilising or maintaining the market price of securities if it is done in conformity with the Stabilisation Rules, or
(b) any action taken during the stabilising period by a person in any jurisdiction, other than the State, for the purpose of stabilising or maintaining the market price of securities, but only if the action taken is, in all material respects, permitted by or is otherwise in accordance with all relevant requirements applicable to such actions in the jurisdiction where such action is effected, including, if those securities are also listed on a stock exchange in that jurisdiction, the rules or other regulatory requirements governing that stock exchange.'

Effect on disclosure of interests in shares

10.40 Sections 67 to 79 of the 1990 Act provide for the compulsory notification of individual and group acquisitions of shares.

Section 3 of the 1999 Act makes it clear that the acquisition or disposal of interest in share capital in connection with permitted stabilising action, can be disregarded for the purpose of notification under s 67 to 79 of the 1990 Act.[1]

---

1 See **22.2** and **27.4**.

Relief for investment companies

10.41   Section 54 of the No 2 Act amends s 253 of the 1990 Act in relation to investment companies.

In order to make Ireland a more attractive centre for international fund management, s 253, as amended, removes a number[1] of company law requirements relating to the offering of securities to the public.

Shareholders' liability

10.42   The immediate liability of the shareholder is to pay for his shares in cash, or, with the consent of the company, in money's worth such as a non-cash asset, in accordance with the terms of the issue.

The full extent of a shareholder's interest, contractual liabilities and rights is dealt with in Parts IV A, IV B, IV C, IV D and Part VII.

Other remedies and protections

10.43   An applicant is not limited solely to his statutory rights under ss 53, 55 and 57. He also has other legal remedies for incorrect pre-contractual information.

When a member of the public is induced to enter into a contract for the purchase of shares by an untrue or misleading statement in the listing particulars or prospectus, it may give rise to either civil or criminal liability.

INVESTORS' REMEDIES FOR MISREPRESENTATIONS

10.44   The remedies available to a misled investor may entail legal action against all or some of the following persons:

(1) the company;
(2) the issuing house;
(3) individuals responsible for producing the statutory documentation, including the directors; and
(4) the experts (if any).

Investors' remedies

10.45   Subscribers for shares have both common-law and statutory remedies. Common-law remedies are based on actionable misrepresentations and rights

---

1 In particular, s 54 disapplies ss 53, 56, 58, 60, 70, 72, 119 and 125 of the 1963 Act; ss 5(2), 6, 19, 20(3) and (4), 22, 23, 24, 25, 30, to 33, 40, 41, 45–51 of the Companies (Amendment) Act 1983, s 14 of the Companies (Amendment) Act 1986 and ss 67–106, s 140 and ss 206–234 of the Companies Act 1990.

in contract (rescission) and the torts of deceit and negligence. Investors' statutory remedies arise under s 49 of the 1963 Act.

Common-law remedies

10.46   Where a prospectus contains an incorrect statement which has induced a person to subscribe for shares on the faith of it, the misled subscriber may rescind (withdraw) from the contract, and, depending on the circumstances, sue for damages.

Rescission

10.47   A subscriber for shares may apply to the court for the contract to be set aside if he was induced to enter into it by incorrect statements of fact in the prospectus, even though these statements were made innocently, eg a false statement made innocently by an 'expert', ie an engineer, accountant or other professional man whose profession gives authority to any statement made by him.[1] Rescission will also be granted if there is a material inaccuracy in a *report* on which the prospectus is based.[2]

In *Re Pacaya Rubber and Produce Co*,[3] Astbury J pointed out that:

> 'If the company does not vouch for the accuracy of such [expert's] reports, it must clearly disassociate itself from them.'

Limits on rescission

10.48   Rescission may not be available in certain circumstances, eg undue delay by the subscriber in attempting to avoid the contract; where he does anything after he becomes aware of the misrepresentation which is inconsistent with the right to repudiate, such as attempting to sell the shares; or where proceedings have been commenced to wind up the company.[4]

10.49   Rescission will only be granted if, by the omission of a material fact, what is stated in the prospectus becomes misleading. For example in *McKeown v Boudard Peveril Gear Co*,[5] Rigby J said:

> 'if a person relies, as a ground for the rescission of a contract, on the omission of a statement he must show that the omission of that statement makes what is stated misleading. It is not that the omission of material facts is an independent ground for rescission, but the omission must be of such a nature as to make the statement actually made misleading.'

Where the representations in a prospectus are not material, ie are only minor or trivial[6] inaccuracies, rescission will also be refused.

---

1 Section 46(3) of the 1963 Act.
2 See *Components Tube Co v Naylor* [1902] 2 IR 1.
3 [1914] 1 Ch 542.
4 *Re Overend, Gurney & Co* (1867) LR 2 HL 325.
5 (1896) 65 LJ Ch 735.
6 For example, failure to disclose the amount of previous allotments – see *Re South of England Natural Gas Petroleum Co Ltd* [1911] Ch 253.

Loss of right to cancel

10.50   The court will not grant rescission if it is impossible to restore the parties to their original positions[1] or where third party rights would be adversely affected. For example, in *Oakes v Turquand and Harding; Peck v Turquand and Harding*,[2] because of the implications for creditors' rights, rescission was refused on grounds that the company had gone into liquidation.

Again, where the shareholder does any act which shows he elects to retain the shares and so affirm the contract, he will lose the right to rescind. Examples would be attempting to sell the shares or attending and voting at general meetings.[3]

Damages for fraud

10.51   Any person induced by fraud to take shares has the right at common law to claim damages in the tort of *deceit*. Such a contract would usually be induced by a fraudulent misrepresentation.

10.52   Where a representation is clearly false, fraudulent and material, made with the intention of inducing a person to take shares, damages will be awarded for the tort of deceit. An example is in *Jury v Stoker and Jackson*,[4] where the facts were as follows:

Jury bought shares in the Cork Milling Co because the prospectus contained a fraudulent misrepresentation that Jackson, from whom the company was purchasing the mill, would be investing £7,500 in the company.

Jackson did not invest the money, and the company failed financially, causing a loss of Jury's investment. The court found for the plaintiff, Sullivan MR stating:

> 'The representation [about Jackson investing £7,500] was false, fraudulent and material, made to induce a man to take shares, and loss has resulted to the plaintiff. The defendant cannot [by way of defence] say "Oh, you might have found out that [the misrepresentation] was wrong if you had gone to the office and checked the instrument yourself ..."
>
> Mr Stoker is answerable to the plaintiff for the loss which he sustained.'

10.53   Want of care can be distinguished from fraud.[5] In *Derry v Peek*,[6] a statutory corporation had authority to provide transport by animal power, and, with the consent of the government, by steam power.

A prospectus issued by the company incorrectly stated that the company had a right to use steam power instead of horse drawn trams. Peek bought shares on the basis of the prospectus. The government subsequently refused their consent to the use of steam power, and the company was wound up.

---

1   See *Northern Bank v Charlton* in **9.10**.
2   (1867) LR 2 HL 325. See also *Houldsworth v City of Glasgow Bank* (1880) 5 App Cas 317.
3   *Sharpley v Louth & East Coast Ry Co* (1876) 2 Ch D 663 (CA).
4   [1882] 9 LR 1R 385 (ChD).
5   It may, however, amount to negligence – see below.
6   (1889) 14 App Cas 337.

Peek sued the directors for damages in deceit (fraud). He succeeded in the Court of Appeal, where Derry, the defendant, appealed to the House of Lords.

The House of Lords decided that Derry had not been guilty of fraud, thus reversing the Court of Appeal decision. This decision is significant for its definition of fraud, Lord Herschell stating:

> 'Fraud is proved when it is shown that a false representation had been made (i) knowingly, or (ii) without belief in its truth, or (iii) recklessly, careless whether it be true or false ... Making a false statement through want of care falls far short of, and is a very different thing from, fraud.'

10.54   Where a representation, though untrue, is nevertheless true 'in the sense in which the representor understood it' he may not be liable for fraud – see *Akerhielm v DeMare*.[1]

A subscriber may not retain the shares and obtain damages against the company.[2] This does not, however, affect his rights of action against those responsible for the fraudulent misrepresentation, eg the directors or promoters.

Damages for negligence

10.55   In principle, subscribers would appear to enjoy the right to claim damages for a negligent[3] misrepresentation against both the company and the persons responsible for issuing the prospectus under the principle enunciated in *Hedley Byrne & Co v Heller & Partners* (see Chapter 34).

Other common-law remedies against the directors and promoters

10.56   Apart from his remedies against the company, a subscriber may also be able to pursue legal action against any person responsible for the incorrect statement in the prospectus. These persons include directors, promoters and experts.

The subscriber can sue the directors, promoters and experts for damages, based on the tort of deceit, in cases where he has been misled by a fraudulent misrepresentation or, indeed, by the concealment of material facts.

Concealment

10.57   In *Aaron's Reefs Ltd v Twiss*,[4] it was held that the concealing of material facts from the prospectus was fraudulent, and the subscriber was entitled to a remedy, Fitzgibbon LJ stating:

---

1   [1959] AC 789 and compare *Arnison v Smith* (1889) 41 Ch D 348.
2   *Houldsworth v City of Glasgow Bank* (1880) 5 App Cas 317.
3   *Securities Trust Ltd v Hugh Moore and Alexander Ltd* [1964] IR 417 (HC).
4   [1895] CA 2 IR 207, a decision subsequently affirmed in the House of Lords – see [1896] AC 273. In *New Brunswick and Canada Railway & Land Co v Muggeridge* (1860) 1 Dr & Sm 383 (ChD), Kindersley V-C stated that those issuing prospectuses 'are bound to state everything with strict and scrupulous accuracy, and not only to abstain from stating as fact that which is not so, but to omit no one fact within their knowledge, the existence of which might in any degree affect the nature, or

'On the question of fraud, in an action by a company ... I do not admit any distinction between ... fraudulent concealment of material facts, ... and actual misrepresentation ...

Though uberima fides, ie the obligation to disclose everything known that could influence an intending subscriber, is not demanded of the authors of a prospectus, no case as yet applied the rule of caveat emptor [to a prospectus]. The duty of disclosure which the authors of a prospectus must discharge is that they must not conceal anything which, if stated, would contradict or even substantially alter any material representation actually made by the prospectus.'

10.58   Fitzgibbon LJ went on to suggest that misrepresentation may occur, even though the statutory disclosure requirements had been met, by saying:

'if a prospectus contains any material representation of fact which is false and fraudulent, it cannot be the law that a reference in the statutory form to a document which would reveal the falsehood can place the framers of the prospectus in the same position as if they had not made the misrepresentation. It is no answer to a plea of false and fraudulent representation to say that the person who made it had supplied the person whom he defrauded with means by which he might have discovered the fraud before he acted upon it.'

Statutory remedies under s 49

10.59   Any person who buys shares or debentures on foot of an '*untrue statement*' in a prospectus (or listing particulars)[1] is given the right to claim damages against those responsible[2] for its issue.

Section 49 of the 1963 Act imposes civil liability on those responsible for the issuing of the prospectus. However, a director or promoter may avoid liability by proving that:

(1) consent to become a director was withdrawn before the prospectus was issued and it was issued without his knowledge or consent; or

(2) the prospectus was issued without his knowledge or consent and on finding this he forthwith gave reasonable public notice of that fact; or

(3) after issue and before allotment he became aware of the mis-statement, withdrew his consent and gave reasonable public notice and reasons for the withdrawal; or

(4) he had reasonable grounds for believing and did believe the statement to be true;

(5) as regards an untrue statement in an expert's report, that it was an accurate copy or extract of the statement or report and he had reasonable grounds to believe that the 'expert' was competent to make the statement and had given the consent required by the Act before the issue of the prospectus.

---

extent, or quality of the privileges and advantages which the prospectus holds out as inducements to take shares.'

1 Article 12, European Communities (Stock Exchange) Regs 1984, SI 1984/282, as amended by SI 1991/18.

2 But not against the company itself.

Position of expert

10.60 An expert can escape liability for a mis-statement made by him if he proves that:

(1) he withdrew his consent to the issue in writing before the registration of the prospectus; or

(2) after registration and before allotment he withdrew his consent, giving reasonable public notice of it and the reason therefor; or

(3) he was competent to make the statement and had reasonable grounds to believe and did believe that the statement was true up to the time of allotment.

A person who has suffered loss or damage because of an untrue statement in a prospectus has an easier evidential task in obtaining compensation under s 49, than in tort, because of the reversal of the burden of proof by s 49.

The measure of damages may be the same as for fraud – see **9.10**.[1]

Persons named in prospectus without authority

10.61 A person named as a director and who does not consent to become one, is entitled to be indemnified by the other directors against all damages and costs for which he is made liable – see s 49(6).

Meaning of untrue statement

10.62 Section 52(1) defines a statement as untrue if it is misleading in the form and content in which it is included.

CRIMINAL LIABILITY FOR MISREPRESENTATIONS

10.63 By virtue of s 50 of the 1963 Act, a person who authorises the issue of a prospectus containing an untrue statement is liable:

(1) on indictment, for up to two years' imprisonment and/or a fine not exceeding £2,500; or

(2) on summary conviction, for up to six months' imprisonment and/or a fine not exceeding £500.

A person may also incur criminal liability for misrepresentation under:

(1) reg 6 of the EC (Stock Exchange) Regulations 1984;

(2) s 44 of the 1963 Act, as amended by s 15 of the 1982 Act; and

(3) s 84 of the Larceny Act 1861.

Defence

10.64 A person will not be liable under s 50 if he can prove that either:

(1) the statement was immaterial; or

---

1 See also *Clark v Urquhart* [1930] AC 28, and *McConnell v Wright* [1903] 1 Ch 546.

(2) he had reasonable grounds to believe, and did, up to the time of the issue of the prospectus, believe that the statement was true.

STATEMENT IN LIEU OF PROSPECTUS

10.65 When a company has not issued a prospectus inviting the public to subscribe for its shares, it is not permitted to commence business or exercise any borrowing powers unless a Statement in Lieu of Prospectus[1] has been delivered to the registrar.

The Second Schedule to the 1963 Act sets out a form of Statement and the particulars which have to be contained in it when delivered to the registrar by a private company in converting to an unlimited public company.

A Statement may also be required from an unlimited public company which does not issue a prospectus.

Apart from these exceptional cases, the requirements of the Companies Acts on prospectuses, and of the 1984 Regulations on listing particulars, are so widespread that the Statement in Lieu has little relevance today.

REGULATION OF INVESTMENT INTERMEDIARIES

10.66 Under the Investment Intermediaries Act 1995, the Central Bank administers a system of regulating investment intermediaries, in the interests of investor protection and the orderly and proper functioning of the national investment markets.

Generally, investment intermediaries, including stockbrokers, must be authorised to transact business.

Under the 1995 Act[2] the supervisory authority was not liable for any loss to investors arising out of the insolvency or default of a regulated firm. However, this gap in investor protection was dealt with on the implementation of the Investor Compensation Act 1998.

The 1998 Act implements the EU Investor Compensation Directive.[3] As a result, under this Act, eligible clients of stockbrokers (and investment firms) may now claim compensation where their intermediary has become insolvent or defaulted.

The clients eligible for protection are private, rather then professional[4] investors. Because of this, the compensation level payable is on the low side; and the directive has been implemented so that the amount is the minimum required, ie 90 per cent of the investor's loss or 20,000 Euros, whichever is the lesser.

1 Section 115(2) of the 1963 Act.
2 Section 53.
3 No 97/9/EC.
4 A professional investor is defined in s 2.

The compensation scheme under the 1998 Act is administered by the Investment Compensation Co Ltd (ICCL), which operates under the supervision of the Central Bank.

Compensation entitlement for a client will be triggered either by a determination of the Central Bank that a firm is unable to meet its obligations arising from claims by clients, or a court decision precluding the making of an investor claim against the intermediaries, for the time being.

Chapter 11

COMMENCEMENT OF BUSINESS BY PUBLIC AND NON-IRISH COMPANIES

INTRODUCTION

11.1 A company registered as a public company will be unable to commence trading or borrow money until it has been issued with a Trading Certificate by the registrar of companies. The registrar will not issue this certificate until he is satisfied that the company has met the statutory requirements regulating the raising of its initial capital from the public.[1]

The Trading Certificate

11.2 The registrar will issue a Trading Certificate only if he is satisfied that the nominal value of the company's allotted share capital exceeds the statutory minimum, and he has received a statutory declaration signed by a director[2] confirming this fact. The declaration must also contain details of:

(1) the amount of the preliminary expenses of the company and the persons by whom any of those expenses have been paid or are payable; and

(2) any amount or benefit paid ... or given to any promoter of the company, and the consideration for it.

Once issued, the Trading Certificate is conclusive evidence that the company is entitled to commence business and to exercise its borrowing powers.[3]

Liability of directors for pre-trading contracts

11.3 When considering early contracts made by a private company, we saw[4] that there are only two categories which may arise. These are contracts:

(1) made on behalf of the company by promoters before the company was incorporated ie 'pre-incorporation' contracts made before the Certificate of Incorporation was issued; and

(2) made after incorporation.

Resulting from s 6(7) of the 1983 Act, however, there are three categories of contract to be considered in the corresponding circumstance for public companies. These contracts are:

(1) pre-incorporation contracts made by promoters, as above; and

---

1 See Chapter 10.
2 Or secretary.
3 Section 6(6) of the Companies (Amendment) Act 1983.
4 In Chapter 9.

(2) contracts made after incorporation but before the issuing of the Trading Certificate. These are known as pre-trading contracts; and

(3) contracts made after the Trading Certificate has been issued.

The law relating to responsibility of promoters is the same for both private and public companies. Section 6(8) of the Companies (Amendment) Act 1983, however, imposes civil[1] liability on directors for pre-trading contracts. This liability can arise where the company fails to honour its contractual obligations within 21 days from being called upon to do so. In these circumstances, the directors are jointly and severally liable to indemnify the other party to the pre-trading contract. The indemnity is for any loss or damage suffered by that party as a result of the company's failure to discharge its obligations.

NON-IRISH COMPANIES

11.4 Companies incorporated outside of Ireland who wish to trade into the State by starting up an establishment there, must comply with Part XI[2] of the 1963 Act. This involves, inter alia, delivering to the registrar within one month of starting up the Irish place of business, the following documents:

(1) certified copies of its *memorandum* and *articles* of association;

(2) a list of *directors* containing specified details of each director;

(3) details of the *company secretary*;

(4) the names and addresses of one or more persons resident in Ireland and authorised to accept service of legal proceedings on behalf of the company, ie the company's authorised *legal representatives*;[3] and

(5) the *address* of the company's principal place of business in Ireland.

Any alterations in (1) to (5) above must be notified to the registrar.

Accounts and publicity

11.5 A non-Irish company trading in Ireland may[4] have to submit accounts to the registrar, and show its country of origin in:

(1) every *prospectus* issued in Ireland;

(2) every place where it carries on business in Ireland; and

(3) on its billheads, letter headings and company publications and notices.[5]

---

1 And criminal – see s 6(7).
2 Comprising ss 351–360.
3 See s 356.
4 See s 354.
5 Section 355.

Cessation of business in Ireland

11.6   If a non-Irish company ceases to have a place of business in the State, it must also notify the registrar.[1]

Irish branches

11.7   The particulars required of companies with a branch, as distinct from an established place of business, in Ireland, are set out in the European Communities (Branch Disclosures) Regulations 1993.[2]

Details of external companies

11.8   The statistics for numbers of non-Irish or external companies show a significant growth in branch operations and a levelling off of established places of business during 1996 and 1997. The official numbers were:[3]

	1997	*1996*
Branches (EU)	607	532
Branches (non-EU)	116	98
Places of Business	2,180	2,148
Total of External Register	2,903	2,778

OTHER BUSINESS ASSOCIATIONS

11.9   Parts VIII[4] and IX[5] of the 1963 Act apply to companies formed and registered under older Companies Acts or other statutes. These companies are now subject to the relevant provisions of the current legislation, which has superseded the older Acts.

European Economic Interest Groupings (EEIGs)

11.10   A legal framework exists[6] which permits groupings of persons, companies and other legal entities to co-operate effectively in economic activities across national frontiers within the EU, whilst at the same time preserving their legal and economic independence.

---

1 Section 357.

2 SI 1993/395.

3 Source – *Companies Report 1997*, Department of Enterprise and Employment (The Stationery Office, July 1998).

4 Sections 324–327.

5 Sections 328–343. This Part includes companies registered under the Joint Stock Companies Act – see ss 329 and 330. The provisions of the Act which apply to chartered companies are outlined in the 1963 Act, Sch 9, as amended by s 250 of the 1990 Act. Section 377 of the 1963 Act makes provision for unregistered companies. Section 334 was amended by s 95 of the 2001 Act.

6 Under the European Communities (European Economic Interest Groupings) Regulations 1989, SI 1989/191.

There are similarities between the structures of an EEIG and a registered company. Instead of a memorandum and articles of association, the contract forming the grouping must be registered with the registrar. Relevant information must also be published in *Iris Oifigiúil* and an annual return furnished to the registrar.

The trading profits and losses of an EEIG belong, not to the grouping, but are returned to the individual members.[1]

There were eight EEIGs registered in Ireland on 31 December 1997.

---

1 An EEIG has some characteristics of a partnership. However, it is recognised by the law as a separate corporate entity.

PART IV A

THE COMPANY'S CONSTITUTIONAL DOCUMENTATION AND THE NATURE OF INVESTORS' LEGAL INTEREST IN IT

Chapter 12

THE MEMORANDUM AND THE ARTICLES OF ASSOCIATION

12.1 Prior to registration, the company's promoters must prepare the prospective company's constitutional documents.[1] These are its memorandum of association and its articles of association.

THE MEMORANDUM OF ASSOCIATION

12.2 The standard clauses in the memorandum deal with a company's name, objects,[2] limitation of liability and capital.[3]

The memorandum concludes by the subscribers to it, in an association clause, '[wishing] to be formed into a company'. When the registrar issues a certificate of incorporation, he has fulfilled this wish by creating a (new) company with a separate legal personality from the subscribers to the memorandum.[4]

The memorandum will also expressly state, 'the liability of the [company] members is limited'.[5] Thus, the two fundamental principles of company law, ie separate legal personality of the company[6] and limitation of liability for its investors/shareholders,[7] are both enshrined within the memorandum.

12.3 The significance of the name clause has already been dealt with in Chapter 7. The company name and this clause can be altered by special resolution.[8]

12.4 The capital clause in the memorandum simply states the authorised share capital of the company and its division into shares. For example, 'The share capital of the company is £200,000, divided into 200,000 shares of £1 each'. The various types of capital and classes of shares will be explained in Chapter 18.

12.5 Much of the litigation concerning the interpretation of the memorandum has centred on the objects clause.

---

1 See **8.10** et seq.
2 And powers.
3 See example in Table B of the 1963 Act.
4 Or any other of its shareholders.
5 Assuming a limited company is being formed.
6 See Chapter 3.
7 See Chapter 4.
8 See **7.3**.

The objects clause and the company's contractual capacity

12.6   A registered company has only the contractual power to enter into transactions authorised[1] by the objects clause in its memorandum.

At common law, any corporate contracts outside the company's objects were void. As Lord Cairns LC said in *Ashbury Railway Carriage & Iron Co v Riche*:[2]

> 'I agree ... that a contract of this kind was not within the words of the memorandum of association. In point of fact it was not a contract in which, as the memorandum of association implies, the limited company were to be the employed, they were the employers. They purchased the concession of a railway – an object not at all within the memorandum of association; and having purchased that, they employed, or they contracted to pay, as persons employing, the plaintiffs in the present action, as the persons who were to construct it. That was reversing entirely the whole hypothesis of the memorandum of association, and was the making of a contract not included within, but foreign to, the words of the memorandum of association.
>
> Those being the results of the documents to which I have referred, I will ask your lordships now to consider the effect of the Act of Parliament – the Companies Act of 1862 – on this state of things ... Your lordships are well aware that this is the Act which put upon its present permanent footing the regulation of joint stock companies, and more especially of those joint stock companies which were to be authorised to trade with a limit to their liability.
>
> The provisions under which that system of limiting liability was inaugurated, were provisions not merely, perhaps I might say not mainly, for the benefit of the shareholders for the time being in the company, but were enactments intended also to provide for the interests of two other very important bodies; in the first place, those who might become shareholders in succession to the persons who were shareholders for the time being; and secondly, the outside public, and more particularly those who might be creditors of companies of this kind ...
>
> I assume the contract in itself to be perfectly legal, to have nothing in it obnoxious to the doctrine involved in the expressions which I have used. The question is not as to the legality of the contract; the question is as to the competency and power of the company to make the contract. Now, I am clearly of the opinion that this contract was entirely, as I have said, beyond the objects in the memorandum of association. If so, it was thereby placed beyond the powers of the company to make the contract.'

12.7   Lord Cairns also made it clear that any contract 'ultra vires' the company's powers cannot be ratified, even with the unanimous agreement of all its shareholders. In this context, he stated:

> 'it is not a question whether the contract ever was ratified or was not ratified. *If it was a contract void at its beginning, it was void because the company could not make the contract.* If every shareholder of the company had been in the room, and every shareholder of the company had said, "That is a contract which we desire to make, which we authorise the directors to make, to which we sanction the placing the seal

---

1   Either expressly or impliedly.
2   (1875) LR 7 H2 653, 44 LJ Exch 185, 33 LT 450.

of the company", the case would not have stood in any different position from that in which it stands now. *The shareholders would thereby, by unanimous consent, have been attempting to do the very thing which, by the Act of Parliament, they were prohibited from doing.'* (author's emphasis)

Company contracts and the memorandum of association are examined more closely in Chapter 36.

Alteration of the objects clause

12.8   Section 10 of the 1963 Act provides that a company may alter the objects clause in its memorandum by special resolution. However, a dissenting minority of no less than 15 per cent of the company's members or debenture holders may petition the court to cancel the alteration – see ss 10(4) to 10(9), as amended by s 85 of the 2001 Act.

Who may object to the alteration?

12.9   The court will only entertain a petition to cancel an alteration of the objects clause, if it is made by the minority in their capacity as members, and not for some other reason. For example, an objection in *Re Munster and Leinster Bank Ltd*[1] was motivated by a desire to preserve an objector's professional fee income rather than being in the general interests of shareholders.

Alteration of the capital clause

12.10   The capital of a company can only be reduced by following the restrictive s 72 procedure, which also involves court approval – see Chapter 19. However, the authorised capital of a company may be increased under s 68 of the 1963 Act, simply by the passing of an ordinary resolution by the members.

Alteration of the liability clause

12.11   The liability clause of a company can also be altered so that a limited company becomes unlimited, or vice versa. The statutory requirements for such change of company status situations have already been mentioned in **8.24** et seq.

Section 27 of the 1963 Act protects all investors by providing that alterations in the memorandum or (articles of association) increasing an existing member's liability to contribute to share capital, will not bind the members without their express agreement, in writing.

---

1   [1930] 1 IR 237.

DISTINCTION BETWEEN THE MEMORANDUM AND ARTICLES OF ASSOCIATION

12.12   In *Ashbury Railway Carriage & Iron Co v Riche*, Lord Cairns LC also referred to the marked and entire difference which existed between the two fundamental contractual documents which form the title deeds of companies. He said:

> 'With regard to the memorandum of association, that is, as it were, the charter, and defines the limitation of the powers of a company to be established under the Act. With regard to the articles of association, those articles play a part subsidiary to the memorandum of association. They accept the memorandum of association as the charter of incorporation of the company, and so accepting it, the articles proceed to define the duties, the rights and the powers of the governing body as between themselves and the company, at large, and the mode and form in which changes in the internal regulations of the company may from time to time be made. With regard, therefore, to the memorandum of association, if you find anything which goes beyond the memorandum, or is not warranted by it, the question will arise whether that which is so done is ultra vires, not only of the directors of the company, but of the company itself. With regard to the articles of association, if you find anything which, still keeping within the memorandum of association, is a violation of the articles of association, or in excess of them, the question will arise whether that is anything more than an act ultra vires the directors, but intra vires the company ...

> Of the internal regulations of the company the members of it are absolute masters, and, provided they pursue the course marked out in the Act, that is to say, holding a general meeting and obtaining the consent of the shareholders, they may alter those regulations from time to time; but all must be done in the way of alteration subject to the conditions in the memorandum of association. The memorandum of association is, as it were, the area beyond which the action of the company cannot go; inside that area the shareholders may make such regulations for their own government as they think fit.'

12.13   Again, in *Roper v Ward and Ors*,[1] Carroll J stated:

> 'in construing the articles, I am guided by the principles that they are subordinate to and controlled by the memorandum of association which is the dominant instrument. While the articles cannot alter or control the memorandum or be used to expand the objects of the company, they can be used to explain it generally or to explain an ambiguity in its terms ...'

Corporate contracts merely ultra vires the directors' powers

12.14   Lord Cairns, in the *Ashbury Railway Co* judgment mentioned above, drew an important distinction between company transactions which were ultra vires the company's objects (and therefore void at common law) and those which were intra vires the memorandum objects clause but ultra vires the directors' powers or authority.

---

1   [1981] 1 ILRM 408 (HC).

A contract which is merely ultra vires the directors' powers may be ratified by the company's members in general meeting if it is intra vires the company's objects. Furthermore, a person dealing with the company need not concern himself with observance of the articles of association because an outsider cannot realistically check that any required formalities, internal to the company, have been observed. This is known as the rule in *Royal British Bank v Turquand.*[1]

The full extent of a company's contractual capacity, at common law and by statute, will be examined in Chapters 36 to 38.

THE ARTICLES OF ASSOCIATION

12.15   As explained in **12.12**, the articles contain regulations governing the internal management of the company. Essentially, they constitute the express contract terms of the legal relationship which exists between the company and its shareholders.

Table A of the Companies Act 1963, contains a model set of articles of association. These articles make provisions for the following broad areas of company organisation:

(1)   share capital and class rights;
(2)   corporate governance, including meetings, voting and election of directors;
(3)   company management, including directors' powers; and
(4)   company contracts.

Ross J in *Clarke v Workman*[2] commented:

> 'Now, what do the articles of association amount to in point of law? They constitute a contract between every shareholder and all the others, and between the company itself and all the shareholders. It is a contract of the most sacred character and it is on the faith of it that each shareholder advances his money.'

The contents of Table A will be considered in more detail in Chapter 14, and Parts IV B, C, D, E and Part VII B.

Alteration of the articles

12.16   The articles can be altered by special resolution (see s 15 of the 1963 Act). Any provision depriving the company of the power to alter its articles is void – *Malleson v National Insurance Corporation.*[3] A company also cannot

---

1   (1856) 6 E & B 327.
2   [1920] 1 IR 107 (HC).
3   [1894] 1 Ch 200.

undertake contractually not to alter its articles – *Southern Foundries Ltd v Shirlaw*.[1] As Porter LJ stated:

> 'A company cannot be precluded from altering its articles, thereby giving itself power to act upon the provisions of the altered articles – but so to act may nevertheless be a breach of contract if it is contrary to a contract validly made before the alteration.'

Where the alteration affects class rights, the approval of more than 75 per cent of that class must be obtained – see **18.24** et seq.

Restrictions on altering the articles

12.17   Because the articles regulate the internal affairs of a company, they can be freely altered by the members. However at common law the courts have intervened to protect minority members when the motivation of the majority is suspect.[2] Members also enjoy statutory protection by s 205 of the 1963 Act.[3]

COLLATERAL SHAREHOLDERS' AGREEMENTS

12.18   A company and its members may also have an additional or collateral contract outside the articles of association. This type of contract is known as a 'shareholders agreement'.

12.19   Shareholders' agreements[4] can deal with such matters as the exercise of voting rights, payment for shares and informal agreement to alter the articles of association.

Shareholders' agreement on exercising their voting rights

12.20   In *Welton v Saffery*,[5] Lord Davey seemed to accept that shareholders may lawfully agree, inter se, to exercise their voting rights in a manner which, if it were dictated by the articles and was thereby binding on the company, would be unlawful.

12.21   Lord Davey said:

> 'Of course, individual shareholders may deal with their own interests by contract in such way as they think fit. But such contracts, whether made by all or some only of the shareholders, would create personal obligations ... against themselves only, and would not become a regulation of the company, or be binding on the transferees of the parties to it, or upon new or non-assenting shareholders. There is

---

1   [1940] 2 All ER 445 (Ch).
2   See **16.4** et seq.
3   See **16.8** et seq.
4   In *Telnor Invest AS v IIU Nominees Ltd and Esat Telecom Holdings* (1999) 6 CLP 315, O'Sullivan J held that whilst a dispute over the interpretation of a shareholders' agreement was being determined by arbitration, the parties were not precluded from seeking interim relief from the court.
5   [1897] AC 299.

no suggestion here of any such private agreement outside the machinery of the Companies Acts.'

Shareholders' agreement not to increase share capital

12.22   Again, in *Russell v Northern Bank Development Corpn*[1] all the shareholders entered into an agreement, to which the company was also a party, 'to regulate the relationship between them with regard to the management and control of the company as long as they remained shareholders'.

Clause 1 of this agreement provided that its terms should have precedence 'between the shareholders over the articles of association'. The agreement also provided that no further share capital was to be created or issued in the company (TBL) without the written consent of the parties to the agreement.

An extraordinary general meeting was called to consider a proposal that the share capital of TBL be increased and allotted on a pro rata basis. Russell, a shareholder, applied for an injunction restraining the other four shareholders from voting upon the resolution.

12.23   Lord Jauncey of Tullichettle stated that the point at issue in this case was whether article 3 of the agreement constituted an unlawful and invalid fetter on the statutory power of TBL to increase its share capital or whether it was no more than an agreement between the shareholders as to the manner of their voting in a given situation. He decided that it was the latter, saying:

> 'I do not doubt that if clause 3 had been embodied in the articles of association so as to be binding on all persons who were or might become shareholders in TBL, it would have been invalid, but it was, of course not so embodied ...
>
> Turning back to clause 3 of the agreement, ... The shareholders agreed only to exercise their voting power in relation to the creation or issue of shares in TBL if they and TBL agreed in writing.
>
> This agreement is purely personal to the shareholders who executed it and ... does not purport to bind future shareholders. It is, in my view, just such a private [shareholders'] agreement as was envisaged by Lord Davey in *Welton v Saffery*.'

Shareholders' agreement as to payment for their shares

12.24   In *Re Pinecord Ltd*,[2] under a shareholders agreement, members sought to permit themselves to set-off any unpaid amounts due on their shares, against any sums which the company might owe them.

The High Court held that such terms in a shareholders' agreement could not allow shareholders to avoid their liabilities for uncalled amounts qua contributories to the company. Thus, a core term in the shareholders' statutory s 25

---

1   [1992] 1 WLR 588.
2   [1995] BCC 483.

contract impacting on the company's capital fund cannot be overridden by an express clause in a voluntary collateral shareholders' agreement.

Shareholders' informal agreement to pass a special resolution

12.25   Section 141(8) of the 1963 Act provides:

'(a)   Notwithstanding anything to the contrary in this Act, in any case in which a company is so authorised by its articles, a resolution in writing signed by all the members for the time being entitled to attend and vote on such a resolution at a general meeting shall be as valid and effective for all purposes as if the resolution has been passed at a general meeting of the company duly convened and held, and if described as a special resolution shall be deemed to be a special resolution within the meaning of this Act.

(b)   Any such resolution shall be deemed to have passed at a meeting held on the date on which it was signed by the last member to sign, and where the resolution states a date as being the date of his signature thereof by any member, the statement shall be prima facie evidence that it was signed by him on that date.'

Section 141(8)(a) and (b) clearly empowers shareholders to agree informally, if unanimous, to alter the articles, provided the informal special resolution is evidenced in writing.

12.26   In *Re Shannon Holdings Ltd*[1] even though the articles stipulated that company meetings be held within the State, where the members agreed to hold a meeting in the USA, Costello J considered this meeting validly held. In the writer's opinion, that decision was correct. Members can by informal unanimous agreement agree to hold the company meetings wherever they like. However, applying the reasoning in the *Welton v Saffery* case above, it is submitted that such shareholders' agreements only bind personally the shareholders who made them; they do not alter the articles of association. To effect an alteration of the articles and bind subsequent shareholders, the informal shareholders' agreement must comply with s 141(8)(a); in particular, it must be evidenced in writing and signed by all members. The registrar would also have to receive a printed copy under s 143(1) and (3).

---

1   (Unreported) 20 May 1993 (HC).

Chapter 13

THE NATURE OF INVESTORS' LEGAL INTERESTS

13.1 A company obtains its capital (and owners) by investing persons acquiring its shares. There is no statutory definition of a share. But this concept has been examined by the judiciary.

WHAT IS A SHARE?

13.2 In *Borland's Trustee v Steel Bros*,[1] the court came close to providing a working definition of the share concept. Here, the company's articles provided that the shares of a member who had become bankrupt should be made available for purchase by the other shareholders at a certain price.

The plaintiff disputed the legality of this provision in the articles, on the grounds, inter alia, that it infringed the rule against perpetuities. The court decided otherwise, effectively holding that because a member's rights and obligations are essential components of his shares and not distinct items of property[2] (ie the funds paid to the company in consideration for the issue of the shares), shares themselves cannot be subject to rules of law which invalidate certain dispositions of property, such as the rule against perpetuities.

In giving judgment, Farwell J said:

> 'A share, according to the plaintiff's argument, is a sum of money which is dealt with in a particular manner by what are called executory limitations. To my mind it is nothing of the sort. A share is the interest of a shareholder in the company measured by a sum of money, for the purpose of liability in the first place, and of interest in the second, but also consisting of a series of mutual covenants entered into by all the shareholders, inter se, in accordance with s 16 of the Companies Act 1862.[3] The contract contained in the articles of association is one of the original incidents of the share. A share is not a sum of money settled in the way suggested, but is an interest measured by a sum of money and made up of various rights contained in the contract, including the right to a sum of money of a more or less amount.'

13.3 If one examines this definition of Farwell J, it is clear that a share consists of:

(1) the interest of the investor in the company; and
(2) a series of mutual provisions entered into by all the shareholders inter se.

---

1 [1901] 1 Ch 279 (approved by Fitzgibbon LJ in *Casey v Bentley* [1902] 1 IR 376).
2 Or limitations imposed on a separate item of property.
3 Now s 25 of the Companies Act 1963 – see Chapter 20.

The interest of the investor in the company

13.4   A share is a 'chose in action', ie a certain form of right or interest which cannot be possessed in a physical sense. The share certificate, issued to an investor, and showing his name, and type and amount of shares held, is evidence of an 'interest' possessed by him in the company.

A shareholder does not possess a 'share' in the property owned by the company. An incorporated association such as a registered company has a legal personality separate from its shareholders. It also owns it own property.[1]

Essential nature

13.5   In *Att-Gen for Ireland v Jameson*,[2] the court held that a shareholder:

> 'is entitled to a share of the company's capital and profits the former ... being measured by a sum of money which is taken as the standard for the ascertainment of his share of the profits. If the company disposes of its assets, or if the latter be realised in a liquidation, he has a right to a proportion of the amount received after the discharge of the company's debts and liabilities.'

A person holding a share or shares does not have any rights over the company's property. For example, in *Att-Gen for Ireland v Jameson*, the court also held that no shareholder: 'has a right to any specific portion of the company's property, and save by, *and to the extent of his voting power* at a general meeting of the company, cannot curtail the free and proper disposition of it ...' (author's emphasis). A shareholder does have rights; the right to a dividend in certain cases; the right to vote at meetings if he holds the appropriate type of share, etc. But the company's property belongs to the company. Notwithstanding this, the courts have decided that a share confers a form of property right in the company itself, rather than its property.

Shareholders property rights in the company itself

13.6   A shareholder, as a member, not only has rights against the company; case-law suggests that he also has rights in the company itself.

The latter type of shareholders' right was explained by Costello J in *Kerry Co-operative Creamery Ltd v An Bord Bainne Co-op Ltd*,[3] thus:

> 'The shareholder has rights which can properly be regarded as property rights, but their nature and extent are to be ascertained by reference to the contract it has entered into with the society whose terms are contained in the society's rules.'[4]

13.7   In *Private Motorists Provident Society and Moore v Attorney General*,[5] the defendant argued that a shareholder (such as Mr Moore) in an incorporated body such as the society, while he had various contractual rights in and against

---

1 See Chapter 4.
2 [1904] 2 IR 644 (ChD).
3 [1990] ILRM 664.
4 The society's equivalent of a company's articles of association.
5 [1984] ILRM 988 (SC).

that body, nevertheless enjoyed no property rights in the society's assets or business.

This argument was not accepted by the Supreme Court, O'Higgins CJ explaining:

> 'it is sufficient that as a shareholder Mr Moore has, to the extent of his investment, an interest in the Society and contractual rights arising therefrom. This interest and those contractual rights are property rights which belong to Mr Moore, and are capable of being harmed by injury done to the Society.'

Accordingly, the Court held that Mr Moore had more than a mere contractual interest, but in fact, possessed a property right in the society itself, which was recognised by the law and capable of being protected by article 40.3 of the Constitution.

13.8 Where shareholders' rights such as those identified by O'Higgins CJ are infringed, it is likely that a shareholder would be able to initiate a personal action as an exception to the rule in *Foss v Harbottle*,[1] or, perhaps more effectively, to seek a remedy under s 205 of the 1963 Act.

Shareholders' series of mutual covenants

13.9 In *IRC v Crossman*,[2] Russell LJ defined a shareholder's interest in the company as being composed of rights and obligations which are defined by the Companies Acts and by the memorandum and articles of association of the company; and a series of mutual provisions entered into by all the shareholders inter se.

The court in *Att Gen for Ireland v Jameson* had also stated that on a shareholder becoming a member of the company and acquiring his rights:

> 'he is deemed to have simultaneously entered into a contract under seal to conform to the regulations contained in the articles of association ... whatever obligations are contained in the articles, he accepts the ownership of the share and the position of a member of the company bound and controlled by them. He cannot divorce his money interest, whatever it may amount to, from these obligations. They are inseparable incidents attached to his rights, and the idea of a share cannot be completed without their inclusion.'

13.10 The 'mutual provisions' and 'rights and obligations' are clearly spelled out in s 25 of the 1963 Act. Section 25 provides that:

> 'the memorandum and articles shall, when registered, bind the company and the members thereof to the same extent as if they respectively had been signed and sealed respectively by each member and contained covenants by each member to observe all the provisions of the memorandum and of the articles.'

As a result of s 25, the members' contract with the company is known as a statutory (or s 25) contract.[3]

---

1 See Chapter 16.
2 [1937] AC 26.
3 See Chapter 20.

The s 25 contract

13.11 The definition of a share is clearly important in a commercial and economic sense. However, from its contractual perspective, the most significant factor is that a shareholder becomes a member of the company, with legal rights and obligations flowing from this relationship. These contractual relations mean that, under s 25, the company's articles of association bind:

(1) the members to the company;
(2) the company to members (individually); and
(3) individual members to other members, each of whom is deemed to have covenanted under seal to observe the articles (and the memorandum).

The 's 25 contract' may be enforced by and against both the company and the individual members.

13.12 The typical matters included in articles of association can be illustrated by Table A. Table A deals with the following important internal company matters:

Share Capital and Shares	articles 2 to 46
Meetings	articles 47 to 74
Directors	articles 75 to 112
Secretary	articles 113 to 114
Dividends and Reserves	articles 116 to 124
Accounts	articles 125 to 129
Capitalisation of Profit	articles 130 to 131
Audit	article 132
Notices	articles 133 to 136
Winding up	article 137

Detailed examination of these articles begins in Chapter 14.

Shareholders' 'top up' statutory rights

13.13 In addition to their contractual rights under their s 25 contracts, members also enjoy further specific statutory rights. These 'top up' statutory rights are mentioned by Pennington[1] when commenting on Farwell J's analysis in the *Borland's Trustee* case. Pennington wrote:

'the concept of a share in this decision is clear. The so-called statutory contract obliges both the company and its members to conform to the terms and conditions contained in the company's memorandum and articles of association in respect of shares. This gives rise to contractual rights and obligations of each member as regards the company and every other member. The aggregate of these rights and obligations of a member is his shareholding, and when divided between the shares he holds, they constitute his shares. In fact, a concept of shares in these terms is incomplete, because many of the important rights and obligations of a member of a registered company under the present law are conferred or imposed on him, not by the statutory contract, but directly by the Companies Act 1985, itself.

1 R. Pennington 'Can shares in companies be defined?' (1989) 10 Co Law 140.

Nevertheless, if account is taken of such statutory rights and obligations and they are aggregated with the member's rights and obligations under the statutory contract, the whole complex of member's rights and obligations constitutes his shareholding.'

13.14 The 'top up' statutory rights conferred on shareholders fall into two categories. These categories are:

(1) rights exercisable by the member alone, ie additional personal or individual rights; and
(2) rights exercisable when the shareholder acts in concert with a member or other members, ie additional statutory (minority) collective rights.

Additional statutory individual members' rights

13.15 In addition to the rights enjoyed by members under the memorandum and articles of association, the Companies Acts confer the following additional statutory rights on shareholders:[1]

(1) to receive a copy of the memorandum and articles of association, and any Act of the Oireachtas which alters the memorandum. The member will be required to pay a small fee – see s 29 of the 1963 Act. Under s 8(2) of the 1963 Act, a member has the right to apply to the court to restrain the company from acting ultra vires;
(2) to receive notice of every general meeting;[2]
(3) to receive copies of balance sheets, profits and loss accounts (group accounts), directors' and auditors' reports.[3]
(4) to inspect and to obtain copies of the minutes of general meetings and resolutions;[4]
(5) to inspect and receive a copy of the statutory registers[5] which must be maintained by the company;
(6) to exercise pre-emption rights or rights of first refusal on a new issue of shares by the company;[6]
(7) not to have his liability to contribute to the capital of the company increased by an alteration of either the memorandum or the articles of association, without his written consent;[7]
(8) to petition the court for relief in cases of oppression by majority shareholders or by the directors, under s 205 of the 1963 Act;[8]
(9) to apply to the court for a disclosure order[9] against the shareholders of a private company, under s 98 of the 1990 Act; and

---

1 This is not meant to be an exhaustive list of such rights. Members' principal individual rights are examined in Chapters 20, 21 and 22.
2 Sections 131–133 of the 1963 Act (and Table A, article 133).
3 See s 159 of the 1963 Act.
4 Ibid, s 143.
5 See Chapter 33.
6 See s 23 of the 1983 Act.
7 See s 27 of the 1983 Act.
8 See Chapter 16.
9 See **22.9** et seq.

(10) to petition the court[1] for relief, if a compromise is agreed between the company and its creditors.

Shareholders' pre-contractual statutory rights

13.16 Investors who purchase shares in a public company on the inducement of a misrepresentation in the prospectus, enjoy specific statutory remedies against promoters and directors under s 49 of the 1963 Act.[2]

Members' additional statutory collective rights

13.17 Certain additional statutory rights are not exercisable by the member alone; these are essentially minority protection rights only being capable of being exercised if a group of minority shareholders co-operate to initate the legal action.

Examples of this category of rights include:

(1) if at least 15 per cent of the shareholders disagree with a special resolution passed to amend the objects clause in the company's memorandum of association, they can apply to the court to cancel the resolution under s 10 of the 1963 Act;

(2) where the majority of shareholders of a particular class of shares agree to vary their own 'class rights',[3] the holders of 10 per cent of the class who did not vote in favour of the resolution may apply to the court to have the variation of their rights cancelled;

(3) members holding at least 10 per cent of the company's shares can requisition the directors to call an extraordinary general meeting under s 132 of the 1963 Act;

(4) members of a plc holding at least 10 per cent of the equity capital, may require the company to investigate significant interests in its shareholdings, under s 83 of the 1990 Act; and

(5) a minority of members may also apply to the court for the appointment of an inspector to investigate the affairs of the company and to prepare and submit a report.

A minority of members who applied successfully to the court for the appointment of an inspector may incur costs of up to £250,000.[4]

MEANING OF INVESTORS' LEGAL INTEREST

13.18 As has been shown in this chapter, once an investor buys shares in a company, he becomes party to a statutory or s 25 contract, under which his

---

1 Under s 279 of the 1963 Act.

2 See **10.59** et seq.

3 See **18.16** et seq. Members may also have individual and collective statutory rights in connection with examinerships and financial arrangements between the company and its creditors – see Chapters 46, 47 and 48.

4 See Chapter 35.

rights and obligations are spelled out in the basic contract documents, the memorandum and the articles of association.

In addition to a shareholder's rights, as expressly contained in the company's memorandum and articles, he also enjoys the specific statutory 'top up' rights illustrated in **13.15** to **13.17**.

Model express contract terms for members

13.19   Table A in the 1963 Act is a model set of articles often adopted[1] in practice by companies.

Table A, Part I contains 138 articles of association labelled as regulations for the management of a public[2] limited company. Table A is, therefore, a model set of members' express contract terms, which we shall begin to examine in the next chapter. It is interesting to note that Sch 1 to the European Communities (Unfair Terms in Consumer Contracts) Regulations 1995[3] exempts from its provisions, 'any contract relating to the incorporation and organisation of companies'.

---

1 Perhaps with some modifications.
2 Table A, Part II shows the few amendments necessary to cater for a private company.
3 SI 1995/27.

Chapter 14

MEMBERS' EXPRESS CONTRACT TERMS

14.1 Using Table A as a model for members' express contract terms, one would expect to see the following matters, inter alia, covered in detail within a company's articles of association:

(1) *Share Capital*: its composition, acquisition, alteration and disposal;
(2) *Communication with members*;
(3) *Members Rights*: in particular their rights related to –
   (a) transferring shares,
   (b) restrictions on the right to transfer shares in private companies,
   (c) transmission of shares,
   (d) voting at company meetings; and
   (e) dividends;
(4) *General meetings*: notices, procedures and voting;
(5) *Corporate Governance*: appointment of directors by members, and division of power between members and directors;
(6) *Company management and directors' powers.*

It should not be forgotten that a shareholder's express contract rights in the articles are supplemented by additional statutory rights – both individual and collective (see **13.15** et seq).

The express contractual rules in Table A on the respective rights and obligations of the company and its shareholders are now introduced.

SHARE CAPITAL AND VARIATION OF 'CLASS RIGHTS'

14.2 Shareholders, as investors, contribute the company's investment capital. Accordingly, articles 1–4 of Table A provides for the company to issue different classes of (investment) share and for the variation of shareholders' 'class rights'.

The meaning and implications of shareholders' 'class rights' will be explained in Chapter 18, including case-law on the apportionment of surplus assets between the ordinary and preference shareholders in the event of a solvent winding up of the company.

14.3 Articles 5, 6 and 10 deal with the power of the company and its directors to grant options, pay commissions or brokerage and to give loans[1] for the purchase of the company's shares.

---

1 Under s 60 of the 1963 Act – see **19.42** et seq.

14.4   Articles 8 and 9 make provision for the issuing of share certificates[1] and for their replacement if defaced, lost or destroyed.

14.5   Section 123 of the 1963 Act makes it clear that the company, when entering the interests of its shareholders in the register of members, need not enter the interest of beneficiaries under a trust. Article 7 reflects the provisions in s 123, but also stipulates that:

> 'this shall not preclude the company from requiring the members[2] to furnish the company with information as to the beneficial ownership of any share when such information is reasonably required by the company.'

The requirements for share certificates are dealt with in **20.35** et seq, and the register of members in **20.18**. The statutory obligations on shareholders to disclose their interests in shares are set out in **22.2** et seq.

ALTERATION OF SHARE CAPITAL

14.6   Articles 44 and 45 of Table A permit the company to increase[3] or diminish its capital by ordinary resolution. However, article 46 reinforces the legal requirements on the preservation of the members' invested capital 'fund' by stipulating that the company may only reduce its capital by means of a special resolution plus the consent of the court.

Chapter 19 explains the formalities that are necessary for a company to comply with the statutory rules[4] for a legal reduction of its capital.

A second set of statutory rules are intended to prevent any indirect repayment of capital to shareholders. These are known as capital maintenance rules and are outlined in **19.21** et seq.

Conversion of shares into stock

14.7   The term 'share' defines the investor's legal interest[5] in the company. It is not the capital of the company as such. Accordingly, articles 40 to 44 enable the company, by ordinary resolution, to convert its share capital into stock, and to re-convert any stock into paid up shares of any denomination.

SANCTIONS AGAINST MEMBERS FOR NON-PAYMENT

14.8   Articles 11 to 14 give the company the power to exercise a lien on a member's shares (and dividends due) for all monies outstanding in respect of his shares.

---

1 As evidence of membership – see **20.35**.
2 Or a transferee of the shares.
3 See **19.59** et seq.
4 Under ss 72–77 of the 1963 Act.
5 See Chapter 13.

The directors' powers to make calls in respect of amounts unpaid on partly paid shares are contained in articles 11 to 21.

If the holder of a partly paid share fails to pay any call, or instalment of a call, the directors may proceed to forfeit his shares under articles 33 to 39. Directors may also deduct any amounts outstanding on shares from any dividends payable to the member – see article 121.

The financial liabilities of shareholders in respect of their shares is dealt with in **21.9** et seq.

RETURN OF CAPITAL ON A SOLVENT WINDING-UP

14.9 Article 137 empowers a liquidator, with the sanction of a special resolution and any other sanctions required by the Act, to divide amongst the members the whole or any part of the assets of the company.

The apportionment of surplus assets between the different classes of share-holders is examined in **18.18** et seq, whereas the apportionment of surplus assets arising on a reduction of a company's capital is considered in **18.25**.

DISPOSAL OF A COMPANY'S SURPLUS CAPITAL

14.10 The articles make express provisions for decision-making in relation to surplus company cash and other assets. Any surplus of company assets may be disposed of by way of dividend payments, creation of reserves and/or the capitalisation of profits.

Dividends

14.11 Articles 116 to 124 deal with dividends (and reserves). Members are only entitled to declare a dividend if recommended to do so by the directors. Hence the policy decision of whether or not to be distribute surplus assets to members by way of declaring a dividend falls to be made by the board, rather than the members theselves.

Since ss 45 to 51 of the Companies (Amendment) Act 1983 came into force, the dividend payable to members as a return on their investment can only be paid out of distributable[1] profits, ie accumulated realised profits less accumulated realised losses. This is to prevent an indirect reduction in the overall shareholders' funds. Thus, losses in previous years must be made good before a company can distribute a current surplus.

The mechanics of paying a dividend to company members are set out in **21.3** et seq.

---

1 See **19.54**.

Members' rights to dividends

14.12   The Companies Acts provide that a dividend must not be paid from the subscribed capital or if the company is insolvent. Otherwise it is a matter for the parties themselves to express the company's policies for distributing surplus assets in the articles of association.

A company does not have to distribute surplus assets to its shareholders as dividends or as bonus shares. In *Burland v Earle*[1] Lord Davey made it clear that there was no legal obligation on a company's internal management to distribute any or all of its surplus assets to the members. In fact, members would have no right to sue for payment of a dividend unless it had been:

(1) recommended by the directors; and
(2) declared (or approved) at an AGM.

Once a dividend has been declared and is payable, a shareholder is deemed to be an ordinary creditor of the company for the amount of his outstanding dividend payment.

Further effects of the declaration of a dividend are dealt with in **21.8**.

Scrip dividends

14.13   If a company's articles of association permit it,[2] members can be offered extra shares in lieu of dividend payments. These shares are known as scrip dividends and involve giving the member a choice. Instead of receiving a cash dividend, he can opt for an appropriate number of shares in the company and they are treated as fully paid up – the amount of the cash dividend waived equalling the market price of the shares issued in lieu of the dividend.

Setting aside profits as reserves

14.14   Article 119 gives the directors the power to set aside reserves out of profits, before recommending any dividend to the members at an AGM.

Capitalisation of profits[3]

14.15   Articles 130, 130A and 131 entitle the directors to recommend that surplus capital (profits) in the company's reserve accounts be capitalised, ie to use this money to make a bonus (free) or rights (partly paid) issue of shares to members. In this way, the directors are able to capitalise profits by giving them to existing shareholders as bonus shares, rather than distributing them by cash as dividends.

14.16   As in the case of dividend payments and reserve creation, *while it is the directors who recommend the capitalisation of profits, it is the members at an AGM who*

---

1 [1902] AC 83.
2 See article 122.
3 Section 51(3) of the 1983 Act defines this term as meaning the application of profits, wholly or partly, in paying up unissued shares in the company to be allotted to members as fully or partly paid bonus shares.

actually make the collective corporate decision to implement the board's recommendation.

COMMUNICATING WITH MEMBERS

14.17   Articles 133 and 134 stipulate that notice may be given to any member, either personally or by post, to his registered address.

Where shares are held in joint names, the company is required to give notice only to the joint holder named first in the register of members, in respect of the share.

MEMBERS' RIGHTS

14.18   Many articles in Table A bestow express rights on members in respect of such matters as assigning their shares, their rights to attend and vote at company meetings, and their limited rights to participate in corporate governance and company management.

MEMBERS' RIGHTS TO TRANSFER THEIR SHARES

14.19   Section 79 of the 1963 Act provides that shares are to be transferable in the manner provided by the articles of the company. Articles 22 to 31 of Table A deal with the transfer and transmission of shares.

Voluntary transfers of shares[1]

14.20   Article 24 gives directors of a plc the power, inter alia, to decline to register a transferee (of a partly paid share) of whom they do not approve.[2] They may also refuse the registration of any share[3] if, in their opinion, its registration would imperil or prejudicially affect the (tax) status of the company in the State.

Restrictions on transferring shares in private companies

14.21   While the nature of public companies and the need for marketability of their shares means the directors' powers to refuse registration of transfers are quite limited, the position is different in respect of private companies.

---

1 See Chapter 22.

2 The directors may also refuse to register the transfer of a partly paid share on which the company has a lien.

3 Ie partly paid or fully paid.

The directors of a private company are given much stronger powers to refuse company membership to transferees. For example, article 3[1] empowers the directors of a private company, 'in their absolute discretion, and without assigning any reason therefor [to] decline to register any transfer of any share, whether or not it is a fully paid share'.

The judicial attitude to the exercise of these wide-ranging directors' 'blocking' powers is examined in **22.21** et seq.

Involuntary transmission of shares

14.22   Table A, articles 29 to 32 provide for the involuntary assignment of shares in the event of the member's death or bankruptcy.

14.23   In *Arulchelvan and Wright v Wright et al*[2] Carroll J held that, as a person is not a member unless his name is on the register of members, so a legal personal representative who is entitled to be registered as a member is not a member until his name is entered in the register.

A personal representative is recognised by article 32 as having title to a deceased's shares. He is also entitled to the same dividends as a registered holder. However, he is not entitled to exercise any right conferred by membership (such as the right to vote), unless he is also a member.

In the *Arulchelvan* case, the legal personal representatives, not being members, could not be counted for the purpose of forming a quorum. As no quorum was present, no proper business could be transacted.

Other involuntary transfers of shares

14.24   In a takeover situation, the bidding company may have a right under s 204 of the 1963 Act to acquire compulsorily[3] the shares of dissenting members.

14.25   Similarly, in granting relief to an applicant under a s 205[4] application for oppression, the court may order the compulsory purchase or selling of shares.

MEMBERS' RIGHT TO VOTE AT GENERAL MEETINGS

14.26   Members are given express rights in the articles to attend and vote[5] at meetings. These are personal or individual rights. However, by exercising their individual rights, members participate in collective corporate decision-making.

---

1 Of Table A, part II.
2 (1997) 4 CLP 230 (HC).
3 See Chapter 48.
4 The court has similar powers under s 10 of the 1963 Act (objections to change in memorandum) and s 15 of the 1983 Act (objection to re-registration of plc as a private company).
5 Assuming they hold ordinary, rather than preference, shares.

MEMBERS' EXPRESS RIGHTS TO PARTICIPATE IN THE CORPORATE DECISION-MAKING PROCESS

14.27   A company is an artificial legal person, owned by its shareholders, and managed on their behalf by a board of directors. The most important forum for interaction between a company's owners and its directors is the general meeting.

General meetings for collective decision-making

14.28   Articles 47 to 51 provide for the holding of Annual and Extraordinary General Meetings. The prescribed amount of notice to be given to members is specified in articles 51 and 52.

Procedures at general meetings

14.29   Articles 53 to 63 deal with the types of business to be transacted, quorum, chairman and voting procedures (ie show of hands or poll).

Voting by members

14.30   Articles 63 to 74 specify which classes of shareholders have a right to vote. A corporate member can appoint a human representative to vote on its behalf – see article 74.

The detailed law relating to company meetings is set out in **15.31** et seq.

MAJORITY RULE AND MINORITY PROTECTION

14.31   The exercise by members of their personal rights to vote, enables them to participate in collective company decision making at general meetings. However, once members have voted on a resolution, the general rule is that the majority view prevails.

The reconciling of majority rule with the protection of minority shareholders' rights is examined in Chapters 16 and 17.

CORPORATE GOVERNANCE AND MEMBERS' EXPRESS CONTRACTUAL RIGHTS

14.32   In the early 1990s, the Bank of Credit and Commerce International (BCCI) collapsed in the UK, ruining many Asian shopkeeper depositors there.

Robert Maxwell was drowned. Following his death, it was discovered that the pension fund assets of the Maxwell Group had also disappeared.

In 1995, Barings' Bank collapsed after an employee made enormous losses trading in futures in its Singapore branch.

Corporate 'scandals', such as those mentioned above, focused public and political attention on the need for a better system of corporate governance.

The Cadbury Report[1] defines corporate governance as the system by which companies are directed and controlled. It states that the shareholders' role in corporate governance 'is to appoint the directors and the [external] auditors, and to satisfy themselves that an appropriate governance structure is in place'.

Appointment of directors by shareholders

14.33   The express rights of the members to appoint[2] directors are detailed in **15.5** et seq.

Consequences for members of appointing directors

14.34   Once the members elect or appoint the board of directors, the latter assume direct control over the day-to-day management of the company. Members, either individually or collectively, do not have the legal right to interfere with the directors in the operational management of the company.

14.35   In *Automatic Self-Cleaning Filter Syndicate Co Ltd v Cunninghame*,[3] the articles of association voted general management and control of the company in the directors 'subject to such regulations as might be made by special resolution'.

The intention of these articles seemed to have been to give the members a general supervisory power over the directors. However, the court took the view that the wording was not strong enough to achieve this effect. It held that the directors could not be compelled to comply with an instruction from the members generally to sell the assets of the company on certain terms when they (the directors) were of the opinion that such terms were not in the best interests of the company. Cozens-Hardy LJ stated:

> 'it seems to me that shareholders have by their express contract mutually stipulated that their common affairs [the company] should be managed by ... directors ..., such directors being liable to be removed only by special resolutions ...'

Relationship between members and directors

14.36   Cozens-Hardy LJ went on to discuss the legal relationship which existed between the members and the directors, saying:

> 'it is a fallacy to say that the relation is that of simple principal and agent ...

---

1 *Report of the Committee on the Financial Aspects of Corporate Governance* (Gee Publications Ltd, 1992).
2 And re-appoint.
3 [1906] 2 Ch 34.

It is not ... a case where you have a master on the one side and a mere servant on the other. You are dealing here ... with parties having individual rights as to which there are natural stipulations [in the statutory contract] for their common benefit, and once you get that [situation] ..., there is no ground for saying that the majority can put an end [unilaterally] to the express stipulations contained in the bargain which they made [the articles of association] ...

I cannot see anything in principle to justify the contention that the directors are bound to comply with the votes or the resolutions of a simple majority at an ordinary meeting of the shareholders.'

14.37   The wording of article 80 in Table A does not ordinarily give the members a general supervisory power over the directors of a company.

Table A provides that the business of the company shall be managed by the directors who may exercise all such powers of the company as are not, by statute, required to be exercised by the company in general meeting subject to such directions[1] as may be given by the company in general meeting.

If members in a company with article 80 wished to control the management powers of its directors, they would need to do so by the passing of a special resolution.[2]

COMPANY MANAGEMENT AND DIRECTORS' POWERS

14.38   The provisions in Table A dealing with directors' powers of management[3] are examined in Chapters 23 and 24.

MONITORING THE DIRECTORS' STEWARDSHIP OF THE COMPANY

14.39   Whilst the members own the company, they have to delegate the management of it to directors over whom they have little practical control. Nevertheless, the Companies Acts recognise this situation and stipulate that directors must keep proper books of account, and have annual accounts prepared.

Each member is entitled, by statutory provisions, to receive the accounts, together with copies of the directors' and auditors' reports, and to have these sent to him at least 21 days before the Annual General Meeting (AGM).

At an AGM, the directors report back to the members on the financial state of the company.

The detailed provisions relating to monitoring the directors' stewardship of the company are contained in Chapters 32 to 35. In this context, the role of the auditor is very important.

---

1 Not being inconsistent with the Companies Acts and Regulations.
2 See **24.2** et seq.
3 Also the role of the company secretary – see **23.15** et seq.

The role of the (external) auditor

14.40 The power of appointing and removing the company's auditors is vested in the shareholders[1] – not the board of directors.

The Cadbury Report saw the auditors' role as vital in a good system of corporate governance. The report stated:

> 'The role of the auditors is to provide the shareholders with an external and objective check on the directors' financial statements which form the basis of that reporting system. Although the reports of the directors are addressed to the shareholders, they are important to a wider audience, not least to employees whose interests boards have a statutory duty to take into account.'

THE APPOINTING OF DIRECTORS AND COMPANY MEETINGS

14.41 The articles in Table A dealing with the appointment of directors[2] and the holding of company meetings[3] are examined in Chapter 15.

---

1 Chapter 34.
2 See **15.5–15.29**.
3 See **15.31** et seq.

PART IV B

THE ARTICLES OF ASSOCIATION AND CORPORATE GOVERNANCE

Chapter 15

APPOINTMENT OF DIRECTORS AND COMPANY MEETINGS

THE UNDERLYING RELATIONSHIPS

15.1 When considering the management of the company, difficulties some-times arise in understanding the underlying relationships between:

(1) the company; and
(2) the directors and investors (or shareholders).

The company

15.2 The company is a separate legal personality on its own account. It is quite distinct from the members (or investors) who own it. The company can own property and enter into contracts in its own right. However, being an artificial creation of the law, a company can only make decisions and act through human agents. The management of a company must therefore be carried out by such agents.

Company management

15.3 It is useful at this stage to refine the term 'management' in the context of company law. The day-to-day management of the company's affairs is the responsibility of its directors and officers. Investors, as owners, have no right to act on behalf of the company in the day-to-day management of its affairs.

A second tier of company management is the taking of decisions to amend the company's memorandum and/or articles of association. Such corporate decisions affecting fundamental constitutional aspects of the company, may impinge directly on investors' contractual rights. Accordingly, investors have a part to play in the voting for and against such changes.

Shareholders' role in corporate governance

15.4 The basic role of company investors in corporate governance under the Companies Acts is to elect or appoint the board of directors. Company members[1] are also entitled to vote at general meetings and thereby participate in the 'democratic' nature of collective decision-making for 'corporate decisions', ie decisions affecting fundamental constitutional aspects of the company, such as amending its memorandum and/or articles of association. They are also empowered to approve (or not) any recommendations made by the directors for the use or disposal of the company's surplus assets.[2]

---

1 Holding ordinary voting shares.
2 See **14.10** et seq.

Shareholders can participate in corporate governance by exercising their voting power, if they are the holders of ordinary shares. Members can vote to appoint, remove or change the board of directors. They will participate in votes on business resolutions at the company's general meetings, some of which will require only a simple majority, whereas other, more fundamental, changes require a 75 per cent majority.

Developments in corporate governance are reviewed in Chapter 54.

APPOINTMENT OF DIRECTORS[1] BY MEMBERS

15.5   Section 181 of the 1963 Act provides that appointment of directors by members must be voted on individually, ie a motion for the appointment of two or more persons as directors by single resolution will be invalid, unless prior approval to proceed on this basis has been obtained from all members present at the meeting.

15.6   Private and public companies must have a minimum of two directors[2] (every company must also have a secretary, who may be one of the directors).

First directors

15.7   The names of the *first directors* must be delivered to the registrar of companies with the memorandum of association.[3]

It is not necessary for directors to have shareholding in a company. In practice, though, many directors will also be members.[4]

If the articles provide for the directors to hold *qualification* shares, ie to purchase a minimum number of shares, they must obtain these share qualifications within two months of their appointment.[5] The first appointees must consent, in writing, to becoming directors of the company.[6]

Subsequent directors

15.8   Appointments subsequent to the first directors must be made in the manner provided by the articles. If no provision is made in the articles, they must be elected by the members in general meeting.

---

1 Principle 5A of the Combined Code also provides that there should be a formal and transparent procedure for the appointment of new directors to a board.
2 Section 174 of the 1963 Act.
3 Section 3 of the 1983 Amendment Act.
4 Particularly of private companies.
5 Or such shorter time as the articles may specify – s 180 of the 1963 Act.
6 See s 179 of the 1963 Act, for details.

Rotation of directors

15.9 Table A[1] provides as follows:

'**92.** At the first annual general meeting of the company all the directors shall retire from office, and at the annual general meeting in every subsequent year, one-third of the directors for the time being, or, if their number is not three or a multiple of three, then the number nearest one-third shall retire from office.

93. The directors to retire in every year shall be those who have been longest in office since their last election but as between persons who became directors on the same day, those to retire shall (unless they otherwise agree among themselves) be determined by lot.

94. A retiring director shall be eligible for re-election.'

Maximum number of directorships

15.10 Section 45(1) of the Companies (Amendment) (No 2) Act 1999 stipulates that a person cannot, at a particular time, be a director (including shadow director) of more than 25 companies.

Section 45(3) to (12) and Sch 2 to this Act contain the detailed rules for calculating the number of 25 valid directorships. Generally, in calculating this maximum number, the following directorships can be excluded:

(1) of any public limited company or public company; and
(2) of a company certified by the registrar under s 44 of the 1999 (No 2) Act (see **8.13**).

Section 45(9) provides that an appointment as a director of a company in breach of the maximum directorships provisions shall be void. In addition, criminal proceedings may be instigated summarily by the registrar.

Increase or reduction in numbers of directors

15.11 Table A, articles 97 and 98 deal with changes in numbers of directors as follows:

'**97.** The company may from time to time by ordinary resolution increase or reduce the number of directors and may also determine in what rotation the increased or reduced number is to go out of office.

98. The directors shall have power at any time and from time to time to appoint any person to be a director, either to fill a casual vacancy or as an addition to the existing directors, but so that the total number of directors shall not any time exceed the number fixed in accordance with these regulations. Any director so appointed shall hold office only until the next following annual general meeting, and shall then be eligible for re-election but shall not be taken into account in determining the directors who are to retire by rotation at such meeting.'

---

1 In the 1963 Act, Sch 1.

Removal of directors

15.12   Again, provision is made in Table A for the members to remove any director and to replace him, the relevant articles providing:

> '**99.** The company may, by ordinary resolution, of which extended notice has been given in accordance with section 142 of the Act, remove any director before the expiration of his period of office notwithstanding anything in these regulations or in any agreement between the company and such director. Such removal shall be without prejudice to any claim such director may have for damages for breach of any contract of service between him and the company.

> **100.** The company may, by ordinary resolution, appoint another person in place of a director removed from office under regulation 99 and without prejudice to the powers of the directors under regulation 98 the company in general meeting may appoint any person to be a director either to fill a casual vacancy or as an additional director. A person appointed in place of a director so removed or to fill such a vacancy shall be subject to retirement at the same time as if he had become a director on the day on which the director in whose place he is appointed was last elected a director.'

The rights of a removed director are dealt with at **15.22**.

Directors' resignation, retirement or removal

15.13   The Companies (Amendment) (No 2) Act 1999 makes it necessary for a company to notify the registrar when a person ceases to act as its director – see **8.14** et seq.

Defects in appointment

15.14   The acts of a director on behalf of the company will be valid, notwithstanding any defects which may afterwards be discovered in his appointment or qualifications.[1]

Disqualification of directors

15.15   Table A, article 91, provides that the office of director must be vacated if the director:

(1)   ceases to be a director by virtue of s 180 of the 1963 Act, ie fails to obtain his qualification shares; or

(2)   is adjudged bankrupt in the State or in Northern Ireland or Great Britain or makes an arrangement or composition with his creditors generally; or

(3)   becomes prohibited from being a director by reason of any order made under s 184 of the Act; or

(4)   becomes of unsound mind; or

(5)   resigns his office by notice in writing to the company; or

---

1   See s 181 of the 1963 Act for an example of a procedural defect in appointing a director.

(6) is convicted of an indictable offence unless the directors otherwise determine; or

(7) is for more than six months absent without permission of the directors from meetings of the directors held during that period.

In Chapter 30, we shall consider disqualification and restriction of directors under the 1990 Act, Part VII of which replaces s 184 in (3) above.

Remuneration of directors

15.16 Directors are not employees of the company. They are elected office holders who control and manage the company's affairs. Accordingly, they are not entitled to remuneration for their services unless, as is usual, there is provision for such payments in the articles.[1] For example, article 76 of Table A provides that:

> 'The remuneration of the directors shall from time to time be determined by the company in general meeting ... The directors may also be paid all travelling, hotel and other expenses properly incurred by them in attending meetings ... or in connection with the business of the company.'

Section 185 of the 1963 Act prohibits tax-free payments to directors.

If remuneration is voted to the directors under the articles, it then constitutes a debt due from the company and may, if necessary, be paid out of capital.[2] Furthermore, the company cannot retrospectively amend its articles to remove the directors' entitlement to accrued remuneration.[3]

Loans to directors

15.17 Section 192[4] specifies the information which must be included in the company's annual accounts in relation to loans made to any director.

Disclosure of directors' salaries and emoluments

15.18 Section 191 contains the particulars of directors' salaries and payments which must be given in the company's annual accounts.

General duty of disclosure on directors (and secretary)

15.19 Every director (and secretary) must give notice to the company, in writing, of relevant loans or emoluments for the purpose of compliance with ss 192 and 191.[5]

---

1 *Woolf v East Nigel Gold Mining Co* (1905) 21 TLR 660.
2 *Re Lundy Granite Co* (1872) 26 LT 673.
3 They may, however, be able to do so prospectively – see *Swabey v Port Darwin Gold Mining Co* (1889) 1 Meg 385 (CA).
4 Of the 1963 Act. See **27.12** et seq.
5 Also with s 190 relating to the register of directors' shareholdings. See Chapter 33.

Particulars of directors to be shown in company letter headings

15.20   Particulars relating to its directors must be shown in all the company's business letters. These particulars are the director's name, initials and nationality, if not Irish.[1]

Assignment of office by directors

15.21   Any transfer by a director, of his office, to another person, even with the agreement of the company,[2] will be of no effect unless and until it is approved by a special resolution of the company. These provisions in s 199[3] are applicable to assignments inter vivos.[4] They are inappropriate where the assignment is made by will or codicil.[5]

REMOVAL OF DIRECTORS

15.22   Section 182 of the 1963 Act gives the members of a company the power to remove any director from office by ordinary resolution, except a director in a private company who was appointed for life.

Extended notice[6] of 28 days must be given of any resolution to remove a director. The detailed procedures are contained in s 182(2) to (7). Under them, the director in question is entitled to make written representations to the meeting in his defence. Section 182(7) also makes it clear that the section does not invalidate the dismissal of a director by the board alone, if such a dismissals procedure is expressly authorised by the articles.

In *Bushell v Faith,*[7] the articles tripled a director's voting power in the event of a poll for his removal under s 303 of the UK's 1985 Act (the equivalent of s 182).

The House of Lords held that the director's shares which carried these weighted voting rights did not infringe s 303 – see also **18.24**.

Natural justice

15.23   When dismissing a director, even under s 182, the company must also comply with the requirements of natural justice. As Walsh J stated in *Glover v BLN Ltd*:[8]

> 'In my view, it was necessarily an implied term of the contract that this inquiry and determination should be fairly conducted . . .

---

1 See s 196.
2 Ie through the board of directors.
3 Of the 1963 Act.
4 Ie between living persons.
5 *Fitzpatrick v Fitzpatricks Footwear Ltd* (Unreported) 18 November 1970 (HC).
6 See s 142.
7 [1970] AC 1099.
8 [1973] IR 388 (SC).

The plaintiff was neither told of the charges against him nor was he given any opportunity of dealing with them before the board of directors arrival at its decision to dismiss him.'

The court, accordingly, held that there had been a breach of natural justice and the plaintiff was entitled to damages for wrongful dismissal.

In the *Glover* case, the plaintiff was an executive director, ie he was an employee of the company as well as an office holder. However, where a non-executive director is dismissed, the rules of natural justice still apply. This was confirmed by *Garvey v Ireland*,[1] which seems to imply a constitutional right to fairness of procedures generally in the making of such decisions.

DIRECTORS' SERVICE CONTRACTS

15.24   There has been a tendency during the last few decades to appoint company executives to the board. Such appointees may be styled 'technical', 'financial', 'personnel' or even managing director. All these executive directors effectively hold two posts. One post is the office of director; the second post is the 'service' or employment contract with the company – a fact acknowledged by s 182(7) which provides, inter alia:

'nothing in this section shall be taken as depriving a person removed thereunder of compensation or damages, – payable to him in respect of the determination of any (other) appointment terminating with that as director.'

The Supreme Court in *Carvill v Irish Industrial Bank Ltd*[2] made it clear that dismissal of [an executive] director under s 182 is without prejudice to any rights he may have to damages for breach of his contract of employment. O'Keeffe J stated:

'Once these words ["subject to the provisions of any contract between him and the company"] appear, it is open to the director to enter into a contract with the managing director *the effect of which may be to deprive the company in general meeting of the power to remove him from office without being liable to pay damages.* The question is whether there is such a contract in the present case.' (author's emphasis)

15.25   The members' power[3] to remove a director by ordinary resolution does not preclude the court from enjoining[4] the removal of a director.

15.26   In *Feighery v Feighery et al*,[5] Laffoy J held that s 205 of the 1963 Act did not empower the court to enjoin the removal of a director by members in violation of s 182. However, in *McGilligan and ANR v O'Grady et al*,[6] Keane J in the Supreme Court refused to follow the decision in the *Feighery* case.

---

1 [1981] IR 25 (SC).
2 [1968] IR 325.
3 In s 182(1).
4 Prohibiting by order.
5 [1999] 1 IR 321, [1999] 1 ILRM 303.
6 [1999] 1 IR 346.

Barron J concurred with Keane J, stating:

> 'no absolute reliance can be placed upon a statutory right given to the general meeting of a company (in this instant, that contained in s 182(1)) when the exercise of that right is alleged to be wrongful; in this case a breach of s 205 of the Companies Act 1963.[1] In all such cases determination of the issue as to the granting of interlocutory relief must be dependent upon the general rules applicable.'

An order for the liquidation of the company terminates the power of the board, and also the directors' individual contracts of employment.

In *Re TN Farrer Ltd*,[2] the articles appointed Farrer (F) governing director for life, or until he should resign or be removed by special resolution.

On the company going into voluntary liquidation, and having acted as director for sixteen years, F sued for damages. The court held the F's employment as governing (managing) director was conditional on the continued existence of the company, and ceased automatically when it wound up. As a result, F could not claim damages for breach of contract.

The managing director's contract

15.27   Article 110 of Table A provides that:

> 'The directors may from time to time appoint one or more of themselves to the office of managing director for such period and on such terms as to remuneration and otherwise as they think fit, and, subject to the terms of any agreement entered into any particular case, may revoke such appointment.'

The directors may confer or delegate any of their powers to the managing director.

A company may be liable in damages if the appointment of a managing director is prematurely terminated, either as a consequence of an alteration of the articles,[3] or his removal from office under s 182, if this action is inconsistent with his contract of service.[4]

1990 Act limitations on directors' service contracts

15.28   Section 28 of the 1990 Act seeks to prevent the possible abuse of s 182 whereby directors could, as a board, agree long-term service contracts for themselves with the company without having to obtain the approval of the shareholders. The significance of these long-term contracts were that if the members did dismiss any directors, the compensation payable to them would usually be based on the unexpired portion of their service contracts.

---

1 See Chapter 16.
2 [1937] 1 Ch 352, 53 TLR 581.
3 *Southern Foundries (1926) Ltd v Shirlaw* [1940] AC 701.
4 Cf *Shindler v Northern Raincoat Ltd* [1960] 1 WLR 1038.

If the effect of a clause in a director's service contract is to extend the contract for a period exceeding five years,[1] then under s 28, that clause is void unless it is first approved by the company in general meeting.[2]

Inspection of directors' service contracts

15.29 A copy of each director's service contract, or, if not in writing, a written memorandum setting out its terms, must be kept by the company for inspection by its members.[3]

Authority of directors

15.30 The authority of the directors to act as agents of the company is examined later in Part VII B.

TYPES OF MEETINGS

15.31 Meetings play a key part in the operation of any company by its human agents, ie its officers and members. There are three different types of meeting. These are:

(1) *company meetings* attended by members and directors;
(2) *board meetings* attended by the directors and secretary. These meetings are dealt with in **23.7**; and
(3) *third party meetings*, ie meetings necessary[4] between company creditors and management. Consideration of third party meetings will be deferred until Parts X A and X B.

COMPANY MEETINGS

15.32 Company meetings fall into the two categories of Annual and Extraordinary General Meetings. In addition, if the interests of a particular class of shareholders are to be affected, the company may have to convene separate 'class meetings' – see **15.57** and **18.24**.

---

1 During which time his employment cannot be terminated by the company giving reasonable notice, or can only be terminated in specified circumstances.
2 See s 28 for the appropriate procedures.
3 Section 50 of the 1990 Act.
4 In the event of a company liquidation.

Annual General Meetings (AGMs)

15.33 The Annual General Meeting (AGM) is the most important meeting of the company investors. It must be held every 12 months, and not more than 15 months must elapse between each meeting.[1]

Notice

15.34 Section 133 sets out the statutory periods of notice for calling company meetings.[2] In respect of AGMs, the minimum period of written notice is 21 days. Any provision in a company's articles specifying a shorter notice period will be void.

15.35 Every member entitled to notice of a meeting must be sent a notice, otherwise a resolution passed at the meeting is void. In *Young v Ladies Imperial Club Ltd*,[3] Lord Sterndale MR stated:

> 'with certain very limited exceptions where a special meeting of a committee or any other body has to be specially convened for a particular purpose, every member of that body ought to have notice of a summons to the meeting.'

In the *Young* case, notice was sent to each member of the committee except one who had previously informed that chairman that she would be unable to attend the meeting. Thus the failure to send the notice was deliberate.

15.36 Where the failure to give notice is accidental, rather than deliberate, the omission need not invalidate the proceedings – see *Re West Canadian Collieries Ltd*.[4] If however, the failure to give notice is due to an error of law, rather than an administrative mistake, this may invalidate proceedings.[5]

Contents of notice

15.37 The notice of a general meeting must disclose all facts necessary to enable a member to decide whether or not to attend. If a director is interested in a proposed transaction, then such interest must be disclosed in the notice.

In *Tiessen v Henderson*,[6] the court granted an order invalidating the resolution in question and restraining the company from carrying it out because the notice of the meeting did not disclose the fact that directors were to receive payments from the transaction. Similarly, in *Rose v McGivern et al*,[7] the plaintiff wrote to members prior to an EGM proposing:

(1) to elect a new board; and

---

1 Except that the company has 18 months to hold the first AGM after the company is formed – see s 131 of the 1963 Act which also makes provision for failure by the directors to call an AGM.
2 Except those at which a special resolution is to be passed which fall to be considered under s 141.
3 [1920] 2 KB 525, 123 LT 191, 36 TLR 392.
4 [1962] Ch 370.
5 See *Musselwhite v CH Musselwhite & Son Ltd* [1962] Ch 964.
6 [1899] 1 Ch 861.
7 [1998] 2 BCLC 593.

(2) to authorise the board to proceed with the demutualisation of the company.

The court held that these proposals in the plaintiff's letter to members could not constitute valid resolutions because (1) was too vague, lacking specificity such as the identity of the persons who were to be elected as new directors.

Waiver of notice

15.38 If all the members, together with the auditors, agree, a meeting called with less than 21 days' notice shall be deemed to have been duly called.[1]

Adjourned AGMs

15.39 Generally, adjourned meetings do not need any particular notice unless:

(1) the articles require it;
(2) new business is to be placed on the agenda; or
(3) the adjournment took place without a date being fixed for the next meeting.

Single-member companies

15.40 The sole member of a single-member company may decide to dispense with the holding of AGMs. If he so decides, all the powers exercisable by the company in general meeting shall be exercisable by the sole member, without the need to hold a general meeting for the purpose.

The conditions under which sole members are given these privileges are set out in regs 8 and 9 of the European Communities (Single-Member Private Limited Companies) Regulations, 1994 – see **8.7**.

Business at AGMs

15.41 Generally, the following items are deemed ordinary business at an AGM:

(1) declaring a dividend;
(2) considering the accounts;
(3) considering the balance sheets;
(4) considering the reports of directors and auditors;
(5) electing replacement directors;
(6) re-appointing retiring auditors;
(7) fixing the remuneration of the auditors.

Consideration of these items give the investors an opportunity of judging the effectiveness of the directors' stewardship of their company – see Part VI.

---

1 Section 133(3).

All other items are special business.[1] So, too, is all business transacted at an Extraordinary General Meeting.

Location of AGM

15.42   Generally, the AGM must be held in Ireland.[2]

Extraordinary General Meetings (EGMs)

15.43   EGMs may be requisitioned by the members under s 132.[3] The directors must call such a meeting if the requisitionists hold at least one-tenth of the paid-up voting capital or, if there is no share capital, hold a minimum of one-tenth of the total voting rights in the company.

The requisition must state the objects of the meeting and be signed by the requisitionists and deposited at the registered office of the company. If the directors do not convene the meeting within 21 days, the requisitionists themselves may do so.

The directors must also call an EGM in the event of a serious loss of capital.[4]

Notice

15.44   Section 133(2)(b) prescribes the following periods of written notice for meetings which are *not* AGMs or a meeting for the passing of a special resolution:

(1) 14 days for public companies (generally); and
(2) 7 days for private or unlimited companies.

If the passing of a special resolution is proposed at the EGM, the minimum notice will be 21 days. The notice should also contain the exact wording of the resolution to be proposed and must be served in accordance with article 51.

Business at EGM

15.45   All items of business at an EGM are classified as special business.[5]

Power to order the holding of a meeting

15.46   If default is made in holding an AGM, the *Director of Corporate Enforcement* may, on the application of any member of the company, call, or direct the calling of, an AGM.[6]

---

1 See article 53 of Table A. Examples would include a proposal to alter the articles under s 15 of the 1963 Act.
2 Section 140 of the 1963 Act.
3 Of the 1963 Act.
4 Under s 40 of the 1983 Amendment Act – see **19.40**.
5 Per article 53 of Table A.
6 Section 131(3) – see **55.8**.

Again, if for any reason it is impracticable to call a meeting, the *court* may, either on its own motion, or on the application of any director or member, order a meeting to be held.[1] In *Angelis v Algemene Bank Netherland (Ireland) Ltd and Others*,[2] it was held that the court will only convene such a meeting where it is otherwise impracticable to convene it. In that case, the requisition served on the directors to convene a meeting was invalid so they were not bound to act on it. Accordingly, the court did not order the meeting because the directors could have convened it if the requisition had been valid. As to the invalidity, Kenny J said:

> 'It seems to me to be probable that the plaintiff agreed to resign as a director of the company and therefore he cannot convene a meeting of directors. By letter dated 14 June 1974 he purported to convene a directors' meeting for the 17 June 1974. If this be read as a requisition to call a meeting of the company, then it was clearly invalid because under s 132 of the Companies Act 1963 the directors have a period of 21 days within which to convene a meeting.'

Any *two or more members* holding at least 10 per cent of the issued capital may also call a meeting, unless the articles provide otherwise – see s 134(b).

Conduct of meetings

15.47   In *Carruth v Imperial Chemical Industries Ltd*,[3] Lord Russell of Killowen made the following comments in the House of Lords on the proper conduct of meetings:

> 'There are many matters relating to the conduct of a meeting which lie entirely in the hands of those persons who are present and constitute the meeting. Thus it rests with the meeting to decide whether notices, resolutions, minutes, accounts, and such like shall be read to the meeting or be taken as read; whether representatives of the press, or any other persons not qualified to be summoned to the meeting, shall be permitted to be present, or if present shall be permitted to remain; whether and when discussion shall be terminated and a vote taken; whether the meeting shall be adjourned. In all these matters, and they are only instances, the meeting decides, and if necessary a vote must be taken to ascertain the wishes of the majority. If no objection is taken by any constituent of the meeting, the meeting must be taken to be assenting to the course adopted.'

Power of majority at meetings

15.48   Where the board of directors act improperly, but their actions can be ratified by a general meeting, the court will not interfere with the internal management of a company acting within its powers, at the suit of a minority shareholder. In *Foss v Harbottle*,[4] Wigram VC said:

---

1   Section 135.
2   (Unreported) 4 July 1974 (HC).
3   [1937] AC 707 (HL).
4   (1843) 2 Hare 461, 67 ER 189.

'[It could not be successfully argued that] it was a matter of course for any individual members of a corporation ... to assume to themselves the right of suing in the name of the corporation. In law the corporation and the aggregate members of the corporation are not the same thing for purposes like this; and the only question can be whether the facts alleged in this case justify a departure from the rule which, prima facie, would require that the corporation should sue in its own name and in its corporate character, or in the name of someone whom the law has appointed to be its representative'.

As there was a board of directors capable of acting and the possibility of calling a general meeting of 'the supreme governing body, the proprietors at a special general meeting assembled, [who] retain the power of exercising the functions conferred upon them by the act of incorporation', there were no special circumstances existing to prevent the company from obtaining redress in its corporate capacity.[1]

Proceedings at general meetings

15.49 The proceedings at general meetings will be regulated by the company's articles of association. As many companies adopt Table A, the contents of articles 53 to 74 are outlined hereunder.

Quorum of members

15.50 Section 134(c) and articles 54 and 55 deal with the quorum required. No business can be transacted at a general meeting unless a quorum of members is *present at the time when the meeting proceeds to business.*

Section 134(c) provides that for a private company, two members constitute a quorum, and for all other companies, three members. These members must be personally present at the meeting – *proxies* cannot be counted for this purpose.

In the case of a single-member company, one member present in person or by proxy will constitute a quorum. This may also apply when an AGM is called by the Director of Corporate Enforcement under s 131(3).

In *Arulchelvan & Wright v Wright et al,*[2] Carroll J held that an unregistered personal representative could not be counted towards forming part of the quorum at an EGM.

Article 55 sets out the procedure to be followed if, within half an hour, there is no quorum present.

In *Byng v London Life Assoc Ltd,*[3] the court held that an inquorate meeting incapable of conducting any business is still a 'meeting' capable of being adjourned.

---

1 But see corporate governance and minority protection in Chapters 16 and 17.
2 [1997] 4 CLP 230.
3 [1989] 5 BCC 227 (CA).

Chairman

15.51 Any member present at the meeting may be elected chairman,[1] unless the articles provide otherwise. However, the articles normally make such provision. For example, under article 56, the chairman of the board of directors is to preside as chairman of every AGM. If he is unavailable, the chairman will be elected from one of the directors present: the decision being made by the directors. If no director is present or willing to act as chairman, the members may choose one of their members to chair the meeting – see article 57.

During the meeting, the chairman must allow the minority of shareholders a reasonable amount of time in which to put forward their case.[2]

Article 61 confers a casting or second vote on the chairman. It is he who will decide on the validity of any disputes as to qualifications of members to vote – article 67.

It is the duty of the chairman to:

(1) preserve order and to regulate proceedings so as to give all persons entitled a reasonable opportunity of voting;
(2) see that the proceedings are conducted properly. In exceptional circumstances, where the articles accord a Chairman sufficient discretion with regard to the conduct of a poll, he may validly take a poll by requiring only those against the motion to cast their votes – see *Duggan v Bank of Ireland*;[3]
(3) take care that the sense of the meeting is properly ascertained with regard to any questions before it;[4]
(4) decide incidental questions arising for decision during the meeting, eg the validity of process.[5]

If the chairman closes the meeting against the wishes of the members, another chairman may be elected. For example, in *National Dwellings Society v Sykes*, the facts were as follows.

At a general meeting called to pass the accounts and re-elect directors, the chairman proposed 'that the accounts be passed'. A member moved an amendment that a committee of enquiry be appointed. The chairman refused to take the amendment, put his original motion to the meeting, who did not approve it. The chairman dissolved the meeting on the failure of his motion to the meeting. The members then appointed a new chairman and passed a motion setting up a committee of inquiry. The court approved the actions of the members.

---

1 Section 134(d).
2 *Wall v London and Northern Assets Corp* [1898] 2 Ch 469.
3 (Unreported) 29 July 1998 (HC).
4 See *National Dwellings Society v Sykes* [1894] 3 Ch 159, 63 LJ Ch 906, 42 WR 696, and *Reg v D'Oyly* (1840) 12 Ad & EL 139.
5 See *Wall v Exchange Investment Corporation* [1926] Ch 143 (CA), and *Oliver v Dalgleish* [1963] 1 WLR 1274.

The chairman may, however, have the power to adjourn the meeting where unruly conduct prevents the continuation of business – see *John v Rees.*[1]

Adjournment

15.52 The chairman may, with the consent of the meeting, or must, if directed by it, adjourn the meeting – article 58.

Voting

15.53 Any resolution put to the vote of the meeting will be decided on a show of hands, *unless* a poll is demanded in accordance with article 59.[2]

Article 63 provides that, subject to the right to vote being attached to the share class, on a show of hands every member present and every proxy shall have one vote.

When the voting is by poll,[3] every member will have one vote for each share which he holds.

In *Kinsella and Others v Alliance and Dublin Consumers Gas Co & Others,*[4] it was held that it was only those persons whose names were entered in the register of members who were entitled to vote at a general meeting.[5]

Voting may be either personally or by proxy.

Proxies

15.54 Any member who is unable to attend a general meeting, is entitled to appoint another person to attend and vote as his proxy. Articles 69 to 71 set out the procedures for the appointment of a proxy. A draft proxy appointment form is contained in article 71.

A body corporate which is a member, may, by resolution of its directors or general meeting, appoint a person to act as its representative at a general meeting.[6]

15.55 It is the duty of the chairman to decide on the validity of proxies. In *Cousins v International Bank Co Ltd,*[7] the court held that a member who has given a proxy may subsequently change his mind, attend the meeting and vote in person. If he does so, his actions will revoke the proxy.

---

1 [1970] Ch 345.
2 See also articles 60 to 62.
3 In *Re Credit Finance Bank plc* (Unreported) 9 June 1982 (HC), it was decided that it is permissible to vote by poll without having a show of hands first.
4 (Unreported) 5 October 1982 (HC).
5 See also articles 64–67 which deal with, inter alia, joint shareholders, incapacity of members and arrears in paying up calls made on shares.
6 Article 74.
7 [1931] 2 Ch 90 (CA).

Informal agreements

15.56 If all the corporators agree to a transaction which was honest and intra vires the company, then, regardless of how informal the manner of the agreement, it binds the company (but see **12.18** and **36.26**).

CLASS MEETINGS

15.57 In *Carruth v ICI Ltd*,[1] Lord Russell of Killowen said:

'Prima facie a separate meeting of a class should be a meeting attended only by members of the class, in order that the discussion of the matters which the meeting has to consider may be carried on unhampered by the presence of others who are not interested to view those matters from the same angle as that of the class; and if the presence of outsiders was retained in spite of the ascertained wish of the constituents of the meeting for their exclusion, it would not, I think, be possible to say that a separate meeting of the class had been duly held.'

RESOLUTIONS

15.58 There are two[2] kinds of resolution: ordinary and special.

Ordinary resolution

15.59 An ordinary resolution is one which is passed by a simple majority of the members present and voting, or by a majority of votes cast where voting is in a poll.

Special resolution

15.60 A special resolution is defined in s 141 as any resolution which:

(1) is passed by not less than three-quarters of the votes actually cast;
(2) at a general meeting;
(3) after at least 21 days' notice of the meeting;
(4) which notice specifies the intention to propose the resolution as a special resolution.

Thus, at the option of the proposer, any resolution could become a special resolution but there are very few proposals which require to be passed as special resolutions. However, under s 141(2), less notice can be given if a majority of the number of members having the right to attend and vote, and holding between them at least 90 per cent of the nominal value of the shares giving such right, agree to the shortened notice.

---

1 [1937] AC 707 (HL).
2 Prior to the Companies Act 1959, there were also extraordinary resolutions – s 141(6) of the 1963 Act.

Unless a poll is demanded, a declaration by the chairman that the resolution is carried shall be conclusive evidence of the fact, without proof of the actual numbers of votes cast in favour of or against the resolution.[1] If, though, the chairman acted fraudulently or made a mistake, the declaration is not conclusive. For example, in *Re Caratal (New) Mines Ltd*,[2] a special resolution was proposed. The chairman then stated 'Those in favour 6; those against 23; but there are 200 voting by proxy, and I declare the resolution carried'. The court held that the declaration was not conclusive and the resolution not passed because those 'voting' by proxy were not permitted to vote on a show of hands.

Unanimous agreement

15.61 A resolution in writing, signed by *all* the members entitled to attend and vote, may be deemed to be the equivalent of a special resolution – see s 141(8).

Similarly, a unanimous agreement of members, obtained without holding a meeting or at a meeting invalidated by some procedural irregularity, may be treated as a binding decision of the company – see *Re Duomatic Ltd*[3] and *Cane v Jones*.[4]

Adjourned meetings

15.62 Where a resolution is passed at an adjourned meeting, it will be deemed to have been passed on the date of the adjourned meeting.[5]

Amendments

15.63 If an amendment is proposed to the resolution before the meeting, it must be voted upon first. If the chairman refuses to allow a prior vote on the amendment, the resolution, if passed, may not be binding.[6]

Extended notice

15.64 Where the 1963 Act requires extended notice for a resolution, it means notice of at least 28 days prior to the meeting must be given.

Notice of special business/special resolutions

15.65 Notice of special business must state the resolution to be passed in sufficient detail for every shareholder to be able to make up his mind whether he will or will not attend, with knowledge of the consequences of his decision.

---

1 Section 141(3).
2 [1902] 2 Ch 498.
3 [1969] 2 Ch 365.
4 [1980] 1 WLR 1451.
5 Section 144.
6 *Henderson v Bank of Australasia* (1890) 45 Ch D 330 (CA).

For example, in *Baillie v Oriental Telephone Co Ltd*,[1] directors of a holding company had from 1907 to 1914 been receiving remuneration as directors of a subsidiary company without the knowledge of the shareholders of the holding company. A special resolution, authorising the directors to retain the remuneration, was proposed and an extraordinary general meeting summoned to pass it. *The notice did not specify the amount of the remuneration, which amounted to £44,876.* The resolution was passed. The court held that the resolution was not binding as the notice was insufficient[2].

Circulars and information accompanying notices must also be accurate and not mislead.[3]

Essentially, there must be no difference in form or substance between the resolution proposed in the notice calling the meeting and the resolution passed at the meeting.

MINUTES OF MEETINGS

15.66   Every company must have minutes prepared recording all the proceedings of general meetings.[4] These minutes must be recorded in book or computer recorded form.

Any minute, if purported to be signed by the chairman of the meeting at which the proceedings were had, or by the chairman of the next succeeding meeting, shall be evidence of the proceedings.

Where minutes have been made of the proceedings at any general meeting of the company then, until the contrary is proved, the meeting shall be deemed to have been duly held and convened, and all proceedings had thereat to have been duly had, and all appointments of directors or liquidators shall be deemed to be valid.

Inspection of minute books

15.67   The books containing the minutes of proceedings of any general meeting must be held at the registered office of the company and open for inspection during business hours.[5]

Supervision by corporate regulator

15.68   Section 19 of the Company Law Enforcement Act 2001 inserts a new subsection 3A in s 145 of the 1963 Act. Under s 145(3A) minute books must be produced to the Director of Corporate Enforcement on request, and he is also

---

1 [1915] 1 Ch 503 (CA). See also *Kaye v Croydon Tramways Co* [1898] 1 Ch 358 (CA).
2 See *Re Moorgate Mercantile Holdings Ltd* [1980] 1 WLR 227 (ChD) where Slade J summarised the relevant principles relating to notices of, and the subsequent amendment of, special resolutions.
3 See *Jackson v Munster Bank Ltd* (1884) 13 LR IR 118.
4 And also meetings of directors and/or committees of directors – see s 145.
5 Section 146.

to be given such facilities for inspecting and copying their contents as he requires.

Section 145(3A) also applied to minute books of board meetings – see **23.10**.

REGISTRATION AND COPIES OF CERTAIN RESOLUTIONS

15.69   Section 143 of the 1963 Act applies to:

(1) special resolutions;
(2) resolutions which have been agreed to by all the members of a company, but which, if not so agreed to, would not have been passed as special resolutions;
(3) resolutions or agreements which have been agreed to by all the members of some class of shareholders but which, if not so agreed to, would not have been effective for their purpose unless they had been passed by some particular majority[1] and all resolutions[2] which effectively bind all the members of any class of shareholders though not agreed to by all those members;
(4) resolutions increasing the share capital of a company;
(5) resolutions that a company be wound up voluntarily passed under s 251(1)(a) or (c);
(6) resolutions attaching rights or restrictions to any share;
(7) resolutions varying any such rights or restrictions;
(8) resolutions classifying any unclassified share;
(9) resolutions converting shares of one class into shares of another class;
(10) resolutions of the directors of a company that an old public limited company be re-registered as a plc.[3]

A printed copy of every resolution or agreement falling within s 143 must, within 15 days after its passing or making, be forwarded to the registrar of companies and be recorded by him.

When special resolutions are required

15.70   Special resolutions are required to make fundamental changes to the company. These fundamental alterations would include:

(1) change of name – s 23(1) as amended by s 87 of the 2001 Act. This change also requires the written approval of the Registrar;
(2) altering its objects – s 10, as amended by s 85 of the 2001 Act;
(3) alteration of, or addition to, its articles – s 15(1) (see Chapter 16);

---

1 Or otherwise in some particular manner.
2 Or agreements.
3 See s 12(3)(a) of the 1983 Amendment Act. A resolution of the directors under s 143(3) must also be sent to the registrar.

(4) reduction of share capital – s 72(2). This change is also subject to confirmation by the court (see Chapter 19);
(5) power to make the liability of its directors unlimited – s 198(1);
(6) resolving that the company be wound up:
    (a) by the court – s 213(a); or
    (b) voluntarily – s 251(1)(b); and
(7) the re-registration of a public company as a private one under s 15 of the 1983 Amendment Act.

DEMOCRATIC CONTROL OF THE COMPANY

15.71   From our examination of the law governing company meetings, it is obvious that, in most instances, a simple majority of members is sufficient to control decision making. In certain, more fundamental, company matters, which require the passing of a special resolution, a 75 per cent majority is required. Once this majority is mustered, the special resolution concerned may be passed. It would appear, therefore, that company control operates under a form of democratic system. This should mean that the wishes of the majority generally prevail. In the next chapter, we shall consider the implications of majority control for minority investors.

Chapter 16

MAJORITY CONTROL AND THE PROTECTION OF MINORITY INVESTORS

THE TAKING OF DECISIONS

16.1 As we saw in the previous chapter, major decisions are taken within the company by the passing of majority resolutions at meetings. Such decisions illustrate the exercise of 'collective' as distinct from 'individual' shareholders' rights.

For example, a simple majority of votes will ensure the passing of an ordinary resolution at a general meeting: a special resolution requires a 75 per cent majority. Thus, a form of democratic system exists which allows majority investors to control many corporate decisions, such as altering the constitutional document which forms the basis of the contract between investors and the company, ie the articles of association.

Alteration of the articles of association

16.2 The articles of association contain the terms of the contract between shareholders and the company. This agreement is known as a 's 25 contract' – see Chapters 13 and 14.

Notwithstanding their fundamental nature, the articles can be altered by special resolution. This is permitted by s 15 of the 1963 Act. Any alteration (or addition) approved by a 75 per cent majority will be as valid as if it had been contained originally in the articles (see **12.16**).

Because of the democratic nature of the company control, a minority of members who voted against the change of articles, may have to accept the decision of the majority.

A member could take action if he was deprived of his individual right to vote. If granted this right, and, after validly exercising it, he is outvoted by the majority of other members, the ordinary shareholder must generally accept his fate. Thus, the majority 'will' prevails where corporate decisions are concerned.

Collective rights versus individual rights

16.3 The distinction between collective and individual members' rights has already been mentioned in **13.14** et seq.

When decisions are taken within the company, for example, to appoint directors, etc these are collective decisions affecting the company as a whole, ie affecting corporate rights. They are not decisions affecting the *individual* rights of shareholders.

Investors have s 25 contracts with the company. They possess *individual* rights under these contracts. If, for example, the directors wrongfully withhold a member's dividend or deprive him of his right to vote, that member can proceed directly against the directors. It is only corporate rights which are subject to majority control. Even in these circumstances, however, both the courts and the legislature have intervened to protect minority members in exceptional cases.

JUDICIAL PROTECTION FOR INDIVIDUAL MINORITY INVESTORS

16.4 Whilst accepting the principle of majority rule, the courts have intervened to protect individual minority members when the motivation of the majority shareholders is suspect.

In *Allen v Gold Reefs of West Africa*,[1] Lindley MR stated:

> '[The power conferred on companies to alter their articles] must, like all other powers, be exercised subject to those general principles of law and equity which are applicable to all powers conferred on majorities and enabling them to bind minorities. It must be exercised, not only in the manner required by law, but also bona fide for the benefit of the company as a whole, and it must not be exceeded.'

The courts have applied a subjective test to ascertain whether or not the majority members were acting 'bona fide for the benefit of the company' – see the *Greenhalgh v Arderne Cinemas* case below.

Bona fide for the benefit of the company as a whole

16.5 An alteration of the articles by special resolution must not discriminate between the majority shareholders and the minority, so as to give the former an advantage over the latter. In *Greenhalgh v Arderne Cinemas*,[2] Evershed MR declared:

> 'It is now plain that "bona fide for the benefit of the company as a whole" means . . . that the shareholder must proceed upon what, *in his honest opinion*, is for the benefit of the company as a whole . . . The phrase, "the company as a whole", does not (at any rate in such a case as the present) mean the company as a commercial entity, distinct from the corporators: it means the corporators as a general body . . . A special resolution of this kind would be liable to be impeached if the effect of it were to discriminate between the majority shareholders and the minority shareholders, so as to give the former an advantage of which the latter were deprived . . . It is therefore not necessary to require that persons voting for a special resolution should, so to speak, dissociate themselves altogether from their own prospects and consider whether the proposal is for the benefit of the company as a going concern.'

---

1 [1900] 1 Ch 656 (CA).
2 [1951] Ch 286 (CA). See also *Clemens v Clemens Brothers Ltd* [1976] 2 All ER 268, which suggests that the majority must act inequitably in relation to the minority.

It appears, therefore, that whether an alteration is for the benefit of the company is for the members to decide. The court will only interfere if no reasonable man would think the alteration was for the benefit of the company. This situation could arise because the alteration discriminated in the majority's favour by giving them some advantage denied to the minority and so amounting to fraud on the minority.

Fraud in this context means action less than circumscribed within the tort of deceit. It could include, for example, an abuse of power corresponding to a breach of fiduciary duty or other inequitable action. In addition, the minority members themselves need not have suffered individual loss – it may have been the company itself that was injured. For example, in *Menier v Hooper's Telegraph Works*,[1] the majority (a rival company) used their voting power to put the company into voluntary liquidation. This left the majority in possession of the company assets. It was held that the action of the majority amounted to an expropriation of the company's property; and accordingly could be restrained by the minority.

Cases of hardship

16.6 An alteration made bona fide and for the benefit of the company as a whole will not be impeached by the court merely because it inflicts hardship on a particular investor. For example, a resolution passed at a general meeting enabling the directors to acquire, at a fair value, the shares of a minority investor who had an interest in a competing business, was permitted as bona fide in the interests of the company.[2]

Other minority remedies

16.7 The minority shareholders may have statutory avenues open to them to overturn an alteration of the articles rather than simply relying on impugning the motivation of the majority. So, for example, they might be able to utilise s 205 of the 1963 Act on the ground that the affairs of the company were being conducted in disregard of their interests.

SECTION 205 REMEDY FOR OPPRESSION BY THE MAJORITY

16.8 Under s 205(1), any (individual) member of a company who complains that the affairs of the company are being conducted or that the powers of the directors of the company are being exercised in a manner oppressive to him or

---

1 (1874) LR 9 Ch App 350. See also other examples of fraud on the minority in the exceptions to the rule in *Foss v Harbottle*, and *G.S. Doherty Ltd v Doherty and Anr* (Unreported) 19 December 1969 (SC).
2 *Sidebottom v Kershaw, Leese & Co* [1920] 1 Ch 154.

any of the members (including himself), or in disregard of his or their interests as members, may apply to the court for an order.

Where the majority failed to purchase the shares of the minority by agreement, and then sought to take the power in its article to do so compulsorily, the court in *Browne v British Abrasive Wheel Co Ltd*,[1] restrained the company from making such an alteration. Any member so affected nowadays would tend to seek a statutory remedy under s 205.

Persons entitled to statutory relief

16.9   Section 205(1) confines the statutory relief contained in it to 'any member'.

In *Re Murph's Restaurant Ltd*,[2] the court noted that whilst oppressive conduct had to be aimed at a petitioner, the loss suffered by him could be incurred in some other capacity, eg qua director; where a member who was also a director was wrongfully excluded from management. A director wrongfully removed under s 182(1) may also rely on s 205(1) – see *McGilligan and Another v O'Grady et al* in **15.26**. Where a petitioner is seeking relief under the second limb (see **16.17**), s 205(1) expressly provides that any loss must be suffered qua member.

In *Re Irish Visiting Motorists' Bureau Ltd*,[3] Kenny J stated:

> 'The shareholders' rights [under s 205] come from the Companies Act, equitable principles which have become part of company law and the memorandum and articles of association viewed as a contract created by membership of the company ... The conduct or exercise of the powers complained of under s 205 must affect the person making the complaint in his character as a member and not as a creditor or a person having commercial dealings with the company ...'

Relief may be sought by minority investors under s 205, even if some other form of remedy[4] is available to the petitioner – see *Re Westwinds Holding Co Ltd*.[5]

Whilst most petitioners will, in fact, be minority members, they need not necessarily be so. For example, in *Irish Press plc v Ingersol Irish Publications Ltd* (see below), the petitioner and respondent each held 50 per cent of the shares.

Any member entitled to petition for relief under s 205 may also petition for the winding up of the company on the grounds mentioned in s 213(g) of the 1963 Act.

---

1 [1919] 1 Ch 290.
2 [1979] ILRM 141.
3 (Unreported) 27 January 1972 (HC).
4 Such as a derivative action.
5 (Unreported) 21 May 1974 (HC).

Whose conduct gives rise to a claim under s 205?

16.10   Section 205(1) caters for two distinct sets of circumstances. The first is where the affairs of the company are being conducted. This generally refers to the *collective action of shareholders* such as when they exercise their power of majority voting, eg to alter the articles of association within the context of corporate governance.

The second circumstance which can give rise to an action under s 205 is where the powers of the directors are being exercised in company management. Sometimes there may be an overlap between the two sets of circumstances – see *Re Clubman Shirts Ltd* (below).

Section 4(4) of the 1990 (Amendment) Act excludes claims under s 205 arising out of the conduct of the company's affairs while it is under the protection of the court and in the control of an examiner – see Part IX.

First limb of culpable conduct – oppression

16.11   The first limb of offending conduct giving rise to relief under s 205 is oppression being exercised either by the majority of members or the directors. In *Re Clubman Shirts Ltd,*[1] the facts were as follows.

The directors of the company, which was in serious financial difficulties, transferred its business to another company under a scheme whereby the shareholders received no payment. Over four years the company had not fulfilled its statutory obligations regarding meetings and returns. The company also refused to give the petitioner, a large shareholder in the company, details of a proposed takeover. The petitioner claimed relief under s 205.

The court held that the irregularities did not amount to oppression, but that the failure to provide adequate information about the disposal of the business did, and on that basis, relief was granted.

O' Hanlon J said:

> 'The petitioner in this case seeks relief under the provisions of s 205 of the Companies Act 1963, alleging that the affairs of [the company] and the powers of the directors of the company are being and have been exercised in a manner oppressive to him as a minority shareholder in the said company. [A number of grounds were put forward by the petitioner, including] that ultimately the directors concluded a transaction during the period between July and October 1980, which apparently *involved handing over the entire business of the company to a newly-formed company called "Clubman Limited", without giving the minority shareholders any information about the details of the transaction, or seeking their approval before taking a step which could well render their shareholding valueless for the future ...*' (author's emphasis)

The judge then considered the meaning of 'oppression' and gave his decision:

---

1   [1983] ILRM 323 (HC).

'My conclusion is that the evidence *tends to show a series of irregularities by the directors in complying with their obligations under the Companies Act 1963, rather than a case of oppression in the sense of s 205 of the Act.* I would not classify as oppression the attempts made from time to time to buy the petitioner's shareholding in the company. In my opinion the directors were entitled to make any offer they thought fit, whether realistic or unrealistic, and to hedge their offers around with conditions if they thought fit to do so. The petitioner, on receipt of the offers, never responded by saying that he was unable to assess the true value of his shares by reason of the wrongful withholding of information by the directors, coupled with a request for such information as he needed to safeguard his interests. Neither did he at any time sell, or consider selling, his shareholding or any part thereof, on the terms offered to him. Consequently any claim for relief under s 205 which is based on these transactions cannot succeed.

Similarly, I would not classify as oppressive conduct within the meaning of the Act, the omission to comply with the various provisions of the Act referable to the holding of general meetings and the furnishing of information and copy documents. *These were examples of negligence, carelessness, irregularity in the conduct of the affairs of the company but the evidence does not suggest that these defaults or any of them formed part of a deliberate scheme to deprive the petitioner of his rights or to cause him loss or damage.*

There remain the events of 1980 to which fuller reference has been made already. In this case the petitioner had genuine ground for complaint although I have some reservations about putting it into the category of oppressive conduct towards a minority. I felt the petitioner has made out a case for limited relief, of a type which the majority shareholders appear to be willing to concede in his favour, and accordingly I would propose to make an order in his favour under s 205 of the Act directing the majority shareholders who are represented in these proceedings to buy out the petitioner's shareholding in the company at a valuation based on the true value of the shares as of 31 July 1980 – this being the time when he should, in my opinion, have been given a fuller opportunity of concurring or not concurring in the course of action embarked upon by the majority shareholders . . .' (author's emphasis)

16.12 The culpable conduct by the majority of members or the directors must relate to corporate governance or the internal management of the company. Furthermore, the motivation of a majority does not necessarily have to be impugned (as required at common law – see **16.4**). Conduct may be oppressive even if dealings are carried out honestly and in good faith. For example, in *Re Irish Visiting Motorists' Bureau Ltd*, Kenny J said:

'The affairs of a company may be conducted or the powers of the directors may be exercised in a manner oppressive to any of the members *although those in charge of the company are acting honestly and in good faith.* If one defines oppression as harsh conduct or depriving a person of rights to which he is entitled, the person whose conduct in question may believe that he is exercising his rights in doing what he does. One of the most terrifying aspects of human history is that many of those whom we now regard as having been oppressors had a fanatical belief in the rightness of what they were doing. *The question then when deciding whether the conduct of the affairs of a company or the passing of a resolution is oppressive is whether judged by objective standards, it is.*' (author's emphasis)

16.13 Cases such as *Re Greenore Trading* and *Irish Press plc v Ingersoll* show that the concept of oppression is easier to recognise and apply when a respondent's conduct is deliberate or dishonest.

16.14 In *Re Greenore Trading*,[1] Keane J followed the judicial definition of oppressive conduct for the corresponding s 210 of the English Companies Act 1948 in *Scottish CWS v Meyer*.[2] He then applied this definition of burdensome harsh and wrongful conduct to the facts of the case before him, concluding that:

> 'The patent misapplication of the company's monies for the purpose of giving Mr Vanlandeghem a dominant position in its affairs seems to me to be properly described as "burdensome, harsh and wrongful" quoad the petitioner.'

Keane J then granted the petitioner relief, ordering that his shares be purchased by Mr Vanlandeghem at a fair price.

16.15 Similarly, in *Irish Press plc v Ingersoll Irish Publications Ltd*,[3] Barron J also invoked the *Scottish CWS v Meyer* case and its definition of oppressive conduct. Barron J said:

> 'What it shows is that where a deliberate plan to damage the interests of a company is carried out by a shareholder in the manner by which it exercises its power to conduct the affairs of the company, such behaviour is oppressive ...
>
> The real complaint was the de facto take over of the companies. This was [achieved by] the placing in position of nominees [to further the interests of the respondent, rather than the company]. That is also oppressive. Neither was done bona fides. Both were done in wilful disregard of the interests of the companies.'

Essentially in this case, repudiation of a management agreement by the respondent was deemed to constitute oppression. The respondent was ordered by the court to sell its shareholding to the petitioner at a price to be determined by the court. In *Re Westwinds Holding Ltd*,[4] fraudulent conduct by one member of a company holding 50 per cent of its shares was held to be oppressive to the other member.

16.16 The Supreme Court has also held that a failure by the majority shareholders to accept offers of compromise in relation to legal proceedings was oppressive conduct within s 205 – see *Crindle Investments v Wymes*.[5]

The second limb – disregard of members' interests as members

16.17 Section 205(1) empowers the court to grant a remedy in two distinct sets of circumstances. The first is where the affairs of the company or the powers

---

1 [1980] ILRM 94 (HC).
2 [1959] AC 329.
3 (Unreported) 15 December 1993 (HC). This decision was appealed to the Supreme Court on narrow grounds – see **16.21**.
4 (Unreported) 21 May 1974 (HC).
5 [1998] 2 IRLM 275.

of the directors have been exercised in an oppressive manner. In *Re Williams Group (Tullamore) Ltd,*[1] Barrington J commented:

> 'If one regards "oppression" as a course of conduct which is "burdensome, harsh and wrongful" or as conduct which involves lack of probity or fair dealing towards some members of the company, there is no history of such a course of conduct in the present company prior to the events giving rise to the present case. On the contrary, the ordinary shareholders appear to have been treated extremely well.
>
> Moreover, in the present case, we are not dealing with a course of conduct but with an individual transaction. It appears however than an isolated transaction can give rise to relief under the Irish section: ...'

The judge noted that s 205 'offers relief not only when the affairs of the company are being conducted in an oppressive manner, but also (and alternatively) where they are being conducted *in disregard of the interests of some member or members*' (author's emphasis).

In this case, the articles of association had provided that, so long as there were preference shareholders, the ordinary shareholders were not entitled to attend and vote at general meetings.

The preference shareholders resolved to issue a new class of shares to both classes of members.

Whilst accepting that the majority of preference shareholders had acted in good faith, Barrington J concluded that the affairs of the company were being conducted in disregard of the interests of the ordinary shareholders. Accordingly, he granted them relief under s 205.

The second limb of relief is, therefore, where the 'affairs of the company' or the powers of the directors are being exercised in disregard of a member's interests as a member. The term 'affairs of the company' essentially means the conduct of the members when acting collectively. The word 'interests' embraces a wider notion of investor protection than 'rights'. Thus, reference to the 'interests' of members may enable the court to grant relief by considering matters outside a petitioner's purely legal rights as a company member.

Hearing court proceedings in camera

16.18   Section 205(7) of the 1963 Act provides that if, in the opinion of the court, the hearing of s 205 proceedings would:

(1) involve the disclosure of information, the publication of which would be seriously prejudicial to the legitimate interests of the company, and stemming from article 34.1 of the Irish Constitution; or

(2) if held in public would fall short of doing justice,

the court may order that proceedings be heard in camera. The onus of proof in (1) and (2) is on the applicant who seeks to have the proceedings held in camera.

---

1 (Unreported) 8 November 1985 (HC).

In *Irish Press plc v Ingersoll Irish Publications Ltd,*[1] the applicants failed to discharge the burden of proof under (1), and thus failed to have the proceedings held in camera. In this case, Finlay CJ summarised the law relating to the hearing of applications under s 205(7) in camera; essentially confining this form of hearing to special limited cases.

Relief available under s 205

16.19 Section 205(3) empowers the court to make such order as it thinks fit, whether:

(1) directing or prohibiting any act;
(2) cancelling or varying any transaction;
(3) regulating the conduct of the company's affairs in future; or
(4) for the purchase of the shares of any members of the company by other members of the company or by the company itself, and, in this event, also making an order authorising the reduction of the company's capital.

Clearly, the court has a wide range of remedies to offer the successful petitioner. As one might expect, a frequently used remedy is (4), ie an order of the court for the purchase of the petitioner's shares.[2] This was the relief granted in the cases of *Re Clubman Shirts Ltd, Greenore Trading Co Ltd* and *Re Westwinds Holding Co Ltd* mentioned in **16.11**, **16.14** and **16.15**.

16.20 In *Re New-Aid Advertising Co Ltd,*[3] Laffoy J considered that a director and majority shareholder in the company had acted oppressively and in disregard of the interests of the petitioner as a member. As the company had no assets, Laffoy J considered that ordering the company to purchase the petitioner's shares, or ordering the winding up of the company itself, were inappropriate remedies. Instead, Laffoy J ordered the majority shareholder involved to personally purchase the petitioner's shares which she valued at £67,200.

The relief granted by the court in *Irish Press Ltd v Ingersoll Irish Publications Ltd* was also an order for the purchase of shares. However, in this case, the court ordered the respondent to sell its shares to the petitioner.

The court may also, when ordering the purchase of a petitioner's shares, also order that a transaction in issue be varied or cancelled. The court does not however, have the power to award damages – see **16.21**.

---

1 [1993] ILRM 747. See also *Re R Ltd* [1989] ILRM 757 (SC).
2 In *Horgan v Murray and Milton* [1998] 1 ILRM 110, the court had to consider, inter alia, the extent to which a minority shareholder is entitled to refuse to accept the appellants' offer to buy his shares. This case is analysed in L. Glennon 'The Residual Nature of the Minority Shareholder Remedy' (2000) 7 CLP 14, at pp 14–21.
3 (1997) 4 CLP 235.

Valuation of minority investor's 'shares'

16.21   In *Re Clubman Shirts Ltd*, the court held that it enjoyed a wide discretion under s 205(3), in arriving at a fair valuation where it orders that shares be purchased. In *Colgan v Colgan & Colgan*,[1] Costello J held that the basis for valuation must be the company's net asset value, ie total assets less total liabilities. Once the net value of the company is calculated, the court will then generally value the minority members' shares on a pro rata basis.

In *Irish Press plc v Ingersoll Irish Publications Ltd*, the High Court decided that if the respondent's oppressive conduct had caused the company a loss, which resulted in the value of its shares reducing, additional compensation may be payable by the respondent to provide for any drop in value of the petitioner's shares.

The decision of Barron J in this case was appealed to the Supreme Court[2] on the grounds, inter alia, that (i) a court had no jurisdiction to award damages as a remedy for a petition brought under s 205, and (ii) the valuation of £2,250,000 placed on the shares was excessive.

16.22   In respect of ground (i), Blaney J held that s 205(3) did not confer jurisdiction upon a court to award damages in a case of oppression.[3] This was because s 205(3) only permitted a court to make such order as it thought fit 'with a view to bringing to an end the matters complained of'. The primary objective of a compensation order was to compensate; not to bring to an end the matters complained of.

Blaney J explained that the duties which shareholders owed, either to the company itself or to other shareholders, were not fiduciary in nature. Such non-fiduciary duties did not give rise to damages or compensation in the event of their breach. The proper remedies for the enforcement of shareholders' non-fiduciary duties were an injunction, declaration, winding up or an order made under s 205(3).

While compensation had been awarded in *Re Greenore Trading*[4] and *Scottish Co-operative Wholesale Society v Meyer*,[5] Blaney J considered that in these cases the element of compensation was incidental to the main relief, which was the purchase of the shares, ie the order to compensate arose indirectly from the court's determination of what would be a fair price for the purchase of the shares of the oppressed shareholder.

In the High Court the trial judge had held that the nature of s 205 relief must be designed (i) to bring to an end the matters complained of, and (ii) also to

---

1   (Unreported) 22 July 1993 (HC). See also **22.29** for the valuation of shares in private companies.
2   *Re Irish Newspapers Ltd and Irish Press Publications Ltd, Irish Press v Ingersoll Irish Publications Ltd et al* [1995] 2 IR 175, (1995) CLP 86.
3   Blaney J also stated that if the *Oireachtas* had intended to include damages as a remedy for oppression under s 205 they could easily have done so.
4   See **16.14**.
5   Ibid.

compensate the petitioner and the companies for the losses sustained. The Supreme Court has made it clear that the latter point is not appropriate in the case of s 205 relief.

16.23   In respect of the second ground of appeal – the valuation of £2,250,000 – the Supreme Court held that it could not disturb primary findings of fact made by a trial judge if there had been credible evidence to support them.

The Supreme Court then concluded, after hearing expert share valuers' evidence, that there had been credible evidence to support the finding of a pre-oppression value of £10 million and a further injection of £13.5 million to turn the companies around. However, since the respondent was no longer obliged to pay £6 million in compensation [awarded in the High Court] this amount should no longer be deducted from the £13.5 million figure. Consequently, as the pre-oppression value of the companies had been £10 million and it would cost £13.5 million to rehabilitate them financially, the Supreme Court held that the respondent shareholding in the companies now had a nil value. Accordingly, the Court ordered that the shareholding in question be transferred for a nominal consideration.

16.24   In *Re London School of Electronics Ltd*,[1] the court suggested that, as a general rule, the date for the valuation of a company which is a going concern, should be the date of the court order. However, the court felt that there would be many occasions when this rule would not be appropriate, and this is reflected in Irish case-law. For example, in *Re Clubman Shirts Ltd*, the valuation date was the date of the oppression, while in *Colgan v Colgan & Colgan* it was fixed by the court for a day some weeks before the date of the court order.

Examinership

16.25   Section 4(4) of the Companies (Amendment) Act 1990 excludes from relief under s 205 claims concerning the conduct of the company's affairs while it is under the protection of the court – see Part IX of this book.

INVESTIGATIONS INTO THE AFFAIRS OF THE COMPANY

16.26   The powers under ss 165 to 173 of the 1963 Act are now replaced and strengthened by Part II of the 1990 Act.

On the application of a minority of the members,[2] the court may appoint one or more inspectors to investigate the affairs of a company.

---

1   [1985] 3 WLR 474.
2   See s 7(1)(a) and (b) of the 1990 Act, and Chapter 35.

PETITIONING FOR THE WINDING UP OF THE COMPANY

16.27 Any member entitled to petition the court under s 205, may also petition for the winding up of the company on the grounds mentioned in s 213(g) of the 1963 Act.

THE RULE IN *FOSS v HARBOTTLE* AND MINORITY INTERESTS

16.28 What is known as the rule in *Foss v Harbottle* also involves consideration of minority interests being adversely affected by fraud in the management of the company.

An investor initiated legal proceedings against the directors of a company in order to compel them to make good losses sustained by the company as a result of their fraud. The legal action by the investor failed, because there was nothing to prevent the company itself from taking the proceedings against the directors.

The policy reasons underlying the rule in *Foss v Harbottle*[1] are that:

(1) litigation at the suit of a minority of the members is futile if the majority do not wish it; and
(2) without the rule, there would be a multiplicity of legal actions.

16.29 As Mellish LJ said in *MacDougall v Gardiner*:[2]

'If the thing complained of is a thing which in substance the majority of the company are entitled to do, or if something has been done irregularly which the majority of the company are entitled to do regularly, or if something has been done illegally which the majority of the company are entitled to do legally, there can be no use in having litigation about it, the ultimate end, of which is only that a meeting has to be called, and then ultimately the majority gets its wishes.'

In this case, the court would not intervene where the chairman's actions in conducting a meeting were culpable. If the chairman was wrong, the company, not a member, was the proper person to sue.

Application of the rule

16.30 The rule in *Foss v Harbottle* is restricted to actions in respect of collective decisions and rights (see **16.3**). In such instances, where a wrong is done to the company which could validly be approved by a majority of the investors in general meeting, the proper plaintiff is the company itself.

The rule in *Foss v Harbottle* has no application where an investor's individual or personal rights are infringed (see **17.4** et seq).

---

1 (1843) 2 Hare 461.
2 (1875) 1 Ch D 13.

Apparent judicial exceptions to the rule

16.31   The following judicial decisions are often cited as exceptions to the rule in *Foss v Harbottle*.

(1)   where the act done is ultra vires the company or *is illegal*;[1]

(2)   where the majority of members have committed a *fraud*[2] on the minority. For example, in *Cook v Deeks*,[3] three directors wrongfully obtained a contract in their own names, when acting on behalf of the company. They then used their voting power (possessing 75 per cent of the ordinary shares) to pass a special resolution wherein the company declared it had no interest in the contract. On being sued by the minority shareholder, the directors were ordered to account to the company for the profits which they had made;

(3)   where the act requires a special resolution but has been done by ordinary resolution – a procedural irregularity.[4] Similarly, if the company meeting has not been convened in time.[5]

If one considers the exceptions outlined above, it will be seen that they are not wrongs done *to* the company, but are wrongs done *by* it.

If the majority act illegally, oppressively, or in breach of proper procedures, it is the company who will be deemed to be so acting. Because of this, the only persons who are in a position to instigate legal action to prevent the wrongdoing by the company, are the minority shareholders. Accordingly, the common law permits them to sue[6] to prevent the company's wrongful acts. Thus, the rule in *Foss v Harbottle* is restricted to wrongs done *against* the company, *not by it*. That is why the author has classified such exceptions as apparent, rather than real. The real exceptions to the rule in *Foss v Harbottle* have been created by statute. In fact, the alternative remedies in s 205 of the 1963 Act now generally provide more relevant and comprehensive grounds for an action by minority investors, than reliance by them on the apparent judicial exceptions to *Foss v Harbottle*.

16.32   In *O'Neill v Ryan, Ryanair and others*,[7] the High Court applied the rule in *Foss v Harbottle* to deny a member's action for compensation in respect of a

---

1   *Cockburn v Newbridge Sanitary Steam Laundry Co* [1915] 1 IR 237.

2   Negligent acts may also be actionable, but only if they confer a benefit on the majority at the expense of the company – see *Daniels v Daniels* [1978] Ch 406 and *Pavlides v Jensen* [1956] Ch 565.

3   [1916] 1 AC 554.

4   Such as a breach of s 181 of the 1963 Act – see *Moylan v Irish Whiting Manufacturers Ltd* (unreported) 14 April 1980 (HC).

5   *Hodgson v National and Local Government Officers Association* [1972] 1 WLR 130.

6   They may also be entitled to be indemnified by the company for all necessarily incurred legal expenses – see *Wallersteiner v Muir (No 2)* [1975] QB 373.

7   [1990] 2 IR 200; a decision also confirmed by the Supreme Court in *DBP Construction Ltd & Ors v ICC* (Unreported) 21 May 1998.

reduction in the value of his shareholding due to an alleged wrong done to the company. This decision was upheld in the Supreme Court.

The plaintiff had proposed bringing an action for oppression under s 205 against the company and its principal shareholders, but those proceedings were settled by pre-trial agreement; one of the defendants buying the plaintiff's shares in the company.

The rule in *Foss v Harbottle* essentially means that where the collective[1] (majority) rights of members are infringed, the appropriate remedy is a matter for internal corporate governance (see **15.48**).

The derivative action

16.33   In the apparent exceptions to the rule in *Foss v Harbottle*, the minority[2] shareholders would be compelled into taking legal action on behalf of the company, because the controlling owners and/or managing agents, the majority shareholders and/or directors, had committed the wrongful act against the company. Because the rights of the minority are derived from the company, the proceedings are known as a *derivative action.*

Where a derivative action succeeds, judgment is made in favour of the company, and not the minority shareholders who sued on its behalf. If the majority of the members are opposed to the litigation, the plaintiff minority shareholder may be debarred from proceeding with their derivative action.[3]

---

1 Where, however the individual or personal rights of a member have (also) been infringed, he may be able to sue on his own behalf – see **17.2** et seq.
2 See also E.J. Boros *Minority Shareholders' Remedies* (Clarendon Press, 1995).
3 See *Smith v Croft (No 2)* [1988] Ch 114, and **17.9**.

Chapter 17

MEMBERS' REMEDIES FOR INFRINGEMENTS OF THEIR RIGHTS

17.1   Members rights' can be classified into four distinct categories. There are:

(1) *Individual or personal rights*
These rights arise from contract terms, topped up by statute – see **13.13**.

(2) *Collective majority rights*
, Collective majority rights generally arise from the members' s 25 contract; in particular, the articles of association.

The passing of ordinary or special resolutions at a general meeting of the company illustrates the exercise by the majority members of their right to participate in corporate decision-making. As a result of the rights of the majority members, it can be stated that corporate decisions are subject to majority control (or rule).

(3) *Minority members' rights*
Such rights fall into the two categories of (a) individual and (b) collective.

(a) Individual minority rights: rights arising at common law[1] and by virtue of s 205 of the 1963 Act.
(b) Collective minority rights: rights which can only be exercised in concert with other members. Such rights are conferred by express statutory provisions – see **13.17**.

MEMBERS' INDIVIDUAL RIGHTS

17.2   Members' individual rights are contained in the articles of association, and 'topped up' by statutory provisions.[2]

Such individual rights are personal to the shareholder in that he can initiate legal action on his own behalf if they are infringed, eg denial of his right to vote. However, if a member is not denied his right to vote, and disagrees with a majority decision of the members made at a general meeting, generally he will have no remedies at law.

Many of the members' rights in the articles are corporate or collective (majority) rights which may be unimpeachable by individual members, ie the majority votes to approve the annual accounts, re-elect directors, appoint the auditors and approve the dividend or a bonus issue of shares recommended by the directors.

17.3   The following would generally be considered as being amongst a member's more important individual contract rights:

---

1 See Chapter 16.
2 See **13.13–13.15**.

(1) the right to vote;[1]
(2) the right to be paid a dividend, once it has been declared;
(3) the right to a return of capital in the event of the solvent winding up of the company;
(4) as explained in **13.3**, a share may also confer an interest in the company and its property which entitles them to bring a personal action when such interests are imperilled or violated.

The specific members rights in (1) to (4) can probably all be categorised as 'class' rights – see **18.16** et seq.

REMEDIES FOR INFRINGEMENT OF MEMBERS' INDIVIDUAL RIGHTS

17.4 Where a member's individual rights are infringed, he can himself take legal action against the directors. This is the situation whether such rights are contractual or statutory in origin. For example, in *Pender v Lushington*,[2] a member was able to sue personally to compel the company to record his vote.

17.5 Other examples of infringement of members' personal rights, either by a majority decision or directors' actions, include:

(1) a decision to enter into a transaction beyond the company's objects;[3]
(2) a decision to involve the company in a transaction contrary to the general law or the Companies Acts;[4]
(3) a members' decision to pay dividends in the form of bonds, even though the articles stipulated that they were to be paid in cash;[5]
(4) a decision by directors to allot shares where the decision is not bona fide in the company's interest or is for an improper purpose;[6]
(5) whether or not a preference dividend was cumulative under the articles and terms of issue[7] or by the company's memorandum of association;[8] and
(6) irregular conduct in the election of directors or other officers.[9]

17.6 A member has a statutory right under s 205 of the 1963 Act to take a personal action for conduct by the directors in disregard of his interests (see **16.8**).

---

1 All shareholders have the right to attend and vote at 'class' meetings. Usually, though, only ordinary shareholders are entitled to attend and vote at General Meetings.
2 (1877) 6 Ch D 70.
3 *Simpson v Westminster Palace Hotel Co* (1860) 8 HL Cas 712.
4 *Hope v International Financial Society* (1876) 4 Ch D 327.
5 *Wood v Odessa Waterworks Co* (1889) 42 Ch D 636.
6 *Fraser v Whalley* (1864) 2 Hem & M 10.
7 *Webb v Earle* (1875) LR 20 Eq 556.
8 *Staples v Eastman Photographics Materials Co* [1896] 2 Ch 33.
9 *Ryan v South Sydney Junior Rugby League Ltd* (1974) 3 ACLR 486.

17.7   When referring to corporate rights, one usually means decisions which can be made collectively by the majority of the members, eg passing ordinary or special resolutions.

If, for example, the directors attempted to deprive the majority of members of their rights to discuss and vote on a particular resolution, the proper remedy would not be litigation. Rather, a group of shareholders owning at least 10 per cent of the shares could requisition the directors to call an Extraordinary General Meeting (EGM).[1] At that meeting, the resolution in question could be debated and decided by the members, who also, if they deemed it necessary, could remove the directors and elect other more helpful persons in their place.[2]

17.8   As Lord Davey stated in *Burland v Earle*:[3]

'It is an elementary principle of the law relating to joint stock companies that the court will not interfere with the internal management [corporate governance] of companies acting within their powers, and, in fact, has no jurisdiction to do so.

Again, it is clear law that in order to redress a wrong done to the company, or to recover moneys or damages alleged to be due to the company, the action should prima facie be brought by the company itself.'

Lord Davey again emphasised the internal corporate governance nature of company wrongs by continuing:

'It should be added that no mere informality or irregularity which can be remedied by the majority will entitle the minority to sue, if the act, when done regularly, would be within the powers of the company and the intention of the majority is clear.'

17.9   To ascertain the intention of the majority, in *Prudential Assurance Co Ltd v Newman Industries Ltd (No 2)*,[4] it was suggested that in a derivative action the judge might grant a sufficient adjournment of the case to enable a general meeting be convened, and that the court then form a view in the light of the proceedings at that meeting.

17.10   A classic application of the rule in *Foss v Harbottle* occurred in the case of *Pavlides v Jenson & Ors*.[5] Here, the directors sold an asset of the company to a third party at a gross undervaluation. An action by a minority shareholder was not allowed by the court since the majority of the members could have ratified the directors' conduct at a general meeting; even resolving not to sue them in respect of it.

17.11   The rule in *Foss v Harbottle* therefore means that individual or minority members collectively cannot pursue derivative actions against the directors on

---

1   Under s 132 of the 1963 Act.
2   Under articles 99 and 100 of Table A.
3   [1902] AC 83.
4   [1982] Ch 204. Procedural problems may, however, arise if fraud by the majority is alleged – see Keane, *Company Law* (Butterworth (Ireland) Ltd, 3rd edn, 2000), at p 319.
5   [1956] Ch 565.

behalf of the company, when the matter in issue can be dealt with at a general meeting by the members exercising their collective majority rights.

The apparent exceptions to the rule in *Foss v Harbottle*

17.12   As explained in **16.31**, the apparent exceptions to the rule in *Foss v Harbottle* are not wrongs committed against either the company or a majority of its members. They are, in fact, wrongs committed by the company against individual or minority members and infringing their personal rights.[1]

REMEDIES FOR INFRINGEMENTS OF MEMBERS' MINORITY RIGHTS

17.13   Even when a remedy is not available to an individual members as a personal right, it is possible for certain corporate decisions made by the majority of shareholders or the actions of the board of directors to involve an infringement of members' minority, rather than their personal,[2] rights. In these circumstances, both common-law and statutory remedies may be available to the minority member(s).

Relief for individual minority members

17.14   At common law, the courts have intervened in corporate governance to protect minority members[3] when the motivation of the majority shareholders can be impugned.[4]

Individual minority members can also utilise s 205 of the 1963 Act against oppressive actions by both the majority of the shareholders and the board of directors.[5]

Relief for minority members acting collectively

17.15   Minority members may invoke s 205 on an individual or collective basis. However, in most instances of statutory minority remedies, a minimum number of members must be mustered to take advantage of the legal right. For example, under s 10 of the 1963 Act, it is only if at least 15 per cent of the members disagree with an amendment of the objects clause by majority vote, that a minority can apply to the court to cancel the special resolution in question.

Other examples of members' statutory collective minority rights are set out in **13.17**.

---

1   See **17.4**.
2   Or individual.
3   Both individually and collectively.
4   See **16.4** et seq.
5   See **16.8** et seq.

FUNDAMENTAL ROLE OF SHAREHOLDERS

17.16   The basic function of shareholders is to provide a company's investment capital.[1]

In Part IV C we examine the composition of a company's investment capital base, and the company law measures designed to protect it. The meaning of shareholders' class rights will also be explained.

---

1 Rather than loan capital.

PART IV C

THE ARTICLES OF ASSOCIATION, SHARE CAPITAL AND CLASS RIGHTS

Chapter 18

CAPITAL, SHARES AND 'CLASS RIGHTS'

DEFINITION OF CAPITAL

18.1 The purpose of issuing shares is to raise capital. Capital may be loosely defined as the money, property and assets used in operating a company. Depending on its source, it may be classified either as investment or loan capital.

Investment capital

18.2 In the context of company law, most persons would tend to view capital as the money which a company possesses as a result of issuing shares to its members. The company, of course, will make use of its investors' monies to buy premises, plant and raw materials and to pursue its business objectives generally. The aggregate fund of the monies contributed by investors, essentially, becomes the major source of a company's capital requirements. This source of corporate funding is styled investment capital.

Balance sheet position

18.3 Because of the separate legal personality of a company, its investment capital is ultimately owed to members. Investment capital is, therefore, shown on the Liabilities, rather than the Assets, side of the company's Balance Sheet.

Loan capital

18.4 A company may not wish to raise all its capital from investors. Instead, it may obtain a loan from a bank. Such finance would have to be repaid. The contract under which the monies are borrowed is known as a debenture. A debenture is, therefore, an acknowledgement of debt issued by a company. Generally, under debentures, the company pays a fixed interest and uses its assets as security. Finance raised by the issue of debentures is known as loan capital.[1]

Capital employed

18.5 The expression 'capital employed' is used to denote the total amount of a company's shareholders' funds plus its long-term borrowings, ie investment capital plus loan capital.

---

1 The respective rights of creditors and company under debentures are dealt with in Part VIII.

Gearing

18.6   The ratio of loan capital to a company's total capital employed is known as 'gearing'. When a company is described as 'highly geared', it indicates that the level of its borrowings is high, compared to its investment[1] capital. A 'lowly geared' company, by contrast, has relatively low borrowings or loan capital.

Fixed and circulating capital

18.7   'Fixed capital' is that held by the company in the form of fixed assets. Fixed assets denote property or machinery which a company owns and uses, but does not buy or sell as part of its regular business, eg machinery used by the company as part of its manufacturing process.

'Circulating capital' refers to capital in the form of cash or debtors, raw materials, finished products and work in progress required for the company to carry on its business.

Working capital

18.8   'Working capital' has a narrow technical meaning. It refers to capital in the form of cash, stocks and debtors (less creditors) used by a company in its day-to-day operations.

Share capital

18.9   The term 'share capital' is widely used to denote the total value of a company's shares. It also includes the types and nature of shares making up the company's capital (see **18.15**).

TYPES OF SHARE CAPITAL

18.10   Money received by the company in return for the issue of its shares, is generally styled 'share capital'. The word 'capital', when used in the context of the share capital of a company, needs to be refined into different categories. These categories are designated as nominal, issued, paid-up, uncalled and reserve (share) capital.

Nominal (or authorised) capital

18.11   By virtue of the capital clause in its memorandum of association, every company 'limited by shares' must set out the amount of capital with which it proposes to be registered. Once the amount of the nominal (or authorised)

---

1 Or *equity* capital, ie that contributed by 'ordinary' shareholders, as distinct from preference shareholders.

capital has been declared in the memorandum, it cannot be increased or reduced unless the appropriate formalities have been observed (see Chapter 19).

The capital clause in the memorandum also provides for the division of the nominal capital into a stated number of shares, each of a fixed amount.

The model capital clause in Table B[1] reads 'The share capital of the company is £200,000 divided into 200,000 shares of £1 each'.

The amount of a company's authorised capital will depend upon its business requirements, both short and long term.

Issued capital

18.12 A company is not required to issue all of its authorised capital immediately. In the example given above from Table B, if that company decides to issue 100,000 shares at £1 each, then £100,000 will be the amount of the issued share capital.

Paid-up and uncalled capital

18.13 The paid-up capital is that part of the issued capital which has been paid up by the investors. For example, if a company wishes, it could issue, say, 100,000 shares of £1 each, and decide that the shareholders would not be called upon to pay the full £1 at once. The company may issue the shares on condition that 60p is paid initially, leaving the balance of 40p to be called up later. In this example, the paid-up capital would amount to £60,000, and the uncalled capital £40,000.

The articles of association[2] will normally give the directors the power to make calls on investors in respect of any monies unpaid on their shares.

Reserve capital

18.14 Reserve capital is explained in s 67 of the 1963 Act, which provides that a limited company may, by special resolution, determine that any portion of its share capital which has not already been called up, shall not be capable of being called up except in the event of the company being wound up.

In *Re Mayfair Property Co, Bartlett v Mayfair Property Co*,[3] members of the company passed a special resolution converting £5 out of each £10 share into reserve capital. The company subsequently borrowed money, giving security for the debentures in the form of a charge over its undertaking and property, including its uncalled capital.

---

1 Of the 1963 Act, Sch 1.
2 See Table A, 1963 Act, articles 15–21 (and Chapter 21).
3 [1898] 2 Ch 28.

The court decided that this charge did not extend to include the reserve capital of £5 per share, ie the reserve capital was only accessible on winding up the company.

Reserve capital is, accordingly, not available to the directors; it is available only for the creditors on the winding up of the company.

CLASSES OF SHARES

18.15 There can be more than one class of share. For example, the articles of association[1] may provide that:

'Without prejudice to any special rights previously conferred on the holders of any existing shares or class of shares, any share in the company may be issued with such preferred, deferred or other special rights or such restrictions, whether in regard to dividend, voting, return of capital or otherwise, as the company may from time to time by ordinary resolution determine.'

Class rights generally

18.16 Each class of share will possess special rights confined to its own class and styled 'class rights'. Class rights often relate to the *voting rights* and/or *dividend payment entitlements* of the holders of a particular class of share.

The two most usual classes of shares are preference and ordinary shares.

Preference shares

18.17 A preference share is a share which entitles its holder to *preference* (over other shares) *when profits have been made available for dividends*. A preference share may indicate a fixed dividend, eg a six per cent preference share. In many cases, there may be preference as to repayment of capital by the company to the shareholder in case of a winding up.

The fixed dividend must be paid to the preference shareholders before the holders of the ordinary shares receive any dividend.

Preference shares may be:

(1) cumulative; this means that if the dividend is not paid in any year or years, the arrears accumulate and must be paid off before the ordinary shares receive dividends; or
(2) non-cumulative; meaning that if no dividend is paid in any year it is lost forever.

There is a presumption that preference shares are cumulative. To be otherwise, they must be expressly stated in the articles as being non-cumulative (see **18.19**).

---

1 See Table A, 1963 Act, article 2.

Preference shareholders' express class rights

18.18   In *Welton v Saffery*,[1] it was held that unless the preference shares are given express rights of preference as to (return of) capital, they are to be dealt with equally with the ordinary shares on the winding up of the company.

However, where preference shares are given express rights of preference as to return of capital, any assets of the company remaining after paying all its debts must be used first to return the capital of the preference shareholders.[2]

In *Re Isle of Thanet Electricity Supply Co Ltd*,[3] the articles expressly conferred on the preference shareholders the right (in priority to the ordinary shareholders) of a 6 per cent dividend and to repayment of capital on a winding up, together with arrears of dividend.

The court held that such preferential rights as set out in the articles were prima facie exhaustive. Accordingly, the preference shareholders in this case were not entitled to share in surplus assets on a winding up. The Irish Supreme Court had taken a different view. In *Re Cork Electric Supply Co Ltd*,[4] Kennedy CJ said:

> 'the right to participate in a distribution of surplus assets on a [solvent] winding up will [only] be taken from preference shareholders by an [express] clause in the articles ... delineating their rights exhaustively to the exclusion of any other rights
> ...
> Upon the construction of the articles ... before us it is to be observed that, while as regards participation in profits the words of exclusion 'but to no further dividend', were carefully inserted. [However], no such limitation was added to the immediately following clause as to priority in payment of capital.'

As a result, Kennedy CJ considered that the preference shareholders were entitled to participate in the distribution of the company's surplus assets (see **18.25**).

18.19   Even though the articles do not expressly provide so, preference shares are presumed to be cumulative, unless there is a clear contrary express provision. Mere omission of the word 'cumulative'[5] in the articles will not render such preference shares non-cumulative.

In *Staples v Eastman Photographic Materials Co*,[6] the company's articles provided that preference shares would be entitled out of net profits each year to a preference dividend of 10 per cent per annum. The court held that the words 'each year' were sufficiently precise to indicate that the shares were meant to be non-cumulative.

---

1   [1897] AC 299.
2   Unless other provisions in the articles expressly stipulated that any arrears of dividends on the preference shares should be paid off first – see *Re W.J. Hall & Co Ltd* [1909] 1 Ch 521.
3   [1949] 2 All ER 1060, [1950] Ch 161.
4   [1932] IR 314 (SC).
5   As in *Foster and (M.B.) Foster & Sons Ltd* (1906) 22 TLR 555.
6   [1896] 2 Ch 303.

Ordinary shares

18.20 Section 155(5)[1] defines equity share capital as a company's 'issued share capital excluding any part thereof which, neither as respects dividend nor as respects capital, carries any right to participate beyond a specified amount in a distribution'. The class of shares to which s 155(5) refers is known as 'ordinary shares'.

Ordinary shareholders only become entitled to dividends if and when:

(1) the company has made a profit; and
(2) the preference shareholders have been paid their fixed dividend.

Ordinary shareholders do, however, have voting rights, and, effectively, have the power to control the company.

Finance raised by ordinary shares is sometimes called 'risk capital', since the holders of these shares are not entitled to dividends nor to return of capital until prior claims have been satisfied. For example, if the company is in financial difficulties, the profits available for dividends may only be enough to pay a dividend on the preference shares; in such circumstances, the ordinary shareholders receive no payment. On the other hand, if the company is prospering, the preference shareholders[2] will be limited to their fixed dividend, while the directors may recommend a dividend of, say, 10 per cent for the ordinary shareholders.

Non-voting ordinary shares

18.21 A company may also issue ordinary shares without voting rights attached. In this way, the directors of the company can raise more capital from investors without diluting control of the company by the existing 'equity' shareholders.

Deferred shares

18.22 Deferred shares are also known as Founders' or Management shares. The rights of these shareholders will depend on the articles. Generally, deferred shareholders would be entitled to participate in dividends after the ordinary shares had been paid a fixed dividend.

Deferred shares are rarely issued now.

Distinctions between preference and ordinary shares

18.23 Ordinary shareholders possess full voting rights. Preference shareholders are not entitled to vote at general meetings, except, perhaps in cases

---

1 Of the 1963 Act.
2 Unless the company has issued a class of share known as *Participating Preference Shares*. Such shareholders may also be entitled to part of the profits in excess of that used to pay the fixed

where their dividend is in arrears and/or their special class rights are being altered. In fact, the fixed dividend payable to preference shareholders is a manner of payment similar to the fixed interest payment made to debenture holders in respect of loan capital.

The possibility of the purchasing back by the company of redeemable[1] preference shares, further strengthens the similarities between this category of investment capital and loan capital.

In the event of a company's liquidation, if its articles of association expressly provide, preference shareholders may be entitled to a return of their capital in priority to the ordinary shareholders.

MEANING OF (SHARE) CLASS RIGHTS

18.24   Class rights refer to the rights which attach to a particular class of shares but not to another class or to shareholders generally.

In *Greenhalgh v Arderne Cinemas Ltd*,[2] Vaisey J said: 'Although the word "class" is not a word of technical art, you cannot put people into the same class if their rights are not capable of being ascertained by a common system of valuation'.

Article 2 of Table A indicates that class rights may be 'such preferred, deferred or other special rights or such restrictions, whether in regard to dividend, voting, return of capital or otherwise'.

In *Cumbrian Newspapers Group Ltd v Cumberland and Westmorland Herald Newspaper and Printing Co Ltd*,[3] Scott J classified provisions in the company's articles conferring (or purporting to confer) rights or benefits on persons, into three categories:

(1) rights or benefits which are annexed to particular shares. These are available to any holder of the shares and could be termed 'membership insider rights'. Such rights would usually include dividend rights, voting and rights to participate in surplus assets on a winding up. However, in *Harman v BML Group Ltd*,[4] the share capital was divided into A and B shares. A provision in the shareholders' agreement that no shareholders' meeting would be quorate unless a B shareholder (or their proxy) was present, was held to constitute a class right;

(2) rights or benefits which are purportedly conferred on a person whether or not he is a member. These are categorised as 'outsider rights'. An example of this category can be seen from *Eley v Positive Government Security Life*

---

dividend of the preference shareholders, always providing this right has been expressly conferred by the articles of association.

1   Defined by s 206 of the Companies Act 1990 as shares which are liable, at the option of the company or the shareholder, to be redeemed. However, even ordinary shares may now be issued as redeemable under the 1990 Act – s 207(1) and Chapter 19.

2   [1945] 2 All ER 719.

3   [1987] Ch 1.

4   [1994] 2 BCLC 674.

Assurance Co Ltd.[1] In this case, the articles provided that Eley was to be the company's solicitor. As this benefit was conferred on Eley in a personal capacity, rather than in his capacity as a shareholder of the company, it could not be regarded as a class right. It did not attach to a class of shares: but was conferred on Eley personally;

(3) rights or benefits conferred on a person for so long as he remains a member or director. For example, the right to appoint a director whilst the member holds at least 10 per cent of the company's shares.

In the *Cumbrian Newspapers* case, the plaintiff was given pre-emption rights[2] under the articles and the right to nominate a director to the board for so long as it held 10 per cent of the ordinary issued shares. The court decided that the provisions were, in fact, class rights, and subject to the protection of s 125 of the UK's Companies Act 1985.

The equivalent statutory protection in Ireland only applies to variations of class rights in plcs – see s 38(11) of the 1983 Amendment Act.

In *Bushell v Faith*,[3] articles of association provided that on a resolution at a general meeting to remove a director, any shares held by that director should carry the (class) right to three votes. This provision was approved by the House of Lords; thereby creating two sub-classes of members, ie shareholders who were directors and those who were not.

Reduction in capital and apportionment of surplus assets

18.25 The courts have had to consider the effects of a reduction of the company's capital on different classes of shareholders.[4] For example, in *Scottish Insurance Corporation Ltd v Wilsons and Clyde Coal Co Ltd*,[5] the assets of a coal mining company had been nationalised, and compensation paid for them.

The company, which had ceased trading, intended to go into liquidation, but first proposed to reduce its capital by paying off the 7 per cent cumulative preference shares. The preference shareholders unsuccessfully objected to the reduction on grounds that it deprived them of the opportunity to share in a distribution of surplus assets on liquidation. The articles stated that on winding up, the preference shares would rank before the ordinary shares 'to extent of repayment of the amounts called up and paid thereon'.

The court held that on a construction of the articles, the preference shareholders were not entitled to a windfall payment arising from surplus assets, and the reduction of capital was not unfair.

In the judgment, Lord Simonds said:

---

1 (1876) 1 Ex D 88.
2 See **22.30**.
3 [1970] AC 1099, [1970] 2 WLR 272, [1970] 1 All ER 1002 – see also **15.22**.
4 See **19.7** et seq.
5 [1949] AC 462 (HL).

'Reading these articles as a whole with such familiarity with the topic as the years have brought, I would not hesitate to say, first that the last thing a preference stockholder would expect to get (I do not speak here of the legal rights) would be a share of surplus assets, and that such a share would be a windfall beyond his reasonable expectations and, secondly, that he had at all times the knowledge, enforced in this case by the unusual reference in art 139 to the payment off of the preference capital, that at least he ran the risk, if the company's circumstances admitted, of such a reduction as is now proposed being submitted for confirmation by the court. Whether a man lends money to a company at 7 per cent or subscribes for its shares carrying a cumulative preferential dividend at that rate, I do not think that he can complain of unfairness if the company, being in a position lawfully to do so, proposes to pay him off.

... It is clear from the authorities, and would be clear without them, that, subject to any relevant provision of the general law, the rights inter se of preference and ordinary shareholders must depend on the terms of the instrument which contains the bargain that they have made with the company and each other. This means, that there is a question of construction to be determined and undesirable though it may be that fine distinctions should be drawn in commercial documents such as articles of association of a company, your Lordships cannot decide that the articles here under review have a particular meaning, because to somewhat similar articles in such cases as *Re William Metcalfe & Sons Ltd* [1933] Ch 142 that meaning has been judicially attributed. Reading the relevant articles, as a whole, I come to the conclusion that arts 159 and 160 are exhaustive of the rights of the preference stockholders in a winding up. The whole tenor of the articles ... is to leave the ordinary stockholders masters of the situation. If there are "surplus assets" it is because the ordinary stockholders have contrived that it should be so, and, though this is not decisive, in determining what the parties meant by their bargain, it is of some weight that it should be in the power of one class so to act that there will or will not be surplus assets.'

18.26   It is interesting to note the reference to the *Metcalfe* case, which is more in the line with the approach taken by the Supreme Court in *Re Cork Electric Supply Co Ltd* (see **18.18**).

Attachment of class rights

18.27   Special rights may be attached to a class of shares by:

(1) the memorandum or (more usually) the articles of association;
(2) the terms of issue of the class of shares; or
(3) a special resolution of the company in general meeting. This method was used to create class rights in *Re Old Silkstone Collieries Ltd*.[1]

---

1 [1954] Ch 169.

VARIATION OF CLASS RIGHTS

18.28   Section 78[1] deals with variation of the rights of special classes of shares. The term 'variation' also includes abrogation or cancellation of class rights. If provision is made in the memorandum or articles for variation of class rights, subject to the consent of any specified proportion of those shareholders, then the class rights can be altered. For example, article 3[2] contains the following 'modification of class rights' clause:

> 'If at any time the share capital is divided into different classes of shares, the rights attached to any class may, whether or not the company is being wound up, be varied or abrogated with the consent in writing of the holders of three-fourths of the issued shares of that class, or with the sanction of a special resolution passed at a separate general meeting of the holders of the shares of the class.'

Objections

18.29   If the holders of 10 per cent or more of the shares in question object to the alteration of their rights, s 78(1) gives them the right to apply to the court to have the variation cancelled. The procedures to be followed when making this appeal to the court are set out in s 78(2) to (5).

Interpretation of class rights

18.30   In *White v Bristol Aeroplane Co*,[3] the court held that the rights of existing shareholders are not varied by the issue of new shares ranking pari passu[4] with them. Article 4[5] reflects this judicial decision by providing:

> 'The rights conferred upon the holders of the shares of any class issued with preferred or other right shall not, unless otherwise expressly provided by the terms of issue of the shares of that class, be deemed to be varied by the creation or issue of further shares ranking *pari passu* therewith.'

Similarly, when the voting power of one class of ordinary (10p) shareholders was diluted by the action of another group of ordinary (50p) shareholders who by resolution subdivided their shares into five 10p shares each, the court in *Greenhalgh v Arderne Cinemas Ltd*[6] held that the rights of the original 10p shareholders, although possibly 'affected as a matter of business', were not varied as a matter of law.

18.31   In *Dimbula Valley (Ceylon) Tea Co Ltd v Laurie*,[7] the reduction of the amount of capital to be returned to the preference shareholders following the

---

1 Of the 1963 Act.
2 Of Table A in the 1963 Act, Sch 1.
3 [1953] Ch 65 (CA).
4 Equally.
5 Of Table A in the 1963 Act, Sch 1.
6 [1946] 1 All ER 512 (CA).
7 [1961] Ch 353.

winding up of the company was, surprisingly, deemed not to affect their class rights.

In this case, it was held that capitalisation of a reserve fund resulting from a revaluation of unrealised fixed assets for the benefit of ordinary shareholders did not encroach upon the rights of preference shareholders to participate in 'surplus assets', but rather had to be equated to payment of a dividend.

From these illustrations, it can be seen that the courts have adopted a rather narrow and literal approach to the interpretation of class rights. Lord Evershed MR and Romer LJ had both sought to explain this judicial approach by suggesting that it was not usually the class rights of the complaining class that were varied or abrogated or affected, but merely the enjoyment of those rights.

The s 38 procedure

18.32   If a company has not made provision in its memorandum or articles to cater for the variation of class rights, s 38[1] effectively makes it mandatory for the procedures in s 78 and art 3 to apply; including the provision for a 10 per cent minority right of objection to the court – see **13.17**.

SHAREHOLDERS' RIGHTS GENERALLY

18.33   Members' 'individual rights' and liabilities arising out of their contracts with the company are dealt with in Part IV D,[2] their 'collective' or corporate rights having already been explained in Part IV B.[3]

---

1 Of the 1983 Act.
2 Chapters 20–23.
3 Chapters 15–17.

Chapter 19

PROTECTION OF A COMPANY'S CAPITAL BASE FOR CREDITORS (AND INVESTORS)

STATUTORY RULES

19.1 One of the main planks of creditor, and indeed, investor[1] protection contained in the Companies Acts, is the legislature's desire to protect a company's share capital, which makes up its capital base. The underlying reason for this was explained by Jessel MR in *Re Exchange Banking Co, Flitcroft's Case*,[2] who stated:

> 'The creditor has no debtor but that impalpable thing, the corporation, which has no property except the assets of the business ...
>
> The creditor, therefore, ... has a right to say that the corporation shall keep its capital and not return it to the shareholders ... If directors ... improperly pay away the [company] assets to the shareholders, they are liable to replace them.'

A company, and its directors acting on its behalf, can quite properly expend contributed capital for any purpose which is intra vires the company.[3] Buckley LJ confirmed this in *Re Horsley and Weight Ltd*.[4] He further stated, however, that:

> 'The company's creditors are entitled to assume that the company *will not* in any way *repay* any paid up share capital to the shareholders except by means of a duly authorised reduction of capital. They are entitled to assume that the company's directors will conduct its affairs in such a manner that no unauthorised repayment will take place.' (author's emphasis)

The statutory rules protecting the share capital[5] base of the company can be divided into two broad categories. The first category consists of the restricted circumstances in which s 72[6] may permit a *direct repayment* to shareholders, or a reduction in their liabilities to the company in respect of their shares, ie restrictions on the direct reduction of share capital.

The second category of statutory rules protecting the capital base is intended to prevent any *indirect repayment* of the share capital to members. These rules are generally referred to as the 'capital maintenance rules'.

---

1 Particularly in public companies where most of the members would not be directors. Effectively, therefore, investors entrust their invested funds in the company to the care of directors over whom, in practice, they may have little control.

2 (1882) 21 Ch D 519.

3 See **23.1**, and Chapter 36.

4 [1982] 3 All ER 1045 (CA).

5 This protection is based upon the supposition that each company will possess a substantial amount of share capital. This is, very often, not the case. Many small private companies will have been formed with only insignificant (£2) amounts of share capital.

6 Of the 1963 Act.

RESTRICTIONS ON THE DIRECT REDUCTION OF SHARE CAPITAL

19.2 A company's articles of association may, like Table A, article 46,[1] provide that the company can, by *special resolution*, reduce its share capital, but only as permitted, and with the consents required, by law.

A company's share capital is viewed in law as a fund, a form of financial buffer out of which creditors may be paid in the event of the company failing. As a result, creditors are protected by the legislature specifying:

(1) the limited circumstances in which share capital may be reduced; and
(2) the procedures to be followed by the company, acting through its directors, to effect a permitted direct reduction of capital.

Share premium fund to be treated as capital

19.3 If a company issues shares of £1 nominal value for, say, £1.25, the extra 25p is deemed to be a premium. Section 62(1)[2] provides that, in these circumstances, a sum equal to the total amount of the premiums in that issue of shares must be kept in a separate account called *the share premium account*.

Permitted use of share premium fund

19.4 Section 62(2) permits the share premium funds to be used:

(1) in *paying up unissued shares* (other than redeemable shares) to be allotted to shareholders as fully paid bonus shares, in writing off:
   (a) the preliminary expenses of the company; or
   (b) the expenses of, or the commission paid or discount allowed, on any issue of shares or debentures; or
(2) in *providing for the premium payable* on redemption of any redeemable preference shares, or of any debentures.

Except in the cases of the limited uses permitted by s 62(2), the share premium fund is to be treated as if it were share capital, and is subject to the statutory restrictions on reduction of capital.

PERMITTED REDUCTION IN SHARE CAPITAL UNDER SECTION 72[3]

19.5 Jessel, MR in *Re Exchange Banking Co, Flitcroft's Case* also said:

'A limited company by its memorandum of association declares that its capital is to be applied for the purposes of the business. It cannot reduce its capital except in the manner and with the safeguards provided by statute ... and it is clearly against

1 Of the 1963 Act.
2 Ibid.
3 Ibid.

the legislature that any portion of the capital should be returned to the shareholders without the statutory conditions being complied with. A limited liability company cannot in any other way make a return of capital ... and even the sanction of every shareholder cannot bring within the powers of the company an act which is not within its powers.'

Sections 72 to 77 of the 1963 Act govern the reduction of a company's capital.

A company may, if authorised by its articles, pass a special resolution reducing its share capital in accordance with s 72(2). A resolution for reducing capital must be confirmed by the court to become effective.

In *Re Halt Garage (1964) Ltd*,[1] the court held that payments of excessive remuneration to directors in three years when there had been no distributable profits in one instance could not be regarded as being anything more than a disguised gift out ot the company's capital,[2] ie an unauthorised reduction.

The power given in s 72 is general. If the company adopts the proper procedure, it can reduce its capital 'in any way'. However, s 72(2) specifies three particular instances in which capital may be reduced. These are for:

(1) the extinction or reduction of the liability on shares in respect of *capital not paid up*;[3] or
(2) the cancellation of paid-up share capital which is 'lost or unrepresented'[4] by available assets; or
(3) the paying-off of any paid-up share capital which is in excess of the needs of the company.

Application to the court

19.6   When the company has passed a resolution for reducing its share capital, it may apply to the court. When the interests to be borne in mind are simply those of shareholders, the court may apply the following criteria:

(1) will the reduction be fair to the interest of members of the public who may be induced to take shares in the company? and
(2) will the reduction be fair and equitable as between the different classes of shareholders?[5]

Fairness between competing class rights

19.7   A useful method for the court to decide what is fair between the different classes of members is to view the consequences of the reduction request in the light of a theoretical winding up of the company. If, therefore, preference shareholders enjoy no special rights as to repayment of capital, a reduction of

---

1 [1982] 3 All ER 1016.
2 See **24.15**.
3 Eg uncalled capital.
4 Eg writing off trading losses, as in *Bannantyne v Direct Spanish Telegraph Co* (1886) 34 ChD 287. Evidence of the loss must be given to the court – see *Re Hoare & Co Ltd* [1904] 2 Ch 208 (CA).
5 *Poole v National Bank of China* [1907] AC 229.

capital should be borne rateably by the preference and ordinary shareholders.[1] However, *if the articles confer preferential rights as to repayment of capital on the preference shareholders, the ordinary shares would be expected to bear the loss first.*[2] The opposite is also the case. If, for example, capital is being returned as surplus to the company's requirements in accordance with s 72(2), it should be returned, firstly, to the preference shareholders.[3] As Costello J stated in *Re Credit Finance Bank plc*:[4]

> 'The reality is, the (restructuring) scheme is fair between the classes of shareholders involved – the preference shareholders and the ordinary shareholders. It is true that the preference shareholders are to be repaid, but this is perfectly permissible.'

19.8   In the *Chatterley-Whitfield Collieries* case, the court held that a company which had issued preference shares carrying a high rate of dividend and a priority to a return of capital on a winding up, was entitled to reduce its capital by buying back those shares. Lord Greene MR stated:

> 'It is a clearly recognised principle that the court, in confirming a reduction by the payment off of capital surplus to the company's needs, will allow or rather require, that the reduction shall be effected in the first instance by payment off of capital which is entitled to priority on a winding up. Apart from special cases where by agreement between classes [of shareholders] the reduction is arranged in a different manner, this is and has for years been the normal and recognised practice of the courts, accepted by the courts and by business men as the fair and equitable method of carrying out a reduction by payment off of surplus capital.'

In *Re Credit Finance Bank plc*, Costello J endorsed Green MR's judgment by stating:

> 'It is true that the preference shareholders are to be repaid [in a scheme to restructure the company's capital] but this is perfectly permissible as the *MacKenzie* case sanctions, namely that where there is a class of shareholders entitled to a preferential repayment of capital on winding up, repayment of such shareholders is permitted . . .'

The *House of Fraser plc v ACGE Investments Ltd & Ors*[5] case confirms the position that preference shareholders cannot complain if the company decides to reduce its capital share by paying them off first.

A result of this permissible treatment of preference shareholders may be that a company has the right to repurchase such shares if it can obtain fresh capital more inexpensively elsewhere.

19.9   The court will also have to be assured that the reduction was carried out in a proper manner. For example, it will satisfy[6] itself that the cause of the

---

1 *Bannantyne v Direct Spanish Telegraph Co* (1886) 34 Ch D 287.
2 *Re Floating Dock Co of St Thomas* [1985] 1 Ch 691.
3 *Prudential Assurance Co v Chatterley-Whitfield Collieries* [1949] AC 512 – see also **18.25**.
4 (Unreported) 19 June 1989 (HC).
5 [1987] BCLC 478 (HL). However, in exceptional cases, a separate class meeting may be necessary – see *Re Northern Engineering Industries plc* [1994] BCC 618.
6 See *Re Jupiter House Investments (Cambridge) Ltd* [1985] 1 WLR 977.

reduction was clearly communicated to the members so that they were in a position to exercise an informed choice. The cause of the reduction may also have to be proved to the court. For example, if capital is reduced because it has been lost, evidence should be adduced to prove the loss.[1] Generally, information should be given to members in a circular[2] accompanying the notice of the meeting.

Where creditors are not affected

19.10   Where only company shareholders are involved, the court will consider whether the reduction of capital was fair and equitable as between the different classes of shareholders.[3] Fair and equitable treatment involves treating shares of the same class equally.

Where there are shares of different classes, the reduction must be carried out in accordance with the special rights of those classes. In *Re Quebrada Railway Land and Copper Co*,[4] North J refused to sanction a proposed reduction of capital, because it seemed to him:

> 'that the proposal that the whole burden of the loss which has occurred shall be thrown upon the ordinary shareholder is not fair as between the two classes of shareholders. The preference shareholders have a preference as regards dividend; but they have no preference as regards [a return of] capital. Prima facia ... all shares ought to be reduced pari passu, that is rateably, and that is not what it is proposed to do.'

19.11   A reduction in capital which involves a variation or repudiation of the rights of a class of shareholders, must either be approved at a separate 'class' meeting of the shareholders affected, or be proved to the court to be fair and equitable – see *Re John Power & Sons Ltd.*[5]

19.12   In *Re Holders Investment Trust*,[6] the court refused to approve a reduction in capital because:

(1) the resolution for class consent was ineffectual, ie it was not validly approved by a separate meeting of the class concerned; and
(2) the reduction had not been shown by the company to be fair and reasonable. When considering whether the majority acted fairly and equitably, the court will look at the scheme to confirm that the majority were acting bona fide.

In *Re John Power & Son Ltd*, Fitzgibbon J had stated: 'What the court has to do is to see, first of all, that the [relevant] provisions of the statute have been complied with; and secondly; that the majority have been acting bona fide' (see **19.13**).

---

1   *Caldwell v Caldwell & Co Ltd* [1916] WN 70.
2   *Re Thorn EMI plc* [1989] BCLC 612.
3   The *Chatterley-Whitfield Colleries* case.
4   (1889) 40 Ch D 363, 58 LJ Ch 332, 60 LJ Ch 482.
5   [1934] IR 412 (SC).
6   [1971] 2 All ER 289.

It is relatively rare for a court to refuse to confirm a capital reduction, so the *Holders Investment Trust* case is exceptional. In Gower's[1] view, this decision confirms the view that in relation to class meetings, it is the interests of the class that must be considered rather than 'the company as a whole'.

Variation of class rights

19.13 If a proposed reduction of share capital is, in effect, a variation of class rights, the court may refuse to confirm the reduction unless the necessary consent of the class had been obtained in the proper manner.[2] In *Re John Power & Sons Ltd*,[3] the court approved the principle that a reduction in capital which is not in accordance with class rights must either:

(1) be approved at a separate meeting of that class; or
(2) be proved to be fair and equitable. When considering whether the majority acted fairly and equitably, the court must look at the scheme, confirm that the majority are acting bona fide, and:

> 'see that the minority is not being overridden by a majority having interests of their own clashing with those of the minority which they seek to coerce . . . and then see the scheme is a reasonable one . . . [to which no] reasonable man might say that he could not approve of it.'

Objections by creditors

19.14 Section 73(2) stipulates that where a proposed reduction of share capital involves either:

(1) diminution of liability in respect of unpaid share capital; or
(2) payment to any shareholder of any paid-up share capital; and
(3) in any other case where the court so directs,

the court shall *settle a list of creditors* in accordance with s 73(2)(a), (b) and (c). Creditors who do not consent to the reduction must be paid off, or their claims secured by payment into court.

19.15 Section 73(3) provides the court with the power to direct that, in the circumstances indicated in (1) and (2) above, s 73(2) shall not apply to any class or classes of creditors. This power is necessary because in instances where no asset out of which their claims could be satisfied is being given up by the company, the creditors should have no right to object to the proposed return of capital. For example, in *Re Meux's Brewery Co Ltd*,[4] the company's capital was made up as follows:

Paid-up Share Capital £1,000,000 (Investment)
Secured Debentures £1,000,000 (Loan)

---

1 L. C. Gower *Principles of Modern Company Law* (6th edn), at p 715.
2 *Re Old Silkstone Collieries Ltd* [1954] Ch 169 – also see Chapter 18.
3 [1934] IR 412 (SC).
4 [1919] 1 Ch 28.

In 1904, losses amounting to £800,000 were incurred. By 1917, this deficiency had been reduced to £640,000 and the company proposed to reduce its capital to £360,000.[1] The debenture-holders, as creditors, objected.

The court held that, as the reduction involved no diminution of unpaid capital, or repayment to shareholders of paid-up capital, creditors were not, prima facie, entitled to object unless they had good grounds for so doing. In this case, the court held that the debenture-holders had no good grounds to object to the proposed reduction.

Court order for reduction

19.16   The court may make an order confirming the reduction on such terms as it thinks fit. Where the court makes such an order, it may also specify in it that the words 'and reduced' be added to the company name.[2]

A copy of the court order and the appropriate minute, showing the reduced share holdings within the company, must be delivered to the registrar of companies.[3] This minute, when registered, shall be deemed to be substituted for the capital clause in the company's memorandum of association.

Liability of shareholders for reduced shares

19.17   Section 76 sets out the liability of members in respect of the reduced shares. Section 76(2) contains some protection for a creditor who had been unaware of the proceedings for reducing the company's capital.

OTHER PERMITTED REDUCTIONS IN SHARE CAPITAL

19.18   Other exceptional examples of reductions in a company's share capital are permitted under ss 15 and 43 of the 1983 Amendment Act.

Re-registration under s 15

19.19   Section 15 applies to a special resolution by a public company to be re-registered as a private one. Section 15(2) gives a minority of shareholders opposed to the re-registration the right to appeal to the court for its cancellation.

When making an order under s 15, the court may, if it thinks fit, provide for the purchase of the shares of dissenting members, and 'for the reduction, accordingly, of the company's capital'.

---

1   £1 million paid-up capital less incurred losses of £640,000.
2   Section 74 of the 1963 Act.
3   Ibid, s 75.

The court has a similar discretion when responding to a petition by a minority of members in cases of oppression under s 205,[1] or to objections to a change of objects clause in the memorandum under s 10 of the 1963 Act.

Forfeiture, etc under s 43

19.20 Section 43(1)[2] provides for the forfeiture, etc of shares held by or on behalf of a public company. Where such shares are forfeited, surrendered or acquired, the company[3] must cancel them and reduce the amount of the share capital by the nominal value of the shares.[4]

STATUTORY CAPITAL MAINTENANCE RULES

19.21 To prevent an *indirect reduction* of share capital, a number of statutory rules exist which deal with the following matters:

(1) redemption of redeemable shares;
(2) restrictions on the acquisition by a company of its own shares or shares in a parent company;
(3) a requirement on the board of directors to call an extraordinary general meeting of the company to consider any serious loss of capital;
(4) the giving of financial assistance (loans) by a company for the purchasing of its own shares;
(5) a prohibition on issuing shares at a discount; and
(6) a requirement that dividends may only be payable out of profits.

We shall now consider each of these statutory requirements separately.

Redemption of redeemable shares

19.22 'Redeemable' shares include any shares which, at the option of the company or the shareholder, are liable to be redeemed.

Under s 207,[5] a company may, if so authorised by its articles, issue redeemable shares. It may also redeem these shares provided it follows the procedures for so doing contained in Part XI.[6]

---

1 See Chapter 16.
2 Of the 1983 Amendment Act – see Chapter 21.
3 Unless the shares or any interest in them is previously disposed of.
4 Section 43(3)(a).
5 Of the 1990 Act.
6 Ibid.

Conditions for redemption

19.23 The conditions applying to the issue and redemption[1] of shares include:

(1) the nominal value of the non-redeemable issued capital must exceed 10 per cent of the value of the company's total issued share capital before redeemable shares can be issued or redeemed;
(2) the redeemable shares must be fully paid up;
(3) the terms of the redemption must provide for payment on redemption; and
(4) generally, these shares must be redeemed out of profits available for distribution.

Cancellation of shares on redemption

19.24 Shares redeemed pursuant to s 207 may be cancelled on redemption. Section 208 provides that where this happens and the shares are:

(1) redeemed wholly out of profits; or
(2) redeemed wholly or partly out of the proceeds of a fresh issue; and
(3) the amount of those proceeds is less than the nominal value of the shares redeemed (the *aggregable* difference); then
(4) a sum equal to the shares redeemed wholly out of profits[2] and, in the case of a redemption out of the proceeds of a fresh issue, the aggregable difference, must be transferred to a reserve fund.

Capital redemption reserve fund

19.25 The reserve fund created as in (4) above is known as a capital reserve fund, and the provisions of the 1963 Act relating to the reduction of capital[3] apply as if this fund was paid-up share capital of the company. In short, the fund is treated in the same way as paid-up share capital for the purposes of statutory restrictions on its reduction.

Payment of a premium on redemption

19.26 Section 206(2)(e) provides that the premium, if any, payable on redemption, must be paid out of profits except in the circumstances detailed in s 206(2). This exceptional case allows a company to pay a premium on redemption out of the proceeds of a fresh issue of shares made specifically for the purposes of the redemption.

---

1 A company also has the power to convert shares into redeemable shares, and dissenting shareholders have a right to object – see s 210. See also s 64 of the 1963 Act for a company's restricted power to issue redeemable preference shares.
2 As in (1) above.
3 Except as provided in s 208 of the 1990 Act.

Treasury shares

19.27 Instead of cancelling redeemed shares and creating a capital redemption reserve fund, a company may instead hold them as treasury shares under s 209. The company may not exercise voting rights, nor pay itself a dividend, in respect of treasury shares which it holds.

Treasury shares may be either cancelled[1] or re-issued.

Re-issuing of treasury shares

19.28 Section 209(5) and (6) set out the detailed procedures to be followed by a company re-issuing treasury shares. Generally, the share capital of the company will not be regarded as having been increased by the re-issue of such shares. In addition, the company, in general meeting, must fix the price range for these shares in advance of their being re-issued for '*off-market*' *purchases*, ie sales otherwise than on a recognised Stock Exchange.

Restrictions on a company purchasing its own shares

19.29 In *Re Balgooley Distillery Co*,[2] the company had produced a large stock of whiskey which it had difficulty in selling. It then sold whiskey to a director in exchange for a number of his paid-up shares. The court held that the contract was valid and intra vires the company.

In *Trevor v Whitworth*,[3] a company, whose articles of association empowered it to do so, purchased its own shares. Here, the House of Lords overruled the *Balgooley Distillery* decision and held that for the company to purchase its own shares was, in effect, a reduction in capital. Accordingly, such a transaction was ultra vires and void, Lord Macnaghten saying:

> 'If the purchase of shares in (the company) was not one of the objects (stated in the memorandum) of that company, how could its capital be properly employed in that purchase?'

The purchase by a company of its own shares was also deemed illegal in *Re Irish Provident Assurance Co Ltd*.[4] In *Bellerby v Rowland & Marwood's Steamship Co Ltd*,[5] the court considered the question of acceptance by a company of a surrender of shares to release the holder from payment. It decided that releasing the shareholder from his liability to pay calls on shares could not be distinguished from a purchase by the company of its own shares. Cozens-Hardy LJ stated:

> 'The real objection to a surrender of shares does not lie in the fact that money has been paid by the company to acquire the shares. The objection is founded on a larger proposition. A company cannot be a shareholder in itself. Every surrender of

---

1 If cancelled, the provisions of s 208 apply – see **19.24**.
2 (1886–87) 17 LR Ir 239.
3 (1887) 12 AC 409.
4 [1913] IR 352 (CA).
5 [1902] 2 Ch 14.

shares, whether fully paid up or not, involves a reduction of capital, which is unlawful, except as sanctioned by the court under the Companies Acts ... Forfeiture is a statutory exception ...'

This common-law 'ban' on a company purchasing its own shares has now been eased by the emergence of statutory exceptions in the 1983 Amendment Act and the 1990 Act.

Section 41 of the 1983 Amendment Act

19.30   Whilst s 41(1) restates the common law prohibition against a company purchasing[1] its own shares, it does allow for the following exceptional cases:

(1)   the *redemption* of redeemable shares;[2]
(2)   the *forfeiture* of shares for failure to pay any sums due to the company under them;[3]
(3)   the acquisition of any shares in a reduction of capital made under s 72;[4]
(4)   the purchase of shares as a result of a court order in response to minority objections;[5] and
(5)   reflecting a further desire by the legislature to extend these exceptional cases, the purchase of shares pursuant to ss 211 to 230 of the 1990 Act.

Let us now focus on this significant widening of companies' powers in 1990.

Purchasing shares under the 1990 Act

19.31   Under the 1990 Act, the purchase of its own shares by a company involves three types of transaction, ie market purchase, non-market purchase and contingent purchase contracts. However, s 211(2) makes it clear that the provisions of ss 207(2), 208 and 209 are to apply to purchases of its own shares in the same way as they apply to the redemption of shares. This ensures the replacement of the share capital purchased by the company with either:

(1)   a fresh issue of shares; or
(2)   a capital redemption reserve fund.

Market purchase

19.32   When a company buys its shares on a *recognised Stock Exchange* and is subject to a *marketing arrangement*, the transaction is styled a market purchase.

A company's shares are subject to a marketing arrangement on a recognised Stock Exchange if they are either:

---

1   Section 44 of the 1983 Amendment Act also regulates the exercising of a lien or the taking of a charge on its own shares by a public company.
2   See **19.22**.
3   See **19.20**.
4   See **19.5**.
5   Under s 10, s 15 or s 205 of the 1963 Act.

(1) listed[1] on that Stock Exchange; or
(2) the company has been afforded facilities for dealings in those shares to take place in that Stock Exchange without prior permission[2] for individual transactions.

Generally, a company can buy its own shares (including redeemable shares) providing it is authorised to do so by a general meeting. This authority may be a general one or limited to a particular contract for the purchase of its shares by the company.

In the case of a *public company*, the authority must:

(1) specify the maximum number of shares which may be acquired; and
(2) state both the maximum and minimum prices which may be paid for the shares.

The company's authority may be varied, revoked or renewed by the company, again in general meeting.[3]

Off-market purchases

19.33   An off-market purchase[4] is basically any purchase which is not a market purchase.

Section 213 provides that a company must not make an off-market purchase of its own shares unless it is authorised to make that contract by special resolution before the contract is entered into.

If the votes of the seller of the shares are responsible for the carrying of the special resolution to buy his shares, then the resolution may be ineffective.[5]

The other formalities involved with an off-market purchase are contained in s 213(4) to (7).

Contingent purchase contracts

19.34   A contingent purchase contract is one which does not amount to a contract by the company to purchase its own shares but under which, at some future time, it may become entitled to or obliged to purchase those shares.[6] A company may only purchase its shares on a contingent basis, if the contract is approved in advance and all the off-market purchase rules are observed.

---

1 Eg see Chapter 10. See also S. Nolan, 'The Redemption and Purchase by Limited Companies of their own Shares and the Changes proposed by [Part XI of the Companies Act 1990]' (1991) 9(1) ILT 9, at pp 9–13.
2 Obtained from the authority governing that Stock Exchange – see s 212(2)(b).
3 Section 215.
4 See s 212(1)(a).
5 See s 213(3).
6 Section 214(1).

Transfer or release of company's right to buy its own shares

19.35 Section 217 provides that any attempted assignment of the rights of a company under any contract authorised under s 213, s 214 or s 215 will be void. The company may, however, relinquish its right under such a contract provided that, in the case of an off-market or contingent purchase, the company's release is authorised by special resolution.

Payments by a company for its own shares

19.36 Generally, payments made by a company in respect of a share purchase or release under ss 213, 214 and 215 must be made out of its distributable profits.

Effect of company's failure to redeem or purchase its own shares

19.37 Section 219(2) makes it clear that a company will not be liable to pay damages for any failure on its part to redeem or purchase shares issued (or converted) under ss 210, 213, 214 and 215.

Purchase by subsidiary of shares in its holding company

19.38 Notwithstanding ss 32 and 60 of the 1963 Act, a subsidiary is now allowed to purchase shares in its holding company. The conditions regulating such transactions are contained in ss 224 and 225.[1]

The European Communities (Public Limited Companies Subsidiaries) Regulations 1997[2] implement EC Directive 92/101 to apply harmonised EU conditions on the purchase of shares in a public company by its subsidiary.

Disclosure of share purchases

19.39 Every company which has purchased shares pursuant to Part XI of the 1990 Act must, within 28 days after the shares were delivered to the company, send prescribed[3] details to the registrar of companies. It must also keep a copy of the contract at its registered office for the 10 years following the performance of the contract.[4]

Under s 230 of the 1990 Act, as amended by s 39 of the 2001 Act, the Stock Exchange must report apparent unlawful purchases by a company of its own shares, to the Director of Corporate Enforcement. The Director may institute criminal proceedings, or refer the matter to the DPP for him to do so – see s 230(4), as amended.

---

1 Of the 1990 Act – see **20.7**.
2 SI 1997/67 – see **20.7**.
3 See s 226.
4 See s 222.

EXTRAORDINARY MEETING FOLLOWING SERIOUS LOSS OF CAPITAL

19.40   The statutory rules preventing reductions in capital considered above are essentially aimed at preventing the re-payment of share capital to the members. Notwithstanding, it must be remembered that if the company's objects include trading, the statutory controls on loss of capital will not prevent a company incurring trading losses. As Buckley LJ commented in *Re Horsley & Weight Ltd*:[1]

> 'a company, and its directors acting on its behalf, can quite properly expend contributed capital for any purpose which is intra vires the company ... it is a misapprehension to suppose that the directors of a company owe a duty to the company's creditors to keep the contributed capital of the company intact.'

In short, company law does not insulate a company's capital base against erosion by losses suffered in the ordinary course of business trading. As a result, s 40[2] of the 1983 Amendment Act seeks to alert shareholders in the event of their company incurring a serious loss of capital.

Section 40 requirements to call a meeting

19.41   Where the net assets of a company fall to half or less of the amount of the company's called-up share capital, the directors must call an extraordinary general meeting of the company.

This meeting must be called within 28 days of a director becoming aware of the short fall in capital. The meeting must be held within a further 28[3] days. The purpose of the meeting will be to consider what measures, if any, should be taken to deal with the serious financial situation.

Directors who fail to convene this meeting shall be guilty of a criminal offence. Section 40 applies to both public and private companies.

OTHER CAPITAL MAINTENANCE RULES

19.42   Other capital maintenance rules concern the giving of financial assistance by a company for the purchasing of its own shares; a prohibition against issuing shares at a discount and a requirement that dividends must only be paid out of profits.

---

1   [1982] 3 All ER 1045 (CA).

2   Implementing art 17 of the Second EC Company Law Directive (Directive 77/91/EEC).

3   Ie within 56 days of the director becoming aware of the drop in capital.

Giving loans by a company for the purchase of its own shares

19.43 In *Charterhouse Investment Trust Ltd v Tempest Diesels Ltd*,[1] a surrender of tax losses by a subsidiary company to another company within the same group, as part of a wider agreement for the sale of its shares to one of its directors, was held not to amount to the giving of financial assistance.

In this case, Hoffmann J stated:

> '... One must examine the commercial realities of the transaction and decide whether it can properly be described as the giving of financial assistance by the company, bearing in mind that the section is a penal one and should not be strained to cover transactions which are not fairly within it.'

After looking at the commercial realities, there was no evidence that the surrender had reduced the price for the shares which the director would otherwise have paid.

Where a company attempts to give financial assistance to another person to enable him to buy the lending company's own shares, this transaction would be viewed as an indirect reduction in capital. Accordingly, such transactions are regulated by s 60 of the 1963 Act, as amended by s 89 of the 2001 Act.

Section 60(1) contains a general ban on a company giving loans or guarantees for the purchase, by any person, of its shares, or those of its holding company.

Conditions for valid loans or guarantees

19.44 Section 60(2)[2] refines the general prohibition against loans and guarantees by providing that s 60(1) will not apply if:

(1) the loan or guarantee was *sanctioned by a special resolution* passed within the previous 12 months; and
(2) the company has furnished with each notice of the meeting a copy of a *statutory declaration* stating:
  (a) the form which the assistance is to take;
  (b) the persons to whom the assistance is to be given;
  (c) the purpose for which the company intends those persons to use the assistance;
  (d) that the declarants have made a full inquiry into the affairs of the company and that, having done so, they have formed the opinion that the company, having carried out the transaction whereby such assistance is to be given, will be able to pay its debts in full as they become due.

Any director making this statutory declaration without reasonable grounds for his opinion, can incur criminal sanctions.[3]

---

1 [1986] BCLC 1. See also *Brady v Brady* [1989] AC 755, [1988] 2 All ER 617 (HL) which concerned the giving of financial assistance to ensure the survival of the company and to free it from management deadlock.
2 See also s 60(15A).
3 Section 60(5).

A copy of the statutory declarations must be forwarded to the Registrar within 21 days from the date the financial assistance is granted (see s 89 of the 2001 Act).

Objections

19.45 Holders of 10 per cent or more of the nominal value of the issued capital may appeal to the court to cancel the special resolution.

Effect of breach of s 60 procedures

19.46 Any transaction in breach of s 60 requirements and procedures will be *voidable* at the company's option against *any person who had notice* of the breach.[1] Where the company is in breach, *every officer* in default will be *criminally liable.*[2]

In *Securities Trust Ltd v Associated Properties Ltd and Estates Development Ltd,*[3] the court held that for a special resolution under s 60 to be valid, *the giving of financial assistance had to be intra vires* the company. In the case, lending money was not one of the objects in the memorandum and an article of association expressly provided that none of the funds of the company could be used for the purchase of its shares. Not surprisingly, therefore, the company's resolution under s 60 was deemed null and void.

The case of *Re Northside Motor Co Ltd; Eddison v Allied Irish Banks*[4] dealt with the directors' statutory declaration. In his judgment, Costello J said:

> 'In my view, if a *resolution and/or statutory declaration are materially inaccurate and misleading,* they fail to comply with ... s 60(2) and (3). As this happened in this case, the guarantee ... was illegal under s 60(1) and the money paid on foot of it recoverable by the liquidator.' (author's emphasis)

Third party notice of breach

19.47 Section 60(14) seems implicitly to render a transaction in breach of s 60 procedures voidable by the company only against a person who had notice of the breach. This assumption was confirmed by the High Court in *Lombard & Ulster Banking Ltd v Bank of Ireland.*[5] In this case, Costello J stated:

> 'even though the transaction was ... one which was rendered illegal by s 60(1), the company is not at liberty to avoid it as the plaintiffs had *no notice* of what had happened.' (author's emphasis)

Again, in *Bank of Ireland Finance v Rockfield Ltd,*[6] the Supreme Court interpreted notice in this context to mean *actual,* as distinct from *constructive,* notice.

---

1 Section 60(14), reinforced by the Supreme Court decision in *Bank of Ireland Finance Ltd v Rockfield Ltd* [1979] IR 21.
2 Section 60(15).
3 (Unreported) 19 November 1980 (HC).
4 (Unreported) 24 July 1985 (HC).
5 (Unreported) 2 June 1987 (HC).
6 [1979] IR 21. Constructive notice in this case was an omission by the plaintiffs to check a matter which they ought to have done. Nevertheless, because it was not actual notice, the plaintiff's action was successful.

Permitted loans under s 60

19.48 Section 60(13) exempts the following three categories of transactions from the s 60 restrictions:

(1) where lending is part of the ordinary business of the company, and the loan is made in the ordinary course of its business;
(2) certain loans for the purchase of fully paid shares by (or for the benefit of) employees, former employees, directors or subsidiary companies;
(3) loans to persons, other than directors, bona fide in the employment of the company or any subsidiary of the company, with a view to enabling those persons to purchase or subscribe for fully paid shares in the company or its holding company.

Restriction on public companies

19.49 Where a public company seeks to avail of the s 60(13) exemptions, it may only do so if its net assets are not reduced[1] as a result of the loan made.

Dividends and debts

19.50 Section 60 does not prohibit the payment of a dividend by the company, or the discharging of any liability lawfully incurred by it.[2]

In *Eccles Hall Ltd v Bank of Nova Scotia*,[3] the liquidator argued that the repayments of debts owed to the company constituted an indirect breach of s 60. However, Murphy J allowed the defence of discharging a liability lawfully incurred by the company.

Prohibition against issuing shares at a discount

19.51 Generally, shares may not be issued at a discount, ie sold at a price less than their nominal value. For example, in *The Ooregum Gold Mining Co of India Ltd v Roper*,[4] the market value of the £1 ordinary shares was 12½p. Because of the low market value of their ordinary shares, the company issued £1 preference shares, crediting 75p as paid, and seeking only 25p per share to render them fully paid up. The court held that the issue was ultra vires the company, and the allottees were liable to pay £1 per share, Lord Macnaghten commenting:

> 'The dominant and cardinal principle of the [Companies] Acts is that the investor shall purchase immunity from liability beyond a certain limit on the terms that there shall be and remain a liability up to the limit [ie the nominal value of the share].'

The common law prohibition against issuing shares at a discount is preserved by s 27 of the 1983 Amendment Act which provides that 'the shares of a company shall not be allotted at a discount'.

---

1 See s 60(15B) and (15C).
2 Section 60(12).
3 (Unreported) 3 February 1995.
4 [1892] AC 125.

Payment by instalments

19.52   Issuing shares at a discount should be distinguished from issuing them for full value, but not necessarily on allotment. If the company does not require payment in full on allotment, the shares are classified as partly paid shares.

Issuing shares at a premium

19.53   There is no prohibition against a company issuing shares at a premium, ie receiving a price greater than the par value. For example, if a company issues £1 ordinary shares at £1.50, then they are issued at a premium of 50p.

When a company issues shares at a premium,[1] a sum equal to the value of the premiums received on those shares must be transferred to a special account known as the *Share Premium Account*. Generally, the fund in the Share Premium Account is to be treated as share capital except that it may be used to allot members of the company bonus shares.[2]

Payment of dividends only out of profits

19.54   At common law, it was possible for a company to pay dividends out of its profits without first making good a previous loss. As Lindley LJ stated:[3]

> 'There is nothing at all in the Acts about how dividends are to be paid, nor how profits are to be reckoned; all that is left ... to the commercial world. It is not a subject for an Act of Parliament to say how accounts are to be kept; what is to be put into a capital account ... and an income account, is left to men of business.'

A change in public policy almost a century later manifested itself in Part IV of the 1983 Amendment Act. Part IV, consisting of ss 45 to 51, enacts rules governing the distribution of profits and assets. The *fundamental rule* in s 45 is that a company must not make a distribution except out of profits available for the purpose. The profits available for this purpose are the company's accumulated realised profits, less its accumulated realised losses.

Accumulated profits less accumulated losses means that losses of previous years must be deducted from any current distributable surplus before arriving at a distributable profits figure.

Any increase in the value of a retained asset cannot be taken into account when reckoning a company's profit because it is not *realised*.

Distribution

19.55   The term 'distribution' is defined in s 51(2) of the 1983 Amendment Act. It includes every distribution of a company's assets to members of the company, whether in cash or otherwise. This includes the payment of

---

1 Whether for cash or otherwise.
2 See s 62 of the 1963 Act, and **19.4**.
3 In *Lee v Neuchatel Asphalte Co* (1889) 41 Ch D 1 (CA).

dividends,[1] it does not, however, because of s 51(2), include distributions made by way of:

(1) an issue of bonus shares;
(2) the redemption of preference shares;
(3) the redemption or purchase of shares out of the proceeds of a fresh issue made for that purpose;
(4) the reduction of share capital by extinguishing or reducing the liability of members on any of its shares which are not paid up; and
(5) a distribution of assets to members of the company on its winding up.

The accumulated profits form the usual source of funding for distributable assets.

The rules on distributable profits apply to both private and public companies. The latter, however, are subject to an additional restriction.

Profits of public companies

19.56 Under s 46(1), a plc may only make a distribution of profits:

(1) if the amount of its net assets (excluding any uncalled share capital) is not less than the aggregate of the company's called-up share capital and its undistributable reserves; and
(2) if, and to the extent that, the distribution does not reduce the amount of those assets to less than that aggregate.

Undistributable reserves are defined in s 46(2). They include any surplus of revalued accumulated unrealised profits over accumulated unrealised losses.

In addition to this assets revaluation reserve, undistributable reserves also include a share premium account and a capital redemption reserve fund (if companies buy back their shares, they must put the same amount as they paid to the shareholders into this reserve in order to maintain the company's capital fund – see **19.24**).

The effect of s 46 is to regulate the valuation of a plc's net worth by ensuring that all assets are considered and their values aggregated.

Specialist companies

19.57 There are special rules in the 1983 Amendment Act for determining the distributable profits of investment[2] and life assurance[3] companies.

---

1 See **14.10** et seq.
2 Section 47.
3 Section 48.

The relevant accounts

19.58 Whether or not a company has distributable profits will have to be determined by reference to the latest properly audited accounts[1] – see Chapter 32.

ALTERATION OF CAPITAL

19.59 A reduction in capital must be distinguished from a diminution of and an increase in capital.

Increase in and diminution of share capital

19.60 By virtue of ss 68 and 69,[2] a company may *increase* its share capital, or, indeed, make other alterations which do not reduce its capital, providing they are authorised by the articles. For example, articles 44 and 45 of Table A provide as follows:

> '**44.** The company may from time to time by *ordinary resolution* increase the share capital by such sum, to be divided into shares of such amount, as the resolution shall prescribe.

> **45.** The company may by *ordinary resolution*:
> (a) consolidate and divide all or any of its share capital into shares of larger amount than its existing shares;
> (b) subdivide its existing shares, or any of them, into shares of smaller amount than is fixed by the memorandum of association subject, nevertheless, to section 68(1)(d) of the Act;
> (c) cancel any shares which, at the date of the passing of the resolution, have not been taken or agreed to be taken by any person.'

The article 45 alterations would be classified as a diminution, rather than a reduction in share capital.

---

1 Section 49.
2 Of the 1963 Act.

PART IV D

SHAREHOLDERS' INDIVIDUAL RIGHTS AND RESPONSIBILITIES

Chapter 20

THE MEMBER'S SECTION 25 CONTRACT

20.1   To become privy to the investory's statutory contract involves a person acquiring rights of membership in the company.

MEMBERSHIP

20.2   There are various ways by which a person can acquire shares in a company. Owning shares, of itself, does not confer membership status on the holder. To become a company member, the shareholder's name must be entered in the register of members.

WHO CAN BECOME MEMBERS?

20.3   Generally, any person of full contractual capacity can become a member. Some exceptional instances exist, though. These include membership by infants and companies, and the status of deceased and/or bankrupt members.

Infants and minors

20.4   Persons aged under 21 years used to be classified as infants for contracting purposes. The Age of Majority Act 1985 reduced this age to 18 and changed the classification to 'minors'.

A minor may enter into a contract to purchase shares. This contract will, however, be voidable at the minor's option.[1] Until such time as he rescinds the contract, the minor will be liable for any obligations arising out of the ownership of his shares, eg meeting a 'call' made upon shareholders by the directors.

A minor must exercise his option to withdraw from the company either before, or within a reasonable time after, attaining majority (18 years).

Notwithstanding the position of a minor at law, a company may provide expressly in the articles that a minor cannot be a member.

Companies

20.5   A company may be a member of *another* company if it is authorised to do so by its memorandum of association. There are, however, limitations on the extent to which a company can become:

---

1   See R. Friel *The Law of Contract* (Round Hall Press, 1995), at Chapter 5.

(1) a member of itself; and

(2) a member of its holding company.

Buying its own shares

20.6 There are restrictions on a company either buying its own shares or giving loans for the purchase of its own shares. These restrictions have already been outlined in Chapter 19 in the context of protecting the capital base of the company (see **19.29** and **19.43**).

Purchasing the shares of its holding company

20.7 Section 224 of the 1990 Act empowers a subsidiary to acquire and hold shares in its holding company. This share holding is subject to the conditions set out in s 224(2). These include:

(1) the consideration for the purchase must be provided out of the profits of the subsidiary available for distribution; and

(2) following the share purchase:

    (a) the profits of the subsidiary available for distribution shall be restricted by a sum equal to the total cost of the shares acquired in its holding company; and

    (b) the subsidiary cannot exercise any voting rights in respect of the acquired shares.

The directors will be liable to repay the cost price of the shares to the subsidiary, if a winding up of that company commences within six months after the purchase and the company is unable to pay its debts.[1]

A return of the transaction must be made to the registrar[2] and, in the case of public companies, the Stock Exchange.[3] Section 228 empowers the Minister to make regulations governing the purchase of companies of their own shares or of shares in their holding company.

The European Communities (Public Limited Companies Subsidiaries) Regulations 1997 (the 1997 Regulations) implement Directive 92/101/EEC, which amends the Second Directive (Formation and Capital of Public Limited Companies) to apply conditions on the purchase of shares in a public limited company by subsidiaries of it.

Part XI of the 1990 Act had already substantially implemented Directive 92/101/EEC.

Regulation 4 of the 1997 Regulations extends the definition of subsidiary of a public limited company for the purposes of s 224 of the 1990 Act.

Regulation 5 applies the conditions relating to acquiring shares by a public limited company itself, to the subscription, acquisition or holding of shares by any subsidiary in its parent plc.

---

1 Section 225.

2 Section 226.

3 See ss 229 and 230.

Regulation 6 extends the provisions of s 14 of the Companies (Amendment) Act 1986, requiring information to be included in the directors' report regarding the acquisition by a company of its own shares, to include the acquisition by a subsidiary company of shares in its parent public limited company.

Section 111 of the 2001 Act disapplies certain provisions in relation to the purchase by a subsidiary of shares in its holding company, if the subsidiary is a member of an approved stock exchange, acting as a professional dealer in the normal course of its business.

Deceased members

20.8   On the death of a shareholder, he ceases to be a member. Ownership of his shares, however, vests automatically in his legal personal representatives.

Bankrupt members

20.9   If a shareholder is made a bankrupt, the Official Assignee in Bankruptcy has the option of taking the shares. If the shares are 'onerous', ie a financial drain on the company, the Official Assignee can[1] disclaim the shares.

HOW PERSONS MAY BECOME MEMBERS

20.10   A person may become a member of a company either by subscribing to the memorandum of association or agreeing to become a member and having his name placed on the register of members.[2]

By subscribing to the memorandum

20.11   Those persons who sign the memorandum of association[3] are deemed to have agreed to become members. When the company's certificate of incorporation is issued by the registrar, the company must enter the subscribers' names in the register of members.[4]

By agreeing to become members

20.12   A person may agree to become a member either by:

(1)   applying[5] for an allotment of shares and being allotted them; or
(2)   taking a transfer of shares from an existing member. Such a transfer may be voluntary or involuntary; or

---

1 Within 12 months of their vesting in him – see Bankruptcy (Ireland) (Amendment) Act 1872, ss 97 and 98.
2 Section 31 of the 1963 Act.
3 Section 31(1) – see also Chapter 8.
4 Section 21(2).
5 See Chapter 10.

(3) by estoppel.

Transfer of shares

20.13 A voluntary transfer of shares takes place when the holder decides to sell them and actually does so. An involuntary transfer occurs when the shareholder dies and the property in his shares passes to his personal representatives.

Directors' powers

20.14 Articles 22 to 28 of Table A[1] provide model internal company guidelines affecting the transfer of shares. They give the directors of public companies the right to decline to register a share transfer. As the purchaser of shares will only become a member when his name is entered on the register of members, the directors of a company may be given the power in its articles to 'block' a new member. For example, article 24 of Table A provides:

> 'The directors *may* decline to register the transfer of a share (not being a fully paid share) to a person of whom they do not approve, and they may also decline to register the transfer of a share on which the company has a lien. The directors may also decline to register any transfer of a share which, in their opinion, may imperil or prejudicially affect the status of the company in the State or which may imperil any tax concession or rebate to which the members of the company are entitled ...'
> (author's emphasis)

The directors of a private company may enjoy even greater powers to refuse membership because of the limit on maximum number of members permitted for private companies. For example, article 3 of Table A, Part II gives the directors of a private company the power 'in their *absolute discretion, and without assigning a reason therefore,* (to) decline to register any transfer of any shares ...' (author's emphasis).

The procedures involved in share transfers will be dealt with in Chapter 22. This will include judicial interpretation of the directors' 'blocking' powers.

Transmission of shares

20.15 The term 'transmission' is used to denote the involuntary transfer of share ownership; in particular in the case of death or bankruptcy of a member.

Articles 29 to 31 of Table A, Part I contain the model guidelines. For example, articles 30 and 31 stipulate that:

> '**30.** Any person becoming entitled to a share in consequence of the *death* or *bankruptcy* of a member may ... elect either to be registered himself as holder of the share or to have some person nominated by him registered as the transferee thereof, but the directors shall, in either case, have the same right to decline or suspend registration as they would have had in the case of a transfer of the share by

---

1 Part I.

that member before his death or bankruptcy, as the case may be. (author's emphasis)

31. If the person entitled elects to be registered himself, he shall deliver or send to the company a notice in writing signed by him stating that he so elects. If he elects to have another person registered, he shall testify his election by executing to that person a transfer of the share ...'

Estoppel

20.16 Any person who allows his name to remain on the register of members, or in other ways holds himself out as a member, may be legally estopped (or prevented) from denying that he is, in fact, a member.

Condition precedent to membership

20.17 In all cases of the acquisition of company membership, mere ownership of shares is not enough. It is the entering of the shareholder's name in the register of members which entitles him to membership. Thus, the entering of a person's name on the register is a condition precedent to becoming a member – see *Kinsella and Others v Alliance & Dublin Consumers Gas Company and Others*.[1]

REGISTER OF MEMBERS

20.18 Every company must maintain a register of members.[2] The register and index must be open to inspection by members and non-members. It is, therefore, possible to obtain details of the membership of a company, and to ascertain their liabilities.

The register is prima facie evidence that the persons named in it are members.[3]

Rectification of the register

20.19 Section 122 of the 1963 Act provides a remedy for any improper entry or omission of entry in the register. The remedy is 'rectification' or correction.

If the name of any person is, without sufficient cause, entered in or omitted from the register, or default is made, the person aggrieved, or any member of the company, may apply to the court for rectification of the register.

Rectification has been ordered by a court:

(1) where a person was wrongfully removed from the register;
(2) where a person was put on the register, but had not agreed to take shares;
(3) where shares had been improperly surrendered;

---

1 (Unreported) 5 October 1982 (HC).
2 See Chapter 33 for its contents.
3 Though not conclusive evidence – see s 124 of the 1963 Act.

(4) where a transfer had been forged.

Notice[1] of any rectification ordered by the court must be given to the registrar.

Trusts not to be entered in the register

20.20   Section 123 provides that no notice of any trust[2] shall be entered on the register or be receivable by the registrar.

Shares may, of course, be held in trust, but if there is a trust, then it is the trustee's name that is put on the register; he is nominally the shareholder and is liable to the company for calls even if the calls exceed the value of the trust property in his hands.

This means that a company is in no way concerned with the relation of its registered holders to anyone else. If they are, in fact, trustees, the company need not enquire whether they are acting within their powers in dealing with the shares. The company looks solely to the registered holders.

Article 7 of Table A, Part I elaborates upon s 123 by providing 'except as required by law, no person shall be recognised by the company as holding any shares upon any trust ...'.

Article 7 also makes it clear that s 123 will not preclude the company from requiring members to furnish the company with information as to the beneficial ownership of any share, when this is reasonably required by the company. This type of information may now be required under Part IV of the 1990 Act.

Even though the company may become aware that there are beneficial interests[3] in shares by reason of disclosure[4] under Part IV, it is prohibited by s 123 from noting any trusts in its register of members. In *Simpson v Molson's Bank*,[5] it was held that the company need not take any notice of a trust, even if it has constructive notice that it exists.

HOW PERSONS RELINQUISH MEMBERSHIP

20.21   A person may cease to be a member in the following ways and circumstances:

(1) by a *transfer of his shares*, duly registered – see Chapter 22. He will, however, be liable to contribute on the 'B' list if winding up commences within 12 months of the sale;[6]

---

1 Section 122(5).
2 Express, implied or constructive.
3 Other than the members'.
4 See Chapter 22 and disclosure orders. Beneficial interests by directors, secretaries and their families must also be disclosed – see **27.24**.
5 [1895] AC 270.
6 See Chapter 50.

(2) by *forfeiture*[1] of his shares through non-payment of *calls*, if permitted by the articles;

(3) by *sale* of the shares by the company under power given by its articles to enforce a *lien*.[2] The former member may remain a debtor of the company for any amount unpaid on his shares, if the articles so provide;

(4) by a valid *surrender*[3] of his shares by the member;

(5) on the *death, bankruptcy* or *mental incapacity*[4] of the member and appropriate notification of disclaimer by the official personal representatives;

(6) by *repudiation* (or cancellation) either:

    (a) by a *minor* under a voidable contract; or

    (b) by any member on grounds of fraud, misrepresentation mistake or irregular allotment.[5]

SIGNIFICANCE OF MEMBERSHIP

20.22 The means by which an investor acquires an interest in a company is by obtaining its shares. He subsequently becomes a member of that company when his name is entered in the register of members. The question now arises as to the significance of membership over mere share ownership.

In *Kinsella and Others v Alliance and Dublin Consumers Gas Company and Others*,[6] the court decided that only persons whose names are entered in the register of members are entitled to vote at a general meeting. In that case, Barron J stated:

> 'Persons entitled to stock (shares) must be registered in the register of shareholders. Until they are, they are not entitled to vote. This is a well established principle and I would be wrong not to follow it ...
>
> The meeting was properly held on the basis of the register of shareholders as it then existed ... In the present case, all reasonable efforts were made to register transfers and the failure to register them is not a ground on which the plaintiffs are entitled to rely ...'

Clearly, membership is significant for investors who wish to exercise important rights attaching to their shares, such as attending company meetings and voting at them.

Corporate majority decisions and individual members' rights

20.23 The Companies Acts permit the majority of the members to control constitutional aspects of a company. We have already explained:

---

1 See Chapter 21.

2 Ibid. A lien is a legal right to keep possession of someone's property and, if necessary, sell it, unless a debt owed by the property owner is paid.

3 Ibid.

4 See Chapter 22.

5 See Chapter 10.

6 (Unreported) 5 October 1982 (HC).

(1) company meetings and resolutions;[1]
(2) the democratic[2] nature of the voting underlying major company decisions.

A result of the democratic nature of corporate control may mean that individual shareholders, if outvoted on an issue, have no grounds for redress. A further extrapolation of this principle is that, if a member feels that the company has suffered a loss, it is the company who must pursue it. This is what the rule in *Foss v Harbottle*[3] entails.

Where, however, collective majority decisions *wrongfully* affect members' individual rights, these individual or minority members are given some protection by:

(1) the apparent judicial exceptions to the rule in *Foss v Harbottle*; and
(2) statutory provisions such as ss 205 and 213[4] of the 1963 Act.

As we focus on shareholders' and members' individual rights, it should not be forgotten that in some cases the exercise of these rights may be adversely affected by this democratic nature of company decision-making.

MEMBERS AND THE MEMORANDUM OF ASSOCIATION

20.24 A shareholder's fundamental right and protection is enshrined in the memorandum of association.[5]

Once the company has been registered and issued with a certificate of incorporation, s 18(2)[6] confirms that 'liability on the part of members to contribute to the assets of the company in the event of its being wound up, is as mentioned in this Act.'

Section 6(2) of that Act further provides that the memorandum of a company limited by shares or by guarantee, must also state (expressly) that the liability of its members is limited – hence clause 3 of the Table B.[7]

The extent of the liability of a member in a company limited by guarantee is set out in s 6(3) of the 1963 Act.

---

1 See Chapter 15.
2 See Chapters 16 and 17.
3 Ibid.
4 Ibid.
5 See **12.1** et seq.
6 Of the 1963 Act.
7 The specimen memorandum in the 1963 Act – see **4.2**.

MEMBERS AND THE ARTICLES OF ASSOCIATION

20.25 The distinction between the memorandum and the articles of association is explained in **12.11** et seq.

As Ross J stated in *Clarke v Workman*,[1] the articles of association 'constitute a contract between every shareholder and all the others, and between the company itself and all the shareholders.'

In *Bratton Seymour Service Co Ltd v Oxborough*,[2] the Court of Appeal refused to imply a term of business efficacy into articles, stating that articles create a contract with distinctive features unlike a normal contract.

Scope of members' express contract terms

20.26 In *Hickman v Kent or Romney Marsh Sheepbreeders' Association*,[3] Astbury J made it clear that:

(1) no articles can constitute a contract between the company and a third person or outsider.[4] Furthermore, in *Securities Trust Ltd v Hugh Moore & Alexander Ltd*,[5] the High Court held that where a third party had suffered loss because of an error in the articles of association supplied to him, the company did not owe him a duty of care in tort; the company's duty of care only extending to a member who was supplied with the articles;

(2) no right purported to be given by an article to a person (whether a member or not) in a capacity other than that of a member,[6] can be enforced against the company. For example, in *Eley v Positive Government Security Life Assurance*,[7] a member acting as the company's solicitor was unable to rely on the company's articles as a contract to provide legal services between the company and himself. Buckley LJ succinctly stated this situation in *Bisgood v Henderson's Transvaal Estates Ltd*.[8] He said:

'The purpose of (the memorandum) and articles is to define the position of the shareholder as [member], not to bind him in his capacity as an individual.'

---

1 [1920] 11R 107 (ChD). See also *Rayfield v Hands* [1960] 1 Ch 1.
2 [1992] BCC 471.
3 [1915] 1 Ch 881.
4 Basically, because there is no privity of contract.
5 [1964] IR 417.
6 For instance as promoter, solicitor or executive director.
7 (1876) 1 Ex D 88.
8 [1908] 1 Ch 743.

Similarly, in *Beattie v E & F Beattie*,[1] the Court of Appeal held that a director who was in dispute with his company was unable to rely on the articles to have the dispute referred to arbitration. However, Beattie might have been successful if he had sued in his capacity as member.[2]

(3) articles regulating the rights and obligations of the members generally as such do create rights and obligations between them and the company respectively.

In *Welton v Saffery*,[3] Lord Herschell, confirming that the articles regulated the rights of members inter se, commented: 'Such rights can only be enforced by or against a member through the company, or through the liquidator representing the company'.

Here Lord Herschell was invoking the legal reasoning underlying the rule in *Foss v Harbottle*[4] which essentially only acknowledges the separate legal personality of a company. There is, however an exception to this rule where a members individual rights are infringed, such as his right to vote. In *Pender v Lushington*,[5] Jessel MR said:

'[Mr Pender] is a member of the company ... and is entitled to have his vote recorded – [this is] an individual [or personal] right to sue ...

[The plaintiff] has a right to say that his vote is a right of property belonging to his interest[6] in the company.'

THE SECTION 25 CONTRACT TERMS

20.27 While a shareholder may enjoy the many specific statutory rights outlined in **13.15**, **13.16** and **13.17**, his basic express contract terms are contained in the company's memorandum and articles of association. This is because of s 25 of the 1963 Act which provides:

's.25(1) – the memorandum and articles shall, when registered, bind the company and the members thereof, to the same extent as if they respectively had been signed and sealed by each member, and contained covenants by each member to observe all the provisions of the memorandum and articles.

s.25(2) – all money payable by any member to the company under the memorandum or articles, shall be a debt due from him to the company.'

Members' important rights outlined

20.28 The more important and, indeed, probably most useful individual rights[7] of a member may include:

---

1 [1938] 1 Ch 708.
2 See Wedderburn 'Shareholders' Rights and the Rule in *Foss v Harbottle*' [1957] CLJ 194, at p 212.
3 [1897] AC 299 (HL).
4 See **16.28** et seq.
5 (1877) 6 Ch D 10.
6 See **13.4** et seq.
7 Including those in the articles and conferred additionally by statute.

(1) *Dividends.* The right to receive a share of the company's distributable profits in the form of a dividend;[1]

(2) *Meetings.* The right to attend and vote at meetings of the company (if the type of share permits);

(3) *Directors.* The right to vote in the election or removal of directors, again if the type of share grants this right;

(4) *Information.* The right to receive a copy of the annual accounts and directors' and auditors' reports, at least 21 days before the AGM;

(5) *Changes in Memorandum and Articles of Association.* The right to vote on these alterations which might be necessary to:
   (a) increase the company's authorised share capital;
   (b) give the directors authority to allot shares; or
   (c) waive members' pre-emption rights;

(6) *Requisitions.* The right to requisition extraordinary general meetings if the statutory minimum number of minority members required can be mustered;

(7) *Rights and Bonus Issues.* The right to participate, in proportion to the number of shares held, in any rights or bonus issues of shares;

(8) *Transfer.* The right to transfer[2] the shares to a third party for consideration (ie by selling them) or by way of gift. This right will, however, be restricted for shareholders of private companies;

(9) *Capital.* The right to receive, on the winding up of the company, their proportion of assets remaining (if any), after all the creditors have been paid.

Many of these rights may be amended or excluded by the articles, unless conferred by statute, eg (4) and (6). Other statutory rights include the shareholders' rights to inspect the register of members, to petition the court to appoint an inspector,[3] to vote to wind up the company voluntarily[4] and to petition the court for relief under s 205 of the 1963 Act, in cases of oppression (see **16.20**). Members' 'top up' statutory rights have already been explained in **13.14** et seq.

Members' duties

20.29 The main duty of a shareholder recognises the fact that he is basically an investor. This duty is his legal obligation to pay the amount which he has agreed to pay on his shares. This may involve payment of the full amount when the contract is agreed, ie when the shares are allotted to him.

Public subscriptions for shares

20.30 The methods of raising capital from the public, making payment for shares and the protection for investors in these transactions have been detailed

---

1 See Chapter 21.
2 See Chapter 22.
3 See Chapter 35.
4 Section 251 of the 1963 Act – see Chapter 49.

in Chapter 10. This chapter also includes rules on the payment for shares by *non-cash consideration.*

Calls

20.31   Part only of a share may be payable on application or purchase. The remaining amount can be payable when a call is made by the directors on the shareholder of a partly paid share – see next chapter.

Types of shares

20.32   Class rights and the differences between types of shares, such as ordinary and preference, were explained when dealing with the composition of the company's capital base, in Chapter 18.

Variation of class rights

20.33   The protections for shareholders in the event of the variation of the rights of their particular class of share were also detailed in Chapter 18.

Amount and numbering of shares

20.34   The memorandum of association must state the amount of the share capital of a limited liability company, divided into shares of a fixed amount, eg 250,000 shares of £1 each.[1]

Unless all the issued shares (or class of shares) are fully paid up and ranking pari passu (equally), each share must be numbered.[2]

Evidence of membership

20.35   A shareholder is furnished with a share certificate as evidence of his s 25 contract, and of his title to the shares. The share certificate contains few details; merely the shareholder's name, number and classes of shares held, etc.

Notwithstanding, as Lord Selborne LC declared in *Oakbank Oil Co v Crum*:[3]

> 'Each party must be taken to have made himself acquainted with the terms of the written contract contained in the articles of association ... He must also in law be taken ... to have understood the terms of the contract according to their proper meaning; and that being so, he must take the consequences, whatever they may be, of the contract which he has made.'

Object of share certificate

20.36   A valid share certificate issued under seal, is prima facie evidence[4] of the investor's title to the shares. As a result, loss of a share certificate can cause

---

1 Section 6(4)(a) of the 1963 Act.
2 See s 80 of the 1963 Act.
3 (1882) 8 App Cas 65.
4 Section 87 of the 1963 Act.

difficulties for a shareholder in dealing with his shares. However, article 8 of Table A provides for the replacement of any share certificate which has been lost, defaced or destroyed.

Effect of certificate

20.37 The certificate has been defined as a statement that the company asserts that the person to whom it is granted is the registered shareholder entitled to the shares included in the certificate, and that the amount certified to be paid has been paid. As a result, the company may be estopped (prevented) from:

(1) disputing the title of the registered holder, as happened in *Re Bahia and San Francisco Ry.*[1]

According to case-law, the company is *not* estopped from denying the title of the registered holder where an *officer* of the company issues a forged certificate. In *Ruben v Great Fingall Consolidated*,[2] Lord Macnaghten stated:

> 'Ruben and Ladenbury are the victims of a wicked fraud ... But their claim against the respondent company is, I think, simply absurd.
> The thing put forward as the foundation of their claim is a piece of paper which purports to be a certificate of shares in the company. This paper is false and fraudulent from beginning to end ... Every statement in the document is a lie. The only thing real about it is the signature of the secretary of the company who was the sole author and perpetrator of the fraud. No one would suggest that this fraudulent certificate could of itself ... bind or affect the company in any way. It is not the company's deed, and there is nothing to prevent the company from saying so ...
> The directors have never said or done anything to represent or lead to the belief that the thing was the company's deed. Without such a representation, there can be no estoppel.
> The secretary *who is a mere servant* ... has no authority to guarantee the genuineness or validity of a document which is not the deed of the company ...' (author's emphasis)

or

(2) alleging that the amount stated as being paid on the shares has not been paid. For example, if the certificate incorrectly states that the shares are fully paid up, the company cannot make a call upon the holder for the amount unpaid.[3]

---

1 (1868) LR3 QB 584. In this case, the registered holder left the share certificate with brokers who forged her signature to a transfer of the shares.

2 [1906] AC 439. The proper shareholder may, however, be able to sue the company for damages if the shares have been sold under the forged certificate to a person who purchases them in good faith.

3 *Burkinshaw v Nicholls* (1878) 3 App Cas 1004. Nor can the company place a transferee of them, without knowledge, on the list of contributories on the company going into liquidation – see *Bloomenthal v Ford* [1897] AC 156.

Comment on case-law

20.38 The decision in *Ruben v Great Fingall Consolidated* in (1) above is based on a nineteenth-century judicial view of the company secretary's role. As pointed out in Chapter 23, the company secretary is no longer viewed as 'a mere servant or clerk', but as a company's chief administrative officer/ executive. Furthermore, there is no common law impediment to holding a company vicariously liable for the fraudulent acts of its employees.[1] Accordingly, it is questionable whether a modern judge would find that a company was not estopped from denying that it was liable for a share certificate issued fraudulently by its secretary – despite the precedent of the *Ruben* case.

Again, the case-law in (2) above – that the company is estopped from making a call on a shareholder where the share certificate wrongly stated that the shares were fully paid up – would result in the issuing of those shares at a discount. This situation is now prohibited by s 27(1) of the 1983 Act.

Where shares are allotted in contravention of s 27(1), the allottee will be liable to pay the company an amount equal to the amount of the discount, plus interest thereon at an appropriate rate.[2]

The term 'allottee' denotes the original purchaser of shares from the company. It is unlikely, therefore, that s 27 could be used by the company as a means of obtaining payment of the discount from a transferee, or at least a person who bought the shares from the allottee in good faith and for value without notice, in the event of the allottee failing to pay them. As a result, the common law position would appear to prevail in favour of transferees,[3] and the company would be estopped from alleging that the amount stated as being paid on the shares had not been paid.

Share warrants

20.39 A share certificate is not a negotiable instrument. If a company issues a share warrant instead of a certificate, the holder can transfer the ownership of his shares by handing over the warrant to a purchaser. Thus, a share warrant is a negotiable instrument like a cheque.

Private companies do not issue share warrants. Whilst s 88 empowers a company to issue share warrants, few, in fact, do so.

CONVERSION OF SHARES INTO STOCK

20.40 Sections 68 and 69 of the 1963 Act give a company the power to alter its share capital structure. In particular, the company may, by ordinary resolution,

---

1 See *Lloyd v Grace Smith & Co* [1912] AC 716.
2 Section 27(2).
3 Some doubts might exist in the case of involuntary transferees and, perhaps, instances where the allottee makes a gift of the shares to the transferee.

convert any paid up shares into stock, and reconvert any stock into paid up shares of any denomination.

Generally, the holders of the stock will have the same rights as if they held the shares from which the stock arose – see Table A, article 42.

Chapter 21

DIVIDENDS AND CALLS ON SHARES

MEMBERS' RIGHTS AND LIABILITIES

21.1 Shareholders enjoy many rights and can incur several liabilities under their s 25 contracts. These have already been summarised in the previous chapter. We now focus on a shareholder's right to dividends and his liability to meet calls for payments on his shares.

MEMBERS' PRINCIPAL RIGHTS

21.2 The principal individual rights enjoyed by shareholders include:

(1) the right to attend and vote[1] at meetings;
(2) statutory rights to accounts and reports,[2] etc;
(3) the right to a dividend, if one is declared; and
(4) the right to receive a proportionate part of any surplus capital remaining after all the creditors have been paid in the event of the company being wound up.[3]

In Chapter 18, we explained which of these rights were enjoyed solely by preference and/or by ordinary shareholders. Generally, both these types of shareholders may be entitled to dividends.

Dividends

21.3 A dividend is the share, received by a shareholder, of the company's profits legally available for distribution[4] to its investors.

Every trading company has the implied power to pay dividends, subject to any restrictions imposed on it by its memorandum of association.

The concept of a dividend is dealt with in **14.11**. We now focus on a member's right to a dividend payment.

Right to a dividend

21.4 Generally, shareholders have no right to a dividend payment, even where the distributable profits are available, if the directors decide not to declare one. For example, article 116 of Table A provides:

---

1 See Chapter 15.
2 See Chapters 32 and 33.
3 See Part X B.
4 See **19.55**.

'The company in general meeting may declare dividends, but no dividend shall exceed the amount recommended by the directors.'

The directors are also empowered by article 117 to pay to members such interim dividends as appear to them to be justified by the profits of the company.

In *Scott v Scott*,[1] a resolution, passed by the company in general meeting, that the directors should pay an interim dividend, was held to be inoperative.

An interim dividend is one passed on a date between two annual general meetings of the company. Clearly, from the judgment in *Scott v Scott*, reinforcing article 117, a majority of investors cannot compel the directors to declare an interim dividend.[2]

Again, article 118 of Table A stipulates that no dividend or interim dividend can legally be paid otherwise than in accordance with Part IV of the 1983 Act.

The provisions of Part IV which apply concern profits[3] available for distribution and restrictions on the distribution of assets.

The fundamental statutory rule is that a company cannot make a distribution except out of its accumulated realised profits, less its accumulated realised losses (see **19.54**).

Again, the directors may, before recommending any dividend, set aside out of the profits of the company such sums as they think proper as a reserve which shall, at the discretion of the directors, be applicable for any purpose to which the profits of the company may be properly applied, and pending such application may, either be employed in the business of the company, or be invested in such investments as the directors may lawfully determine. The directors may also, without placing the same to reserve, carry forward any profits which they may think it prudent not to divide.[4]

Amount of dividend payable

21.5   The dividends on preference shares are usually paid at a fixed rate, eg six per cent, whereas dividends paid to ordinary shareholders will vary according to the amount of the distributable profit. If there is only sufficient distributable profit to pay the fixed dividends to the preference shareholders, then the ordinary shareholders will not receive any dividend.

If the company has incurred a trading loss, it will not be able to pay dividends to either preference or ordinary shareholders.

The articles usually stipulate the amounts to be paid. For example, article 120 of Table A provides that, subject to the rights of special classes such as preference shareholders, 'all dividends shall be declared and paid according to the amounts paid (or credited as paid)' on the relevant shares.

1 [1943] 1 All ER 582.
2 Except, perhaps, in the case of fraud: *Thairlwall v Great Northern Rly Co* [1910] 2 KB 509.
3 Sections 45 and 45A – see **19.54**.
4 Article 119 of Table A – see **14.14**.

Mode of payment

21.6 The mode of payment for dividends is normally determined by the articles. For example, article 123 of Table A provides that any dividend payable in cash in respect of any shares may be paid by cheque or warrant sent through the post to the registered address of the member.

Shares in lieu of dividends

21.7 Members can also be offered extra shares in lieu of dividend payments (see **14.13** and **14.15**).

Effect of declaration of dividend

21.8 The declaration of a dividend creates a contract debt from the company to the shareholder. Because the articles of association bind the investors in a s 25 contract[1] as if they had covenanted under seal, the debt is in the nature of a specialty debt, and thus not barred for a period of 12 years.[2]

Dividends are no longer debts owed by the company if a winding up occurs. In this event, the shareholder's right to sue for his arrears of dividend is deferred until the debts of the company's trading creditors have been satisfied.[3]

FINANCIAL LIABILITIES OF MEMBERS

21.9 When a member has paid the full nominal value for his shares, then, on the winding up of the company, he incurs no further liability – his liability being limited to the amount, if any, unpaid on his shares.[4]

Where any share is issued with less than the nominal value paid on allotment, it is partly paid. Generally, the company is entitled to require the unpaid amount of shares to be paid at any time. However, the articles usually make provision for such payments 'by instalments' to be made.

Whilst normally payment for shares is required in full, in the case of a newly formed company, the directors may consider that payment of the full value of each share is not required at once. Such issued 'partly paid' shares therefore are paid for by instalments. A request by the company to the shareholders for a part payment is known as a *call*. For example, the issuing company may require 50p per £1 share paid on allotment, followed by two further calls of 25p each.

---

1 See previous chapter.
2 *Re Belfast Empire Theatre of Varieties* [1963] IR 41.
3 *Wilson (Inspector of Taxes) v Dunnes Stores (Cork) Ltd* (Unreported) 22 January 1976 (HC) – see also Part X A.
4 See Chapter 4.

Making a call for payment

21.10 An example of a procedure for the making of calls is to be found in Table A, articles 15 to 21.

Article 15 empowers the directors from time to time to make calls upon the investors in respect of any money unpaid on their shares (whether on account of the nominal value or by way of premium).

A call is made at the time the directors' resolution was passed.[1]

Calls should be made by directors equally on all shareholders. In *Alexander v Automatic Telephone Co*,[2] it was held to be an abuse of power, when directors made calls on shareholders other than themselves.

In *Galloway v Halle Concerts Society*,[3] Sargant J stated:

'Prima facie ... there is ... an implied condition of equality between shareholders in a company, and ... prima facie it is entirely improper for the directors to make a call on some members of a class of shareholders ... without making a similar call on all the other members of that class.'

Article 20 of Table A allows directors:

'on the issue of shares, [to] differentiate between the holders as to the amount of calls to be paid and the times of payment.'

Such powers must be used by the directors in good faith and for the benefit of the company.

Limits

21.11 There is a limit on the amount that can be called, ie no call shall exceed one-quarter of the nominal value of the share or be payable at less than one month from the date fixed for the payment of the last preceding call, and each member shall (subject to receiving at least 14 days' notice specifying the time or times and place of payment) pay to the company at the time or times and place so specified the amount called on his shares. A call may be revoked or postponed as the directors may determine.

Early payment of calls

21.12 Article 21 permits the early or advance payment of calls, and allows the directors to pay interest of up to five per cent on the money advanced.

Late payment

21.13 Under article 18, a member may be liable to pay interest not exceeding five per cent for late payments, although the directors can waive payment of this interest.

---

1 See article 16 of Table A.
2 [1900] 2 Ch 56.
3 [1915] 2 Ch 233.

Non-payment of calls

21.14 The company has sanctions against investors who do not meet calls made on them. These sanctions are:

(1) forfeiture;
(2) surrender; and
(3) lien.

Forfeiture of shares

21.15 A company can take the powers in its articles to forfeit shares as illustrated by articles 33 to 39 of Table A.

Notice of forfeiture

21.16 If an investor fails to pay any call[1] on the day appointed for payment thereof, the directors may, at any time whilst any part of the call remains unpaid, serve a notice on him requiring payment of so much of the call as is unpaid together with any interest which may have accrued.

The notice must name a further day (not earlier than 14 days from the date of service of the notice) on or before which the payment required by the notice is to be made, and shall warn that, in the event of non-payment at or before the time appointed, the shares in respect of which the call was made will be liable to be forfeited.

If the requirements of the notice are not complied with, the shares in question may be forfeited by resolution of the directors.[2]

Effect of forfeiture

21.17 A forfeited share may be sold or reissued on such terms as the directors think fit. An investor whose shares have been forfeited ceases to be a member of the company. Notwithstanding, article 37 imposes a liability on him to pay calls due at the date of forfeiture, unless these unpaid calls have been paid by a subsequent holder of them.

Section 43(1) of the 1983 Act imposes a time limit on a plc within which to sell shares which have been forfeited or surrendered. These shares must be sold within three years. If not, they must be cancelled. This action would have the effect of reducing the amount of the plc's nominal share capital.[3]

Surrender of shares

21.18 An investor is only allowed[4] to voluntarily surrender his shares where they could have been forfeited and it is desired to avoid the formalities attached

---

1 Or instalment of a call.
2 See article 35.
3 See Chapter 19.
4 If there is authority in the articles.

to forfeiture. Otherwise, a surrender would be classified as an unlawful reduction of the company's capital.

Lien on members' shares

21.19   A lien is a legal right to hold another person's goods/assets, and keep them until a debt owed by that person has been paid.

Normally, the articles[1] give the company a 'non-possessory' lien on the members' shares for non-payment of calls. For example, article 11 of Table A provides:

> 'The company shall have a first and paramount lien on every share (not being a fully paid share) for all monies (whether immediately payable or not) called or payable at a fixed time in respect of that share; but the directors may at any time declare any share to be wholly or in part exempt from the provisions of this regulation. The company's lien on a share shall extend to all dividends payable thereon.'

The company may enforce its security by selling the shares under powers given to it in articles 12 and 13.

If the proceeds of the sale exceed the amount owed on the shares, the balance must be paid to the member – see article 14.

Notice of other interests

21.20   Cases such as *Bradford Banking Co v Briggs*[2] and *Rearden v Provincial Bank of Ireland*[3] suggest that, although no notice of any trust or equitable interest in its shares is registerable[4] by the company, it must, nevertheless, take notice of such interests when a question of priorities to title arises between the company and a third party. This situation could arise in circumstances involving the exercise of a company's lien over an investor's shares.

Because of the possibilities of problems arising relating to third party interests, the remedy of forfeiture would seem to be a much more effective and practical remedy for non-payment of calls, than the exercising of a lien on the defaulting member's shares.

---

1   Section 44 of the 1983 Act also restricts a plc taking a lien or charge on its own shares.
2   (1986) 12 App Cas 29.
3   [1896] 1 IR 532 (ChD).
4   See **22.2** et seq.

Chapter 22

DISCLOSURE AND TRANSFERS OF SHAREHOLDERS' INTERESTS

THE REGISTER

22.1 We shall see[1] that the interests of directors, secretaries and their families in the shares and debentures of the company must be noted in a register of directors' and secretaries' interests.

DISCLOSURE OF INTERESTS IN SHARES

22.2 The disclosure regime under the 1990 Act is contained in Part IV. It involves the *disclosure* of interests in shares in the following circumstances:

(1) share dealings by directors, secretaries and their families;
(2) in the case of individual and group acquisitions:
    (a) the disclosure of interests exceeding five per cent in the voting shares of a plc held by any person;
    (b) the notification of interests of concert parties in the shares of a plc;
    (c) the keeping of a register of notified interests of shares in a plc.

Share dealings by directors, secretaries and their families

22.3 The 1990 Act requires the disclosure of beneficial interests of directors, secretaries and their families – see Chapter 27. This requirement applies to both public and private companies.

Disclosure of significant interests in shares of a plc

22.4 Any person holding an interest in voting shares exceeding five per cent of the company's issued share capital, must notify a plc of their significant share holding in it.[2]

A person is deemed to be interested in any shares:[3]

(1) in which his spouse or minor child has an interest;
(2) held by a body corporate if:
    (a) the body corporate or its directors are accustomed to act in accordance with his directions or instructions; or
    (b) he has the control of one-third or more of the voting power at that body corporate's general meetings;

---

1 In Chapter 27.
2 Disposal of a significant share holding is also notifiable – see ss 72 and 73.
3 For notification purposes – see ss 72 and 73.

(3) held under a concert party agreement of which he is a member (see **22.8**).

Register of significant interests

22.5   Section 80 provides for the keeping of a register of notified significant (five per cent) interests in shares by every plc. This register must be updated within three days of a new notification being received.

There are detailed procedures contained in s 80 for the maintenance of this register.

Investigations of interests in shares

22.6   If a plc knows, or has reasonable cause to believe, that a person was interested in its voting shares during the preceding three years, it may, by written notice, ask him to confirm or deny the holding. If he confirms the holding, the company may require him to provide further details.[1]

If the recipient of a notice fails to give the information within such a time period as the company may specify, the company may apply to the court for an order directing that the rights attaching to the shares in question be restricted.[2]

A plc must include in its s 80 register of significant interests, information which it receives in response to notification enquiries made by it. The information must be entered in a separate part of the register.[3]

Members of a public limited company holding at least 10 per cent of the voting paid-up share capital can also require the company to investigate any interests in its voting shares.[4]

After the investigation has been completed, the company must make available a report to its investors at its registered office. Interim reports must be made available at three-monthly intervals until a final report is made.[5]

The register of significant interests, and any company investigation report required by s 84, must be made available for inspection to members and other persons. Copies of such documents must also be made available by the company on payment of a fee.[6]

---

1 Section 81. The penalty for failure to supply this information is detailed in s 85, as amended by the Schedule, Part 2, of the 2001 Act.
2 Section 85.
3 Section 82.
4 Section 83.
5 Section 84.
6 Section 88.

Notification of thresholds to Stock Exchange

22.7 The 1990 Act also implemented the EU Major Holdings Directive[1] whose objective is to harmonise the rules relating to information publishable when a major holding in a listed company is acquired or sold.

If a person acquires or disposes of an interest in an Irish public limited company which results in an ownership threshold of 10 per cent, 25 per cent, 50 per cent or 75 per cent being exceeded or reduced below, that person must, in addition, to notifying the company of the change in interest, also notify the Stock Exchange.

The Stock Exchange is required to publish the information within three days of the receipt of the declaration.[2]

The exchange is required to report breaches of notification to the Director of Corporate Enforcement.[3] The Director may initiate proceedings for breach of s 91, or can refer the matter to the DPP for him to do so.

Notification of interests of concert parties

22.8 A concert party is an arrangement whereby several people or companies work together to acquire another (target) company through a takeover bid.[4]

Parties acting in concert must keep each other informed[5] of all relevant facts in relation to interests held in a plc.

They must also notify the company of the names and addresses of the parties to their takeover agreement.[6] Thus, disclosure is now required by parties acting in concert both to each other and to the company.

Disclosure orders for interests in private companies

22.9 A disclosure order is defined in s 98 of the 1990 Act as an order of the court which obliges:

(1) any person whom the court believes to have or to be able to obtain any information as to:
    (a) persons interested at present, or at any time during a period specified in the order, in the shares or debentures of a company;
    (b) the names and addresses of any of those persons;
    (c) the name and address of any person who acts or has acted on behalf of any of those persons in relation to the shares or debentures,

---

1 Directive 88/627/EEC of 12 December 1988.
2 Section 91. See also ss 92–96 which deal with, inter alia, obligation of professional secrecy, immunity from suit and the application and amendment of the 1984 Regulations mentioned in Chapter 10. Section 94 was amended by the Schedule, Part 2 of the 2001 Act.
3 Section 92, as amended by s 36 of the 2001 Act.
4 See s 73 for detailed statutory definition.
5 See ss 74 and 75.
6 See s 74(4) and (5).

to give such information to the court; or

(2) any person whom the court believes to be, or at any time during a period specified in the order to have been, interested in shares or debentures of a company to confirm that fact or (as the case may be) to indicate whether or not it is the case and, where he holds any interest[1] in such shares or debentures, to give such further information as the court may require; or

(3) any person interested specified in the order, to disclose the information required in (1) above.

Exempted companies

22.10   Section 97 provides that a disclosure order will *not* be available against the following companies:

(1) plcs;

(2) building, industrial and provident societies; and

(3) any body corporate which is prohibited by statute or otherwise from making any distribution of its income or property among its members while it is a going concern or when it is in liquidation.

Who can apply for a disclosure order?

22.11   Any person who has a financial interest in a company may apply to the court for a disclosure order.

A person with a financial interest is defined as a member, contributory, creditor, employee, co-adventurer, examiner, lessor, lessee, licensor, licensee, liquidator or receiver in relation to the company or a related company.

The court will only make the disclosure order if:

(1) it deems it just and equitable to do so; and

(2) it is of the opinion that the financial interest of the applicant is or will be prejudiced by the non-disclosure of any interest in the shares or debentures of the company.

Notice of the order must be sent to the parties specified in s 102. These include the registrar of companies.

Scope of disclosure order

22.12   Section 100 sets out details of what information must be disclosed by the addressee of a disclosure order. The interests to be disclosed under s 100 include those of beneficiary under a trust and of a person, who, though not a shareholder, can influence and control the exercise of the rights of the named shareholder.

---

1 Or has, during that period, held any interest.

Where information on interests held in shares, etc is furnished to the applicant for a disclosure order, or to a company, the court may impose such restrictions[1] on the publication of this information as it thinks fit.

Contravention of disclosure order

22.13   Where the addressee fails to comply with the terms of a disclosure order, his rights under the non-disclosed shares become unenforceable, unless the court is satisfied that his failure to comply was accidental or due to some other sufficient cause.[2]

TRANSFER OF SHARES

22.14   A transfer of shares may take place voluntarily or involuntarily, ie compulsorily. An example of a voluntary transfer is where the shareholder sells the shares or makes a gift of them. An involuntary transfer is one that takes place automatically on the death, bankruptcy or insanity of the member.

Sections 81 to 84 of the 1963 Act make it clear that there are two distinct stages in the process of completing both voluntary and involuntary transfers of shares. These stages are:

(1) assignment of his interest by the holder to the transferee; and
(2) registration of the transferee as a member of the company, ie the entering of his name in the register of members.

Assignment of interest

22.15   Sections 81 and 82 provide that it shall not be lawful for any company to register a transfer of shares (or debentures) unless a proper instrument of transfer has been delivered to the company. In other words, if, and when, the seller completes the proper instrument of transfer, ie a Stock Transfer Form, this first stage of the transaction is in order and complete.

The Stock Transfer Form

22.16   Section 79 of the 1963 Act classifies shares as personal (rather than real) estate and 'transferable in the manner provided in the articles of the company'.

Articles 22 and 23 of Table A provide:

> '**22.** The instrument of transfer of any share shall be executed by or on behalf of the transferor and transferee, and the transferor shall be deemed to remain the holder of the share until the name of the transferee is entered in the register in respect thereof.

---

1 Section 103(4).
2 Section 104.

23. Subject to such of the restrictions of these regulations as may be applicable, any member may transfer all or any of his shares by instrument in writing in any usual or common form or any other form which the directors may approve.'

Whilst article 23 permits the use of 'any other form which the directors may approve', under the Stock Transfer Act 1963, there is a standard 'Stock Transfer Form' used for the transfer of shares. However, it is the contents of the form that are essential, and any form embodying these contents would probably suffice.

Contents[1]

22.17   The main details required by the Stock Transfer Form include:

(1) amount of the consideration money;
(2) full name of undertaking, ie the company whose shares are being transferred;
(3) full description of security, eg ordinary shares;
(4) number or amount of shares;
(5) the name(s) of registered holder(s). The address should be given if there is only one holder. If the transfer is not being made by the registered holders, the capacity of the person(s) making the transfer must be indicated, eg on the death of the member, his shares would be transferred by the executors[2] named in his will;
(6) the name(s) and address(es) of the person(s) to whom the security is transferred;
(7) signature(s) of transferor(s) to the following declaration: 'I/We hereby transfer the above security out of the name(s) aforesaid to the person(s) named ...'.

The transfer also requests that such entries be made in the register of members as is necessary to give effect to the transfer.

There are also parts[3] of the form which must be stamped by the selling and buying brokers and the certifying Stock Exchange.

The effect of the computerised CREST system on the Stock Transfer Form is mentioned in **22.41**.

Procedure

22.18   The transferor signs the completed Stock Transfer Form and delivers it to the transferee (or his brokers), together with the original share certificates.[4]

---

1 See P. Egan, A. Gilvarry and M. Graham *Irish Company Secretarial Precedents* (Jordans, 1993), at pp 98 and 99, for example of Stock Transfer Form.
2 See **22.44**.
3 There is also a section dealing with a certificate required where the transfer is not liable to ad valorem stamp duty.
4 Or instead, a Stock Transfer Form certificated as provided for in s 85 of the 1963 Act. This may be necessary if the seller is retaining some shares or where there are several transferees.

The share transfer is then completed by insertion of the name of the transferee, who may be the person who now owns the shares beneficially, or his nominee. Following this, the transfer form is lodged with the company secretary or the registrar who performs the function of registration. In a company with articles in the form of Table A (see article 24), the directors may refuse to register the transfer of shares.

Consequences

22.19 As between the parties, the transaction will be completed on the exchange of the share certificates and transfer form for the consideration, unless the contract for the purchase of the shares expressly provides otherwise. Assuming that it does not, the transaction is at the end of phase 1. The legal position of both parties is now clearly stated in article 22 of Table A which stipulates that 'the transferor shall be deemed to remain the holder of the share until the name of the transferee is entered in the register of members'. In other words, despite the transfer of ownership of the shares, the transferor still remains the member.

Registration of the transferee

22.20 The transfer is complete as between the transferor and transferee at the end of phase 1. However, the transfer is not complete as between the company and the parties at that stage: registration of the transferee's name is required for this.

Section 83 of the 1963 Act places the onus on the company to enter the name of the transferee in its register of members 'on the application of the transferor'. As illustrated in the outline contents of the Stock Transfer Form above (see **22.17**), this form includes a request by the transferor to the company to make the necessary entries in the register to give effect to the transfer. However, the directors are not bound to approve the proposed transfer.

Directors' powers to refuse registration in private companies

22.21 As we saw in **14.20**, the directors of private companies are given the power by article 3 of Table A, Part II, 'in their absolute discretion, and without assigning any reasons therefor, [to] decline to register the transfer of any share'.

In *Re Smith and Fawcett Ltd,*[1] the articles gave directors absolute discretion to refuse to register any transfer of shares. Fawcett died. His executor applied to have the deceased's shares registered in his name. Smith refused to register a transfer of the full holding, but offered to register part and to buy the balance.

---

1 [1942] 1 All ER 524, [1942] Ch 304. Smith and Fawcett each held 50 per cent of the issued share capital of the company.

The court held that the power to refuse registration need not be limited to matters personal to the transferee, and that the only limitation on that power was that, being fiduciary, it must be exercised bona fide in the interests of the company. The court then concluded that it could see no reason for saying that the director's action was *not* bona fide in this case.

Lord Greene MR stated in his judgment:

'The language of the article in the present case does not point out any particular matter as being the only matter to which the directors are to pay attention in deciding whether or not they will allow the transfer to be registered. The article does not, for instance, say, as is to be found in some articles, that they may refuse to register any transfer of shares to a person not already a member of the company [ie an outsider] or to a transferee of whom they do not approve. Where articles are framed with some such limitation on the discretionary power of refusal as I have mentioned in these two examples, it follows on plain principles [of interpretation] that if the directors go outside [the articles] ... the directors will have exceeded their powers ... The question, therefore, simply is whether on the true construction of the particular article the directors are limited by anything except their bona fide view as to the interests of the company. In the present case, the article is drafted in the widest possible terms, and I decline to write into that clear language any limitation other than a limitation, which is implicit by law, that a fiduciary power of this kind must be exercised bona fide in the interests of the company. Subject to that qualification, an article in this form appears to me to give the directors what it says, namely, an absolute and uncontrolled discretion.'

22.22   Lord Greene also said that:

'The principles to be applied in cases where the articles of a company confer a discretion on directors with regard to the acceptance of transfers of shares are ... free from doubt. [The directors] must exercise their discretion bona fide in what they consider – not what a court may consider – is in the interests of the company, and not for any collateral purpose.'

Directors need not give reasons for refusal

22.23   In the absence of evidence of mala fides,[1] the court will refuse to intervene in the exercise by directors of their discretion. Furthermore, from the wording of article 3 it is clear that the directors of a private company need not give reasons for declining to register a transferee. For example, in *Re Hafner, Olhausen v Powderly*,[2] Black J confirmed that, '[The directors] are not bound to assign their reasons, and the court is not entitled to infer merely from their omission to do so, that their reasons were not legitimate'.

However, having confirmed that directors need not give reasons for refusing to register a transfer, Black J also admitted that, 'like many another settled rule ... it is not proof against possible exceptions'.

---

1 See *Re Coalport China Co* [1895] 2 Chapter 404.
2 [1943] IR 426. If, however, the directors do give reasons for refusal to register the transferee, the court is at liberty to consider the validity of these reasons – see *Tett v Phoenix Property Co* [1984] BCLC 599.

22.24   In *Re Dublin North City Milling Co*,[1] Meredith MR approved of the judgment of Lindley LJ,[2] who had stated:

> 'I have not the slightest doubt that the court has ample power to control the refusal of directors [to give reasons for their decisions] provided there is some evidence which justifies the court in coming to the conclusion that they have not done their duty [bona fide].'

Thus, to impugn the directors' motive for refusing to give reasons, a rejected transferee must allege and prove mala fides on the part of directors in refusing his application. This was successfully achieved in *Re Hafner*.

22.25   In *Clark v Workman*,[3] the directors, after approving the proposed transfer of a controlling interest in the company, failed to refute an unsubstantiated allegation that the transferees intended to use the assets of the company to finance their own business. Because the directors failed to answer the allegation, the court overturned their approval of the proposed transfer.

22.26   By contrast, the directors in *Popely v Planarrive Ltd*[4] exercised their absolute discretion in refusing to register shares in the plaintiff's name which would have given him control of the company. Evidence was adduced to the court showing that the plaintiff's actions had made him a less than ideal person to gain control of the company.[5]

The court held that as any reasonable board would have taken the same decision, the directors had acted bona fide and in the best interest of the company in refusing to register the plaintiff as a member.

Section 205 relief?

22.27   If the transferor of shares can prove that the directors exercised their powers to refuse registration of the transferee in an oppressive manner, or in disregard of his interests as a member, he may be able to petition for relief under s 205.

Where a transferee of shares is not registered, the transferor holds the shares in trust for the transferee.[6] He also remains a member and can therefore, if he wishes,[7] assist the transferee by seeking relief under s 205. Section 205(6) makes it clear that 'any trustee' may apply to the court for relief under s 205.

If the directors did not furnish reasons for their decision in response to a s 205 action, it seems likely that the court would rule against them.

---

1 [1909] 1 IR 179.
2 In *Re Coalport China Co* [1895] 2 Ch 404.
3 [1920] 1 IR 107.
4 [1997] 1 BCLC 8.
5 For example, he had interfered with the company's business and involved it in unnecessary and unsuccessful litigation.
6 See **22.36** et seq.
7 He may also be contractually bound to do so if the contract for the sale of shares contained such an express provision.

Again, the unregistered transferee has an equitable interest in the shares. Consequently, he may be able to pursue relief under s 205(1) in his own right because the section also extends to embrace 'persons beneficially interested in the shares'.

Accordingly, both transferor and transferee[1] probably have rights to seek relief from the courts for non-registration on grounds of oppression or disregard of their interests as members.

Time limit for directors' decision

22.28 The directors must, within two months after the date on which the transfer documentation was lodged with the company, send the rejected transferee notice of their refusal to register him as a member – see s 84 of the 1963 Act (although article 27 of Table A, by allowing companies to close their registers for up to 30 days per annum, may extend this two-month period of notice).

Where the directors fail to communicate their decision to a transferee within the statutory two-month period, it is likely that their powers to decline his registration will be deemed to have lapsed[2] (see also **22.34**).

In *Popely v Planarrive Ltd*,[3] the directors refused to register Popely as a member because to do so would have given him control of the company. The company's articles, whilst giving the directors absolute discretion to refuse registration of a transferee, also stipulated that they should communicate their decision to the applicant within two months.

The directors made their decision to refuse registration within the two-month period, but failed to notify the plaintiff within this time limit. As a result, Popely sought rectification of the register of members under the UK equivalent of s 122 of the 1963 Act.

The court held that the two-month time limit in the articles only applied to the exercise of the directors' powers. Failure to exercise them with the two months would have made them lapse. However, as the directors had exercised their powers in this case they were still valid, and the plaintiff was refused rectification of the register (but see **22.34**).

Valuing shares in private companies

22.29 The methods used in valuing shares also emphasise the differences between public and private companies.

---

1 See *Re Swaledale Cleaners Ltd* [1968] I WLR 1710.
2 Section 205(6) permits a transferee to be treated as a full member for the purpose of seeking relief under s 205.
3 [1997] 1 BCLC 8.

Shares in plcs are valued according to their prevailing market valuation on the Stock Exchange. This price level accurately reflects the market forces of supply and demand.

By contrast, there is no public market for any dealings in the shares of private companies.

The articles of most private companies would usually provide that their shares were to be valued by the auditor, and in carrying out this function he would be deemed to be acting as an expert and not as an arbitrator.

In *Dean v Prince*,[1] the court had to consider the principles on which an auditor should find a 'fair value' of a private company.

Dean, Prince and Cowen were each shareholders and directors of a company which was incurring financial losses. Dean, the majority shareholder, died. Under the articles the surviving directors were obliged to buy his shares at a valuation certified to be 'fair' by the auditor, acting as expert.

Mrs Dean disagreed with the auditor's valuation and Harmon J overturned it. On appeal the auditor's original valuation was upheld, the court deciding that:

(1) the controlling interest should not be valued at a premium in this instance; and
(2) as the loss making company was on the verge of insolvency, it was appropriate to value it on a 'break-up' basis and not as a viable going concern.

In *Colgan v Colgan and Colgan*,[2] Costello J confirmed that in a quasi-partnership company, majority shareholdings should not be entitled to a premium. Instead, all shareholdings (majority and minority) should be valued on a pro rata basis.

O'Hanlon J, in *Re Clubman Shirts Ltd*,[3] like Lord Denning in *Dean v Prince*, also took the view that a company trading at a loss should properly be valued on a break-up[4] basis rather than as a going concern.

Pre-emption rights

22.30   The personal quasi-partnership nature of a private company requires a certain amount of control to be retained over the admission of new members to the 'business' or the company. As a result, in addition to the directors' power to refuse registration under article 3, many articles will also contain pre-emption rights, ie rights of first refusal, whereby a member wishing to sell his shares must first notify the board, and arrange for the shares to be offered to the other members in proportion to their existing shareholdings. The articles may also stipulate that the selling price should be calculated by the company's auditor.

---

1 [1954] Ch 409 (CA).
2 (Unreported) 22 July 1993 (HC).
3 [1993] ILRM 323.
4 Ie a net asset valuation basis. Valuation of shares in the context of relief under s 205 of the 1963 Act is dealt with in **16.21** et seq.

Under a pre-emption rights clause, it is only in the event of the existing members not wishing to purchase the shares that the seller may then offer them for sale to 'outsiders'.

The courts have enforced articles containing pre-emption rights in *Lee & Co (Dublin) Ltd v Egan (Wholesale) Ltd*[1] and in *Re Champion Publications Ltd.*[2]

Section 23 of the 1983 Act introduced the concept of statutory pre-emption rights for shareholders of both private and public companies.[3]

Summary – private company share transfers

22.31 If a shareholder wishes to dispose of his shares in a private limited company, he must make application to the company by means of a duly executed transfer form. But the directors are not bound to approve the proposed transfer. It will be recalled that one of the three distinguishing features of a private limited company is that it restricts the right to transfer its shares. In other words, the company's shares are not freely marketable on the stock market in the same way as the shares of a public company. Thus, if the directors do not approve of the transferee, they will refuse the holder's application to transfer his shares to him, and their decision is final. No reasons need be given for their refusal, provided that the directors are acting in good faith and for the benefit of the company.

Directors' powers to refuse registration in plcs

22.32 Unlike the shares in a private company, those in a plc are generally freely transferable. However, here, too, the directors possess the power to refuse registration of a transfer, but their power of refusal is less than that enjoyed by the directors of private companies. For example, under article 24[4] of Table A, the directors of a plc have a discretion to decline to register the transferee. In *Re Dublin North City Milling Co Ltd,*[5] the articles provided that the directors, on behalf of the company, may decline to register any transfer. A shareholder purchased additional shares in the company and the directors refused to register the transfer. In his judgment, Meredith J said:

> 'I dislike mystery, but I think the law is wise in refusing to compel directors to disclose their reasons for accepting or declining a transfer. The directors have kept themselves within the rule, and the reasons operating on their minds are not disclosed, and I cannot speculate or guess as to what they were. There could not have been anything dishonourable, or anything approaching personal unfitness on the part of [the shareholder]. But I am of opinion that the law allows the directors to hold their tongues. It allows them to say that everything was done honestly and bona fide in the interests of their company; and they have

---

1 (Unreported) 27 April 1978 (HC).
2 (Unreported) 4 June 1991 (HC).
3 See **10.25**.
4 See **14.20**.
5 [1909] 1 IR 179.

unanimously decided that it is not for the interest or advantage of the company that these shares should be transferred to [the shareholder] and according to my view I have no power to make them say more.

If [the shareholder] had made a clear, definite charge against the directors of corruption, or conspiracy, or dishonesty, I should have had them examined before me; and if I came to the conclusion that they had not acted fairly and honestly, I should compel them to register the transfer. There is no proof that these directors did not act in the way that they were entitled to act under the articles.'

Meredith J concluded that, even though the transferee was already a member,[1] the board had acted bona fide.

From this judgment, it would appear that the courts are reluctant to interfere in instances where directors are exercising the powers to refuse registration under either article 24 or article 3 of Table A.

Notice of refusal to register

22.33 Section 84 of the 1963 Act stipulates that, if the company refuses to register a transfer, it must, within two months after the date on which the transfer is lodged with it, send the transferee notice of the refusal.

If the company does not issue this notice of refusal under s 84, its right to refuse registration will probably be considered unenforceable.

Delays

22.34 In *Re Sussex Brick Co*,[2] it was held that where default or unnecessary delay takes place in entering the transferee's name in the register, the court can order both rectification of the register and payment of damages, even if the company is being wound up (see also **22.28**).

Consequences of non-registration

22.35 There is no implied condition in a contract for the sale of shares that the company will register the purchaser as a member.[3]

Until a share transfer is registered, the transferor holds them as nominee for the transferee. This is a trust relationship which is recognised in equity but not in law. Section 123 of the 1963 Act specifies that no notice of a trust shall be entered on the register of members.

The transferor will be obliged to account to the transferee for any benefit he may receive.

---

1 In *Tangney v Clarence Hotel Co Ltd* [1933] IR 51 (HC), it was held that a restriction on transfer to an undesirable person could not be applied to a person who was already a member of the company.
2 [1904] 1 Ch 598.
3 *Casey v Bentley* [1902] 1 IR 376 (CA).

Non-registration and subsequent transfers

22.36 When only phase 1 of the transfer process is completed, the company having refused to register the transferee, the rights of the parties are:

(1) the transferor, as the registered holder of the shares, is the legal owner; and
(2) the transferee, whilst beneficially entitled to the shares, has merely an equitable interest.

Competing claims

22.37 Disputes can arise between the registered holder of the shares and a claimant asserting a prior equity, or between two competing equitable interests in the shares.

Generally, all rights of a registered holder, as legal owner of the shares, will prevail over a prior equitable claimant, if the registered holder gave valuable consideration for the shares and had no notice of the prior equitable interest.[1]

Where there is a conflict between two equitable interests in the same shares, the rules of equity apply as follows:

(1) where the equities are equal, the first to register has priority;
(2) where the equities are equal and neither is registered, the first in time prevails.

It is therefore important that shares are registered as soon as possible. Such registration will only prevail, however, if the transferee is a purchaser for value without prior notice of the equities, ie the third party interests. Thus, the interest of a recipient of the shares as a gift would not be protected by registration.

To be without prior notice of equities means that there must have been no reason in the manner of the conduct of the transaction which would have put a reasonable transferee on enquiry. For example, if the transferee is handed the original share certificates or good forgeries of them, there would be no apparent reason to put him on enquiry. As a result, the company may be estopped from denying the validity of a forged certificate – see **20.37**.

Whilst the handing over of share certificates is not absolutely necessary, if they are missing, the transferee is put on enquiry. In fact, companies would normally refuse to register share transfers where the original share certificates do not accompany the completed Stock Transfer Form – see article 25 of Table A.

---

1 See also **39.15**.

Forged transfers

22.38 If a transfer is forged, and the company registers the transferee, the true owner remains entitled to be put back on the register.[1] Where the company issues a certificate on foot of the forged transfer, and any person acts on the faith of it and suffers damage, the company may be liable.

Certification of transfer

22.39 If a shareholder wishes to transfer only part of his holding, a new share certificate will be required. Section 85 of the 1963 Act provides for this situation by making available to the company a procedure by which it can certificate the transfer of shares. For example, if A has 10,000 shares and sells 5,000 to B, he can deliver the certificate and transfer form to the company. The company will then stamp on the transfer form (before it is handed to B) 'certificate for 10,000 shares has been lodged at the company's office'.

On registration of the transfer, the company prepares two new certificates for 5,000 shares each for A and B.

A 'certified transfer' under s 85 is, of course, accepted by the Stock Exchange as a good delivery of the shares.

Rights issues[2] and voluntary share transfers

22.40 Where a company makes a rights issue of new shares, they generally include a renounceable letter by means of which the recipients can sell and transfer them.

The letter usually states that the allottee is entitled to a certain number of shares upon acceptance but it will have printed on it a letter of renunciation and an application for registration. If the allottee wishes to sell his rights or gift them to somebody else, he signs the renunciation form and delivers it to the transferee. The latter can also sign and pass it on to someone else.

Eventually, the application for registration will be completed and sent to the company.

Computerised transfers of shares

22.41 In July 1996, a new computerised system for settling sales and purchases of shares was introduced into both the UK and Irish Stock Exchanges. This system is known as CREST.

In Ireland, CREST has replaced the former Talisman system which involved the use of a nominee stock exchange company called Sepon Ltd.

---

1 *Sheffield Corporation v Barclay* [1905] AC 392. However, the company can claim an indemnity from the person responsible for perpetrating the fraudulent transfer.
2 See Chapter 10.

CREST is intended to bring the systems in the UK and Ireland up to the best international standards. It will achieve this aim by making settlement cheaper, faster and more secure.

Under CREST, each investor, if he elects, will be able to hold his share certificates in electronic form as a computer record, rather than on paper.

The introduction of CREST meant that ss 79 and 81 of the 1963 Act and s 2(1) of the Stock Transfer Act 1963 needed to be amended. This was done by reg 4(1) of the Companies Act 1990 (Uncertificated Securities) Regulations 1996[1] (the 1996 Regulations). Regulation 4(1) now permits the evidencing and transferring of title to securities without a written instrument, provided the procedures set out in the 1996 Regulations are followed.

A new vocabulary

22.42 In the 1996 Regulations, the computer based system and procedures are known as the *relevant system*. The legal framework underlying the operation of the relevant system, together with the criteria which the operator and the relevant system must meet, are contained in these lengthy regulations.

A unit of a security which may be transferred is referred to as an *uncertificated unit*.

A security, the units of which may become uncertificated, is known as a *participating security*.

An issuer which issues a participating security may be referred to as a *participating issuer*. Instructions sent by means of the relevant system will be known as *dematerialised instructions*.

The 1996 Regulations outlined

22.43 Chapter II of the 1996 Regulations deals with a range of matters relating to transfers of title to securities (including transfers of uncertified holdings, transfers from uncertificated to certificated holdings and vice-versa) through a dematerialised system; the recording and registration of these transfers and the obligations imposed on participating issuers.

Chapter III provides for the approval of an operator by the Minister or recognition by him of an operator already approved by a competent authority of a Member State of the EU. The Minister may delegate these approval and supervisory functions to a designated body, if he so wishes.

Provision is made in Chapter IV to prevent persons sending dematerialised instructions from denying particular matters relating to them. This chapter also compels persons receiving such instructions to accept, with certain exceptions, that the information contained in them, and matters relating to them, are correct.

---

1 SI 1996/68. Section 11 of the Electronic Commerce Act 2000 confirms that nothing in that Act is to prejudice the operation of the 1996 Regulations.

Chapter V details certain notices to be issued in respect of minority shareholdings resulting from a take-over situation, whilst supplementary provisions designed to overcome evidential problems which may arise in relation to system entries, are included in Chapter VI.

The *Schedule* to the Regulations sets out the requirements for approval and continuing operation of a person as an operator within the CREST system.

The practical consequence of the new stock exchange system is that much of the administrative work associated with share transfers is devolved to the exchange's member firms.

Involuntary share transfers

22.44   Sections 81 and 82 of the 1963 Act make provision for the involuntary transfer of shares and the registration of persons as members, who become entitled to this status by operation of the law. For example, on the death of a member, his shares vest in his personal representatives: on a member's bankruptcy, they vest in the Official Assignee in Bankruptcy.

Articles 29 to 32 of Table A set out the requirements for the personal representatives and Official Assignee. They must either:

(1)   elect to be entered on the register themselves; or
(2)   have some other person nominated by them registered as the transferee of the shares in question.

The two stages of assignment and registration are also involved in these cases, and the directors have the same rights to decline or suspend registration as they enjoyed against the original members (see also **14.22** to **14.25**).

Compulsory purchase of shares

22.45   When a company is in financial difficulties, the remedy may mean reconstruction, takeover or merger. These corporate remedies can affect the individual rights of shareholders. For example, if at least 80 per cent of the investors accept a takeover bid, then the acquiring company may compel the minority to transfer their shares on the same terms – see Chapter 48.

SHARE WARRANTS

22.46   There is another way that the membership of a company can be transferred. This is through the use of share warrants. Under s 88,[1] a company may, where the articles so permit, issue a warrant stating that the bearer is entitled to the shares specified therein. Transfer is effected by mere delivery.[2]

---

1   Of the 1963 Act.
2   Section 88(3).

As a result, share warrants, unlike share certificates, are negotiable instruments. However, few companies issue share warrants.

PART IV E

THE ARTICLES OF ASSOCIATION AND COMPANY MANAGEMENT

Chapter 23

THE ROLE OF THE DIRECTORS AS MANAGING AGENTS

23.1   Article 80 of Table A makes it clear that 'the business of the company shall be managed by the directors [as its human managing agents]'.

The directors may exercise all the powers of the company to borrow money, and charge or mortgage company property and uncalled capital as security for amounts borrowed.[1] The directors may delegate all their own powers to any company or firm by power of attorney.[2]

Directors are office holders, not employees

23.2   In *Re Forest of Dean Coal Mining Co*,[3] Jessel MR said:

> 'It does not matter what you call [directors], so long as you understand what their true position is, which is that they are merely commercial men, managing a trading concern for the benefit of themselves and all other shareholders in it.'

Section 2 of the 1963 Act defines directors as including any person occupying the position of director, by whatever name called.

Section 27 of the 1990 Act introduced the new concept of a shadow director into Irish law. A shadow director is a person in accordance with whose directions or instructions the directors of a company are accustomed to act.

A director is an office holder, not an employee of the company. He may, however, be both a director and an employee. As Kenny J said in *Dairy Lee Ltd; Stakelum v Canning*:[4]

> 'A director holds his office under articles of association of the company and so, as a director is not an employee or a clerk or servant of the copany. Article 85 of the articles in Table A which applied to this company, permits him to hold any other office or place of profit under the company in conjunction with his office of director for such period and on such terms as to remuneration and otherwise as the directors may determine. The result is that a director may be employed by the company not as a director but as a salaried employee.'

The term executive director is used to denote a director who is also a full-time employee/manager of the company. A non-executive director is simply an office holder. He does not also have a contract of employment with the company.

---

1 Article 79.
2 Article 81.
3 (1878) 10 Ch D 450.
4 [1976] IR 314 (HC).

The function of directors is not to act as employees of the company. Their role is essentially to manage it. When carrying out their managerial role they act at times like trustees, at other times like ordinary agents. For example, in *Great Eastern Railway v Turner*,[1] Lord Selborne stated:

> 'The directors are mere trustees or agents of the company – trustees of the company's money and property – agents in the transactions which they enter into on behalf of the company.'

DIRECTORS AS QUASI-TRUSTEES OF COMPANY ASSETS

23.3 In *Smith v Anderson*,[2] James LJ said:

> 'A trustee is . . . the owner of property and deals with it as a principal, as owner and as a master, subject only to an equitable obligation to account to some persons to whom he stands in the relation to trustee . . . The office of director is that of a paid servant of the company. A director never enters into a contract for himself, but for his principal . . . He cannot sue on such contracts, nor be sued on them (unless he exceeds his authority).'

Where ordinary trustees of a settlement hold shares as part of trust investments and, arising from this, secure their own appointment as directors, their resulting powers of trusteeship may be different. For example, in *Re Butt, Butt v Kelsen*,[3] it was held in these circumstances that although all the beneficiaries under a trust may, if of full age, be able to compel the trustees to exercise their voting rights as members in a certain way, they cannot similarly compel trustee directors to use their powers as directors as if such powers were part of trust property.

Generally, therefore, directors are not ordinary trustees because:

(1) the company's property and monies are owned by the company – not by the directors; and
(2) their duties of care and skill (competency levels) are lower than those required of trustees. As a result, their position may more correctly be described as that of 'quasi-trustees'.

23.4 As quasi-trustees, directors stand in a fiduciary position in relation to the company and owe the following specific duties to it:

(1) they must account for their control over the company's property – any money improperly paid out must be refunded;
(2) they must exercise their powers honestly in the interests of the company and not themselves (see Chapter 24);
(3) they must not make any secret profit for themselves when acting for the company; and

---

1 (1872) LR 8 Ch D 247.
2 (1880) 15 Ch D 247.
3 [1952] 1 All ER 167, [1952] Ch 197.

(4) they must not be interested in a contract with the company unless the articles permit it.

Specific duties (1), (3) and (4) are examined in Chapter 25.

At common law, the directors owe these duties to the company, and not to the individual shareholders who own it.[1]

DIRECTORS AS HUMAN MANAGING AGENTS OF THE COMPANY

23.5 Directors are empowered under company law to negotiate and conclude contracts on behalf of the company.

When directors act as agents of the company in corporate transactions, they generally incur no personal liability under such contracts. It is the company, as principal, which will be liable under them.

At common law, directors will become liable under such contracts only if, when negotiating them, they exceeded the powers given to them by the memorandum and articles of association. They may also be liable for breach of warranty of authority (in agency law) in respect of corporate transactions.

Directors' duties as quasi-trustees and company managing agents

23.6 Directors' specific fiduciary duties as quasi-trustees, and the levels of skill or competency expected from them when acting as managing agents of the company are detailed in Chapters 25 and 26.

DIRECTORS' (BOARD) MEETINGS

23.7 Articles 101 to 104 of Table A contain a set of rules governing the holding of board meetings.[2]

Proceedings[3] at board meetings

23.8 The proceedings of directors will usually be provided for in the articles of association. For example, article 101 provides that:

---

1 *Percival v Wright* [1902] 2 Ch 421. However, the 'insider trading' permitted by directors as a consequence of this decision is now prohibited by ss 107–121 of the 1990 Act – see Chapter 27.
2 The provisions in the articles for the appointment, removal and disqualification of directors have already been detailed in Chapter 15.
3 See also G. Casey and S. T. Leonowicz, 'Directors' Meetings; Modern Technology and Best Practice' (1999) 6 CLP 127.

'the directors may meet together for the dispatch of business, adjourn and otherwise regulate their meetings, as they think fit. Questions arising at any meeting shall be decided by a majority of votes. Where there is an equality of votes, the chairman shall have a second or casting vote. A director may, and the secretary on the requisition of a director shall, at any time summon a meeting of the directors.'

The quorum necessary may be fixed by the directors, and unless so fixed, shall be two.[1] The directors themselves decide on their chairman[2] and they can change the chair as they wish.

Reasonable notice of forthcoming board meetings must be given to directors, even though Table A is silent on this matter. The notice must also contain *an agenda showing what business it is proposed to transact* at the meeting, including any *proposed resolutions.*

Informal board meetings

23.9   Article 109 of Table A supplies a useful means of avoiding the need to hold formal meetings where the board is of one mind. Under this article, a resolution in writing, signed by all the directors, shall be as valid as if it had been passed at a meeting of the directors duly convened and held. With such a preponderance of private companies registered in Ireland, informal board meetings are by no means uncommon. However, the difficulties to which this lack of formality can lead were graphically illustrated in *Re Aston Colour Print Ltd.*[3]

In this case, Kelly J held that even if a board meeting was held on an informal basis, there must have been some appreciation by the directors that they were, in fact, attending a board meeting. In this instance, the chairman believed that the meeting was an ordinary meeting which subsequently became a board meeting. The financial controller, who also attended, did not consider he was at a board meeting. If an informal meeting is to be a board meeting, it should be chaired by the chairman of the board properly so appointed.[4] Decisions taken and resolutions passed should be recorded clearly in the minutes.

Minutes

23.10   Minutes of proceedings at directors' meetings must be kept in accordance with s 145 of the 1963 Act.[5] In the *Aston Colour Print* case, the minutes did not record that a decision to appoint an examiner to the company had been made. Instead, the minute simply stated 'no choice but to examine or liquidate'.

---

1 Article 102.
2 Article 104.
3 (1997) 4 CLP 125. See also article by C. T. Canniffe 'More than mere formalities' (1997) 4 CLP 280, at pp 280–283.
4 That was not the case here.
5 Minute books must be produced, on request, for inspection, to the Director of Corporate Enforcement – see **15.68**.

23.11   In *Re PMPA Garage (Longmile) Ltd (No 1)*[1] Murphy J summarised the current practice of minute recording when he said:

> 'one would not expect to find in any case – the divergent views of directors and managers ... The Longmile [minute book] records, as does probably most minute books of comparable companies, show the basic decisions which must be taken in accordance with the requirements of the Companies Acts.'

23.12   The case of *Municipal Mutual Insurance Ltd v Harrop et al*[2] concerned the amendment of a pension scheme, whose rules provided that it could be altered at any time by resolution of the board of directors with the concurrence of the trustees.

The company's articles of association provided that a resolution of the board could be passed at a duly convened meeting of the board or by written resolution signed by all the directors.

Five directors orally indicated their agreement to the proposed pension scheme change; two directors abstained without comment. The minutes of the following board meeting recorded that the directors had endorsed the proposed change.

Rimer J held that the oral assent of the directors was not sufficient to amount to the passing of a resolution. However, the subsequent signing of the minutes of the earlier meeting by the chairman amounted to a ratification of improperly passed resolutions at that meeting.

Committees

23.13   Articles 105 to 107 deal with the appointment of sub-committees of the board of management. Article 107 gives the chairman of a committee a second or casting vote. Apart from any such provision, motions are carried on majority decision.

Chairman's and managing director's roles

23.14   The board of directors may, and often does, appoint a managing director of the company, delegating certain of their powers to him, principally the day-to-day management of the company. A managing director is answerable to the board and they may dismiss him or otherwise amend his delegated powers.[3] As mentioned in Chapter 37, there is a significant different between the roles of a chairman of a board of directors and the managing director. The chairman is not, per se, a salaried employee of the company. He is an office holder. By contrast, the managing director has a contract of employment[4] with the company and, in the event of his dismissal, has recourse to the range of

---

1   [1992] ILRM 337.
2   [1998] BCLC 540.
3   Article 112.
4   See Chapter 15.

rights and remedies available to any fixed-term contract employee in labour law.

The role of the company secretary

23.15 Article 113 provides for the appointment of the company secretary by the directors – not the members. Even though not appointed by the members, a company secretary, as its chief administrative officer, has a most important role to play in ensuring compliance by the directors and the company with their statutory and other legal obligations. The term 'company officer' extends to include the company secretary (see ss 174 and 175 of the 1963 Act).

The traditional judicial attitude[1] to the company secretary was that:

> 'he is a mere servant, his position is that he is to do what he is told, and no person can assume that he has any authority to represent anything at all . . .'

In 1902, Lord MacNaghten[2] described his duties as 'of a limited and of a somewhat humble character'. This judicial attitude changed in 1971 following the Court of Appeal's decision in *Panorama Developments Ltd v Fidelis Furnishing Fabrics Ltd.*[3] As a result of this decision, the secretary is no longer regarded as a mere clerk, but as the chief administrative officer of the company with ostensible authority to enter into many contracts on the company's behalf.

Function as chief administrative officer

23.16 While the functions of the secretary are not defined in the Companies Acts, it is clear that he is the official with special responsibility for ensuring compliance with the companies legislation. In particular, the secretary will:

(1) keep the registered books of the company, including the registers of:
    (a) members,[4]
    (b) directors and secretaries,[5]
    (c) directors' and secretaries' shareholdings[6] (including those of spouses and children),
    (d) debenture-holders.[7]
    A register of charges[8] must be kept centrally by the registrar of companies for each company.
    Section 378[9] allows the registered books to be kept in book form or in any other manner, whilst s 4 of the 1977 Amendment Act permits the use of computers, etc, for the maintenance of certain company records;

---

1 Per Lord Esher in *Barnett Hoares & Co v South London Tramways Co* (1887) 18 QBD 815 (CA).
2 In *George Whitechurch Ltd v Cavanagh* [1902] AC 117.
3 [1971] 2 All ER 16.
4 Sections 117–124 of the 1963 Act.
5 Section 195, as amended by s 8 of the 1982 Amendment Act, s 51 of the 1990 Act and s 91 of the 2001 Act.
6 Section 190, as amended by ss 53–66 of the 1990 Act.
7 Sections 91–93 of the 1963 Act.
8 Sections 103–110 of the 1963 Act – Chapter 41 of this book.
9 Of the 1963 Act.

(2) making the proper returns to the registrar, eg the annual return;[1]
(3) notifying the registrar of any changes to the memorandum or the articles of association;
(4) giving the required period of notice for meetings to members;
(5) preparing and recording the minutes of general meetings and meetings of the board of directors;
(6) issuing share certificates and dealing with the transfer of shares;
(7) witnessing the use of the seal of the company; and
(8) delivering particulars of charges entered into by the company to the registrar.

The role of the company secretary in corporate governance is mentioned in **54.5**. In large public companies, an external company may be employed to carry out some of these functions, and the secretary's duties may be expanded into managerial functions.

Authority of the secretary

23.17 The extent of the authority of a company secretary to act as agent for the company is dealt with in Part VII B.

23.18 The increasing recognition given to the role of the company secretary is emphasised further by the introduction of qualifications for the secretaries of public companies by the 1990 Act. Section 236 provides that it shall be the duty of the directors to take all reasonable steps to secure that the secretary of the company is a person who appears to them to have the requisite knowledge and experience to discharge the function of secretary of the company and who:

(1) on the commencement of this section held the office of secretary of the company; or
(2) for at least three years of the five years immediately preceding his appointment as secretary held the office of secretary of a company; or
(3) is a member of a body for the time being recognised for the purposes of this section by the Minister; or
(4) is a person who, by virtue of his holding or having held any other position or his being a member of any other body, appears to the directors to be capable of discharging that function.

On 31 December 1996, the following two bodies were recognised by the Minister under s 236(c):

(1) the Institute of Chartered Secretaries and Administrators (ICSA);
(2) the Irish Institute of Secretaries and Administrators.

In September 1997, the Irish Institute of Secretaries merged with the ICSA. Consequently, there is now only one recognised body, namely ICSA.

It should be noted, though, that it is not obligatory for a secretary of a plc to be a member of a recognised body.

---

1 See Part VI.

Appointment of secretary

23.19   Every company must have a secretary, who may be one of the directors.[1] The first secretary is the person[2] named as such in the statement delivered to the registrar.[3] Subsequent appointments will be made by the directors, and any secretary[4] so appointed may be removed by them.[5]

DIRECTORS' DUTIES

23.20   Articles 83 to 87[6] deal with avoidance and regulation of conflict of interest situations arising between the director's personal interests and those of the company for whom he is acting. Otherwise, the articles are silent on the nature and extent of directors' duties in carrying out their responsiblities as managing agents of the company.

Where the articles are less exhaustive or silent

23.21   The articles, as detailed internal company 'rules', emphasise the roles of members as owners and directors as the company's managing agents. However, the articles, while stating the management powers of the directors quite clearly, are less exhaustive in terms of directors' duties and their legal liabilities generally. The articles are also silent on the question of defining directors.[7] Many of the 'gaps' in the articles have been filled by judicial decisions and recently by significant statutory developments. In the absence of express duties and liabilities in the articles, the courts have developed a series of implied duties for directors embracing:

(1) fiduciary responsibilities; and
(2) competency elements, ie duties of care and skill.

The common-law directors' fiduciary duties and duties of care and skill have been strengthened and extended by statutory developments such as s 202 of the 1990 Act, ie the directors' statutory duty to keep proper books of account. Failure to discharge this legal duty could lead to a director being held personally liable for the debts of the company.

These judicial and statutory developments will be examined in Parts V A and B. But first we shall consider the limits imposed by judicial decisions on the exercise by company directors of their powers.

---

1 Section 175 of the 1963 Act.
2 Or body corporate.
3 Under s 3 of the 1982 Amendment Act.
4 Or joint secretaries.
5 See articles 113 and 114 of Table A.
6 Article 138 also provides for an indemnity to any company officer who has successfully defended any proceedings taken against them whilst acting for the company.
7 See **23.2**.

Chapter 24

LIMITATIONS ON DIRECTORS' POWERS OF MANAGEMENT

24.1   As explained in Chapters 14 to 16, the articles of association provide for a division of power between members and directors.

DIVISION OF POWER BETWEEN MEMBERS AND DIRECTORS

24.2   In *Howard Smith Ltd v Ampol Petroleum Ltd,*[1] Lord Wilberforce explained this division of power thus:

> 'The constitution of a limited company normally provides for directors with powers of management, and shareholders, with defined voting powers having power to appoint the directors, and to take in general meeting, by majority vote, decisions on matters not reserved for management ... it is established that directors, within their management powers, may take decisions against the wishes of the majority of shareholders and indeed that the majority of shareholders cannot control them in the exercise of these powers while they remain in office.'

The law bestows freedom on the directors to exercise the powers conferred upon them. However, this freedom is granted to the directors as fiduciaries.[2] Accordingly, their power is subject to the control that courts normally exercise over the use of fiduciary powers. This judicial control imposes *limits on the purpose* for which directors' powers may be exercised.

24.3   The directors' general powers of management are conferred by article 80 of Table A. The members, in law,[3] cannot hold meetings to instruct directors on how to manage the company. For, as Buckley LJ stated in *Gramophone & Typewriter Ltd v Stanley:*[4]

> 'The directors are not servants to obey directions given by the shareholders as individuals; they are not agents appointed by and bound to serve the shareholders in their proposal.
>
>   They are the persons who may by the [articles] be entrusted with the control of the business, and, if so entrusted, they can be disposed from that control only by the statutory majority which can alter the articles.'

In *Breckland Group Holdings Ltd v London & Suffolk Properties Ltd,*[5] Harman J held that the general meeting could not interfere with the management of the company, regardless of the wishes of the board or the shareholders' agreement.

---

1   [1974] AC 831.

2   The directors are managing the company on behalf of its owners, the shareholders.

3   In commercial practice it may be otherwise.

4   [1908] 2 KB 89 (CA).

5   (1988) 4 BCC 542 (ChD). Harman J reviews the case-law on interpretation of article 80 in the course of his judgment.

24.4   Thus, if members wish to control the exercise of management powers by directors, they should muster a majority to pass a special resolution altering the articles.[1] Usually, unless the articles expressly provide otherwise, members of registered companies do not posses a general supervisory power over directors.[2]

Article 80 of Table A expressly empowers the directors to manage the company. This power is subject to little express restraint in the articles. Over the last half century, however, many judicial decisions have 'mapped out' the boundaries or limitations on the exercise of directors' powers.

DIRECTORS MUST ACT IN THE BEST INTERESTS OF THE COMPANY

24.5   In *Re Smith & Fawcett Ltd*,[3] Lord Greene MR said that directors must exercise the powers conferred upon them 'bona fide in what they consider – not what a court may consider – is in the [best] interests of the company'.

Generally, directors will fulfil their obligation to act in the best interests of the company if, when taking part in corporate decision-making, they act *in good faith and for a proper purpose.*

Directors must act in good faith and for a proper purpose

24.6   In *Re Smith & Fawcett Ltd*, the judicial test of good faith was suggested as 'did the directors do what they honestly believed to be right [for the company]?'.

Ross J clarified the meaning of the bona fides concept for directors in *Clark v Workman* stating:

> 'In all cases, bona fides is the test of the valid exercise of powers by trustees. An opportunity for deliberation in the full light of the facts and circumstances is implicitly required.'

Ross J also stated that the obligations on majority members 'to act bona fide for the benefit of the company as a whole apply with augmented force when [similar] powers are being exercised by directors'. Thus, the implication is that the *company as a whole* refers to the corporators as a general body.[4] This aspect of the fiduciary duty of directors was explained by Henchy J in *G & S Doherty Ltd v Doherty*,[5] when he stated:

> 'directors . . . must exercise their powers bona fide for the company as a whole, that is to say, the shareholders as a whole' (as stipulated in the *Greenhalgh* case (see **16.5** above)).

---

1 See *John Shaw and Sons (Salford) Ltd v Shaw* [1935] All ER 456.
2 *Automatic Self-Cleansing Filter Syndicate Co Ltd v Cunninghame* [1906] 2 Ch 34.
3 [1942] Ch 304.
4 See judgment of Evershed MR in *Greenhalgh v Arderne Cinemas.*
5 (Unreported) 19 June 1969 (HC).

24.7   In *Howard Smith Ltd v Ampol Petroleum Ltd*, the directors were empowered by the company's articles of association to 'allot or otherwise dispose of shares on such term and conditions ... as the directors may think fit'. The directors used this power to issue shares in order to block a proposed takeover of the company.

Lord Wilberforce, while accepting that the directors had acted 'intra vires' said:

> 'But, intra vires though the issue may have been, the directors' power under this article is a fiduciary power; and it remains the case that an exercise of such a power though formally valid, may be attacked on the ground that it was not exercised for the purpose for which it was granted.'

The court decided that the use of their powers to issue shares for the purpose of granting a new majority was improper, Lord Wilberforce stating:

> 'The right to dispose of shares at a given price is essentially an individual right to be exercised on individual decision and on which a majority, in the absence of oppression or similar impropriety, is entitled to prevail. Directors are, of course, entitled to offer advice and bound to supply information relevant to the making of such a decision but to use their fiduciary power solely for the purpose of shifting the power to decide to whom and at what price shares are to be sold, cannot be related to any purpose for which the power over the share capital was conferred upon them. That this is the position in law was, in effect, recognised by the majority directors themselves when they attempted to justify the issue as made primarily in order to obtain much needed capital for the company. And once this primary purpose was rejected, as it was by Street J, there is nothing legitimate left as a basis for their action except honest behaviour. That is not, in itself, enough.'

Directors' actions in takeover situations

24.8   In *Dawson International plc v Coats Patons plc*,[1] Lord Cullen considered whether or not directors were under a fiduciary duty to current shareholders with regard to disposal of their shares in a takeover situation. He decided that no fiduciary duty is owed by the directors in such circumstances, saying:

> 'I see no good reason why it should be supposed that directors are, in general, under a fiduciary duty to shareholders, and in particular current shareholders, with respect to the disposal of their shares in the most advantageous way. The directors are not normally the agents of the current shareholders. They are not normally entrusted with the management of their shares. The cases and other authorities to which I was referred do not seem to me to establish any such fiduciary duty. It is contrary to statements in the standard textbooks such as *Palmer's Company Law* 23rd ed, para. 64-02. The absence of such duty is demonstrated by the remarkable case of *Percival v Wright* [1902]. I think it is important to emphasise that *what I am being asked to consider is the alleged fiduciary duty of directors to current shareholders as sellers of their shares. This must not be confused with their duty to consider the interests of shareholders in the discharge of their duty to the company.* What is in the interests of current shareholders as sellers of their shares may not necessarily coincide with what is in the interests of the company. The creation of parallel

---

1   [1989] BCLC 233.

duties could lead to conflict. *Directors have but one master, the company . . .*'

In this case the court held that a contract between Dawson International plc and the directors of the defendant company that they would recommend their takeover bid to the shareholders was valid, Lord Cullen also stating:

> 'I do not accept as a general proposition that a company can have no interest in the change of identity of its shareholders in a takeover . . . *there will be cases in which its agents, the directors, will see the takeover of its shares by a particular bidder as beneficial [or damaging] to the company.*' (author's emphasis)

24.9 In *Hogg v Cramphorn Ltd*,[1] directors issued voting shares to a trust for the company's employees as a strategy to block a hostile take-over bid. The court held that while the directors' action was ultra vires their fiduciary powers,[2] the issuing of the shares was intra vires the company's powers and could be ratified by the members in general meeting; which it was.

24.10 In *Clark v Workman*, the directors of a private company had express power under its articles to approve the transfer of shares. The directors approved the transfer of a controlling interest which involved, according to Ross J, 'a complete transformation of the company'. He then held that the directors' action was wrongful and inconsistent with, 'their fiduciary duty to the company in respect of which the chairman had fettered himself by a promise to the transferee so that he was disqualified from acting bona fide in the interests of the company'.

Directors' actions in disregard of members' interests generally

24.11 Directors of a private company may not be required to give reasons for refusing to register a transferee of shares – see **22.23**.[3]

24.12 Generally, where the powers of the directors in managing the company are used in disregard of members' interests, or in an oppressive manner, any member may pursue a remedy under s 205 of the 1963 Act – see **16.8**.

Directors and interests of company employees

24.13 Cases such as *Re Lee Behrens & Co Ltd*, and *Parke v Daily News Ltd*[4] suggested that at common law, the interest of the company equated with that of the 'collective' interests of all its members – past, present and future. It did not extend to embrace the interests of company employees.

Section 52(1) of the 1990 Act now stipulates that directors owe a duty to consider 'the interests of the company's employees in general, as well as the interests of its members'.

---

1 [1967] Ch 254.
2 The directors had a discretionary power under article 10 to decide to whom the allotment of 5,707 shares should be made. However, these shares would not have been issued to the employees but for the threatened takeover.
3 Of this book.
4 See **36.8**, which deals with, inter alia, the extent of a company's implied powers to pay pensions to employees.

Section 52(2) seems to restrict the directors' duty to the company alone. It will be interesting to see how the Irish judiciary treat future cases of gratuitous payments to company employees where the donor company is being wound up, in the light of s 52.

Directors and interests of company creditors

24.14　In *Re Frederick Inns*,[1] Blaney J suggested that directors can normally only validly exercise company power on behalf of the general body of shareholders. When a company becomes insolvent though, the interests of creditors intrude. Creditors' interests then become prospectively entitled to displace those of the general body of shareholders. Accordingly, where companies are in actual or imminent insolvency, their directors must take into account the interests of company creditors. The principle upon which Blaney J relied emanated from a judgment by Street CJ in the Australian case of *Kinsela v Russell Kinsela Property Ltd*.[2] The consequences of this line of judicial reasoning on abuses of a company powers by its directors are examined in **38.12**.

In *Jones v Gunn*, McGuinness J stated that the directors of an insolvent company owe a fiduciary duty to the company's general creditors – see **38.22**.

Directors and payment of their own remuneration

24.15　In *Re Halt Garage (1964) Ltd*,[3] the liquidator of the company sought to recover remuneration paid to directors in three years when there had been no distributable profits. The liquidator claimed that the amount paid to the directors exceeded reasonable remuneration.

The court held that the directors were entitled to continue to pay themselves their salaries, at a time when the company was incurring losses prior to its ultimate insolvency.

Oliver J decided that payments to one director were not so blatantly excessive or unreasonable to conclude that they were disguised distributions to a shareholder out of capital. As regards payments to his wife (who for three years had been so ill that she was unable to contribute anything to the company's prosperity), Oliver J held that payments in excess of a modest weekly sum 'could not be regarded as being anything more than disguised gifts out of capital'.

24.16　The question of conflict of interest arose in the case of *Guinness plc v Saunders*.[4] Here a payment of £5.2 million made to Mr Saunders by a committee of three directors (including himself) and not authorised by the full board, as required by article 91, was held by him as a constructive trustee and had to be returned to the company.

1　[1991] ILRM 582 (HC) and [1994] 1 ILRM 387 (SC).
2　(1986) 4 NSWLR 722. Also applied, again by Blaney J, in *Parkes v Hong Kong & Shanghai Bank Corp* [1990] 1 ILRM 342 – see Parts VII A and B.
3　[1982] 3 All ER 1016.
4　[1990] 1 All ER 652, [1990] 2 AC 663 (HL).

24.17   The company's objects clause in *Re Horsley & Weight Ltd*[1] expressly permitted the purchase of pensions for directors and employees. Two shareholders owning all the shares, who were directors (their wives were also directors but took no part in company management), bought a pension policy in 1975 for a fifth director who was about to retire.

In 1977, the company went into insolvent liquidation, and the liquidator brought an action against the two directors who had bought the pension, for *misfeasance*.

The unauthorised purchase of the pension by the directors without a formal board meeting was deemed invalid, but it was ratified by the fact that they were the company's sole shareholders. Accordingly, the liquidator's claim failed.

In his judgment, Buckley LJ said:

> 'the purchase of the pension policy was, in my view, intra vires the company. It was not, however, within the powers of Mr Campbell Dick and Mr Frank Horsley acting, not as members of the board of directors, but as individual directors. Unless the act was effectually ratified it cannot bind the company. They were, however, the only two shareholders. A company is bound in a matter which is intra vires the company by the unanimous agreement of its members (per Lord Davey in *Salomon v A. Salomon & Co Ltd* [1897] AC 22 at p 57; even where that agreement is given informally (see *Parker and Cooper Ltd v Reading* [1926] Ch 975). That both Mr Campbell-Dick and Mr Frank Horsley assented to the transaction in question in the present case is beyond dispute. They both initialled the proposal form and they both signed the cheques for the premiums. Their good faith has not been impugned, nor, in my view, does the evidence support any suggestion that in effecting the policy they did not honestly apply their minds to the question whether it was a fair and proper thing for the company in the light of the company's financial state as known to them at the time. In my judgment, their assent made the transaction binding on the company and unassailable by the liquidator.'

DIRECTORS' GENERAL FIDUCIARY DUTY

24.18   As explained in **24.4**, because the articles gave excessive power to directors, the courts were called upon to circumscribe them. One result of the judicial decisions mentioned in this chapter is the imposition of a general fiduciary duty on directors to act in the best interests of the company.

Acting in the best interests of the company for directors means that when making decisions on behalf of the company, they are under a duty to act in good faith and for a proper purpose.[2]

In addition to this general fiduciary duty, directors also owe a number of specific duties to the company.

---

1 [1982] 3 All ER 1045, [1982] Chapter 442 (CA).
2 See **24.6**.

DIRECTORS' SPECIFIC DUTIES

24.19 Because of directors' positions (i) as quasi trustees of the company's property, and (ii) as agents for the company in negotiating and concluding corporate contracts, a number of specific duties have been imposed upon them at common law and by statute.

The specific duties of non-executive directors as office holders can be classified under the headings of

(1) fiduciary duties (or honesty requirements);
(2) duties of care and skill (competency requirements); and
(3) statutory duties.

The specific duties encompassed under (1) to (3) will be examined in Chapters 25 to 27.

EXTRA DUTIES OF EXECUTIVE DIRECTORS

24.20 In addition to these duties of non-executive directors, executive directors, as company employees, will owe the usual duties owed by an employee to his employer. For example, at common law, most employees will owe their employer implied duties which include the following:

(1) to render personal services;
(2) to carry out their work with reasonable care and skill; and
(3) to behave with good faith.

In respect of an employee's duty of good faith, Neill LJ[1] cited with approval the following passage from the judgment of Cross J in *Printers and Finishers Ltd v Holloway*:[2]

> 'If [an employer] is right in thinking that there are features in his process which can fairly be regarded as trade secrets ... then the proper way for [an employer to protect himself] would be by exacting covenants from their employees restricting their field of activity after they have left their employment, not by asking the court to extend the general equitable doctrine on breaking confidence, beyond all reasonable grounds.'

If a company wishes to limit the use by an executive director of confidential information following his resignation, as his employer it would be well advised to follow Cross J's comment and exact a restrictive covenant from him.

The use of confidential information by directors generally is examined in Chapter 25, in the context of directors' and secret profits.

---

1 In *Faccenda Chicken Ltd v Fowler* [1986] All ER 617.
2 [1965] 1 WLR 1.

PART V A

DIRECTORS' COMMON LAW AND STATUTORY DUTIES

Chapter 25

DIRECTORS' SPECIFIC FIDUCIARY DUTIES

25.1 As explained in Chapters 23 and 24, directors act as the human managing agents of a company. By limiting the use of their powers, the courts have effectively imposed a general fiduciary duty upon directors to act in the 'best interests' of the company. Arising out of their fiduciary roles as quasi trustees of company property and assets, directors, at common law, are also deemed to owe the following specific fiduciary duties[1] to the company:

(1) directors must account for their control over company assets;
(2) directors must not make secret profits;
(3) directors must avoid conflicts of interests; and
(4) directors must not fetter their discretion.

We shall now examine each of these four specific fiduciary duties.

DIRECTORS MUST ACCOUNT FOR THEIR CONTROL OVER COMPANY ASSETS

25.2 Directors must account for their control over the company's assets: any monies improperly paid out must be refunded by them.

25.3 In *Alexander v Automatic Telephone Co*,[2] the directors called up payments from all company shareholders, but paid up nothing themselves on shares of that class held by them. The court held that the directors were in breach of trust and must pay up the same amount on their shares as all other shareholders.

Directors are, therefore, trustees of the company when exercising its powers of issuing and allotting shares, making calls on shares and approving transferees of them.

25.4 Similarly, in *Bishopsgate Investment Management Ltd v Maxwell*,[3] the signing of blank transfer forms in respect of securities owned by the company, which were then assigned without consideration and without authority of the full board of directors, constituted a misapplication of the company's assets.

In fact any ultra vires disposition of company assets would probably render the directors liable to account[4] for them.

25.5 In *Jackson v Munster Bank Ltd*,[5] the court held that even though a director himself does not commit a breach of trust, if he becomes aware of breach of

---

1 They also owe a competency-based duty of care and skill at common law – see Chapter 26.
2 [1900] 2 Ch 56.
3 [1993] BCC 120 (CA).
4 See *Re George Newman & Co* [1895] 1 Ch 674 (CA).
5 (1885) 15 LR IR 356.

duty by fellow directors, he is under a duty to take remedial action. As Chatterton VC said:

> 'It was [the defendant director's] bounden duty to have gone at once into an investigation of [the unlawful] transactions, and to have put a stop to them, and I can listen to no excuse for his not having done so. If no better course was open to him, he was, in my opinion, bound to institute a suit in Chancery to put a stop to those proceedings. He did nothing of the kind. I am clear that [the defendant] is liable from February 1883 ...'

25.6 If directors remove company property or withdraw company assets they may be pursued in misfeasance proceedings under s 298 of the 1963 Act, and compelled by the court to return the property or to repay the monies with interest.[1]

25.7 In *Re David Ireland & Co Ltd*,[2] the liquidator of the company brought an action under (what is now) s 298 of the 1963 Act. The liquidator had brought the action to recover monies which he alleged the directors had expended ultra vires and in breach of trust. In their defence, the directors were able to prove that no loss had actually been sustained by the company.

The court held that notwithstanding the fact that the company had suffered no loss, when a director has managed the affairs of a company in such a neglectful way that the assets of the company can only be ascertained by means of a court action, there is a right to sue, quite irrespective of whether the misconduct has caused pecuniary loss.

25.8 In the Court of Appeal judgment, Holmes LJ held:

> 'I have no reason to doubt, and in any case I am bound to assume, that the directors, by the neglect of the duty they owed the company, allowed its business and accounts to be so mixed up with the affairs of David Ireland as to have misled the liquidator, and to have made it necessary, in the interests of the company, to obtain a judicial decision on the questions raised by him in his application under s 165 [now s 298 of the 1963 Act].
>
> Had the judge in this state of things jurisdiction to order the directors to pay the liquidator's costs, although he failed in the object of the litigation? This is the narrow point arising in this appeal ...'

The liquidator had won his case in the High Court. Porter MR awarded him costs because the directors had been guilty of gross neglect throughout the proceedings in relation to dealings with David Ireland and his accounts, and held that such gross neglect and breach of duty were the cause of the litigation which, in consequence thereof, became unavoidable.

The Court of Appeal dismissed the case. Holmes LJ concluded:

> 'although judges are rightly reluctant to visit with costs breaches of trust which do not affect the value of the trust property, or where the deficiency caused thereby is afterwards made good, the jurisdiction to do so exists in cases like the present; and as this is the only matter for our consideration, the appeal must be dismissed.'

---

1 See Chapter 29.
2 [1905] 1 IR 133.

25.9 Almost a century after this case was heard, it should be remembered that there is now a statutory duty on directors to maintain proper books of account – see next chapter.

25.10 A liquidator also instituted misfeasance proceedings against the directors in *Re Mont Clare Hotels Ltd.*[1]

The liquidator's case failed because he was unable to establish gross negligence by the directors. However, one of the directors, whose actions were largely to blame for the legal proceedings being instituted in the first place, was refused an application to pay his legal costs out of the company's assets.

25.11 Directors may also fail in their duty to account for control over the company's assets, if they benefit themselves by selling property to a relative for less than its market value.[2]

Third parties and company assets

25.12 Third parties dealing with the company may also need to be aware of the distinction between a company's assets and those of its members and directors. For example, in *A.L. Underwood Ltd v Bank of Liverpool*,[3] the bank was liable for conversion to the company because, having been put on enquiry, it had failed to distinguish between the assets of Underwood, in his personal capacity, and those of his company.

Theft of company property

25.13 Directors and shareholders can also be found guilty of stealing company property – see *R v Philippou* in **4.13**.

Statutory strengthening of this duty

25.14 In order to reinforce directors quasi-trustee relationship with the company, strengthen their common law duty to account for company's assets and to avoid conflicts of interest, the 1990 Act introduced a regulatory regime for, inter alia:

(1) substantial property transactions involving the directors and company assets;[4]
(2) granting of loans and credit to directors and connected persons;[5] and
(3) disclosure of transactions involving directors and connected persons, in the accounts.[6]

---

1 (Unreported) 2 December 1986 (HC).
2 See *Daniels v Daniels* [1978] Ch 406.
3 See **4.12** for the facts.
4 See Chapter 27.
5 Ibid.
6 Ibid.

DIRECTORS MUST NOT MAKE A SECRET PROFIT

25.15 A director in not permitted at common law to use his privileged position of control within the company to make a secret profit for himself at the company's expense.

If a director makes a secret profit out of his position, he may have to account for it to the company, even though the profit itself could not have been earned by the company.

The fundamental agency principle

25.16 It is a fundamental principle of agency law that an agent must not make a secret profit from a transaction he negotiates or conducts for his principal. Because directors are 'quasi' trustees, they are not permitted to make secret profits out of their positions as directors. As Lord Russell of Killowen stated in *Regal (Hastings) Ltd v Gulliver*:[1]

> 'The rule of equity which insists on those, who by use of a fiduciary position make a profit, being liable to account for that profit, in no way depends on fraud, or absence of bona fides; or upon such questions or considerations as whether the profit would or should otherwise have gone to the plaintiff, or whether the profiteer was under a duty to obtain the source of the profit for the plaintiff, or whether he took a risk or acted as he did for the benefit of the plaintiff, or whether the plaintiff has in fact been damaged or benefited by his action. *The liability arises from the mere fact of a profit having, in the stated circumstances, been made.* The profiteer, however honest and well intentioned, cannot escape the risk of being called upon to account ...
>
> It now remains to consider whether those in acting as directors of Regal stood in a fiduciary relationship to the company. Directors of a limited company are the creatures of statute and occupy a position peculiar to themselves. In some respects they resemble trustees, in others they do not. In some respects they resemble agents, in others they do not. In some respects they resemble managing partners, in others they do not ...
>
> In the result, I am of opinion that the directors standing in a fiduciary relationship to Regal in regard to the exercise of their powers as directors, and having obtained these shares by reason and only by reason of the fact that they were directors of Regal and in the course of the execution of that office, are accountable for the profits which they have made out of them. The equitable rule laid down in *Keech v Sandford*[2] and *Ex parte James*[3] and similar authorities applies to them in full force. It was contended that these cases were distinguishable by reason of the fact that it was impossible for Regal to get the shares owing to lack of funds, and that the directors in taking the shares were really acting as members of the public. I cannot accept this argument.' (author's emphasis)

25.17 Lord Russell's judgment in this case was emphatically supported by that of Lord Porter, who said:

---

1 [1942] 1 All ER 378.

2 (1726) S & L Cas Ch 61.

3 (1803) 8 Ves JR 337.

'The legal proposition may, I think, be broadly stated by saying that one occupying a position of trust must not make a profit which he can acquire only by use of his fiduciary position, or, if he does, he must account for the profit so made. For this proposition the cases of *Keech v Sandford* and *Ex parte James* (1803) are sufficient authority ...

Directors, no doubt, are not trustees, but they occupy a fiduciary position towards the company whose board they form. Their liability in this respect does not depend upon breach of duty but upon the proposition that a director must not make a profit out of property acquired by reason of his relationship to the company of which he is director. It matters not that he could not have acquired the property for the company itself – the profit which he makes is the company's even though the property by means of which he made it was not and could not have been acquired on its behalf ...'

Diverting business opportunities

25.18   Even where it is clear that a person would not contract with the company, a director who took a contract personally was held liable to account to the company for the profit he made, even though the company could not have made that profit itself.

This is what happened in *Industrial Development Consultants Ltd v Cooley*,[1] when Roskill J stated:

'It is an overriding principle of equity that a man must not be allowed to put himself in a position in which his fiduciary duty and his personal interests conflict.'

25.19   In *Peso Silver Mines Ltd (NPL) v Cropper*,[2] it was held that:

(1) the company directors had acted in good faith when rejecting an offer of mining claims because of the company's strained financial position; and
(2) the subsequent acquisition of those mining claims by the managing director, even without seeking shareholder approval, was a proper and valid exercise of directors' powers, *because the company's interest in the claims had ceased.*

This decision was referred to by Laskin J in *Canadian Aero Service v O'Malley*.[3] Laskin J said:

'There is a considerable gulf between the Peso case and the present one on the facts as found in each and on the issues that they respectively raise ... What is before this court is not a situation where various opportunities were offered to a company which was open to all of them, but rather a case where it had devoted itself to originating and bringing to fruition a particular business deal which was ultimately captured by former senior officers who had been in charge of the matter for the company.

It is a mistake, in my opinion, to seek to encase the principle stated and applied in *Peso*, by adoption from *Regal (Hastings) Ltd v Gulliver*, in the straight-jacket of

---

1 [1972] 1 WLR 443.
2 (1966) 58 DLR (2nd) 1. The case of *Cook v Deeks* is yet another example of diverting business opportunities – see **16.31**.
3 (1974) 40 DLR (3d) 371.

special knowledge acquired while acting as directors or senior officers, let alone limiting to benefits acquired by reason of and during the holding of those offices.

   As in other cases in this developing branch of the law, the particular facts determine the shape of the principle of decision without setting fixed limits to it. So it is in the present case.'

Laskin J then sought to introduce a less rigid approach in his decision, saying:

'I am not to be taken as laying down any rule of liability to be read as if it were a statute. The general standards of loyalty, good faith and avoidance of a conflict of duty and self-interest to which the conduct of a director or senior officer must conform must be tested in each case by many factors which it would be reckless to attempt to enumerate exhaustively. Among them are the factor of position of office held, the nature of the corporate opportunity, its ripeness, its specificness and the director's or managerial officer's relation to it, the amount of knowledge possessed, the circumstances in which it was obtained and whether it was special or indeed even private, the factor of time in the continuation of fiduciary duty where the alleged breach occurs after termination of the relationship with the company and the circumstances under which the relationship was terminated, that is, whether by retirement or resignation or discharge ...'

On facts quite similar to those in *Industrial Development Consultants Ltd v Cooley*, directors who had diverted a business or corporate opportunity from the company to themselves were also held by Laskin J to be liable for damages for breach of duty.

25.20   The case of *Island Export Finance Ltd v Umunna*[1] seems to endorse the more flexible judicial approach to corporate business opportunities enunciated by Laskin J (above). This more flexible approach takes into account other factors such as the office held, the nature of the business opportunity, etc. Accordingly, in this case, a director who resigned his office was not liable to account for profits earned by him on contracts made after his resignation, even though the contracts were of the same nature and made with the same person as an earlier contract concluded with the company. In this instance, though, unlike *Cooley*, the director had not resigned to obtain the contracts.[2]

Executive and non-executive directors

25.21   There is a tendency, in cases such as *Industrial Development Consultants Ltd v Cooley*, to blur the distinctions between the office of director and director's role as an employee under a contract of employment with the company. For example, all employees are under an implied duty not to disclose confidential information, nor to solicit business from their employer's customers. Any employee who solicits orders from his employer's customers intending to meet the orders personally, rather than *qua* employee, would be in breach of an implied duty to serve his employer faithfully.[3] Accordingly, it could be argued that the managing director in the *Cooley* case was in breach of his duty to serve

---

1 [1986] BCLC 460 (QBD). See also *Moore v McGlynn* [1894] 1 IR 74.
2 Nor had he made use of confidential information acquired whilst acting for the company.
3 *Arclex Optical Corporation v McMurry* [1958] Ir Jur Rep 65 (HC).

the company (his employer) faithfully as an executive director, rather than of a specific fiduciary duty arising out of his holding of the office of director.[1]

Directors' use of 'insider' information in share dealings

25.22   The court decision in *Percival v Wright*[2] that directors owed their fiduciary duties to the company alone (and not its shareholders), had the effect of permitting directors to profit from inside knowledge when dealing in a company's shares.

25.23   This unsatisfactory situation is now remedied by the *insider dealings* provisions contained in ss 107 to 121[3] of the 1990 Act. Furthermore, ss 53 to 61[4] require disclosure by directors, shadow directors and company secretaries of their interests in shares and debentures of the company.

25.24   In addition, it is rendered a criminal offence[5] for directors or their agents to deal in options to buy or sell shares in and debentures of the company or associated companies.

DIRECTORS MUST AVOID CONFLICTS OF INTEREST

25.25   Directors are expected at all times to act in the best interests[6] of the company, and to avoid situations where conflicts of interest may arise.

In *Aberdeen Railway Co v Blaikie Bros*,[7] Lord Cranworth LC said:

> '... It is a rule of universal application, that no one having [fiduciary] duties to discharge, shall be allowed to enter into engagements in which he has, or can have a personal interest conflicting, or which possibly may conflict with the interests of those whom he is bound to protect.'

Disapplication of this duty

25.26   The members of a company may, by ordinary resolution, relax this duty to avoid conflict of interests (and also the duty prohibiting secret profits), providing there has been a full and frank disclosure of all material facts.

25.27   As Upjohn LJ stated in *Boulting v Association of Cinematograph, Television & Allied Technicians*,[8] when explaining how what he labelled as the rules against

---

1 See **24.20**.
2 See **23.4**. In exceptional circumstances, where mutual trust existed between the parties, a director might be held to owe a fiduciary duty to an individual shareholder – see *Crindle Investments v Wymes* [1998] 4 IR 567.
3 See Chapter 27.
4 Ibid.
5 By s 31 of the 1990 Act.
6 See Chapter 24.
7 (1854) 1 Macq 461 (HL).
8 [1963] 2 QB 606.

[secret] profiting and against conflict of interest (which he treated as a single rule) could be relaxed:

> 'The rule ... is one essentially for the protection of the person to whom the duty is owed. Thus the company is entitled to the undivided loyalty of its directors ... But the person entitled to the benefit of the rule may relax it, provided he is ... *sui iuris* and fully understands not only what he is doing but also what his legal rights are, and that he is in part surrendering them. Thus the company may, in its articles of association, permit directors to be interested in contracts with the company. It may go further, and articles may validly permit directors to be present at board meetings and even to vote when proposed contracts in which they are interested are being discussed; provided, of course, that they make full disclosure of their interests.'

Section 194 of the 1963 Act

25.28   Section 194(1) places a statutory duty on a director 'who is in any way ... interested ... in a proposed contract with the company, to declare the nature of his interest at a meeting of the directors ...'. Section 47 of the 1990 Act extends this disclosure duty to loans, credit transactions and guarantees.

25.29   In *Hopkins v Shannon Transport Ltd,*[1] the court confirmed that the board must consist of independent directors.

Section 194(2) to (5) deals with the manner of making the disclosure declaration required by s 194(1). These subsections provide for both specific and general notice situations.

Section 194 is supplemented by Table A, articles 83 to 87. For example, article 84 prevents a director from voting on certain proposed contracts in which he has a personal interest. This article also specifies four types of contracts in which a director may be interested and can still vote.[2] These exceptional contracts include 'any contract by a director to subscribe for ... shares or debentures of the company'.

Consequences of failure to make statutory disclosure

25.30   When a director fails to give notice as required by s 194 he:

(1)   may be accountable to the company for any secret profit obtained from the impugned transaction(s);
(2)   will lose the benefit of any express provisions in the articles relieving him of liability for non-disclosure; and
(3)   commits an offence and may be fined.

In addition, the impugned contract(s) is voidable at the option of the company.

Ratification of a conflict of interest

25.31   If a director had an undisclosed interest in a contract to which the company is a party, it is permissible at common law for the members to ratify the

---

1   (Unreported) 10 July 1972 (HC). See also **9.5**.
2   And also be counted in the quorum for the meeting.

director's breach of his duty to disclose. As Sir Richard Baggallay said in *North-West Transportation Co Ltd v Beatty*:[1]

> 'The general principles applicable to cases of this kind are well-established … a director of a company is precluded from dealing, on behalf of the company, with himself, and from entering into engagements in which he has a personal interest conflicting, or which possibly may conflict, with the interests of those whom he is bound by fiduciary duty to protect … Any such dealing or engagement may, however, be affirmed or adopted by the company, provided such affirmance or adoption is not brought about by unfair or improper means, and is not illegal or fraudulent or oppressive towards those shareholders who oppose it.'

In *Movitex Ltd v Bulfield*,[2] Vinelott J made it clear that once a director makes full disclosure to a company's members, and they consent to his having the interest, then 'the conflict between duty and interest is dissolved'. To the extent that the company in general meeting gives its informed consent to the transaction, there is no breach [of the self dealing rule]; the conflict of duty and interest is avoided.

25.32 A director interested in a transaction who is also a member can, *qua* member, vote[3] at the general meeting in favour of ratifying the transaction in question.

25.33 Members cannot, though, ratify an ultra vires contract – see **36.26**.

Executive directors' service contracts

25.34 Under s 28 of the 1990 Act, any clause in an executive director's service contract seeking to extend it for longer than five years, is void, unless first approved by the members in general meeting (see **15.28**).

Section 50 of the 1990 Act makes special provisions for inspection of executive directors' service contracts by company members.[4]

CONNECTED PERSONS AND SHADOW DIRECTORS

25.35 Sections 26 and 27 of the 1990 Act define connected persons and shadow directors.

The regulatory regime introduced by Part III[5] of the 1990 Act in relation to transactions involving directors, also applies to company deals involving connected persons and shadow directors.[6]

1 (1887) 12 App Cas 589.
2 (1986) 2 BCC 99.
3 *North-West Transportation Co Ltd v Beatty*, cited above.
4 Section 50 also applies to service contracts held by directors with subsidiaries of the company.
5 Sections 25–52 of the Act.
6 See **27.4–27.6**.

DIRECTORS MUST NOT FETTER THEIR DISCRETION

25.36 It is a fundamental principle of company law that a director must act in the best interests[1] of the company. Because of this principle, in *Clark v Workman*,[2] the court decided that, in acting for the company, a director must not forego his independence by entering into a prior contract with an outsider as to how he might use his vote. In this case, Ross J said:

> '[The directors] were bound to consider the interests of all the shareholders, unfettered by any undertaking or promise to any intending purchaser. They were bound to consider all offers, by whomsoever made and they were bound to weigh and consider the desirability of admitting the persons or companies who proposed to come into their concern. If they failed in any of these matters, they disabled themselves from performing their duty to the shareholders and nothing that they did would in the eye of the law be held to have been done in good faith ...'

In *Fulham Football Club Ltd v Cabra Estates plc*,[3] the Court of Appeal held that a board of directors had not fettered their discretion when they acted bona fide in giving undertakings in return for substantial benefits accruing to the company.

Special circumstances may also arise in connection with a proposed takeover of the company.[4]

---

1 See **24.5** et seq.
2 [1920] 1 1R 107 (ChD).
3 [1994] 1 BCLC 363.
4 See **24.8** et seq.

Chapter 26

DIRECTORS' DUTIES OF CARE AND SKILL

26.1 The fiduciary duties of directors set out in Chapter 25 generally relate to the honesty norms expected of directors. Duties of care and skill, by contrast, relate to the competency levels or commercial skills required from directors.

26.2 At common law, no greater degree of skill or competence is expected from a director than may be reasonable to expect from a person of his knowledge and experience. The leading case is *Re City Equitable Fire Insce Co.*[1]

NEGLIGENCE AND THE SUBJECTIVE TEST OF COMPETENCE

26.3 The facts of the *City Equitable* case are as follows. A company was being wound up when it was discovered that there was a shortage of funds to the extent of over £1,200,000, largely due to the managing director's fraud. Under the articles of the company it was provided that the directors, the auditor, the secretary and the other officers should not be liable for frauds of any of the other directors, etc, except where their own wilful neglect or default was concerned. On a misfeasance summons under s 125 of the Companies (Consolidation) Act 1908, the liquidator sought to make the respondent directors, all of whom (except the managing director) had admittedly acted honestly throughout, liable for negligence in respect of losses occasioned by investments and loans, and of payment of dividends out of capital.

26.4 The standard of care for negligence actions generally is an objective test, ie the conduct of a reasonable man. In this case, however, Romer J did not consider the objective standard of a 'reasonable director', to be appropriate for negligence actions against company directors. Instead, he decided that the proper standard of competence to be expected from directors was a subjective one to be judged against the defendant director's particular personal knowledge and experience. Romer J said:

> 'The care that [a director] is bound to take has been described ... as "reasonable care" to be measured by the care an ordinary man might be expected to take in the circumstances on his own behalf ... A director need not exhibit in the performance of his duties a greater degree of skill than may reasonably be expected from a person of his knowledge and experience ... [ie a subjective test]. It is perhaps only another way of stating the same proposition to say that directors are not liable for mere errors of judgment.'

---

1 [1925] Ch 407.

Romer LJ's judgment reflected the reasoning in *Re Brazilian Rubber Planations and Estates Ltd*[1] of Neville J, who said:

> 'A director's duty has been laid down as requiring him to act with such care as is reasonably to be expected from him, having regard to his knowledge and experience. He is, I think, not bound to bring any special qualifications to his office. He may undertake the management of a rubber company in complete ignorance of everything connected with rubber, without incurring responsibility for the mistakes which may result from such ignorance.
>
> Such reasonable care must, I think, be measured by the care an ordinary man might be expected to take in the same circumstances on his own behalf. He is clearly, I think, not responsible for damages occasioned by errors of judgment.'

26.5   Lindley MR in *Lagunas Nitrate Co v Lagunas Syndicate*[2] stated:

> 'The amount of care to be taken [by directors] is difficult to define ... Their negligence must not be the omission to take all possible care; it is much more blameable than that; it must be in a business sense culpable and gross.'

26.6   Costello J commented in Re *Mont Clare Hotels Ltd; Jackson v Mortell*[3] thus:

> '... it is not every act of negligence that amounts to a misfeasance in law ... something more than mere carelessness is required, some act that, perhaps, may amount to gross negligence[4] in failing to carry out a duty owed by a director to his company.'

A director who lost company assets (diamonds) while on a business trip and who had not insured them, was held grossly negligent in *Re Simmon Box (Diamonds) Ltd* [2000] BCC 275. He was found liable for misfeasance and ordered to contribute towards the assets of the insolvent company.

26.7   At common law, therefore, a company director is not required to possess any special qualifications or expertise in the business in which the company is engaged. However, if a director does happen to have special knowledge or qualifications relevant to the company and its business, then, applying Romer J's subjective test, he will be expected to give the company the benefit of this knowledge when acting as its director.

26.8   The subjective nature of a director's standard of care in negligence is well illustrated by the case of *Dorchester Finance Co v Stebbing*.[5] Here two non-executive directors, P and H, were held liable in negligence for signing blank cheques which allowed the managing director, Stebbing,[6] to misappropriate the company's money. P and H both had considerable accountancy and business experience, a factor which was very relevant to making a subjective decision as to their negligence.

---

1   [1911] 1 Ch 425.
2   [1899] 2 Ch 392.
3   (Unreported) 2 December 1986 (HC) – see also **25.10**, and Chapter 29.
4   Is gross carelessness not negligence, but recklessness? We shall consider this point in **26.10**.
5   [1989] BCLC 498.
6   Stebbing was also held to be negligent.

STATUTORY NEGLIGENCE?

26.9 The Companies Act 1990, s 204 can render company directors personally liable for failure to maintain proper books of account. This form of tortious
liability for breach of statutory duty can arise from incompetence as well as
dishonesty.[1]

RECKLESS TRADING AND THE OBJECTIVE TEST OF COMPETENCE

26.10 The idea of reckless trading was introduced into Irish law by the 1990
Act. The concept is defined in s 297A (1) and (2) of the 1963 Act.[2]

The statutory definition incorporates two tests.

The first test of reckless trading bears similarities to negligence with an
objective test of competence. The second test is based on fraud or deceit, and
involves a subjective element.

The objective competence test for knowledge

26.11 Section 297A(2)(a) provides that an:

> 'officer of a company shall be deemed to have been knowingly a party to the
> carrying on of any business of the company in a reckless manner if: (a) he was a
> party to the carrying on of such business and, having regard to the general
> knowledge, skill and experience that may reasonably be expected of a person in his
> position, he ought to have known that his actions or those of the company, would
> cause loss to the creditors of the company, or any of them.'

26.12 Essentially, the objective test of competence is intended to be used by a
court to decide whether or not it should *impute knowledge* for the purpose of
deeming a defendant director '*knowingly* a party to the carrying on of any
business of the company in a reckless manner'. The test in limb (a) breaks new
legal ground by importing an objective test of general knowledge, skill and
experience' that may reasonably be expected of a director. This test replaces a
director's common-law subjective test of skill. The effect of this reform should
be to raise the competence levels expected from all directors.

26.13 In *Re Hefferon Kearns Ltd (No 2)*,[3] Lynch J, when applying the objective
test, equated recklessness with gross carelessness.[4] The criteria he applied was
'would a *reasonable man* have described the defendant's actions as reckless?'

This author must diverge from Lynch J's analysis here.

---

1 See **28.3** et seq.
2 Which was amended by the 1990 Act.
3 [1993] 3 IR 191 (HC) – see also Chapter 28.
4 Correctly, in this writer's view.

26.14   The definition outlined in **26.11** indicates that:

(1) a new minimum level of general knowledge, skill and experience, ie a minimum competence level for company directors, is now prescribed for reckless trading; and

(2) as a result, the proper test for imputing knowledge is now: 'Would a director having the minimum competence levels in (1) have reasonably described the defendant's actions as reckless?'

Lynch J also considered that the word 'knowingly' had an effect on the definition of reckless. Because of it, recklessness required knowledge, or imputed knowledge, that the defendant's action would cause a loss to creditors; it would not be sufficient simply to show that there might have been some worry or uncertainty as to the ability to pay all the creditors. The judge continued:

> 'I think [knowingly] requires that the director is party to carrying on business in a manner which [he] knows very well involves an obvious and serious risk or loss or damage to others and yet ignores that risk because he does not really care because his selfish desire to keep his own company alive overrides any concern which he ought to have for others.'

26.15   Lynch J is saying here that the word 'knowingly' essentially means that the plaintiff must adduce proof of actual, rather than imputed knowledge.

The legislation does not require this interpretation because in it the word 'knowingly' is preceded by the words 'deemed to have been'.

The intention of the statutory definition seems to be that the court should apply the objective test of the reasonable director to decide whether or not to impute knowledge to a defendant. In other words the legislature has sought to raise directors' liability for reckless trading to 'ordinary' negligence (the reasonable director yardstick) when introducing the objective competence test. Lynch J, however, seems to have interpreted this definition too narrowly by effectively not applying the objective director test for imputing knowledge. One must, however, have sympathy for Lynch J when endeavouring to 'unscramble' the intention of the legislature in this particular instance.

At common law, there are both subjective and objective tests for recklessness: the objective test being that a person will be deemed to have acted recklessly if he does not appreciate the risks attendant to his actions where such risks would have been appreciated (or foreseen) by a reasonable man.[1]

In a South African case,[2] the judicial interpretation of their equivalent provision was 'did the defendant act recklessly when judged by the standards of a reasonable businessman?'.

At common law, recklessness has also been equated with gross carelessness or gross negligence. What renders the Irish objective test confusing is the added direction to apply the standards 'not of a reasonable businessman', but of a

---

1   *R v Caldwell* [1982] AC 341.
2   *State v Goertz* (1980) (1) SA 269.

'reasonably qualified director' (see **26.13**). This added statutory direction, in the author's view, virtually creates a new tort of 'Negligent Trading'.[1] If this is the intention of the *Oireachtas*, it might be a good idea for a future Companies Amendment Act to make it clear that:

(1) the subjective test was the appropriate one for trading in a reckless manner;
(2) the objective test created the new tort of 'negligent trading'; and
(3) the defence of 'acting honestly and responsibly' in s 297A(2)(b) should be limited to the tort of reckless trading only (ie the present subjective test).

The subjective test for honesty

26.16 Section 297A(2)(b) sets out an alternative test for proof of knowledge of reckless trading.

This test is applicable to cases where the defendant was party to the contracting of a debt, rather than party to the carrying on of the business generally.

26.17 Under the subjective test, a court will decide to impute knowledge of reckless trading to a defendant if:

'he was a party to the contracting a debt by the company and did not honestly believe, on reasonable grounds, that the company would be able to pay the debt when it fell due for payment as well as all its debts (taking into account the contingent and prospective liabilities).'

This subjective test was referred to by Lynch J in the *Hefferon Kearns Ltd (No 2)* case as:

'a very wide ranging and indeed draconian measure and could apply in the case of virtually every company which becomes insolvent and has to cease trading for that reason. If, for example, a company became insolvent because of the domino effect of the insolvency of a large debtor, it would be reasonable for the directors to continue trading for a time thereafter to assess the situation and almost inevitably they would incur some debts which would fall within paragraph [b] before finally closing down. It would not be in the interests of the community that whenever there might appear to be any significant danger that a company was going to become insolvent, the directors should immediately cease trading and close down the business. Many businesses, which might well have survived by continuing to trade coupled with remedial measures, could be lost to the community.'

As a result of this subjective test, all directors should be very careful as to the decisions they make when their company gets into financial difficulties.

---

1 For example, see *Re D'Jan of London Ltd* [1993] BCC 646, where a director was held to be negligent for signing an insurance proposal without first reading it. However, the court relieved him of liability under the UK equivalent of s 391 of the 1963 Act, because he had acted honestly and reasonably.

DEGREE OF DILIGENCE

26.18   Another aspect of a director's duty of care referred to by Romer J in the *City Equitable* case was the degree of diligence which had to be exercised by a director in relation to the company's business affairs.

In his judgment, Romer J accepted that a non-executive director is not bound to give continuous attention to the affairs of his company. Nor need he attend all board meetings. To cite Romer J again:

> '[The director's] duties are of an intermittent nature to be performed at periodical board meetings, and at meetings of any committee of the board upon which he happens to be placed. He *is not, however, bound to attend all such meetings,* though he ought to attend whenever, in the circumstances, he is reasonably able to do so.'

26.19   Unless a director is bound under a contract of employment to perform specific duties (ie is an executive director), he is essentially only liable for 'sins' of commission. He is not generally liable to be held negligent simply for failing to take part in the conduct of the company's business. However, as Neville J said in the *Brazilian Rubber Plantations*[1] case:

> '[While a director of a company] is not, I think, bound to take any definite part in the conduct of the company's business, so far as he does undertake it he must use reasonable care in its dispatch.'

26.20   In the *Marquis of Bute's Case,*[2] the Marquis had only attended one board meeting in 38 years. As he had received notices of board meetings all this time, and the company appeared to be managed normally, the Marquis was held not to be in breach of his duty of care/diligence. This case can be distinguished from *Jackson v Munster Bank Ltd*[3] because here the director concerned was made aware of wrongdoings by fellow directors and consequently, in light of this special knowledge, was under a duty to act.

26.21   Finally, if directors do attend board meetings they are under a duty to stay awake during them – see *Land Credit Company of Ireland v Lord Fermoy.*[4]

Delegation of management duties

26.22   The Companies Acts always envisaged companies being managed by non-executive directors who would delegate the day-to-day operations of the company's business to official managers and employees. As Romer J said:

> 'In order to ascertain the duties that a person appointed to the board of an established company undertakes to perform, it is necessary to consider not only the nature of the company's business, but also the manner in which the work of the company is, in fact, distributed between the directors and the other officials of the company, provided always that this distribution is a reasonable one in the

1   See **26.4**.
2   [1892] 2 Ch 100.
3   See **25.5**.
4   (1870) 5 Ch App 763.

circumstances, and is not inconsistent with any express provisions of the articles of association ... In respect of all duties that, having regard to the exigencies of business, and the articles of association, may properly be left to some other official, a director is, in the absence of grounds for suspicion, justified in trusting that official to perform such duties honestly ...'

26.23   Earlier, in the case of *Dovey v Cory*,[1] Lord Halsbury LC, commenting on the extent to which directors could rely on company officials, said:

'The charge of neglect appears to rest on the assertion that Mr Cory, like the other directors, did not attend to any details of business not brought before them by the general manager or the chairman [who were both defrauding the company], and the argument raises a serious question as to the responsibility of all persons holding positions like that of directors, how far they are called upon to distrust and be on their guard against the possibility of fraud being committed by their subordinates of every degree. It is obvious if there is such a duty it must render anything like an intelligent devolution of labour impossible ... I cannot think that it can be expected of a director that he should be watching either the inferior officers of the [company] or verifying the calculations of the auditors himself. The business of life could not go on if people could not trust those who are into a position of trust for the express purpose of attending to details of management.'

Company monies

26.24   Table A, article 88 stipulates that all cheques, etc and receipts issued for money paid by and to the company, shall be signed, drawn and issued by such persons as 'the directors from time to time by resolution determine'.

Signing of cheques by directors

26.25   On the signing of cheques by directors, Romer J in *City Equitable* said:

'A director who signs a cheque that appears to be drawn for a legitimate purpose is not responsible for seeing that the money is, in fact, required for that purpose or that it is subsequently applied for that purpose, assuming, of course, that the cheque comes before him for signature in the regular way having regard to the usual practice of the company ...

A director must of necessity trust to the officials of the company to perform properly and honestly the duties allocated to those officials ...'

A director cannot however, absolve himself of all responsibility simply by delegating work to company officials. For, as Romer J also stated:

'Before any director actually signs, or at any rate parts with a cheque signed by him, he should satisfy himself that a resolution has been passed by the board, or committee of the board, as the case may be, authorising the signature of the cheque. In the case where a cheque has to be signed between the meetings, he must, of course, obtain the confirmation of the board subsequently to his signature ...

The authority given by the board or committee should not be for the signing of numerous cheques to an aggregate amount, but a proper list of the individual

---

1 [1901] AC 477.

cheques, mentioning the payee and the amount of each, should be read out at the board or committee meeting and subsequently transcribed into the minutes of the meeting.'

In *Dorchester Finance Co v Stebbing*,[1] two directors were held to be negligent for signing blank cheques which enabled the managing director to misappropriate the company's monies.

Identification of company's assets

26.26 In the *City Equitable* case, owing to the managing director's (MD's) fraud, a large amount of the company's assets had disappeared.

Items were shown in the balance sheet as 'loans at call or at short notice' and 'cash at bank or in hand'; the latter item included £73,000 in the hands of the company's stockbrokers, of which the MD was a partner.

On these matters, Romer J stated:

'It is the duty of each director to see that the *company's moneys* are from time to time in a *proper state of investment*, except in so far as the company's articles of association may justify him in delegating that duty to others ... *Before presenting their annual report and balance-sheet to their shareholders, and before recommending a dividend, directors should have a complete and detailed list of the company's assets and investments prepared for their own use and information, ought not to be satisfied as to the value of their company's assets merely by the assurance of their chairman, however apparently distinguished and honourable, nor with the expression of the belief of their auditors, however competent and trustworthy.*'

The directors were held to be negligent. However, because the company's articles limited their liability to 'wilful neglect or default', they were able to escape liability.[2]

Section 202 of the 1990 Act now regulates very precisely matters such as the identification of company assets and liabilities – see **26.28**.

Investment of company assets

26.27 Romer J's judgment also dealt with directors' duties in respect of the investment of company assets. He acknowledged that this function had to be delegated to officials, saying:

'It is not the duty of a director of such a company as the City Equitable to see in person to the safe custody of securities. That is one of the matters which the directors must almost of necessity leave to some official who is at the office daily, such as the manager, accountant or secretary. When an investment is made through the brokers it would be quite impracticable for the directors to receive actual delivery of the securities. So, too, when investments are sold, delay and great

---

1 See **26.8**.
2 Section 200 of the 1963 Act would seem to render such a provision in the articles of an Irish company void. In the UK, s 310(3)(a) of their 1985 Act now provides that their equivalent of s 200 does not prevent a company purchasing directors' and officers' (or auditors') liability insurance.

inconvenience would result if the delivery of the securities to the brokers had to await a meeting of the board or of a committee of directors ...'

Keeping proper books of account

26.28 The common-law rule on delegating of book-keeping must be viewed in the light of s 202 of the 1990 Act. Under s 202, every company must keep proper books of account. The detailed statutory requirements in this regard are detailed in **27.42** to **27.47**.

A director can incur unlimited personal liability for company debts if the company is in breach of s 202. However, the Act allows a director to prove in defence that 'he had reasonable grounds for believing that a *competent* and *reliable* person was charged with the duty [of compliance with s 202].

Thus, while all directors are now under a statutory duty to ensure proper books of account are kept, they are permitted to delegate[1] this work, by resolution of the board, to a competent and reliable executive (such as the finance director).

Monitoring compliance with s 202

26.29 Section 194 of the 1990 Act imposes a duty on auditors to monitor whether or not a company is complying with s 202 – see **34.22**.

Preparation of annual accounts

26.30 Section 148 of the 1963 Act imposes a duty on directors 'to lay before the annual general meeting' a profit and loss account and balance sheet.

The annual accounts[2] must be signed by at least two directors. Reports of the directors and independent auditors[3] must be attached to the accounts.

Duty in the event of a serious loss of capital

26.31 Where the company suffers a serious loss of capital, under s 40 of the 1983 Amendment Act, the directors must call an extraordinary general meeting to discuss the situation with the members – see **19.40**.

TYPICAL DUTIES DELEGATED BY DIRECTORS

26.32 The typical director envisaged by the companies legislation is of the non-executive variety. Accordingly it is accepted that much of the day-to-day responsibility for operating the company, and, indeed, for detailed compliance

---

1 See s 202(10)(a) of the 1990 Act.
2 See Chapter 32.
3 See Chapter 34.

with the Companies Acts requirements, will be delegated by the board to executive directors, managers and employees. Much of the directors' responsibility for company law compliance will be delegated to the company secretary.

26.33 The typical compliance duties which might be delegated by the directors include:

(1) preparation and maintenance of the basic financial records and books of account;
(2) maintenance of the statutory registers[1] such as the registers of:
    (a) members,
    (b) significant interests,
    (c) directors and secretaries,
    (d) directors interests, and
    (e) debenture holders;
(3) maintenance of statutory books and minutes;[2] and
(4) preparation and filing of the annual return.

A company secretary would usually be responsible for items (2) to (4) above as well as notifying the registrar of any special resolutions under s 143 of the 1963 Act.

26.34 The directors have the power to appoint and to remove the company secretary. They cannot, however, without the approval of the members, appoint or remove the company's auditor.

---

1 See Chapter 33.
2 Ibid.

Chapter 27

STATUTORY STRENGTHENING OF DIRECTORS' DUTIES

THE COMPANIES ACT 1990

27.1   The Companies Act 1990 was of great significance to the law relating to directors. Reflecting the traditional focus of litigation involving directors, the Act introduced a new regulatory regime to strengthen directors' fiduciary duties (or honesty requirements). The new statutory provisions also increased directors' duties of care and skill. These aspects of the Act will be considered in this chapter. Its sections increasing the liability of directors will be examined in Part V B, including the new sanctions of restriction and disqualification orders.

STRENGTHENING OF DIRECTORS' HONESTY REQUIREMENTS

27.2   The sections of the 1990 Act strengthening directors' common law fiduciary duties include ss 28 to 47 regulating transactions involving directors, and ss 53 to 66 requiring disclosure of share dealings by directors, secretaries and their families.

The insider dealing rules introduced by ss 107 to 121 are also most relevant to share dealings where a company director is involved.

TRANSACTIONS INVOLVING DIRECTORS (AND OTHERS)

27.3   Part III of the 1990 Act seeks to regulate a number of different transactions involving directors, connected persons and shadow directors. Sections 25 to 27, as amended, contain the relevant definitions, including those of 'connected persons' and 'shadow directors'.

Connected persons

27.4   Under s 26, as amended by s 76 of the 2001 Act, a person (not already a director) is connected with a director of a company if, and only if, he is:

(1) the director's spouse, parent, brother, sister or child;
(2) a trustee acting for him, his family or company; or
(3) the director's partner, within the meaning of s 1(1) of the Partnership Act 1890.

Where another company is controlled by a director, either alone or together with any other directors or connected persons, that company is also a connected person. Such a company is generally one where the director, either alone or with others, can control more than 50 per cent of the voting shares.

Prima facie, the sole member of a single-member private company, is a person connected to a director of that company – see s 26(3).

Shadow directors

27.5   Section 27 introduces the term 'shadow director' to Irish law, defining it as 'a person in accordance with whose directions or instructions the directors of a company are accustomed to act'. The definition does not include a person giving professional advice to the directors.

The qualifications within the definition above are important; there must be 'directions or instructions' (as opposed to, for example, comment, suggestion or simple advice, including especially advice given 'in a professional capacity'), while some degree of regularity, or at least repetition, is implied by the need for the directors to be 'accustomed to act' on the shadow director's input. It will thus be apparent that the bona fide independent professional adviser should not find himself liable as a shadow director – as long as he confines his input to giving advice only.

Recently, similar qualifications in the UK's legislation received judicial scrutiny.

In *Secretary of State for Industry v Deverell and Another*,[1] two individuals were held to be shadow directors of a company.[2] The judge at first instance held that shadow directorship could not be established where the individual had provided merely 'advice' (rather than the defined 'directions or instructions') and that the board being 'accustomed to act' on such input meant both a pattern and that the advice was accepted and acted upon with little or no independent judgement.

The Court of Appeal considered that both tests were too strict. Instead, it determined the essence of shadow directorship should be the establishment of influence:

(1) in at least the corporate governance of the company (but not necessarily over all its activities);

(2) rendered as any form of 'guidance'(which would not exclude non-professional 'advice' as an alternative to the more specific 'directions or instructions'); and

(3) upon which the board was accustomed to act but without necessarily surrendering its authority or discretion.

Similarly, Murphy J, in *Re Vehicle Imports Ltd*,[3] refused to make an order under s 150 (see Chapter 30) against the spouse of a respondent director who had no involvement in the day-to-day running of the company.

In *Re Vehicle Imports Ltd*, Murphy J applied the restriction provision of s 150 to a shadow director, although granting him a stay of 21 days in which to make an application under s 152 (see **30.10**), if he deemed it fit to do so, because some

---

1 [2000] 2 WLR 907.
2 And thus liable to disqualification.
3 *Bar Review*, Vol 6, Issue 4, January 2001, and (2001) 8(3) CLP 72.

doubts had existed as to whether or not the person in question was a shadow director. However, in *Re Gasco Ltd*,[1] the person who owned 50 per cent of the share capital did not replace two directors who had resigned. Instead he employed two persons to manage the company.

McCracken J held that from the time that 50 per cent shareholder replaced the directors with the two managers, he had become a shadow director.[2]

The position of a shadow director might usefully be contrasted with a de facto (constructive) director. The former would normally not be an active, visible member of the board, while the latter, despite a lack of appointment, would generally be very visible and active.

While the conduct and intentions of persons acting as shadow and de facto directors may be very different, both may be made liable in tort for the debts of the company, as if they had been properly appointed de jure directors.

Disclosure of interest in proposed contracts

27.6   Under s 194[3](1) of the 1963 Act, it:

> 'shall be the duty of a director ... who is in any way, whether directly or indirectly, interested in a contract or proposed contract with the company, to declare the nature of his interest at a meeting[4] of the directors of the company.'

Shadow directors must also disclose such interests, in writing, to the board.[5]

If a director (or shadow director) fails to disclose his interest in accordance with s 194, the contract is voidable and the director must account to the company for the personal profits he has made.[6]

Section 194 was extended by s 47 of the 1990 Act to require disclosure by directors of loans, quasi-loans, etc – see **27.20**.

SPECIFIC TRANSACTIONS REGULATED

27.7   Part III of the 1990 Act makes provision for specific transactions which may give rise to potential conflict between a director's personal interest and that of the company.

These specific contracts include:

(1)   contracts of employment or directors' service contracts;
(2)   property transactions between the company and its directors;
(3)   loans to directors;
(4)   contracts entered into by the company with a third party in which the director has an interest.

---

1   (2001) 8(3) CLP 72.
2   And amenable to a restriction declaration under s 150 of the 1990 Act.
3   As amended by ss 27 and 47 of the 1990 Act.
4   Section 194(2)–(7) deals with the procedural requirements for such a board meeting.
5   See s 27(3) of the 1990 Act.
6   See also **25.28**.

Directors' service contracts

27.8   The limitations on extending directors' service contracts, imposed by ss 28 and 50 of the 1990 Act, have already been detailed in **25.34**.

The effect of these sections is to protect the company, and indirectly its investors, against a breach of his fiduciary duty by a director who might otherwise have placed his own personal interests above those of the company.

Substantial property transactions with directors

27.9   A property transaction is substantial if its value is the lower of £10,000 or 10 per cent of the company's net[1] assets shown in the most recent statutory accounts, but in no case less than £1,000.[2]

No transfer of any substantial non-cash asset, or any interest therein, can take place between a company and a director of the company, or of its holding company, or a person connected with such a director, unless it has first been approved by a resolution of the members in general meeting.

Effect of breach of s 29

27.10   Any arrangement[3] to transfer a non-cash asset made in contravention of s 29 is voidable at the option of the company, unless restitution to the company is no longer possible or avoidance would affect an innocent third party or the approval of the company in general meeting has been given within a reasonable period after the transaction.

Unless a director can show that he did not know the relevant circumstances[4] constituting a contravention, the director concerned and any director authorising such a transaction will be liable to repay to the company any gain he made and to indemnify the company for any loss it suffers.

Penalising the dealing in options to trade in certain shares and debentures

27.11   Section 30 of the 1990 Act makes it a criminal offence for directors, or any person acting on behalf of, or at the instigation of, a director, to deal in options to buy or sell 'relevant'[5] shares in, or debentures of, the company or associated companies.

A new s 30(3A) was inserted by s 102 of the 2001 Act to ensure that there was no conflict between Revenue-approved savings-related share option schemes and s 30.

---

1   The aggregate of the assets less the aggregate of all liabilities, including provisions for liabilities and charges.
2   See s 29(2).
3   And any transaction resulting from such an arrangement.
4   Or that he took all reasonable steps to secure the company's compliance with s 29 – see s 29(5).
5   Defined in s 30(2).

Prohibition of loans and credit to directors and connected persons

27.12 The 1963 Act did not prohibit the making of loans by companies to their directors, nor the granting of guarantees in respect of loans to directors by third parties. However, s 192[1] required particulars of such loans to be given in the company accounts, and then laid before the investors at the annual general meeting.

The 1963 Act did not provide for sanctions in the event of non-disclosure, s 192(3) simply placing a duty on the auditors, so far as they were reasonably able to do so, to include the required particulars in their report.

The 1990 Act introduces a much stricter regime. Sections 31 to 38 of that Act strictly regulate the provisions of loans, 'quasi-loans'[2] and other forms of credit granted by companies to their directors and persons connected with them. Unlike the 1963 Act, the 1990 legislation provides for criminal penalties and civil remedies in cases of non-compliance.

Section 75 of the 2001 Act added a new subsection 3A to s 25, which excludes certain leases for nominal rents being classified as credit transactions.

General prohibition on granting of credit to directors

27.13 Section 31(1) provides that, subject to the exceptional transactions specified in ss 32 to 37, all companies are prohibited from:

(1) making a loan or quasi-loan to a director of the company or of its holding company or to a person connected with such a director; or

(2) entering into a credit transaction as creditor for a director or a person so connected; or

(3) entering into any guarantee or providing any security in connection with a loan, quasi-loan or credit transaction made by a third party to such a director or a person so connected.

'Permitted' credit transactions

27.14 The exceptional transactions permitted by ss 32 to 37 are set out below.

Transactions below a certain value

27.15 Section 32 permits a company to 'lend' money to any of its directors or persons connected with them up to a maximum of 10 per cent of the net asset value[3] of the company.

Where the total amount outstanding to a company under such an arrangement exceeds 10 per cent of the net assets (in particular if the value of the relevant

---

1 Of the 1963 Act, as amended.

2 Defined in s 25(2)(a), (b) and (c). An example of a quasi-loan might be where a company allows a director to use its credit card for his personal purchases. The company pays the price of any purchases; in effect creating a loan to be repaid by the director.

3 Determined by reference to the last set of audited accounts – see s 29(2).

assets has fallen) and the directors become aware or ought reasonably to become aware that there exists such a situation, it is the duty of the company, its directors and any persons for whom the arrangements were made to amend the terms of the arrangements concerned within two months so that the total amount outstanding under the arrangements again falls within 10 per cent of the net asset value.[1] If the terms of the arrangements are not amended within two months, the arrangements are voidable by the company, unless s 38 applies (see **27.18**).

Intra-group loans and transactions

27.16   Section 78 of the Company Law Enforcement Act, 2001 substituted a new s 34 in the 1990 Act. Under the new s 34, a mechanism is introduced whereby companies may guarantee and provide security in connection with loans in favour of directors and persons connected with directors.

Section 34 provides for a validation procedure which permits the giving of guarantees and the provision of security, while at the same time ensuring that shareholders' and creditors' interests are protected. This validation procedure allows companies to give guarantees to and provide security in connection with leases, etc made by third parties to directors or connected persons. The new section is modelled on s 60(2) of the Companies Act 1963 (see **19.44**). The validation procedure is based on the requirement that the guarantee or security is given on the authority of a special resolution of the company and that the members voting on such a resolution have been provided by the directors of the company with certain facts and guarantees as to the company's financial state and ability to meet any debts which may arise from the giving of the guarantee or security in question.

Section 79 of the 2001 Act amended s 35 of the 1990 Act, which exempts transactions between a subsidiary and its holding company from the prohibition on the making of loans, etc contained in s 31 of the Act, where the transaction is made in favour of the holding company. The effect of this amendment is to extend the exemption afforded by the section to cover all companies, both holding and subsidiary, within a group of companies.

Business transactions and advances on directors' expenses

27.17   By virtue of s 37, a company can trade on a normal basis with its directors and persons connected with them. Such transactions must be in the ordinary course of business and the credit terms must be no more favourable than would be reasonable for the company to offer to a third party of the same financial standing. Thus a director can be a trade debtor of his company in respect of purchases of the company's ordinary goods and services.

Section 36 permits a company to provide its directors with advances to meet expenses to be properly incurred by them on the company's behalf. If these advances are not used, they must be refunded within six months.

---

1 Section 33(1) and (2), as amended by s 77 of the 2001 Act.

Civil[1] remedies for the making of prohibited loans, etc

27.18   Section 38(1) renders a transaction prohibited by s 31 voidable, unless this is not possible. In any event, the director concerned is liable to repay to the company any gain he has made and to indemnify it for any loss or damage resulting from the prohibited transaction.

Personal liability for company debts

27.19   If a company is being wound up and unable to pay its debts, and the court considers that loans to directors have contributed materially to the company's insolvency, or substantially impeded its orderly winding up, the court, on the application of the liquidator, any creditor or contributory, may declare that director personally liable, without limitation of liability, for the debts and liabilities of the company.

In deciding whether to make such an order under s 39(1), the court will take into account amounts paid back prior to the winding up and will consider the extent to which the loans in question contributed to the insolvency or impeded the orderly winding up of the company.

DISCLOSURE OF TRANSACTIONS INVOLVING DIRECTORS, AND OTHERS, IN THE ACCOUNTS

27.20   Sections 41 to 47 of the 1990 Act contain the requirements for disclosure by companies of transactions involving directors and persons connected with them.

A company must disclose, in its accounts, particulars of transactions entered into or subsisting during the accounting period, by the company[2] to a director,[3] or to any person connected with the director.

Under s 41(8), the disclosure requirement applies whether or not:

(1) the transaction or arrangement was prohibited by s 31;
(2) the director (or connected person) was of this status at the time the transaction was made; and
(3) the company making the loan was a subsidiary company and the loan was to a director of its holding company.

When disclosure is not required

27.21   The general disclosure requirements are exempted in the cases of:

(1) licensed banks[4] or their holding companies in respect of loans to directors;

---

1 An officer of the company who authorises or permits the breach of s 31 will also be guilty of a criminal offence – see s 40.
2 Or its subsidiary.
3 Including a director of a holding company.
4 Section 41(6).

(2) certain inter-company transactions;[1]

(3) directors' service contracts.[2]

Specific 'low value' transactions are also exempted from disclosure by s 45, eg loans etc, if the outstanding balance did not exceed £2,500 for each category of transaction during the year.

Particulars to be disclosed in companies' accounts

27.22 Section 42 sets out the particulars to be included in the accounts. In respect of each transaction,[3] the names of the persons involved, together with particulars of the principal terms, are to be disclosed in the annual accounts and, in the case of loans, the amounts outstanding at the start and end of the year, interest due, provisions made (if any) and the percentage of the company's net assets at the year end tied up in such loans. These general requirements relate to all companies, except licensed banks. Special rules for disclosure by licensed banks are contained in ss 44 and 45.

Where the particulars required by ss 41 to 43 are not supplied, under s 46 the auditors must include in their report such particulars so far as they are reasonably able to. This duty on auditors is similar to that in s 192(3) of the 1963 Act, which required disclosure in the auditors' report of loans to directors to the extent that these were not included in the accounts.

DISCLOSURE OF DIRECTORS' AND OTHERS' INTERESTS IN SHARES AND DEBENTURES

27.23 Sections 53 to 66 of the 1990 Act contain detailed provisions requiring disclosure by directors, shadow directors and company secretaries, of their interests in shares and debentures of the company.[4]

Chapter 2 (ss 67 to 96) provides for the notification of individual and group acquisitions of voting shares in plcs – see **22.2** et seq.

Share dealings by directors, secretaries and their families

27.24 Sections 54, 55 and 64 define the nature of interests to be disclosed. Generally, ss 53 to 66 require disclosure of beneficial interests of directors and secretaries for all companies.

Under s 53(1), directors, etc, must notify the company, *in writing*, of:

(1) interests held[5] on taking up the office;

---

1 Section 41(7)(a).

2 Section 41(7)(b).

3 And also any agreement reached during the year for such a transaction.

4 Or other companies within the group. See S. Nolan, 'Disclosure of Interests in Securities under Part IV of the Companies Act 1990' (2000) 7 CLP 31, at pp 31–36.

5 Including those of his spouse or minor child.

(2) purchases and sales of shares and debentures[1] while holding that office.

Sanction for non-compliance

27.25 Section 53(7) provides a criminal sanction for non-compliance with s 53(1) and (2).

Register of directors' and other interests

27.26 Every company must keep a register[2] of interests notified under ss 53 to 58. Sections 60 to 62 contain the detailed provisions relating to this register, which must be open to inspection by members or the public.[3]

Disclosure of interests in directors' report or accounts

27.27 The notified information on directors' etc interests must be included in the directors' report or as a note to the accounts – see s 63.

A public company is also under a duty to notify the Stock Exchange of any information it receives on shares or debentures held by a director, shadow director or secretary.[4]

The Director of Corporate Enforcement can appoint inspectors to investigate share dealings – see s 66 of the 1990 Act, as amended by the 2001 Act, Schedule, Part 2.

INSIDER DEALING BY CONNECTED PERSONS

27.28 In *Percival v Wright* (see **25.22**), the directors bought investors' shares without disclosing to the vendors that the board were in negotiations on a take-over bid for the company which valued the shares at a price much higher than the directors paid the investors. The court refused to overturn these transactions, holding that the directors' fiduciary duty was owed to the company, and not the individual shareholders.

The insider dealing provisions in the 1990 Act now extend the directors' duty of disclosure to protect potential investors in the company. This protection is against the use by 'insiders' such as directors, of privileged information which:

(1) they obtained by virtue of being connected with the company; and
(2) is unpublished and could materially affect the trading price of the shares in question, if published, ie is 'price-sensitive'.

---

1 Of the company, its holding company or subsidiary. The number of shares and the amount of the debentures must be given.
2 Section 59.
3 Section 60(8).
4 Section 65.

Persons who are closely connected with a company (insiders) and use 'price-sensitive' privileged information about that company to benefit themselves in share dealings with 'outsiders', would engage in the practice known as 'insider dealing'.

The Stock Exchange Listing Agreement required directors of listed companies[1] to ensure that share dealings did not take place between parties, one of which did not have price-sensitive information, which was in the possession of the other. Sections 107 to 121 of the 1990 Act now make insider dealing unlawful.

Unlawful dealing in securities by insiders

27.29   Section 108 makes it unlawful for a person who is, or has been during the preceding six months, connected with a company to deal in any securities of that company if, by reason of his connection with the company, he is in possession of unpublished price-sensitive information.

Section 107 defines both 'dealing' and 'securities'; the latter including, of course, shares and debentures.

Lawful dealings

27.30   The 1990 Act essentially makes it unlawful for *connected persons* to engage in dealings in securities, *unless* they give at least 21 days' notice to the Stock Exchange and the dealing takes place 7 to 14 days after the publication of the company's results.[2]

Connected persons

27.31   Section 108(11) makes it clear that a person is connected with a company and thus an insider if he is:

(1) an officer of the company, or other group company (subsidiary, holding company or fellow subsidiary); or
(2) a shareholder of the company or other group company; or
(3) a person who occupies a position which could reasonably be expected to give him access to inside information, ie persons having a professional, business or other relationship with the company or other group companies;
(4) an officer of a substantial shareholder (five per cent) in the company or other group company.

Section 107 contains a wide definition of 'officers'. It includes a director, secretary, or employee, liquidator, auditor, receiver, examiner or any person arranging a compromise between the company and its creditors.

---

1 See **10.15**.
2 Interim or final – see s 108(10).

Other companies and tippees

27.32   Persons connected with other companies[1] and individuals who receive 'tips'[2] or information from connected persons, can also be deemed to be 'insiders' for the purposes of insider dealing.

Liability for insider dealing

27.33   Under s 109, the insider will be liable to compensate any other party who sustained a loss[3] by virtue of his unlawful actions. The insider will also be liable to account to the company for any profit made by him out of dealing in the securities.

Time limits

27.34   An action for recovery of profit or loss must be commenced within two years after the date of the completion of the unlawful transaction.[4]

Criminal sanctions

27.35   Exceptionally heavy criminal sanctions are imposed by ss 111 to 114; the maximum being imprisonment for 10 years and/or a fine of £200,000.

Exempt transactions

27.36   Section 110 provides that certain transactions are exempt from the insider dealing provisions of s 108. These include securities acquired:

(1)   under a will or an intestacy;
(2)   under an approved employee profit-sharing scheme;
(3)   under the following transactions entered in good faith:
    (a)   obtaining a share qualification by a director;
    (b)   fulfilling obligations by a person under an underwriting agreement;
    (c)   by personal representatives, trustees, liquidators, receivers or examiners in the performance of their duties;
    (d)   by way of, or arising out of, mortgages or charges, pledges or liens on documents of title to securities.

Section 110 was amended by s 103 of the 2001 Act to remove any conflict between s 108 and Revenue-approved savings-related share option schemes.

Securities acquired in conformity with price stabilisation rules are also exempt – see **10.39**.

---

1 Section 108(2).
2 Section 108(3).
3 Based on the share price differences arising out of the existence of the price-sensitive information.
4 Section 109(4).

Stock Exchange supervision of insider dealing regulations

27.37 The Stock Exchange is expected to 'police' the insider dealing rules and to report any apparent offences to the Director of Public Prosecutions (DPP).

The obligation to report to the DPP and the Director of Corporate Enforcement is imposed upon both the relevant authority of the exchange and its members. Relevant authority is defined in s 108 as the Stock Exchange's:

(1) board of directors, committee of management or other management body; or
(2) manager, however described.

During 1999, two complaints of insider dealing were referred by the Irish Stock Exchange to the DPP.

The Director of Corporate Enforcement and the court are also empowered, under s 115(3), (5) and (6), to direct a Stock Exchange authority to investigate a complaint of an alleged offence, and to make a report to the DPP.

Section 38 of the 2001 Act makes it clear that the obligation of professional secrecy imposed on Stock Exchange officials by s 118 of the 1990 Act does not prohibit the disclosure of information concerning suspected breaches to the Director.

The Director may institute criminal proceedings or refer the matter to the DPP for him to do so – see s 115, as amended by s 37 of the 2001 Act.

Annual report

27.38 The Stock Exchange must present an annual report[1] to the Minister on its supervision of the insider dealing rules.

EU dimension

27.39 Section 116,[2] as amended by the 2001 Act, Schedule, Part 2, contains provisions intended to encourage co-operation between member state national stock exchanges in combating insider dealing.

---

1 Section 120.
2 And s 119.

FRAUDULENT TRADING

27.40   The statutory[1] liability for fraudulent trading extends the duty of honesty owed by directors (and others) to creditors, as well as the company.

Any person guilty of fraudulent trading may be personally responsible, without limitation of liability, for all the debts and other liabilities of the company.

RECKLESS TRADING (SUBJECTIVE TEST)

27.41   The subjective test[2] for reckless trading contained in s 297A(2)(b) of the 1963 Act is[3] intended to make available to company creditors a deceit-based remedy with a less demanding evidential requirement[4] than fraud – see Chapter 28.

RAISING OF DIRECTORS' COMPETENCE LEVELS

27.42   At common law, the test of competence for directors is subjective. A director need not exhibit in the performance of his duties a greater degree of skill than may reasonably be expected from a person of his knowledge and experience. Here again, the 1990 Act has increased the duties of directors, particularly the 'proper books of account' and reckless trading provisions.

Keeping proper books of account

27.43   Section 202 of the 1990 Act requires proper books of account to be kept, whether in the form of documents, or otherwise.

Purpose of books of account

27.44   Every company must keep proper books of account that:

(1)   correctly record and explain the transactions of the company;
(2)   will at any time enable the financial position of the company to be determined with reasonable accuracy;
(3)   will enable the directors to ensure that any balance sheet, profit and loss account or income and expenditure account of the company complies with the requirements of the Companies Acts; and
(4)   will enable the accounts of the company to be readily and properly audited.

---

1   Section 138 of the 1990 Act – see **28.34**.
2   See **26.15** et seq.
3   In this author's opinion.
4   Albeit in more limited circumstances.

Contents of books of account

27.45 Proper books of account are required to contain:

(1) entries from day to day of all sums of money received and expended by the company and the matters in respect of which the receipt and expenditure take place;
(2) a record of the assets and liabilities of the company;
(3) if the company's business involves dealing in goods:
  (a) a record of all goods purchased, and of all goods sold (except those sold for cash by way of ordinary retail trade), showing the goods and the sellers and buyers in sufficient detail to enable the goods and the sellers and buyers to be identified, and a record of all the invoices relating to such purchases and sales;
  (b) statements of stock held by the company at the end of each financial year and all records of stocktaking from which any such statement of stock has been, or is to be, prepared; and
(4) if the company's business involves the provision of services, a record of the services provided and of all the invoices relating thereto.

Criteria for proper books of account

27.46 If books of account are kept on a continuous and consistent basis, comply with the purpose and contents outlined above, give a true and fair view of the state of affairs of the company (see **32.27**), and explain its transactions, then they will be deemed to comply with s 202.

Personal liability of directors and officers

27.47 Directors and officers can incur both criminal and civil liabilities for failure to keep proper books of account, including unlimited personal liability for the debts of the company.[1]

Reckless trading (objective test)

27.48 The concept of 'reckless trading' was introduced by s 138 of the 1990 Act.

Unlike fraudulent trading, reckless trading is confined to officers of the company, including directors, shadow directors, secretaries and auditors. All these officers can now be made personally liable to contribute to the assets of the company, thereby providing a further source of funds for creditors of insolvent companies.

The statutory definition[2] of 'reckless trading' in s 297A(1) and (2)[3] includes two tests. An officer of a company shall be deemed to have been knowingly a party to the carrying on of any business of the company in a reckless manner if:

---

1 See next chapter.
2 Section 297A of the 1963 Act was inserted by s 138 of the 1990 Act.
3 Of the 1963 Act.

'(a) he was a party to the carrying on of such business and, having regard to the *general knowledge, skill and experience that may reasonably be expected of a person in his position,* he ought to have known that his actions or those of the company would cause loss to the creditors of the company, or any of them; or

(b) he was a party to the contracting of a debt by the company and did not honestly believe on reasonable grounds that the company would be able to pay the debt when it fell due for payment as well as all its other debts (taking into account the contingent and prospective liabilities).'

The test in limb (a) breaks new legal ground by importing an *objective* test of 'general knowledge, skill and experience' that may reasonably be expected of a director. This test replaces a director's common law subjective test of skill. The effect of this reform must be to raise the competency levels expected from all directors – see **26.1** to **26.14**.

PART V B

LEGAL LIABILITIES OF COMPANY DIRECTORS AND OFFICERS

Chapter 28

TORTIOUS LIABILITY OF COMPANY DIRECTORS

28.1   Torts which can be committed by directors can be classified into two main groups, depending upon whether the tortious conduct was based on dishonesty or a lack of competence.

TORTS BASED ON DISHONEST CONDUCT

28.2   We have seen[1] that the principle of honesty underlies directors' fiduciary duties. When a director is dishonest in carrying out his duties, he may incur a legal liability under the tort of deceit; for example, by fraudulently misrepresenting the company's profits to a bank when negotiating a loan on its behalf.

28.3   Section 297 of the 1963 Act creates the specific statutory tort of fraudulent trading, whilst the principle underpinning the subjective test of reckless trading in the 1990 Act is also deceit or fraud.

In actions for fraudulent trading, a liquidator must prove an actual intent[2] to defraud creditors on the part of a defendant director. This tort, being based on deceit or dishonesty, involves proof of moral turpitude akin to mens rea in criminal offences.

Where, however, an action is based on negligence, proof of moral turpitude is unnecessary. This tort is based on standards of competence. Thus proof of intention is not generally essential or relevant in negligence actions.

An element of dishonesty or deceit may also be involved where a director is in breach of a restriction or disqualification[3] order.

TORTS BASED ON INCOMPETENT CONDUCT

28.4   The tort of negligence is based on incompetence rather than dishonesty. In ordinary negligence actions, the standard of care (or competence) is measured by application of a 'reasonable man' test.

As pointed out in **26.3** et seq, the test required to make a director negligent at common law was that of gross carelessness, which is essentially

---

1 In Chapter 25.
2 The insertion of the words 'shall be deemed to have been' before 'knowingly' in s 297A(2) of the 1990 Act is evidence of the intention of the *Oireachtas* to ensure that imputed, as well as actual, knowledge will suffice to succeed in an action for reckless trading, under both objective and subjective tests – see **26.10** et seq and **28.27**.
3 See Chapter 30.

recklessness.[1] The objective test of recklessness in the 1990 Act is intended to raise directors' standards of care to 'ordinary' negligence by applying a 'reasonable director' test.

Again, the new s 204[2] liability for failure to maintain books of account is essentially 'competence' based.

Statutory interpretation

28.5 A tort is a civil wrong which arises, not exclusively from agreement, but from breach of a duty imposed by either common law or statute. The main remedy for a tort is an action for unliquidated damages.

Many of the specific instances of statutory liability imposed upon directors under the Companies Acts are torts. Accordingly, it is appropriate for a court to apply principles of statutory interpretation[3] which have evolved in tort law generally when considering them. For example, the concept of strict liability for breach of statutory duty.

28.6 Let us now focus on the more important[4] statutory 'company law' torts imposing upon directors unlimited liability to pay damages. These are:

(1) failure to maintain proper books of account. The first court decision dealing with this form of liability was not very encouraging for company creditors. However, a subsequent Supreme Court decision may help change this situation;
(2) reckless and fraudulent trading; and
(3) breach of restriction or disqualification order.

THE TORT OF FAILURE TO MAINTAIN PROPER BOOKS OF ACCOUNT

28.7 The duty to maintain proper books of account arises under s 202(1) of the 1990 Act. The types of books and their contents are prescribed in s 202(2), (3), and (4) and have been detailed in **27.42** et seq.

Who can initiate legal action

28.8 The liquidator, or any creditor or contributor of the company may apply to the court to declare any officers personally liable for the debts of the company.

---

1 At common law.
2 Of the 1990 Act.
3 And evidential developments such as res ipsa loquitur.
4 See also **27.19**.

Liability for breach of s 202

28.9   Section 204 imposes civil liability on officers[1] where:

(1)   a company that *is being wound up and is unable to pay its debts* has breached s 202; and
(2)   the court considers that the *breach has either*:
   (a)   contributed to the company's inability to pay all of its debts, or
   (b)   has *resulted in substantial uncertainty* as to the assets and liabilities of the company, *or*
   (c)   has substantially *impeded its orderly winding up*.

Let us now examine these three bases of tortious liability.

Contributing to the company's inability to pay all its debts

28.10   The court must be satisfied that the breach of s 202 contributed to the company's inability to pay all its debts.

Resulting in substantial uncertainty as to the assets and liabilities of the company

28.11   Any person who operates a company without keeping proper books of account should know that this (mal-) practice will result in uncertainty as to the assets and liabilities of the company. (In fact, this may well be the very reason for a conscious and dishonest decision by the directors *not* to maintain books of account.)

Because of this, it could be argued that a court should treat any failure to keep proper books as prima facie:

(1)   contributing to the company's inability to pay all its debts (basis (2)(a) above); and
(2)   resulting in substantial uncertainty as to the assets and liabilities of the company (basis (2)(b) above).

Substantially impeding the orderly winding-up of the company

28.12   This heading resulted in an award of £91,000 against the defendant in the *Mantruck Services* case because of the extra work generated for the liquidator and his staff (see below).

Defence

28.13   Section 204(4) allows an officer to plead in defence that he had taken all reasonable steps to secure compliance by the company, or that he had delegated this duty. However, there are conditions. The delegatee must be a

---

1 Or former officers – see also s 204(6). The obligation to keep books of account is a joint and separate liability on each director – see Murphy J's judgment in *Re Vehicle Imports Ltd* (2001) 8(3) CLP 72.

'competent and reliable person, acting under the supervision or control of a director who had been formally allocated [this] responsibility'.

Judicial interpretation of ss 202 and 204

28.14   The first opportunity for judicial interpretation of ss 202 and 204 arose in the case of *Mantruck Services Ltd (in liquidation); Mehigan v Duignan*.[1] In this case, Shanley J found that:

(1) (a)   the company was in breach of s 202 in failing to keep proper books of account;
    (b)   the company was unable to pay its debts at the date of its winding up;
(2)   the breaches of s 202 resulted in:
    (a)   substantial uncertainty as to the assets and liabilities of the company; and
    (b)   substantially impeded the orderly winding up of the company; and
(3)   the respondent knowingly and wilfully authorised and permitted the breach of s 202, and could not avail of any defence.

Exercising the court's discretion

28.15   When exercising its discretion under s 204, Shanley J felt the court must consider the extent to which the breach of s 202 resulted in financial loss and, if it did, whether or not such losses were reasonably foreseeable by the officer as a consequence of his action. He then held that, although it was not possible to separate out liabilities prior to winding up which resulted from the breach of s 202, the liquidator had spent 80 per cent of his time seeking to remedy the deficiencies in the books of the company. The cost of that proportion of the liquidator's time was £91,240 and was a loss reasonably foreseeable by the respondent as a consequence of his actions. Accordingly, Shanley J declared the respondent to be personally liable to the company for the £91,240.

There can be no doubt that Shanley J was correct in finding the defendant personally liable for the extra work undertaken by the liquidator under liability basis (3), because it had been clearly necessary for the orderly winding up of the company, and as such was easily proved.

Proof of loss

28.16   Shanley J also found that the breaches of s 202 had resulted in substantial uncertainty as to the assets and liabilities of the company. However, before exercising the court's discretion to declare the defendant liable under this heading, Shanley J stated that this discretion must be exercised in a 'responsible but also in a constitutional fashion'. This meant the court must have regard to the extent to which the contravention of s 202 resulted in financial loss and, if it did, whether such losses were reasonably foreseeable by the officer as a consequence of the contravention, Shanley J then held that as it

---

1   [1997] 1 IR 340.

was not possible to separate out liabilities of the company, the defendant incurred no liability for the substantial uncertainty as to the assets and liabilities of the company which resulted from the breach of s 204.

28.17 A counter argument[1] would be that once the court was satisfied that the breach of s 204 resulted in substantial uncertainty as to company assets, it should be the wrongdoer who committed the breach who would suffer evidentially – not the creditors whom ss 202 to 204 were enacted to protect. Accordingly, under this heading of liability, the court could achieve a more just result by treating the consequences of the breach as prima facie causing loss to company creditors, unless the defendant(s) (who was under a statutory duty to keep the books) can prove otherwise. Is this not what the wording in s 204(1)(a) and (b) intends when setting out this form of creditor protection? If the Oireachtas had intended the court to apply the further test of whether there had been financial loss suffered by the defendant, surely express provision would have been made for it, as the legislature did in s 297A(3)(b) in respect of reckless and fraudulent trading actions.

A case of strict liability?

28.18 Because the Oireachtas did not expressly provide for the proof of financial loss (as it did in the reckless and fraudulent trading provisions), is it not likely that it intended breach of s 202 to be a case of strict liability?[2]

To put it simply, if the Oireachtas bestows the privilege of incorporation, it is entitled to make persons who grossly abuse it strictly liable for losses which company creditors suffer. As Leigh[3] comments, 'the courts and Parliament were commonly astute to devise doctrines to overcome evidentiary problems and ... strict liability should be seen in this light'. Let us now consider foreseeability, causation and culpability in this context.

Foreseeability (or intention)

28.19 Culpable conduct like fraudulent and reckless trading necessarily involves proof of foreseeability and/or intention by a plaintiff. The legislature makes provision for this (see **28.41**).

Section 204 involves, not positive conduct, but a failure by a director to carry out a duty imposed on him by law. Here, intention is irrelevant. The tort is simply breach of a positive statutory duty (but see **28.21**).

Causation

28.20 In both fraudulent and reckless trading, a plaintiff will have to prove causation. In the case of reckless trading, for example, not all company creditors are likely to have suffered loss.

---

1 The comments on Shanley J's judgment are based upon a conference paper delivered by the author at the University of Limerick on 8 March 1999.
2 To use the tort and criminal law analogy.
3 L.H. Leigh *Strict and Vicarious Liability* (Sweet and Maxwell, 1982).

The legislature makes no provision for company creditors to prove causation in the case of s 204 liability. This is not unreasonable because of the opportunity for fraud and the difficulties of proof associated with a lack of company accounting records. It would therefore seem pragmatic and realistic to conclude that offending directors are strictly liable to the general body of company creditors.

Culpability

28.21 Foreseeability and culpability can be linked. The legislature requires the proof of fault in fraudulent and reckless trading actions which are based on deceit. The directors must have been personally involved. There is no such requirement for breach of s 202 which is based on competence. All directors will be (strictly) liable unless they can avail of the statutory defence in s 204(4).

As auditors are required to advise the Registrar under s 194 if proper books of account have not been kept, there is the potential here also for them to incur a liability for professional negligence if they fail to do so.

The punitive nature of civil liability and constitutional rights

28.22 Shanley J in the *Mantruck Services* case accepted that the 1990 Act required *no causal relationship* between the contravention of s 202 and the declaration of unlimited liability on an officer for the debts of the insolvent company under s 204. However, he was influenced by the High Court decision in *O'Keeffe v Ferris, Ireland and the Attorney-General*, where Murphy J stated that:

> 'in exercising its discretion under section 297(1) of the 1963 Act, (the fraudulent trading provisions), the court would exercise its powers not merely in a responsible but also in a constitutional fashion. If the Constitution does require that in civil proceedings the burden imposed on defendants should in general be commensurate with the loss suffered by the plaintiff (or the class whom the plaintiff represents) then it must be assumed that the subsection will be so construed and applied.'

Shanley J then decided that the factors of proof of causation, culpability and duration were relevant to the exercise of the court's discretion under s 204.

The Supreme Court decision in *O'Keeffe v Ferris and Ors*,[1] clarifying the power of the Oireachtas to enact punitive civil liability provisions, placed some doubts on Shanley J's restrictive interpretation of s 204.

In this case, O'Flaherty J approved of Lord Denning MR's comments in *Cyona Distributors Ltd* [1967] Ch 889 when he stated:

> 'In my judgment that section is deliberately framed in wide terms so as to enable the court (to bring fraudulent persons to book) ...
>
> The court order may be compensatory. Or it may be punitive. The court has full power to direct its destination.'

---

1 [1997] 3 IR 463 (see **28.40**).

O'Flaherty J stated that Irish law recognises that in civil proceedings, punitive damages may be awarded on occasion, without trenching the Constitution in any respect. However, a court should ensure that any sanction imposed (the culpability rather than the causation element), was proportionate to the wrong doing (see also **28.39**).

Illustrating legal alternatives

28.23   It is, perhaps, easiest to illustrate the post *Mantruck Services* position by using a simple example.

Suppose a company is being wound up. The liquidator finds that its financial position is thus:

Assets   –   £50,000
Liabilities – £250,000
Shortfall   – £200,000

If a court applied Shanley J's judgment in similar circumstances to the *Mantruck Services* case, the company's loss of £200,000 would be borne by its unpaid creditors, notwithstanding the fact that the directors were in breach of s 202.

To apply the strict liability (causation) principle in the same case would mean that the company loss of £200,000 is, in effect, transferred from the creditors to the directors who were in breach of their statutory duty to keep proper accounts under s 202.

The court can still use the culpability concept to apportion the £200,000 loss among the individual directors.

The strict liability causation principle approach was, in fact, taken by Geoghegan J in *Re Ashclad Ltd (In Liquidation)*.[1]

In this case Geoghegan J found, inter alia, that:

(1)   proper books of account had not been kept;
(2)   as a consequence of deficiencies in cash, there was quite obviously substantial uncertainty as to the company's assets and liabilities;
(3)   the company's orderly winding up was being impeded;
(4)   as a matter of probability, at least £100,000 had been wrongly withdrawn from the company and appropriated for other purposes; and
(5)   the extra work necessitated by the liquidator cost £12,000.

Geoghegan J then ordered that the respondents should be made personally liable, to the extent of £112,000, for the company's debts.

---

1   (2000) 7 CLP 153, and *Bar Review*, Vol 6, Issue 6, April 2001.

THE TORT OF RECKLESS TRADING

28.24　The Cork Committee[1] recommended the introduction of liability for wrongful trading. This was implemented in the United Kingdom in 1985 and is now contained in s 214 of the Insolvency Act 1986.

The legislature in Ireland adopted a weaker concept in terms of creditor protection and introduced a new statutory liability for reckless trading.

Who can sue and be sued

28.25　Officers' liability for reckless trading was originally enacted by s 33 of the 1990 Amendment Act. This was then repealed by s 138 of the 1990 Act which effectively inserted s 297A in the 1963 Act.

Section 297A (1) provides that if, either:

(1) in the course of winding up a company; or
(2) during examinership proceedings, it appears that an officer committed reckless trading,

the court, on the application of the receiver, examiner, liquidator or any other creditor or contributory of the company, may declare that such officer shall be personally liable, without limitation of liability, for all or any of the debts or other liabilities of the company which the court may direct.

What constitutes reckless trading?

28.26　The concept of reckless trading is set out in s 297A(1)(a) and (2) of the 1963 Act. Whilst reckless trading is not actually defined, s 297A(2)(a) and (b) give two broad alternative tests for ascertaining whether conduct is reckless or not. Objective or subjective criteria in these tests may therefore be used by a court.

The objective test of foreseeability and culpability

28.27　Section 297A(2)(a) contains the objective test. It would impose liability if a director or officer was party to the carrying on of the business in such a manner that, having regard to the general knowledge, skill and experience that may reasonably be expected of a person in his position, he ought to have known that his actions or those of the company would cause loss to the creditors.

The purpose of this section is to enable the court to apply an objective test to the decision making process for imputing knowledge of reckless trading – see **26.10**.

1　*Report of the Review Committee on Insolvency Law and Practice* (Chaired by Sir Kenneth Cork) (HMSO, 1982, Cmnd 8558).

The objective test and the **Hefferon Kearns** *case*

28.28 The reckless trading provisions were considered in *Re Hefferon Kearns Ltd (No 2); Dublin Heating Co Ltd v Hefferon and Others.*[1]

Hefferon Kearns Ltd (the company) was a construction company in which the four defendants were the only members and directors. The company commenced trading in January 1989. Its initial trading losses were:

	Losses after	Amount in £000s
1989	6 months	73
1989[2]	12 months	8
1990	2 months	23
	4 months	39
	6 months	72

During May 1990, two directors personally borrowed £45,000 which they used to discharge company debts.

The directors expected to reduce the losses in summer 1990 (as they had done the previous year) but due to a dispute over contract payments, this did not happen. Instead, losses increased, and the August management accounts (when produced on 1 October) showed the company with a balance sheet deficit in excess of £400,000.

A meeting of creditors was called and it was resolved to have an examiner appointed. The examiner proposed a scheme of arrangement. It was a condition of the scheme that there should be no reckless trading proceedings taken against the directors. However, the plaintiff, who was owed £41,000, decided to sue, and this caused the scheme to collapse.

Lynch J, in this case, when applying the objective test, equated recklessness with gross carelessness. The criteria he applied was 'would a reasonable man have described the defendant's actions as reckless?'.[3] Again, the word 'knowingly' has an effect on the definition of reckless. Because of it, recklessness required knowledge, or imputed knowledge, that the defendant's action would cause a loss to creditors; it would not be sufficient simply to show that there might have been some worry or uncertainty as to the ability to pay all the creditors.[4]

Applying this objective test of recklessness to the facts of the case, the judge considered them mainly against the first director, T. Hefferon, who was then de facto managing director.

Lynch J then found that, as Hefferon had reasonable grounds for believing that extra monies might be received to pay the company's creditors, he did not know that his actions would cause them loss.

---

1 [1993] 3 IR 191 (HC).
2 Directors had obtained bi-monthly management accounts from 1 January 1990.
3 See **26.13** et seq.
4 See **26.14** where author suggests the legislature might have intended to create a new tort of 'negligent trading' with the objective test.

Thus, in applying the objective test to the facts, Lynch J held that there was no evidence to show that T. Hefferon had traded recklessly within the objective test criteria.

Critique

28.29   As explained in **26.14**, the author considers that Lynch J should have applied an objective test using the criteria of 'a reasonably competent director'. The question posed should have been 'Would a reasonably competent director have reasonably described Mr T. Hefferon's actions as reckless?' (see **26.13**).

The subjective test for imputing knowledge and blame

28.30   Under the subjective test of recklessness in s 297A(2)(b), a director will be liable if:

> 'he was party to the contracting of a debt *but did not honestly believe, on reasonable grounds, that the company would be able to pay the debt* when it fell due for payment (including all contingent and prospective liabilities).'

The subjective test and the **Hefferon Kearns** case

28.31   A court may consider both tests to decide whether a director's conduct is reckless. In this instance where a person did not honestly believe, on reasonable grounds, that the company would be able to pay its debts as they fell due, he would be guilty of reckless trading. Lynch J held that by continuing to trade after the board meeting on 27 September, T. Hefferon, 'was ... a party to the contracting of debts, by the company, when *he knew that those debts ... could not be paid by the company as they fell due*'.

Accordingly, Lynch J found T. Hefferon, according to the subjective test, had traded recklessly. However, he also found that Mr Hefferon had acted honestly and reasonably in the circumstances.

Defence

28.32   Section 297A(6) provides that where the court finds that an officer has acted honestly and responsibly in relation to the affairs of the company, it may relieve him of liability. In the *Hefferon Kearns* case, Lynch J, after finding that T. Hefferon had traded recklessly, absolved him from liability under s 297A(2)(b), because he had acted honestly and reasonably.

Causation and proof of loss

28.33   A successful applicant to the court when proving reckless conduct, must also prove that he had suffered[1] loss or damage resulting from the defendant's conduct – see s 297A(3)(b).

---

1 The court also cannot grant a declaration unless the company is unable to pay its debts under s 214 of the 1963 Act.

Because of the narrow definition of this tort, not all company creditors will be able to prove loss. As a remedy, therefore, it is probably of use only to creditors who dealt with the company shortly before its liquidation, ie when the company was technically insolvent.

As pointed out in **28.17**, no such requirement to prove causation has been imposed on plaintiffs seeking redress on grounds of a failure to keep proper books of account under ss 202 and 204 of the 1990 Act.

THE TORT OF FRAUDULENT TRADING

28.34   Fraudulent trading is defined in s 297A(1)(b) of the 1963 Act as being knowingly a party to the carrying on of any business of the company with intent to defraud creditors[1] of the company or for any fraudulent purpose.

Who may sue and be sued

28.35   Section 297A(1) provides that if either

(1) in the course of winding up the company; or
(2) during examinership proceedings, any person was knowingly a party to carrying on the business of the company in a fraudulent manner,

then the court, may entertain an application from the same persons as entitled to pursue a reckless trading claim – see **28.25**.

What constitutes fraudulent trading

28.36   In *Re Kelly's Carpetdrome Ltd*,[2] inadequate books of account were kept, financial records destroyed and company assets and stocks siphoned off. Costello J imposed personal liability for company debts, not only on company officers and members, but also on an outsider because, 'he ran the company and the directors did his bidding[3] at every opportunity that he required them to do so'.

Two sets of books were kept in *Re Aluminum Fabricators Ltd*[4] with the intention of defrauding company creditors, including the Revenue Commissioners, by enabling the controllers to siphon off company assets for their own purposes. Not surprisingly, Hanlon J held that those responsible were personally liable for the debts of the company.

28.37   In *Re Contract Packaging Ltd*,[5] a number of deposit accounts were excluded from the company's records, and the money in them siphoned off by some of the directors.

---

1 Or creditors of any other person.
2 (Unreported) 1 July 1983 (HC).
3 He would now be a shadow director as defined in s 27 of the 1990 Act.
4 [1984] ILRM 399.
5 (Unreported) 16 January 1992 (HC).

There was also a VAT fraud involving the creation of second invoices seeking VAT credits, and company business[1] was diverted to another company controlled by one of the directors. Flood J imposed personal liability on the directors involved, for fraudulent trading.

28.38   The 'carrying on' of a business can include a single transaction. This was made clear in *Re Hunting Lodges Ltd.*[2] In this case, the directors arranged for the sale of the company's main asset (a public house), at a time when the company was insolvent. Part of the purchase price was paid secretly to the directors 'under the table', essentially to defraud the Revenue Commissioners as company creditors.[3]

Carroll J held that this single transaction constituted the carrying on of the business in a fraudulent manner, stating, 'it is not necessary that there should be a common agreed fraudulent interest. If each of the participants act for a fraudulent purpose, then each may be liable'.

In *Morris v Banque Arabe et al (No 2)*,[4] Neuberger J held that in s 213(2) of the UK's Insolvency Act 1986, where it was sought to make a person who was not an officer of the company liable for being knowingly a party to the carrying on of the company's business with intent to defraud creditors, it was only necessary to show that the person had participated in the fraudulent acts of the company. It was not necessary to show that such a person carried on, or assisted in carrying on, the company's business.

Culpability and apportionment of personal liability

28.39   Carroll J relied on the judgement of Maugham J in *Re William C Leith Bros Ltd*[5] in accepting that the imposition of civil liability for fraudulent trading can be punitive. Accordingly, in *Re Hunting Lodges Ltd*, she apportioned the extent of the directors' personal liability on the basis of their individual culpability: an action now reinforced by the Supreme Court decision in *O'Keeffe v Ferris and Others*.

Constitutionality of fraudulent trading provision

28.40   Because of the punitive nature of the fraudulent trading provision, the plaintiff in *O'Keeffe v Ferris, Ireland and the Attorney General*[6] sought a declaration that it was unconstitutional, because it created a criminal offence. Murphy J found in the High Court that the provision in question neither created a

---

1 And also the equitable ownership of the company's premises.
2 [1985] ILRM 75.
3 It also does not matter that only one creditor has been defrauded – see *Re Gerald Cooper Chemicals Ltd* [1978] 1 Ch 262.
4 [2000] TLR 749.
5 [1932] 2 Ch 71.
6 [1993] 3 IR 165.

criminal offence, nor infringed the Constitution: a decision upheld on appeal by the Supreme Court in February 1997.[1]

The Supreme Court held that none of the indicia of a criminal offence were present, but that the plaintiff's case was put on the basis that civil proceedings were really a disguise for an attempt by the Oireachtas to impose a criminal sanction in a civil context.

The court rejected this construction. It held that the fraudulent trading provisions are within the power of the Oireachtas to enact, with a view to protecting creditors and others who may fall victim to persons engaged in corporate fraud; O'Flaherty J stating:

> 'It is true that fraud is an ingredient in many criminal offences, but it is also an ingredient in various civil wrongs.'[2]

O'Flaherty J also clarified the punitive element of the sanction permitted by the legislation, saying it takes the following two forms:

(1) the loss of the protection of limited liability in the case of shareholders, and
(2) the fact that a wrongdoer may have to repay more than he got out of his wrongdoing.

In respect of (2), O'Flaherty J confirmed that:

> 'any sanction imposed should be proportionate to the wrongdoing that has been made out. But it is [also] clear that our law recognises the fact that punitive or exemplary damages may be awarded on occasion.'

As mentioned in **28.22**, this Supreme Court decision may also have implications for the future judicial interpretation of s 204 of the 1990 Act.

Causation and proof of loss

28.41   As in the case of reckless trading, the court, as required by s 297A(3), will only impose personal liability for fraudulent trading when satisfied that the applicant creditor(s) has suffered foreseeable loss or damage resulting from the defendant's conduct. In cases of serious and blatant fraud, such as continuous siphoning off of company funds, or other misappropriation of company assets, a liquidator should have little difficulty proving foreseeability in the circumstances. The effect of such erosion of the company's financial position is so fundamental that it is easily seen to impact upon all its creditors, both existing and future. In *Re Kemp*,[3] it was held that it did not matter that the creditor was not owed a present debt at the time of the fraud.

---

1   *O'Keeffe v Ferris & Ors* [1997] 3 IR 463.
2   See *Northern Bank Finance v Charlton* [1979] IR 199.
3   [1988] BCLC 217 (CA).

Where the creditors only allege that the company or its officers preferred one or more creditors over others, it was held in *Re Sarflax Ltd*[1] that this conduct did not constitute fraud within the corresponding UK legislative provisions.

Time limits

28.42   Under the Statute of Limitations 1957, the limitation period[2] for cases of fraudulent trading (and misfeasance proceedings) is six years from the date of the alleged offence.

TORTIOUS LIABILITY OF DIRECTORS FOR BREACH OF RESTRICTION OR DISQUALIFICATION ORDERS

28.43   The law relating to the imposition of restriction and disqualification orders is outlined in Chapter 30. Directors (and managers) can incur tortious liability arising out of a breach of either of these sanctions.

28.44   Where a person breaches a restriction or a disqualification order:

(1) the company will be entitled to recover from him as a simple contract debt any consideration given to him by the company for an act done or services provided, while he was acting in contravention of the order, eg remuneration paid to him;

(2) where the company is wound up while he is acting, or within a period of twelve months since his involvement, and if it is unable to pay its debts, *that person may be made personally liable for all or part of the company's debts incurred while he was so acting.*[3] An application may be made by a liquidator or a creditor to render that person liable.

Other directors and minimum capital requirements under s 150(3)

28.45   The other directors of a company, *which does not comply with the capital requirements of s 150(3)* after it is notified by a person on whom a restriction order has been placed, are also at risk financially. If the company is wound up and is unable to pay all its debts, its officers who knew or ought to have known of the restriction may be personally liable for all the debts of the company.[4]

Acting under the direction of a disqualified person

28.46   Any person who acts on an instruction from a person whom he knows is disqualified will be guilty of an offence which on conviction could lead to that

---

1 [1979] 1 Ch 529.
2 *Southern Mineral Oil Ltd (In Liquidation) v Cooney (No 2)* [1997] 1 IR 237.
3 Section 163 of the 1990 Act.
4 See s 163(4).

person himself being disqualified. In addition he may also be held liable for the debts of a company while he was acting on the instruction of the disqualified person.[1]

CIVIL REMEDIES FOR COMMISSION OF TORT

28.47 In the next chapter we shall focus on the civil remedies[2] available against directors and others who may have committed a 'company law' tort.

---

1 Sections 164 and 165.
2 Both substantive and procedural.

Chapter 29

CIVIL REMEDIES AGAINST DIRECTORS

29.1 Directors can incur a legal liability to pay compensation or to contribute personally to the assets of the company, by breaching their common-law or statutory duties, or behaving in a reckless, fraudulent or other culpable manner.

In this chapter, we highlight the main grounds for civil actions against directors[1] by the company, its creditors, members and others.

REMEDIES OF THE COMPANY AGAINST ITS DIRECTORS

29.2 A breach of duty by a director is a wrong against the company. The company itself has the right to take legal action against the offending director(s). However, as the company is controlled by the directors who may have committed the wrong against it, there may be practical difficulties in the company pursing legal action against its directors whilst they retain control of it. This situation is implicitly recognised in cases of statutory duties, where most remedies apply in the course of the winding up of the company.

If sufficient independent shareholders were aware of the directors' breach of duty, then they could replace the board by passing an ordinary resolution at a general meeting. The new directors could then pursue the company's rights of action against the (former) offending directors.

A change in ownership of the company might also lead to action being taken on its behalf by a new board against its former directors for breaches of their duties to the company.

29.3 The type of remedy will vary according to the nature of the breach of duty.[2] For example, the director may have to account for a personal gain or secret profit as in *Industrial Development Consultants Ltd v Cooley*,[3] or he may be required to indemnify the company against loss caused by his incompetence in negotiating an ultra vires or unlawful contract on behalf of the company.

Members may waive breach of duty

29.4 Since directors' duties are owed to the company, the members may, after full disclosure of the breach in question to a general meeting, *waive (or forgive) a director's breach of duty.* For example, in *Multinational Gas Petrochemical Co v*

---

1 And others.
2 See Chapters 25 to 27.
3 See **25.18** et seq.

Multinational Gas and Petrochemical Services Ltd,[1] the court confirmed that members can, by resolution, waive a director's breach of duty. Such a company resolution may also be a bar to a liquidator pursuing that breach of duty against the director(s). However, members cannot ratify an ultra vires or unlawful contract – see **12.7**.

Difficulties facing minority shareholders

29.5 Because of the rule in *Foss v Harbottle,*[2] where directors are in breach of their duties to the company, the proper person to sue is the company itself. This means, in practice, that the majority of shareholders must agree to bring the action. If the directors hold the majority of the shares or are in control of the company, they may feel secure or immune from the risk of being sued.

REMEDIES OF SHAREHOLDERS AGAINST DIRECTORS

29.6 The rule in *Foss v Harbottle* only applies to wrongs done to the company: it does not prevent any shareholder suing for wrongs done to him personally by the company, its directors or a majority of its members. For example, in *Pender v Lushington,*[3] a member successfully sued and compelled the company to record his vote.[4]

Under s 205 of the 1963 Act, any member of a company can complain to the court that the powers of the directors are being exercised in a manner oppressive to him. Such a member may also petition the court to wind up the company.[5]

When granting relief under s 205 in *Irish Press Ltd v Ingersoll Irish Publications Ltd,*[6] the court ordered the respondent to sell its shares to the petitioner.

Section 23(11) of the Companies (Amendment) Act 1983 makes directors directly liable to shareholders for all losses or damage or expenses incurred by them when new shares have been allotted in violation of existing shareholders' statutory pre-emption rights.

REMEDIES OF CREDITORS AGAINST DIRECTORS

29.7 Because of the difficulties facing a company in taking legal action against its own directors, most serious civil actions against directors will arise when the

---

1 [1983] Ch 258. There may also be limited relief available to directors under s 391 of the 1963 Act, and the company's articles of association. See article 138 of Table A.
2 See **17.7** et seq.
3 (1877) 6 Ch D 70.
4 This is one example of the 'apparent' exceptions to the rule in *Foss v Harbottle* – see also *Cook v Deeks* [1916] 1 AC 554.
5 Under s 213 of the 1963 Act.
6 (Unreported) 16 December 1993 (HC).

company is in financial trouble. Actions can be taken by creditors personally against directors, or, more usually, by a liquidator on behalf of all the company creditors. These actions are generally based on the notion of statutory liability being imposed on directors for culpable conduct, as a means of protecting company creditors.

DIRECTORS' LIABILITY IN TORT FOR INSOLVENT COMPANY'S DEBTS

29.8 Directors mainly face potential unlimited liability for company debts by statutory provision under specific torts.[1] In these circumstances, the directors' tortious liability arises when the company is in the course of being wound up.[2] The main torts are:

(1) failure to keep proper books of account and breach of s 202 of the 1990 Act;
(2) reckless trading;
(3) fraudulent trading;
(4) where a director makes a declaration of *solvency*:
  (a) under s 60(5) of the 1963 Act in connection with the *giving of financial assistance* for the purchase of shares in the company, and the company is wound up within 12 months, or
  (b) under s 256(8) of the 1963 Act prior to a *voluntary* winding up, the director may incur unlimited liability for the debts of the company;
(5) when a company has made a loan[3] to a director covered by s 32 of the 1990 Act (ie exceeds 10 per cent of the net asset value of the company), and the company is subsequently wound up; and
(6) where a person has acted as a director whilst a restricted or disqualified person, or took instructions from such a person, he can incur unlimited liability for company debts under s 163 of the 1990 Act, when the company is subsequently wound up.

Any officer who knew that a restricted person was acting as a director may also be liable – see s 163(4).

VOLUNTARY CONTRACTUAL ASSUMPTION BY DIRECTORS OF UNLIMITED LIABILITY

29.9 Sections 197 and 198 of the 1963 Act provide that the liability of the directors, or of the managing director, may, if so provided by the memorandum and articles of association, be unlimited.

---

1 See Chapter 28.
2 Exceptionally, in the cases of reckless and fraudulent trading, liability can additionally arise in respect of companies under examinership, but not being wound up – see s 297A of the 1963 Act.
3 See **27.12** et seq.

LIABILITY OF DIRECTORS FOR TRANSACTIONS OF SOLVENT COMPANIES

29.10   Generally, contracts negotiated on behalf of the company are the responsibility of the company. It is only in exceptional cases that the director may incur a legal liability for individual corporate transactions.

Ultra vires and unauthorised transactions

29.11   Directors can incur personal liability to the company for ultra vires or unauthorised transactions.[1] Here again though, the members, after full disclosure in general meeting, may waive the company's right of action.

Personal contractual liability

29.12   Where a director, for example, gives a personal guarantee to induce a bank to loan the company money, he will incur personal liability under the guarantee if the company defaults with repayment(s).

TORTIOUS LIABILITY OF DIRECTORS GENERALLY

When considering the tortious liability of company directors, it is useful to distinguish between common-law and statutory torts.

Common law and statutory deceit

29.13   At common law, a director of a solvent company can commit the tort of deceit if, for example, he fraudulently misrepresents the profits of the company when negotiating a loan on its behalf from a bank. Generally, though, it is the company, rather than its directors, which is responsible for corporate torts. Of course, if a director himself commits or gives instructions for the commission of a tort, he may be jointly liable with the company. As this conduct by directors would be rare, actions against a solvent company's directors on grounds of common-law deceit would be infrequent. However, s 297 of the 1963 Act created a tort of statutory deceit – making it possible to bring an action against the directors of an *insolvent* company for *fraudulent* trading.

Common-law and statutory negligence

29.14   Actions against directors of solvent companies based on the tort of negligence are also impractical, not least because of the subjective standard of care (low competency level) expected from directors. For the unqualified

---

1 The outsider or creditor being protected by either s 8 of the 1963 Act, or reg 6 of the European Communities (Companies) Regulations 1973, SI 1973/163 – see Chapters 36 and 38.

director to be negligent at common law, he must have acted with gross carelessness (recklessly!). Because of the low standards expected from directors at common law, the legislature introduced the tort of reckless trading. The objective test in s 297A of the 1963 Act is, as this author argues in **26.14**, an attempt to create the new tort of negligent trading, but this new tort is only actionable if the company is being wound up (see Chapter 26).

The s 204 tort of failure to maintain proper books of account is another example of statute-based negligence – on this occasion akin to strict liability because of the limited defence available against it – see **28.13**. Other examples of statutory liabilities based on the negligence concept are set out in **29.8**.

It should be remembered, though, that whilst the statutory torts supplement common-law remedies in certain specified company law situations, they do not replace them.

STATUTORY LIABILITY FOR INDIVIDUAL TRANSACTIONS

29.15   There are a number of instances where the legislature imposes liability on directors for transactions involving the company, its creditors and others. Some examples are set out in **29.16** to **29.18**.

Liability to the company

29.16   Where a director fails to disclose his interest in a proposed contract in accordance with s 194 of the 1963 Act, the contract is voidable and he must account to the company for the personal profits he has made.

Again, if the company loses money on the transfer of a non-cash asset (of at least £1,000), and there is a breach of s 29 of the 1990 Act, the director concerned and any director authorising such a transaction will be liable under s 29(4) to repay the gain to the company and to indemnify it for any loss it suffers. Section 38 imposes similar liabilities on directors in respect of loans etc prohibited by s 31 of the 1990 Act.

A director of a subsidiary company which has bought shares in its holding company may also incur personal liability.[1]

Liability to company creditors[2]

29.17   Where an officer issues a business letter, cheque or invoice showing the name of the company incorrectly, that officer will be subject to a fine and also be liable for the debts of the company in the transaction involved, if the company fails to honour its obligations under them.

---

1 See **20.7**.
2 Section 36 of the 1963 Act imposes personal liability on company shareholders when trading with fewer than the statutory minimum number of members.

Liability to others

29.18   In the case of insider dealing, the director or other insider involved will be liable to compensate any other party who sustained a loss on the sale or purchase of shares – see s 109 of the 1990 Act.

PROCEDURAL REMEDY

29.19   Section 298 of the 1963 Act (as amended by s 142 of the 1990 Act and s 50 of the 2001 Act), gives a court power to assess damages against directors of an insolvent company. The s 298 remedy of misfeasance proceedings only operates during the winding up of a company.

Misfeasance proceedings

29.20   Misfeasance proceedings may be initiated by the liquidator, the Director of Corporate Enforcement or any creditor or contributory of the insolvent company against 'any person who has taken part in the formation or promotion of the company, or any past or present officer, liquidator, receiver or examiner of the company'.

Conduct falling under s 298

29.21   The circumstances in which persons may be held liable under s 298 are if they have misapplied or retained or become liable or accountable for any money or property of the company, or have been guilty of any misfeasance or other breach of duty or trust in relation to the company.

Examples of circumstances where the courts have held officers liable include:

(1)   where promoters/directors had sold their own property to the company without full disclosure,[1] or had made other secret profits;[2]
(2)   where directors used the funds of the company for an ultra vires purpose;[3] and
(3)   where directors paid dividends out of the company's capital.[4] In such a case, they are entitled to be indemnified by each shareholder who received the dividends, knowing them to be paid out of capital.[5]

Remedies available to the court

29.22   Section 298(2) provides that the court may examine the conduct of the promoter, officer, liquidator, receiver or examiner, and compel him:

---

1   *Cavendish Bentinck v Fenn* (1887) 12 App Cas 652, 36 WR 441 (HL). Affirming *sub nom Re Cape Breton Co* [1885] 29 Ch D 795.
2   The *Pearson* case (1877) 5 Ch D 336.
3   *Coats v Grassland* (1904) 20 J & R 800.
4   *Re Exchange Banking Co, Flitcroft's Case* (1882) 21 Ch D 519.
5   *Moxham v Grant* [1900] 1 QB 88.

(1) to repay or restore the money or property or any part thereof respectively with interest at such rate as the court thinks just; or

(2) to contribute such sum to the assets of the company by way of compensation in respect of the misapplication, retainer, misfeasance or other breach of duty or trust, as the court thinks just.

In *Re Contract Packaging Ltd*,[1] directors found to be in breach of their fiduciary duties were ordered by Flood J under s 298(2)(a), to convey to the liquidator a house which they held in trust for the company.

A court has discretion as to the amount to be paid as compensation under s 298(a)(b).[2] No set-off may be allowable against a claim for misfeasance.[3]

Limits on misfeasance proceedings

29.23 In *Re Etic Ltd*,[4] the liquidator initiated a misfeasance summons against the company secretary seeking recovery of monies taken by him from the company for expenses and for sums overdrawn on account of his salary.

The court held that as this was a claim for a debt due from the secretary not involving any breach of fiduciary duty to the company, no order on the summons ought to be made.

This decision was approved in *Re SM Barker Ltd*[5] by Gavan Duffy J, who said:

'I cannot express the principle to be applied more tersely than in the words of Mr Justice Maugham, as he then was, in *In re Etic* [when he said]: "The conclusion at which I have arrived is that this section is ... *limited to cases where there has been something in the nature of a breach of duty by an officer of the company as such which has caused pecuniary loss to the company*".'

Limited to actions against officers[6]

29.24 The decision in *Re SM Barker Ltd*, was referred to by Keane J in *Re Greendale Developments Ltd (No 2)*.[7] Keane J said:

'The ratio of the decision [in *SM Barker Ltd*] is that shareholders in a company cannot be made amenable under misfeasance proceedings for profits made by them, not in their capacity as directors of the company, but as shareholders.'

Keane J then concluded that as the acts of the first respondent were performed by him in his capacity as a director,[8] the liquidator was entitled to bring proceedings against him under s 298.

---

1 (Unreported) 16 January 1992 (HC).
2 *Re Home and Colonial Insurance Co Ltd* [1930] 1 Ch 102.
3 *Ex parte Pelly* (1882) 21 Ch D 492 (CA), and *Re Greendale Developments Ltd (No 2)* [1998] 1 IR 8.
4 [1928] 1 Ch 861.
5 [1950] IR 122.
6 And the other persons specified in **29.20**.
7 [1998] 1 IR 8.
8 Ie as an officer of the company.

Applicable only to cases of breach of duty owed to the company

29.25   The judicial decisions *In re Etic, SM Barker Ltd* and *Greendale Developments Ltd*,[1] confirm that only losses caused by a breach of directors' (or officers') duties to the company, can be recovered by way of misfeasance proceedings.

Scope for slight expansion

29.26   The English Court of Appeal in *West Mercia Safetywear Ltd v Dodds*[2] held that a director of an insolvent company must have regard to the interests of its creditors. This decision was also taken by Blaney J in the *Frederick Inns*[3] case. Blaney J stated:

> 'Because of the insolvency of the companies, the shareholders no longer had any interest. The only parties with an interest were creditors.'

It might therefore be argued that if the directors of a company, at a time when the company is in serious financial difficulty, deal with its property in a way that is prejudicial to the interest of company creditors, they may be in breach of their fiduciary duty (which ostensibly is only owed to the company), rendering them susceptible to s 298 proceedings, notwithstanding the limits in **29.25**.

Section 298 is a procedural remedy only

29.27   Section 298 does not bestow any new course of action; it simply gives a summary remedy.[4] As a result, it is not available where the company has a right of action at common law for negligence[5] against an officer. However, in *Re Mont Clare Hotels Ltd; Jackson v Mortell*,[6] it was held that where an officer had conducted the affairs of the company, giving the impression that there was a prima facie case of misfeasance, he may be liable for the costs of unsuccessful proceedings brought against him under s 298.[7]

SECURITY FOR COSTS BY COMPANY

29.28   Under s 390 of the 1963 Act, a judge may require a plaintiff company to give security for legal costs. Keane J, in *Bula Ltd v Tara Mines Ltd*[8] held that the

---

1   The facts of the *Greendale Developments* case are set out in **36.26**.
2   [1988] BCLC 250; reflecting judicial developments already seen in *Lonhro Ltd v Shell Petroleum Co Ltd* [1980] 1 WLR 627 (HL), and *Kinsela v Russell Kinsela Property Ltd* (1986) 4 NSW LR 722, 10 ACLR 395.
3   [1994] 1 ILRM 387 (SC).
4   *Coventry and Dixons* case (1880) 14 Ch D 660 (CA).
5   *Re B Johnson & Co (Builders) Ltd* [1955] Ch 634 (CA).
6   (Unreported) 2 December 1986 (HC). See **25.7** et seq.
7   See also *Re David Ireland & Co Ltd* [1905] 1 IR 133, where the assets of the company could only be ascertained by a court action.
8   (Unreported) 26 March 2001 (SC). See also *Lismore Homes Ltd (In Receivership) v Bank of Ireland Finance Ltd* [1999] 1 IR 501, where the plaintiffs failed to establish a prima facie case that an order for security of costs should not be made in favour of a fifth defendant.

court has a discretion to make an order granting security for costs, not only under s 390, but also under Ord 58, r 17 of the Rules of the Supreme Court.

The court's discretion must be exercised so as to ensure that the requirements of justice are met in a particular case. When considering the grounds for an appeal, the court is not pre-judging the ultimate determination of that appeal.

In *Hot Radio v IRTC*,[1] the Supreme Court upheld an earlier High Court order for security of costs against a company which challenged the awarding of radio licences. This case, and *Windmaster v Airogen*,[2] also considered the measure (or amounts) of security which should be provided under s 390.

Similarly, in *Ochre Ridge Ltd v Cork Bonded Warehouses & Ors*,[3] O'Neill J considered, inter alia, the effect on the plaintiff company's solvency if it were to lose the action. He then refused the application that the plaintiff company should provide security for the defendant's costs.

HOW DIRECTORS CAN PROTECT THEMSELVES AGAINST CIVIL ACTIONS

29.29 Directors can protect themselves against the financial consequences of many of the sources of potential legal liabilities identified in this chapter, by effecting directors' and officers' professional indemnity insurance cover.

---

1 (2000) 7(10) CLP, [2000] 10 ICLMD.
2 Ibid. High Court, 7 July 2000.
3 (2001) 8(3) CLP 74.

court has in the exercise of an order granting so to do, for cases I until under $380 . . . also . . . any Ord 58 , r 2(2) the Order . . the Sery of the court.

The . . . . have . . . . Court had . . . . the par . . . . . damages . . . to the . . . the circumstances . . . . What . . . . might . . . . . attempt to . . . impo . . . there . . not proper . . . the matter . determine the of the . ap . . .de

In the case of Will . . the . . . . one ought to con . . . . that the court . . . . to grant . . . . . to as . . . against company who in . . . a breach . . . drag . . under . . . forms . . . The conduct of the . . . . Brown . . . the . . . . or . . . to mean that the result . . . . the c . . . provided . . . .

A number . . . of writs issued . . . . complaint . . . unable . . . either on the . . . until . . . . to . . . . the plaintiff . . . . . . should prevent . . . .

HOW DIRECTORS CAN PROTECT THEMSELVES AGAINST CIVIL ACTIONS

17.29 Directors . . . . against . . . the . . . . in one of the sources of potential . . . . . liabilities identified in this chapter . . . effecting directors and . . . . cover.

Chapter 30

RESTRICTION AND DISQUALIFICATION OF DIRECTORS

THE COMPANIES ACT 1990

30.1 Under the 1963 Act, there was only one section which dealt with restricting persons from acting as directors. This was the little used s 184, whose provisions were limited to:

(1) circumstances where a person was found guilty of fraud or dishonesty; and
(2) in the case of companies in liquidation, where a person was found guilty of fraudulent trading.

Section 184 has now been replaced by Part VII of the Companies Act 1990.

Part VII of the 1990 Act introduced radical reforms in the treatment of directors and other officers who are found to have abused the privilege of trading with limited liability. These reforms are based on the recommendations of the Cork Committee[1] which stated, inter alia, that:

> 'to provide proper safeguards to the general public the law must also provide that those whose conduct has shown them to be unfit to manage the affairs of a company with limited liability shall, for a specific period, be prohibited from doing so.'

Part VII effectively implements the Cork Committee's recommendation by providing for the restriction and disqualification of directors.[2]

PART VII OF THE 1990 ACT

30.2 Part VII is divided into three chapters. These chapters deal with:

(1) *restrictions*[3] on directors of insolvent companies;
(2) *disqualification*[4] of directors; and
(3) *enforcement* provisions.[5]

---

1 *Report of the Review Committee on Insolvency Law and Practice* (chaired by Sir Kenneth Cork) (HMSO, 1982, Cmnd 8558).
2 See articles by H. Linnane 'Restrictions on and Disqualification of Directors' (1994) ILT 132, and B.P. Farren 'Restrictions on Directors of Insolvent Companies' *Bar Review*, Vol 2, Issue 8, June 1997, at p 349.
3 Sections 149–158.
4 Sections 159 and 160.
5 Sections 161–169.

Restrictions on directors

30.3 Directors of insolvent companies which are wound up may only act as directors of other companies in restricted circumstances. The term 'director' may include non-executive and shadow directors – see *Re Vehicle Imports Ltd*[1] and *Re Gasco Ltd*.[2]

The provisions of Chapter 1 come into effect where, under s 149(1), *a company is being wound up and*:

(a) it is proved to the court at the commencement of the winding up that it is unable to satisfy its debts; or

(b) the liquidator certifies, or it is otherwise proved, to the court during the course of the winding up, that it is unable to pay its debts.

In *Re Verit Hotel and Leisure (Ireland) Ltd; Carway v Attorney General*,[3] the constitutionality of s 149(1)(b) was raised. This case made it clear that the fact that a s 150 (restriction) declaration might affect a person's ability to earn a livelihood was not a reason for declaring s 149(1)(b) unconstitutional. Carroll J held that nothing in s 149 warranted the interpretation that the liquidator's certificate was to be conclusive evidence of insolvency. Once this was established, the plaintiff's claim failed.

Any director or 'shadow director' of such a company (or anyone who was such within 12 months prior to the commencement of the winding up) is not to act as a director or secretary or be concerned in the promotion or management of any company for a period of five years, unless the company meets the specified[4] requirements as to its paid-up capital.

The five-year period commences whenever the court says it is to commence. The public interest that unsuitable persons should not be directors will overcome a delay in serving notice of intention to proceed – see *Duignan v Carway*.[5]

Effect of s 150 restriction declaration

30.4 Directors who are affected by these provisions[6] cannot act as directors of other companies during the five-year period unless, in the case of a public limited company, the nominal value of the allotted share capital is at least £250,000 or, in the case of a private company, £50,000 and in either case each allotted share and any premium is fully paid up in cash. The liquidator applied to the court to have two directors restricted in *Re E.P. Nolan Contractors (Longford) Ltd*[7] because the directors had failed to keep proper records, failed to hold annual meetings or to file annual returns. During the case, further

---

1 (2001) 8(3) CLP 72.
2 Ibid.
3 [1997] 1 ILRM 110.
4 Section 150(1), as amended by s 41 of the 2001 Act.
5 *Bar Review,* Vol 6, Issue 4, January 2001.
6 Eleven persons were restricted during 1994, 57 during 1995 and 128 during 1999.
7 *The Irish Times,* 22 June 1996, (1996) 3 CLP 214.

irregularities came to light. As a result, the court restricted the two directors for five years.

Directors of a company which had traded for six months while insolvent, before going into voluntary liquidation, were restricted for the mandatory period of five years in *Business Communications Ltd v Baxter & Parson*.[1]

In this case, Murphy J stated that Chapter 1 of the 1990 Act contained provisions of the utmost importance to the commercial community generally, and in particular, to those who had undertaken the duties of a company director. He also considered that a much stricter burden of proof was required to satisfy the court that directors ought not to be disqualified than was needed for their restriction.

Murphy J's comments on the mandatory nature of s 150 were approved by McGuinness J in *Re Squash (Ireland) Ltd*[2] – see **30.8**.

30.5 The failure by a director of his statutory obligation to submit a statement of affairs to the official liquidator of his company, and his failure to give a satisfactory explanation for so acting, was deemed sufficient reason by Carroll J to make a declaration under s 150 in the matter of *Re Dunleckney Ltd*.[3]

In the same case, the question of whether s 150 was of retrospective effect also arose.

The company had been struck off the register of companies on 6 November 1990 for failing to file annual returns. However, on a petition by the Revenue Commissioners, the company was restored to the register on 21 October 1991.

A winding up of the company was also ordered on 21 October 1991, and an official liquidator appointed.

The director involved claimed that s 150 did not have retrospective effect, despite the restoration of the company to the register. Carroll J disagreed with this contention; holding that when the office copy of the order returning the company to the register was delivered on 6 December 1992, the company, under s 311(8) of the 1963 Act, was deemed to have continued in existence as if it had not been struck off the register. Accordingly, Part VII, which came into operation on 1 August 1991, applied to the company which was not wound up until 21 October 1991.

30.6 In *Re Mantruck Services Ltd; Mehigan v Duignan* (see **28.14**), the respondent director was restricted for five years and not entitled to exemptions under s 150(2) (below).

An application can be made under s 150(1) by the Director of Corporate Enforcement, a liquidator or a receiver.

---

1 (1995) 2 CLP 237.
2 (2001) 8(3) CLP 72 (SC), *Bar Review* Vol 6, Issue 7, May 2001.
3 *The Irish Times Law Reports*, 19 April 1999, (1999) 6 CLP 150.

Exemption and relief

30.7 Under s 150(2), a restriction declaration is not to be made where the court is satisfied that:

(1) the person concerned has acted honestly and responsibly in relation to the conduct of the affairs of the company and there is no other reason why it would be just and equitable to subject him to such restriction; or
(2) the person concerned was a director solely because he was nominated as such by a financial institution in connection with the giving of credit to, or the purchase of shares in, the company by that institution.

In *Re Costello Doors Ltd*,[1] Murphy J reviewed the factors which would influence the court's discretion under s 150(2)(a). In particular, he stated that the maintenance of proper books and accounts and the employment of two full time book keepers (and other experienced staff) would 'go a long way to discharge the onus of showing that the directors had behaved responsibly.'

The court held, in *Re Cavan Crystal Group Ltd*,[2] that the directors, other than the managing director who had been responsible for falsifying VAT and PAYE returns, had acted honestly and responsibly, and as a result, they were not restricted.

When must directors have acted honestly and responsibly

30.8 The question of when the directors had acted honestly and responsibly was considered in a number of cases.

In a different context, Murphy J in *Re Hefferon Kearns Ltd (No 1)*,[3] had held that s 33 of the Companies (Amendment) Act, 1990, which first introduced liability for reckless trading, was not retrospective in its effect.

Carroll J, in the *Dunleckney Ltd* case, had to consider whether actions which took place prior to 1 August 1991[4] should be taken into account in deciding whether the director concerned had acted honestly and responsibly in relation to the affairs of the company.

Carroll J held, in a similar manner to Murphy J, that the intention of the legislature was that s 150 liability was prospective only. Accordingly, it was the conduct of the company's affairs after 1 August 1991 (only) which had to be considered in determining whether the director had acted honestly and responsibly, and not conduct prior to this date.[5]

---

1 (1995) 2 CLP 238.
2 (1996) 3 CLP 226.
3 [1992] ILRM 51, [1993] 3 IR 177.
4 The date s 150 came into force.
5 In fact, the relevant period for this case was from 1 August 1991 to 21 October 1991, and the director concerned (Mr John Keenan) had not acted at all in relation to the company's affairs during that period.

Similarly, in *La Moselle Clothing Ltd (In Liquidation) and Rosegem Ltd v Djamel Soualhi*,[1] Shanley J stated that acting honestly and responsibly in relation to the conduct of the affairs of the company, arguably did not apply to any period after the commencement of a winding up or receivership, when the director concerned might have no further role or involvement in the management of the company's affairs. However, before deciding whether or not to make a restriction declaration under s 150, the court was allowed to consider any relevant conduct of a director after the commencement of a winding up or receivership; for example any failure by that director to co-operate with the liquidator or receiver.

In *Re Squash (Ireland) Ltd*, the Supreme Court considered the meaning of irresponsible conduct.

McGuinness J stated:

> 'Commercial errors may have occurred, misjudgments may well have been made, but to categorise conduct as irresponsible, I feel that one must go further than this.'

She then quoted, with approval, Shanley J's decision in the *La Moselle Clothing* case, and endorsed the following criteria for irresponsible conduct identified by him.

Guidelines on irresponsible conduct

The guidelines endorsed by McGuinness J were:

(1) the extent to which the director has/has not complied with any obligation under the Companies Acts;
(2) the extent to which his conduct would be regarded as so incompetent as to amount to irresponsibility;
(3) the extent of his responsibility for the company's insolvency;
(4) the extent of his responsibility for the net deficiency in the company's assets at the time of its winding up, or thereafter; and
(5) the extent to which, in his conduct of the affairs of the company, he has displayed a lack of commercial probity or want of proper standards.

Applying these criteria to the facts, McGuinness J held that while the directors of Squash (Ireland) Ltd were open to criticism, such criticism was insufficient to be categorised as irresponsible. Accordingly, she reversed a High Court order restricting two directors.

When it would be unjust and inequitable to restrict a director

30.9 In the *Dunleckney* case, Carroll J also considered the second limb of s 150(2)(a), ie whether there was any other reason why it would have been unjust and inequitable to restrict the director concerned (Mr Keenan).

---

1 [1998] 2 ILRM 345 (HC).

Carroll J concluded that Mr Keenan had not filed a statement of affairs and had given no reason in his replying affidavit for his failure to comply with this statutory obligation.

The official receiver stated that it appeared that no books or records had been maintained by the company; nevertheless, his investigations did not reveal any (extra) items which would have been disclosed if Mr Keenan had submitted the statement of affairs. Furthermore, the liquidator confirmed that Mr Keenan had co-operated with him.

In response to the liquidator's comments, Carroll J felt that it was not the function of a liquidator to excuse a director from his statutory liability. She then identified payments of £1,750 and £1,500 made out of company funds which, while made prior to 1 August 1991, appeared to be a debt due to the company with a continuing obligation on Mr Keenan to repay it. No explanation was given by Mr Keenan as to why he had failed to repay this debt[1] to the company.

Taking these aspects of Mr Keenan's conduct into account Carroll J did not consider that he merited relief under the second limb of s 150(2)(a).

Application for relief under s 152

30.10   A person may, within one year after having a restriction declaration made against him, apply to the court for relief, either in a whole or in part.

A court may, if it deems it just and equitable to do so, grant an applicant such relief on whatever terms and conditions it thinks fit.

In *Robinson v Forrest*,[2] by the time of the (second) hearing, the applicant had paid £200,000 to reduce the company's debts and had started another company employing several people and trading successfully. Laffoy J held that it was just and equitable to grant the relief sought.

REGISTER OF RESTRICTED PERSONS

30.11   The register of companies must keep a register of restricted persons – see s 153.

Duties of liquidators and receivers

30.12   There is no obligation on the liquidator to notify the persons affected by these provisions of the fact that they are so affected. If, however, it appears to him that the interests of another company or its creditors may be placed in jeopardy, under s 151 a liquidator must inform the court that a restricted person is acting as a director or promoter of that other company. In fulfilling this duty, the liquidator will have access to a list of restricted persons, as a

---

1   Recovery of which, Carroll J said, was a matter for the official liquidator to pursue.
2   [1999] 1 IR 426.

current register of such persons must be maintained by the registrar of companies.[1]

Section 154 makes it clear that the provisions of Chapter 1 applying to liquidators and winding up proceedings, also apply to receivers and receiverships.

Effect of restriction declarations on companies

30.13 A person who is declared a restricted person by the court must give 14 days' notice to a company appointing him as a director, notifying it that he is a restricted person.[2]

Restrictions on the company

30.14 Section 155 imposes a number of restrictions on any company where a restricted person is an officer. These restrictions preclude such a company from making use of the machinery provided under s 60 of the 1963 Act (whereby a company may provide financial assistance for the purchase of its own shares) and subjecting it to the same restrictions as are imposed by the 1983 Act on public limited companies in making allotments of shares other than for cash.

Where such a company allots a share which is not fully paid up, it is to be treated as if the whole of its nominal value and any premium had been received, but the allottee is liable to pay the company, in cash, the full amount which should have been received less the amount of any consideration paid.[3]

Relief for the company

30.15 Section 157 gives the court the power to grant relief to the company, or any person adversely affected by these restrictions. However, no such relief will be granted if the company was properly notified in advance by the restricted person.

Disqualification of directors

30.16 The second form of restraint imposed upon directors is a disqualification order.

Disqualification order

30.17 A disqualification order is an order made by the court, disqualifying a person from acting[4] as:

---

1 Under s 153.
2 Section 155(5).
3 Section 156.
4 Or being appointed to act – see s 159.

'... an auditor, director or other officer, receiver, liquidator or examiner, or be in any way, whether directly or indirectly, concerned or take part in the promotion, formation or management of any company or any society registered under the Industrial and Provident Societies Acts, 1893 to 1978.'

Whilst a restriction declaration may impose conditions under which a person can act as a director or secretary, a disqualification order extends to prevent a person being employed by a company in a management position.

Disqualification may be either mandatory or discretionary.

Mandatory disqualification

30.18   Where a person is convicted on indictment of any indictable offence in relation to a company or one involving fraud or dishonesty, he shall be deemed to be disqualified for five years from the date of the conviction.[1]

The court, on the application of the prosecutor, has the discretion to vary the five-year disqualification period.

At 31 December 1997, one person was disqualified.[2] He was a former managing dierctor of a garage who was found to have defrauded companies by purporting to sell cars which had never existed. He was disqualified for a period of five years from 23 October 1996.

Discretionary disqualification

30.19   Discretionary disqualification may occur following an application to the court. The court may make an order where:

(1)   a person has been guilty of *any* fraud in relation to a company, its members or creditors, while acting as promoter, auditor, officer, receiver, liquidator or examiner of the company;
(2)   a person has been guilty, while acting in any of the roles mentioned in (1) of a breach of his duty as such;
(3)   a person has been declared personally liable for a company's debts because of fraudulent or reckless trading;
(4)   a person's conduct in any of the roles mentioned in (1) makes him unfit to be concerned in the management of a company – see **30.20**;
(5)   in consequence of an inspector's report under the Companies Acts a person is similarly unfit;
(6)   a person has been persistently in default in making returns, giving notices or filing documents with the registrar; or
(7)   a person has been guilty of two or more offences under s 202(10) (for failing to keep proper books of account – see **32.12**).

---

1 Section 160(1)(b).
2 *Companies Report 1997*, Department of Enterprise, Trade and Employment (The Stationery Office, July 1998). This report also records a total of 108 persons restricted at 31 December 1997.

A person is presumed conclusively to have been persistently in default for the purpose of (6) if he has been found guilty of three or more such defaults.[1]

The court, as an alternative to disqualification, can restrict a director – see s 160(9A) inserted by s 42 of the 2001 Act.

Section 160(1A) and (1B), (2)(h) and (i) also provide for conduct resulting in disqualification, including being disqualified under the law of another State.

Conduct which makes a person unfit to be concerned in the management of a company

30.20   In the United Kingdom, judges have made some general comments on the type of conduct which they consider would make a person unfit to be concerned in the management of a company.

In *Re Bath Glass Ltd*,[2] Gibson J suggested that it would be necessary to show 'a serious failure or serious failures' of duty, 'whether deliberately or through incompetence'.

In *Re Lo-Line Electric Motors Ltd*,[3] Browne Wilkinson VC commented:

> 'ordinary commercial misjudgement is, in itself, not sufficient to justify disqualification. In the normal case, the conduct complained of must display a lack of commercial probity, although I have no doubt that in an extreme case of gross negligence or total incompetence, disqualification could be appropriate.'

However, in *Re Sevenoaks Stations (Retail) Ltd*,[4] Dillon LJ did not consider that it was necessary for incompetence to be 'total'. Dillon LJ thought that incompetence or negligence 'in a very marked degree' should be sufficient grounds for disqualification. Arden J said in *Re Firedart Ltd*:[5]

> 'In my judgment there are a number of matters which if proved would generally lead me to the conclusion that a director was unfit to be concerned in the management of a company. They include: trading while insolvent; taking personal benefits over and above any proper remuneration; failing to keep proper accounting records.'

Morritt LJ considered that persistent failure to co-operate with the liquidator and the official receiver would be regarded as unfitness in the case of *Secretary of State for Trade and Industry v McTighe (No 2)*.[6]

In *Re Polly Peck International plc (No 2)*,[7] Lindsay J dealt at length with the nature of misconduct which should lead to disqualification under the UK legislation. In particular, Lindsay J said that any breach of duty designed to benefit the

---

1 Section 160(2) and (3). See also s 160(9). Section 160 has been amended by the Schedule, Part 2 of the 2001 Act.
2 [1988] BCLC 329.
3 [1988] Ch 477, [1988] 3 WLR 26, [1988] 2 All ER 692, [1988] BCLC 698.
4 [1991] Ch 164, [1990] 3 WLR 1165, [1991] 3 All ER 578, [1991] BCLC 325, [1990] BCC 765.
5 [1994] 2 BCLC 340.
6 [1996] 2 BCLC 477.
7 [1994] 1 BCLC 574.

offending director was likely to be regarded as serious enough to warrant disqualification, but a breach of duty which was not intended to benefit the director, may not merit disqualification.

Laffoy J held in *Re NC*[1] that admission of past misconduct (while not admitting any specific misconduct), made a person unfit to be concerned in the management of a company.

Who may apply for the making of a disqualification order?

30.21 An application for the making of a disqualification order may be made in any proceedings, civil or criminal, or independently under s 160. Such an application may be made by the Director of Public Prosecutions, the Director of Corporate Enforcement (DCE) or any member, contributory, officer, employee, receiver, liquidator, examiner or creditor of the relevant company. However, only the DPP or the DCE may apply on ground (5) and only the DPP, the DCE or the registrar under ground (6) – see s 42(e) of the 2001 Act, inserting s 160(6A).

Relief from disqualification order

30.22 Any disqualified person has the right to apply to the court for relief, which the court is empowered to grant on whatever terms and conditions it deems fit.

Enforcement and sanctions

30.23 When a person breaches the terms of either a restriction or disqualification order, he is liable to the following sanctions:

(1) a person who is already subject to a restriction order becomes subject to a disqualification order for five years from the date of conviction;
(2) a person who is already subject to a disqualification order will have his period of disqualification extended by a period of 10 years from the date of his conviction or such other period as the court may decide;
(3) where a restricted person is or becomes a director of another company, which goes into insolvent liquidation during his restriction period, this can lead to the making of a disqualification order on that person;
(4) where a person is found to be guilty of breaching his restriction or disqualification, he will not be permitted to apply to the court for relief from his disqualification order.[2]

Civil consequences

30.24 Where a person breaches a restriction or a disqualification order there are further civil consequences which have been detailed in **28.43** et seq.

---

1 (2000) 7 CLP 203.
2 Sections 161 and 162.

Register of orders

30.25 The registrar of companies is required to keep a register of disqualification orders, having been furnished with particulars by an officer of the court.[1]

Undischarged bankrupts

30.26 Section 183 of the 1963 Act dealing with an undischarged bankrupt acting as director has been replaced by a new section which prohibits an undischarged bankrupt acting as an officer, auditor, liquidator or examiner of a company or even acting in the management of a company. If an undischarged bankrupt is convicted of an offence, he, too, may become the subject of a disqualification order.[2]

Section 40 of the 2001 Act inserted an additional s 183A in the 1963 Act.

Under s 183A, where the Director of Corporate Enforcement has reason to believe that a director of a company is an undischarged bankrupt, he may examine him as to his financial solvency, both within the State and elsewhere.

The court, on the application of the Director, may make a disqualification order against a director on the ground that he is an undischarged bankrupt.[3]

---

1 Sections 167 and 168.
2 Section 169.
3 Section 183A(3).

Chapter 31

CRIMINAL LIABILITIES OF DIRECTORS AND OFFICERS

31.1   In *Lennard's Carrying Co Ltd v Asiatic Petroleum Co Ltd*,[1] Viscount Haldane LC emphasised that fact that a company is a lifeless person. He stated:

> 'A corporation is an abstraction. It has no mind of its own any more than it has a body of its own; its active and directing will must consequently be sought in the person of somebody who for some purposes may be called an agent, *but who is really the directing mind and will of the corporation, the very ego and centre of the personality of the corporation.*'

Lord Haldane's analysis of the 'directing mind and will' of a corporate body received approval from McCarthy J in *Taylor v Smith and Others*.[2]

It has been shown in Chapter 5 of this book how the 'directing mind and will concept' has been developed to allow a court to impute 'mens rea' to the 'lifeless' company: thereby facilitating the imposition of criminal liability on a corporation.

When a court ascribes criminal responsibility to a company, it is imposing a form of vicarious liability.

VICARIOUS LIABILITY IN CIVIL AND CRIMINAL LAW

31.2   Perhaps the best example of vicarious liability in tort is that of an employer being held to be legally liable for torts committed by its employees in the course of their employment.

31.3   In *Lister v Romford Ice and Cold Storage Co Ltd*,[3] the House of Lords held that an employer's insurance company was entitled to recover damages[4] it had paid on his behalf, from the negligent employee. Thus employer and employee are joint (and several) tortfeasors in cases of civil vicarious liability.

If one were to extend this notion of joint liability to criminal law, it could be argued that as the directors constitute the directing mind and will of a company,[5] then they should also be (jointly) criminally liable for the wrongful action of the company's employees. The common law, however, has been slow to move in this direction of ascribing criminal responsibility to a company's

---

1   [1915] AC 705.
2   (Unreported) 5 July 1990 (SC).
3   [1957] AC 555. An employer is jointly and severally liable with his employee for torts committed by the latter in the course of the employment. By contrast, a principal is generally not vicariously liable for torts committed by an independent contractor – but there are exceptions to this rule.
4   In practice, many employers' liability insurers forgo their rights of recovery against negligent employees.
5   Controlling it like a puppet.

directors and officers for the wrongful actions of the company's employees. The cases of *R v Alcinder and Ors* (1990) and *R v P and O European Ferries (Dover) Ltd*,[1] which arose out of the Herald of Free Enterprise ferry disaster at Zeebrugge, illustrate the cautious attitude of the court to incriminating company directors and officers.

IMPOSING CRIMINAL LIABILITY ON DIRECTORS BY STATUTE

31.4 While it would appear that the courts have been slow in imposing criminal liability on company directors and officers, the legislature has not demonstrated the same reticence.

Many of the statutory torts committable by directors are accompanied in the Companies Acts by parallel criminal liabilities. For example, the tortious liability for failure to maintain proper books of account[2] is accompanied by s 205 of the 1990 Act which imposes a parallel criminal liability carrying a maximum penalty of £10,000 fine and/or five years' imprisonment.

Similarly, while s 297A of the 1963 Act deals with the tort of fraudulent trading,[3] s 297 makes provision for the parallel criminal offence carrying a maximum penalty of £50,000 fine and/or seven years' imprisonment. For persons to be convicted under s 297, they must have been 'knowingly a party to the carrying on of the business of a company with intent to defraud creditors'. In short, for directors to be successfully prosecuted under s 297, it would have to be proved that they personally possessed the appropriate 'mens rea'. Such criminal liability is not, therefore, truly vicarious.

Schedule of statutory offences

31.5 The more serious of the statutory criminal offences which may be committed by directors under the Companies Acts include:

Nature of Offence	Source	
Fraudulent trading	s 297	1963 Act
Insider dealing	s 114	1990 Act
Failing to notify the company in writing of interests[4] in its shares or debentures	s 53	1990 Act

---

1 See **5.8** et seq.
2 See **28.7**.
3 And reckless trading.
4 Including those of his spouse and children – see s 64 of the 1990 Act. A director also commits an offence if he fails to disclose payments made to him in connection with company shares or fails to disclose his interest in company contracts – see ss 188 and 194 of the 1963 Act.

Failure to ensure notification by agent of acquisition or disposal of company shares or debentures	s 58	1990 Act
Misleading statements to company auditors	s 197	1990 Act
Failure to ensure that proper books of account[1] are maintained	s 202	1990 Act
Failure to keep proper books of account in a company which is subsequently wound up	s 203	1990 Act
Failure to co-operate with an inspector looking into the affairs of the company	s 10	1990 Act
Incorrect statements in a prospectus	ss 44, 46 and 50	1963 Act
Offences prior to and during winding up (16 offences listed in s 293), eg non-co-operation with liquidator	s 293	1963 Act
Frauds committed by officers of companies which have gone into liquidation	s 295	1963 Act
Furnishing false information	s 242	1990 Act, as amended by s 106 of 2001 Act
Destruction, mutilation or falsification of company documents	s 243	1990 Act
Breach of restriction declaration	s 161	1990 Act
Breach[2] of disqualification order	s 161	1990 Act

Section 110 of the 2001 Act provides for the giving of relevant information by a trial judge to juries in cases concerning offences under the Companies Acts.

Personal involvement of accused director

31.6 An examination of these statutory offences will show that in most instances, the offending director or officer must have been personally involved

---

1 There are other offences in relation to the preparation of accounts. See ss 148, 149 and 158 of the 1963 Act and s 22 of the 1986 Amendment Act.
2 Any person who acts under the direction of a disqualified director also commits a criminal offence – see s 164 of the 1990 Act.

in the wrongful actions to incur the criminal liability. In fact, recent developments in the UK courts show that directors who themselves are involved in the day-to-day operations[1] of smaller companies can be held to be criminally liable with the company itself. For example, in *R v OLL Ltd*,[2] a company was found guilty of manslaughter, fined £60,000, and its managing director jailed for three years.

31.7 The concept of company directors being held criminally responsible for their own[3] actions is not new. This idea is encapsulated neatly in s 299 of the 1963 Act. Section 299 provides that:

> 'If it appears to the court ... that any past or present officer, or any member, of the company has been guilty of an offence in relation to the company for which he is [personally] criminally liable, the court may ... direct the liquidator to refer the matter to the DPP.'

The requirement of personal involvement or responsibility is also reflected in the definition of 'officer in default'; see s 383 of the 1963 Act, as amended by s 100 of the 2001 Act.

STATUTORY CRIMES OF OMISSION

31.8 It is long established in tort law that a person (such as a director) can incur a legal liability for breach of a statutory duty – see, for example, **28.7** et seq.

The same principle can apply in criminal law. For example, under s 203 of the 1990 Act, every officer of a company being wound up which has not kept proper books of account, will be liable to criminal prosecution unless he can show that:

(1) he took all reasonable steps to secure compliance by the company with s 202; or
(2) he has reasonable grounds for believing that he had delegated this duty to a competent person – see **26.28**.

31.9 Again, an annual return must be completed and sent to the registrar of companies within a specified time from the company's annual general meeting. Section 127(2) of the 1963 Act imposes criminal liability on 'the company and every officer who is in default', where the company's annual return is not submitted.[4]

31.10 There are other offences of omission in the Companies Acts. These include:

(1) failure by a director or company secretary to notify share dealings by themselves and their families under ss 53 to 66 of the 1990 Act;

---

1 In other words, executive directors.
2 See **5.10**.
3 But not being held vicariously liable for crimes committed by company employees in the course of their employment.
4 The registrar also has the power to strike the company off the register – see Chapter 53.

(2) failure by a director or company secretary to give appropriate information to the company to maintain and update its register of directors and secretaries – see s 51 of the 1990 Act;
(3) failure to co-operate with an inspector investigating the affairs of the company – see s 10(5) of the 1990 Act and Chapter 35.

Non-compliance and disqualification

31.11 Any person who has been persistently in default in relation to such matters as making returns, giving notice of filing documents with the registrar of companies, may be disqualified[1] from acting as a director.

DIFFICULTIES IN IMPOSING VICARIOUS CRIMINAL LIABILITY ON DIRECTORS

31.12 With many torts, negligence in particular, the state of mind or intention of the tortfeasor is irrelevant. Accordingly there is little theoretical difficulty in making both employer and employee jointly liable in negligence for the same act. Thus, vicarious liability in tort can involve both joint and several liability.[2]

By contrast, in criminal offences the state of mind (or mens rea) of the wrongdoer is a constituent part of the offence. While in some instances the courts will, at common law, impute mens rea[3] to make a company liable for the criminal actions of its employees, the courts, and indeed the legislature, are reluctant to take the same step and impute criminal responsibility upon company directors (or officers), in the absence of them personally possessing the necessary mens rea. Thus, the managing director of a small company who is involved at a low working level may be criminally liable[4] while the directors of a large corporation, who are far removed from its day-to-day operational tasks, are not likely to be ascribed the necessary mens rea to render them vicariously criminally liable for employees' wrongful actions.[5]

31.13 Furthermore, any employees who committed the criminal acts while on company business would have been employees of the company – not of its directors: a further difficulty in attempting to import a form of vicarious criminal liability for company directors into our common law jurisprudence.

---

1 See **30.19** et seq.
2 See **31.3**.
3 See Chapter 5.
4 As in *R v OLL Ltd* in **31.6**.
5 As in the 'Herald of Free Enterprise' cases cited in **31.3**.

Extending the imposition of criminal liability on directors

31.14   In a conference paper delivered in March 1999,[1] Friel suggested that 'the argument for imposing criminal liability on corporate directors for the criminal acts undertaken by companies under their control seems irresistible.' Friel then gave the following hypothetical situations.

Situation 1

Acme Ltd has just completed a production run of a product line. It is preparing the products for distribution into the marketplace. It discovers that the product is defective in that, under certain, admittedly rare, circumstances the product can malfunction causing potential fatality to the consumer. An economic analysis of cost/benefit indicates that the company should not withdraw the product, but instead 'tough it out'. The chances of the defect causing damage is small, the risk of fatality even smaller. By denying liability, and fighting cases all the way, compensation payments can be minimised. The company decides to circulate the product.

Situation 2

Acme Ltd has a number of customers whom it considers are troublesome in terms of late payment on invoices, small uneconomic orders and such like. Acme decides to remedy this by deliberately invoicing these companies for more than the amount of product actually supplied.

Conclusion

31.15   In both these situations Friel submitted that the controlling mind of the corporation can, should and must be found guilty of a criminal act. The fact that the criminal act is conducted through the medium of a corporation should not act as a shield to criminal liability for the directors. Friel concludes that:

> 'The time has come for enforcement agencies in this jurisdiction to press the issue. Of course one of the major difficulties will be, in medium to large corporations,[2] securing sufficient evidence to show a clear controlling mind but this is no different in many ways from standard investigative work as to the author of a crime. It may require specialised assistance beyond that traditionally associated with company enforcement but the time may have come for such an approach.'

31.16   A close analysis of these two hypothetical cases and Friel's conclusion reinforces the principle that the directors and officers of a company must have some personal involvement with the corporate crime, before they can incur a criminal liability for it. This personal involvement, though, might consist of the directors actually making the policy decision[3] to 'tough it out' on behalf of the company and not withdraw the product in Situation 1, and instructing the

---

1   R. Friel 'Company directors and the criminal law', University of Limerick. (See the version of this paper published in (1999) 6 CLP 191, at pp 191–197 and, (1999) 6 CLP 226, at pp 226–229.
2   As in the 'Herald of Free Enterprise' cases.
3   There could be evidence of this decision in board minutes.

accounts department to deliberately invoice troublesome customers for excessive amounts in Situation 2. Directors and officers, in each situation, if privy to these company policy decisions, would be likely to be ascribed with the necessary 'mens rea' to render them criminally liable for these two examples of corporate wrongdoing.

The actus reus may be committed by directors' agents

31.17   In many instances of corporate crimes, the actus reus will have been committed by (relatively) junior company employees. For example, in the two hypothetical situations in **31.14**, once the directors, as the company's directing mind and will, make the policy decisions to circulate the defective product and to fraudulently invoice customers, it should be no defence to criminal changes against them that the actual offences were carried out by their subordinates,[1] acting on their instructions.

Where, however, senior management have expressly instructed company employees not to breach a statutory prohibition and they ignore this command; while the employees' actions may render the company criminally liable, the directors' instructions in this situation should be a valid defence to criminal charges made personally against the directors and managers. The case of *Re Supply of Ready Mixed Concrete (No 2)* illustrates this form of criminal liability – see **5.12**.

DIRECTORS AND OFFICERS MUST POSSESS ACTUAL MENS REA

31.18   While we have seen in Chapter 5 that the mens rea of company employees may be attributed to a company to render it vicariously liable in criminal law, the courts (and the legislature) do not similarly impute mens rea to directors and officers so as to render them criminally responsible for corporate crimes.

Directors and officers generally must posses actual 'mens rea' to be found guilty of corporate crimes. In the case of breaches of statutory duty, a director or officer will be unable to plead lack of knowledge of such duties as a defence.

The position under the Companies Acts regarding vicarious liability is therefore very similar in both tort and criminal law. Generally, it is only in cases where a director is personally involved in the commission of a corporate tort or crime that he will be held vicariously liable.[2] However, in a wider context than the Companies Acts, criminal vicarious liability may attach to regulatory offences,[3] even in the absence of mens rea.

---

1 In effect, acting as their agents for this purpose.
2 Either in civil or in criminal law.
3 See **5.23** et seq, and F. McAuley and J.P. McCutcheon *Criminal Liability* (Round Hall Sweet & Maxwell, 2000), at pp 361–379.

PART VI

MONITORING THE DIRECTORS' STEWARDSHIP OF THE COMPANY

Chapter 32

FINANCIAL RECORDS, ACCOUNTS AND REPORTS

32.1 While the shareholders may ultimately own a company, nevertheless they are debarred, as members, from managing it. Company management is delegated by the members to a board of directors (see **23.1**), who might be expected to take their interests as owners into account.

Shareholders and stakeholders

32.2 The Hampel Report[1] recognised that a company must have regard to various stakeholders' interests as well as the interests of its shareholders. Hampel comments:

> 'a company must develop relationships relevant to its success. These will depend on the nature of the company's business, and will include those with employees, customers, suppliers, credit providers, local communities and government. It is management's responsibility to develop policies which address these matters ...'

Protecting the interests of shareholders

32.3 Whilst identifying stakeholders and their interests, the Hampel Report makes it clear that in the final analysis, it is the interests of shareholders which are paramount. The Report states:

> 'The directors' relationship with the shareholders is different in kind from their relationships with other stakeholders' interests. The shareholders elect the directors. As the CBI put it in their evidence to us, the directors are responsible for relations with stakeholders; but they are accountable to the shareholders. This is not simply a technical point.'

In pointing out that the directors are accountable to the shareholders for their stewardship of the company, the Hampel Report is simply stating their position implied under the Companies Acts.

DIRECTORS' RESPONSIBILITIES UNDER THE COMPANIES ACTS

32.4 Directors are ultimately responsible for the preparation and maintenance of the company's financial records, minutes of meetings, statutory registers and the submission to the registrar of the annual return. So far as financial records are concerned, directors must ensure that proper books of

---

1 *Report of the Committee on Corporate Governance* (chaired by Sir Ronald Hampel) (Gee Publications Ltd, 1998).

account are kept. They can now incur unlimited liability for company debts if they have failed to comply with this statutory duty.[1]

Directors are required to lay before the members at the annual general meeting a profit and loss account and a balance sheet.

The members' annual accounts are required to have a report by the directors[2] attached to them. Essentially, under the Companies Acts, the directors are responsible for keeping proper accounting records which disclose with reasonable accuracy at any time the financial position of the company and which enable them to ensure that the financial statements comply with the statutory requirements.

Directors would also have a general responsibility for taking such steps as are reasonably open to them for safeguarding the assets of the company and to prevent and detect fraud and other irregularities.

Monitoring transactions between the directors and the company

32.5   The Companies Act 1990 has strengthened the directors' fiduciary duties at common law, by regulating a number of specific transactions involving directors and their families (see Chapter 27).

DIRECTORS' RESPONSIBILITIES AND CORPORATE GOVERNANCE

32.6   The reports of the Cadbury,[3] Greenbury[4] and Hampel Committees are all concerned, to a greater or lesser degree, with the problem of improving the accountability of directors to shareholders.[5]

32.7   In Ireland, ss 67 and 68 of the Company Law Enforcement Act 2001, whilst providing for the establishment of the Company Law Review Group as a statutory body, includes in its proposed functions advising the Minister concerning the application of company law in promoting enterprise and enhancing corporate governance. We shall look more closely at this development in Chapter 54.

Let us now focus on directors' basic responsibilities under company law.

---

1 See **28.7**.
2 And by the auditors – see Chapter 34.
3 *Report of the Committee on Financial Aspects of Corporate Governance* (chaired by Sir Adrian Cadbury) (Gee Publications Ltd, 1992).
4 *Directors' Remuneration* (Report of a study group chaired by Sir Richard Greenbury) (Gee Publications Ltd, 1995).
5 See **34.40**.

BASIC FINANCIAL RECORDS

32.8   Prior to the 1963 Act, Irish companies were not legally required to keep proper books of account, although many would have done so as a matter of good commercial practice. However, s 147(1) of the 1963 Act provided that all companies had to keep basic financial records in the form of proper books of account showing:

(1)   all income and expenditure;
(2)   all sales and purchases; and
(3)   the assets of the company.

BOOKS OF ACCOUNT

32.9   Section 147 has now been superseded by the more detailed and onerous requirements of s 202 of the 1990 Act. As a director could be held liable for the debts of the company if proper books of account are not kept, the requirements of s 202 have been dealt with in Chapter 27.

The books of account must be kept at the registered office of the company or at such other places as the directors think fit.[1] The books must be kept by the company for at least six years.

Section 202(4) stipulates that proper books of account shall only be deemed to be kept if they comply with subsections (1), (2) and (3),[2] and give a *true and fair view* of the state of affairs of the company and *explain its transactions.*

Books of account must be available for inspection at all reasonable times, without charge, by the officers (but not members) of the company and 'by any other persons entitled pursuant to the Companies Acts, to inspect the books of account of the company'.

32.10   In *Healy v Healy Homes Ltd,*[3] Kenny J held that a director of a company, when exercising his right to inspect the books of account, is entitled to be accompanied by an accountant, and, if necessary, make copies of these records. In his judgment, Kenny J stated:

> 'a director's right to inspect the books of account necessarily involves that an accountant nominated by him may do this ... when he is accompanied by the director or when the accountant has been given a written authority to do so ...'

The accountant may also be required to give a written undertaking that he will treat the knowledge gleaned from the books of account as confidential, using it only for the purpose of giving confidential advice to the director who employed him in relation to the matter with which he has been retained.

---

1   See s 202(5)–(10).
2   See **27.43–27.47**.
3   [1973] IR 309 (HC).

Sanctions for breach of s 202

32.11   The 1990 Act provides for both criminal and civil sanctions in respect of breaches of s 202.

Criminal sanctions

32.12   Section 202(10) makes it a criminal offence where a director 'fails to take all reasonable steps to secure compliance by the company . . . or has, by his own wilful act been the cause of any default by the company'.

Defences

32.13   Section 202(10) sets out two defences to a director in these circumstances. First, if he can prove that he took all reasonable steps to secure compliance with s 202(1) to (4), he will have a good defence. Secondly, he may also escape responsibility if he can prove that he had reasonable grounds for believing, and did believe, that the task of keeping proper books of account had been delegated to an appropriate officer who was in a position to carry it out.

Officers

32.14   Section 203 includes similar provisions to impose criminal liability on 'officers' of the company. However, unlike s 202(10), s 203 will operate against officers only if:

(1)   the company being wound up and unable to pay its debts has contravened s 202; and
(2)   the contraventions have:
    (a)   contributed to the inability of the company to pay all its debts; or
    (b)   resulted in substantial uncertainty as to the assets and liabilities of the company; or
    (c)   substantially impeded the orderly winding up of the company.

An officer charged under s 203, may avail of the same two defences open to directors under s 202(10).

The maximum punishment for an officer is a £10,000 fine and/or five years' imprisonment.

Other criminal sanctions

32.15   Section 293(1) of the 1963 Act and s 243(1) of the 1990 Act create statutory offences relating to the hiding, concealment, destruction, mutilation and falsification of books of account by company officers.

Civil liability of officers for debts of the company

32.16   Under s 204 of the 1990 Act, officers of the company may incur civil liability for the debts of the company. This is a most important new remedy available to company creditors, against directors and other officers. Accordingly, s 204 has been dealt with in Chapter 28 in the context of directors' liabilities to company creditors. This chapter includes an analysis of the *Mantruck Services Ltd* case – the first arising under s 204 (see **28.7** et seq).

THE ANNUAL ACCOUNTS

32.17 Investors do not generally have the right[1] to inspect their company's primary financial records. Accordingly, s 148 of the 1963 Act is an important plank in the context of investor protection.

Section 148 imposes a duty on directors to prepare annually a profit and loss account and a balance sheet. These accounts must be laid before the annual general meeting of the company and signed by at least two directors on behalf of the board.[2]

Reports by the directors and an independent auditor must be attached to the company accounts. Copies of the balance sheet with directors' and auditors' reports must be forwarded to members[3] at least 21 days before the AGM.

Group accounts

32.18 The preparation of group accounts for limited companies is governed by the European Communities (Companies) (Group Accounts) Regulations 1992 (the 1992 Regulations).[4]

Under the 1992 Regulations, parent undertakings must prepare consolidated group accounts[5] detailing the state of affairs of the group as a whole. They must lay these group accounts before the AGM at the same time as their own accounts.

A parent undertaking is defined in the 1992 Regulations as one which has one or more subsidiary undertakings. 'Subsidiary undertaking' is also defined in reg 4: the definition using both ownership *and* control as criteria.

The 1992 Regulations also deal with the form, format and contents of group accounts. They also include accounting principles to be used in the cases of acquisitions and mergers.

---

1 Unless granted by the articles of association, which would be rare.
2 Section 156 of the 1963 Act.
3 Special provision is made for single-member companies in reg 8 of the European Communities (Single-Member Private Limited Companies) Regulations 1994.
4 SI 1992/201. These regulations implemented the Seventh EU Company Law Directive.
5 In addition to their own accounts.

Failure to prepare annual accounts

32.19 If the directors fail to prepare either individual company or group accounts, they are liable to criminal prosecution.[1]

Preparation of annual accounts

32.20 Section 149[2] of the 1963 Act deals with the content and form of company accounts. It has now, however, for most practical purposes, been replaced by provisions in the Companies (Amendment) Act 1986.

The 1986 Act applies generally to all limited[3] companies engaged in trading operations. When implementing the Fourth EC Company Law Directive,[4] it introduces a distinction between accounts prepared for company members, and 'filed' accounts. As illustrated (in **32.40**), less information may have to be made available to the public than to shareholders.

Shareholders' accounts and filed accounts

32.21 Two sets of accounts may now be prepared under the 1986 Act. The first set are those which must be prepared for the AGM. These are *shareholders' accounts*, and must give a true and fair view of the profit[5] for the year and the state of affairs at the balance sheet date.

The second set of accounts must be filed in the Companies Registration Office by annexing them to the annual return.[6] These are *filed accounts*.

Under the 1986 Act, specified accounting principles are to be followed in the preparation of the accounts. Specified formats are also prescribed for the accounts. Certain information must be disclosed by way of notes to the accounts. 'Medium-sized' and small companies enjoy certain disclosure exemptions in respect of their accounts. Notwithstanding, each profit and loss account and balance sheet filed must give a true and fair view of the company's financial position. The requirement of accounts to give a true and fair view of the profit or loss and balance sheet of a company is described in the Act[7] as an 'overriding' or fundamental requirement.

---

1 See ss 148(3) and 158(7) of the 1963 Act. The fines were increased to £500 in the Companies (Amendment) Act 1982, Sch 1.
2 But not subsection (7).
3 See s 2 which specifies the types of companies which are outside the scope of this Act. These include unlimited companies. However, if the shareholders of any unlimited company are all limited liability companies, it must follow the accounts requirements for limited liability companies – see reg 7 of the European Communities (Accounts) Regulations 1993.
4 Directive 78/660/EEC.
5 Or loss.
6 See next chapter.
7 In s 3(4).

Form and content of accounts

32.22 Prior to the 1986 Act, there had been few regulations on the format of accounts, although certain balance sheet groupings and disclosures were required by the 1963 Act, Sch 6.

The 1986 Act[1] changed this situation by prescribing statutory formats for the balance sheet and profit and loss accounts.

Formats

32.23 The formats to be followed are set out in Part I of the Schedule to the 1986 Act.

There are two types of format for the balance sheet, giving a choice between a vertical (list) and a horizontal layout.

Balance sheet layout

32.24 A balance sheet is drawn up in the vertical form when assets are shown at the top of the page, followed by liabilities, and capital at the bottom. In the horizontal form, liabilities and capital are shown on the left hand side of the page.

Format 1 in the Schedule is the vertical form and the more up to date and common format used. Information required by it includes details of:

A. Fixed Assets

    I.   Intangible assets

        1. Development costs
        2. Concessions, patents, licences, trade marks and similar rights and assets
        3. Goodwill
        4. Payments on account

    II. Tangible assets

        1. Land and buildings
        2. Plant and machinery
        3. Fixtures, fittings, tools and equipment
        4. Payments on account and assets in course of construction

    III. Financial assets

        1. Shares in group companies
        2. Own shares
        3. Shares in related companies
        4. Loans to related companies
        5. Other investments other than loans
        6. Other loans

---

1 Section 4.

B. Current Assets

    I.   Stock

        1. Raw materials and consumables
        2. Work in progress
        3. Finished goods and goods for resale
        4. Payments on account

    II. Debtors

        1. Trade debtors
        2. Amounts owed by group companies
        3. Amounts owed by related companies
        4. Other debtors
        5. Called up share capital not paid
        6. Prepayments and accrued income

    III. Investments

        1. Shares in group companies
        2. Own shares
        3. Other investments

    IV. Cash at bank and in hand

C. Creditors: amounts falling due within one year
        1. Debenture loans
        2. Bank loans and overdrafts
        3. Payments received on account
        4. Trade creditors
        5. Bills of exchange payable
        6. Amounts owed to group companies
        7. Amounts owed to related companies
        8. Other creditors including tax and social welfare
        9. Accruals and deferred income

D. Net current assets (liabilities)

E. Total assets less current liabilities

F. Creditors: amounts falling due after more than one year under Headings 1 to 9 in C above.

G. Provisions for liabilities and charges

    I.   Pensions and similar obligations
    II. Taxation, including deferred taxation
    III. Other provisions

H. Capital and reserves

    I.   Called up share capital
    II. Share premium account
    III. Revaluation reserve

    IV. Other reserves

        1. The capital redemption reserve fund
        2. Reserve for own shares
        3. Reserves provided for by the articles of association
        4. Other reserves

    V. Profit and loss account.

All assets must be classified as either fixed or current. They must then be valued in accordance with statutory rules – see **32.29**.

Profit and loss account layout

32.25 Choices of format also have to be made when preparing the profit and loss account. There are four formats which allow two methods of aggregating costs in the trading and profit and loss account, both of which can be in either vertical or horizontal form.

Every profit and loss account must show the amount of the profit or loss of the company on ordinary activities before taxation. This account must also show:

(1) separately, the aggregate amount of the dividends paid and the aggregate amount of the dividends proposed to be paid;
(2) any transfer between the profit and loss account and reserves;
(3) any increase or reduction in the balance on the profit and loss account since the immediately preceding financial year;
(4) the profit or loss brought forward at the beginning of the year; and
(5) the profit or loss carried forward at the end of the year.

Profit and loss account formats 1 and 3 use a functional approach whilst formats 2 and 4 show receipts and expenditure by their nature, rather than their function. For example, the following details are required under Format 1:

1. Turnover
2. Cost of sales
3. Gross profit or loss
4. Distribution costs
5. Administrative expenses
6. Other operating income
7. Income from shares in group companies
8. Income from shares in related companies
9. Income from other financial assets
10. Other interest receivable and similar income
11. Amounts written off, financial assets and investments held as current assets
12. Interest payable and similar charges
13. Tax or profit or loss on ordinary activities
14. Profit or loss on ordinary activities after taxation
15. Extraordinary income
16. Extraordinary charges
17. Extraordinary profit or loss

18. Tax on extraordinary profit or loss
19. Other taxes not shown under the above items
20. Profit or loss for the financial year.

Vertical and horizontal layouts

32.26 Both balance sheet and profit and loss accounts can be prepared in either vertical or horizontal layout. Whichever format is chosen, however, must be adopted in following years unless the directors are of the opinion that there are special reasons for a change.[1]

Accounting principles

32.27 The Statements of Standard Accounting Practice (SSAPs) are rules laid down on behalf of the accountancy bodies for the preparation of financial statements.

If an SSAP has been issued, accounts which do not comply with it may be presumed not to be true and fair. In *Lloyd Cheyham & Co Ltd v Littlejohn & Co*,[2] it was held that compliance with SSAP No 2[3] was strong (but not conclusive) evidence that accounts prepared presented a 'true and fair' view of the company. Furthermore, Wolfe J stated:

> 'third parties on reading the accounts are entitled to assume that they have been drawn up in accordance with approved practice, unless there is some indication in the accounts which clearly states that this is not the case.'

SSAP 2 had identified four fundamental accounting principles which must be followed if accounts are to show a true and fair view. These principles were:

(1) going concern;
(2) accruals;
(3) consistency; and
(4) prudence.

32.28 These principles are now included in s 5 of the 1986 Act, which provides that the amounts to be included in the accounts of a company shall be determined in accordance with the following principles:

(1) the company shall be presumed to be carrying on business as a going concern;
(2) accounting policies shall be applied consistently from one financial year to the next;
(3) the amount of any item in the accounts shall be determined on a prudent basis and in particular:
     (a) only profits realised at the balance sheet date shall be included in the profit and loss account; and

---

1 See s 4(3) and (4).
2 [1987] BCLC 303 (QBD).
3 Issued in November 1971 and dealing with Disclosures of Accounting Policies.

(b) all liabilities and losses which have arisen or are likely to arise in respect of the financial year to which the accounts relate, or a previous financial year, shall be taken into account, including those liabilities and losses which only become apparent between the balance sheet date and the date on which the accounts are signed;

(4) all income and charges relating to the financial year to which the accounts relate shall be taken into account without regard to the date of receipt or payment; and

(5) in determining the aggregate amount of any item the amount of each individual asset or liability that falls to be taken into account shall be determined separately.

If it appears to the directors of a company that there are special reasons for departing from any of the principles specified in s 5, they may so depart, but particulars of the departure, the reasons for it and its effect on the balance sheet and profit and loss account of the company shall be stated in a note to the accounts, for the financial year concerned, of the company.[1]

Valuation rules

32.29 A company's accounts are often prepared on the historic cost principle. This involves valuing assets at their purchase price. Because of factors such as inflation, assets may be undervalued in accounts using the historic cost basis. An alternative method, known as current cost or replacement cost accounting, may give a more accurate view of a company's current worth.

A company may opt for either method under the 1986 Act. Part II of the Schedule sets out the rules to be followed where the historic cost method is used. If the company opts for the current cost method, Part III of the Schedule contains alternative accounting rules permitting certain assets to be revalued according to current cost, market value or any basis which appears to the directors to be appropriate in the circumstances of the company. However, if the current cost basis is used, the historical cost of assets must always be disclosed or ascertainable.[2] In *Carroll Industries plc v O'Cualacháin*,[3] Carroll J held that accounts prepared for taxation purposes must follow an historic[4] cost approach. In other cases, a company could choose either of the two methods.

Fixed and current assets

32.30 All assets are classified under the 1986 Act as either fixed or current – see AI to III and BI to IV of the prescribed balance sheet format illustrated at **32.24**.

---

1 Section 6.
2 See para 21(3) and (4) of the Schedule.
3 [1988] IR 705.
4 A current cost accounting basis may, in some circumstances, produce a smaller amount of taxable profits.

Part IV of the Schedule clarifies that fixed assets are those intended for use on a continuing basis in the company's activities. Assets not intended for such use are taken to be current assets.

Each individual asset, whether fixed or current, must be valued separately.

Parts II and III of the Schedule contain the detailed historical costs and current cost accounting rules for valuing fixed and current assets respectively.

Revaluation reserve

32.31 Any profit or loss arising on the revaluation of an asset under the current cost method must be credited or debited to a separate reserve. This reserve is styled the 'revaluation reserve'.[1]

Information required by way of notes to the accounts

32.32 Part IV of the Schedule to the 1986 Act prescribes additional information to be given as notes to the accounts or in a separate document annexed to them.

Balance sheet

32.33 Paragraphs 26 to 37 require information which either supplements information given with respect to any balance sheet item or is otherwise relevant to assessing the company's state of affairs in the light of the information so given. Paragraphs 26 to 37 deal with such matters as:

(1) share capital and debentures;
(2) fixed assets;
(3) financial assets and investments held as current assets;
(4) reserves and provisions;
(5) provisions for taxation;
(6) details of indebtedness;
(7) guarantees and other financial commitments.

Profit and loss account

32.34 Paragraphs 39 to 43 require supplementary information in relation to the profit and loss account. This information deals with matters such as:

(1) separate statement of certain items of income and expenditure;
(2) particulars of tax and turnover;
(3) particulars of staff, including:
    (a) the average number of persons employed by the company in the financial year; and
    (b) the average number employed within each category of persons employed by the company.

---

1 See para 22 of the Schedule.

Details of subsidiaries

32.35   Under s 16 of the 1986 Act, the company must also include a note to the accounts giving full information regarding subsidiary and associated companies.

Other information required in accounts

32.36   The 1963 Act requires particulars of directors' salaries and other payments to be given in the accounts or a statement annexed thereto. The 1990 Act provides for disclosure of transactions involving directors, and others, in the accounts.

Directors' salaries, etc

32.37   Section 191(1) of the 1963 Act prescribes the following information requirements for payments to directors:

(1)   the aggregate amount of directors' emoluments;
(2)   the aggregate amount of directors' and past directors' pensions;
(3)   the aggregate amount of any compensation to directors or past directors for loss of office.

'Emoluments' is defined in s 191(2). It includes fees, commissions and sums paid to directors by way of expenses allowances insofar as those sums are charged to income tax.

Disclosures of transactions involving directors, and others

32.38   Sections 41 to 47 of the Companies Act 1990 provide for disclosures in respect of transactions involving directors. Directors' interests in shares, etc. must also be disclosed in their report or as a note to the accounts – see **27.20**.

Medium-sized and small private companies

32.39   Medium-sized and small private companies are defined in ss 8 and 9 of the 1986 Act.

Section 8, as amended by reg 4 of the European Communities (Accounts) Regulations 1993,[1] sets out the following criteria for defining medium and small private companies.

---

1 SI 1993/396.

Tests to be satisfied

32.40   Companies have to satisfy *two* of the following three criteria:

	Medium-sized (not exceeding)	*Small* (not exceeding)
Balance sheet total	£6 million	£1.5 million
Turnover for the year	£12 million	£3 million
Average number of employees in the year	250	50

Some relief from disclosure is provided for medium-sized and small private[1] companies. These reliefs relate to the format of the accounts and the content of the notes to the accounts. They are detailed in ss 10, 11 and 12 of the Act.

Generally, both medium-sized and small companies are permitted to prepare 'shortened' profit and loss accounts for their members. In addition, a small company may also prepare an 'abridged' balance sheet. Both these types of company enjoy more concessions in relation to 'filed' accounts.

The information requirements for the annual return and the concessions available to small and medium-sized companies are detailed in **33.18** et seq.

Directors' report

32.41   Section 158 of the 1963 Act requires that a directors' report be attached to the balance sheet of every company. This report must deal with:

(1) the state of affairs of the company, or, in the case of a holding company, of the company and its subsidiaries; and
(2) the proposed dividend; and
(3) the amount to be carried to reserves; and
(4) any change in the nature of the company's or its subsidiaries' business.

The report must also give a list of its subsidiaries and the nature of their businesses and a list of any bodies in which it holds more than 20 per cent in nominal value of shares carrying voting rights. It must also state where each subsidiary or body mentioned above is incorporated.

The report must also contain a statement of the measures taken by the directors to secure compliance with s 202 of the 1990 Act relating to keeping proper books of account. The exact location of those books must also be stated – s 158(6A), added by s 90 of the 2001 Act.

Under s 26 of the Electoral Act 1997, particulars of all donations made by the company exceeding £4,000 must be included in the directors' report (and the annual return).

---

1 Public companies do not qualify for size exemptions. These would therefore all be classified as large companies.

The Safety, Health and Welfare at Work Act 1989 places a duty on directors to include in their report 'an evaluation of the extent to which the policy set out in the safety statement was fulfilled'.

Expanded directors' report

32.42 The directors' report was expanded by ss 13 and 14 of the 1986 Act, to require inclusion of the following matters:

(1) a fair review of the development of the business of the company and of its subsidiaries, if any, during the financial year ending with the relevant balance sheet date;

(2) particulars of any important events affecting the company or any of its subsidiaries, if any, which have occurred since the end of that year;

(3) an indication of likely future developments in the business of the company and of its subsidiaries, if any; and

(4) an indication of the activities, if any, of the company and its subsidiaries, if any, in the field of research and development.

Section 14 requires detailed information on any shares in the company which are acquired by:

(1) forfeiture or surrender in lieu of forfeiture;[1]

(2) the nominee of the company or a person given financial assistance by the company to buy its shares; or

(3) where any shares are made subject to a lien or other charge.[2]

Extra statement for directors of small or medium-sized companies

32.43 By virtue of s 18(2) of the 1986 Act, a copy of a balance sheet annexed to the annual return[3] must contain a statement by the directors that:

(1) they have relied on specified exemptions for small or medium-sized companies; and

(2) they have done so on the ground that the company is entitled to the benefit of those exemptions as a small company or (as the case may be) as a medium-sized company.

Auditors' report

32.44 The auditors of a company must report to the members on the accounts examined by them, and on every balance sheet, profit and loss and group accounts laid before the company in general meeting.[4]

The auditors' report has to be read at the AGM and open to inspection by any member.

---

1 See **21.15** et seq.
2 See s 14(d).
3 See **33.13**.
4 Section 193(1) of the 1990 Act.

Contents of auditors' report

32.45 Section 193(4) of the 1990 Act provides that the auditors' report must state whether:

(1) the auditors have obtained all the information and explanations which, to the best of their knowledge and belief, are necessary for the purposes of the audit;
(2) in their opinion, proper books of account have been kept by the company;
(3) in their opinion, proper returns adequate for their audit have been received from branches of the company not visited by them;
(4) the company's balance sheet and profit and loss accounts are in agreement with the books of account and returns;
(5) if relevant, the company's group accounts have been prepared in accordance with the provisions of the Companies Acts and give a true and fair view of the company's[1] affairs and profit or loss for its financial year;
(6) in their opinion, a serious loss of capital as defined in s 40[2] has occurred.

Auditors must also notify the registrar if they find that proper books have not been kept.

Expanded auditors' report

32.46 Section 15 of the 1986 Act provides that the auditors have a duty, in preparing their report, to consider whether the information given in the report of the directors of the company relating to the financial year concerned is consistent with the accounts prepared by the company for that year, and the auditors must state in the report whether, in their opinion, such information is consistent with those accounts.

Special auditors' reports

32.47 Where the auditors of a medium-sized or small company are satisfied that the directors are entitled to rely on the filing concessions and that the accounts are properly prepared pursuant to the exemption provisions, the auditors must provide the directors with a written report stating:

(1) that the directors are entitled to file those accounts; and
(2) that the accounts are properly prepared as aforesaid.[3]

This written report must be accompanied by the auditors' report on the shareholders' accounts. These two reports together constitute the special report of the auditors required by s 18(3) of the 1986 Act. This special auditors' report must be filed with the company's balance sheet.

The auditors may also be requested to comment[4] on the profits available for distribution.

---

1 And its subsidiaries – see s 193(4)(e) and (f).
2 Of the Companies (Amendment) Act 1983 – see **19.41**.
3 Section 18(4) of the 1986 Act.
4 Under s 49(3) of the 1983 Act.

Exemption from requirement to have accounts audited

32.48 The 1997 Partnership 2000 agreement between the social partners[1] crystallised into reality in the Companies (Amendment) (No 2) Act, 1999. Part III of this Act exempts certain private companies from the requirement to have their accounts audited.

To qualify for exemption, companies must comply with ss 31 to 33. In particular, only certain private companies will qualify, namely those:

(1) whose turnover does not exceed £250,000;
(2) whose balance sheet total does not exceed £1,500,000;
(3) whose average number of persons employed does not exceed 50; and
(4) who are not a group company, insurance company, bank or a company specified in the Second Schedule to the 1999 Act – for example, investment business firm.

The directors must be of the opinion that the company satisfies the statutory conditions and resolve to avail of the exemption. The directors' decision to avail of the exemption must be recorded in the board minutes.

Under s 33, a company cannot avail of the exemption if any member(s) holding not less than 10 per cent of the voting rights (not being rights exercisable only in special circumstances) requests the company not to avail of the exemption. A member must do this by notice served not later than one month before the end of the preceeding financial year under s 33(1) to (3).

If a company avails itself of the exemption in a financial year, s 33(4) and (5) stipulates that its balance sheet must include a statement from the directors that:

(1) the company is availing of the exemption;
(2) the company satisfies the conditions;
(3) no notice under s 33(1) to (3) has been received from relevant members:
(4) the directors acknowledge the obligations of the company under the Companies Acts to keep proper books of accounts and prepare accounts which give a true and fair view of the state of affairs of the company at the end of its financial year and of its profit or loss for such a year and otherwise comply with the provisions of those Acts relating to the accounts. This statement must be immediately above the directors' signatures.

Where a company removes an auditor (because it is availing of the exemption), the auditor must serve notice on the company that there are no circumstances connected with the removal which should be brought to the notice of members/creditors, or if there are such circumstances, a statement of same – see s 34.

A copy of the auditor's notice must be given to the registrar and if the auditor has stated that there are circumstances to be brought to the attention of

---

1 Government, industry, employers and trade unions.

member/creditors, the company must forward a copy of it to all members/ creditors entitled to receive a copy of the accounts under the Companies Acts.

If the exemption ceases to have effect, the directors (failing which the members in general meeting) must appoint an auditor 'as soon as may be'. The auditor then holds office until the next general meeting at which accounts are laid – see s 35.

Profits available for distribution

32.49 At common law, a company could pay dividends out of the profits of any one year, without first making good the losses of previous years. This situation was altered by s 45 of the 1983 Act.

The rules on distribution of company profits are subject to the profit figure being based on properly prepared audited annual accounts – see s 49. In particular, s 49(3) provides that the following requirements apply where the last annual accounts constitute the only relevant accounts for a distribution of profits:

(1) the auditors must have stated in their report whether, in their opinion, the accounts were *properly prepared* ie unqualified;
(2) if the auditors' report is *not unqualified*, the auditors must have included a *statement* indicating that the distribution is in breach of the 1983 Act; and
(3) a copy of the accounts, auditors' report and statement, if any, indicating the illegality of the distribution, must have been delivered to the registrar.

Dividends

32.50 A dividend is the portion, received by a shareholder, of the company's distributable assets which have been divided among the members.

Most companies are formed with the objective of earning profits for their members. The company pays the shareholders dividends out of the distributable profits earned by it.

The payment of dividends is dealt with in Chapter 21 of this book as a shareholders' right.

When the directors propose payment of an attractive dividend to its shareholders at the AGM it is an indication of good management by them. As a result, the shareholders are more likely to approve the annual accounts.

Approval of annual accounts

32.51   When the accounts have been discussed at the AGM, it is usual that a resolution be proposed that they be 'adopted' or approved. When this resolution is passed, it can be regarded as a vote of confidence by the investors in the directors' management of their investment – the company.

If the investors were to reject the accounts, by not agreeing to approve them, this would be a most serious matter for the directors. It would, essentially, be an expression of the investors' lack of confidence in them.

Chapter 33

REGISTERED OFFICE, STATUTORY REGISTERS, BOOKS AND THE ANNUAL RETURN

REGISTERED OFFICE

33.1 A company must, at all times, maintain a registered office[1] in Ireland, to which all communications and notices may be addressed.[2] This requirement is necessary because the company, whilst being a legal person, is artificial and has no physical existence.

Particulars of the registered office must be delivered to the registrar prior to incorporation of the company. The registrar must also be notified of any change in its situation, within 14 days of the date of the change.

Service of proceedings on a company

33.2 Section 379(1) of the 1963 Act permits a document to be served on a company by leaving it at, or sending it by post to, the company's registered office.

Registers and documents to be kept at the registered office

33.3 The following statutory documents will usually be kept at the registered office:

(1) The Register of Members;
(2) Minute Books of General Meetings;
(3) Books of Account;
(4) Register of Directors and Secretary;
(5) Register of Directors' and Secretary's interests in shares;
(6) Register of Debenture Holders;
(7) Copies of instruments which create charges.

MAINTAINING REGISTERS

33.4 As was shown in the previous chapter, each company must record transactions in proper books of account. In addition, they must also keep registers. The objective of keeping these registers is to record its members' investments and its creditors' loans and other debts. Maintaining registers also assists in the orderly conducting of each company's affairs.

---

1 Section 113 of the 1963 Act.
2 A company need not necessarily carry on its business from its registered office.

STATUTORY REGISTERS

33.5   The Companies Acts make it compulsory for each company to maintain several registers. These include the register of members.

The register of members

33.6   Section 116(1)[1] of the 1963 Act makes it necessary for every company to record the following particulars in its register of members:

(1)   the name and address of each member;
(2)   in the case of a company having share capital, a statement of the shares held by each member distinguishing each share by its number (so long as it has a number) and the amount paid or agreed to be considered as paid on each share;
(3)   the date at which each person was entered in the register as a member;
(4)   the date at which any person ceased to be a member.

If there are more than 50 members, the register should be indexed.[2] Any member may inspect the register during business hours without charge; non-members must pay an appropriate charge. This facility must be available for at least two hours every day.[3] A copy may also be requested.

A company may close the register for 30 days in any year so long as it advertises the fact.[4] This will enable companies without computer facilities to make up a list of dividend recipients.

The register of members may be located elsewhere than in the registered office. In fact, public companies quite often contract out the management of their register.

Other aspects of the register of members have been dealt with in Chapters 20 and 22.

Extra registers for plcs

33.7   A plc must also keep a *register of significant interests* under s 80 of the 1990 Act. This register is to record the acquisition and disposal of shareholdings in excess of five per cent of the company's shares by individuals acting alone or in concert.[5]

Again, s 81 empowers a plc to investigate the ownership of its shares. If it obtains relevant information, it must be recorded in a register of interests disclosed under s 81 – see Chapter 22.

---

1 As amended by s 20 of the Companies (Amendment) Act 1982.
2 1963 Act, s 117.
3 Ibid, s 119.
4 Ibid, s 121.
5 See ss 67–71 of the 1990 Act.

Register of directors and secretaries

33.8 The register of directors and secretaries must contain the following information:[1]

(1) present and former Christian names and surnames; and date of birth;
(2) residential address;
(3) nationality, if not Irish;
(4) business occupation;
(5) particulars of other directorships held currently or within the previous 10 years.

Similar disclosure obligations apply in relation to shadow directors as to ordinary directors.

The position is altered in the case of a company secretary because a body corporate may act as company secretary. The register must contain the following particulars relating to the secretary or, where there are two secretaries, in respect of each of them:

(1) in the case of an individual, his present Christian name and surname, any former Christian name and surname and his usual residential address; and
(2) in the case of a body corporate, the corporate name and registered office.

Any changes in this register must be notified to the registrar within 14 days.[2]

Companies are obliged to permit inspection of this register.

Section 195 of the 1963 Act has also been amended by s 47 of the Companies (Amendment) (No 2) Act 1999.

Under s 195 (as amended), a person who has ceased to be a director of a company which fails to notify the registrar that he has ceased to be its director or secretary, may serve notice on the company requesting it to notify that matter forthwith, in the appropriate form, to the registrar. Details of this notification procedure are contained in new subsections 11A to 11E of s 195.

On the registrar receiving a copy of a resigning director's notice of cessation under subsections 11(A) and 11(B), it may afford him good grounds for believing that the company is not carrying on business and thereby constitute a cause for striking off the company.

Register of directors' interests in shares and debentures of the company

33.9 This register must be maintained by all companies[3] and show details of holdings which have to be notified[4] under s 53.

---

1 Section 195 of the 1963 Act, as amended by s 51 of the 1990 Act and s 91 of the 2001 Act.
2 Section 8 of the Companies (Amendment) Act 1982. If an appointee was disqualified in another jurisdiction, details must be given to the registrar – see s 195(8), inserted by s 91(a) of the 2001 Act.
3 Section 59 of the 1990 Act.
4 By directors, secretaries and their families – see s 64.

Whenever the company grants to a director or secretary a right to subscribe for shares in or debentures of the company, appropriate details must be included in this register.

The interests recorded in this register must be disclosed in the directors' report or in a note to the company's accounts.[1]

Register of debenture-holders

33.10 A debenture[2] is a contract of loan: an acknowledgement of a debt by a limited company.

Every company must keep a register[3] of holders of debentures of the company, and enter in it the:

(1) names and addresses of the debenture-holders; and
(2) the amount of debentures currently held by each.

Section 92 of the 1963 Act gives debenture-holders (and members) rights to inspect this register and to obtain copies of it and of any trust deed for securing an issue of debentures.

Debentures can be secured by a charge on the company's assets. If so, they may have to be registered under s 99. The registrar will give a certificate of registration which is conclusive evidence that s 99 has been complied with.

The *registrar* also maintains, *in relation to each company*, a register of charges[4] which is open to inspection by any person.

STATUTORY BOOKS AND MINUTES

33.11 Where a director discloses his interest in any contract made by or with the company, a copy of every declaration made and notice given under s 194[5] must be entered in a book which is kept for that purpose. This book must be open for inspection by company officers, investors and auditors, and must be produced at every general meeting of the company.

Section 194 also applies to the interests of shadow directors.[6]

Minute books

33.12 Books must be maintained by companies, recording the minutes of all proceedings of general meetings and meetings of its directors or committees of directors.[7]

---

1 Section 63 – see also previous chapter.
2 Debentures pay a fixed interest and are often long-dated – see Part VIII.
3 Section 91 of the 1963 Act.
4 See s 103 of the 1963 Act.
5 Of the 1963 Act.
6 Companies Act 1990, s 27.
7 Section 145 of the 1963 Act.

Investors are given a statutory right by s 146 to inspect the minute books recording the proceedings at general meetings.

ANNUAL RETURN

33.13   Section 125 of the 1963 Act, as amended by s 59 of the 2001 Act, makes it compulsory for every company having a share capital to make an annual return to the registrar of companies.

Information to be included in annual return

33.14   The information to be included in the annual return of a company having a share capital was prescribed in Part I of the Fifth Schedule to the 1963 Act. It included:

(1)   the address of the registered office of the company;
(2)   (a)   if the register of members is kept elsewhere than at the registered office of the company, the address of the place where it is kept;
     (b)   if any register of holders of debentures of the company is kept elsewhere than at the registered office of the company, the address of the place where it is kept;
(3)   a summary, distinguishing between shares issued for cash and shares issued as fully or partly paid up otherwise than in cash, specifying the following particulars:
     (a)   the amount of the share capital of the company and the number of shares into which it is divided;
     (b)   the number of shares taken from the incorporation of the company up to the date of the return;
     (c)   the amount called up on each share;
     (d)   the total amount of calls received;
     (e)   the total amount of calls unpaid;
     (f)   the total amount of the sum, if any, paid by way of commission in respect of any shares or debentures;
     (g)   the discount allowed on the issue of any shares issued at a discount or so much of that discount as has not been written off at the date on which the return is made;
     (h)   the total amount of the sums, if any, allowed by way of discount in respect of any debentures since the date of the last return;
     (i)   the total number of shares forfeited;
(4)   particulars of the total amount of the indebtedness of the company in respect of all mortgages and charges which are required to be registered with the registrar of companies;
(5)   a list:
     (a)   containing the names[1] and addresses of all persons who, on the 14th day after the company's annual general meeting for the year, are members of the company, and of persons who have ceased to be

---

1   In alphabetical order or with an index attached.

members since the date of the last return or, in the case of the first return, since the incorporation of the company;

(b) stating the number of shares held by each of the existing members at the date of the return, specifying shares transferred since the date of the last return (or, in the case of the first return, since the incorporation of the company) by persons who are still members and have ceased to be members respectively and the dates of registration of the transfers;

(6) particulars[1] relating to the persons who, at the date of the return, are the directors of the company and any person who is the secretary of the company.

Under the Electoral Act 1997, details of all donations made by the company which exceed £4,000 must also be included in the annual return.

Part II of the Fifth Schedule prescribed the format in which the information contained within the annual return is to be presented.

The Fifth Schedule was repealed by s 63(2) of the 2001 Act. Under s 125(1), as amended by the 2001 Act, the return is to be made in the form prescribed in regulations made by the Minister.

The annual return date

33.15   Section 127 of the 1963 Act was revised by s 60 of the 2001 Act.

The revised s 127 introduced the concept of an annual return date. This concept breaks the link between time limits for filing returns and the holding of annual general meetings.

The annual return date is defined in s 127(5) and (6). In respect of existing companies, for example, the annual return date is the anniversary of the date to which the most recent annual return, delivered to the registrar, was made up.

Companies may change their annual return dates – see s 127(9) and (10).

Where a company fails to meet the annual return date deadline, both itself and its officers can incur criminal sanctions.[2]

The introduction of the annual return date has had consequences for groups of companies and the financial year of holding companies and subsidiaries.

Section 61 of the 2001 Act amends s 153(2) of the 1963 Act, giving the Minister the power to direct that the annual return date of the subsidiary accords with that of the holding company.

Section 127(3) allows the court, if it is satisfied that it would be just to do so, to grant an extension of time for the filing of an annual return.

---

1 Such as are required to be contained in the register of directors and secretaries.
2 See s 127(10). Definitions of 'annual return' and 'annual return date' were inserted in s 2(1) of the 1963 Act by s 84 of the 2001 Act.

Documents to be attached to the annual return

33.16 The following documents are required by s 7[1] to be submitted with the annual return:

(1) a certified copy of every *balance sheet, profit and loss account* and other documents and reports required by law to be attached to the balance sheet, ie filed accounts; and

(2) a certified copy of the *auditors' report.*

Section 7 was amended by s 64 of the 2001 Act to create a link between the age of the accounts and the date to which the annual return has been made up. Generally the accounts must be made up to a date not earlier than 9 months before the date covered by the annual return.

The amended s 7 also makes it clear that the accounts annexed need not now be certified as having been laid before an AGM.

Private companies did not need to attach filed accounts to their annual returns under the 1963 Act. The 1986 Amendment Act removes this exemption. However, in doing so, it grants concessions to 'medium-sized' and 'small' private companies.

Medium-sized and small private companies

33.17 The criteria for defining medium-sized and small companies were set out in the previous chapter.

Concessions for medium-sized private companies

33.18 These companies are permitted[2] to annex an *abridged balance sheet.* An abridged balance sheet is less detailed than either Format 1 or 2 in the Schedule to the 1986 Amendment Act. The precise items to be omitted are specified in s 11(2).

Section 11(1) also permits[3] a company to attach a *shortened form of profit and loss account.* The items to be combined into one heading of 'gross profit or loss' are specified in s 11(1).

Section 12(2) also exempts medium-sized companies from the requirement to disclose particulars of turnover by way of note to the filed accounts, abridged or otherwise.

Concessions for small private companies

33.19 Section 10(1) of the 1986 Amendment Act permits small companies to prepare an *abridged balance sheet* for the purposes of both the shareholders and the filed accounts, subject to the requirement that it gives a 'true and fair' view of the company's state of affairs at the end of the year. The items to be deleted from the balance sheet are indicated in s 10(1). Using the horizontal layout in

---

1 Of the 1986 Amendment Act.
2 Section 11(2).
3 The directors may, if they wish, forego these concessions and annex full accounts.

Format 2 of the Schedule, an abridged balance sheet under s 10(1) would require the following information:

Assets	Liabilities
A. *Fixed Assets*	A. *Capital and Reserves*
I. Intangible Assets	I. Called up share capital
II. Tangible Assets	II. Share Premium Account
III. Financial Assets	III. Revaluation reserve
B. *Current Assets*	IV. Other Reserves
I. Stocks	V. Profit and Loss Account
II. Debtors	B. *Provisions for Liabilities/Charges*
III. Investments	
IV. Cash at Bank and in Hand	C. *Creditors*

Because of s 10(2), it is not necessary for a small company to annex either the profit and loss account, and/or the directors' report, to the filed accounts. All a small company, therefore, need attach to its annual return are the abridged balance sheet and the special auditors' report.[1]

Section 12 exemptions in relation to notes to the accounts

33.20   Section 12(1) exempts small companies from complying with paras 23 to 44 of the Schedule relating to notes to the accounts with the exception of:

Para	24	Details of accounting policies
	26	Information regarding share capital and debentures
	27	Allotments of shares
	33	Provision for taxation
	34	Details of indebtedness
	44	Details of foreign exchange; changes in accounting policy or errors in accounts.

Summary of 1986 Act concessions for medium-sized and small companies

33.21   The 1986 Act, whilst removing the exemption on filing accounts which private companies had enjoyed under s 128,[2] nevertheless has granted concessions to medium-sized and small companies in respect of both filed and shareholders' accounts. For example, medium-sized companies need file only a shortened profit and loss account and an abridged balance sheet.[3] They can also prepare a shortened profit and loss account for their shareholders.

Small companies are exempted from filing a profit and loss account and need only prepare a shortened balance sheet for filing[4] and for their members.[5]

---

1 See previous chapter.
2 Of the 1963 Act.
3 Under s 11(2).
4 Sections 10(2) and 12(1).
5 Section 10(1).

Large companies

33.22   Private companies not qualifying as medium-sized or small companies can be classified as large companies. So, too, can all public limited companies.

Large[1] limited liability companies are not entitled to any concessions from the requirements of the 1986 Act. Accordingly, they must prepare full balance sheet and profit and loss accounts, and annex all other documents, notes and reports, to both their shareholders and their filed accounts. These accounts will also have to be accompanied by expanded directors' and auditors' reports.[2]

Certificates to be attached by private companies

33.23   A private company must send a *certificate* with the annual return[3] confirming that the company has not invited the public to subscribe for its shares or debentures, and that its membership numbers do not exceed the 50 maximum in s 33.[4]

Time limit for filing of annual return

33.24   The annual return had to be completed within 60 days of the AGM and then immediately sent to the registrar. However, this provision was repealed by s 60 of the 2001 Act. Under the amended s 127, the annual return must be made up to a date not later than the annual return date, and filed with the registrar within 28 days.

There are serious sanctions available against both the company and its officers in the case of defaults in making returns. These sanctions may be brought and prosecuted by the registrar – see ss 125 and 127 of the 1963 Act and s 12[5] of the Companies (Amendment) Act 1982. Section 12 gives the registrar the power to strike off the register a company which fails to make annual returns for two consecutive years.

The maximum fine in s 125 was increased to £1,000 by s 244 of the 1990 Act.

Section 46 of the Companies (Amendment) (No 2) Act 1999 amended the 1982 Act. Under the amended s 12 of the 1982 Act, the registrar is given the power to have a company struck off if it fails in any one year to file an annual return – see Chapter 53.

Sections 62 and 66 of the 2001 Act also facilitate the registrar in taking criminal sanctions against offending companies and persons – again, see Chapter 53.

---

1   Except those excluded under s 2(1) and not enjoying the partial exemptions under s 2(2) and (3) of the 1986 Act.
2   See previous chapter and ss 18 and 15 of the 1986 Act.
3   Signed by both a director and the secretary.
4   Of the 1963 Act.
5   As amended by s 245 of the 1990 Act.

Chapter 34

THE AUDITOR'S ROLE AND RESPONSIBILITY

THE AUDITOR

34.1   An auditor is an independent professional who examines the books and financial records of a company.

Every company must appoint an auditor whose task it is to examine the books of account, annual accounts, group accounts (if any) and directors' report. He then makes a report on his findings to the members – the investors who own the company.

APPOINTMENT OF AUDITORS

34.2   The articles usually provide for the appointment of auditors and the auditing of the accounts of the company. For example, Table A, article 130 states:

> 'Auditors shall be appointed and their duties regulated in accordance with ss 160 to 163 of the Act.'

First auditors

34.3   The first auditors may be appointed by the directors[1] at any time before the first AGM. However, their appointment is subject to the power of the members in general meeting to remove them.

Subsequent auditors

34.4   As the function of the auditor is to check the books and accounts on behalf of the company owners, it is the investors in general meeting who have the powers to appoint and remove an auditor, and to fix his fee.

Section 160(1) provides that every company shall, at each general meeting, appoint an auditor(s) to hold office until the conclusion of the next AGM.

Retiring auditors

34.5   At any general meeting, a retiring auditor,[2] however appointed, will be re-appointed without any resolution being passed unless:

(1) he is not qualified for re-appointment; or

---

1   Section 160(6) of the 1963 Act.
2   See s 160(2) and (3) of the 1963 Act.

(2) a resolution has been passed at that meeting appointing somebody instead of him or providing expressly that he shall not be re-appointed; or
(3) he has given the company notice in writing of his unwillingness to be re-appointed.

Appointment by Minister

34.6 Where, at an AGM, no auditors are appointed, or re-appointed, the Minister may appoint a person to fill the vacancy.

Qualifications for appointment

34.7 Generally, under s 187(1) of the 1990 Act, a person will not be qualified to act as an auditor of a company[1] unless:

(1) he is a member of a body of accountants recognised by the Minister and holds a valid practising certificate from such a body; or
(2) he holds an accountancy qualification that is, in the opinion of the Minister, of no lesser standard and which would entitle him to be granted a practising certificate by that body if he were a member of it, and is for the time being authorised by the Minister to be appointed;[2] and
(3) the particulars required by ss 199 and 200[3] in respect of them have been forwarded to the registrar.

Part 8 of the Company Law Enforcement Act 2001 provides for the amendment of Part X of the 1990 Act, relating to accounts and audit. The 2001 Act amendments are intended to facilitate the Director of Corporate Enforcement in ensuring the compliance of auditors with their statutory obligations under the Companies Acts. In addition, provisions are included for the reporting by auditors of instances where they suspect that breaches of the Acts may have occurred in their client companies.

Section 72 of the 2001 Act amends s 187 of the 1990 Act, which concerns the qualification of persons for appointment as auditors. The effects of the amendments are twofold.

First, subsection (1)(a)(iii) of s 187 is amended to provide that a person who is qualified to act as an auditor by virtue of his or her membership of a recognised accountancy body must hold a valid practising certificate from the body in question. In this context, it is clearly appropriate that the body in question has issued a practising certificate averring the member's fitness to practise. A provision amending s 187(1)(a)(iii) to this effect was introduced by regulations made by the Minister (reg 3 of SI 1992/259) but as there was some doubt as to whether this would be open to legal challenge, the opportunity was taken in this Act to enshrine the requirement in primary legislation.

---

1 Or as a public auditor.
2 See additional categories in s 187(1)(a)(iii)–(vi).
3 Of the 1990 Act.

Secondly, the section introduces provisions to allow the Director of Corporate Enforcement to quickly establish a person's qualifications to act as auditor and, where the person is not so qualified, to facilitate prosecution. Provision is made whereby a person acting as an auditor or purporting to be qualified to so act is required to furnish the Director with evidence of his or her qualifications; failure to do so constitutes an offence. In addition, where a prosecution is taken against a person for acting as an auditor while not qualified to do so, a certificate in writing from a recognised accountancy body to the effect that the person is not a member of the body will be admissible as prima facie evidence of such non-membership. This will obviate the need to call witnesses from the various recognised accountancy bodies to attend in court to give direct evidence.

Section 73 of the 2001 Act amends s 192 of the 1990 Act which relates to conditions which may be imposed on accountancy bodies recognised for the purposes of the Companies Acts (ie whose members may be qualified to act as auditors). The amendment requires that such bodies notify the Director of Corporate Enforcement where a disciplinary committee or tribunal of the body has reason to believe that a member may have committed an indictable offence under the Companies Acts. This formalises and gives legal effect to existing procedures whereby such bodies notify the Department of Enterprise, Trade and Employment when, in the course of investigating complaints and monitoring members' compliance with codes of conduct, they discover evidence of any such breaches.

Section 74 amends s 194 of the 1990 Act to extend the reporting requirements of auditors as set out in that section.

Under s 194(5), if auditors form the opinion that there are reasonable grounds for believing that an indictable offence under the Companies Acts has been committed, they must notify the Director of Corporate Enforcement.

Recognition of accountancy bodies

34.8   The full set of rules governing qualification for auditing purposes and the information to be furnished to the registrar of companies is contained in Part X of the 1990 Act and the Companies Act 1990 (Auditors) Regulations.[1]

At the end of 1995, the following bodies of accountants were recognised by the Minister for Enterprise and Employment for auditing purposes under s 191 of the Companies Act 1990:

(1)   The Institute of Chartered Accountants in Ireland;
(2)   The Institute of Certified Public Accountants in Ireland;
(3)   The Chartered Association of Certified Accountants;
(4)   The Institute of Chartered Accountants in England and Wales;
(5)   The Institute of Chartered Accountants of Scotland.

---

1 SI 1992/259.

A further body, the Institute of Incorporated Public Accountants Limited, was recognised by the Minister in April 1996. In addition, an application for recognition was received by the Minister from the Association of International Accountants. This body had already been recognised by the UK authorities.

Registration of auditors

34.9 Section 198 of the 1990 Act required the registrar to maintain a register of persons notified to him to be qualified for appointment as auditors. Accordingly, details of those members of the recognised bodies who are qualified to act as auditor of a limited company are retained in the Companies Registration Office and are available for public inspection on payment of the appropriate fee. Particulars of each member qualified for appointment as auditor of a company are submitted to the registrar on an annual basis. This is one of the conditions of recognition for accountancy bodies.

Each of the recognised bodies is also required to submit an annual report to the Minister giving details of the number of complaints received and the number and outcome of cases dealt with by its investigation, disciplinary, and appeals committees pertaining to members practising as auditors in the State. By the time the Companies Report for 1995 was issued by the Department of Enterprise and Employment, none of the five recognised bodies had supplied the required reports for the year 1995 and only one had supplied a report for 1994.

Individually recognised auditors

34.10 Fifty-nine individuals had obtained Ministerial authorisation[1] prior to 3 February 1983 and were authorised to continue as auditors on 31 December 1995.

Prosecution

34.11 During 1997, three persons were fined £100, £350 and £500 for acting as an auditor without being qualified to do so.

Persons disqualified from acting as auditors

34.12 Section 187(2) provides that the persons who are disqualified from being appointed as auditors include:

(1) an officer or servant of the company;
(2) a person who has been an officer or servant of the company within a period in respect of which accounts would fall to be audited by him if he were appointed auditor of the company;
(3) a parent, spouse, brother, sister or child of an officer of the company;
(4) a person who is a partner of or in the employment of an officer of the company;

---

1 Granted under s 199 of the 1990 Act.

(5) a person who is disqualified from acting as an auditor of the company's holding company or any of its subsidiaries.

In addition, any former directors who are the subject of a disqualification[1] order, are also disqualified from being appointed to act as auditor of any company.

REMUNERATION OF AUDITORS

34.13 Generally, whoever appoints the auditor has the power to negotiate and agree his remuneration for the period of the appointment. Nevertheless, when the members appoint the auditors at the AGM, they usually authorise the directors to negotiate his remuneration and expenses.

TERMINATION OF AUDITOR'S APPOINTMENT

34.14 The auditor may voluntarily resign, or be removed and replaced against his wishes.

Resignation of an auditor

34.15 An auditor can resign before the expiry of his term of office if he serves written notice[2] on the company stating his intention to resign.

The notice must contain a statement of the circumstances giving rise to his resignation and a statement as to whether or not the auditor considers his reasons should be brought to the notice of the members or creditors of the company.

A similar procedure must be followed by an auditor who is unwilling to be re-appointed as auditor.

A resigning auditor is empowered[3] to requisition a general meeting of the company and to address it. He is also entitled to attend and be heard at:

(1) the annual general meeting at which, but for his resignation, his term of office would have expired; and
(2) any general meeting at which it is proposed to fill the vacancy caused by his resignation.

Removal and replacement of an auditor

34.16 Section 160(5) of the 1963 Act empowers the members of a company, by ordinary resolution at a general meeting, to remove an auditor[4] and appoint

---

1 See s 195 of the 1990 Act.
2 Complying with the requirements of s 185(2), (3) and (4) of the 1990 Act.
3 By s 186 of the 1990 Act.
4 Other than the first auditor(s).

in his place any other person who has been nominated for appointment by any member of the company (and who is qualified to be an auditor and of whose nomination notice has been given).

Extended notice

34.17   Extended notice[1] is required for:

(1) a resolution at an annual general meeting of a company appointing as auditor a person other than a retiring auditor or providing expressly that a retiring auditor shall not be re-appointed;
(2) a resolution at a general meeting of a company removing an auditor before the expiration of his term of office; and
(3) a resolution at a general meeting of a company filling a casual vacancy in the office of auditor.

An auditor is entitled to have his representations sent to members at the company's expense, prior to the meeting at which he is to be removed. He is also entitled to attend and address this meeting.

GENERAL POSITION OF AUDITORS

34.18   The relationship between an auditor and a company is not one of employer and employee. Instead, it is that of a professional independent accountant and his client.

Again, whilst an auditor is not ostensibly an officer of the company, where he has been guilty of fraud or breach of duty[2] in relation to the company's books and accounts, he may be treated as an 'officer' for both criminal and civil proceedings, eg the term 'officer' in s 138 of the 1990 Act includes 'any auditor, liquidator, receiver or shadow director'. Section 138 renders officers liable for reckless trading.

Auditors are not normally deemed to be the agents of the company.[3] They are, however, agents for the shareholders although members are not necessarily bound by notice of all matters given to or discovered by the auditors,[4] eg their knowledge of fraudulent acts of the directors.

AUDITORS' RIGHTS

34.19   Section 193(3) of the 1990 Act gives every auditor a statutory right of access at all reasonable times to the books, accounts and vouchers of the company. Auditors are also entitled to require from company officers and

---

1 Within the meaning of s 142 – see **15.64**.
2 *R v Shacter* [1960] 1 All ER 61 (CCA).
3 *Re Transplanters (Holding Co) Ltd* [1958] 2 All ER 711.
4 *Spackman v Evans* (1868) LR 3 HL 171.

employees such information and explanations[1] that are within their knowledge or can be procured by them if they think these are necessary for the proper discharging of their duties as auditors. The auditors are entitled to attend any[2] general meeting of the company and to receive all notices of, and other communications relating to, any general meeting which any investor in the company is entitled to receive and to be heard at any general meeting which they attend on any part of the business of the meeting which concerns them as auditors.[3]

AUDITORS' DUTIES

34.20 Under the Companies Acts, the auditor is responsible for forming an independent opinion on the financial statements presented by the directors. The auditor audits these statements and reports on them to the members at the annual general meeting.

The auditors' report must state, inter alia, whether they have obtained all the information and explanations from the directors and managers which they consider necessary for the purposes of the audit.

The contents of the auditors' report, including expanded and special auditors' reports, are outlined in **32.44** et seq.

34.21 In *Nelson Guarantee Corporation Ltd v Hodgson*,[4] McCarthy J stated:

> 'The duties of an auditor must be determined by the contract and by no other test, for the relationship between an auditor and a company engaging him is solely a matter of contract ...'

The main task facing auditors is to make a report[5] to the investors on the accounts examined by them, and on every balance sheet and profit and loss account, and all group accounts, laid before the company in general meeting during their tenure of office.

In preparing his report, s 193(6) of the 1990 Act places the auditor under a general duty to carry out the audit with *professional integrity*. Whilst this statutory duty is not explained in detail, one would expect compliance with it to include the maintenance of auditing standards at least equal to the levels required by the professional accounting bodies.[6]

The auditors are also under a duty to make themselves acquainted with the company's articles of association.

---

1 Section 196 also gives auditors powers to obtain information from subsidiary companies.
2 Section 193(6).
3 The auditors of a single-member company may request the holding of an AGM – see reg 8(3) of the European Communities (Single-Member Private Limited Companies) Regulations 1994.
4 [1958] NZLR 609 (Supreme Court of New Zealand).
5 Section 193(1).
6 Such as in the Statements of Standard Accounting Practice (SSAP) – see Chapter 32. They would also be expected to have an adequate knowledge of the Companies Acts 1963–2001.

In the *Nelson Guarantee* case, McCarthy J also suggested the following five principles as applying to the duties of an auditor:

(1) that the primary purpose in the engagement of an auditor is to obtain a report to the shareholders on the accounts of the company and the primary duty of the auditor is to make that report;
(2) that, in carrying out this primary duty, an auditor has to exercise reasonable care and skill in making inquiries and investigations which may include investigations and reports upon the conduct of employees of the company;
(3) that an auditor is never bound to exercise more than reasonable care and skill;
(4) that what is reasonable care and skill in any particular case must depend upon the circumstances of that case;
(5) that, where there is cause for suspicion, more care is necessary but the test is still that of reasonable care and skill in the light of all the circumstances including those circumstances which arouse suspicion.

If proper books of account are not being kept

34.22   If the auditors form the opinion that proper books of account[1] are not being kept, and the breach is major or significant, they must:

(1) serve a notice on the company as soon as may be stating their opinion; and
(2) not later than seven days after the service of such notice on the company, notify the registrar of companies, in the prescribed form, of the notice.

If the breach is minor or immaterial, or the situation has been rectified by the directors, the auditors need not serve the notices required above – see s 194(1) of the 1990 Act.

Section 74 of the Company Law Enforcement Act 2001 amends s 194. Section 74 provides for the copying of s 194 notifications by the registrar to the Director of Corporate Enforcement to support the Director's role of investigating suspected offences under the Companies Acts. It also provides that, where auditors notify the Registrar of Companies of the failure of a client company to keep proper books of account, they shall be obliged to furnish the Director with such information about the matter as the Director may require. This is to facilitate the Director in taking prosecutions for offences under s 202 of the 1990 Act. The amendments effected by this section also impose an obligation on auditors to report suspicions or breaches of the Companies Acts on the part of client companies or their officers to the Director and to report suspicions that companies are being used for fraudulent purposes both to the Director and to the Gardái. By virtue of their examination of a company's books, auditors may sometimes discover evidence suggesting that offences such as these have been or are being committed by the company. The purpose of these amendments is to impose a clear reporting obligation on auditors in such

---

1 As required by s 202 of the 1990 Act.

circumstances. The new subsection (6) of s 194 introduced by this section affords legal protection and immunity to auditors when complying with the reporting requirement of the section.

Directors' emoluments

34.23 If details of the directors' emoluments are not included in the accounts, as required by s 191 of the 1963 Act, it is the duty of the auditors to include in their report a statement giving the required particulars, insofar as they are reasonably able to do so.[1]

Auditors and the 1983 Act

34.24 Under the Companies (Amendment) Act 1983, the auditors are required to report on the *s 40 maintenance of capital provision.*[2] They may also be required to comment on several other matters, including profits available for distribution,[3] allotment of shares by a plc otherwise than for cash,[4] and the transfer of a non-cash asset to a plc by a shareholder.[5]

Again, on the re-registration of a private limited company as a plc, the registrar of companies must be furnished with a written statement[6] from the auditor expressing his opinion that the company's net assets are not less than the aggregate of its called-up share capital and undistributable reserves (as defined by s 46(2)).

PENALTIES FOR FALSE STATEMENTS TO AUDITORS

34.25 Section 197 of the 1990 Act authorises the imposition of heavy criminal sanctions against officers who are convicted of giving false or misleading information to the company auditors.

CIVIL LIABILITY OF AUDITORS

34.26 When considering the civil liability of auditors in respect of mistakes made by them in carrying out their duties, one must consider the standard of care owed by them, and to whom it is owed.

---

1 Section 191(8) of the 1963 Act.
2 See **19.40**.
3 See s 49(3) and (6), and **19.54** and **32.49**.
4 See s 30(5)–(8), and (12), and **10.32**.
5 Section 32, and **10.32**.
6 See s 9(3) of the 1983 Act, and **8.29**.

Auditors' standard of care

34.27   An auditor must carry out his work with professional integrity[1] – this is now a statutory requirement. Earlier, in judicial parlance, Hanna J almost implied this general duty when stating[2] that:

> '... the duty upon an auditor is, under the circumstances of the particular case and of his employment, to exercise such skill and care as a diligent, skilled and cautious auditor would exercise according to the practice of the profession.'

An auditor who has been, or ought to have been, put on enquiry, is under a duty to make an exhaustive investigation of the matter in question.[3]

Auditors' liability under contract

34.28   Generally, where an auditor fails to perform his duties competently,[4] he will be liable to the company for any losses it may sustain as a result of his breach of contract.

Again, an auditor, if formally appointed by the articles or under s 160 of the 1963 Act, may be an 'officer' of the company[5] and liable to be proceeded against for misfeasance under s 298 of the 1963 Act.

Other examples where auditors may be liable to pay damages as company 'officers' include situations where there has been reckless trading (see **28.24**) and failure by the company to keep proper books of account.

In *Mutual Reinsurance Co Ltd v Peat, Marwick Mitchell & Co*,[6] a firm of auditors (formally appointed) were held to be 'officers' of the company and entitled to rely upon an indemnity[7] for 'officers' in the company's articles of association.

In *Re Western Counties Steam Bakeries v Milling Co*,[8] the auditors were not formally appointed by the general meeting and the court held that 'informally' appointed auditors could not be made liable as 'officers' of the company.

Contracting out of liability

34.29   Any provision,[9] whether contained in the articles or in any contract with the company, exempting an auditor from, or indemnifying him against, any liability which would attach to him in respect of any negligence, default, breach of duty or breach of trust of which he may be guilty in relation to the company, is *void.*

---

1 See **34.21**.
2 In *Leech v Stokes* [1937] IR 787.
3 *Re Thomas Gerrard & Son Ltd* [1968] Ch 455.
4 Ie with reasonable care and skill.
5 *R v Shacter* [1960] 1 All ER 61.
6 (1997) 4 CLP 128.
7 Broadly similar to that contained in article 138 of Table A.
8 [1897] 1 Ch 617.
9 Section 200 of the 1963 Act as amended by 1983 Act, Sch 1, para 16.

An auditor may, however, be indemnified against the costs of defending such proceedings if the judgment is given in his favour.[1]

Auditors' liability in tort

34.30 A firm of auditors prepared accounts with the knowledge that they would be shown to a third person with the purpose of inducing him to invest in shares of that company. The third party invested in the company.

It turned out that the accounts had been incorrectly prepared by the auditors. The company was wound up within a year. The third party investor suffered a financial loss as a result.

In *Candler v Crane, Christmas & Co*,[2] it was held that, in these circumstances, the auditors did not owe a duty of care to third parties with whom they had no contractual obligation. As a result, the plaintiff investor was unable to recover his loss from the auditors in tort.

34.31 The law changed following the decision in *Hedley Byrne & Co v Heller & Partners*.[3] In this case, the court extended the auditors' duty beyond their contract with the company, to include a non-contractual duty of care in negligence to third parties such as potential investors relying upon the accounts to decide whether or not to buy that company's shares.

Irish cases such as *Kelly v Haughey Boland & Co*[4] and *John Sisk & Son v Flinn*[5] recognised this extended version of actionable auditor's negligence in Ireland. However, in the UK, the House of Lords decision in *Caparo Industries plc v Dickman*[6] seemed to restrict the auditors' duty of care to the company itself. The court felt that there was nothing in the statutory duties of an auditor to suggest that they were intended to protect the interests of the public at large or potential investors in the company. It also considered that the auditors' statutory duty was owed to the shareholders as a body, and not as individual shareholders.[7]

34.32 The facts in the *Caparo* case were as follows. Caparo Industries plc owned shares in a public company, Fidelity plc, whose accounts for the year ended 31 March 1984 showed profits far short of the predicted figure, which resulted in a dramatic drop in the quoted share price. After receipt of the audited accounts for the year ended 31 March 1984, Caparo purchased more shares in Fidelity and later that year made a successful takeover bid for the company. Following the takeover, Caparo brought an action against the

---

1 See s 200(b).
2 [1951] 2 KB 164.
3 [1964] AC 465.
4 [1989] ILRM 373. See also *Securities Trust Ltd v Hugh Moore and Alexander Ltd* in **20.26**.
5 (Unreported) 18 July 1984 (HC). Also *Golden Vale Co-op Ltd v Barrett* (Unreported) 16 March 1987.
6 [1990] 1 All ER 568, [1990] 2 AC 605, [1990] 2 WLR 358 (HL).
7 The interests of the individual shareholders could be protected indirectly by the company bringing an action against the auditors for professional negligence.

auditors of the company, alleging that Fidelity's accounts were inaccurate and misleading in that they showed a pre-tax profit of £1.2 million when in fact there had been a loss of over £0.4 million, that the auditors had been negligent in auditing the accounts, that Caparo had purchased further shares and made their takeover bid in reliance on the audited accounts, that they had thereby suffered loss, and that the auditors owed them a duty of care to prevent that loss either as potential bidders for Fidelity because they ought to have foreseen that the 1984 results made Fidelity vulnerable to a takeover bid from one quarter or another, or as an existing shareholder of Fidelity interested in buying more shares.

The House of Lords held that the defendant auditors did not owe Caparo a duty of care. Such a duty of care would only be owed when the following three-pronged test[1] of foreseeability, proximity, and fairness is satisfied:

(1) *foreseeability*: when making the statement, the defendant (D) should reasonably have foreseen that the Plaintiff (P) might suffer that loss if the statement proved to be wrong;

(2) *proximity*: there must, in relation to the statement, be a sufficient relationship between D and P. Such a relationship will exist if, at the time he made the statement, D knew:

   (a) that the statement would be communicated to P, either as an individual or as a member of an identifiable class,

   (b) that the statement would be so communicated specifically in connection with a particular transaction, or a transaction of a particular kind, and

   (c) that P would be very likely to rely on it in deciding whether or not to enter into that transaction, or a transaction of that kind;

(3) *fairness*: the court must consider it to be fair, just and reasonable that the law should impose the specified duty of care of D for the benefit of P.

Examples of post-*Caparo* liability in the UK

34.33 Before looking at some post-*Caparo* cases, it is instructive to examine part of the reasoning of Lord Bridge of Harwich in the House of Lords. Lord Bridge said:

> 'One of the most important distinctions in negligence always to be observed lies in the law's essentially different approach to the different kinds of damage which one party may have suffered in consequence of the acts or omissions of another. It is one thing to owe a duty of care to avoid causing injury to the person or property of others. It is quite another to avoid causing others to suffer purely economic loss . . .
>
> The salient feature of all these cases [which his Lordship discussed and which included the *Hedley Byrne* case and *Smith v Eric S Bush* and *Harris v Wyre Forest DC* [1990] 1 AC 831] is that the defendant giving advice or information was fully aware of the nature of the transaction which the plaintiff had in contemplation, knew

---

1 In suggesting this three-pronged test, the House of Lords accepted that there would often be an overlap between the three elements, that the elements themselves were 'labels' rather than precisely applicable definitions, and that there was a necessary element of pragmatism in applying the test to any given set of circumstances. So far as audited accounts were concerned, while it

that the advice or information would be communicated to him directly or indirectly and knew that it was likely that the plaintiff would rely on that advice or information in deciding whether or not to engage in the transaction in contemplation. In these circumstances the defendant could clearly be expected, subject always to the effect of any disclaimer of responsibility, specifically to anticipate that the plaintiff would rely on the advice or information given by the defendant for the very purpose for which he did in the event rely on it. So also the plaintiff, subject again to the effect of any disclaimer, would in that situation reasonably suppose that he was entitled to rely on the advice or information communicated to him for the very purpose for which he required it. The situation is entirely different where a statement is put into more or less general circulation and may foreseeably be relied on by strangers to the maker of the statement for any one of a variety of different purposes which the maker of the statement has no specific reason to anticipate. To hold the maker of the statement to be under a duty of care in respect of the accuracy of the statement to all and sundry for any purpose for which they may choose to rely on it is not only to subject him, in the classic words of Cardozo CJ to "liability in an indeterminate amount for an indeterminate time to an indeterminate class" (see *Ultramares Corporation v Touche* (1931) 174 NE 441 at p 444); it is also to confer on the world at large a quite unwarranted entitlement to appropriate for their own purposes the benefit of the expert knowledge or professional expertise attributed to the maker of the statement. Hence, looking only at the circumstances of these decided cases where a duty of care in respect of negligent statements has been held to exist, I should expect to find that the "limit or control mechanism ... imposed upon the liability of a wrongdoer towards those who have suffered economic damage in consequence of his negligence" (*Candlewood Navigation Corporation Ltd v Mitsui OSK Lines Ltd* [1986] AC 1 at p 25) rested in the necessity to prove, in this category of the tort of negligence, as an essential ingredient of the "proximity" between the plaintiff and the defendant, that the defendant knew that his statement would be communicated to the plaintiff, either as an individual or as a member of an identifiable class, specifically in connection with a particular transaction or transactions of a particular kind (eg in a prospectus inviting investment) and that the plaintiff would be very likely to rely on it for the purpose of deciding whether or not to enter upon that transaction or upon a transaction of that kind ...'

If, for example, during the course of a contested takeover bid, the directors and financial advisers of the target company make express representations (in the form of a profit forecast), after an identified bidder has emerged, intending that the bidder would rely on these representations, then they owe such a bidder a duty of care in negligence. This is what the court decided in the *Morgan Crucible* case.

In *Morgan Crucible Co Plc v Hill Samuel Co Ltd*,[1] during the course of a takeover bid, the directors and managers issued a profits forecast, which was supported by a letter from the auditors stating that the forecast had been properly compiled in accordance with stated accounting policies.

---

cannot fairly be said that the purpose of the statutory provisions as to publication is solely to assist members and debenture holders to an informed supervision and appraisal of the stewardship of the company's directors, that is nevertheless the original, central and primary purpose of these provisions.

1 [1991] Ch 295.

As the auditors, in giving advice, were fully aware of the nature of the transaction which the company directors had in contemplation, the Court of Appeal, distinguishing *Caparo*, held that the auditors owed a duty of care.

In *ADT Ltd v BDO Binder Hamlyn*,[1] accountants who attended a meeting between the vendor and the intending purchasers of shares, and who gave a (specific) verbal assurance to the purchasers that the accounts were accurate, were held liable in negligence when they were found not to be.

Auditors of a subsidiary company may also owe a duty of care to its parent company.

In *Baring's plc v Cooper & Lybrand*,[2] the Court of Appeal held that the auditors of a subsidary's accounts owed a duty of care, not only to the subsidiary, but also to the parent company.

POST-*CAPARO* LIABILITY IN IRISH LAW

34.34 As outlined in **34.31**, the extension of auditors' liability to tortious actions in Ireland can also be traced back to the *Hedley Byrne* case. As a result of this case a person such as an auditor may be liable for financial loss resulting from a negligent statement. However, to succeed in his negligence action against a company's auditors, a plaintiff must prove that:

(1) there was a sufficient degree of proximity; and
(2) the defendant who made the statement did so in a professional capacity which made it reasonably foreseeable that the plaintiff would rely on it; and
(3) the plaintiff did actually rely on the inaccurate statement and, as a result, suffered a loss which was reasonably foreseeable.

Takeovers, *Caparo* and Irish law

34.35 So far as auditors' liability in takeover situations is concerned, the law in Ireland was that a general duty towards potential investors is owed, once the financial position disclosed in the audited accounts is such as to make the company susceptible to a take over bid.[3] As Quill[4] states:

'Subsequently decisions [to *Caparo*] in respect of negligent misstatements causing economic loss have continued to utilise the *Hedley Byrne* formulation, and the Irish judiciary have shown no inclination to use the more restrained approach in *Caparo*
. . .

This means that auditors in Ireland are exposed to a broader obligation than their English counterparts ... In order to avoid liability [Irish auditors] will have [to show] for example, that reliance [on the negligent statement] was

---

1 [1996] BCC 80.8
2 [1997] 1 BCLC 427.
3 See *Kelly v Haughey Boland & Co* [1989] ILRM 373.
4 E. Quill *Torts in Ireland* (Gill Macmillan, 1999), at Chapter 2.

unreasonable (eg because the plaintiff has access to independent advice), or the plaintiff was not misled (as occurred in *Kelly v Haughey Boland*), or that there was no breach of duty.'

However, Keane CJ in *Glencar Exploration plc v Mayo County Council*,[1] advocated a *Caparo*-style 'fairness test' (see **34.32**); an approach followed by Morris J in *Wildgust and Others v Bank of Ireland and Others*.[2] This negligent misstatement case did not relate directly to auditors' liability. Nevertheless, it is further evidence of a change in Irish judicial attitudes to the imposition of *Caparo*-style restrictions on negligence actions.

Contracting out of liability for negligent acts

34.36 Generally, auditors cannot 'contract out' of their liability to third parties. This is because no contract exists between the auditors and such 'company outsiders'. As a result, a disclaimer in the auditors' contract with the company may not be a defence[3] against a third party action for damages based on their negligent acts – always assuming a duty of care is owed to them.

Auditors' concern over size of potential liability

34.37 Following the collapse of the PMPA Insurance Company in 1983, its outstanding claims liabilities were transferred to a new company, Primor plc. Two High Court decisions empowered Primor plc to pursue a claim for £175 million damages, plus interest, against the joint auditors of PMPA. During December 1995, the Supreme Court[4] overturned the two High Court decisions, dismissing what would have been Ireland's largest tortious claim because of unjustified delay by the plaintiffs.

Again, the failure of the Insurance Corporation of Ireland Insurance Co (ICI) led to the transfer of its outstanding liabilities to ICAROM plc.

ICAROM plc (and Allied Irish Banks), like Primor plc, sought damages against ICI's accountants. The case was settled out of court for an amount thought to be £77 million during 1993. In the same year, the six largest accounting firms in the UK paid up to eight per cent of their audit fees in legal claims.[5]

34.38 From the size of these awards/settlements levels, it is understandable that the issue of legal liability is one of major concern to the auditing profession in Ireland (and the UK). In these two EU Member States, legal actions against auditors are particularly prevalent, with amounts of awards of damages running

1 (Unreported) 19 July 2001 (SC).
2 (Unreported) 17 August 2001 (HC).
3 See *John Sisk & Son v Flinn* where a qualification to the accounts succeeded as a defence against a third party.
4 In *Primor plc v Stokes Kennedy Crowley; Primor plc v Oliver Freaney & Co, The Irish Times*, 20 December 1995, [1996] 2 IR 459.
5 P. Boyle 'Accountants face rise in litigation' *Irish Press*, 22 February 1994.

very high. By contrast, in Germany,[1] auditors are entitled to limit their liabilities arising out of an audit to DM500,000 (about £200,000), thereby reducing the incentive for litigation.

In December 1996, a conference was held in Brussels to consider a Green Paper on the role and liability of auditors within the EU. It will be interesting to see whether political developments at an EU level can reduce legal liability and litigation levels for auditors in Ireland. In any event, by 2001 Irish judicial attitudes to limiting the scope of negligence actions seemed to be moving closer to the UK position (see **34.35**).

CORPORATE GOVERNANCE AND INTERNAL COMPANY CONTROLS

34.39   During the 1990s, reports from the Cadbury, Greenbury and Hampel Committees resulted in the adoption of a non-statutory 'Combined Code' for listed companies. This code of good practice in corporate governance essentially seeks to give shareholders more information on directors' actions in running a company. This trend towards the prescribing of non-statutory guidelines to ensure more transparency in, and monitoring of, company management by the directors, is reinforced by the Turnbull Report 1999.[2]

The Turnbull Report considers, inter alia, that, 'the board should maintain a sound system of internal controls to safeguard shareholders' investment and the company's assets.' Thus, the limited degree of monitoring by auditors of directors' stewardship, prescribed in the Companies Acts, is being significantly supplemented for listed companies by non-statutory guidelines.

THE PUBLIC ACCOUNTS COMMITTEE

34.40   On 11 July 2000 the Minister for Enterprise, Trade and Employment published the report of the Review Group[3] on Auditing, whose establishment was initially recommended by the Committee of Public Accounts in their DIRT Inquiry report.

The Review Group report deals with the following four main issues:

(1) the role of the auditor in ensuring compliance with statutory provisions;
(2) the auditing of financial institutions;
(3) auditor independence; and
(4) the regulation of the auditing and accountancy profession.

---

1 Germany has a fundamentally different legal system to the UK and Ireland, being civil law, rather than common-law based.
2 See Chapter 54.
3 Available from Government Publications Sales Office, Molesworth St, Dublin 2.

Audit committees

34.41 The Review Group on Auditing (RGA) had also investigated the role and status of audit committees, and made several specific recommendations to improve their independence and effectiveness.

The most significant recommendation was that, 'boards of directors of plcs, financial institutions and public interest companies, should be required by legislation to establish audit committees, the membership of which is made up of [independent] non-executive directors'. The RGA further recommended that audit committees should prepare an annual report for presentation to shareholders, which should include their view on the directors' compliance report.

The RGA also considered that shareholders should approve the appointment of the company's auditors and set their fees, on the basis of a recommendation from the [statutory] audit committee, rather than the management, as is currently the case.

Internal auditors

34.42 The RGA recommended that, in addition to a statutory audit committee, companies should also have a properly resourced internal audit function set up independently of management and the external auditor.

Future of Review Group recommendations

34.43 Before bringing the report to Cabinet for decision, the Minister invited public comment on the report's contents and its recommendations. It is likely, therefore, that the Government will reform aspects of auditing in the near future.

Chapter 35

INVESTIGATIONS INTO A COMPANY'S AFFAIRS AND OWNERSHIP

APPOINTMENT OF INSPECTORS

35.1   Under ss 165 to 173 of the 1963 Act, the Minister had the power to appoint inspectors to investigate the affairs of a company.

Only four investigations were instigated by the Minister under the 1963 Act. Not surprisingly, therefore, ss 165 to 173 have been replaced by more effective provisions in the Companies Act 1990.

Generally, the directors, as a company's managing agents, enjoy almost complete control over the company's internal affairs. As a result, investors, and indeed, creditors, could encounter great difficulty in obtaining information concerning the company, if the directors chose not to be of help to them. Part II of the 1990 Act now allows members and creditors to apply to the courts seeking an investigation into the affairs of the company.

Section 7 empowers the courts to appoint inspectors who can investigate the company's affairs. Section 14 authorises the Minister to appoint inspectors to investigate a company's ownership without prior recourse to the courts.

Section 14 was amended by the Company Law Enforcement Act 2001 so that the Ministers function was transferred to the Director of Corporate Enforcement (DCE) – see **55.6**.

INVESTIGATION OF A COMPANY'S AFFAIRS

35.2   Sections 7 and 8 transfer the power of ordering an investigation into the affairs of a company from the Minister to the court.

The court may appoint one or more *inspectors* to investigate the affairs of the company as directed by the court and to submit a report. The term 'affairs of the company' was judicially defined[1] as including the company's goodwill, its profits and losses, and its contracts and assets. This definition also embraces a company's shareholdings in, and ability to control the affairs of, a subsidiary or subsidiaries.

WHO CAN APPLY FOR APPOINTMENT OF INSPECTORS?

35.3   Section 7(1) permits the following persons to apply to the court for the appointment of inspectors to investigate a company:

---

1 In *R v Board of Trade ex parte St Martin's Preserving Co Ltd* [1965] 1 QB 603.

(1) in the case of a company having a share capital, either not less than 100 members or a member or members holding not less than one-tenth of the paid-up share capital of the company;

(2) in the case of a company not having a share capital, not less than one-fifth in number of the persons on the company's register of members;

(3) the company;

(4) a director of the company;

(5) a creditor of the company.

The court may require applicant(s) to give security of up to £250,000 for payment of the costs of the investigation – see s 20 of the Company Law Enforcement Act 2001 (the 2001 Act).

Applications by the Minister

35.4 Section 8 (as amended by s 21 of the 2001 Act) empowers the court to appoint inspectors on the application of the Director of Corporate Enforcement (the Director). Before it does so, however, the court must be satisfied that there are circumstances suggesting:

(1) that the company's affairs are being or have been conducted with intent to defraud its creditors or for other fraudulent or unlawful purposes or in a manner which is unfairly prejudicial to the interest of its members;

(2) that persons connected with the formation or the management of the company's affairs have been guilty of fraud, misfeasance or other misconduct towards it or its members; or

(3) that the company's members have not been given all the information relating to its affairs which they might reasonably expect.

On 16 September 1991, the High Court, on the application of the Minister, appointed Messrs Aidan Barry, accountant, and Ciaran Foley, barrister, as inspectors under s 8 to investigate the affairs of Siúcre Éireann cpt and certain related companies. The inspectors furnished their final report to the court on 25 February 1992.

Since 2001, an inspector may be an officer of the Director.

DUTIES OF COMPANY OFFICERS AND AGENTS

35.5 All officers and agents are under a duty to assist appointed inspectors by:

(1) producing all relevant books and documents; and/or

(2) meeting the inspectors, when required; and

(3) giving the inspectors all the assistance which they are reasonably able to give.

Any answer given by a person to an inspector may be used against him.

POWERS OF INSPECTORS

35.6 Section 10 of the 1990 Act deals with inspectors' powers; in particular, those to obtain the documents and other evidence necessary for them to discharge their duties.

In *Chestvale Properties Ltd v Glackin*,[1] the court held that Part II of the 1990 Act operated retrospectively, therefore inspectors appointed under it were empowered to obtain and examine documents and other evidence which existed prior to the implementation of Part II.

Section 7(4) makes provision for the court, when appointing an inspector under ss 7 or 8, to give such directions as it thinks fit 'with a view to ensuring that the investigation is carried out as quickly and as inexpensively as possible'.

In *Re Countyglen plc*,[2] it was decided that implementation of a court order under s 7(4) did not constitute the administration of justice. Consequently, there was no duty on inspectors to carry out their investigations in public.

Under s 10(1) and (2), company officers and agents must produce all the books and documents of the company being investigated, plus the books and documents of a related[3] company which are within their custody or power. In *Bula v Tara Mines*,[4] it was held that a document is within the power of a person if he has an enforceable legal right to obtain sight of it from the person who holds the document.

An inspector may be entitled to demand documents, even when their ownership is vested in other companies – see *Desmond v Glackin (No 2)* at **35.21**.

A company officer or agent will not be permitted to argue as a defence that compliance with an inspector's request to produce books or documents will breach an existing contractual obligation. For example, in *Glackin v Trustee Savings Bank*[5] the court held that a bank may not use the defence of breach of its duty of confidentiality towards its customer to refuse compliance with an inspector's request for information. As Costello J said, contractual arrangements between the bank and its customer are 'overridden' by the statutory duties [of disclosure] imposed on them. However, in *Haughey v Moriarty v Ors*,[6] the court decided that it was not appropriate to compel banking institutions to produce information relating to customers' accounts to a tribunal of inquiry, without first notifying the customer and allowing him to challenge the discovery order.

Section 23 of the Company Law Enforcement Act 2001 amends s 10 of the 1990 Act in three respects.

---

1 [1993] 3 IR 35.
2 [1995] 1 IR 220.
3 Which is also being investigated – see **35.12**.
4 [1994] 1 ILRM 111.
5 [1993] 3 IR 55.
6 [1999] 3 IR 3 (HC), [1999] 3 IR 28 (SC).

First, an amended s 10(1) provides for the protection of a lien on company books or documents so that their production to inspectors would not prejudice any such right claimed over them by the parties producing them to the inspectors. This would facilitate the work of inspectors by limiting the scope for legal objections to the production of books or documents to an inspector where a person holds a lien.

Secondly, two new subsections (5) and (6) are substituted in the 1990 Act. The amended s 10(5) and (6) are included to reflect a decision of the Supreme Court[1] that the provision at subsection (5) that a person who refuses to co-operate with an inspector may be punished 'in like manner as if he had been guilty of contempt of court' was unconstitutional. The subsections have been re-drafted to remove the objectionable element while retaining the provision that the inspectors may seek the court's assistance with recalcitrant companies or company officers. Finally, s 10(7) is amended to extend the definition of 'agents' to include accountants, book-keepers and taxation advisers employed by the company.

Secret transactions

35.7   Section 10(3) gives inspectors power to obtain details of any 'secret' bank accounts and/or improper corporate transactions that may have taken place under the directors' stewardship.

Examination on oath

35.8   Under s 10(4), an inspector has the power to compel attendance and to examine under oath any company officer or agent or both, and to administer the oath personally. The definition of 'officer' and 'agent' in s 10(7) includes past, as well as present, officers and agents. The term 'agents' includes the company's bankers, solicitors and auditors.

35.9   The decision in *Re Countyglen plc* (above) makes it clear that there is no obligation on an inspector to carry out such an enquiry in public.

A company officer or agent cannot refuse to give an inspector evidence under oath by pleading as a defence that the information had already been submitted to the inspector in a statutory declaration.

In *Probits v Glackin*,[2] the Supreme Court affirmed O'Hanlon J's judgment that an inspector was not required to show a prima facie case for disbelieving averments[3] contained in a statutory declaration before requiring further evidence to corroborate such averments.

---

1 In *Desmond v Glackin (No 2)* [1993] 3 IR 106 (SC).
2 [1993] 3 IR 134.
3 An averment is an allegation or an affirmation in pleadings.

Non-disclosure of privileged information

35.10 Section 23(1) contains a statutory defence to permit non-disclosure of information[1] requested, on the grounds of legal professional privilege.

The right against self-incrimination

35.11 Company agents and officers are not entitled to refuse to answer questions put by inspectors nor to refuse to provide the inspectors with documents requested by them, on the grounds that such answers or documents might incriminate them. In *Heaney v Ireland,*[2] O'Flaherty J, when addressing the issue of statutory interference with a citizen's right against self-incrimination, cited Lord Mustill, who, in *R v Director of Serious Fraud Office ex parte Smith*[3] said, 'statutory interference with the right [against self-incrimination] is almost as old as the right itself'. O'Flaherty J then illustrated the concept with a selection of examples of statutory interference with the right against self-incrimination. These examples included the Companies Acts 1963 to 1990.

O'Flaherty J also illustrated the penalties associated with these statutory examples of interference, before concluding, 'They evoke a legislative intent to abrogate, to various extents, the right to silence … subject only to the Constitution'.

McGuinness J, following *Heaney v Ireland* in *Gilligan v CAB,*[4] also held that the privilege against self-incrimination was not an absolute right and might be qualified by the state in the pursuance of the maintenance of public peace and order.[5] McGuinness J further held that the appropriate test to employ, in determining whether the curtailment of a person's constitutional right by way of statute was proportionate to the curtailment's purpose, was whether:

(1) it was rationally connected to the objectives [of the statute] and not arbitrary, unfair or irrational;
(2) the right was curtailed as little as possible; and
(3) the curtailment was such that its effect on rights was proportional to the objective.

If inspectors hold an oral hearing the persons examined are entitled to fair procedures,[6] including the right to cross-examine witnesses.

---

1 Or refusal to produce any document.
2 [1996] 1 IR 580 SC.
3 [1993] AC 1.
4 [1998] 3 IR 185.
5 McGuinness J also held that in construing the constitutional validity of statutes, the court must assume the statute is constitutional, and not declare an impugned enactment to be invalid when it is possible to construe it in accordance with the Constitution. Furthermore, there is also the presumption that the Oireachtas intended the whole proceedings involved to be conducted in accordance with the principles of constitutional justice.
6 See *Re Haughey* [1971] IR 217, and *Kiely v Minister for Social Welfare* [1977] IR 267.

The constitutional protection available to employees to invoke the right against self-incrimination and the constitutional guarantee of fair procedures, was considered by the Supreme Court in *Re National Irish Bank Ltd (No 1).*[1]

In this case, the court upheld the High Court decision of Shanley J that persons (employees) from whom information, documents and evidence was sought by inspectors were not entitled to refuse to answer questions put by inspectors, nor to refuse to provide the documents required, on the grounds of self-incrimination. However, the Supreme Court mollified the employees' positions by holding that confessions obtained by inspectors as a result of the exercise of their powers under s 10, would not generally be admissible at a subsequent criminal trial, unless the trial judge was satisfied that the confession was voluntary.

In *Re National Irish Bank Ltd (No 2),*[2] Kelly J held that the entitlement to the transcript of an interview at the information gathering stage[3] of an inspector's work was personal to the individual interviewee, and did not extend to the bank.

Section 11(2) empowers an inspector, at any time in the course of his investigation, and without the necessity of making an interim report, to inform the court of matters coming to his knowledge as a result of the investigation, tending to show that a criminal offence has been committed. When making such a determination, the principle of natural justice must be followed. Thus, any party concerned must be given an opportunity of being heard – see *Desmond v Glackin (No 2)* in **35.21**.

Related companies

35.12 With the approval of the court, the inspector may have his power extended under s 9 to include an investigation into related companies.

In *Lyons, Keleghan and Murphy v Curran,*[4] the inspector, Mr Curran, appointed under s 14 (see **35.20**) extended his investigation to a company, Talmino, not named in his warrant of appointment, and without obtaining prior approval from the court under s 9.

The applicants sought to have the inspector's final report quashed on the grounds that there was no authority or power to investigate Talmino.

Blaney J held that the inspector had both the power and a duty to investigate Talmino under the terms of his appointment. He stated:

'In my opinion Section 9 applies to a situation different from that in which the respondent found himself in Talmino. The respondent had to investigate Talmino

---

1 [1999] 3 IR 145 (HC), [1999] 3 IR 169 (SC).
2 [1999] 2 ILRM 443 (HC).
3 Kelly J also stated that an interviewee had no entitlement to invoke the panoply of *Re Haughey* rights, at this preliminary stage of the investigative procedure.
4 [1993] ILRM 375.

in order to fulfil the purpose for which he was appointed. That is very different from the position of an inspector availing of Section 9. Such an inspector simply 'thinks' it is necessary for the purposes of his investigation to investigate also the membership of another body corporate. He does not *know* that it is necessary, which was the respondent's position.' (author's emphasis)

Section 22 of the 2001 Act inserts a new s 9(2) in the 1990 Act widening the definition of a related company.

INSPECTOR'S SANCTIONS

35.13   If any company officer or agent refuses to co-operate with an inspector, he may certify their refusal to the court. The court will then enquire into the matter, and, if necessary, punish the offender as if he had been guilty of contempt of court.

The court can also compel attendance before an inspector, the production of particular books or documents, or the answering of a particular question.

INSPECTOR'S REPORTS

35.14   Inspectors, if directed by the court, may have to submit interim reports to it. In any event, they must prepare a final report on the conclusion of their investigations, and for the court.

Copies

35.15   Section 11(3) makes provision for copies of the report to be made available to a number of interested parties,[1] including the Director, the company itself, auditors, shareholders, the applicants for the investigation and any person whose conduct has been referred to in the report.

The court may also decide that the inspector's report be printed and published. The inspector's report may be used in civil proceedings as evidence of the facts or of the inspector's opinion.

Section 18, as amended by s 28 of the 2001 Act, now provides that a statement made, or answer given to a question put by an inspector, may be used in evidence against any individual making or concurring in making it.

Acting upon the inspector's report

35.16   Having considered the inspector's report, the court can make any order it deems fit. Such orders might include:[2]

(1) an order for the winding up of the company; or

---

1 Section 11(3) was extended by s 24 of the 2000 Act.
2 Section 12(1).

(2) an order for the purpose of remedying any disability suffered by any person whose interests were adversely affected by the conduct of the affairs of the company.

The Director also has the power to present a petition for the winding up of the company, following an inspector's report.

Confidentiality of information obtained

35.17 The question of confidentiality of information obtained became a major political/legal issue in September 1999 in connection with the Ansbacher accounts and 120 persons named in the report of an authorised officer.

Section 21 basically prohibited publication or disclosure to the public, unless required with a view to the institution of legal proceedings.[1] A person who published unauthorised information would be committing a criminal offence.[2]

Limited circulation of information was, however, allowed to a 'competent authority' as defined in s 21(3). This definition included the 'Minister'.

In *Desmond v Glackin (No 2)*, the Court held that where a Minister obtained information from his agent which might be of assistance to another Minister in the exercise of his duties, there was no principle of law or of common sense which would prohibit such Minister passing on the relevant information to a ministerial colleague.

The circumstances in which information obtained by an inspector could be published, were widened in 1999. This occurred when s 21(2) of the 1990 Act was amended by s 53 of the Companies (Amendment) (No 2) Act 1999.

Under the amended s 21(2),[3] the information obtained by an inspector may now also be published or disclosed:

(1) for the purpose of the performance by a tribunal (to which the Tribunals of Inquiry (Evidence) Acts, 1921 to 1998, apply) of any of its functions;

(2) for the purpose of assisting or facilitating the performance by any Minister of the Government of any of his functions;

(3) for the purpose of assisting or facilitating any accountancy or other professional organisation in the performance of its disciplinary functions with respect to any of its members;

(4) for the purpose of the performance by the Irish Takeover Panel or any stock exchange established in the State of any of its functions in relation to the body or any other person who, in its opinion, is connected with the body; and

(5) for the purposes of complying with the requirements of procedural fairness, to be made to:

---

1 See s 21(1)(a)–(e).
2 Section 21(2).
3 Section 21(3) is also amended to include certain authorities established outside of the State – see s 53(3).

(a) any company in relation to which an inspector has been appointed under s 14 or any person required by the Minister to give any information under s 15, or

(b) any body in relation to which a person has been authorised under s 19 to exercise the powers conferred by that section or any person named in a report prepared by a person so authorised.

These amendments are retrospective – see s 53(4) of the 1999 (No 2) Act.

Admissibility of inspectors' reports

35.18 Section 18 provides for the admissibility in evidence against a person of certain questions put to him by an inspector.[1]

Section 22 of the 1990 Act specifically provides that a copy of an inspector's report is to be admissible in any civil proceedings as evidence:

(1) of the facts set out therein without further proof, unless the contrary is shown; and

(2) of the opinion of the inspector in relation to any matter contained in the report.

In *Countyglen plc v Carway*,[2] Laffoy J held that the interim and final reports of the inspector were admissible in actions to give all findings of primary fact, clearly expressed as such, the status of proven fact, unless disproved. However, it was implicit in s 22 that a court should not infringe the constitutional rights of a party to fair procedures.

EXPENSES OF INVESTIGATION INTO COMPANY'S AFFAIRS

35.19 The costs of the investigation will be paid initially by the relevant Minister.[3] However, the court may order the company, or the applicant, to reimburse the Minister. If this were to happen, s 13(1), as amended by s 25 of the 2001 Act, limits the amount payable by an applicant to £250,000.

In *Minister for Justice v Siúcre Éireann, Greencore plc*,[4] it was held that the Minister should, prima facie, be reimbursed the expenses by the company investigated. However, because Siúcre Éireann was controlled by the Minister for Finance prior to its 'privatisation', Lynch J decided that it would be unjust to penalise purchasers of shares by making that company reimburse the expenses.

If property is restored to any person as a result of the investigation, he may be ordered to contribute up to 10 per cent of its value towards the costs of the investigation.

---

1 Particularly when exercising his powers under s 10 or s 10 as applied by ss 14 and 17.
2 [1998] 2 IR 540.
3 See s 13(3A)(a) and (b) for definition of 'relevant Minister'.
4 [1992] 2 IR 215.

Any person convicted or ordered to pay damages may also be ordered to repay all or part of the costs of the investigation.

INVESTIGATION BY AN INSPECTOR INTO THE OWNERSHIP OF A COMPANY

35.20   Section 14, as amended, *gives the Director of Corporate Enforcement the power* to appoint one or more inspectors to investigate and report on the membership of any company. The purpose of this investigation is to determine the true persons who are financially interested in the success or failure of the company or who are able to control or influence company decisions. This power should enable the Director to unveil some of the secrecy which surrounds nominee shareholdings.

The Director also has the power to investigate a company's ownership without appointing an inspector (see **35.23**).

When appointing an inspector under s 14, the Director can specify the period of time or the specific matters to be investigated, in particular the enquiry may be limited to matters connected with particular shares or debentures.

An appointment may be made by the Director[1] where there are circumstances suggesting that it is necessary in the public interest – see s 14(2).

The initial appointments of inspectors under these powers were made during 1991.

35.21   The Minister for Industry and Commerce utilised these powers in September 1991. Then he decided to initiate an investigation into suspected irregularities which involved the purchase of shares in Sugar Distribution (Holdings) Ltd and their resale to Siúcre Éireann cpt at a substantial profit. This subsequently became known as the Greencore investigation.

The Minister appointed Maurice Curran, solicitor, under s 14, as an inspector to investigate the beneficial ownership of certain companies associated with Siúcre Éireann cpt and of certain of its debentures.

During October 1991, the Minister appointed John Glackin, solicitor, as an inspector to investigate the true ownership and control of Hoddle Investments Ltd and Chestvale Properties Ltd arising out of the sale of a Ballsbridge site to Telecom Éireann, again at a substantial profit.

In *Desmond v Glackin (No 2)*,[2] the court held that the Minister must exercise his discretion to appoint an inspector in good faith.

Section 26 of the 2001 Act adds subsections (6), (7) and (8) to s 14 of the 1990 Act.

---

1 The exercise of this power may be subject to judicial review – see *Dunnes Stores (Ireland) Ltd v Maloney* [1999] 3 IR 542, [1999] 1 ILRM 119.
2 [1993] 3 IR 67 (HC); [1993] 3 IR 106 (SC).

Section 14, as amended, now provides for the recoupment of costs of investigations ordered by the court.

Inspector's powers

35.22 An inspector appointed by the Director has essentially the same powers[1] as those available to inspectors appointed by the court. The inspector's powers extend to examining the existence of arrangements which, though not legally binding, were observed in practice and relevant to the investigation.

An inspector appointed under s 14(1) has the power (and duty) to investigate the membership of a company for the purpose of ascertaining those persons interested in its financial success or failure. In *Desmond v Glackin (No 2)*, the Supreme Court confirmed that where shares of a company are held by a trustee or by a corporate shareholder, the inspector is, irrespective of s 9, empowered to ascertain the identity of persons beneficially entitled to those shares.

The Director has the power to direct the publication of part or all of the report.

DIRECTOR'S POWERS TO INVESTIGATE COMPANY OWNERSHIP

35.23 Section 15, as amended, gives the Director the power, without appointing an inspector, to require any person whom he has reason to believe to have, or to be able to obtain for him, information as to the ownership of shares or debentures, to supply that information to him. This may be a less expensive and faster method of investigating company ownership than appointing an inspector.

'Ownership' is defined widely in s 15(2). Section 19 authorised the Minister to direct a body corporate to produce specified books and documents to him or to any authorised officer.

In addition to requesting his own officers to carry out this work, the Minister could appoint outsiders to carry out this function, and such outsiders shall have the same rights, duties and obligations as officers.

On 14 December 1993, the Minister appointed Mr Peter Fisher, accountant, as an authorised officer under s 19 to examine the books and documents of Countyglen plc. The authorised officer's report was submitted to the Minister on 23 December 1993, who immediately applied to the court for the appointment of an inspector under s 8. Arising out of this application, the High Court appointed Mr Frank Clarke, barrister, as an inspector to enquire further into certain of the affairs of County Glen plc.

In *Dunnes Stores (Ireland) Ltd et al v Ryan et al*,[2] Kinlen J held that where an authorised officer appointed under s 19 had demanded information which was

---

1 With appropriate amendments – s 14(5).
2 (1999) 6 CLP 314.

not specific enough and did not allow sufficient compliance time, he had acted ultra vires. Laffoy J in *Dunnes Stores (Ireland) Ltd v Maloney*[1] also held that the range of documents demanded by the Minister was excessive.

On appeal, the Supeme Court[2] ordered that the High Court's order in *Dunnes Stores v Ryan et al* be set aside, as the constitutional issue could not be determined in isolation from the other issues in this case.

The Supreme Court ordered a full re-hearing in the High Court, which took place in June 2000.

The second High Court decision found that the Minister's reasons for the appointment of an authorised officer to examine the books and records of two Dunnes Stores companies, were unreasonable and irrational and in excess of her powers under the 1990 Act. The court rejected the claim that the Minister had acted in bad faith in making the appointment.

The Minister appealed this second High Court decision and the Supreme Court heard it in July 2001: the five-judge court reserving its judgment on 2 July 2001.[3]

Section 29 of the 2001 Act substituted a new s 19 in the 1990 Act.

The replacement s 19 provides for the exercise by the Director of Corporate Enforcement of the power[4] to examine books and documents and otherwise amends the existing provisions of the section to facilitate their more effective application. In particular, subsection (2) has been extended to allow the production of books and documents other than those of the company whose books are being examined but which may contain information relating to that company's books. Also, certain terminology used in subsection (5) has been clarified to permit a broader interpretation, thereby facilitating the work of the Director.[5]

A new provision has been included at subsection (8) to the effect that a person who furnishes false or misleading answers to questions put to him under the section is guilty of an offence. This should discourage persons from attempting to mislead the Director or his agent in an examination of books and documents under this section and provide a sanction where any person does so. A new provision has also been included at subsection (9), whereby the time limit of 6 years for the retention of books and documents under s 202 of the 1990 Act is effectively extended to ensure that books and documents, the production of which has been demanded under the section, may not be destroyed notwithstanding the elapse of that period. A provision similar to that inserted in s 14 of the 1990 Act (by s 26 of the 2001 Act) for the recovery of costs of an examination

---

1 [1999] 3 IR 542, [1999] 1 ILRM 119.
2 See *Bar Review*, Vol 6, Issue 4, January 2001.
3 Reported in *The Irish Times*, 3 July 2001.
4 See amended s 19(4) for restrictions on the director's use of this power.
5 The director can also apply for a court order directing compliance with s 19(3)(b) – see s 371A of the 1963 Act, inserted by s 97 of the 2001 Act.

of books and documents under s 19 is also included by the provisions in subsections (10), (11) and (12).

Section 19 also provides for the insertion of a new s 19A into the 1990 Act. The effect of this section is to create an offence where a person, who knows or suspects that the Director of Corporate Enforcement is investigating an offence under the Companies Acts, destroys or conceals any documentary evidence that may relate to that offence. Section 19A(2) also creates a presumption that a person who destroys or conceals documentary evidence in this way is aware of the fact that the evidence may have been relevant to an investigation of the Director unless a court or jury is satisfied that there is reasonable doubt as to the person's knowledge in this regard.

Powers to enter and search premises

35.24   If the authorised officer, inspector or other person acting on behalf of the Minister could demonstrate reasonable grounds to suspect that there are, on any premises, books or documents which give information in relation to the ownership of shares and debentures, then, under s 20, he had the right to seek an order from the District Court for the Gardai, together with other named persons, to enter and search the premises for the purposes of obtaining the documents.

Section 30 of the 2001 Act substituted a new s 20 in the 1990 Act. The replacement section 20 extends the grounds on which a search warrant may be sought to include a suspicion that there are on any premises any books, documents or other things which may constitute evidence of the commission of an offence under the Companies Acts. The extension is required to facilitate the investigative role of the Director of Corporate Enforcement in respect of offences under the Companies Acts. The new section also extends the period provided in subsection (3) for which books, documents, etc seized under a warrant may be retained. The period is increased from three to six months and provision is made for an application to a district judge for a further extension beyond six months. This reflects the fact that material which may be seized under a warrant issued under this section may be voluminous and complex and may take a considerable time to analyse and decipher. Subsection (4) also introduced a new provision whereby a person may be required to operate any computer at a premises searched under warrant or to facilitate its operation by the officer authorised in the warrant for the purpose of retrieving relevant information.

Privacy of information

35.25   Section 21 provided for the confidentiality of information obtained by the Minister as a result of using his powers under s 19 and/or s 20. There were also provisions in s 23 relating to *privileged* information.

Sections 20 and 21 of the 1990 Act were amended by s 53 of the Companies (Amendment) (No 2) Act 1999. The amended s 21 widens the circumstances in which information obtained under ss 19 and 20 can be published.

Under s 21(2), as amended, no information, book or document shall be published without the consent, in writing, of the body investigated, except to a competent authority (defined in s 21(3), unless the disclosure or publication is, in the opinion of the Minister, required in the ten specific circumstances set out in s 21(1)(a) to (j) inclusive. These circumstances include for the purpose of the performance by a tribunal of any of its functions. This change is retrospective – see s 21(4) and **35.17**.

Sections 21 and 23 of the 1990 Act were also amended by ss 31 and 32 of the 2001 Act.

The amended s 21(1) now reflects the fact that since 2001 it is the Director, rather than the Minister, who is the corporate regulator, and who will decide whether or not it is appropriate to disclose information obtained by an inspector.

Section 32 substitutes a new s 23(2) in the 1990 Act. Under the amended s 23(2), an inspector will now have access to documents relating to a company whose books are being examined under s 19, where such documents are held by a bank, whether or not the company under examination is a customer of that bank. This will ensure that an examination of books and documents under s 19 may be as comprehensive as possible and that any relevant documents relating to the company which may be in the hands of a third party, including a bank, may be examined under the section. In addition, a definition of 'customer' is provided for the purposes of clarity of meaning in a new s 23(4).

Retention of certain powers by Minister

Section 34 of the 2001 Act provides for the power to examine books and documents of certain companies to be retained by the Minister and/or her authorised officer, in certain circumstances.

Power to impose restrictions on shares

35.26 If it appears to the Director that there is difficulty in finding out the relevant facts about the ownership of any share, the Director may, by notice in writing, direct that the shares shall, until further notice, be subject to restrictions. Those restrictions are that:

(1) any transfer of the shares or rights to the shares shall be void;
(2) no voting rights shall be exercised in respect of the shares;
(3) the shareholder will not be entitled to participate in any rights issue;
(4) no dividend shall be paid in respect of the shares, whether in respect of capital or otherwise.

Any person aggrieved by the Director's action can appeal to the court.[1]

The consequences of the Director's action are dealt with in s 16(3) to (18). The court may, for example, on the application of the Director, order the restricted shares to be sold.[2]

In such circumstances, the proceeds of the sale, less the related costs of the sale, will be paid into court for the benefit of the person who is beneficially interested in the shares. Such person may apply to the court for the proceeds to be paid to him.[3]

Section 16 was amended by s 27 of the 2001 Act so as to remove the exemption of companies in liquidation from certain of its provisions.

Criminal offence

35.27　Any person who exercises rights in relation to shares or debentures which are restricted, will be guilty of a criminal offence.[4]

Lifting of restrictions on shares

35.28　The restrictions can be lifted by order of the court or a direction by the Director under s 16(6).

The restrictions will only be lifted if:

(1)　the relevant facts about the shares have been disclosed to the company, and no unfair advantage had accrued to any person as a result of the earlier non-disclosure; or
(2)　the shares are to be sold and the court or the Director approves the sale.

LIMITS ON INVESTIGATING FOREIGN COMPANIES

35.29　Inspectors may be appointed by the court[5] to investigate foreign companies who carried on or are engaged in business within the State.

The court does not have the power to make a winding up order nor the Director to seek such an order as a result of the inspector's report.

Section 33 of the 2001 Act inserted s 23A in the 1990 Act, giving the Director power to assist overseas company law authorities.

1　Section 16(5).
2　Section 16(8).
3　Section 16(9).
4　See s 16(14)–(17).
5　Section 17.

TRANSFER OF MINISTER'S POWERS TO DIRECTOR

35.30   Many of the Minister's powers under ss 11, 12, 14, 15 and 16 of the 1990
Act have been transferred to the Director – see 2001 Act, Schedule, Part 2.

COMPANY CONTRACTS AND THE MEMORANDUM OF ASSOCIATION

Chapter 36

A COMPANY'S CONTRACTUAL CAPACITY AND THE ULTRA VIRES DOCTRINE

CONSTITUTIONAL DOCUMENTS

36.1   We saw in Chapter 3 that a company is recognised as a distinct but artificial person in law. Being an artificial legal person, a company's 'powers of contracting' have to be contained within its constitutional documents. Of particular relevance is the objects clause in a company's memorandum of association.

The memorandum of every company *must* state its objects.[1] The stating of the company's objects in its memorandum achieves the dual aim of protecting:

(1)   the *investors*[2] (shareholders), who can elicit the purposes to which the capital they have contributed is being applied; and
(2)   external persons such as *creditors*, dealing with the company, who can discover from the memorandum, a public document, the extent of the company's (including borrowing) powers.

If a company acts outside the scope of its powers it is deemed to be acting 'ultra vires' (see **12.6**).

Constructive notice

36.2   The thinking underlying the common law doctrine of ultra vires was that the memorandum of association, once approved and registered with the registrar of companies, became a public document.

Since the public had access to public documents, no company creditor could later plead that he did not know of the limitations of the company's trading powers; he should have checked them out first before doing business with that company. Creditors were deemed to have constructive notice of the contents of public documents.

The corollary to the creditors' position is that the company must restrict its trading activities to the objects stated in its memorandum. If it goes outside of those objects, or begins to trade in areas not foreseen by the drafters of the objects clause, then the company is acting 'ultra vires', or 'outside of its powers'.

In *Attorney-General v G.E. Ry Co*,[3] it was held that the doctrine of ultra vires:

---

1   Section 6(1)(c) of the 1963 Act.
2   Under s 29 of the 1963 Act, a company must forward a member a copy of the memorandum (and articles), if requested by him, subject to the payment of a small charge.
3   (1880) 5 App Cas 473.

'ought to be reasonably ... understood and applied, and ... whatever may fairly be regarded as incidental to, or consequential upon, those things which the legislature has authorised, ought not (unless expressly prohibited) to be held, by judicial construction, to be "ultra vires".'[1]

EFFECT OF ULTRA VIRES TRANSACTIONS

36.3   In *Ashbury Railway Carriage Co Ltd v Riche,*[2] it was judicially decided that an ultra vires contract was void, and not even the subsequent assent of the whole body of shareholders could ratify it. Persons dealing with the company were deemed to have constructive notice of its powers, even if they have not inspected its memorandum of association. As a result, at common law, third parties would have no rights against the company[3] under an ultra vires contract. For example, in *Re Jon Beauforte (London) Ltd,*[4] a company's objects clause empowered it to transact business as costumiers and gown makers. It subsequently diverted into the business of making veneered panels, which were ultra vires.

The company decided to build a factory to manufacture veneer panels. Builders (and other suppliers) were contracted to build the factory. Neither the builders nor any of the suppliers of goods and materials for the factory knew that the building of the factory was ultra vires. Nevertheless, the court held that none of them could prove for their debts in the company's liquidation, as they had acquired no contractual rights under their ultra vires contracts.

Effect of doctrine on drafting of objects clauses

36.4   The severe consequences at common law for company contracts deemed ultra vires by the courts, led to objects clauses becoming lengthy – quite different to the succinct model in Table B.[5]

EVOLUTION OF THE MODERN OBJECTS CLAUSES

36.5   In the earlier cases, it was sometimes held by the courts that the company had a *main object*[6] and, possibly, several subsidiary objects. The main object was generally to be found in the first paragraph of the objects clause.

In *Re German Date Coffee Co Ltd,*[7] it was held that as the main object was no longer capable of achievement, the *substratum* of the company was gone; the company was not empowered to carry out its subsidiary objects and had to be wound up.

---

1 Per Lord Selborne LC.
2 (1875) LR 7 HL 653.
3 They might, however, enjoy rights of recovery against the directors – see Part V B.
4 [1953] Ch 131.
5 See 1963 Act at p 701.
6 Eg in *Ashbury Railway Carriage Co Ltd v Riche* (1875) LR 7 HL 653.
7 (1882) 20 Ch D 169 (CA).

However, a company will not be wound up if the substratum or main object has not become impossible to achieve.[1] The 'main objects' rule will not be applied by the courts if the memorandum states that each of the objects is to be regarded as a main (or independent) object. The validity of this approach originated in the case of *Cotman v Brougham.*[2]

The effects of these cases on object clauses had been to make them give the company power to undertake a number of trading purposes, and to declare that each individual head of trading was an independent main object.

There were other UK cases which shaped the drafting of present day objects clauses.[3] However, because of the reform initiated in Ireland by s 8 of the 1963 Act, these cases are not being dealt with in the text, except for one: the *Bell Houses*[4] case.

Bell Houses (or catch-all) clauses

36.6   The *Bell Houses* case upheld the validity of the following objects clause:

> 'to carry on any other trade or business whatsoever, which can, in the opinion of the directors, be advantageously carried on by the company in connection with, or ancillary to, any of the above businesses or the general business of the company.'

The Court of Appeal's ruling effectively allows a company to undertake any business which the directors, acting in good faith, thought might be advantageously carried on. This type of 'catch-all' clause virtually overturns the effectiveness of the ultra vires rule.

COMPANY POWERS

36.7   In addition to the various separate objects contained in the 'objects' clause, the modern memorandum would also generally contain a number of powers which are considered reasonably conducive to the furtherance of the company's objects.[5] These might include the powers:

(1)   to sell the undertaking of the company for shares in another company or other consideration;

(2)   to take shares in another company;

(3)   to borrow money and to issue bills of exchange. This is implied in the case of a trading company, but an express power removes any difficulty if there is a doubt as to whether the company answers that description;

(4)   to amalgamate or enter into profit-sharing agreements with other companies, and to borrow money jointly with other companies;

(5)   to acquire similar businesses;

---

1 As in *Re Kitson & Co Ltd* [1946] 1 All ER 435 (CA).
2 [1918] AC 514 (HC).
3 But see L. MacCann 'The Capacity of the Company' *Irish Law Times*, April 1992, pp 79–86.
4 *Bell Houses Ltd v City Wall Properties Ltd* [1966] 2 All ER 674 (CA).
5 Many of these express powers would probably be implied.

(6) to sell or otherwise dispose of any part of the property of the company.

Implied powers

36.8   Powers not expressly taken in the memorandum of association may be implied if deemed necessary to achieve the objects of the company. For example, a trading company[1] would have the implied power to borrow money for the purposes of its trading (see **38.1**)

Trading companies also enjoy implied power to sell land[2] and to give pensions to their employees.[3] However, *Re Lee, Behrens & Co Ltd*[4] laid down the following three conditions necessary to justify the payment of pensions or gratuities:

(1) the transaction must be reasonably incidental to the carrying on of the company's business;
(2) it must be a bona fide transaction; and
(3) the pension or gratuity payment must have been made for the benefit of and to promote the prosperity of the company.

In *Re W & M Roith Ltd*,[5] the memorandum and articles of a company were altered to give the directors power to pay pensions to the dependents of any person who had served the company.

Shortly afterwards a director was made general manager for life. One of the terms of his service contract was that if he died while in office, the company would pay his widow a pension for the remainder of her life.

The general manager, who had been in poor health, died shortly after taking up his appointment. The company went into liquidation, and the liquidator refused to pay the pension to the widow, on the grounds that it was ultra vires.

The court held that the liquidator was correct. The pension arrangement made for the manager was not reasonably incidental to the carrying on of the company's business, and was not bona fide for the benefit of and to promote the prosperity of the company.

Express power to make gratuitous payments

36.9   It appeared from the *Roith* case that where gratuitous transactions[6] were involved, they would be deemed ultra vires the company unless the three tests set out by Eve J in *Re Lee, Behrens & Co Ltd* were satisfied.

---

1 But not a non-trading company. This would have to take an express power to borrow – see **38.1**.
2 *Re Kingsbury Collieries Ltd and Moore's Contract* [1907] 2 Ch 259.
3 *Cyclists Touring Club v Hopkinson* [1910] 1 Ch 179.
4 [1932] 2 Ch 46.
5 [1967] 1 All ER 427.
6 Such as donations, gifts, acting as guarantor or giving security for the indebtedness of another party.

These three tests were deemed not to apply to express powers by Pennycuick J in *Charterbridge Corporation v Lloyd's Bank*:[1] an approach endorsed by the Court of Appeal in *Re Horsley & Weight Ltd.*[2] In fact, Slade LJ in *Rolled Steel Products (Holdings) Ltd v British Steel Corporation*[3] considered that Eve J's three tests:

> 'should, in my opinion, now be recognised as being of no assistance and indeed positively misleading when the relevant question is whether a particular gratuitous transaction is within a company's corporate capacity.'

The UK position appears to be that if gratuitous payments are within the scope of the objects clause, but are improperly paid, then this is a breach of the directors' fiduciary duty[4] rather than being ultra vires the objects clause.

The real significance of the *Rolled Steel Products* judgment, therefore, is that it relegates an abuse of a company's powers to be simply a matter ultra vires the directors' authority rather than ultra vires the company's contractual capacity – such a transaction would now be binding on the company, unless the recipient was aware of the directors' breach of duty – see Chapters 37 and 38.

Implied power to make gratuitous payments

36.10   In *Re Lee, Behrens & Co Ltd*,[5] the directors decided that the company should covenant to pay a pension to the widow of the former managing director. The court held this transaction ultra vires and void because it was not:

(1) for the benefit of the company; or
(2) reasonably incidental to its business.

Again, in *Parke v Daily News Ltd*,[6] the company had sold the major part of its business and proposed to distribute the purchase price amongst former employees. The court held that such a gratuitous payment was ultra vires, void, and incapable of ratification by the majority of shareholders. Once again, the proposed payment was not reasonably incidental to, or consequential upon, the company's business.

36.11   It might be argued that gratuitous payments generally are in the interests of a company by generating a certain amount of good will. This argument, however, will not succeed where the donor company is being wound up, as in *Hutton v West Cork Railway Co*[7] and in *Re Frederick Inns*.[8]

The *Frederick Inns* case involved the Belton group of companies which owned and managed nine public houses in Dublin. The corporate structure used for this enterprise was a holding company, Motels Ltd, and nine subsidiary

---

1 [1970] Ch 62.
2 [1982] 3 All ER 1045.
3 [1986] Ch 246 (CA).
4 Or, perhaps, in agency law terms, a breach of warranty of authority.
5 [1932] 2 Ch 46.
6 [1962] Ch 927. A similar approach was taken by Carroll J in *Roper v Ward* [1981] IRLM 408.
7 (1883) 23 Ch D 654 (CA).
8 [1991] ILRM 582 (HC); [1994] 1 ILRM 387 (SC).

companies. The case was concerned with the holding company, Motels Ltd, and three specific subsidiaries, namely:

(1) Frederick Inns Ltd;
(2) The Rendezvous Ltd; and
(3) The Graduate Ltd.

Since the late 1970s, the group was in a position of constantly owing money to the Revenue Commissioners in respect of VAT, PAYE/PRSI and Corporation Profits Tax.

By June 1984, the group's liabilities to the Revenue Commissioners had risen to £2.8 million.

On 12 June 1984, the Collector General sent each of the ten companies ten separate letters demanding the amount due from it and giving notice that, in the event of failure to pay, the letter would be used as evidence[1] that the company was unable to pay its debts, and a petition for winding up would be issued.

Subsequent to these letters, negotiations took place between representatives of the Revenue Commissioners and some of the group's directors. These negotiations resulted in an arrangement whereby the three subsidiaries identified above would be sold, and £1.4 million paid to the Revenue out of the proceeds.

This arrangement was duly carried out, with one variation: £1.2 million was paid to the Revenue Commissioners instead of the £1.4 million.

The £1.2 million was made up of the following contributions:

Frederick Inns Ltd	£200,000
The Rendezvous Ltd	£100,000
The Graduate Ltd	£123,000 approx
Motels Ltd	£777,000 approx
Total	£1,200,000

All four companies were insolvent when each of the instalments was paid. The Revenue Commissioners were aware of these facts.

The Revenue Commissioners applied the £1.2 million received to reducing the amounts owing by *all ten* companies in the group.

36.12   In the High Court, Lardner J held that each of the companies in the group was a separate legal entity, and that the Revenue Commissioners were not entitled to treat the group as one single entity. He stated:

'Insofar as payments to the Revenue . . . were intended to be applied in reduction of the tax liabilities of other companies in the group, they can only be regarded as voluntary payments made without consideration for the benefit of third parties

---

1 For the purpose of s 214 of the 1963 Act.

and ... in the absence of any evidence that such excess payments were for the benefit of the paying companies, they are clearly ultra vires.'

Specifically, Lardner J gave the following reasons for his finding the excess payments of tax ultra vires. He said:

'payment ... of any sum in excess of its (own) tax liability was ultra vires the paying company insofar as:

(a)   it effected a gratuitous reduction or alienation of its assets and
(b)   it was done when the company was insolvent.'

On appeal, the Supreme Court upheld Lardner J's decision.

Power to lend money

36.13   In the appeal to the Supreme Court, it was submitted that an express power to lend money in the memorandum of association of Frederick Inns Ltd could be relied upon.

The express power read as follows:

'To advance and lend money from time to time either with or without mortgage or other security at such rates of interest and generally upon such terms and conditions and in such manner as may be thought expedient.'

Blaney J's response was:

'I reject this submission also. The four companies did not lend any monies to the other six. What they did was to pay part of their debts which was something very different.'

Other express powers

36.14   It would not be unusual to include an express power 'to pay pensions to employees of the company and to their wives and other dependants.' For example, art 89 of Table A confers express power or authority on directors to pay a gratuity or pension to executive directors or their widows.

An objects clause often concludes with a general 'catch-all' power to do 'all such business and things as may be incidental or conducive to the attainment of the above objects, or any of them'. However, such a power should be interpreted as authorising the company only to do that which is incidental or conducive to the main object(s)[1] of the company. This is because objects are the activities which a company was formed to carry out; powers merely assist in the attainment of these objects.

---

1   Unless there is a 'Bell Houses' type catch-all clause in the memorandum – see **36.6**.

IMPROPER USE OF COMPANY'S POWERS

36.15 In *Re Introductions Ltd*,[1] the court held that on a construction of the company's memorandum of association, the borrowing of money was a power and not an object. Thus, money borrowed to fund an activity not stated in the objects clause was an ultra vires transaction and, as the lending bank was aware of the purpose for which the funds lent were to be used, the transaction was unenforceable by them against the company.

A major change to this type of judicial thinking was brought about by *Rolled Steel Products (Holdings) Ltd v British Steel Corporation.* The decision in this case classified the use of an express power *as an internal matter between the directors and shareholders, and of no relevance to the ultra vires rule and the interests of third party or external company creditors who were without notice.*

The express power in question was:

> 'to lend and advance money or give credit to such persons . . . and on such terms as may be expedient, and in particular, to customers of . . . and others having dealings with the company and to give guarantees or become security for any such persons, firms or companies.'

Two of Rolled Steel Products Ltd's directors authorised a guarantee by the plaintiff company of the debts of another company controlled by one of the directors.

Browne-Wilkinson LJ considered that no question of ultra vires (the memorandum's powers) arose, and the matter was merely an internal abuse or exceeding of the directors' authority. In other words, the improper use of an express power is to be treated as a matter for the articles, rather than the memorandum, of association (see **38.10** and **38.21**).

INVESTORS AND THE ULTRA VIRES DOCTRINE

36.16 In *Anglo Overseas Agencies Ltd v Green*,[2] Salmon J said that:

> 'The principal purpose of (the main objects) rule is that (investors) may know how the money they invest is to be used.'

The original idea was that the ultra vires rule would protect investors, as enunciated by Salmon J. However, the development of lengthy object clauses, including express powers and catch-all objects and powers as illustrated above, has eroded the effectiveness of the ultra vires doctrine in protecting investors. It is arguable, however, whether such protection is really necessary for investors.

In Ireland, most companies are private. In many of these, the investors will also be the directors and actually making decisions on behalf of the company.

---

1 [1970] Ch 199.
2 [1961] 1 QB 1.

In public companies, the objects clause is an internal matter affecting investors and directors. Each investor is entitled to a copy of the memorandum, and, if sufficient interest is mustered, investors can alter the objects clause.

Alteration of objects clause

36.17 Section 10(1)[1] allows the company, by special resolution, to amend the provisions of its memorandum by:

(1) abandoning;
(2) restricting; or
(3) amending any existing object; or
(4) by adopting a new object.

Thus, the majority of shareholders have it within their power to restrict or amend their company's objects clause if they consider it gives too much discretion to the directors. They can also apply to the court, under s 8(2) of the 1963 Act, to restrain a company from carrying out an ultra vires act. Ultimately, of course, the majority of investors can remove the directors if they are dissatisfied with the manner of their transacting the business of the company.

CREDITORS AND THE ULTRA VIRES DOCTRINE

36.18 Where the company entered into an ultra vires contract with a third party, at common law this transaction was void. This meant that neither the company nor the third party could acquire rights or incur liabilities under it. The *Re Jon Beauforte (London) Ltd* case (see **36.3**) illustrated this fact, and, particularly the unjust nature of a third party or creditor's legal position. The legislature has attempted to protect the creditors' legal position by enacting s 8 in the 1963 Act.

Section 8 protection

36.19 To mitigate the harshness of the common law position, s 8(1) of the 1963 Act modifies the ultra vires rule thus:

> 'Any act or thing done by a company which if the company had been empowered to do the same would have been lawfully and effectively done, shall, notwithstanding that the company had no power to do such act or thing, *be effective in favour of any person relying on such act or thing who is not shown to have been actually aware*, at the time when he so relied thereon, that such act or thing was not within the powers of the company, but any director or officer of the company who was responsible for the doing by the company of such act or thing shall be liable to the company for any loss or damage suffered by the company in consequence thereof.' (author's emphasis)

---

1 Of the 1963 Act – see **12.8**.

Essentially, s 8(1) gives third party protection against ultra vires contracts provided that:

(1) such contracts are 'lawfully and effectively done'; and
(2) the person[1] relying on the contract 'is not shown to be actually aware, . . . that the act was ultra vires'.

Acts lawfully and effectively done

36.20   The usual interpretation of this requirement would be that the ultra vires act must otherwise be in accordance with company and general law. However, the *Frederick Inns* case (see **36.11**) seems to have distinguished between 'lawful' and 'effectively done'.

In that case, Blaney J raised two separate questions, namely:

(1) is the transaction within the power or capacity of the company? (lawful) – an example of an unlawful contract arose in *Re Greendale Developments Ltd.*[2] Here, Keane J decided that payments made by a company in circumstances where the company received no benefit in return were fundamentally illegal and ultra vires (the objects clause); and
(2) if the transaction is lawful, has that power been validly exercised so as to bind the company? (effectively done).

He then decided that the transaction was within the power of the company, but that this power had not been validly exercised by the directors,[3] saying:

> 'It is clear that it could not be held that the payments by the four companies were "lawfully and effectively done". At the time the payments were made, the four companies were under the management of their directors pending imminent liquidation. Because of the insolvency of the companies the shareholders no longer had any interest. The only parties with an interest were the creditors. The payments made could not have been lawful [and effective] because they were made in total disregard of their interests. And since the payments were not lawfully [and effectively] made, the Revenue Commissioners cannot rely on s 8 of the Companies Act 1963 to remedy the fact that the payments were ultra vires.'[4]

Person relying on s 8 must not be actually aware

36.21   The intention of s 8 is to overturn the constructive notice which the third party was deemed to have of a company's objects in its public constitution, or memorandum of association.

---

1 The wording of s 8(1) is wide enough to include both internal interests of directors and external interests of creditors.
2 [1998] 1 IR 8 – the facts are set out in **36.26**.
3 The directors can only validly exercise powers on behalf of the general body of shareholders. When a company is insolvent, the interests of the creditors intrude. Creditors then become prospectively entitled to displace the normal power of the shareholders (and consequently directors) to deal with the company's assets. This seems to be the line of reasoning underlying Blaney J's decision (see **38.12**).
4 Bracketed words inserted by author.

Because of s 8, it will no longer be necessary for those dealing with companies to read their objects clauses. If a contract is ultra vires, such persons would be protected by s 8 as they were not actually aware of this fact.

However, where a person enters into an ultra vires contract with a company, having firstly read that company's memorandum and failing to realise that the transaction in question was ultra vires, s 8(1) will not protect him. As Keane J stated in *Northern Bank Finance Co Ltd v Quinn and Achates Investment Co*:[1]

> 'I see no reason in logic or justice why the legislature should have intended to afford the same protection to persons who had actually read the memorandum and simply failed to appreciate the lack of vires.'

36.22   Keane J's decision has been criticised on the basis that he did not distinguish between actual 'notice' and actual 'knowledge'.

If the wording of s 8(1) had been restricted to a person 'who is not shown to have been given notice', then perhaps Keane J's decision would be more appropriate. However, s 8(1) clearly provides that once the third party 'is not shown to have been actually[2] aware' he is entitled to protection.

In the *Northern Bank Finance Co* case, the third party, because his agent failed to appreciate fully the objects in question, was, in fact, actually unaware. In this writer's opinion, third parties who attempt to read and understand a company's objects clause, should not be unreasonably denied protection under s 8(1) simply because they failed to comprehend its full significance.

Regulation 6 protection for company creditors

36.23   Regulation 6 of the European Communities (Companies) Regulations 1973[3] implemented art 9 of the First EU Directive on Company Law.[4]

Regulation 6(1) reads as follows:

> 'In favour of a person dealing with a company in *good faith*, any transaction entered into by an *organ of the company*, being its board of directors or any *person registered* under these regulations as a person authorised to bind the company, shall be deemed to be within the capacity of the company and any limitation of the powers of that board or person, whether imposed by the memorandum or articles of association or otherwise, may not be relied upon as against any person so dealing with the company.
>
>   Regulation 6(2) provides that "any such person shall be presumed to have acted in good faith unless the contrary is proved".' (author's emphasis)

Regulation 6(3) clarifies the registration procedure mentioned in reg 6(1). The registration of a person authorised to bind the company shall be effected by delivering to the registrar of companies a notice giving the name and description of the person concerned.

---

1   [1979] ILRM 221.
2   Not constructively.
3   SI 1973/163.
4   Directive 68/151/EEC.

Clearly, under reg 6, an outsider may enforce an ultra vires transaction against the company, provided it was negotiated with the board of directors or a registered person, and, at the time of entering into the contract, the outsider was unaware that it was beyond the powers or capacity of the company and its authorised agents.

Regulation 6 and s 8 compared[1]

36.24 In reg 6(1), the person seeking to enforce the ultra vires contract must have dealt with the company in *good faith*. In s 8, he need only be 'actually unaware'. The criterion of good faith may imply a duty to investigate, even though reg 6(2) imports a presumption of good faith on the part of the third party. Under s 8, the ultra vires contract must simply be negotiated by the company. The protection under reg 6 is limited to contracts negotiated by 'its board of directors or any person registered under the 1973 regulations'.

In the *Frederick Inns* case, Blaney J stated:

> 'I think it is clear that none of the companies had any person registered under the regulations as a person authorised to bind the company. The payment appears to have been agreed to be made as a result of informal meetings between accountants acting on behalf of the companies and Mr Burke on behalf of the Revenue Commissioners. In these circumstances, ... the Revenue Commissioners cannot rely on Regulation 6 as validating the payment.'

Again, s 8(1) mentions only contracts which are ultra vires the company's memorandum (objects); the wording of reg 6 is wide enough to embrace contracts which are either ultra vires the memorandum or ultra vires the directors' authority in the articles.[2]

Finally, reg 6 only applies to limited companies.

Regulation 10

36.25 Regulation 10 of the 1973 Regulations also protects persons, where documents should have been published in *Iris Oifigiúil*, but were not. These documents cannot be relied upon by the company against a third party.

Informal company agreements and ultra vires contracts

36.26 Kingsmill Moore J held, in *Buchanan Ltd v McVey*,[3] that if all the corporators agree to a transaction which was honest and intra vires the company, then, regardless of how informal the manner of the agreement, it binds the company. The judgment was cited with approval by Keane J in *Re*

---

1 For a more detailed comparison, see L. MacCann 'The Capacity of the Company (Part II)', *Irish Law Times*, July 1992, pp 151–159. MacCann considered that Keane J did not distinguish between 'actual notice' and 'actual knowledge' in the *Northern Bank Finance Co* case – see **36.21**. See also P. Ussher 'Company Law – Validation of Ultra Vires Transactions' [1981] DULJ 76.
2 See next chapter.
3 [1954] IR 89.

Greendale Developments Ltd (No 2).[1] In that case, payments were made by the company for the benefit of the respondents in circumstances where the company received no benefit in return. Keane J therefore held that such payments were ultra vires the company, and this fundamental illegality could not be cured even by all the shareholders assenting to each and every one of the payments in question. Furthermore, the company liquidator had the right to pursue recovery of such payments by misfeasance proceedings.[2]

Position of company under ultra vires contracts

36.27 Section 8 and reg 6 only benefit the other parties to the ultra vires contract. The company itself cannot enforce an ultra vires contract against the other party. However, it may have an *action for damages against any director or officer* of the company who was responsible for the ultra vires transaction under s 8(1).

---

1 [1998] 1 IR 8.
2 See **29.19** *et seq.* See also J. Meade 'Ultra vires or Directors' abuses: When can shareholders right a wrong' (1999) 6 CLP 198, at pp 198–202.

PART VII B

COMPANY CONTRACTS AND THE ARTICLES OF ASSOCIATION

Chapter 37

COMPANY CONTRACTS AND THE AUTHORITY OF ITS HUMAN AGENTS

FORM OF COMPANY CONTRACTS

37.1   A company is recognised by law as a legal person with almost the same powers as a human being to enter into contracts.

Notwithstanding its artificial existence, a company may enter into oral or written contracts. However, the company can only negotiate its contracts by means of human agents. As Denning LJ stated in *Bolton & Co Ltd v T. J. Graham & Sons Ltd*:[1]

> '. . . companies may in many ways be likened to human bodies. They have a brain and a nerve centre which control what they do. They also have hands that hold the tools and act in accordance with directions from the centre.
>
>   Some of the people in the company are mere servants and agents who are nothing more than hands to do the work and cannot be said to represent the directing mind or the will. Others are directors or managers who represent the directing mind and will of the company, and control what they do. The state of mind of these managers is the state of mind of the company and is treated by the law as such.'

These comments, made in the context of illustrating the criminal aspects of a company's activities, also show that, for all practical purposes, a company can only negotiate contracts by human persons acting under its authority, express or implied.[2]

A bill of exchange can be made, accepted or endorsed on behalf of the company by any person acting under its authority.[3]

A document or proceeding requiring authentication by a company, may be signed by a director, secretary or other authorised officer of the company, and need not be under its common seal.

The seal

37.2   The company's seal must be used only with the authority of the directors or of a committee of directors authorised by the directors on that behalf, and every instrument to which the seal is affixed must be signed by a director and countersigned by the secretary or by a second director or by some other person appointed by the directors for the purpose.[4]

---

1 [1957] 1 QB 159.
2 Section 38 of the 1963 Act.
3 Section 39.
4 Article 115 of Table A.

A company will generally not be bound if the seal is affixed without proper authority.

THE COMPANY'S HUMAN AGENTS

37.3 As mentioned in Chapter 1, the company has neither mind nor body, so cannot operate or enter into contracts without the assistance of human agents. These human agents will normally be the company's directors, officers, managers and other employees. Before considering the role of these intermediaries, it is useful to outline some relevant principles of the law underpinning these relationships. The area of law concerned is that of agency.

Agency law principles

37.4 Generally, only people who are parties to a contract can acquire rights and incur liabilities under it. This principle is known as privity of contract. The technical term 'privity' means, essentially, that a person will not be bound by any deal made by another, unless he personally took part in its negotiation.

Definition of agent

37.5 An agent, quite simply, is a person authorised to act on behalf of another. Accordingly, the law of agency contains the legal rules governing the relationships that arise when one person is authorised by another to perform certain legal tasks on his behalf, eg a manager on behalf of the company.

Fridman[1] suggests the following description of what agency involves:

> 'Agency is the relationship that exists between two persons where one, called the agent, is considered in law to represent the other, called the principal, in such a way as to be able to affect the principal's legal position in respect of strangers to the relationship by the making of contracts.'

The 'strangers' to the contract are usually termed 'third parties'. Thus, an agent is a person who is employed for the purpose of bringing his principal into contractual relations with third parties.

In the context of company contracts, the company is the principal; directors, officers and employees act as its agents in negotiating contracts on the company's behalf, with third parties (outsiders).

Authority of agent

37.6 There are three broad categories of agent, depending upon the amount or extent of authority vested in them by their principal.

These categories are:

---

1 G.H.L. Fridman *The Law of Agency* (Butterworths, 1971).

(1) *Universal Agents* – here the agent has an unlimited authority to act on behalf of his principal. In effect, he can bind his principal as if he were the principal himself. Such agents must be appointed by deed – a power of attorney. These appointments are relatively rare in commercial transactions. However, the board of directors of a company is, collectively, its universal agent. So, too, would be a managing director to whom the board delegated all of its powers (see **37.15**).

(2) *General Agents* – these agents have authority or power to bind their principals within certain limits. A company director has been held to be a general agent in *Hammond Properties Ltd v Gajdis*,[1] as has the manager of a public house in *Watteau v Fenwick*.[2]

(3) *Special Agents* – this type of agent has authority for only a specific purpose or occasion and is delegated limited powers.[3]

Most human agents negotiating contracts on behalf of companies would probably fall into the category of general agents, although the company may also employ special agents in connection with 'one-off' or specialist transactions. To discover the true nature of an agent's relationship with the principal, one must examine the extent of his authority.

Actual and ostensible authority

37.7 The actual extent of the agent's authority will depend upon:

(1) the express terms of his appointment by his principal; or

(2) the existence of authority implied by the law for particular legal relationships (usual authority).

Implied, or ostensible,[4] authority may exceed the agent's actual authority from his principal, thereby rendering the principal liable in contracts made by his agent outside the limits of his actual authority.

37.8 In *Watteau v Fenwick*, the manager of a public house was prohibited from ordering tobacco by his employer (principal). However, he ignored this prohibition and ordered tobacco on credit.

His employer was held liable to pay the seller because public house managers would usually have authority to place orders of this kind. The agent, therefore, had ostensible authority.

A principal is generally bound to third parties by the acts of his agents, whether within their actual, usual or ostensible authority.

---

1 [1968] 3 All ER 267.
2 [1893] 1 QB 346.
3 Eg an estate agent, solicitor, barrister, stockbroker, etc.
4 Sometimes also styled 'apparent' authority.

Usual authority of company's agents

37.9   Actual authority is that which the company's agent actually possesses by virtue of the express terms of his appointment. Usual authority is that which is generally possessed by a particular class of agent.

As the standard set of articles of association in Table A are widely used by companies,[1] it would be customary to refer to Table A to ascertain the usual authority of many of the company's agents, including its board of directors.

Board of directors

37.10   Article 80 of Table A provides that:

> 'the business of the company shall be managed by the directors ... subject to such directions ... as may be given by the company in general meeting: but no direction given by the company in general meeting shall invalidate any prior act of the directors which would have been valid if that direction had not been given.'

The directors may also 'exercise' all the powers of the company to borrow money,[2] and to mortgage or charge its undertaking, property and uncalled capital.

Internal limits on borrowing powers and lender protection

37.11   Article 79, in standard form, places a limit[3] on the directors' exercise of the company's borrowing powers. This upper limit is the nominal amount of the share capital of the company, unless the company, in general meeting, sanctions a loan exceeding this amount.

Suppose the directors of a company borrow money on the company's behalf in excess of the internal maximum limit, without obtaining prior authority from the shareholders by way of a resolution. What is the effect of this 'internal management' defect on the loan transaction?

37.12   These were the basis of the facts in the famous case of *Royal British Bank v Turquand*,[4] where Jervis CJ said:

> 'The (third) party here, on reading the deed of settlement would find, not a prohibition from borrowing, but a permission to do so on certain conditions. Finding that the authority might be made complete by a resolution, *he would have a right to infer the fact of a resolution* authorising that which, on the face of the document, appeared to be legitimately done. Consequently, persons dealing with a company are not concerned to inquire whether all matters of internal management have been complied with, if everything is apparently regular.' (author's emphasis)

---

1 Either with or without alteration.
2 Article 79. Article 81 gives the directors the authority, by power of attorney, to delegate such powers as they think fit to any company, firm or person.
3 Apart from temporary loans obtained from the company's bankers in the ordinary course of business.
4 (1856) 6 E & B 327.

This is known as the rule in the *Turquand* case or the Internal or Indoor Management rule.[1]

The rule in the *Turquand* case is an example of judicial creditor protection. It was applied in *Ulster Investment Bank Ltd v Euro Estates Ltd*[2] by Carroll J who stated:

> 'while persons dealing with a company are assumed to have read the public documents of the company, ... They need not inquire into the regularity of the internal proceedings and may assume that all is being done regularly.'

Again, in *Allied Irish Banks Ltd v Ardmore Studios International (1972) Ltd*,[3] Finlay J upheld the plaintiff's contention that 'a person dealing with a limited liability company, and doing so bona fides, was not required to enquire into irregularities in the internal management of the company'.

Exceptions to the rule in Turquand*'s case*

37.13 The rule does not apply when:

(1) it is *known*[4] that the rules of internal management have not been complied with; or
(2) the document upon which the person dealing with the company relies is a forgery;[5] or
(3) an agent of the company has done something beyond any authority given him, or which he was held out as having,[6] ie an agent clearly exceeds his ostensible authority; or
(4) the person dealing with the company has been put on enquiry;[7] or
(5) the person dealing with the company is not an outsider. In *Hely-Hutchinson v Brayhead Ltd*,[8] however, the judgment suggests that where an insider like a director is dealing with the company qua outsider, he may still be able to claim the protection of the rule in the *Turquand* case.

Protection of lenders[9] *under art 79*

37.14 Article 79 also provides for instances where directors exceed their borrowing powers. In fact, the relevant wording reflects and develops the principle underlying the *Turquand* case by providing that:

> '... no debt incurred ... in excess of [the internal] limit, shall be invalid or ineffectual, *except* in the case of express notice to the lender ... at the time when the

---

1 See G. McCormack 'The Indoor Management Rule in Ireland' *Law Society Gazette*, January/February 1985, at pp 17–20.
2 [1982] ILRM 57 (HC). See also *Cox v Dublin City Distillery (No 2)* [1915] 1 IR 345.
3 (Unreported) 30 May 1973 (HC).
4 *Howard v Patent Ivory Manufacturing Co* (1883) 38 Ch D 156, and *AL Underwood Ltd v Bank of Liverpool and Martin* [1924] 1 KB 775.
5 *Ruben v Great Fingall Consolidated* [1906] AC 439, but see **20.37** and **20.38**.
6 *Kreditbank Cassel v Schenkers* [1927] 1 KB 826.
7 *Houghton & Co v Nothard, Lowe and Wills Ltd* [1927] 1 KB 246.
8 [1967] 2 All ER 14.
9 The 'mechanics' of company borrowing and creditors' rights generally are dealt with in Part VIII.

debt was incurred. ... that the [internal] limit had been ... exceeded.' (author's emphasis)

Managing director

37.15 Articles 110 and 111 authorise the directors to appoint one (or more) of themselves to the office of managing director, and to confer upon him 'any of the powers exercisable by them'. Essentially therefore, the board can delegate all of its authority to a managing director, who in turn, will be able to negotiate contracts on behalf of the company.

Chairman

37.16 A company chairman usually has no executive authority, unless expressly appointed an executive chairman. The chairman's usual authority would be to chair company and directors' meetings and to sign the minutes of a previous meeting.

Individual directors

37.17 Individual directors' usual authority would be limited to witnessing the affixing of the company seal to a document.[1] However, they may also have contracts of employment with the company making them executive directors and thereby greatly increasing their actual authority.[2]

Company secretary

37.18 The development of the company secretary's role has already been detailed in **23.15**. Since the *Panorama Developments* case, his ostensible authority to act on behalf of the company has greatly increased.

Shareholders

37.19 A shareholder has no usual authority to enter into contracts on behalf of the company.[3]

Third party protection and the doctrine of ostensible authority

37.20 In *Freeman & Lockyer v Buckhurst Park Properties (Mangal) Ltd,*[4] K and H formed the defendant company to purchase and resell a large estate. K, H and two nominees were appointed directors of the company. The articles provided for the appointment of a managing director, but none was appointed and K acted throughout as managing director with the knowledge of the board. K employed a firm of architects, the plaintiffs, to do certain work connected with developing the estate. The plaintiffs did this and then claimed from the

---

1 Article 115 of Table A.
2 The ostensible authority of non-executive directors would also be much wider than their actual authority.
3 See Chapters 3 and 4.
4 [1964] 2 QB 480 – see also the *Ulster Factors* case in **38.13**.

company for payment of their fee. The court held that the company was bound by acts done by a managing director within his ostensible or apparent authority and therefore liable to pay the fee.

Conditions necessary

37.21 In the *Freeman & Lockyer* case, Diplock LJ stated that the relevant law can be summarised by stating four conditions which must be fulfilled to entitle a contractor or third party to enforce against a company a contract entered into on behalf of the company by an agent who had no actual authority to do so. It must be shown:

(1) that a representation that the agent had authority to enter on behalf of the company into a contract of the kind sought to be enforced was made to the third party;
(2) that such representation was made by a person (or persons) who had 'actual' authority to manage the business of the company either generally or in respect of those matters to which the contract relates;
(3) that the third party was induced by such representation to enter into the contract, and in fact relied upon it; and
(4) that under its memorandum or articles of association the company was not deprived of the capacity either to enter into a contract of the kind sought to be enforced or to delegate authority to enter into a contract of that kind to the agent.

Managing directors and chairmen

37.22 In the *Freeman & Lockyer* case, a person who had acted as managing director without being formally appointed, but with the knowledge of the board, was deemed to have the full (ostensible) authority of that office holder.

Again, in *Hely-Hutchinson v Brayhead Ltd* (see **37.13**), a person who was chairman of a company also acted as its de facto managing director; the board acquiescing afterwards by approving contracts negotiated by him. This person was deemed to have implied authority to do all such things as fall within the usual remit of a managing director's authority.

Thus, the authority of a managing director may be inferred from a course of dealings or from the conduct of the parties.

37.23 In *Kilgobbin Mink and Stud Farms Ltd v National Credit Co Ltd*,[1] Hamilton J seemed to extend the doctrine of ostensible authority to include a request made by a chairman and controlling shareholder to pay monies due to the company into the bank account of another company also controlled by himself.

This decision might have been easier to reconcile with established precedents had the request been made by a managing director (possessing wide usual authority) rather than a chairman (with limited usual authority – see **37.16**). Again, it raises questions relating to the separate personality of the

---

1 (Unreported) 16 February 1978 (HC).

company. Accordingly, perhaps it should be interpreted narrowly as relating to its own peculiar facts.

Directors and managers

37.24   The doctrine of ostensible authority would seem to possess the potential to expand and encompass the activities of non-executive and executive directors, eg those styled finance and technical directors, senior (line) managers,[1] middle and junior management and, indeed, all employees. The ostensible authority of junior employees would, of course, be quite limited.

The company secretary

37.25   In the *Panorama Developments* case,[2] the company secretary hired cars for his own use by fraudulently representing that they were for the company. The court held that the company was liable as the secretary has ostensible (or apparent) authority to make a contract on the company's behalf for the hire of cars. However, in *UBAF Ltd v European American Banking Corp*,[3] it was held that the secretary had no apparent authority to make representations on the company's behalf in relation to a syndicated loan.

The secretary's ostensible authority is not as wide as that, for example, of a managing director. Perhaps it would be safe to assume he has only ostensible authority to bind the company in contracts relating to administration/internal management aspects of the company's affairs.[4]

Estoppel, ostensible authority and company contracts are discussed further in **38.21**.

The ultra vires doctrine and company agents

37.26   At common law, because of the doctrine of constructive notice, a contract which was ultra vires the company's objects was void. As a result, the other party possessed no rights under it against the company.

Because of the s 8 and reg 6 protection, detailed in Chapter 36, the other party can now enforce an ultra vires contract against the company. The doctrine of constructive notice has been virtually overturned by those statutory reforms whose aim was to protect company creditors.

This chapter has focused on company contracts entered into by human agents which were ultra vires the agents' authority, though not necessarily the company's objects. Where, for example, a company is empowered to borrow money, but the directors exceed an internal ceiling on borrowing, such a

---

1 Cf. the ostensible authority of a public house manager in *Watteau v Fenwick* [1893] 1 QB 346.
2 See **23.15**.
3 [1984] QB 713.
4 The *Panorama Developments* case included elements of agency by estoppel and fraud. In his judgment, Lord Denning MR said: 'Mr Bayne was a fraud. But it was the company which put him in a position in which he was able to commit the fraud. So the defendants are liable'.

transaction is intra vires the company but ultra vires the directors. The judicial rule in *Turquand*'s case protects the innocent third party lender in these circumstances; so, too, does article 79 of Table A (see **37.14**).

Generally, if a company agent enters into any contract in excess of his actual authority, it is ultra vires the agent. The doctrine of ostensible authority, developed by judicial decisions, has the effect of rendering some such unauthorised transactions intra vires the agent's authority and enforceable against the company.

In the next chapter, we shall focus on recent judicial developments in the protection of creditors against ultra vires actions by a company's directors.

Chapter 38

TRENDS IN JUDICIAL PROTECTION FOR CREDITORS AGAINST ULTRA VIRES ACTIONS BY DIRECTORS

38.1 A most important power for any company is the power of borrowing money and of giving security for any such loans. At common law, it is necessary to distinguish between trading and non-trading companies when considering the power to borrow and obtain loan capital.

TRADING COMPANIES

In *General Auction, Estate and Monetary Co v Smith*,[1] the court confirmed that because the plaintiff was a trading company, it had implied power to borrow money for the purpose of its business, and to charge its assets as security for such borrowings or loans.

NON-TRADING COMPANIES

38.2 A company formed for a non-trading purpose does not have implied power to borrow. As a result, non-trading companies need to be given express borrowing power in their memorandum of association.

A typical express objects clause empowering a non-trading company to borrow might read thus:

> 'To borrow and raise money in such manner as the company shall think fit, and in particular, by the issue of debentures and debenture stock, mortgages, charges, perpetual or otherwise, charged [secured] upon all or any of the company's property (both present and future) and undertaking, including its uncalled capital.'

PROPERTY WHICH CANNOT BE CHARGED

38.3 Whilst a company may charge its uncalled capital if the memorandum or articles allow it;[2] it cannot borrow on the security of either its:

(1) reserve capital;[3] or
(2) books.

---

1 [1891] 3 Ch 432.
2 See *Newton v Anglo-Australian Investment Cos Debentureholders* [1895] AC 244. Article 79 of Table A expressly allows this.
3 *Re Mayfair Property Co, Bartlett v Mayfair Property Co* [1898] 2 Ch 28.

If a company charges all its undertaking, the liquidator, on a winding up order, has a better right of access to the company's books than a receiver appointed by the debentureholders.[1]

COMPANY BORROWING BY THE DIRECTORS

38.4   Article 79 of Table A gives the directors the authority to exercise 'all the powers of the company to borrow money [and to charge its property]'.

Internal limits on directors' authority

38.5   Article 79 also stipulates that the directors are not authorised to borrow an amount 'exceeding the nominal amount of the company's share capital' without the prior approval of the shareholders at a general meeting.

Protection for lenders without notice

38.6   Article 79 further provides that a third party lender will be unaffected by the directors exceeding their authority (acting ultra vires), unless they had express notice of that fact at the time when the debt was incurred.

BORROWING ULTRA VIRES THE DIRECTORS' AUTHORITY ONLY

38.7   It is clear from article 79, the *Turquand* case, reg 6 and the agency doctrine of ostensible authority, that a lender without notice is now well protected by judicial and statutory developments (see Chapter 37). However, borrowing that is not merely ultra vires the directors' authority, but is also ultra vires the company's objects and powers is in a different category.

BORROWING ULTRA VIRES THE COMPANY'S OBJECTS

38.8   At common law, if a company borrowed money for a purpose beyond its authority in the objects clause of its memorandum, such a contract was ultra vires and void ab initio.[2] This meant that any securities or charges given were also void and the lender could not sue the company.[3]

---

1 *Engel v South Metropolitan Brewing and Bottling Co* [1892] 1 Ch 442.
2 See **12.6**.
3 He could, however, sue the directors for breach of their warranty of authority.

STATUTORY PROTECTION FOR LENDERS AND OTHER CREDITORS

38.9 The lender's disadvantageous position at common law has been remedied to a large extent by s 8 of the 1963 Act and reg 6 – see **36.18** et seq.

When considering creditor protection against contracts which are ultra vires the company, recent judicial developments make it necessary to distinguish between contracts ultra vires:

(1) the objects clause;
(2) a company's powers; and
(3) the articles of association.

Modern judicial analysis is tending to render breaches of express powers by directors solely an internal matter (ie ultra vires the directors' authority and the articles only), whether or not they are also outside of the company's objects.

CURRENT JUDICIAL REASONING ON ABUSES OF POWERS

38.10 This modern judicial analysis of the ultra vires doctrine can be traced back to the *Rolled Steel Products* case (see **36.15**). In this case, Slade J applied agency law principles in restating the doctrine.

Slade J essentially drew a distinction between directors' actual and ostensible authority in their capacity as agents of the company. He stated the traditional ultra vires doctrine thus:

> 'at least in default of the unanimous consent of all the shareholders … the directors of a company will not have actual authority from the company to exercise any express or implied power, other than for the purpose of the company as set out in its memorandum of association.'

Directors' ostensible authority

38.11 Slade J broke new ground in his judgment by expressly introducing the ostensible authority concept, stating:

> 'a company holds its directors out as having ostensible authority to bind the company to any transaction which falls within the powers expressly or impliedly conferred on it by its memorandum of association. Unless he is put on notice to the contrary, a person dealing in good faith with a company which is carrying on an intra vires business, is entitled to assume that its directors are properly exercising such powers … If, however, a person dealing with a company is on notice that the directors are exercising the relevant power for purposes other than the purposes of the company, he cannot rely on the ostensible authority of the directors and on ordinary agency principles, cannot hold the company to the transactions.'

This part of Slade J's judgment reflects agency law principles like those applied in the *Turquand* and the *Freeman and Lockyer* cases. Browne-Wilkinson LJ in the *Rolled Steel Products* case also said:

'(1) To be ultra vires, a transaction has to be outside the capacity of the company, not merely in excess or abuse of the powers of the company.

(2) The question whether a transaction is outside the capacity of a company depends solely upon whether, on the true construction of its memorandum of association, the transaction is capable of falling within the objects of the company as opposed to being a proper exercise of [its] powers.'

Two important developments seem to follow from the *Rolled Steel Products* judgment. First, the use of the term 'ultra vires' should now be restricted to instances where the act in question is beyond the capacity of the company as stated in the objects clause in its memorandum. Strictly speaking, the term 'ultra vires' should not be used to describe the acts of directors which consist merely of an abuse of their powers.

Secondly, a consequence of this judgment should be to reduce the significance of the ultra vires doctrine. The reason for this result is that the court did not apply the traditional differences between objects and powers (whereby powers had to be exercised to further an object, otherwise the transaction would be ultra vires). Instead, the Court of Appeal decided that if a power is not exercised for a purpose in the objects clause of the memorandum, then, as long as it is capable of being so exercised, it will be merely a breach of the directors' ostensible authority as company agents. To illustrate the significance of this development, for example, a director's ostensible authority to borrow money and give guarantees will almost always be capable of being exercised in furtherance of an object in a company's memorandum. Judicial reasoning along these lines would have resulted in a different decision in the *Re Introductions Ltd* case (**36.15**).

Developments in Irish law

38.12 Let us now consider related developments regarding ultra vires contracts in Irish law. For example the High and Supreme Courts, in the *Frederick Inns* cases, found that payments by a group company were ultra vires the paying company, ie outside its contractual capacity.

When s 8 of the 1963 Act was pleaded by the creditors, the Supreme Court held that this was not applicable because the payments were not 'effectively' made (see **36.20**).

The meaning of 'not effectively made' appears to be an abuse by directors of their powers, ie a matter merely ultra vires the directors' authority rather than wholly outside of the company's objects and it's contractual capacity.[1] In fact, the distinction in these circumstances between a transaction ultra vires the

---

1 This is judicial reasoning along the same lines as that in the *Rolled Steel Products* case – see **36.15**.

company (memorandum) and one merely ultra vires the directors' authority, had already been accepted by the Irish courts.

In *Parkes & Sons Ltd v Hong Kong and Shanghai Banking Corporation (HKSB)*,[1] Blaney J, referring to *West Mercia Safetyware Ltd (In Liquidation) v Dodd*,[2] where the defendant was aware that the company was insolvent when (as a director) he transferred its money, stated, 'While a disposition [of company assets] is such circumstances may constitute a breach of duty on the part of directors, it does not follow that it would be ultra vires the company'.

Thus, the fact that a company is insolvent at a time of making a disposition of its assets does not, of itself, render that disposition ultra vires the powers of that company. Such a disposition, however, while intra vires the company, may be ultra vires the directors' powers. For example, in the *Hong Kong Banking* case, Blaney J also approved of the statement of Street CJ in *Kinsela v Russell Kinsela Pty Ltd*,[3] that when a company becomes insolvent, the interest of the creditors intrude and they become prospectively entitled, through the mechanism of liquidation, to displace the power of the shareholders and the directors to deal with the company's assets. Thus, the directors of an insolvent company owe a fiduciary duty to its creditors.

In the *West Mercia* case, the defendant, Dodd (a director) was guilty of breach of duty when, for his own purposes, he caused £4,000 of company assets to be transferred in disregard of the interests of the general creditors of the insolvent company.

In the *Hong Kong Banking* case, Blaney J distinguished the *West Mercia* decision because, in that case, Mr Dodd was aware at the time of the disposition of its property that the company was insolvent. In the *Hong Kong Banking* case, Blaney J essentially held that as the defendant was not actually aware the company was insolvent when the guarantee and mortgage in question were granted, he was therefore not acting in breach of his fiduciary duty which he owed to the company's creditors.

38.13   The *Frederick Inns* decision was distinguished by Laffoy J in *Ulster Factors Ltd v Entoglen Ltd and George Moloney*,[4] a case also concerning payment of the debts of a third party by a company which itself subsequently was wound up.

In the *Frederick Inns* case, the claim that the company's payment of another's debt was ultra vires succeeded against the Revenue Commissioners. The Commissioners were unable to rely on s 8 protection because they knew that all the paying companies were insolvent at the time the payments were made.

In the *Ulster Factors* case, Laffoy J stated that there was no evidence to suggest that the company was insolvent when the payment was made in June 1990, therefore the plaintiff did not lose the protection of s 8 of the 1963 Act.

---

1   [1990] ILRM 341.
2   [1988] BCLC 250.
3   4 NSWLR 722, 10 ACLR 395.
4   (1997) 4 CLP 124.

Furthermore, there was no obligation on the plaintiff to satisfy himself that the payment was intra vires; even if such a payment was ultra vires, constructive knowledge of a breach of trust by the directors cannot be imputed to the plaintiff for failing to make enquiries as to vires.

The defendants, in addition to their defence of 'ultra vires', also pleaded that the payment of the debt of the third party was made without the authority of the company because the individual within the company responsible for making the payment had no actual authority to do so. As to this defence, Laffoy J found that the plaintiff had established the four conditions necessary in the *Freeman and Lockyer* case[1] and accordingly the company agent had ostensible authority to make the payment.

The significance of current judicial developments

38.14 The deeper modern judicial analysis outlined in **38.10** is likely to categorise breaches of express company powers by directors as solely an internal corporate matter. Consequently, where the directors are in breach of the company's objects clause, in future such defective contracts may be treated as being simply ultra vires the directors' powers,[2] rather than being also ultra vires the company's objects. As a result, will gaps in the statutory protection against ultra vires contracts, such as (i) constructive notice[3] (which may invalidate s 8 protection), and (ii) non-registration of the company's agent as required under reg 6,[4] any longer be effective as defences against third party creditors?

SYNTHESISING UK AND IRISH DEVELOPMENTS

38.15 Perhaps the best method of rationalising the parallel developments in UK and Irish jurisdictions is to revert to basic agency law, and to consider the whole ultra vires doctrine in that context.

Corporate contracts and agency law

38.16 In *Ashbury Railway Carriage Co v Riche*,[5] the court held that a company had only the contractual capacity (vires) to enter into contracts expressly or impliedly authorised by its memorandum. Any ultra vires contracts were void. In agency terminology, the House of Lords decided that a company had only actual and usual authority to enter into contracts for activities authorised by its memorandum.

---

1 See **37.20** See also H. Linnane 'Corporate capacity and ostensible authority and their "inextricable" entwinement on display' (2000) 7 CLP 37, at pp 37–42.
2 An internal matter.
3 See the case of *Northern Bank Finance Etc v Quinn & Ors* at **36.21**.
4 This happened in the *Frederick Inns* case.
5 (1875) LR 7 HL 653.

Could all the members ratify an ultra vires contract? The House of Lords also decided that when a contract was outside the memorandum, it was ultra vires and could not be ratified,[1] even with the unanimous consent of all the shareholders. This approach was followed by Keane J in *Re Greendale Developments Ltd (No 2).* A principal must have had contractual capacity both at the date of the contract and at the date of ratification.[2]

At common law, therefore, when a company (acting through its directors) enters into a contract which exceeds its actual authority (as expressed in the memorandum), it is void, and the third party acquires no rights against the company under it. However, the directors[3] who negotiated an ultra vires contract would be liable to the third party for breach of their warranty of authority.

Statutory intervention

38.17   The basic common-law ultra vires doctrine was reformed by s 8 of the 1963 Act and reg 6.[4] As a result, corporate contracts outside the company's actual authority are now intra vires and valid, subject to the few 'gaps' identified above in the statutory protection of third party company creditors.

Directors' authority and agency law

38.18   Cases such as *Re Introductions Ltd* and *Jon Beauforte (London) Ltd,* indicated that the judiciary considered directors needed actual express authority to validly exercise certain implied powers. Accordingly, if a director exceeded this actual express authority, the company, as principal, was not liable to the third party.[5]

The significance of the *Rolled Steel Products Ltd* case is that it extended the directors' agency powers, so that a director now has ostensible authority to bind the company in any transaction which a bona fide third party might reasonably assume to be within the powers, expressly or impliedly, conferred upon a company by its memorandum.[6]

The application of the ostensible authority principle in this context is not new. The principle of ostensible authority had already underpinned leading court decisions such as the *Turquand* and the *Freeman and Lockyer* cases.

This type of judicial interpretation and analysis is to be welcomed. For, as Browne-Wilkinson LJ said in the *Rolled Steel Products* case:[7]

---

1 There were also problems at common law relating to ratification of intra vires pre-incorporation contracts, which are now remedied by s 37 of the 1963 Act – see **9.17**.
2 *Boston Deep Sea Fishing & Ice Co v Farnham* [1957] 1 WLR 1051.
3 Even if they had acted in good faith in believing that they had the necessary authority.
4 See **36.18** et seq.
5 See **36.8** and **36.9**.
6 See **36.15**.
7 Recently cited with approval by Neill LJ in *Crédit Suisse v Allerdale Borough Council* [1997] QB 306.

'If the transaction is outside the objects, in law it is wholly void. But the objects of a company and the powers conferred on a company to carry out those objects are two different things ... If the concept that a company can not do anything which is not authorised by law had been pursued with ruthless logic, the result might have been reached that a company could not (ie had not capacity) to do anything otherwise than in due exercise of its powers. But such ruthless logic has not been pursued and it is clear that a transaction falling within the objects of the company is capable of conferring rights on third parties even though the transaction was an abuse of the powers of the company'.

Thus, it would appear that a third party without notice may now enjoy protection at common law by being able to enforce against companies, any contracts negotiated on their behalf by directors acting outside of their actual or ostensible authority. But what is the position if the directors are (also) in breach of a fiduciary duty.

Breach of fiduciary duty and agency law

38.19 Judicial decisions in the following cases have been mentioned in **38.12**: the *Frederick Inns* case; *Parkes & Sons Ltd v HKSB Corporation*; *West Mercia Safetyware v Dodd*; *Kinsela v Russell Kinsela*; and *Ulster Factors Ltd v Entoglen Ltd and George Moloney*.

These judicial decisions show no significant differences in treatment between breaches of fiduciary duty and instances where directors have exceeded their actual authority. For example, in *Parkes & Sons Ltd v HKSB Corporation*, Blaney J stated, 'While a dispositon [of company assets] ... may constitute a breach of duty on the part of directors, it does not [necessarily] follow that it would be ultra vires the company'.

In the *Frederick Inns* case, while s 8 saved an ultra vires contract, nevertheless the outsider was unable to enforce the contract because it was 'not effectively made' by the directors, ie because the directors had abused their powers. But would this abuse of powers not be within the directors' ostensible authority? The answer is probably in the affirmative.

Limits to ostensible authority principle

38.20 A fundamental requirement to recovering against any principal for breach of his agent's ostensible authority is lack of notice. In the *Rolled Steel* case, Shenkman, the main director involved, was also the company's majority shareholder. Shenkman authorised a guarantee by Rolled Steel Products Ltd of the debts of Scottish Steel Sheet Ltd, a company in which Shenkman owned all the share capital.

Rolled Steel argued that as all the contracting parties knew that Shenkman only issued the guarantee to support his other company, Scottish Steel; the transaction was ultra vires. In his judgment, Slade LJ concluded:

'the relevant transactions of 22 January 1969 were not beyond the corporate capacity of the plaintiff and thus were not ultra vires in the proper sense of that phrase. However, the entering into the guarantee and, to the extent of the sum guaranteed, the debenture was beyond the authority of the directors, because they were entered into in furtherance of purposes not authorised by the plaintiff's memorandum. Despite this lack of authority; they might have been capable of conferring rights on Colvilles if Colvilles had not known of this lack of authority. Colvilles, however. did not have such knowledge and so acquired no rights under these transactions.'

In the *Frederick Inns* case, the Revenue Commissioners effectively were denied the protection of s 8 because they know that all the paying companies were insolvent at the time that the payments were made. By contrast, because the plaintiff was unaware of the company's insolvent state in the *Ulster Factors* case, he was deemed entitled to the protection of s 8.

ESTOPPEL, OSTENSIBLE AUTHORITY AND CORPORATE CONTRACTS

38.21　In an important passage of his judgment in the *Freeman and Lockyer* case, Lord Diplock explained clearly the distinctions between actual and ostensible authority. He said:

> 'An "actual" authority is a legal relationship between principal and agent created by a consensual agreement to which they alone are parties. Its scope is to be ascertained by applying ordinary principles of construction of contracts, including any proper implication from the express words used, the usages of the trade, or the course of business between the parties. To this agreement the contractor[1] is a stranger; he may be totally ignorant of the absence of any authority on the part of the agent. Nevertheless, if the agent does enter into a contract pursuant to the "actual" authority, it does create contractual rights and liabilities between the principal and the contractor. It may be that this rule relating to "undisclosed principals" which is peculiar to English law, can be rationalised as avoiding circuity of action, for the principal could in equity compel the agent to lend his name in an action to enforce the contract against the contractor, and would, at common law be liable to indemnify the agent in respect of the performance of the obligations assumed by agent under the contract.
>
> An "apparent" or "ostensible" authority, on the other hand, is a legal relationship between the principal and the contractor created by the representation, made by the principal to the contractor, intended to be and in fact acted on by the contractor, that the agent is a stranger. He need not be (although he generally is) aware of the existence of the representation. The representation, when acted on by the contractor by entering into a contact with the agent, operates as an estoppel, preventing the principal from asserting that he is not bound by the contract. It is irrelevant whether the agent had actual authority to enter into the contract.'

In Chapter 37 we have shown how little actual authority a non-executive company director possesses. In fact, a junior official may have far greater actual

---

1　Reference to the contractor in the company law context means the third party creditor seeking to enforce the contract against the company.

authority to bind the company. Lord Denning[1] described agency by estoppel giving rise to 'apparent' or 'ostensible' authority as, 'the authority of an agent as it appears to others'. Costello J,[2] quoting part of Lord Diplock's judgment, explained that, 'the doctrine of ostensible authority is an application of the principle of estoppel as a result of which a person is not permitted to resist an inference which a reasonable man would draw from his words or conduct'.

There is however, a limitation on this principle, explained by Henchy J[3] when he said:

> 'Ostensible authority, is founded on a representation made by the principal to the third party which is intended to convey, and does convey to the third party, that the arrangement entered into under the apparent authority of the agent, will be binding on the principal.'

If a contractor deals with a non-executive company director in good faith, can he enforce such a contract against the company even if it is clearly in excess of the non-executive director's actual authority?

It is appropriate to refer to Lord Diplock's judgment again when he said:

> 'The commonest form of representation by a principal creating an "apparent" authority of an agent is by conduct, viz, by permitting the agent to act in the management or conduct of the principal's business. Thus, if in the case of a company the board of directors who have "actual" authority to manage the company's business permit the agent to act in the management or conduct of the company's business, they thereby represent to all persons dealing with such agent that he has authority to enter on behalf of the corporation into contracts of a kind which an agent authorised to do acts of the kind which he is in fact permitted to do normally enters into the ordinary course of such business. Prima facie it falls within the "actual"[4] authority of the board of directors, and the company is estopped from denying to anyone who has entered into a contract with the agent in reliance on such "apparent" authority, that the agent had authority to contract on behalf of the company.'

A closer examination of cases such as *Freeman & Lockyer v Buckhurst Park Properties (Mangal) Ltd* and *Hely-Hutchinson v Brayhead Ltd* indicates that where a board allows a person to act as managing director without being formally appointed to the position, then the company will be estopped from denying that such a person had the actual or usual authority normally associated with that position, against third party without notice.

If the board were to acquiesce in the negotiating of company contracts by a non-executive director (far in excess of his actual authority), Lord Diplock's judgment in the *Freeman and Lockyer* case suggests that the company in question should be estopped from denying that the non-executive director in question had ostensible authority to bind it.

---

1 In *Hely-Hutchinson v Brayhead Ltd* [1968] 1 QB 549, [1967] 2 All ER 14, [1967] 2 WLR 1312.
2 In *EES v Crown Shipping (Ireland) Ltd* [1991] ILRM 97.
3 In *Kett v Shannon and England* [1987] I ILRM 364 (SC).
4 Perhaps 'usual' authority would be more appropriate in this context.

Persons dealing with company secretaries have already received increased protection at common law by the decision in *Panorama Developments (Guildford) Ltd v Fidelis Furnishing Fabrics Ltd.*[1] This decision is based upon a revised judicial perception of the ostensible authority of company secretaries.

Third parties dealing with executive directors and other authorised agents[2] of companies now enjoy greater judicial protection as a result of the developments in ostensible authority arising from cases such as *Rolled Steel Products* and *Ulster Factors Ltd v Entoglen.*

A combination of the doctrines of estoppel and ostensible authority, as enunciated by Lord Diplock in the *Freeman and Lockyer* case, offers similar scope[3] for increased judicial protection of third parties dealing with company agents acting outside of their actual authority. The type of company agent envisaged here would include non-executive directors, managers and employees generally.

Directors of insolvent companies

38.22 When a company becomes insolvent, we have seen[4] that the interests of the creditors displace the power of the shareholders and the directors to deal with company assets.

McGuinness J, in *Jones v Gunn,*[5] held, inter alia, that where a company is clearly insolvent, even if not in liquidation, the directors owe a fiduciary duty to the general creditors and may not make payments which benefit either closely connected companies or themselves to the detriment of general and independent creditors.

Whether or not a director has ostensible authority[6] in these circumstances would appear to depend upon whether or not he knew the company was insolvent at the time of the transaction – see comments of Blaney J and Laffoy J in *Parkes & Sons Ltd HKSB Corporation* and the *Ulster Factors* cases in **38.12** and **38.13**.

---

1 [1971] 2 QB 711.
2 Perhaps abusing their powers.
3 Subject to the filling of the four essential requirements set out in **37.21**.
4 In **38.12**.
5 [1997] 2 ILRM 245 (HC).
6 And was acting 'effectively' for the purposes of s 8 protection – see **36.20**.

PART VIII

CREDITORS' RIGHTS AGAINST THE COMPANY AND ITS OFFICERS

Chapter 39

COMPANY CREDITORS AND CHARGES

CREDITORS

39.1   In Chapter 2, the twin objectives of company law are identified. These objectives are the protection of two classes of persons, ie investors and creditors.

Investors provide the investment capital of the company by purchasing shares and becoming members. It is the members who actually own the company. Shareholders have an interest in the company which they own.

Creditors are persons to whom the company is indebted. This indebtedness may have arisen out of a trading transaction. More frequently, however, when the term creditor is used in company law, it refers to a person who has loaned money to the company, often taking security for the loan in the form of a charge on the company's assets. Creditors may, therefore, be unsecured or secured.

Secured creditors are usually known as debenture-holders (see **39.10**).

Creditors, unlike shareholders, do not have an interest in the company; instead they have a claim against the company for repayment of the monies owed to them.

Creditors' rights generally

39.2   The contractual rights of shareholders have already been examined in Parts IV A to IV E. The statutory rules (see Part IV C, Chapter 19) relating to maintenance of company capital, whilst offering some protection to investors, are designed primarily to protect the interests of company creditors: creditors being given a right to object to a permitted reduction of capital under s 72 of the 1963 Act.

Not only are creditors given the right to object to changes in the company's capital structure which affect their interest; they are also given the right to object to certain major corporate decisions. By virtue of s 8(2) of the 1963 Act, any debenture-holder may apply to the court to restrain the company from acting ultra vires. Again, s 10(3) and (7) entitle certain debenture-holders to apply to the court to block a proposed alteration of the company's objects clause.

Apart from bestowing separate rights on creditors to take action when their financial interest in the company is threatened, the Companies Acts also provide for much of the information which has to be made available to members, to be also provided for creditors.

Company information for creditors

39.3   The general requirements for companies to deliver information to the registrar of companies and/or publish it in *Iris Oifigiúil*, renders certain company information public and therefore accessible to both members and creditors. For example, any person can obtain details of all company charges, by inspecting the register of charges. This register is maintained by the registrar of companies.

Copies of a company's memorandum and articles of association – its constitutional documents – must also be forwarded to the registrar. Consequently, these are 'public documents'. Creditors can inspect these documents and extract such information as they consider necessary.

Again, in addition to sending them to members, s 159 provides that a company must send a copy of its balance sheet and directors' and auditors' reports to every debenture holder.

The companies legislation, therefore, provides for minimum levels of information to be made available to creditors, both indirectly and directly, to assist them negotiate and manage their transactions with the company.

39.4   In Chapter 2, we identified the range of creditors' or third party interests arising out of company transactions. We shall now focus on the distinctions between the different types of creditor.

For all practical purposes, company creditors can be classified into the following categories:

(1) unsecured; or
(2) preferential; or
(3) secured.

Unsecured creditors

39.5   A wide range of third party interests fall under this heading. For example, where a company buys raw material from suppliers it is likely that the latter will be an unsecured creditor of the company until paid. Where builders and painters are employed to repair and paint the company premises, these parties will also be unsecured creditors until the prices agreed for their services have been remitted to them.

Even employees can be classified as unsecured creditors for arrears of wages and salaries, although their rights have been elevated to that of preferential creditors for at least part of their outstanding salaries and holiday pay in s 285 of the 1963 Act.

Preferential creditors

39.6 Section 285[1] lists a series of unsecured debts which are elevated to preferential status, ie they rank above the unsecured creditors and creditors whose debts are secured by a floating (but not a fixed) charge.

Section 285 grants priority on certain amounts due in respect of:[2]

(1) various claims by employees and unpaid taxes due to the Revenue Commissioners; and,
(2) damages for personal injuries to employees.

Secured creditors

39.7 Creditors who possess some mortgage, charge or lien on the company's property are termed 'secured'. The most common situation giving rise to a secured transaction with a company is when the latter wishes to raise funds by loan capital, ie by borrowing money, often from a bank.

A COMPANY'S BORROWING POWERS

39.8 All trading companies have, by implication, the power to borrow money to finance the company's business. In many cases, the power to borrow will be specifically granted by the memorandum of association. It might be thought that a sole trader or a partnership would find it easier to borrow money since the trader or the partners in a firm are personally liable. This is not so. By the device of a 'floating charge' (see **39.18**) a company may borrow money, and give as security a general charge over the whole of the company's assets. This general security does not interfere with the company's trading transactions, and only 'crystallises' into a fixed charge in certain circumstances.

As stated above, a power to borrow money is an implied prerogative of every trading company, but the memorandum or the articles may restrict this power by setting out the purposes for which money may be borrowed. They may direct how the directors can exercise this power. Any borrowing which is not covered by the power given is, prima facie, ultra vires.

A non-trading company cannot borrow money unless the power to do so is conferred by the memorandum of association. If borrowing is beyond the powers of the company, the lender is the one who finds himself in difficulty, not the company. The lending and the borrowing constitute a contract between the company and the lender, but if the borrowing is beyond the powers granted to the company, the contract is void.

39.9 At common law, the lender was not entitled to sue the company for non-payment under an ultra vires lending contract. In Chapters 36 to 38, it was

---

1 As amended by s 10 of the 1982 Act.
2 See **50.52** for fuller details.

shown how creditors are now protected against lending which is ultra vires the company's memorandum of association by s 8 of the 1963 Act and reg 6 of the European Communities (Companies) Regulations 1973. These statutory reforms will allow most lenders to pursue repayment of their loans to a company, even if the transaction was ultra vires.

A lender's contract may be intra vires the company's objects but outside the authority of the directors or managers who negotiated the loan. Where, for example, the directors borrow money in excess of a limit in the company's articles, this transaction would be intra vires the company but ultra vires the directors' powers. The judicial rule in the *Turquand* case may also protect a lender in these circumstances.

Recent judicial developments summarised in **38.11** seem to indicate that for the purposes of redress by creditors, the defence of ultra vires is now hardly likely to be an effective one for any company, whether the contract is for borrowing money, or for the provision of any goods or services.

When a company borrows money, the written terms of the transaction are contained in a document called a debenture. The creditor who lends the company the money is known as a debenture-holder.

DEBENTURES

39.10   Whilst, strictly speaking, a debenture is the document by which the company acknowledges its indebtedness under a loan, the term is also used generally to describe the loan transaction.

Chitty J, in *Levy v Abercorris Slate and Slab Company*,[1] described a debenture as:

> 'a document which either creates a debt or acknowledges it, and any document which fulfils either of these conditions is a debenture. I cannot find any precise legal definition of the term ...'

Debentures and shares

39.11   Because debentures are not capital, the rules of capital maintenance do not apply to them. Accordingly:

(1)   a company's capacity to purchase its own debentures is not restricted, unlike the purchase of its own shares; and

(2)   interest due on debentures may be paid out of capital, whereas dividends on shares can only be paid out of distributable profits; and

(3)   unlike shares, debentures may be issued at a discount – see s 99(9) of the 1963 Act. However, such debentures cannot subsequently be exchanged for fully paid shares of an equal nominal value.

---

1   (1887) 37 Ch D 260.

Despite these fundamental differences between shares and debentures, there are also similarities. For example, a typical debenture will be one of a series similar to a class of shares. Debentures are transferable in the same manner as shares. Debentures may be issued to the public. If so, a prospectus may be required. Debentures may also be quoted on the Stock Exchange.

Because shares and debentures are both essentially vehicles of investment in a company, potential investors will be concerned with balancing the potential for capital appreciation in shares and the degree of risk associated with them, with the yield and security offered by debentures (and, indeed, preference shares).

The types and forms of debentures are dealt with in Chapter 41.

Security for company borrowing

39.12 When a company has the power to borrow, it also has the power to charge its property as security for repayment of the loan.[1]

Debentures can be issued with or without security. For example, s 2(1) of the 1963 Act defines a debenture as 'including stocks, bonds and any other securities of a company, whether constituting a charge on the assets or not'.

Debentures, once issued by the company, are often classified under the generic name of 'charges'.

CHARGES

39.13 A charge may be broadly defined as a guarantee of security for a loan, for which assets of the company are pledged as collateral. It includes a mortgage.

Unless registered[2] with the registrar of companies within 21 days of its creation, the security conferred on the company's asset will be void against the liquidator and any creditor of the company.

Thus, if a charge securing any issue of debentures is not registered within 21 days, the lender loses out. The company has the money loaned, but a failure to register by the company will render the charge or security for the loan invalid.

However, on the charge becoming void, s 99(1) provides that the monies secured became immediately repayable.

---

1 See **38.1**.
2 Sections 99–102 of the 1963 Act, as amended. Section 106 sets out circumstances where the time for registration of a charge may be extended – see Chapter 41.

MORTGAGES AND FIXED CHARGES

39.14   Money borrowed by a company may be secured by a range of charges, including:

(1) charges by way of legal (or equitable) mortgage;
(2) fixed charges; and
(3) floating charges.

Charges by way of mortgage

39.15   A legal mortgage is where the company, as mortgagor, executes a deed transferring the ownership of the property to the lender (mortgagee). The company retains an equitable right in the property. On repayment of the loan and interest, the company will be able to recover ownership of the property.

Where, instead of transferring the ownership of the property, the company merely deposits the title deeds with the lender, this would constitute an equitable rather than a legal mortgage. Here, the lender possesses an equitable, instead of a legal, interest in the charged property.

Legal and equitable interests

39.16   Where a person holds a legal interest, eg the registered owner of land, his title is good against all other persons. However, when a person has an equitable title to land and goods, his interest might be defeated by a subsequent bona fide purchaser for value without notice of his interest.

All charges are equitable. What the chargee obtains is not ownership (or legal title), but the equitable right to claim the charged property in satisfaction of his secured debt, if unpaid. In legal theory, therefore, a legal mortgage would not be technically classified as a charge. However, in practice it often is.

Fixed charges

39.17   A fixed charge is one which attaches to a specific asset belonging to the company, eg a factory, plant and machinery. Although the company can deal with the asset in the usual course of its business, it is subject to the charge at all times. In short, the charge is attached to a specific and named asset.

The asset must be sufficiently identified and any necessary formalities observed for the creation of the charge. Essentially, a fixed charge prevents the company from selling or otherwise disposing of the specified property without the consent of the holders of the charge.

FLOATING CHARGES

39.18   A floating charge is a charge on a class[1] of assets present and future, which, in the ordinary course of business, changes from time to time, eg the stock, or a fleet of motor vehicles. The company is free to deal with that class of assets until the holders of the charge take steps to enforce their security. A floating charge 'floats like a cloud over the assets' but does not settle on them unless and until certain circumstances intervene to threaten those assets, when it 'crystallises' and becomes fixed as a charge on the assets. Thus, in the case of *Re Yorkshire Woolcombers Association*,[2] the characteristics of a floating charge were said to be:

(1)   a charge on both present and future assets;
(2)   the assets are constantly changing from time to time in the ordinary course of the business; and
(3)   until the holder of the charge takes some steps to enforce the security, it floats.

A floating charge is, therefore, an equitable interest on some or all of the present and future property of the company: it is, however, subject to the company's power to deal with the assets in the course of its business. As Henchy J stated succinctly in *Re Keenan Bros Ltd:*[3]

> 'A floating charge, so long as it remains floating, avoids the restricting (and in some cases, paralysing) effect on the use of the assets of the company resulting from a fixed charge. While a charge remains a floating one, the company may, unless there is agreement to the contrary, deal with its assets in the ordinary course of business just as if there were no floating charge ...'

Until the charge crystallises, the company can utilise its assets in the ordinary course of business. Any assets disposed of in this way cease to be subject to the floating charge, whilst any new assets of the same type acquired by the company become subject to it.

Crystallisation of a floating charge

39.19   A floating charge remains suspended until such time as it 'crystallises'. To quote Henchy J[4] again:

> 'Crystallisation occurs on the happening of some event, such as the appointment of a liquidator which shows that the company is no longer in business, or until the chargee intervenes. At that point, the floating charge is said to crystallise and the rights of the chargee become the same as if he had got a fixed charge; thereafter the company cannot deal with the assets in question except subject to the charge.'

Thus, crystallisation of a floating charge will occur:

---

1   Rather than a specific.
2   [1903] 2 Ch 284.
3   [1985] IR 401 (SC).
4   Ibid.

(1) if winding up of the company commences; or

(2) if the company defaults *and* the debenture-holders take steps to enforce their security either by appointing a receiver or applying to the court to do so.

In the absence of express provision in the debenture to the contrary, crystallisation will not occur automatically, simply because the company ceases to carry on business.

When a floating charge crystallises

39.20 A floating charge crystallises and becomes fixed when the company defaults[1] on its obligations under the terms of the debenture, or on the commencement of the winding up of the company itself.

In *Halpin v Cremin,*[2] the court held that merely taking steps to appoint a receiver by the lender, will not, of itself, be sufficient to cause a floating charge to crystallise.

In *Re Brightlife Ltd,*[3] Hoffmann J confirmed that the parties to a debenture can stipulate whatever events they wish to cause crystallisation. He said, 'I do not think that it is open to the courts to restrict the contractual freedom of parties to a floating charge [on grounds of public policy]'.

Under this freedom of contract, the lender and the company may agree to 'automatic' crystallisation clauses in a debenture. Such clauses would seek to cause crystallisation on an event occurring other than the appointment of a receiver, the cessation of trading or the winding up of the company. Automatic crystallisation might, for example, include the mere giving of notice by the debentureholder or any attempt by the company to create a subsequent charge over the same assets.

Hoffmann J considered it 'wholly inappropriate' for the courts to interfere with automatic crystallisation clauses on grounds of public policy.

Whilst the express terms in a debenture will often stipulate events giving rise to crystallisation, the most frequent cause of crystallisation is likely to be the appointment of a receiver. Most debentures will give the debenture-holder the express right to appoint a receiver without firstly applying to the court – see **42.4**.

Effect of crystallisation

39.21 On crystallisation, the floating charge becomes a fixed charge. As a result, equitable ownership of the assets which were subject to the floating charge is involuntarily transferred to the debenture-holder. Thereafter, the

---

1 Usually leading to the appointment of a receiver over its assets.

2 [1954] IR 19 (HC).

3 [1987] 2 WLR 197.

company can only deal in these assets with the express approval of the debenture-holder.

Whilst crystallisation, in effect, automatically transfers title in the (formerly floating) assets to the debenture-holder; nevertheless the title which he enjoys can be no better than that of the transferor (company) itself.[1]

Post-crystallisation company debts

39.22 A post-crystallisation creditor has no right to set off in respect of a company's debts which become due after the crystallisation of a floating charge if to allow him such a right would give him priority over the pre-existing debenture-holder.[2]

De-crystallisation of a floating charge

39.23 A floating charge, which crystallises on the appointment of a receiver, may de-crystallise if the company becomes subject to the protection of the court and an examiner is appointed.

In *Re Holidair Ltd*,[3] Blaney J stated:

'Once the examiner is appointed, the receiver could no longer act [because of s 5(2)(b) of the 1990 Amendment Act].[4] It would accordingly have been pointless to keep the book debts frozen. The receiver would have had no right to collect them.

... Furthermore, it is no injustice to the debentureholders who appointed the receiver since the companies are continuing to trade and so continuing to create new book debts to replace those that may be paid and the proceeds of which may be used by the companies.'

---

1 *Tempany v Hynes* [1976] IR 101 (SC).
2 See *Lynch v Ardmore Studios (Ireland) Ltd and Hayes* [1966] IR 33.
3 [1994] 1 ILRM 481.
4 See Chapters 45 and 46.

Chapter 40

INEFFECTIVE CHARGES AND DISPOSITIONS OF COMPANY ASSETS

40.1 If a company creates a charge over its assets shortly before becoming insolvent, this security may be ineffective. For example, even a fixed charge may be ineffective if deemed a fraudulent preference under s 286 of the 1963 Act.[1] Sections 288 and 289[2] make provision for the avoidance of certain floating charges on the liquidation of the company. In addition, a charge may become ineffective by the holder's interest being relegated below the interests of other chargees by virtue of s 98 of the 1963 Act, negative pledge and reservation of title clauses and s 174 of the Finance Act 1995. Furthermore, unprofitable trading may gradually reduce the amount of assets subject to a floating charge.

STATUTORY RESTRICTIONS ON PREFERRING CREDITORS

40.2 Any charge made within six months[3] (two years for connected persons) may be deemed invalid as a fraudulent preference under s 286.

Floating charges created within 12 months (two years for connected persons) prior to the commencement of a winding up, will be deemed prima facie invalid under ss 288 and 289.

Fraudulent preferences

40.3 The twin objectives of the fraudulent preference concept are:

(1) to recapture property which has been transferred to one creditor in preference to the other creditors; and
(2) to encourage a higher level of commercial morality and a greater confidence in the credit system.

Section 286(1) provides that:

'Any conveyance, mortgage, delivery of goods, payment or other act [such a creating a fixed charge over it] relating to property made or done by a company which is unable to pay its debts as they become due in favour of any creditor, ... with a view to giving such creditor ... a preference over other creditors, shall, if the winding up of the company commences within 6 months ... be deemed a fraudulent preference of its [general] creditors and be invalid accordingly.'

---

1 Supplemented by s 139 of the 1990 Act.
2 Of the 1963 Act.
3 Of the commencement of the winding up of the company.

1990 reforms

40.4   Section 286 was amended by s 135 of the 1990 Act. The 1990 Act introduced two types of creditors who might be preferred. There were 'unconnected' and 'connected' persons. Under s 286(3), any fraudulent preference in favour of a connected person which was made within two years before the commencement of the winding up, will, unless the contrary is shown, be deemed a fraudulent preference and accordingly invalid.

Connected persons and onus of proof

40.5   'Connected persons' are defined in s 286(5). The term includes directors, shadow directors, relations of directors and related companies.

The onus of proving that a disposition of company property to a connected person is not fraudulent is on the connected person. Such a person would therefore have to adduce sufficient evidence to convince a court that the transaction was 'at arms length' and had not been entered into with the intention of preferring that (connected) person over the company's other creditors.

Transactions with unconnected persons

40.6   A disposition of company property to an unconnected person will not be rendered invalid under s 286(1) unless the liquidator can prove that the intention of the company was to prefer one creditor over another. In *Re Olderfleet Shipbuilding Co Ltd*,[1] Powell J cited A.L. Smith LJ,[2] who explained, 'I have always understood that to ascertain whether there has been a fraudulent preference it is necessary to consider what the dominant or real motive was; whether it is to defraud some creditors by preferring others, or for some other motive'.

In the *Olderfleet Shipbuilding* case, a company in financial difficulties obtained credit, subject to a debenture and the depositing of title deeds to some of the company's property as security.

Arising out of an action by the liquidator under what is now s 286, the court essentially held that the borrowing of this money was an honest and bona fide, but unfortunately unsuccessful, attempt by the directors to assist the company out of its financial difficulties. Accordingly, the charge was not a fraudulent preference.

In *Corran Construction Co Ltd v Bank of Ireland Ltd*,[3] one month[4] before its liquidation, the plaintiff company deposited title deeds with the bank by way of

---

1 [1922] 1 IR 26.
2 In *New, Prance and Garrard's Trustee v Hunting* [1897] 2 QB 19 (CA); affirmed by House of Lords in *Sharp (Official Receiver) v Jackson & Ors* [1899] AC 419.
3 [1976–97] ILRM 175.
4 The bank had an earlier equitable mortgage, but it had not been registered under s 99 of the 1963 Act.

equitable mortgage. The liquidator subsequently sought to have this charge avoided under s 286. McWilliam J turned down the liquidator's claim, stating that the liquidator had not established a dominant intention to prefer; the member-directors' decision had been influenced by pressure applied by the bank to give a fresh mortgage. Accordingly, the charge held by the bank was valid.

Again, in *Parkes & Sons Ltd v Hong Kong and Shanghai Banking Corporation*,[1] Costello J held that a threat from the bank to put in a receiver was the dominant motive in giving a charge, notwithstanding that the company's controlling director gained indirectly himself by having pressure taken off his personal guarantees. Blaney J concluded, 'In my opinion, it has not been established that the facts are such that I should infer that [his] dominant motive was to reduce[2] his [personal] liability on the guarantees'.

Thus, while a liquidator need not prove fraud; nevertheless, to avoid a charge on the company's assets under s 286, he may have to prove that the decisionmakers within the company acted without pressure from company creditors. For, as Porter MR said in *Re Daly & Co*,[3] 'where pressure exists so as to overbear the volition of the debtor, a payment is not made with a view to prefer the creditor exerting it, but because the debtor cannot help it'.

A court will examine all the evidence, and then decide on the dominant intention of the company's decision makers. For example, in *Station Motors Ltd & AIB*,[4] Carroll J found that payments made into the company's overdrawn account were made with the dominant intention[5] of preferring the bank as a direct creditor and the directors themselves (indirectly) as personal guarantors' of the company's debts.

Another case where the liquidator succeeded in having a charge deemed invalid under s 286(1) was *Kelleher v Continental Irish Meat Ltd*.[6] Here, Costello J found, inter alia:

> 'In some instances no explanation was given for this [irregular] conduct. Such explanations that were offered . . . I find entirely unconvincing . . . It is clear that the plaintiff and the general manager were engaged in a subterfuge . . . The inference to be drawn from [the general manager's] conduct is irresistible. He demonstrated a quite extraordinary zeal in furthering the plaintiff's interest . . . He wanted to help the plaintiff to retrieve the loss he was facing, and his substantial and dominant intention in entering into the sale of the company's goods to him, was to prefer him.'

---

1 [1990] ILRM 341.

2 The mere fact that a preference is shown does not mean that it is fraudulent. Proof must also be adduced of a dominant intention to prefer a particular creditor – *Re M Kushler Ltd* [1943] Ch 248 (but see *Station Motors Ltd v AIB* below).

3 [1887–1888] 19 LR IR 83.

4 [1985] ILRM 756, [1985] IR 1.

5 A court can draw an inference of intention to prefer in the absence of direct evidence of such intention.

6 (Unreported) 9 May 1978 (HC).

Not surprisingly, Costello J held that the liquidator had discharged his onus of proof and therefore the receiver had better title to the goods in question than the plaintiff.

Limits to scope of s 286

40.7 In *Parkes & Sons Ltd v HKSB Corporation* (see above), Blaney J also decided that the giving of credit by a third party to a creditor of an insolvent company, in circumstances which would constitute a fraudulent preference if given by an insolvent company, cannot amount to a fraudulent preference under s 286 because the act of preferring must be 'made or done by ... a company [itself]' or be against its property.

Again, in *Re Welding Plant Ltd; Cooney v Dargan*,[1] McWilliam J stated:

'Turning to the words of s 286, a transaction must be done by or against the company [itself] ...

Whatever may be the position between the [directors] and the [bank], I am of the opinion that payment by the [directors] which was appropriated by the [bank] to meet the debt due by the company, does not constitute an act relating to property done by or against the company. [Accordingly] no [company] creditor has been prejudiced by the payment ... and [therefore] the [liquidator] is not entitled to recover it.'

To reduce the company's overdraft, the directors in the *Welding Plant Ltd* case proposed to purchase property from the company. It was agreed that the bank would loan the purchase money to the directors. The sum of £21,000 in respect of this loan was paid over to the company and used to discharge some of its debts. However, the sale of the company's property to the directors was never completed.

The court ruled that:

(1) the attempted property purchase transaction between the directors and the company was invalid under s 286 because the directors, knowing the financial situation of the company was hopeless, intended, as guarantors[2] of the debt due to the bank, to prefer themselves over other creditors by obtaining from the company property of the value of the debt they owed to the bank; and

(2) the payment by the directors of £21,000, which had been appropriated by the bank to meet the company's debt, was valid under s 286 because it was not an act done by or against the company – see McWilliam J's comments above.

---

1 (Unreported) 27 June and 25 July 1984 (HC).
2 As the ownership in the company's property was never transferred to the directors under this incomplete sale, they were treated by the court as guarantors who had paid the company's debts to the extent of £21,000.

Transfers to trustees

40.8 Section 286(2) provides that 'any conveyance or assignment by a company of all its property to trustees for the benefit of all its creditors, shall be void to all intents'.

Purchases from company creditors

40.9 Section 286(4) makes it clear that s 286(1) and (3) will not affect the rights of any person acquiring title to disposed property 'in good faith and for valuable consideration', through, or under, a creditor of the company.

Position of a preferred creditor

40.10 Section 287 of the 1963 Act sets out the liabilities and rights of a person who was deemed preferred under s 286. Generally, the person preferred will be subject to the same rights and liabilities as if he had undertaken to be personally liable as surety for the debt to the extent of the charge on the property, or the value of his interest, whichever is the less.

Section 287(2) provides for the calculation of the value of a preferred person's interests.

Other fraudulent transfers of company assets

40.11 Section 286 of the 1963 Act has been supplemented by s 139 of the 1990 Act.

Power of the court to order return of assets

40.12 Under s 139, where any property of the company has been transferred or charged and results in the perpetration of a fraud on the company, its creditors or members, the court, if it deems it just or equitable, can order the return of the assets or payment of their value, to the liquidator of the company.

The court, in deciding to make such an order against the person in possession of the improperly transferred assets, is to have regard to the rights of any bona fide purchaser for value without notice – see s 139(4).

Avoidance of floating charges

40.13 While s 286 may affect both fixed and floating charges, ss 288 and 289 of the 1963 Act are confined to floating charges.

Under ss 288 and 289, floating charges created within 12 months of the company's liquidation will be invalid unless the lender or company officer can prove that the company was solvent immediately after the creation of the charge.

The period of 12 months is extended to two years where a floating charge is created in favour of a connected person.

Meaning of solvency

40.14   Where a floating charge is created (or caught) within the time limits in ss 288 and 289, the recipient must prove that the company was solvent immediately after charge was created; otherwise his security will be avoided.

In *Re Creation Printing Co Ltd; Crowley v Northern Bank Finance Corporation Ltd and Kelso,*[1] Kenny J said:

> 'the burden of establishing that the company was solvent at the date of [creation of] the debenture rests on the debenture-holder. The charge is avoided unless something is proved ...
>
> Although the solvency of a company is a question of fact, some guidelines as to how this question is to be approached are given be decided cases ... the test to be applied in determining this question is whether immediately after the debenture was given, the company was able to pay its debts as they became due. The question is not whether its assets exceed in estimated value its liabilities, or whether a business man would have regarded it as solvent. The question whether a company was solvent on a specified date is one of fact and it involves many difficult inferences. If there is, or is likely to be, a large deficiency of assets when the liquidation starts, the temptation to hold that the company was not solvent when the charge was given is strong. But the deficiency may have been caused by some change in economic or market conditions happening after the charge was given. So an examination of the financial history of the company, both before and after the charges were given, is necessary ... When considering whether a company was solvent immediately after it had created a particular floating charge, in circumstances where its directors intended that the company would continue to carry on its business after that time, the fixed and moveable assets of the company are not to be taken into account. However, the capacity of the company immediately after the creation of the particular charge to borrow money on the security of another charge on its assets must be taken into account. This necessarily involves the court in an inquiry as to whether any creditor would advance money to the company on the security of another and later floating charge which would rank in priority after the particular debenture whose validity is in question. If a sum could be borrowed on the security of such a subsequent charge, it should be taken into the reckoning which has to be made when determining the company's solvency ....'

Saving floating charges where (present) consideration given

40.15   Section 288(1) and (2) stipulate that a floating charge will not be invalid in respect of money, goods or services actually supplied to the company in consideration for the charge. However, the interest rate payable in these circumstances will not be that agreed by the parties, but the 5 per cent rate fixed by s 288(1).

---

1   [1981] IR 353 (SC).

Essentially, therefore, ss 288 and 289 only apply to floating charges given for past consideration. For example, in *Lakeglen Construction Ltd,*[1] a floating charge, given to unsecured creditors in respect of past loans of money to the company, was deemed invalid. In this case, the company issued a debenture in favour of some of its creditors, which included a charge on its book debts. The company was insolvent at the date of the execution of the debenture, and was also wound up within the succeeding 12 months.

The liquidator took legal action seeking a direction by the court as to whether the charge on book debts was fixed or floating.

Costello J held that the charge was a floating one, and accordingly was invalid by virtue of s 288.

A delay in the creation of a floating charge may have the effect of making the consideration given for it, past.

A delay of two years and three months in *Smurfit Paribas Bank Ltd v AAB Export Finance Ltd (No 2)*[2] was deemed to be unreasonable and therefore past; while in *Re Daniel Murphy Ltd*[3] a delay of 55 days was considered by the court to be reasonable in the circumstances.

RELEGATION OF CHARGEHOLDERS' RIGHTS

40.16 A chargeholder may also lose his rights because of the priority rules (see Chapter 41).

Priority of charges generally

40.17 A charge may become ineffective because it is lower in priority to another charge on the same assets. For example, the holder of a legal mortgage will rank before a previously acquired equitable interest in the same property, where it was acquired by a bona fide purchaser for value without notice. Again, a floating charge will be postponed to any subsequently created fixed charge.[4] In addition, any charge not registered under s 99 of the 1963 Act will lose all entitlement to priority which it might otherwise possess.

---

1 [1980] IR 347.
2 [1991] 2 IR 19.
3 [1964] IR 1.
4 Because debenture-holders with a floating charge have implicitly authorised the company to deal with the assets charged, their interests may be postponed to a subsequent fixed charge on the property if the fixed chargee had no notice of their prior floating charge. Registration of the charge will constitute constructive notice.

Other matters which may render a floating charge ineffective include s 98 of the 1963 Act, negative pledge and reservation of title clauses and s 117 of the Finance Act 1995.

We shall focus on these essentially 'priority' rules in the next chapter.

Chapter 41

DEBENTURES, REGISTRATION AND PRIORITY OF CHARGES

THE DEBENTURE

41.1   There are two principal ways by which a company can raise capital. These are by the issue of shares to investors and by the issue of debentures to lenders of money. The rights of investors[1] are very different to the rights of lenders, who are (usually) secured creditors of the company. The contract evidencing the loan between the lender and the borrowing company is known as a debenture.

TYPES OF DEBENTURES

41.2   If the company decides to raise money by the issue of debentures, it may be either:

(1) a *single* debenture between the company and a particular lender; or
(2) a whole *series* of debentures issued by the company to members of the public. Such debentures will usually have the same terms and rank pari passu (equally), although they need not necessarily each be issued for the same amount.

Where a series of debentures is issued to the public, the statutory provisions relating to prospectuses will apply. If the debentures are listed on the Stock Exchange, the Exchange's regulations will apply – see Chapter 10.

Registered and bearer debentures

41.3   A debenture is usually registered in the books of the company in the name of the person who has lent the money to the company. But a company may issue 'bearer debentures' which are transferable by delivery under the rules relating to negotiable instruments.

Redeemable and perpetual debentures

41.4   Some debentures are issued for a fixed period of time. When this elapses, the lender may call for redemption of the loan, ie repayment of it. These types of debenture are styled *redeemable*. By contrast, a *perpetual* debenture is one in which the principal sum only becomes repayable at the winding up of the company – see s 94. It is also possible to issue debentures payable on demand.

---

1 See Parts IV A–D of this book.

FORMS OF DEBENTURE

41.5   A debenture is an instrument issued by the company, by which it agrees to repay a loan at a specified time. Before repayment, the company will agree to pay interest in the agreed manner and amount, charging the company's property as security for those payments and promising to comply with the various conditions contained in, or endorsed on, the instrument.

The charge

41.6   An example of the wording of an instrument creating the charge might be:

> 'The company has agreed with the lender to charge all its undertaking property and assets whatsoever and wheresoever both present and future including its uncalled capital for the time being and goodwill with payment to the lender of all moneys due or to become due by the company to the lender either as principal or surety to the lender.'[1]

The conditions

41.7   The conditions might also include additional details of fixed and/or floating charges including a negative pledge[2] clause.

If the debenture is one of a series, a condition will be included that all debentures are to rank pari passu.

'Pari passu' means that all the debentures of the series are to be paid rateably, so that if there are insufficient company funds to repay them all, each receives a similar proportion. If the debentures were not expressly 'pari passu', each would be payable according to the date of issue or, if all issued at the same time, in numerical order.

Again, the conditions will generally stipulate the circumstances in which the principal loan becomes immediately payable, eg:

(1)   if the company makes default for a period of, say, 14 days, in the payment of interest; or
(2)   if a receiver is appointed.

The conditions will usually also give the debenture holder the power to appoint a receiver[3] and manager. Without this express power, they could not appoint a receiver without first applying to the court.

---

1 See Specimen Bank 'All Monies' debentures giving a fixed and floating charge in *Jordans Irish Company Secretarial Precedents* (Jordans, 1993), at pp 162–166.
2 See below.
3 See next chapter.

Interpretation of wording

41.8 A debenture may describe the property and the type of charge. The fact that a particular charge is described as a fixed charge is not conclusive evidence that it is so. The court, on the construction of the document as a whole, may hold it to be a floating charge. This happened in *Re Lakeglen Construction Ltd,*[1] where future book debts were held to be a floating charge. However, in *Re Keenan Bros Ltd (in Liquidation),*[2] the Supreme Court classified book debts as a fixed charge when the debenture expressed them to be so and restricted the borrower's freedom to deal with them by requiring it to pay all monies it received in respect of those debts into separate designated accounts. Again, in *Re A.H. Masser Ltd,*[3] the High Court, following the same reasoning as the Supreme Court, held that the debenture placed such restrictions on the use of book debts that they were in the nature of a fixed charge.

41.9 In *Re Holidair Ltd,*[4] the Supreme Court approved *Re Keenan* and confirmed that, when determining whether a charge is fixed or floating, the instrument as a whole must be considered.

When book debts are being considered, the significant question is whether the company can deal with its book debts in the ordinary way. Whilst the debenture provided for payment of book debts to be made into selected banks, it did not provide for any restriction on the withdrawal of monies from these bank accounts. In this case, therefore, the charge on the book debts was a floating one.

The significance of these distinctions has now lessened due to statutory intervention in the Finance Acts – see **41.27**.

Trustees for the debenture-holders

41.10 When a series of debentures is issued to the public, the company will enter into an agreement with trustees to act on behalf of the debenture-holders and watch over their interest.

There is great value in appointing such trustees, since by this method, the trustee can act immediately instead of having to await separate instructions from the individual debenture-holders. If property of the company has been used as security to cover the loans of the debenture-holders, the trustee will usually call for the title deeds to such property.

The trust deed will provide, inter alia, for payment of remuneration to the trustees and the calling by them of meetings of debenture-holders.

The principal function of the trustees is to ensure that the terms of the debenture are honoured by the company, and to safeguard generally the

---

1 [1980] IR 347 (HC).
2 [1985] ILRM 641.
3 (Unreported) 6 October 1986 (HC).
4 [1994] 1 ILRM 481.

interests of the debenture-holders. Whilst so acting, the trustees must carry out their functions prudently and competently. Any clauses in the trust deed seeking to exempt the trustees from, or to indemnify them against, liability for breach of trust or failure to exercise proper care and diligence, may be void – see s 93 of the 1963 Act.

REGISTRATION OF CHARGES SECURING DEBENTURES

41.11 A person proposing to lend money to a company on the security of its assets, will need to know if those same assets have already been charged. In order to make this information available to potential lenders, s 99 of the 1963 Act provides that all charges created by a company must be registered with the registrar of companies, within 21 days[1] of their creation. However, in *Bank of Ireland Finance Ltd v D.J. Daly*,[2] McMahon J held that a charge arising by operation of the law, such as an unpaid vendor's lien arising on the purchase of property by a company, did not require registration under s 99.

Consequences of non-registration

41.12 A charge not registered under s 99 will be void against the liquidator or any creditor of the company, and money secured becomes immediately repayable to the lender. The failure to register is without prejudice to the lender's rights against the borrowing company.

Specific charges which must be registered

41.13 Section 99(2) specifies the range of charges which must be registered. They are any charge:

(1) To secure any issue of debentures. In *Re Valley Ice Cream (Ireland) Ltd*,[3] where a clause in a debenture irrevocably obliged the borrower to procure a mortgage over leased equipment in favour of the lender when the existing leases had expired, McCracken J held that this (fixed) charge required registration.

(2) On uncalled share capital of the company.

(3) Created or evidenced by an instrument which, if executed by an individual, would require registration as a bill of sale. Section 4 of the Bills of Sale (Ireland) Act 1879, defines a bill of sale as including transfers and other assurances of personal chattels but not including assignments of any ship or vessel.

---

1 The exact time when a charge is created is ascertained by examining the facts and contractual documents as a whole – see *Re Olderfleet Shipbuilding Co Ltd* [1922] I IR 26, and *Re Daniel Murphy Ltd* [1964] IR 1.
2 [1978] IR 79.
3 (Unreported) 22 July 1998 (HC).

In *Kruppstahl AG v Quitmann Products Ltd*,[1] unworked steel being used by the defendants in their manufacturing process was the subject of a floating charge.

The plaintiff had supplied the raw steel under a contract for sale which included a retention of title clause. On a receiver being appointed over the defendants' property, the plaintiffs sought a return of the unworked (new) steel.

Gannon J held that:

(i) the plaintiffs were entitled to a return of any unworked steel in the defendant's possession, which had not been paid for, on foot of the retention of title clause in the contract for the sale of goods; and

(ii) the steel delivered on foot of the contract constituted 'personal chattels' within the meaning of s 4 of the 1879 Act, and therefore, in relation to the worked steel, any floating charge created in respect of it would be void for want of registration under s 99(2)(c).

Again, in *Re South Coast Boatyard: Barbour v Burke*,[2] the Supreme Court held that 'yachts' were not 'ships' but 'vessels' within the meaning of s 99(2)(c), Kenny J stating:

'If any [person] went to Dun Laoghaire during the sailing season ... he would never dream of calling any of the yachts there, irrespective of their size, ships [however] the yachts are certainly vessels [so] the agreement [a charge on a vessel] did not require registration as a bill of sale.'

(4) On land or any interest therein, but not including a charge for any rent or periodical sum issuing out of land. Where a bank agrees to lend money to a company in return for a deposit of the title deeds to some of its property, this creates an equitable mortgage which is registrable. As Keane J stated in *Re Farm Fresh Frozen Foods Ltd*:[3]

'in the present case, the documents of title came into possession of the bank as equitable mortgages, and were not held by them ... on foot of any lien which survived the avoidance of the equitable mortgage, for non-registration.'

By contrast, in the *Kum Tong Restaurant* case (see below) McWilliam J had to point out that:

'as from the date of the contract for sale, the vendors interest in the land sold is converted into personality, that in equity the lands [belong] to the purchaser from the date of the contract, and [therefore] the vendor is only entitled to the purchase money with a lien on the lands for it.'

---

1 [1982] ILRM 551 (HC).
2 [1980] ILRM 186 (SC).
3 [1980] ILRM 131 (HC).

(5) On a company's book debts. In *Re Kum Tong Restaurant (Dublin) Ltd; Byrne v Allied Irish Banks*,[1] the bank loaned the company money in return for an undertaking by it to lodge the proceeds of the sale of their premises, which they were selling, with the bank as security for the loan.

The company, which had been in financial difficulties, was wound up before the property sale was completed, and the liquidator alleged that the bank's charge on the proceeds of the sale [of land] was void for non-registration. McWilliam J held that the security was a charge, not on book debts, but on the proceeds of a sale, and he was satisfied that the purchase price was not a book debt within the meaning in s 99(2)(c).

Much of the case-law on book debts has been concerned with whether they constituted fixed or floating charges – see **41.8**.

(6) Floating over the company's undertaking and property. Floating charges have been explained in **39.18** et seq. In certain circumstances a 'reservation of title' clause may require registration as a floating charge. Gannon J in *Kruppstahl AG v Quitmann Products Ltd* held that an equitable interest in the nature of a floating charge had been created which was void for want of registration.

(7) On calls made but not paid.

(8) On a ship or aircraft, or any shares in them. In the *South Coast Boatyard* case, Kenny J also said of the vessels in Dun Laoghaire harbour, 'any [person] would say that the British Rail vessel was a ship, the yachts were yachts and the boats were boats'.

(9) On goodwill, on a patent or a licence under a patent, on a trademark or on copyright or a licence under a copyright. It is the duty of the borrowing company to register the charge, but registration may be effected by any interested party.

Examples of non-registrable charges

41.14　Charges falling outside the categories specified in s 99(2)(a) to (i) (1 to 9 above) need not be registered. The most important types of non-registrable charges are those arising by operation of the law. In particular:

(1) unpaid vendor's liens;[2]
(2) bankers' liens,[3] confirmed by Keane J in the *Farm Fresh Frozen Foods* case above; and
(3) charges on the proceeds of the sale of land – see the *Kum Tong* case above.

1　[1978] IR 446 (HC).
2　See **41.11**.
3　Bankers enjoy a right to detain documents belonging to their customers until the latter's entire indebtedness to them has been discharged. This right is known as a general lien.

Register of charges

41.15 The registrar of companies must keep,[1] in relation to each company, a register of charges notified to him. This register is open to inspection by any person, and contains the following particulars of a company's debentures:

(1) the total amount secured by the whole series; and
(2) the dates of the resolutions authorising the issue of the series, and the date of the covering deed, if any, by which the security is created or defined; and
(3) a general description of the property charged; and
(4) the names of the trustees, if any, for the debenture-holders.

The registrar will issue a certificate confirming that he has received the required particulars of the charge. This certificate is conclusive evidence that the statutory registration requirements have been complied with.[2]

If and when the debt in relation to the charge has been repaid, the registrar, on evidence being supplied to him, may enter on the register a memorandum of satisfaction that the undertaking or property has been released[3] from the charge.

Extension of registration time and correction of errors in the register

41.16 Section 106 of the 1963 Act allows the company, or any person interested in the charge, to apply to the court to:

(1) extend the time for registration of the charge; or
(2) rectify any omission or mis-statement of any particulars which were delivered.

Any order granted by the court under s 106 may be made subject to a condition that it is not to affect the rights of secured creditors or a liquidator acquired against the property prior to registration.[4]

41.17 The circumstances in which a court can exercise this discretion are set out in s 106(1).

In *Re International Retail Ltd*, Kenny J confirmed the invariable practice of the courts of England and Ireland to require on applications under s 106, 'evidence that no winding up of the company is pending or contemplated and that no judgments have been registered against it which are unpaid, before [exercising their discretion to extend] the time for registration'.

The reasoning behind this practice is to ensure the protection of a company's unsecured creditors, because once the company is wound up, all its creditors have an interest in its property. Thus, a court will not exercise its discretion

---

1 Sections 103–105 of the 1963 Act.
2 Section 104. See **41.19**.
3 See s 105.
4 See *Re International Retail Ltd* (Unreported) 19 September 1979 (HC).

under s 106 if the company is actually being wound up.[1] Even in the case of a solvent company, the order extending the time for registration may be made subject to or without prejudice to the rights of secured creditors or liquidator existing prior to the time of actual registration.

Priorities following late registration

41.18 Generally a charge registered under s 106 will have priority over an earlier unregistered charge. However, if the charge registered late is made expressly subject to the rights of a prior mortgage, the registered chargee will be deemed to have foregone his right of priority – see *Re Clarets Ltd; Spain v McCann and Stonehurst Bank (Ireland) Ltd.*[2]

Conclusiveness of certificate of registration and constructive notice

41.19 Section 104 of the 1963 Act provides that the registrar will certify the amount of any charge registered under s 99, and the certificate 'shall be conclusive evidence that the requirements as to registration have been complied with'.

In *Lombard and Ulster Banking (Ireland) Ltd v Amurec (In Liquidation),*[3] the defendants loaned money on an undated mortgage in 1972. They then inserted a date in 1974 and registered the mortgage within 21 days of that date. Hamilton J stated:

> 'The evidence clearly establishes ... that the prescribed particulars were not delivered to ... the registrar ... within 21 days after the date of its creation ... [but] the wording of s 104 is clear and unambiguous ... I have [therefore] no alternative but to hold that the charge is a valid one and is void against the liquidator.'

Consequently, once the registrar issues his certificate under s 104, it is almost impervious to challenge in the courts. If, however, inaccurate details are registered, the court will give effect to the actual terms of the debenture.[4]

Lenders to companies are deemed to have constructive notice of registered charges. However, the notice imputed to a lender is simply the particulars of such charges which require compulsory registration under ss 99 and 103. In *Welch v Bowmaker (Ireland) Ltd and ANR,*[5] the Supreme Court held that a chargee did not have constructive notice of a negative pledge clause, Henchy J saying:

> 'If [such an extension] of the doctrine of constructive notice is to be made, the necessary change in the law would need to be made prospectively, and therefore, more properly by statute.'

---

1 See *Re Telford Motors Ltd; Doody v Mercantile Credit Co of Ireland* (Unreported) 27 January 1978 (HC).
2 [1978] ILRM 215.
3 (1978) 112 ILTR 1 (HC).
4 *Re Shannonside Holdings Ltd* (Unreported) 20 May 1993.
5 [1980] IR 2511 (SC) – see also **41.28**.

The case of *Coveney v Persse*[1] seems to suggest that subsequent chargees would only be bound by a negative pledge clause if it was registered, and they had actually inspected the clause in the Companies Office records.

Register of debenture-holders

41.20   Every company which issues a series of debentures must keep a register of holders, entering in it the names and addresses of each debenture-holder and the amount of debentures currently held by each. This register may be kept on computer records.[2]

Debenture-holders are given rights by s 92 to inspect the register and to obtain copies from it and the trust deed.

TRANSFER OF DEBENTURES

41.21   Generally, debentures may be transferred in a similar manner to shares: ss 79 to 90[3] provide for the transfer and evidence of title to *both* shares and debentures. Section 81 makes it clear that it shall not be lawful to register a transfer of shares or debentures unless a proper instrument of transfer has been delivered to the company. Section 83 provides for registration of the transfer by the company at the request of the transferor.[4]

Transfer generally 'subject to equities'

41.22   When a debenture is transferred, unless the contrary is expressly provided for in the debenture,[5] the transferee takes the debenture 'subject to equities', ie subject to any rights enjoyed by others. Thus, the transferee will not be in a better position than the transferor.[6]

If there are rights enjoyed by others in the property or assets charged, then the law must provide for the resolution of disputes relating to their claims. This is done through the rules relating to priority.

Priority of charges

41.23   A legal mortgage will rank before a previous equitable interest where it was acquired by a bona fide purchaser for value without notice of the earlier interest.

---

1 [1910] IR 194.
2 See s 91 of the 1963 Act and s 4 of the 1977 Act.
3 Of the 1963 Act.
4 See Chapter 22.
5 See *Hilger Analytical Ltd v Rank Precision Industries and Others* [1984] BCLC 301.
6 *Re China Steamship Co ex parte Mackenzie* (1869) LR 7 Eq 240.

Priority is governed between equitable charges by the date or order of their creation, the charge created first ranking in priority. This rule has been modified in relation to floating charges and subsequent fixed charges.

A floating charge will be postponed to any subsequently created fixed charge regardless of notice, because the nature of a floating charge permits the company to deal with the assets which are subject to the charge.[1]

Effect of registration on priorities

41.24   Any charge which is not registered within 21 days, in accordance with s 99 of the 1963 Act, is void. As a result, it will lose all entitlement to priority which it might otherwise possess.

Registration gives constructive notice to subsequent chargees (see **41.18**). In *Wilson v Kelland*,[2] however, it was held that registration of a charge, while it gave constructive notice of the charge, did not give the same notice of the terms contained in the deed creating it.

Generally, a registered charge will have priority over an earlier unregistered charge (which is void), even if the later chargee had notice of the earlier unregistered charge. However, if the subsequent chargee expressly agrees to subordinating his rights to those of the earlier unregistered chargee, the latter can regain priority by obtaining late registration of his charge under s 106.[3]

OTHER INSTANCES OF LOSS OF PRIORITY

41.25   In addition to the priority rules summarised in **41.23** and **41.24**, a chargeholder may lose his priority by virtue of s 98 of the 1963 Act; by s 174 of the Finance Act 1995; and because of a negative pledge or reservation of title clause.

Loss of priority under s 98

41.26   Under s 98, the receiver of a solvent company must use any assets he obtains on foot of a floating (but not a fixed) charge to pay the preferential[4] creditors. It is only when he has paid these creditors that he can use the remaining balance to pay the holder of a floating charge.

In *Re Eisc Teo*,[5] Lardner J considered that the receivers statutory duty under s 98:

> 'was not terminated or affected by the circumstances either (i) that a winding up order was made three months after the appointment of the receiver, or (ii) that the receiver did not, in fact, require to make any payment out of assets [which formed] the subject of the floating charge.'

1 See negative pledge clauses (discussed at **41.28**).
2 [1910] 2 Ch 306.
3 See **41.16**.
4 See **50.52**.
5 [1991] ILRM 760 (see also **43.8**).

Where a debenture has created both fixed and floating charges, s 98 does not apply to the proceeds of the sale of assets subject to the fixed charge. In such circumstances, Murphy J held in *United Bars Ltd v Revenue Commissioners*[1] that a receiver left with a financial surplus was obliged to pay this money to the company, rather than to a preferential creditor of it – the Revenue Commissioners.

The Finance Act 1995

41.27 Although a floating charge has some advantage to a lender, in view of the range of factors mentioned above which can imperil the security of assets subject to the charge, it is clear that the fixed charge offers a superior form of security. Because of this, disputes have arisen as to whether a particular charge in a debenture is fixed or floating, particularly in the case of book debts.[2]

Disputes over whether charges are fixed or floating can be of special concern to the preferential creditors; in particular the Revenue Commissioners. Section 115 of the Finance Act 1986 stipulated that even if book debts were deemed to be fixed charges, they would no longer be entitled to priority over debts to the Revenue Commissioners. Section 115 was amended by s 174 of the Finance Act 1995. Under s 174, where a person holds a fixed charge on book debts, he may be liable to pay tax if the company fails to pay any amount for which it is liable.

Negative pledge clauses

41.28 A negative pledge is an express contractual undertaking given by the borrowing or chargor company that it will not create any further charges on its assets, without the chargee's express permission.

As a negative pledge clause does not require registration under s 99 of the 1963 Act, subsequent chargees will not be deemed to have constructive notice of it.[3]

An examiner is not bound by a negative pledge.[4]

Reservation of title clauses

41.29 Reservation of title clauses are also known as 'Romalpa' clauses since the case of *Aluminium Industry Vaassen BV v Romalpa Aluminium Ltd.*[5]

Where a seller of goods to the company 'reserves title' to their goods until payment, a floating charge may not, on crystallisation, attach to those specified

---

1 [1991] I IR 391. Murphy J applied the principle in *Re Lewis Merthyr Consolidated Colliery* [1929] 1 Ch 489 that the combining of a floating charge does not bring [s 98] into operation as against the assets expressed in the fixed charge (see also **43.8**).
2 See **41.8**.
3 See **41.19**.
4 See **45.37**.
5 [1978] I WLR 676.

goods, because the supplier has a better claim than the borrowing company to those goods. For example, where a floating chargee has a charge over raw material to be used by the company, he may find that on crystallisation of his charge, it does not attach to the raw material in question because the supplier of the goods has retained title to them until he has been paid, by a reservation of title clause. Such a clause may even allow the supplier, if unpaid, to remove the goods from the company's premises, in priority to the floating chargee's rights.[1]

The unpaid seller may lose his rights if the goods become mixed, eg where wool supplied became woven into carpets. Again, if the unpaid seller had reserved merely 'equitable' (rather than legal) ownership of the goods, his interest may require registration[2] as a charge under s 99 of the 1963 Act – see **41.13**.

A detailed analysis of the law relating to Romalpa clauses is more properly the province of a book on commercial[3] contracts.

RE-ISSUE OF DEBENTURES

41.30 Debentures which have been redeemed by the company may be re-issued under s 95 of the 1963 Act. The re-issued debentures will rank pari passu with the original issue unless:

(1) the articles or any contract provide to the contrary; or
(2) the company has carried out some act showing its intention that the debentures be cancelled.

Subject to the saving of rights of certain mortgagees, on the re-issue of redeemed debentures, the transferee shall be entitled to the same priorities as if the debentures had never been redeemed.[4]

DEBENTURE STOCK

41.31 Debenture stock is also a debt, generally secured by a trust deed. It is sub-divisible, and is often issued frequently in a series of transferable debenture stocks that are registered and transferred in a similar manner to shares. In fact, the distinction between a debt secured by debenture and debenture stock[5] is rather like that between shares and stock (see **20.40**).

---

1 See, for example, *Somers v James Allen (Ireland) Ltd* [1984] ILRM 437.
2 *Re Bond Worth* [1979] 3 All ER 919. Problems may also arise for the unpaid seller if the goods are re-sold and he seeks to claim the proceeds of the sale – see *Re W.J. Hickey Ltd (in Receivership) Uniacke v Cassidy Electrical Supply Co Ltd* [1988] IR 126 (HC).
3 See, for example, M. Forde *Commercial Law in Ireland* (Butterworth (Ireland) Ltd, Dublin, 1997), at pp 206 et seq, and G. McCormack *Reservation of Title* (Sweet & Maxwell, 2nd edn, 1995).
4 See ss 95 and 96.
5 The liability of the company is regarded as a liability to pay an annuity rather than as a liability to repay a loan forever under a perpetual debenture.

DEBENTURE-HOLDERS' REMEDIES

41.32 Whilst, in theory, debentures can be issued without security, in commercial practice few are.

In the next chapter, we shall focus on the rights of both unsecured and secured creditors against the company.

DEBTS DUE FROM DEBENTURE-HOLDERS

41.33 If the holder of debentures owes money to the company, and the company, in turn, cannot pay him monies due under the debenture in full, the holder cannot normally set off his debt against the debenture. Such transactions should generally be kept separate and distinct.

However, where a floating chargee is owed money by the company, Kenny J held in *Re Russell Murphy*[1] that a right of set off may operate over the assets subject to the charge, before the charge crystallises.

---

1 [1976] IR 15.

Chapter 42

CREDITORS' REMEDIES AGAINST THE COMPANY – CONSEQUENCES OF RECEIVERSHIP

RIGHTS OF ACTION

42.1 If a creditor, at any stage of his transaction with the company, considers some event has occurred which makes it less likely that the company will be able to (re)pay him the monies owed, he has certain legal rights of action. These rights of action will depend on whether the creditor is unsecured or secured.

UNSECURED CREDITORS' REMEDIES

42.2 An unsecured debenture-holder would be in a similar position to an ordinary trade creditor of the company. The fact that the company's indebtedness to him arose from a loan rather than from the supply of goods or services, is immaterial.

An unsecured debenture-holder has a choice of remedy. He can sue for recovery of outstanding principal and interest; obtain judgment, and if the judgment is not paid, levy execution against the company's property.

An unsecured lender (and creditor) can also, if he wishes, petition under s 213 for the winding up of the company.

When a creditor, who is owed at least £1,000, leaves a written demand for payment of it at the registered office of the company, and the company does not pay it within three weeks, that creditor may be able to petition the court to wind up the company under s 213 of the 1963 Act. The grounds for the petition would be that the company is unable to pay its debts.

This is a drastic remedy for the unsecured creditor. It is further complicated by the fact that unsecured creditors are discriminated against on the liquidation of a company. Creditors whose debts are secured by fixed charges, preferential creditors and floating chargees, are entitled to be paid out of the assets of a liquidated company, in priority to the unsecured creditors.

Because of their low priority in the distribution of company assets, unsecured creditors are unlikely to be paid out of the liquidated assets of an insolvent company. Their most realistic source of redress would, therefore, be to sue the company's officers.[1]

Secured creditors (or debenture-holders) are in a much stronger legal position to obtain repayment of their debts from the company, without having to seek its winding up.

---

1 See Chapters 28 and 29.

SECURED DEBENTURE-HOLDERS' REMEDIES AGAINST SOLVENT COMPANIES

42.3 As an alternative to petitioning for the winding up of the company, a debenture-holder will have several other remedies available to him. These are often set out in the debenture deed, and include the rights:

(1) to take possession of the charged property and, subsequently, sell it without the assistance of the court;
(2) to apply for a court order to sell the charged property in their possession;
(3) to receive and apply the income from the possessed property to discharge the loan; or
(4) to appoint a *receiver* under the terms of the debenture, or apply to the court to appoint one.

The appointment of a receiver is the most frequently used remedy.

Appointment of receiver

42.4 A receiver may be appointed either by a mortgagee, by debenture-holders (or trustees on their behalf), or by the court.

The most common form of appointment is that made directly by the debenture-holder(s); most instruments containing a condition empowering the debenture-holders to appoint a receiver without recourse to a court order.

Power is usually also given to the trustees to appoint a receiver, or, alternatively, to approve the appointment of a receiver nominated by the holders of the majority in value of the outstanding debentures in the series.

Appointment under a fixed charge

42.5 A debenture with a fixed charge will normally set out the circumstances when a power of sale[1] will arise, eg if payment of interest on the loan is in arrears or if winding up commences. The receiver appointed by the trustees will collect the income from the charged property until it can be sold.

Appointment under a floating charge

42.6 Generally, default by the company on repayment of either principal or interest will crystallise a floating charge and convert it into a fixed charge.

If expressly provided for in the trust deed, the receiver may be appointed without an application to the court.

---

1 A power of sale and the power to appoint a receiver is conferred on mortgagees and registered chargees whose mortgages are created by deed – see ss 17–23 of the Conveyancing Act 1881.

Jeopardy

42.7 In *Angelis v Algemene Bank Nederland (Ireland) Ltd*,[1] Kenny J seems to suggest that the debenture-holders can also appoint a receiver directly whenever their security is in jeopardy. Kenny J stated:

> 'It is not necessary to cite authority for the proposition that when the assets charged by a debenture are in danger of seizure, a debenture holder may immediately appoint a receiver.'

Appointment by the court

42.8 If the debenture does not contain a provision for the direct appointment of a receiver, the holders may petition the court[2] to do so on one of the following grounds:

(1) that the principal sum or interest payable is in arrears;
(2) that an event has occurred on which, under the terms of issue of the debentures, the security becomes enforceable against the company; or
(3) whilst there has been no actual breach of a condition in the debenture of the company, nevertheless, that the chargee's security is in jeopardy or imperilled, eg when liquidation is likely because creditors are pressing for payment.

Qualifications of receiver

42.9 Any fit person may be appointed a receiver. In practice, the appointee will usually be an experienced accountant. The following persons are, however, prohibited from being appointed as receiver by ss 314 and 315 of the 1963 Act, as amended by s 170 of the 1990 Act:

(1) any body corporate;
(2) an undischarged bankrupt;
(3) a person who is, or who has within 12 months of the commencement of the receivership been, an officer (including auditors) or servant of the company;
(4) a parent, spouse, brother, sister or child of an officer of the company;
(5) a person who is a partner of or in the employment of an officer or servant of the company;
(6) a person who is not qualified for appointment as receiver of the property of a related company.

In *The Wise Finance Co Ltd v O'Regan*,[3] the court held that a company's secretary was ineligible to act as that company's receiver.

---

1 (Unreported) 4 July 1974 (HC). In Lynch, Marshall and O'Ferrall *Corporate Insolvency and Rescue* (Butterworths, 1996), the authors question this proposition – see pp 124 and 125.
2 See *Alexander Hull & Co Ltd v O'Carroll, Kent & Co* (1955) 89 ILTR 70.
3 (Unreported) 26 June 1998 (HC).

Notice of appointment

42.10 The person who appoints the receiver under a debenture, or who obtains a court order for his appointment, must, within seven days of appointment, publish notice of it in *Iris Oifigiúil* and in at least one local daily newspaper. Section 107(1)[1] also makes provision for the registrar of companies to be notified at the same time.

Invoices and letterheads

42.11 Where a receiver of the property of a company has been appointed, every invoice, order for goods or business letter issued by or on behalf of the company or the receiver or the liquidator of the company, being a document in which the name of the company appears, must contain a statement that a receiver has been appointed.[2]

Notifications and information

42.12 Section 319 of the 1963 Act also stipulates that where a receiver of substantially the whole of the property of a company is appointed on behalf of debenture-holders secured by a floating charge:

(1) the receiver must immediately send notice to the company of his appointment;
(2) the company must then, within 14 days[3] after receipt of the notice, make out and submit to the receiver a statement in the prescribed form as to the affairs of the company; and
(3) within two months after receipt of the statement, the receiver must forward to the registrar of companies, to the court, to the company, to any trustees for the debenture-holders on whose behalf he was appointed and, so far as he is aware of their addresses, to all such debenture-holders, a copy of the statement and of any comments he sees fit to make on it.

Section 319 was amended by s 52 of the Company Law Enforcement Act 2001.

The insertion of a new s 319(2A) requires a receiver to file a statement with the registrar as to whether, in his opinion, the company is solvent at the end of the receivership. The registrar is required to copy every such statement to the Director of Corporate Enforcement. This is intended to allow the Director to monitor the state of companies that have undergone receiverships. Receiverships often precede liquidation or, where liquidation does not ensue, the company may be left insolvent. In either instance, the Director needs to be aware of the situation in order to discharge his functions in respect of such companies and their officers.

A new s 319(7) requires the registrar to inform the Director of the appointments of receivers which are notified to the registrar. This enables the Director

---

1 Of the 1963 Act.
2 Section 317(1) of the 1963 Act.
3 Or such longer period as may be allowed by the receiver or the court.

to discharge his general supervisory function in this respect. Many receiverships last for a considerable period and the Director might wish to make enquires of a receiver during the course of the receivership as to its progress and the likely outcome, ie whether the company is likely to be solvent at the end of the process.

Finally, a new s 319(8) makes it a criminal offence for a receiver to fail to comply with the amended s 319.

Section 53 of the 2001 Act inserted a new s 323A into the 1963 Act.

Section 323A empowers the Director to require a receiver to produce his books and answer any questions in relation to them or to the conduct of a receivership. However, such a request from the Director may not be made in respect of books relating to a receivership which had concluded more than six years prior to the request.

The receiver's specific statutory tasks are detailed in **43.10**.

Powers of receivers and managers

42.13   If it is necessary to carry on the company's business in addition to realising the chargees' security, the appointee must be expressly appointed receiver and manager. This would be the case where the creditors' security embraced the entire undertaking and business of the company, rather than being confined to a single asset. Section 323 of the 1963 Act stipulates that unless the contrary intention appears, any reference in the Act to a receiver of the property (or part of it) of a company, includes a reference to the receiver and manager of that property.

The typical powers of a receiver and manager appointed by the debenture-holders might be:

(1) to take possession of, collect and get in the property charged by the debentures, and, for that purpose, to take all the proceedings in the name of the company or otherwise as may seem expedient;

(2) to carry on or concur in carrying on the business of the company, and, for that purpose, to raise money on the premises charged in priority to the debentures or otherwise;

(3) to sell or concur in selling any of the property charged by the debentures after giving to the company at least seven days' notice of his intention to sell, and to carry any such sale into effect by conveying in the name or on behalf of the company or otherwise;

(4) to make any arrangement or compromise which he or they shall think expedient in the interest of the debenture-holders.

A receiver/manager may also be granted express powers[1] to:

---

1 Receivers/managers will also possess such ancillary powers as are incidental to the exercise of their express powers.

(1) borrow money for the company's business; and/or

(2) dismiss and employ staff; and/or

(3) insure and repair company property.

Although a receiver/manager clearly has the authority to manage the business of the company, such powers are conferred on him solely for the purpose of realising the charged property and not for rescuing the company. As Richardson J commented in *First City Corporation Ltd v Downsview Nominees Ltd*:[1]

> 'While in practice receiverships are sometimes used to achieve a moratorium and rehabilitation of the company's business, that is legitimate only where it is an incident of the receiver's proper role. The receiver is there to enforce the security and only for that purpose to trade. He is not a white knight.'

Application to court for directions or objections

42.14   Section 316(1)[2] of the 1963 Act gives the following persons the right to apply to the court for directions in relation to any matter connected with the exercise of the receiver's powers:

(1) the receiver himself;

(2) an officer of the company;

(3) a member of the company;

(4) employees of the company comprising at least half in number of the persons employed in a full-time capacity by the company;

(5) a creditor or creditors of the company owed at least £10,000 in aggregate;

(6) a liquidator;

(7) a contributory,

and, on any application, the court may give such directions, or make such order declaring the rights of persons before the court or otherwise, as the court thinks just.

An application by any of these persons,[3] other than by the receiver himself, would have to be supported by such evidence that the applicant is being unfairly prejudiced by any actual or proposed action or omission of the receiver, as the court may require.

Application of monies realised

42.15   All monies received or realised by a receiver must[4] be applied in or towards satisfaction pari passu of the debts due to the debenture-holders.

---

1 [1990] 3 NZLR 265.

2 As amended by s 171 of the 1990 Act.

3 An application to the court by a director and shareholder under s 316, seeking further information as to the receiver's fees and accounts, was refused by Budd J in *Kinsella v Somers, Bar Review*, Vol 5, Issue 8, June 2000.

4 Subject to the order of application of receipts in s 24(8) of the Conveyancing Act 1881.

EFFECT OF APPOINTMENT OF A RECEIVER

42.16   When a receiver is appointed by the debenture-holders, the following effects flow immediately from the appointment:

(1)   any floating charge crystallises and becomes a fixed charge on the assets over which it was created;

(2)   the powers of the directors to control the management of the company are suspended. This suspension, however, only relates to powers over assets over which the receiver is appointed. Directors retain their powers where these are exercisable over assets not controlled by the receiver (see **42.25**);[1]

(3)   the receiver may, if the interests of the debenture-holders so require, sell the property charged, or make any compromise which he considers expedient in the interests of the debenture-holders (see **43.6**);

(4)   contracts of employment between the company and its employees may not be automatically terminated.[2] A receiver has, however, the power to terminate such contracts of employment, if he considers this action necessary (see **42.24**);

(5)   other existing contracts of the company remain valid and binding on it (see **42.21**).

THE STATUS OF A RECEIVER

42.17   When a receiver has been appointed, a fundamental matter which must be clarified is whether he is an agent of the company or an officer of the court. The answer to this question depends on the manner of his appointment.

Receivers appointed by the debenture-holders

42.18   A receiver appointed by a debenture-holder or holders would, in the absence of express provision to the contrary, be the agent of the debenture-holder(s). However, to protect the debenture-holders against being held liable for the actions of a receiver appointed by them, most debenture instruments would contain a clause making any receiver appointed on the basis of it, the agent of the company. As a result, the company, not the debenture-holders, will be responsible for the receiver's wrongful acts (if any). It will also be liable to pay him his remuneration.

---

1   *Wymes v Crowley* (Unreported) 27 February 1987 (HC). The directors' powers are automatically reinstated if, and when, the receivership ends – see next chapter.

2   At common law, contracts of employment were automatically terminated by the appointment of a receiver. The European Communities (Safeguarding of Employees' Rights on Transfer of Undertakings) Regulations 1980, SI 1980/306, changes the common law position; at least in the context of transfers of undertakings. The decision in *Griffiths v Secretary of State for Social Services* also seems to revise the common law position – see **42.24**.

Despite the fact that the receiver is, in effect, the company's agent, it is an extraordinary type of agency. For, as Costello J said in *Irish Oil and Cake Mills Ltd v Donnelly*,[1] 'the agency here is ... very different from the ordinary agency arising everyday in commercial transactions'.

Unlike ordinary agents, a receiver may choose to repudiate some of his principal's (the company's) obligations – see **42.16**, **42.21** and **42.24**.

Receivers appointed by the court

42.19 Whilst most receivers will be appointed by the debenture-holders, occasionally, one will be appointed by the court.

A receiver appointed by the court is an officer and agent of the court. As the court cannot be liable, at common law the receiver is personally liable on his contracts, and entitled to be indemnified out of the assets of the company in priority[2] to the rights of the debenture-holders.

The receiver and company contracts

42.20 The appointment of a receiver can have implications for both existing and new company contracts.

Existing contracts

42.21 Generally, existing contracts remain binding on the company, although a receiver cannot be held liable under them. In fact, the receiver can repudiate or cancel such contracts unless to do so would:

(1) adversely affect the subsequent realisation of the company's assets; or
(2) injure the company's good will[3] if it were to trade again.

When the receiver decides that existing contracts are to be continued and performed by the company, he does not thereby incur a personal liability[4] in respect of them. This position differs for new contracts.

New contracts

42.22 Section 316(2) of the 1963 Act renders the receiver personally liable on any new contract entered into by him in the performance of his functions, unless the contract expressly provides that the receiver is not to be liable.

Section 316 further provides that if the receiver is held liable for a new company contract, he will be entitled to an indemnity out of the company assets.

---

1 (Unreported) 27 March 1983 (HC).
2 *Burt, Boulton & Hayward v Bull* [1895] 1 QB 276.
3 *Re Newdigate Clothing Co Ltd* [1912] 1 Ch 468.
4 Unless the receiver expressly accepts personal responsibility for the continuation of the existing company contract.

Substituting new for existing contracts

42.23   A supplier of goods or services to the company may insist on payment of his arrears as a condition for the continuation of his obligation to supply under a new contract. For example, in *W & L Crowe Ltd & Anor v E.S.B.*,[1] it was held that the E.S.B. were entitled to refuse to enter into a new contract with the receiver to supply power to the company, unless the monies owed to them under their existing contract were paid. The E.S.B. were also not prepared to accept the receiver's undertaking to accept personal responsibility for electricity bills under the new contract proposed.

Contracts of employment

42.24   Where a receiver is appointed by the court, the contracts of employees are automatically terminated. If this happens, the dismissed employees may be able to sue for damages for wrongful dismissal.[2]

Where the receiver is appointed directly by the debenture-holders, it was held in *Griffiths v Secretary of State for Social Services*,[3] that an employee's contract of employment was not automatically terminated, unless his continued employment (as managing director) was inconsistent with the role and functions of the appointee (see also **48.21**).

Directors' powers

42.25   While the directors' powers in respect of the assets subject to the charge are suspended on the appointment of the receiver, nevertheless, the directors do remain in office and can exercise any powers which have not passed to the receiver.

Where a receiver is appointed over all the assets and undertaking of the company, the directors' powers are virtually extinguished. Nevertheless, even in these circumstances, directors may retain residual decision-making powers, such as the power to initiate legal proceedings in the name of the company. In *Newhart Developments Ltd v Co-operative Commercial Bank*,[4] the court upheld the directors right to initiate proceedings in this manner, largely because they provided a personal indemnity for the costs of the litigation in the event of it being unsuccessful.

The *Newhart Developments* case[5] thus upheld the directors' residual right, because (and on the condition that) it did not interfere with the receiver's work of realising the charged assets, nor deprive the debenture-holders of any part of their security.

---

1   (Unreported) 9 May 1984 (HC).
2   *Reid v Explosives Co Ltd* (1887) 19 QBD 264.
3   [1974] QB 468.
4   [1978] QB 814, [1978] 2 All ER 896 (CA).
5   In *Tudor Grange Holdings Ltd v Citibank NA* [1992] Ch 53, Browne-Wilkinson VC thought that this case should only be followed where the directors undertook to provide a personal indemnity to meet any award of costs against the company.

It is also likely that the courts would uphold the directors' rights to:

(1) challenge the validity of the receiver's appointment – see *Paramount Acceptance Co Ltd v Souster*;[1]

(2) oppose a petition to wind up the company – see *Re Reprographic Exports (Euromat) Ltd*;[2]

(3) cause the company to sue the receiver for breach of duty – see *Watts v Midland Bank plc*;[3] and

(4) obtain whatever information they might need from the receiver to enable them to discharge their residual duties. For example, notwithstanding the appointment of a receiver, the directors may still have the residual duty of preparing annual accounts for the members and the registrar, and the receiver, on request, would have to supply the directors with the relevant information to enable them carry out such residual duties.

Keane J, in *Lascomme Ltd Ballyglass House v United Dominions Trust & Gilligan*,[4] allowed directors to exercise their residual powers to maintain proceedings against the lender who had appointed the receiver and manager over company property. The learned judge did, however, point out that the directors' residual powers could not be used in a manner which would interfere with the receiver's ability to deal with, or dispose of, the charged property.

---

1 [1981] 2 NZLR 38.
2 (1978) 122 SJ 400.
3 [1986] BCLC 15.
4 [1994] ILRM 227 (HC).

Chapter 43

THE RECEIVER'S RIGHTS AND DUTIES – PREMATURE ENDING OF HIS POWERS

RIGHTS OF RECEIVER

43.1 The rights of a receiver may be considered under the headings of remuneration, indemnity and relief from liability for defects in his appointment.

Remuneration

43.2 Section 318[1] deals with the remuneration of the receiver. The remuneration of the receiver is normally a matter for the receiver and the person appointing him. However, the court may, on application by a liquidator, creditor or member of the company, fix the receiver's remuneration. This provision applies even where the remuneration has already been agreed between the receiver and the person appointing him.

Indemnification

43.3 A prudent receiver will seek to have included, in his contract with debenture-holders, a clause indemnifying him against any claims or proceedings which might be brought against him as a result of the receivership.

In addition, receivers are entitled[2] to an indemnity out of company assets if they incur a personal liability for company contracts.

Defective appointment

43.4 Where it is discovered subsequently that there was a defect in the charge purporting to appoint a receiver, s 316(3) gives the court the power, if it thinks fit, to order that the receiver is wholly or partially relieved from liability for his actions under the defective appointment.

RECEIVER'S DUTIES

43.5 Receivers, irrespective of the method of their appointment, are regarded as being in a fiduciary relationship with those who appointed them. Consequently, the receiver's relationship with the debenture-holders is a

---

1 Of the 1963 Act.
2 Ibid, s 316 – see previous chapter.

fiduciary one, and he must exercise his powers of receivership[1] in *good faith and for their proper purposes.*

Duty when selling property

43.6   Whilst the receiver's primary duty is owed to the debenture-holders as agent of the company, he owes a secondary duty to the company (and to a guarantor of its indebtedness).[2] This common law duty has been strengthened by s 316A(1)[3] of the 1963 Act which provides that a receiver, on selling company property, must exercise 'all reasonable care to obtain the best price reasonably obtainable for the property as at the time of the sale'.

Section 316A(2) further provides that if a receiver is in breach of s 316A(1), he will lose any rights he might have had to be compensated or indemnified by the company for his breach of statutory duty.

In *Re Edenfell Holdings Ltd,*[4] Laffoy J stated if a receiver was in breach of s 316A, then on the authority of *Holohan v Friends Provident and Century Life Office,*[5] a contract made in pursuance of such breach was not properly made and the completion of it had to be restricted by injunction.

The Supreme Court[6] allowed an appeal by the receiver holding, inter alia, that:

(1) the receiver had exercised all reasonable care and was entitled to act as he did;
(2) the fact that the purchaser paid less than the accepted value of the lands would only have been a material factor had there been another conditional offer before the receiver; and
(3) had the receiver rejected the offer, he could have incurred greater financial liabilities for the company and ended up without a purchaser.

Even if a receiver sells property in breach of s 316A, McCracken J confirmed in *Ruby Property Co Ltd et al v Kilty & Another*[7] that a bona fide purchaser for value of such property obtains a good title to it.

Sale of non-cash assets

43.7   Section 316A(3) prohibits a receiver from selling a non-cash asset of the requisite value to an officer of the company unless he has given at least 14 days' notice of his intention to do so to all creditors of the company who are known to him or who have been intimated to him.

---

1 He must also exercise a general duty of care by, for example, obtaining the best possible price which the circumstances of a sale permit – see *McGowan v Gannon* [1983] ILRM 516.
2 *Standard Chartered Bank Ltd v Walker* [1982] 3 All ER 938.
3 As amended by s 172 of the 1990 Act.
4 (1997) 4 CLP 233, [1999] I IR 443 (HC).
5 [1996] IR 1.
6 [1999] I IR 458.
7 (2000) 7 CLP 155.

Duties in applying the proceeds of sale of assets

43.8   Section 98 of the 1963 Act makes provision for the payment by a receiver of the debts of preferential creditors, when he has been appointed under a floating charge.

Under s 98, when a receiver is appointed on behalf of debenture-holders under a floating charge or possession is taken by or on behalf of the debenture-holders of any property under a charge, then, even if the company is not at that time being liquidated, the preferential debts under s 285 must be paid out of the assets coming into the hands of the receiver in priority to any principal or interest payable under the debentures. Any preferential payments made by the receiver under this section can, of course, be recouped, so far as may be, out of the assets of the company available for the general creditors.

Where the receiver sells assets which are the subject of a fixed charge or a legal mortgage, his duty is to apply the proceeds in the discharge of the monies due to the debenture-holders. Any surplus is payable to the company, as s 98 only applies to assets subject to a floating charge (see **41.26**).

In *Re Eisc Teo*,[1] Lardner J held that:

(1)   the receiver's duty under s 98 to pay the preferential creditors out of the proceeds of the sale of assets subject to the floating charge was not terminated by the subsequent appointment of a liquidator;

(2)   s 98 applied to a receiver once a claim for principal and interest had been made under a debenture – this claim existed at the time the receiver was appointed and it was irrelevant that the proceeds of the floating charge were surplus to requirements; and

(3)   the fact that the preferential creditors would obtain a priority whether under s 98 or s 285 should not be a factor in determining the statutory duty of a receiver.

Lardner J's analysis in (2) and (3) was approved in *Re Manning Furniture Ltd*,[2] where McCracken J held that the receiver had a duty to pay the preferential creditors out of assets coming into his hands, despite the fact that the proceeds of the floating charge were not used to discharge monies due under the debenture in question.

Where, however, a receiver does not realise or take possession of the assets which are the subject of a floating charge; instead simply realising the assets subject to a fixed charge (only), he is not obliged to pay the preferential creditors under s 98 because to do so would confer on these creditors an unwarranted entitlement that they would not have enjoyed in the event of the company's liquidation – see *United Bars Ltd v Revenue Commissioners*.[3] Section 98

---

1   [1991] ILRM 760.
2   [1996] I ILRM 13.
3   See **41.26**.

may also be disapplied in the case of a company being placed[1] under the protection of the court – see **43.23** and Chapters 45 and 46.

Duty to report misconduct

43.9	Section 299(2) of the 1963 Act imposes a duty on liquidators to report criminal behaviour by company officers and members to the Director of Public Prosecutions, and to assist him to prosecute the offenders. This duty was extended to receivers by s 179 of the 1990 Act.

Receiver's specific statutory tasks

43.10	Sections 319 and 320 specify the procedures to be adopted when a receiver, appointed on behalf of holders of debentures secured by a floating charge, *takes over the whole, or substantially the whole, of the property of a company.* Such a receiver is required by the Act to take the following steps.

Notification

43.11	The receiver must notify the company immediately of his appointment.

Statement of particulars

43.12	Within 14 days after receipt of the notice or such longer period as he, or the court, may allow, the receiver must obtain from the company a statement showing particulars of:

(1)	the assets;
(2)	the debts and liabilities;
(3)	the names and residences of the creditors;
(4)	the securities held by the respective creditors;
(5)	the dates on which the various securities were given;
(6)	such other information as may be prescribed.

Verification of particulars

43.13	The statement of particulars must be submitted and verified by the affidavit (or statutory declaration where the appointment is under a deed) of one or more of the directors of the company and by the secretary at the date of the appointment. In addition, the receiver may require any of the following persons to submit and verify the statements:

(1)	present or past officers of the company;
(2)	anyone who has taken part in the formation of the company within a year of the receiver's appointment;
(3)	persons employed by the company within the past year and who are, in the opinion of the receiver, capable of giving the information required;

---

1 Or likely to be placed.

(4) anyone employed within the preceding year as an officer in another company which itself took part in the management of the main company.

Any person making the statement and affidavit (or statutory declaration) is entitled to be paid by the receiver, out of his receipts, any costs and expenses which the receiver considers reasonable. He may appeal to the court if dissatisfied.

Persons not complying with these verification requirements are liable to criminal sanctions of up to three years' imprisonment and/or a fine not exceeding £5,000.

Copies to registrar and debenture-holders

43.14 Within two months of receipt of this statement of particulars, the receiver must send copies of it, together with any comments he sees fit to make, to the registrar of companies, the court,[1] the company, to any trustees for the debenture-holders on whose behalf he was appointed and, so far as he is aware of their addresses, to all debenture-holders.

Delivering of half-yearly returns to the registrar

43.15 Section 321 of the 1963 Act provides that every receiver, within one month after the expiration of six months from the date of his appointment and every subsequent six months (and again within one month of ceasing to act as receiver), must send to the registrar of companies an abstract in the prescribed form showing:

(1) the assets of the company of which he has taken possession, since his appointment;
(2) their estimated value;
(3) the proceeds of sale of any such assets since his appointment;
(4) his receipts and payments during the period of six months, or for the broken period when he ceases to act;
(5) the aggregate amounts of his receipts and payments during all preceding periods since his appointment.

In addition to making these returns, the receiver must, of course, render proper accounts of his receipts and payments to the persons to whom he is responsible, in accordance with the terms of his appointment.

Sections 319 and 320 (at **43.10**) apply where the receiver takes over the whole of the company's property. Where a receiver is appointed *other than over substantially all of the company's assets* so that ss 319 and 320 do not apply, he still must file half-yearly accounts with the registrar of companies containing the same particulars as those required under s 319. On ceasing to act, a receiver must file a final return.

---

1 If appointed by the court.

Enforcement of receiver's duty to make returns

43.16   The court is empowered under s 322, on an application being made, to direct a receiver to make good any default in making returns. In particular, s 322 specifies the receiver's default:

(1) in failing to file, deliver or make any return,[1] account or other documents within 14 days after the service on him of a notice requiring him to do so; or

(2) in failing to provide proper accounts, to vouch his receipts and payments and to pay over the balance due to the liquidator of the company.

Applications for the purpose of (1) above may be made to the court by any member or creditor of the company or by the registrar of companies, and on the grounds in (2) by the liquidator. The court may provide for the costs of the application to be borne by the receiver.

Liabilities of receivers

43.17   The main legal liabilities of receivers are likely to arise out of contracts entered into by them on behalf of the company. Their liability for existing and new company contracts has been explained in **42.20**.

Application to the court for directions

43.18   If a receiver is unsure as to the legality of a course of action, he has the right, under s 316 of the 1963 Act, to apply to the court for directions (see **42.14**).

PREMATURE TERMINATION OF RECEIVER'S POWERS

43.19   A receiver's powers may be brought to an end before he has accomplished his task of utilising or realising the company's assets under his control to pay the debenture-holders. This premature termination of a receiver's powers may be brought about either voluntarily or involuntarily. A receiver may resign voluntarily. He may also be involuntarily removed by the court.

Resignation

43.20   Section 322C[2] of the 1963 Act makes provision for the resignation of a receiver. A receiver of the property of a company appointed under the powers contained in any instrument may resign, provided he has given one month's notice to:

---

1 Or to give any notice which he is required to deliver.
2 As inserted by s 177 of the 1990 Act.

(1) the holders of floating charges over all or any part of the property of the company;

(2) the company or its liquidator; and

(3) the holders of any fixed charge over all or any part of the property of the company.

If any receiver resigns without giving the notice prescribed by s 322C, he will be liable to a maximum fine of £1,000.

Removal

43.21 In addition to voluntary resignation, the Act also provides for the involuntary removal of a receiver. Section 322A(1)[1] empowers the court, on cause shown, to remove[2] a receiver and appoint another in his place.

The court may also remove a receiver on the application of the liquidator – see **43.24**.

RECEIVERS, EXAMINERS AND LIQUIDATORS

43.22 A *receiver* is an appointee of the secured creditors[3] (debenture-holders). His primary function is to take over (and, if necessary, sell) the assets of the company which have been mortgaged or charged by it as security for repayment of the debenture-holders' loan.

The exercising of his rights over the charged assets by the receiver may, but not necessarily must, result in the winding up of the company.

An *examiner*[4] is appointed by the court, usually at the request of the company's officers, who are seeking his appointment to protect the company against its secured creditors. The examiner's function is to examine the financial affairs and prospects of the company, and to report back to the court on its prospects for survival, ie how it can avoid liquidation.

A *liquidator*[5] may be appointed by either investors or creditors. His task is to terminate the 'life' of the company by winding it up, liquidating its assets and distributing them in accordance with the law.

---

1 Inserted by s 175 of the 1990 Act.

2 Section 322A(2) sets out the procedure to be followed. This includes giving the receiver at least seven days' notice before the hearing of such proceedings.

3 Or by the court on their behalf.

4 See Part IX.

5 See Part X B.

Effect on receiver of appointment of examiner

43.23   Section 6(1) of the Companies (Amendment) Act 1990[1] provides that where, at the date of the presentation of a petition to appoint an examiner to a company, a receiver is already in control of the whole or any part of the property or undertaking of that company, the court may make such order as it thinks fit, including an order as to any or all of the following matters:

(1) that the receiver shall cease to act as such from a date specified by the court;

(2) that the receiver shall, from a date specified by the court, act as such only in respect of certain assets specified by the court;

(3) directing the receiver to deliver all books, papers and other records, which relate to the property or undertaking of the company and are in his possession or control, to the examiner within a period to be specified by the court;

(4) directing the receiver to give the examiner full particulars of all his dealings with the property or undertaking of the company.

The Supreme Court has held that the appointment of an examiner will de-crystallise a floating charge over a company's book debts.[2]

Effect on receiver of appointment of liquidator

43.24   The subsequent appointment of a liquidator over a company whose property is under the control of a receiver, does not automatically affect the receivership. However, s 322B[3] of the 1963 Act gives a court the power to terminate or limit the receivership on the application of the liquidator.

On the application of a liquidator, in these circumstances, the court may:

(1) order that the receiver shall cease to act as such from a date specified by the court, and prohibit the appointment of a new receiver; or

(2) order that the receiver shall act as such only in respect of certain assets specified by the court.

The court may, on receipt of an application made either by the liquidator or by the receiver, cancel or amend an order made under s 322B(1).

---

1 As amended by s 6 of the Companies (Amendment) (No 2) Act 1999. This section also applies to provisional liquidators.
2 See **39.23**.
3 Inserted by s 176 of the 1990 Act.

Chapter 44

UNSATISFIED CREDITORS' REMEDIES AGAINST THE INSOLVENT COMPANY'S MEMBERS AND OFFICERS

CREDITORS' REMEDIES AGAINST INSOLVENT COMPANIES

44.1 Because of the separate legal personality[1] of the company, the general rule is that creditors of the company only have redress against company assets to obtain (re)payment of any monies owing to them by the company.

Any unsecured or secured creditor owed at least £1,000 has the right to petition for the winding up of the company. When a company is liquidated, the law provides for priority of payment to secured over unsecured creditors. For example, after the holders of any fixed charges have realised their security, the liquidator will use the remaining company assets realised to repay the company's creditors in the following order:

(1) preferential creditors;
(2) creditors secured by floating charges;
(3) unsecured creditors.

As mentioned in Chapter 2, in many company liquidations, the Revenue Commissioners, though preferential creditors, are often left unpaid because of the lack of company assets. In this context, the likelihood of floating chargees and unsecured creditors being paid is very slim. In many liquidations, the unsecured creditors will not be paid.

UNSATISFIED CREDITORS' REMEDIES AGAINST THE MEMBERS

44.2 The reason why the unsatisfied creditors remain unpaid during (and after) a liquidation is clearly the insufficiency of company assets to pay them. Can these unsatisfied creditors now seek to reclaim their monies from the company's members?

In Chapter 4, we explained how the principle of limited liability protected the members of a company from being held liable for the debts of the company which they own. Once every member has fully paid up the nominal value of each share he holds, then his liability to company creditors is generally extinguished. Thus, the principle of limited liability, allied to the separate personality of the company, confers an immunity on members against claims by unsatisfied creditors of the company.

As was illustrated in Chapter 6, corporate personality is likened to a veil. This veil of incorporation prevents unsatisfied creditors from pursuing legal action

---

1 See Chapter 3.

against company members, even though the identities of the members and the number of shares which they hold can be ascertained.

It is only in exceptional cases that unsatisfied company creditors can successfully pursue a claim against the members. These exceptional cases have arisen as a result of the courts and the legislature[1] 'lifting' the veil of incorporation.

The rare instances where unsatisfied creditors are able to pursue company members might be where the company was originally formed or used for a fraudulent purpose. Members of companies which traded with less than the minimum number of members required by s 36 of the 1963 Act, may also be held personally responsible for the company's unpaid debts.

Immunity of members

44.3   The Joint Stock Companies Act 1844 and the Limited Liability Act 1855 permitted the registration of companies as separate legal persons with limited liability for their investors. The purpose of these Acts was to encourage enterprise by offering the protection of limited liability to investors or company members. The few exceptional cases where investors' immunity against unsatisfied company creditors' claims have been breached by the 'lifting of the veil' during the past 150 years, would seem to suggest that the nineteenth century legislation has been most successful in protecting investors against claims by unsatisfied creditors of the company.

UNSATISFIED CREDITORS' CLAIMS AGAINST DIRECTORS AND OFFICERS

44.4   Although investors, as company members, are protected, essentially, against claims made by unsatisfied creditors of the company, the legislature has opened up new avenues of redress for creditors against the managing agents of the company, ie its directors and officers.

In Ireland, of the 147,058 companies registered at 31 December 1995, 134,769 (92 per cent) were private limited companies. Many directors of private companies will also be major[2] shareholders in them. Accordingly, it is worth noting that even though a private company member may be protected, qua member, against the claims of unsatisfied company creditors, that same individual, as a director, or officer, might be held liable[3] for the debts of the company.

---

1   See Chapter 6 for details.
2   Possibly controlling shareholders.
3   Qua director or officer.

Directors' and officers' liabilities towards creditors

44.5 The right of an unsatisfied company creditor to pursue directors and officers depends on whether or not these managing agents are legally liable for the debts of the company.

We have already detailed the duties and liabilities of company directors and officers in Chapters 25 to 29. From the perspective of an unsatisfied creditor of the company, perhaps the most important likely sources[1] of redress will arise out of either a director's failure to keep proper books of account; reckless or fraudulent trading; or breach of a restriction or disqualification order.

Failure to keep proper books of account

44.6 Section 204(1) of the 1990 Act provides that when a company is being wound up, is unable to pay all of its debts and has failed to keep proper books of account, and the court considers that such contravention has contributed to the company's inability to pay all of its debts or has resulted in substantial uncertainty as to the assets and liabilities of the company or has substantially impeded the orderly winding up thereof, the court, on the application of the liquidator or any creditor or contributory of the company, may declare that any one or more of the officers and former officers of the company who are in default shall be personally liable, without any limitation of liability, for all, or part of the debts of the company.

Directors' and officers' liability under s 204 has already been analysed in **28.7** et seq, including the implications of the *Mantruck Services* case.

The advantage of s 204 to an unsatisfied creditor is that he, or the liquidator, can seek to supplement the paucity of company assets by making the directors and officers personally liable for the company's debts.

Reckless and fraudulent trading

44.7 Section 138 of the 1990 Act also provides that:

'If in the course of winding up of a company or in the course of proceedings under the Companies (Amendment) Act 1990, it appears that—

(a) any person was, while an officer of the company, knowingly a party to the carrying on of any business of the company in a reckless manner; or

(b) any person was knowingly a party to the carrying on of any business of the company with intent to defraud creditors of the company, or creditors of any other person or for any fraudulent purpose;

the court, on the application of the receiver, examiner, liquidator or any creditor or contributory of the company, may, if it thinks it proper to do so, declare that such person shall be personally responsible, without any limitation of liability, for all or any part of the debts or other liabilities of the company as the court may direct.'

---

1 See Part V B for other examples of statutory redress.

Thus, the company assets available to meet the claims of unsatisfied creditors can be supplemented by obtaining contributions:

(1) from officers of the company who were knowingly privy to the carrying on of any business of the company in a reckless manner; or

(2) any person who was knowingly a party to fraudulent trading.

The case-law on these statutory reckless and fraudulent trading provisions was examined in Chapter 28.

Restriction and disqualification

44.8   Any director who has been acting in breach of a restriction declaration or disqualification order, may be made personally liable for all or part of the company's debts[1] – thereby providing a further source of funding for unsatisfied company creditors.

The post-1990 legal environment

44.9   The Companies Act 1990 has greatly increased the potential liability of a company's human managing agents towards the unsatisfied creditors of the company. As a result, such creditors now enjoy a much greater chance of recovering some, if not all, of their unsatisfied claims against the company from its directors and officers. The fact that directors and officers can effect insurance to indemnify themselves against many of these potential claims, further improves the creditors' position. In fact, the likely reaction of unpaid company creditors will be to pursue the directors and officers, rather than the members, for recovery of their unsatisfied claims against the company. This reaction is a practical acknowledgement of the strength of the veil of incorporation and the effectiveness of the investors' immunity from liability for the debts of their companies.

---

1 See **28.43**.

PART IX

PROTECTION AVAILABLE TO A COMPANY AGAINST ITS CREDITORS

Chapter 45

EXAMINERSHIP AND ITS EFFECTS ON CREDITORS' RIGHTS

THE EFFECT OF EXAMINERSHIP

45.1   The prospect of losing a valuable beef trade outlet as a result of a United Nations embargo on trade with Iraq led to financial difficulties for companies within the Goodman International Group.[1] To protect these companies from their creditors, special sittings of the Oireachtas took place in August 1990, to process the parliamentary stages of the Companies (Amendment) Act 1990.[2] The 1990 Amendment Act provided for the placing of a company facing temporary financial difficulties under the protection of the court, whilst an examiner is appointed to look into its affairs.

The effect of the process of examinership is to allow a company in difficulty the opportunity of obtaining court protection from its creditors for some time whilst the examiner attempts to put in place a financial rescue package to save the company.

If the examiner considers that the company is viable, he may propose a scheme of arrangement involving the creditors accepting less than the amounts owed to them by the company. The court will have to approve such a scheme before it becomes binding.

Where the examiner forms the opinion that the company has no chance of survival, he is likely to propose its winding up.

We now focus on the detailed provisions in the 1990 legislation, as amended by the Companies (Amendment) (No 2) Act 1999 (the 1999 Act).

POWER OF THE COURT

45.2   Where it appears to the court that:

(1) a company is or is likely to be unable to pay its debts; and
(2) no resolution subsists for the winding up of the company; and
(3) no order has been made for the winding up of the company,

---

1 In August 1990, this group's debts were estimated to be about £450 million. Many of the creditors were foreign banks whose loans were unsecured.

2 This Act was, in effect, an early enactment of Part IX of the Companies Bill which was being processed at the time. This Bill subsequently became the Companies Act 1990. Sections 180 and 181 of the 1990 Act amended the 1990 Amendment Act, revising the practical working of examinership in the light of several months' experience.

it may appoint an examiner to the company for the purpose of examining the state of the company's affairs.[1]

In particular, the court may make an order if it considers that such action would be likely to facilitate the survival of the company, either whole or part, as a going concern.

The 1990 Act did not include criteria to guide the court in assessing whether a company is likely to survive. In *Re Atlantic Magnetics Ltd*,[2] Finlay CJ suggested:

> 'does the evidence lead to the conclusion that in all the circumstances, it appears worthwhile to order an investigation by the examiner into the company's affairs and see can it survive, there being some reasonable prospect of survival.'

Keane J, in *Re Butler Engineering Ltd*,[3] refined the term 'some reasonable prospect of survival' to 'an identifiable possibility' that the company will survive as a going concern if an examiner is appointed; a refinement approved by Budd J in *Re Westport Property Construction Co Ltd*.[4]

In *Re Cavan Crystal Glass Ltd*,[5] Kelly J approved a test of some reasonable prospect of survival,[6] and agreed with Keane J in *Re Butler's Engineering Ltd* that the onus was on the petitioner to establish that there was an identifiable possibility that the company could survive as a going concern if a protection order was granted. Kelly J did not grant the order.

On appeal, the Supreme Court reversed his decision in an ex tempore hearing, O'Flaherty J stating, inter alia, 'there has been good deal of support forthcoming for the company. It employs ... 80 people and the workforce are giving the application their support. The hope is that this may expand when the busy season begins ...'.

The appointment of an examiner in the *Cavan Crystal* case illustrated clearly the conclusion of the Company Law Review Group[7] that the criteria for the appointment of an examiner were not sufficiently onerous.

To remedy this situation, s 5 of the 1999 (Amendment) (No 2) Act (the 1999 Act) substitutes a new s 2(2) in the 1990 Amendment Act, as follows:

> '(2) The court shall not make an order ... unless it is satisfied that there is a reasonable prospect of the survival of the company and the whole or any part of its undertaking as a going concern.'

The same criteria are now to be applied to related companies – see s 6 of the 1990 Act, as amended (see **45.7**).

---

1 And performing the appropriate duties in relation to the company – see s 2 of the 1990 Amendment Act, as amended by s 181 of the 1990 Act.
2 [1993] 2 IR 561 (SC).
3 (Unreported) 1 March 1996 (HC).
4 (Unreported) 13 September 1996 (HC).
5 [1998] 3 IR 570. See also *Re Advanced Technology College Ltd* (1997) 4 CLP 126.
6 Originally enunciated by Lardner J in the High Court hearing of *Re Atlantic Magnetics Ltd*, and later widened by Finlay CJ in the Supreme Court.
7 First Report.

In *Re Tuskar Resources plc,*[1] McCracken J decided that the court cannot appoint an examiner to a purely holding company, because it has no undertaking to continue as a going concern.

Independent accountant's report

45.3 Section 7 of the 1999 Act also makes provision for the presentation of a pre-petition report in relation to the company. As a result, it will be necessary to furnish a report prepared by an independent accountant on any application to court. This report will include, inter alia:

(1) a statement of affairs of the company showing its assets, debts and liabilities;
(2) a statement of opinion by the accountant that the company has a reasonable prospect of survival;
(3) details of the extent of the funding required to keep the company trading during the examinership period and the sources of that funding;
(4) a recommendation as to which debts incurred before the presentation of the petition should be paid during the course of examination; and
(5) such other matters as he thinks fit.

The independent accountant is required to be either the auditor of the company or a person who is qualified to be appointed as examiner of the company. In the *Tuskar Resources* case, it was noted that there might be circumstances where the appointment of the independent accountant as examiner would be undesirable.

Section 11 of the 1999 Act inserts a new s 3B in the 1990 Amendment Act, dealing with the supplying of copies of the independent accountant's report to interested parties.

Duty of petitioner to act in good faith

45.4 In order to make it less easy to obtain the protection of the court, s 13 of the 1999 Act inserts a new s 4A in the 1990 Amendment Act. The aim of s 4A is to impose a statutory duty of good faith on a petitioner. In future, therefore, a court will refuse to appoint an examiner if the petitioner[2] has:

(1) failed to disclose any material information; or
(2) failed to exercise utmost good faith.

In *Re Aston Colour Print Ltd,*[3] Kelly J had already made it clear that even though a petition was presented without mala fides, it must be properly presented to the court. Here, because a directors' resolution was invalid, the petition was struck out and the interim examiner discharged.

---

1 [2001] 5 ICLMD, (2001) 8 CLP 5 (HC).
2 Or independent accountant.
3 (1997) 4 CLP 125.

Creditors' right to be heard

45.5   Section 10 of the 1999 Act inserts a new s 3B into the 1990 Act.

Section 3B makes it clear that all creditors will have a right to be heard by the court before it makes a decision to appoint an examiner.

When a company is unable to pay its debts

45.6   In deciding whether to make an order under s 2, the court may also have regard to whether the company has sought from its creditors significant extensions of time for the payment of its debts, from which it could reasonably be inferred that the company was likely to be unable to pay its debts.

A company will be deemed to be unable to pay its debts if:

(1) it is unable to pay its debts as they fall due;
(2) the value of its assets is less than the amount of its liabilities, taking into account its contingent and prospective liabilities; or
(3) s 214(a) or (b) of the 1963 Act applies to the company – see Chapter 49.

For example, during February 1997, an interim examiner (see **45.9**) was appointed over Bell Lines. In the petition to appoint him, the court was informed that the company had a surplus of assets over liabilities of £8 million. However, without access to further working capital which it required, the company was in a position where it was likely that it would be unable to pay its debts as they fell due. Nevertheless, it was felt that Bell Lines was capable of surviving as a going concern.

The court appointed the interim examiner to facilitate the orderly re-structuring of the company.

Related companies

45.7   Where the court appoints an examiner to a company, it may, at the same or any time thereafter, make an order:

(1) appointing the examiner to be examiner to a related company; or
(2) conferring on the examiner, in relation to such company, all or any of the powers or duties conferred on him in relation to the original company.

Section 4(5) of the 1990 Amendment Act stipulates that a company will be related to another company if:

(1) that other company[1] is its holding company or subsidiary; or
(2) more than half in nominal value of its equity share capital is held by the other company and companies related to that other company; or
(3) more than half in nominal value of the equity share capital of each of them is held by members of the other; or

---

1 Which must be an Irish registered company – see the *Tuskar Resources* case; the definition excludes overseas companies.

(4) that other company or companies related to that other company are entitled to control the exercise of more than one half of the voting power at any general meeting of the company; or

(5) the businesses of the companies have been so carried on that the separate business of each company, or a substantial part thereof, is not readily identifiable; or

(6) if there is another corporate body to which both companies are related.

45.8 Before deciding to appoint the examiner to a related company, the court will have regard to whether the making of the order would be likely to facilitate the survival of the company, or of the related company, or both (see **45.2**).

A related company to which an examiner is appointed will also be deemed to be under the protection of the court for the period beginning on the date of the making of an order and continuing for the period during which the company to which it is related is under protection.

Where an examiner is appointed to two or more related companies, he will have the same powers and duties in relation to each company, taken separately, unless the court directs otherwise.

Interim examiner and interim protection

45.9 The court has the power, if it considers it necessary, to appoint an interim examiner pending an adjourned hearing of a petition.

Section 9 of the 1999 Act inserts an additional s 3A(1) to (8) in the 1990 Act. Section 3A of the amended 1990 Act, makes provision for interim protection pending the preparation of the independent accountant's report.

Under s 3A if, for exceptional circumstances outside the control of the petitioner, it is not possible to prepare the independent report, a company may still be put into court protection for a period not exceeding 10 days, pending preparation of the report. If a petition is presented by a creditor, the directors of the company will be obliged to co-operate with the creditor in the preparation of the report. Any liabilities incurred during this interim period cannot be certified as liabilities having special priority.

Security for costs

45.10 The court may refuse to hear a petition to appoint an examiner presented by a contingent or prospective creditor until such security for costs has been given as the court thinks reasonable, and until a prima facie case for the protection of the court has been established.

Examiner's liability for company contracts

45.11 The legal position of an examiner resembles that of a receiver. For example, under s 13(6), he is personally liable on any contract entered into by him in the performance of his duties (whether the contract is entered into by him in the name of the company or in his own name as examiner or otherwise) unless the contract provides that he is not to be personally liable on such contract.

Right to indemnity

45.12   Section 13(6) also provides that if the examiner does incur a personal liability for company contracts, he will be entitled to an indemnity in respect of that liability, out of the assets of the company.

Qualifications of an examiner

45.13   A person will only be qualified to act as an examiner of a company, if he is qualified to act as its liquidator – see **50.5**.

WHO CAN PETITION THE COURT?

45.14   Generally, the following[1] may petition the court to appoint an examiner:

(1) the company; or
(2) the directors of the company; or
(3) a creditor, or contingent or prospective creditor (including an employee), of the company; or
(4) members of the company holding, at the date of the presentation of a petition, not less than one-tenth of such of the paid-up capital of the company as carries at that date the right of voting at general meetings of the company; or
(5) by all or any of those parties, together, or separately.

The petition presented to the court must nominate a person to be appointed as examiner.[2]

The petition must also be accompanied:

(1) by a consent signed by the person nominated to be examiner; and
(2) if proposals for a compromise[3] or scheme of arrangement in relation to the company's affairs have been prepared for submission to interested parties for their approval, by a copy of the proposals.

Section 3 of the 1990 Amendment Act is revised by s 6 of the 1999 Act in respect of banks and other specified companies. Under the amended s 3, a petition to appoint an examiner may be presented generally only by the Central Bank alone, or the Central Bank and/or the other specified companies acting together.

---

1 See s 3 of the 1990 Amendment Act, as amended by s 180 of the 1990 Act.
2 Paragraphs (b) and (c) of s 3(3) were repealed by s 30 of the 1999 Act.
3 See Part X A.

Notification of examiner's appointment

45.15   Section 12, as amended by s 20 of the 1999 Act, deals with notification of examiners appointment. Section 12(1) prescribes that notice of the petition to appoint an examiner must be delivered in the appropriate form, *by the petitioner*, to the registrar of companies.

By the examiner

45.16   Section 12(2) imposes a duty on the examiner to immediately notify the public of:

(1) his appointment and the date thereof; and
(2) the date, if any, set for the hearing of the matters arising out of his report (see **46.2**).

The examiner must notify the public by publishing the notices in *Iris Oifigiúil* and in at least two local daily newspapers. The time limits for publishing these notices are:

(1) 21 days after his appointment, in the case of *Iris Oifigiúil*; and
(2) three days after this appointment, for the local daily newspapers. He must also send the registrar of companies a copy of the order appointing him within three days.

In letterheadings, etc

45.16A   Every invoice, order for goods or business letter issued by or on behalf of the company, being a document on or in which the name of the company appears, must immediately after the name, include the words 'in examination (under the Companies (Amendment) Act 1990)'.

Special court hearing

45.17   Section 21 of the 1999 Act inserted a new s 13A to the 1990 Amendment Act. Section 13A deals with the holding of a special court hearing following the discovery of irregularities in the report of the independent accountant, or otherwise.

The full procedures for such a hearing to be held, where there has been a substantial disappearance of company property or other serious irregularities in relation to the company's officers, are detailed in s 13A(1) to (10).

Creditors are entitled to attend and be heard at such a special hearing.

CONSEQUENCES OF EXAMINERSHIP

45.18   Section 5(1) of the 1990 Amendment Act provided that for three months[1] after the presentation of the petition, the company was deemed to be under the protection of the court.

---

1 Or such extension as is permitted by s 18(3) and (4) of the 1990 Amendment Act.

Section 5, as amended by the 1999 Act, reduces the protection period from three months to 70 days. This reduced protection period is reasonable because the court will now, generally, have had the independent accountant's report available at the time of hearing the petition. This report will include an opinion on the prospect of the company's survival and on the funding of an examination period.

Company protections

45.19 When a company is deemed to be under the protection of the court, the immunities enjoyed by it under s 5(2) of the 1990 Act include:

(1) no proceedings for the winding up of the company may be commenced or resolution for winding up passed in relation to that company. Any resolution so passed shall be of no effect;

(2) no receiver over any part of the property or undertaking of the company may be appointed, or, if so appointed before the presentation of a petition shall, subject to s 6 (see **45.25**), be able to act;

(3) no attachment, sequestration, distress or execution can be put into force against the property or effects of the company, except with the consent of the examiner;

(4) where any claim against the company is secured by a charge on the whole or any part of the property, effects or income of the company, no action may be taken to realise the whole or any part of such security, except with the consent of the examiner;

(5) no steps may be taken to repossess goods in the company's possession under any hire-purchase agreement except with the consent of the examiner;

(6) where any person other than the company, such as a guarantor, is liable to pay all or any part of the debts of the company:

    (a) no attachment, sequestration, distress or execution can be put into force against the property or effects of such person in respect of the debts of the company; and

    (b) no proceedings of any sort may be commenced against such person in respect of the debts of the company;

(7) no order for relief against oppression will be made under s 205 of the 1963 Act against the company in respect of complaints as to the conduct of the affairs of the company or the exercise of the powers of the directors prior to the presentation of the petition;

(8) no set off between separate bank accounts of the company can be effected, except with the consent of the examiner.

45.20 The Company Law Review Group identified a number of problem areas arising out of these immunities. In particular, the areas of guarantees, pre-petition debts, set-offs and leased assets.

Guarantors

45.21   Section 5(2)(f) protects a guarantor of the company's debts, as well as the company itself, during the protection period. However, it has been affected by s 25 of the 1999 Act which implements the recommendations of the Company Law Review Group.

Section 25 of the 1999 Act inserts an additional s 25A(1) and (2) in s 25 of the 1990 Amendment Act.

Under s 25A of the 1990 Amendment Act, a company creditor can still take legal action against the guarantor after the examinership has ended. However, the guarantor will remain liable to the creditor for the full amount of the debt guaranteed, notwithstanding any write-down of it in a compromise or scheme of arrangement between the company and its creditors.

If the creditor does seek to enforce his rights against the guarantor, he must transfer to him any rights he has to vote at a meeting in respect of the proposals for the compromise or scheme of arrangement.

Pre-petition debts

45.22   While s 5 of the 1990 Act barred creditors from enforcing their rights for payment of debts against a company under the protection of the court, it did not affect the voluntary discharging of such debts by the company. The Company Law Review Group considered that such rights of voluntary payment of pre-petition debts could lead to serious abuses of creditors' rights.

The 1999 Act has introduced restrictions on payment of such debts; inserting a new s 5A(1) and (2) into the 1990 Amendment Act. Under s 5A(1), no voluntary payment may be made by the company during examinership, unless the report of the independent accountant recommended it. In addition, s 5A(2) grants the court the power to authorise the payment of pre-petition debts during the protection period, if it can be proved that a failure to discharge them, in whole or in part, would considerably reduce the prospects of the company surviving as a going concern.

Set off

45.23   The presentation of a petition will no longer restrict a banker's right to set off between separate bank accounts of the company, because s 5(2)(h) of the 1990 Act has been deleted.

Leased assets and creditors

45.24   The protection of creditors under leases was not specifically provided for in the 1990 Act. However, again following a recommendation of the Company Law Review Group, a section dealing with leases was included by the 1999 Act. This is s 26 which inserts a new s 25B(1) to (4) in the 1990 Act.

Under the new s 25B, certain lessors[1] cannot be compelled (in a scheme of arrangement)[2] to accept a reduction in any rent falling due following the completion of the examinership process. Arrears of rent arising during, or prior to the protection period, may be part of a scheme of arrangement.

Section 25B(3) makes it clear that the lessor or owner of property concerned may waive these post-examination rights, provided their consent is evidenced in writing.

Receivers

45.25   Section 6(1) of the Act clarifies the effect of the appointment of an examiner on an existing receivership.[3]

Provisional liquidators

45.26   Where an examiner is appointed to a company and a provisional liquidator stands appointed to that company, the court may make such order as it thinks fit, including an order as to any or all of the following matters:

(1) that the provisional liquidator be appointed as examiner of the company;
(2) appointing some other person as examiner of the company;
(3) that the provisional liquidator shall cease to act as such from the date specified by the court;
(4) directing the provisional liquidator to deliver all books, papers and other records, which relate to the property or undertaking of the company or any part thereof and are in his possession or control, to the examiner within a period to be specified by the court;
(5) directing the provisional liquidator to give the examiner full particulars of all his dealings with the property or undertaking of the company.

POWERS OF EXAMINER

45.27   Sections 7 and 8 of the 1990 Amendment Act deal specifically with the powers of an examiner.

Essentially, s 7 confers on an examiner the powers and rights of an auditor of the company. An examiner may seek the production of documents and evidence, without reference to the court. He may also attend meetings, convene and chair board meetings, and take appropriate remedial action if he discovers detrimental conduct (see **45.33**) by the company or its agents. He may certify expenses and apply to the court for specific directions.

With the consent of the court, an examiner may also be empowered to:

---

1 Ie of land or of a substantial lease – see s 25B(4).
2 Or in a compromise.
3 See **43.23**.

(1) deal with company property that is subject to a charge;
(2) seek a transfer of the directors' powers. These would include their power to borrow on the company's behalf.

Murphy J clarified the powers of the examiner over directors in *Re Edenpark Construction Ltd.*[1] He stated:

'in the absence of some particular order of the High Court, the examiner may not usurp the functions of the board of directors ... and it is the board or its officials who will continue to manage the business of the company during the period of protection and the continuance of the examinership.'

Further powers of the court over company management

45.28 If the examiner finds:

(1) that the affairs of the company are being conducted, or are likely to be conducted, in a manner which is calculated or likely to prejudice the interests of the company or of its employees or of its creditors as a whole; or
(2) that it is expedient, for the purpose of preserving the assets or of safeguarding the interests of the company or its employees or its creditors as a whole, that the carrying on of the business of the company by its directors or management should be curtailed or regulated in any particular respect; or
(3) that the company, or its directors, have resolved that such an order should be sought; or
(4) any other matter in relation to the company the court thinks relevant,

he may apply to the court. The court may then, if it considers it is just and equitable to do so, make an order under s 9 that all or any of the functions or powers which are vested in or exercisable by the directors shall be performable or exercisable only by the examiner. Such an order may provide that the examiner shall have all or any of the powers that he would have if he were a liquidator appointed by the court in respect of the company.

Seeking the production of documents and evidence

45.29 Officers and agents of the company are under a duty by s 8 to produce for the examiner all books and documents which are in their custody or power, to attend before him when required and otherwise to give to him all assistance in connection with his functions which they are reasonably able to give.

If the examiner considers that a person, other than an officer or agent, may be in possession of any information, he may require that person to produce any books or documents in his custody or power relating to the company, to attend before him and otherwise to give to him all assistance which he is reasonably able to give.

---

1 (Unreported) 17 December 1993 (HC).

Examination on oath

45.30 An examiner may examine, on oath, officers, agents or any other persons, in relation to the company's affairs. He may also:

(1) administer an oath; and
(2) reduce the answer of such persons to writing, and require their signatures of them.

Any person who refuses to produce books, etc when requested to do so by the examiner, will be liable to punishment as if he had been guilty of contempt of court.

'Agents' include bankers, solicitors and auditors of the company.

Directors' statement of affairs

45.31 Within seven days of the appointment of an examiner, the directors had to submit[1] to him a statement of affairs of the company. However, this requirement in s 14 of the 1990 Act was repealed by s 30 of the 1999 Act.

Meetings

45.32 An examiner is entitled to reasonable notice of, to attend and be heard at, all meetings of the board of directors of a company and all general meetings of the company to which he is appointed.

An examiner also has the power to convene, set the agenda for, and preside at meetings of the board of directors and general meetings of the company and to propose motions or resolutions and to give reports to such meetings.

Discovery of detrimental conduct

45.33 Section 8(3) gives an examiner power to require a director to produce for him all documents in the director's possession or control, relating to an unauthorised bank account. An unauthorised bank account is one into or out of which there has been paid:

(1) any money which has resulted from or been used in the financing of any transaction, arrangement or agreement, particulars of which have not been disclosed in the accounts of any company as required by law; or
(2) any money which has been in any way connected with any act or omission which, on the part of that director, constituted misconduct (whether fraudulent or not) towards that company or its investors.

The powers of an examiner to compel the production of books and documents under s 8(5) and 8(5A) of the 1990 Act were amended by s 19 of the 1999 Act. Section 19 substitutes two new subsections 8(5) and 8(5A).

Under s 8(5) and (5A), the examiner may certify refusal of a person to co-operate to the court, whose wide discretion is spelled out in s 8(5A).

---

1 Section 14(1).

Remedies

45.34 Section 7(5) gives the examiner full power to take whatever steps are necessary to halt, prevent or rectify any detrimental conduct by the company's officers, employees, investors or creditors. This can include avoidance of some company contracts – see **45.37**.

Certification of expenses

45.35 Section 29(2) provides that, unless the court otherwise orders, the remuneration, costs and expenses of an examiner shall be paid and the examiner shall be entitled to be indemnified in respect of them out of the revenue of the business of the company or the proceeds of realisation of its assets (including investments).

Whilst an examiner, insofar as is reasonably possible, should make use of the staff and services of the company, he may, if necessary, appoint or employ persons to assist him.

Section 10(1) makes it clear that any liabilities incurred during the 'protection period'[1] will be treated as expenses properly incurred for the purpose of s 29. Such liabilities are those certified by the examiner, to have been incurred in circumstances where, in the opinion of the examiner, the survival of the company as a going concern during the protection period would otherwise have been seriously prejudiced.

45.36 In *Re Edenpark Construction Ltd*, (see **45.27**) Murphy J only took into account liabilities incurred by the company after the appointment of the examiner. He excluded any costs arising out of the presentation of the petition to appoint the examiner. The result of this judgment was a reduction of 20 per cent in the fees presented by the examiner.

Sections 10 and 29 were also considered by the Supreme Court in *Re Don Bluth Entertainment Ltd and Related Companies*.[2] Here, it was held that certified expenses, properly incurred by an examiner under ss 29 or 10, rank in priority to both unsecured and secured creditors – but see **45.40**.

Cancellation of company contracts

45.37 Section 7(5) of the 1990 Amendment Act empowers an examiner to repudiate or rectify any act, course of conduct or contract which, in his opinion, was likely to be to the detriment of the company.

In *Re Holidair Ltd*,[3] secured creditors pleaded that, as the company was prohibited from borrowing without the permission of the debenture-holder because of a negative pledge clause, an examiner was similarly bound. The

---

1 Ie the time the company is under the protection of the court.
2 *The Irish Times Law Reports*, 4 July 1994.
3 [1994] I IR 416, 1 ILRM 481.

court decided against the creditors, and held that the examiner had the power under s 7(5) to halt, prevent or rectify the negative pledge clause, because its enforcement was 'likely to be to the detriment of the company, notwithstanding that the debenture was registered by the company prior to the company's examinership' (and, indeed, the 1990 Act itself).

The Review Group was concerned that s 7(5), as interpreted in the *Holidair Ltd* case, 'clearly undermines the reliability of contracts entered into with Irish companies'. To overcome this problem, the Group recommended that s 7(5) powers be limited to contracts entered into during the course of its examination only.

Section 18[1] of the 1999 Act reforms s 7(5) of the 1990 Act by inserting subsections 7(5A), 7(5B) and 7(5C).

Section 7(5A) now makes it clear that an examiner will not be entitled to repudiate a contract which has been entered into by the company prior to the period of protection by the court.

However, under s 7(5B) and (5C), if the examiner serves a notice on a party to a contract with the company that a certain provision would be likely to prejudice the survival of the company, such a provision will have no effect. These special provisions are restrictions upon the company:

(1) to borrow monies or otherwise obtain credit; or
(2) to create or permit to subsist any mortgage, charge, lien or other encumbrance over the company's property.

Now, as a result of the amendments to s 7(5) of the 1990 Act by s 18 of the 1999 Act, with the exception of certain negative pledges,[2] only contracts entered into during the examinership period can be repudiated by the examiner.

Applications to the court for directions

45.38   Sections 7(6) and (7) and 13(7) make provision for questions arising in the course of the examinership to be determined by application to the court.

Power to deal with charged property

45.39   Section 11(1) empowers the examiner, with the approval of the court, to dispose of property already secured by a floating charge. However, the court will have to be satisfied that the exercise of his power by the examiner is likely to facilitate the survival of the company, or any part of it, as a going concern, before it authorises him to take priority over the floating charge.[3]

---

1 Section 18 does not amend s 20 of the 1990 Act, which related to cancellation of contracts in particular circumstances.
2 By continuing to allow an examiner to repudiate pre-examinership negative pledges, s 18 of the 1999 Act permits the examiner to borrow in order to rescue the company under protection.
3 See s 11(1) and (3).

Fixed charge and mortgage holders, and the owners of goods held under a hire-purchase agreement, are dealt with in s 11(2) and (4). In these cases, if property or goods are sold by the examiner, the court can determine the open market value of the company asset sold, and order the company to make good any deficiency in price to the holder of the security.

The right to seek a transfer of the directors' powers

45.40   As mentioned above, s 9 gives the court further powers to transfer 'all or any' of the directors' powers to the examiner. These powers include the right to borrow money on the company's behalf. The court may, when sanctioning the transfer of directors' borrowing powers, also order that such borrowings may be certified as 'expenses' of the examinership under s 10. If this is done, it will give a 'certified lender' priority over earlier secured creditors.

EFFECT OF EXAMINERSHIP ON CREDITORS' RIGHTS

45.41   The whole purpose of the examinership process is to give the company temporary protection against creditors exercising their legal rights and remedies against the company's assets.

The effects of the appointment of an examiner on a receiver have already been outlined (see **43.23**). Let us now consider the individual positions of the various types of creditors.

Costs of examinership paramount

45.42   Section 29(3) gives first priority to the remuneration, costs and expenses of an examiner which have been sanctioned by order of the court. Such costs must be paid in full before any other claim, secured or unsecured, under any compromise or scheme of arrangement or in any receivership or winding up of the company.

In *Re Atlantic Magnetics Ltd,*[1] the Supreme Court held that the costs[2] of examinership take priority over fixed, as well as floating charges.

In *Re Springline,*[3] the High Court held that, notwithstanding s 29(3), an examiner's remuneration and costs do not have priority over those of an official liquidator. This decision was reversed in the Supreme Court.[4] As a result, the examiner's remuneration etc under s 29 takes priority over that of the official liquidator, where the company under court protection is subsequently wound up.

---

1   [1993] 2 IR 561.
2   Incurred under ss 29 and 10 – see the *Don Bluth* case (at **45.36**). They also take priority over the rights of fixed charge holders, etc, in s 11(2) and (4).
3   *The Irish Times Law Reports,* 22 December 1997, [1998] 1 ILRM 301 (HC).
4   *The Irish Times Law Reports,* 17 August 1998, [1999] 1 IR 478 (SC), [1999] 1 ILRM 15.

The Supreme Court decision in *Re Springline* has found statutory expression in s 28 of the 1999 Act, which adds s 29(3A) and 29(3B) to the 1990 Act.

Secured creditors

45.43 Section 5(2)(d) provides that a secured creditor can take no action to realise the whole or any part of the charged assets, except with the consent of the examiner.

In *Re Holidair Ltd*,[1] a bank's instruction to the borrowing company to lodge the proceeds of its book debts into a designated bank account after an examiner was appointed, was held to be a breach of s 5(2)(d).

This Supreme Court judgment also suggests that floating charges which have crystallised, will de-crystallise on the appointment of an examiner, and that an examiner can ignore a negative pledge clause.

Where an examiner is given the power to borrow money and to certify such borrowings as 'expenses' under s 10, these expenses will rank before earlier secured creditors, whether fixed or floating. Because of this threat to their underlying security, secured lenders in the United Meat Packers examinership[2] refused to lend further monies to the company to enable it to survive during the protection period. As a result, the examiner was unable to facilitate the continued survival of the company. This, in turn, led to a withdrawal of the court's protection for the company.

The idea behind s 10 was to guarantee payment to suppliers and employees for goods and services provided during the examination process. However, the effect of s 29 was to give such unsecured creditors priority over examinership secured creditors.

The Company Law Review Group identified this anomalous position and proposed that expenses under s 10 should rank after fixed, but before floating, charges. Section 28 of the 1999 Act introduces such a change into the law by inserting new subsections (3A) and (3B) into s 29 of the 1990 Act.

Unsecured creditors

45.44 Unsecured creditors' remedies of petitioning for the winding up of the company or initiating legal proceedings against it to obtain judgment for its debt, cannot[3] be utilised while the company is under the protection of the court.

---

1 [1994] 1 ILRM 481.
2 (Unreported) 2 March 1992 (HC); 13 March 1992 (SC).
3 See s 5(2) and (3) of the 1990 Amendment Act.

Chapter 46

THE EXAMINER'S REPORT AND THE FUTURE OF THE COMPANY

46.1 The duties of an examiner detailed in ss 14, 15, 16 and 17 of the 1990 Act have all been replaced by s 30 of the 1999 Act.

FORMULATING A RESCUE PACKAGE

46.2 Section 22 of the 1999 Act now takes into account the existence of the independent accountant's report, and changes s 18 of the 1990 Act. Under the amended s 18(1) to (9), the examiner's duty on appointment is, first and foremost, to formulate proposals for a compromise or scheme of arrangement and to report back to the court within 35 days (or such longer period as the court may allow – which might mean an extension for another 30 days). In addition, this period can be further extended where time is required by the court to make a decision regarding the confirmation hearing on the proposals for a scheme.

An examiner must also carry out such other duties as the court may direct.

STATUTORY MEETINGS

46.3 Under s 18(2), the examiner must convene and preside at such meetings of the members and creditors as he thinks proper for the purposes of s 23 (see **46.10**).

EXAMINER'S REPORT

46.4 Having discussed his proposals with the members and creditors, the examiner submits his report to the court within the statutory time limits.

Contents of examiner's report

46.5 An examiner's report under s 18 must include the following details:[1]

(1) the proposals placed before the required meetings;
(2) any modification of those proposals adopted at any of those meetings;
(3) the outcome of each of the required meetings;
(4) the recommendation of the committee of creditors, if any;

---

1 Section 19.

(5) a statement of the assets and liabilities of the company as at the date of his report;

(6) a list of the creditors of the company, the amount owing to each creditor, the nature and value of any security held by any such creditor, and the priority status of preferential creditors;

(7) a list of the officers of the company;

(8) his recommendations;

(9) such other matters as the examiner deems appropriate or the court directs.

Copies of the report must be delivered to the company, and other interested parties, on receipt of their written request.[1]

Avoidance of certain company contracts

46.6 Where a compromise or scheme of arrangement is being devised by the examiner as a 'rescue package', the company may, subject to the approval of the court under s 20, affirm or repudiate any contract under which some element of performance, other than the payment of money, remains outstanding either by the company or the other contracting party.

Any contracting party who suffers loss or damage as a result of such avoidance under s 20(1) will be deemed to be an unsecured creditor for the value of his loss or damage.

The proposed rescue package

46.7 Section 22 sets out the requirements in relation to an examiner's proposals to 'rescue' the company. Proposals for a compromise or scheme of arrangement must:

(1) specify each class[2] of members and creditors of the company;

(2) specify any class of members and creditors whose interests or claims will not be impaired by the proposals;

(3) specify any class of members and creditors whose interests or claims will be impaired by the proposals;

(4) provide equal treatment for each claim or interest of a particular class unless the holder of a particular claim or interest agrees to less favourable treatment;

(5) provide for the implementation of the proposals;

(6) if the examiner considers it necessary or desirable to do so to facilitate the survival of the company as a going concern, specify whatever changes should be made in relation to the management or direction of the company, or in the memorandum or articles of the company;

---

1 Section 18(5). See also s 18(6)–(8).

2 Ie 'those persons whose rights are not so dissimilar as to make it impossible for them to consult together with a view to their common interest' per Bowen LJ in *Re Sovereign Life Assurance v Dodd* [1892] 2 QB 573.

(7) include such other matters as he thinks appropriate.

A statement of the assets and liabilities of the company at the date of the proposals must be attached. There must also be attached a description of the financial outcome of a winding up of the company for each class of members and creditors.

Impairment

46.8 A creditor's claim against the company will be impaired if he receives less in payment than the full amount due to him on the appointment of the examiner.

In *Re Jetmara Teo*,[1] it was held that where the creditors claim is to be paid in full, but only by means of instalments, that claim will be deemed to be impaired for the purposes of s 24(2)(c) of the 1990 Amendment Act. Section 24(2) gives an impaired creditor the right to be heard by the court when the examiner presents his proposals to it for confirmation (see **46.12**).

A member's interest in the company is impaired if:

(1) the nominal value of his shareholding in the company is reduced;
(2) he is entitled to a fixed dividend in respect of his shareholding in the company, and the amount of that dividend is reduced;
(3) he is deprived of all or any part of the rights accruing to him by virtue of his shareholding in the company;
(4) his percentage interest in the total issued share capital of the company is reduced; or
(5) he is deprived of his shareholding in the company.

Committee of creditors

46.9 Under s 21, an examiner may, and if so directed by the court, must, appoint a committee of creditors to assist him in the performance of his functions.

The committee of creditors must consist of not more than five members, including the holders of the three largest unsecured claims who are willing to serve.

The examiner will have to provide the committee with a copy of any rescue proposals. The committee may express an opinion on the proposals on its own behalf or on behalf of the creditors or classes of creditors whom it represents.

When the examiner has put together his proposed rescue package, he must call a meeting of all members and creditors to consider it.

---

1 (Unreported) 10 May 1991 (HC).

Plenary meetings

46.10   At plenary meetings of members and creditors summoned under s 23,[1] the examiner's proposals can be modified, but only with his consent.

Proposals will be deemed to have been accepted by a meeting of members, or of a class of members, if a majority of the votes validly cast at that meeting, whether in person or by proxy, are cast in favour of the resolution for the proposals.

The examiner's proposals shall be deemed to have been accepted by a meeting of creditors or of a class of creditors when a majority in number representing a majority in value of the claims represented at that meeting have voted, either in person or by proxy, in favour of the resolution for the proposals.

Confirmation by the court

46.11   Section 24 makes it necessary for the examiner to present his proposals for a compromise or scheme of arrangement to the court for its confirmation. The court can confirm these proposals, or approve them subject to modification. It may also refuse to approve them.

The criteria to be applied by the court were considered in *Re Wogan's (Drogheda) Ltd (No 2)*[2] and *Re Goodman International.*[3] They include the finding of defects, such as the right of a proposed investor to withdraw unilaterally from the scheme at any time.

The court will not confirm any proposals unless:

(1)   it can be shown that at least one class of members and one class of creditors whose interests or claims would be impaired by implementation of the proposals have accepted the proposals; or
(2)   the proposals are fair and equitable in relation to any class of members or creditors that has not accepted the proposals and whose interests or claims would be impaired by implementation; and
(3)   the proposals are not unfairly prejudicial to the interests of any interested party.

The court will also refuse to confirm the proposals if their primary purpose is the avoidance of payment of tax due or if they would favour the creditors or members of a related company.

Objections

46.12   At the court hearing to consider the examiner's proposals, any member or creditor who claims that his rights would be impaired, may object to confirmation of the rescue package by the court on the grounds set out in s 25. These grounds are:

1   Procedural matters are detailed in s 23(4A)–(9).
2   (Unreported) 7 May 1992 (HC).
3   (Unreported) 28 January 1991 (HC).

(1) irregularities in or at the plenary meetings of members or creditors;

(2) that acceptance of the proposals by the meeting was obtained by improper means;

(3) that the proposals were put forward for an improper purpose;

(4) that the proposals unfairly prejudice the interests of the objector(s).

If the court upholds such an objection, it may order that the decision in question be set aside. The court may then order that another plenary meeting be convened.

Special provisions were introduced in 1999 with respect to guarantees and leases – see **45.21** and **45.24**.

Court's decision

46.13 Once the court confirms the examiner's proposals, they become binding on all creditors and members, and on the company.

If the court refuses to confirm the proposed rescue package, it may order the winding up of the company or make any other order it deems fit.

Revocation on grounds of fraud

46.14 Section 27 entitles the company, or any interested party, within 180 days after the confirmation of the proposals by the court, to apply to the court for revocation of confirmation on the grounds that it was procured by fraud. The court, if satisfied that such was the case, may revoke the confirmation on such terms and conditions as it thinks fit.[1]

CESSATION OF PROTECTION ORDER

46.15 When a compromise or scheme of arrangement confirmed by the court comes into effect, the protection of the court for the company will cease. So, too, will the examiner's appointment – see s 26.

WHEN A RESCUE FAILS

46.16 Under s 18(9), if the examiner is unable to formulate proposals for a rescue package, he may apply to the court for a grant of directions in the matter. The court may make such order as it thinks fit, including, if it considers it just and equitable to do so, an order for the winding up of the company.

Similarly, at a court hearing under s 24 (see **46.11**), the court may also order the winding up of the company – see s 24(11).

---

1 Section 27(2) provides for delivery of a copy of such order to the registrar of companies and others.

PART X A

FINANCIAL ARRANGEMENTS AND RESTRUCTURING; CHANGE(S) IN COMPANY OWNERSHIP

Chapter 47

FINANCIAL ARRANGEMENTS BETWEEN THE COMPANY, ITS CREDITORS AND MEMBERS

PAYMENT OF OUTSTANDING COMPANY DEBTS

47.1 In Part IX, we looked at a recent legal development which permits a company to protect itself against its creditors by petitioning the court to appoint an examiner; an official who, if he considers the company could be saved as a going concern, is entitled to place a financial rescue package for the company before the court, for its approval. In this way, a company could be maintained as a going concern by coming to a compromise or arrangement with its creditors, in respect of their debts.

Apart from examinership, s 201 of the 1963 Act also facilitates a company coming to an arrangement with its creditors over payment of outstanding company debts.

SECTION 201 SCHEMES OF ARRANGEMENT AND COMPROMISES

47.2 An arrangement can be defined as a scheme drawn up by a company to offer ways of paying its debts so as to avoid winding up proceedings.

Section 201 makes provision for the court to sanction a proposed compromise or arrangement between a company and its members and/or creditors.

In *Re Savoy Hotel Ltd*,[1] the court made it clear that it would not approve a proposed arrangement unless it was supported by the company itself.

In *Re National Farmers Union (NFU) Development Trust*,[2] over 85 per cent of the members voted in favour of a scheme in which their rights were surrendered without compensation. The court held that the scheme was neither a compromise nor an arrangement, because both these processes required a measure of 'give and take' from both sides.

A compromise is, essentially, an agreement between two sides, where each gives way a little to settle a dispute. A compromise can only be reached when the parties had previously been in dispute. An arrangement does not require the existence of a prior dispute. In fact, s 201(7) defines an 'arrangement' as including a reorganisation of the share capital of the company by the consolidation of shares of different classes or by the division of shares into shares of different classes or by both those methods.

---

1 [1981] 3 All ER 646.
2 [1973] 1 All ER 135.

Who may apply to the court?

47.3 The company itself, or any creditor[1] or member of the company may apply to the court to sanction a proposed arrangement under s 201. However, creditors or members may need, at least, the approval of the company if they wish to apply to the court on their own – see *NFU Development Trust* case (in **47.2**).

The applicant(s) will submit a document to the court detailing the terms of the scheme, and enclosing a copy of the explanatory statement to be issued to members and creditors before the appropriate meeting(s) (see **47.4**). On receipt of this application, the court may, on such terms as seems just, stay all proceedings against the company for as long as it thinks fit.

When the application is successful, the court will order the holding of meetings between the interested parties to discuss the proposed scheme of arrangement.

The statutory meetings

47.4 Section 201(1) stipulates that the court may:

'order a meeting of the creditors or class of creditors, or of the members of the company or class of members, as the case may be, to be summoned in such manner as the court directs.'

In fact, the court will not approve[2] a scheme, unless proper class meetings have been held.

Class meetings

47.5 All unsecured creditors will generally form a single class unless some of them are to be treated differently from the rest. In such circumstances, separate class meetings will have to be held.

In *Pye (Ireland) Ltd,*[3] a substantial unsecured creditor was also a substantial shareholder. Because there was not a separate class meeting held for unsecured creditors who were also shareholders, the court refused to sanction the scheme.

Information for members and creditors

47.6 Every notice summoning the relevant meeting(s) which is sent to a creditor or member, must also include a statement[4] explaining the effect of the arrangement; in particular, stating any material interests of the directors of the company, whether as directors or as members or as creditors of the company or otherwise, and the effect on them of the compromise.

---

1 Or liquidator when the company is being wound up.
2 *Re Hellenic & General Trust Ltd* [1975] 3 All ER 382.
3 (Unreported) 11 March 1985 (HC).
4 Section 202(1)(b) and (3) also provide for the disclosure and notification of certain information in advertisements.

This statement must also disclose whether the directors are being treated differently to other persons holding similar interests.

Where the proposed compromise affects the rights of debenture-holders of a company, the statement must give the same explanation in relation to the trustees of any deed for securing the issue of the debentures as it is required to give in relation to the company's directors.[1]

Approval of members and creditors

47.7 After the holding of the required meetings and class meetings, the scheme will need to obtain the support of interested parties before being sent to the court for its approval.

The scheme must be approved by:

(1) a majority in number of those voting at each meeting of:
    (a) creditors; or
    (b) class of creditors; or
    (c) members; or
    (d) class of members; and
(2) who represent 75 per cent in value of the relevant shares or amounts owed.

When these approvals have been obtained, a further application is made to the court for its approval of the scheme.

COURT SANCTION OF SCHEME

47.8 The detailed scheme and the responses of the interested parties will be considered by the court. Even if a class of members does not vote in favour, the court may still sanction the scheme if it is satisfied that one class, eg ordinary shareholders, has no interest whatever in the remaining company assets.[2]

Once the court sanctions the arrangement, it then becomes binding on all interested parties. However, as Murnaghan J stated in *Re John Power & Sons Ltd:*[3]

> 'the sanction to be given by the court must be a real sanction ... no majority ... can carry an arrangement which a fair and impartial mind would not sanction.'

In *Re Ocean Steam Navigation Co Ltd*,[4] Simonds J made it clear that the court would only sanction a scheme if it was intra vires the company's objects.

Objections by minorities

47.9 While the scheme is being considered, s 203(1)(e) empowers the court to make provision for dissenting minorities.

---

1 Section 202(2).
2 As happened in *Tea Corporation Ltd; Sorsbie v Tea Corporation Ltd* [1904] 1 Ch 12 (CA).
3 [1934] IR 412.
4 [1939] Ch 41.

AMALGAMATIONS

47.10 An amalgamation is where two or more companies join together to form a single new company.

Section 203 also makes it clear that the court can, if necessary, also approve a scheme for the reconstruction or amalgamation of any two or more companies whilst considering a proposal under s 201. In this event, the court order may provide for any of the following:

(1) the transfer to a new 'transferee' company of the whole or any part of the undertaking and of the property or liabilities of any 'transferor' company;
(2) the allotting or appropriation by the transferee company of any shares, debentures, or other like interests in that company[1];
(3) the continuation by or against the transferee company of any legal proceedings pending, by or against any transferor company;
(4) the dissolution, without winding up, of any transferor company;
(5) such incidental, consequential and supplemental matters as are necessary to secure that the reconstruction or amalgamation will be fully and effectively carried out.

Registration of the court order

47.11 The approval of the court for either a scheme of arrangement or amalgamation will not take effect until an office copy of its order has been delivered to the registrar of companies.

A copy of the court order must also be attached to every copy of the memorandum of association issued after the order was made.

USES FOR SCHEMES OF ARRANGEMENT

47.12 A scheme of arrangement is a useful instrument for making changes to the rights of members and creditors in the light of a company's financial difficulties. For example, it has been used to vary the rights attached to debentures and preference shares, and to reconstruct the capital of a company. However, the court will not permit the s 201 procedure to be used to circumvent the safeguards for minority interests available generally,[2] where there is a reduction of capital or a variation of class rights.

The usefulness of s 201 schemes of arrangement has diminished as a result of the examinership procedures detailed in Chapters 45 and 46.

---

1 Which under the arrangement are to be allotted or appropriated by the transferee company 'to or for any person' – see s 203(1)(b).
2 See Chapter 19.

Reconstructions

47.13 A reconstruction of a company takes place when it restructures its finances by transferring its assets to a new company. The s 201 procedure can also be used[1] to facilitate reconstruction and amalgamation of companies.

Where the scheme provides for the transfer of company assets to a new company, with little other change, this process is often referred to as 'reconstruction'. For example, in addition to effecting compromises or arrangements with creditors and members,[2] ss 201 and 203 will permit the transferring of their rights to another transferee company which then issues shares or takes over liabilities in return for the cancellation of existing rights against the first company. Section 260 provides for reconstruction, where the first company is already in voluntary liquidation (see **47.15**).

Amalgamations

47.14 Sections 201 and 203 can also be used to amalgamate two companies as an alternative to a takeover under s 204.[3] In *Re Hellenic & General Trust Ltd*,[4] the court would not permit a scheme of arrangement to circumvent provisions similar to those in s 204, which were designed to protect dissenting members from having their shares compulsorily acquired.

Similarly, where a scheme involves a reconstruction which could have been effected under s 260, the court will only sanction it if any dissenting shareholders are given the same protection[5] as detailed in **47.18**.

RECONSTRUCTIONS UNDER SECTION 260

47.15 Section 260 of the 1963 Act gives the liquidator, in a members' voluntary winding up situation, the power to sell the 'whole or part of' the business or property of a company, and to accept shares in the transferee company, as consideration for that sale. In fact, s 260(1) stipulates that the liquidator may enter into:

> 'any other arrangement whereby the members of the transferor company may, in lieu of receiving cash, shares, policies or other like interests, or in addition thereto, participate in the profits of or receive any other benefit from the transferee company.'

---

1 Under s 203.
2 By changing their rights in or against the company.
3 In this event, the Mergers, Takeovers and Monopolies (Control) Act 1978 may also apply – see s 14 and Chapter 48.
4 [1975] 3 All ER 382.
5 See *Re Anglo-Continental Supply Co Ltd* [1922] 2 Ch 723.

Procedure

47.16 Under s 260, if a company is being, or is proposed to be, wound up voluntarily, and its property intended to be transferred or sold to another company, the liquidator of the first company (the transferor company) may, with the sanction of a *special resolution* of that company, receive in compensation for the transfer or sale, 'shares, policies or other like interests in the transferee company, for distribution among the members of the transferor company'.

Any sale or arrangement under s 260(1) will be binding on the members of the transferor company.[1]

Effect of winding-up order

47.17 If an order is made within a year for the winding up of the company by the court, the special resolution becomes invalid unless sanctioned by the court.[2] This allows for the protection of creditors who might otherwise be prejudiced by the reconstruction.

Dissenting members' rights

47.18 If any member who did not vote for the special resolution expresses his dissent in writing, addressed to the liquidator, and leaves it at the registered office of the company within seven days after the passing of the special resolution, he may require the liquidator either:

(1) to abstain from carrying the resolution into effect; or
(2) to purchase his interest, 'at a price to be determined by agreement or by arbitration'.[3]

The arbitration procedure is that laid down in the Companies Clauses Consolidation Act 1845.[4]

If the liquidator elects to purchase the dissenting member's interest, the purchase money must be paid before the company is dissolved.[5]

A company cannot, by provisions in either its memorandum or articles of association, deprive dissenting shareholders of these rights.

SECTION 260 AND A CREDITORS' VOLUNTARY WINDING-UP

47.19 In a members' voluntary winding-up, the company is in a position to pay all its creditors in full. This is not the position, however, in a creditors'

---

1 Section 260(2).
2 Section 260(5).
3 Section 260(3).
4 Section 260(6).
5 Section 260(4).

voluntary winding-up. Because of this, s 271 stipulates that the liquidator cannot proceed with a s 260 reconstruction unless he also obtains the sanction of either the court or the creditors.[1]

AMALGAMATIONS GENERALLY

47.20   An amalgamation results in the joining together of two (or more) companies to form a single new company. As illustrated above, an amalgamation may be carried out under ss 201 to 203, as a scheme of arrangement with creditors, or under s 260 in the course of a voluntary liquidation.

A takeover or merger may also result in an amalgamation. However, in these cases, the reason for the takeover may have nothing to do with the creditors of the company. Takeovers often take place because the bidding company sees a company of profit-making potential and wishes to acquire a controlling interest in it. As takeovers and mergers are, essentially, changes of company ownership and control, rather than arrangements with company creditors, we shall deal with them separately in Chapter 48.

---

1 Through their representatives on the committee of inspection – see s 268.

Chapter 48

COMPANY TAKEOVERS AND MERGERS

INTRODUCTION

48.1 The term 'takeover' is usually used to describe a bid to purchase the majority or all of the shares in a 'target' company by another company.

If the bid is not contested, the transaction will be described as a merger. This would happen, for example, where a private company with few controlling shareholders 'agrees' to the proposed takeover. However, a takeover bid may be contested where one public company seeks to take over a second public company with a multiplicity of shareholders.

TAKEOVER PROCEDURE

48.2 Generally, the bidding company will offer to purchase all the shares in the target company either for cash or in exchange for its own shares. This offer will be conditional on acceptance by a stated percentage of the shareholders. When that percentage acceptance level has been reached, the offer becomes unconditional and binding on the acquiring company.

POWER TO COMPULSORILY ACQUIRE SHARES OF MINORITY

48.3 In some instances, a minority of shareholders in the target company may not wish to sell their shares. This could be problematic for a bidding company which wants to acquire a wholly owned subsidiary. In these circumstances, s 204 of the 1963 Act, gives the bidding company the power to acquire shares of dissenting members, when the bid has been accepted by a majority of 80 per cent.

In *Re Fitzwilton plc*,[1] the Supreme Court upheld Kelly J's High Court decision that s 204 does not require, for its applicability, that the holders of the 80 per cent majority of countable shares must be independent of, or disinterested in, the transferee company.

If, within four months, the offer of the bidding company is accepted by holders of not less than 80 per cent in value of the shares affected,[2] the bidding company may buy the shares of any dissenting member by giving him two months' notice after the end of the four-month period.

---

1 [2000] 2 ILRM 263.
2 Excluding those already held by the bidding company at the date of the offer – see s 204(2).

If the bidding company wishes to compulsorily acquire shares, under s 204(1), it must offer the dissenting minority the same terms as the majority have already accepted.[1]

Rights of dissentient members

48.4   Once a member has received notice from the bidding company that it wishes to compulsorily purchase his shares, he has the right to apply to the court, within one month, seeking an order disallowing the purchase.

Section 204(1) gives the court power to disallow the compulsory purchase if it thinks fit to do so. Generally, once the takeover bid is fair and the procedural requirements of s 204 have been followed, the court will be reluctant to grant relief[2] to the dissenting shareholder. In *Securities Trust Ltd v Associated Properties Ltd*,[3] it was suggested that the dissenting members should also have been given particulars of the takeover, including the method of carrying it out and its consequences. However, the onus remains on the dissenting shareholder to convince the court that the wishes of the majority should be overturned.[4]

Onus of proof

48.5   The burden of showing that the compulsory purchase of the dissentients' shares is unfair, lies on the applicant.[5] In *Re Sussex Brick Co*,[6] Vaisey J stated that it was difficult to 'predicate unfairness' where the good faith of the transferee company is not challenged, and there is no case of intentional misleading of the offeree shareholders. The fact that an applicant may be able to demonstrate that the takeover scheme is open to criticism or is capable of improvement, is not enough to discharge the onus of proof which lies on the applicant.[7]

In *Re Grierson, Oldham and Adams Ltd*,[8] the court held that the test of the fairness of an offer is not whether it is fair to the individual shareholder, but whether it is fair to the body of shareholders as a whole. In that case, where holders of 99 per cent of the shares had approved the scheme and the price was slightly above market value, it was held that there was no unfairness.

The market price of the shares on the Stock Exchange is cogent, but not conclusive, proof of the true value of shares.[9]

---

1 See *Re Carlton Holdings* [1971] 2 All ER 1082, [1971] 1 WLR 918.
2 *McCormick v Cameo Investments Ltd* [1978] 1 ILRM 191 (HC).
3 (Unreported) 19 November 1980 (HC).
4 See *Duggan v Stoneworth Investment Ltd* [2000] 1 IR 563.
5 *Re Hoare & Co Ltd* (1933) 150 LT 374.
6 [1961] 1 All ER 772.
7 Ibid.
8 [1967] 1 All ER 192.
9 Ibid.

Proving unfairness

48.6 Generally, the dissenting shareholders must establish affirmatively that, notwithstanding the view of the majority, the scheme is unfair. Thus, the onus is on an applicant to adduce evidence showing the takeover scheme to be patently and obviously unfair. This was done in the case of *Re Bugle Press Ltd.*[1]

In this case, a company had three shareholders. Two of these shareholders (A and B) each held 45 per cent of the shares: the third (C) 10 per cent. A and B formed a new company. This company then made an offer for the shares of the old company. A and B accepted the takeover bid. The new company then served notice[2] on C, who had dissented.

C opposed the compulsory purchase of his shares on the ground that it was an expropriation of his interest because the two shareholders of the new company were the persons who held 90 per cent of the shares in the old company. The Court of Appeal accepted C's evidence and held that the bidding company could not compulsorily acquire his shares, Harman J stating:

> 'In my judgment this is a barefaced attempt to evade that fundamental rule of company law which forbids the majority of shareholders, unless the articles so provide, to expropriate a minority. It would be all too simple if all one had to do was to form a £2 company and sell to it one's shares and then force the outsider to comply. If the point had been taken earlier, I, for one, should have been prepared to hold that this case never came within s 209 at all. Indeed, no serious attempt to comply with the section has ever been made here. ...
>
> [The applicant proves his case] ... quite simply by showing that the transferee company is nothing but a little hut built round his two co-shareholders and that the so-called scheme was made by themselves as directors of the company with themselves as shareholders and the whole thing, therefore, is seen to be a hollow sham. It is then for the company to show that nevertheless there is some good reason why the scheme should be allowed to go on. The company, whether because they do not wish to go into the witness-box and be cross examined or for some other reason, do not file any evidence at all ... There is in my judgment no case to answer. The applicant has only to shout and the walls of this Jericho fall flat. I am surprised that it was thought that so elementary a device would receive the court's approval ...'

Dissentients' opportunity to sell

48.7 Section 204(4) gives the dissentients an opportunity to sell their shares to the bidding company, even where that company does not wish to exercise its powers of compulsory purchase under s 204(1).

This offer to buy under s 204(4) must be on the same terms as the remaining 80 per cent were acquired.

---

1 [1960] 3 All ER 791 (CA).
2 Under s 209 of the Companies Act 1948, the UK equivalent of s 204.

LEGAL CONTROLS OVER PROFITEERING

48.8   Takeovers and mergers present an opportunity for directors and shareholders to make sizeable profits. Accordingly, there are a number of controls in place to prevent conflict of interest situations arising and secret profits being earned. These controls[1] include ss 187 and 188 of the 1963 Act which deal with compensation for loss of office by directors following a transfer of the company's shares, undertaking or property.

Compensation for loss of office on mergers, etc

48.9   Section 187 of the 1963 Act makes it necessary for directors to obtain the approval of the company in general meeting, for any payments of compensation to them for loss of office on the merger, takeover or amalgamation of the company.

Where a director receives such compensation without approval of the general meeting, he holds the amount received in trust for the company.

Section 188 contains provisions imposing a duty on directors to disclose payments to be made to them in connection with the transfer of shares, where the transfer involves an offer being made to the general body of shareholders. Where a director is in breach of s 188, he will be subject to a fine of £125. Any amounts received by him will be deemed as being held in trust for persons who sold their shares as a result of the offer.

The duty of directors in a takeover situation is considered in **24.6** et seq.

The City Code on Takeovers and Mergers

48.10   As mentioned in **48.1**, it is the prior agreement of the parties to an amalgamation of companies that distinguishes the process of merger from that of takeover. Mergers are usually the result of an agreed takeover bid, perhaps with the directors being involved in negotiations on behalf of the members.

In a takeover, there are likely to be unrepresented dissenting shareholders who may need protection.

In the case of a takeover bid for shares of public companies listed on the Stock Exchange, the City Code on Takeovers and Mergers applied. This non-statutory code of practice operated amongst investment banks and intermediaries.

---

1 The fiduciary duties of directors are also relevant – see Chapter 25. So, too, are the statutory rules on insider dealing detailed in **27.28** et seq. The statutory restrictions which prohibit a company from giving financial assistance for the purchase of its own shares could also prevent a company assisting a 'friendly' third party to out-bid the bidding companies. These restrictions are dealt with in Chapter 19.

The main purpose of the Code[1] was to ensure that, in a takeover bid, all shareholders were treated in the same way. Information given to them had to be adequate, accurate and made available to all shareholders concerned.

The operation of the Code was supervised by a panel, who could give rulings on disputed issues which arose in the course of takeover bids.

The City Code and s 204

48.11 The Code generally supplemented the statutory takeover rules in s 204 until the Irish Takeover Panel began exercising its functions on 1 July 1997.

THE IRISH TAKEOVER PANEL

48.12 The Irish Takeover Panel Act 1997 provides for the appointment of a Takeover Panel to monitor and supervise takeovers and certain other transactions in relation to securities, mainly in public companies quoted on the Irish Stock Exchange.

The designation of a Takeover Panel has two main objectives:

(1) to protect shareholders in situations where takeovers or other relevant transactions (eg substantial acquisitioning of shares) are contemplated and/or put into effect; and
(2) to provide support and credibility for the Irish financial market following the separation of the Irish Stock Exchange from London.

The Irish Panel published its takeover rules just prior to assuming its regulatory functions.

Whilst the 'voluntary' self-regulatory regime administered by the London Panel only applied to Irish listed companies, the statutory based rules of the Irish Panel will also apply to Irish companies quoted on the Exploration Securities or the Developing Companies Markets.[2]

'Takeover' is defined as an agreement or transaction whereby control of a company is, or may be, acquired. 'Control' means the holding, directly or indirectly, of securities of a company, which confers not less than 30 per cent of the voting rights in that company.

48.13 Under the 1997 Act,[3] the Panel has a general power to make appropriate rules. In particular, the Act obliges the Panel to make rules on the following three issues:

---

1 Which consists of General Principles, Detailed Rules and Practice Notes in the form of specific rulings.
2 See **10.17**.
3 See N. Hyland, 'The Irish Takeover Panel Act 1997', *Bar Review*, Vol 2, Issue 9, July 1997, at p 408.

(1) the requirement that a person or persons acting in concert who acquire control of a company make a 'mandatory offer' for the remaining securities of the company. The rule made by the Panel for this purpose is similar to the City Code's mandatory offer rule;
(2) the interaction between the rules and the requirements of the mergers legislation (see **48.23**); and
(3) the speed with which a person or persons acting in concert may make a 'substantial acquisition of securities' below the control threshold. The rules made by the Panel for this purpose follow the form of the London rules.

Generally, as expected, the Irish Panel's General Principles and Rules on Takeovers are broadly similar to the London City Code which they replaced.

Section 92 of the 2001 Act makes it clear that nothing in ss 201 to 204 of the 1963 Act prejudices the jurisdiction of the Irish Takeover Panel under the 1997 Act.

Rulings and directions

48.14 The Irish Panel has the power, of its own accord or at the request of an interested person, to make a ruling as to whether any activity or proposed activity complies with the general principles and the rules. To ensure that the general principles and the rules are complied with, the Panel also has an extensive power to give a direction to any party to a takeover to do or refrain from doing any act.

If the Panel believes that a ruling or direction made by it has not been complied with, it may apply to the High Court for an order enforcing the ruling or direction.

Appeals

48.15 An appeal against a rule, ruling or direction of the Irish Panel is normally only by way of an application to the High Court for a judicial review.

In addition to the investor protection granted by the General Principles and Rules of the Irish Takeover Panel, shareholders in certain companies may be further protected by the European Communities (Mergers and Divisions of Companies) Regulations 1987.

THE EUROPEAN COMMUNITIES (MERGERS AND DIVISIONS OF COMPANIES) REGULATIONS 1987

48.16   These Regulations, SI 1987/137, implement the Third[1] and Sixth[2] EU Company Law Directives. They apply only to plcs and to some unregistered companies.

The Regulations define mergers and divisions. Both involve the transfer of the assets and liabilities of plcs (transferor companies) to other public companies (acquiring companies), or, in some cases, to companies formed specifically for the purpose of the merger or division.

The transfer of the assets and liabilities of the transferor company must be in exchange for shares in the acquiring company, with or without additional cash payment.

Procedure

48.17   Generally, the directors of the companies involved must draw up draft terms of the merger or division. These must be approved by a special resolution passed at a general meeting or class meetings of each company.

The court has the power to make an order for the protection of the interests of dissenting shareholders.

The Regulations also provide for the directors to draw up written explanatory reports, and for companies to appoint an independent person to examine the draft terms indicating, inter alia, whether or not the proposed merger or division is fair and reasonable.

Liability of directors and independent persons

48.18   The directors and independent persons may incur personal liability[3] for any losses suffered by shareholders as a result of untrue statements in the draft terms, or any reports prepared by them. They may also be liable for losses caused by misconduct in the preparation for, or implementation of, the transactions involved.

Confirmation by the court

48.19   When all the shareholders involved have given their approval, application must be made to the court by all companies involved, for an order confirming the draft terms.

Creditors have a right to object to the making of a court order confirming the draft terms. On hearing them, the court may dispose of the consent of creditors

---

1 Directive 78/855/EEC.
2 Directive 82/891/EEC.
3 They may also be subjected to criminal sanctions.

on condition that the company pays their debts. The court may also order the acquiring company to purchase the shares of dissenting shareholders at a price fixed by the court.

If the transaction is caught by the Mergers, Takeovers and Monopolies (Control) Act 1978, the court may delay the making of its order 'until the Minister's intention is clear' (see **48.24**).

Copy to registrar

48.20   A copy of the confirmation order must be delivered to the registrar and notice of such delivery published in *Iris Oifigiúil* within 14 days.

The European Communities (Safeguarding of Employees' Rights on Transfer of Undertakings) Regulations 1980

48.21   These 1980 Regulations[1] implement the EU's Acquired Rights Directive[2] and transfer automatically to the transferee company any obligations to employees arising under collective agreements entered into by the transferor company.

Notwithstanding these Regulations, there is some doubt as to whether a receiver and manager appointed over the assets of a transferee undertaking would be liable for company obligations. For, as McLoughlin J stated in *Ardmore Studios (Ireland) Ltd v Lynch*,[3] '[When a receiver/manager acts] as agent for the company, the company is made responsible for his acts, but it is not a corollary to this that [the receiver] is bound[4] by all company contracts entered into by the company before the date of [the receiver's] appointment'. However, it must be recognised that this judgment pre-dates the 1980 Regulations.

Under the equivalent UK regulations, it was held in *Bernadone v Pall Mall Services Group and Others; Martin v Lancashire CC*,[5] that the transferor's:

(1)   employers' liability in tort towards an employee was transferred; and
(2)   employers' liability insurers, having received a premium for this risk, were required to indemnify the transferee employer.

Controlling the economic impact of mergers and takeovers

48.22   In the *Irish Independent Business Supplement* of 10 July 1997, a strategic merger was mentioned between United Drug and Dublin Drug. On p 12 it was reported:

> 'The board have agreed a share swap which values Dublin Drug at £15·1 million, but the acquisition is conditional on acceptance by at least 80% of Dublin Drug

---

1   SI 1980/306.
2   77/187/EEC of 14 February 1977.
3   [1965] IR 1.
4   See also **42.24**.
5   (2000) *The Times*, May 26 (CA).

shareholders *and* regulatory clearance under the Merger Act and Competition Act.' (author's emphasis)

This newspaper report illustrates clearly that mergers are not simply a matter for the respective shareholders and company law; aspects of competition law have to be considered as well.

The State has an interest in ensuring that takeovers or mergers do not result in monopoly conditions prevailing within a market, thereby harming the consumer by reducing competition. The Mergers, Takeovers and Monopolies (Control) Act 1978[1] gives the government powers to act to prevent such a situation arising.

The Mergers, Takeovers and Monopolies (Control) Act 1978 (the 1978 Act)

48.23 The 1978 Act enables the Minister to prohibit, or to permit subject to conditions, certain takeovers and mergers which would impede competition.

A merger is defined in s 1(3)(a) as arising where 'two or more enterprises, at least one of which carries on business in the State, come under common control'. Common control means one enterprise obtaining the right to appoint or remove a majority of the board of the other; or acquiring a substantial part of the assets of the other so as to result in the buyer being in a position to substantially replace the vendor in the business in which the latter was engaged immediately before the acquisition. Common control can also exist after the acquisition of a substantial bloc (about 25 per cent) of voting shares.

The 1978 Act, generally, only applies to mergers and takeovers where the turnover of the two enterprises exceeds £20 million.[2] However, if the Minister considers the public interest warrants it, he may declare that the Act is to apply to a particular merger or takeover which does not reach the statutory minimum turnover[3] threshold.

Procedure

48.24 Every takeover or merger is deferred until the Minister has had the time to consider whether or not he should make an order prohibiting it on grounds of being anti-competitive.

A circular is available from the Department setting out the relevant information which has to be submitted to the Minister.

The initial notification to the Minister must be made within one month of there having been a viable offer, which if accepted, would bring the enterprises

---

1 As amended by the Restrictive Practices (Amendment) Act 1987.
2 This threshold does not apply to newspapers because of the Mergers, Takeovers and Monopolies (Control) Act (Newspapers) Order 1979, SI 1979/17.
3 Or assets. The gross assets threshold for the two (or more) enterprises involved is £10 million. These thresholds are regularly revised upwards.

under common control.[1] As a result, the ownership of the assets involved in a takeover or merger will not be transferred until:

(1) the Minister has confirmed that he will not be making a prohibition order; or
(2) the Minister has made a conditional order; or
(3) three months have elapsed from the date of notification of all the information required by the Minister. If, however, within the first month, the Minister requires further information, the three months will not start to run until the Minister receives that information.

The criteria to be used by the Minister in deciding whether to make a prohibition order are set out in the Act. They include such factors as continuity of supplies or services, level of employment, regional development, rationalisation of operations, research and development, increased production, access to markets and the interests of shareholders, employees and consumers.

Section 14 of the Competition Act 1991 empowers the Minister, where he is of the opinion that there is an abuse of a dominant position,[2] to request the Competition Authority to carry out an investigation on his behalf. The Minister will then consider the findings of the Authority's report, before making his decision.

The Competition Act 1991

48.25 Section 4(1) of the Competition Act 1991 is modelled on art 85 of the Treaty of Rome. It defines a number of prohibited anti-competitive agreements which have as their object the prevention or distortion of competition or trade within the State.

Section 4(1) prohibits and declares void any of the anti-competitive agreements indicated in it. As mentioned in **48.29**, s 4 has been deemed to embrace agreements for a merger or takeover, with or without restrictive covenants or 'non-compete' clauses.

Section 4(2) established the Competition Authority (CA) with a view to monitoring such agreements. With effect from 23 June 1997, the CA is located at Parnell House, 14 Parnell Street, Dublin 1, telephone 01–804–5400.

The CA has the power to grant a licence in the case of any agreement or category of agreement. Before granting a licence, the CA may invite any Minister concerned with the matter to offer such observations as he may wish to make.

---

1 See T. O'Connor 'Notifying the Irish Regulatory Authorities of a Merger or Takeover' (1994) *Commercial Law Practitioner* 156, at pp 156–158.
2 As defined in s 5 of the Competition Act 1991.

Powers of the Competition Authority

48.26 The CA may confirm that an agreement is not, in its opinion, a prohibited one. This statement would be classified as a *certificate*. The CA may also state that even though the agreement submitted offends s 4(1), it approves of it on grounds of the resulting benefits. This type of statement is styled a *licence*.

A licence may have conditions attached and be for a limited period of time. Effectively, a licence legalises a prohibited agreement under s 4(1).

Sanctions available to aggrieved persons

48.27 Section 6 of the 1991 Act gives any person who is 'aggrieved' as a result of an agreement prohibited by s 4(1), the right to institute legal proceedings for damages (including exemplary damages) and other judicial remedies against any undertaking which is a party to such an agreement.

Defences

48.28 If a CA certificate is in place, an aggrieved person, whilst entitled to initiate legal proceedings, will not be awarded damages.

When a CA licence has been issued, an aggrieved person is debarred from mounting a legal challenge to the terms of the agreement.

The 1978 and 1991 Acts

48.29 In the *Woodchester* case,[1] the CA stated that, in its view, a merger was not automatically outside the scope of the Competition Act[2] by virtue of its having been approved by the Minister under the Mergers, Takeovers and Monopolies (Control) Act 1978. (The Collins Report has since recommended that the 'double jeopardy' result from the Woodchester decision be repealed so that mergers would be outside the scope of the Competition Act – see **48.32**.)

The CA, however, indicated that unless the market following the merger was likely to be fairly concentrated, it would not regard the merger as offending s 4(1) of the Competition Act. Even where the market was to be concentrated, the CA considered that it would not deem a merger offensive in the absence of barriers to entry by new firms, or if there was a significant level of competition from imports. Some of these indicators from the CA appeared in draft quasi legislative form during 1997 (see **48.30**).

The first merger to be found offensive by the CA[3] under s 4 of the Competition Act, was the proposed acquisition of the entire share capital of Cooley Distillery

---

1 Competition Authority Decision No 6 of 4 August 1992.
2 For further information, see T. O'Connor *Competition Law Source Book* (Round Hall, Sweet & Maxwell, 1996), vols 1 and 2, and B. Clarke *Takeovers and Mergers Law in Ireland* (Round Hall, Sweet & Maxwell, 1999).
3 See Decision No 285 of 25 February 1994.

by Irish Distillers Group plc. This case further highlighted the question as to whether proposed mergers needed to be notified to both the Minister under the 1978 Act and the CA under the 1991 Act. There appears to be an overlap between these Acts which may involve parallel notifications[1] of mergers. This overlapping situation may be eased somewhat by the CA granting notification exemptions for categories of acquisitions which do not contravene the 1991 Act. Guidelines in connection with such exemptions are being issued under the Competition (Amendment) Act 1996.

The Competition (Amendment) Act 1996[2]

48.30   Under the Competition (Amendment) Act 1996, the CA is empowered to issue notification exemption certificates for *categories of agreements* which, in its opinion, do not contravene the law. These are known as 'category certificates' and constitute a form of 'negative block clearances'.

During May 1997, the CA published a draft list of conditions which companies must meet if they require an automatic approval for a merger[3] agreement. Generally, under these proposed conditions, following a merger the combined market share of the four largest companies in the market should be less than 40%, unless there are no significant barriers on entry to that market, or there is a reasonable prospect of future competition from imports.

The CA also proposes accepting the practice of including a 'non-compete' provision in merger and buy out agreements. For example, in the case of a standard business, the seller can be restrained from competing for a maximum of two years. This period of restraint can be extended up to five years in the event of the business involving significant and secret technical knowledge.

In order to qualify for a 'category certificate', a non-compete agreement must also be confined to the geographical area within which the business operates.

The current draft certificate in respect of agreements involving a merger and/or a sale of business is available on www.irlgov.ie/compauth/dec489/htm.

Abuse of a dominant position

48.31   Section 5 of the Competition Act 1991 (by analogy with art 86 of the Treaty of Rome) prohibits any abuse by an undertaking of a dominant position. The acquisition of one competitor by another may lead to an abuse of a dominant position.

---

1 See P. Massey and P. O'Hare *Competition Law and Policy in Ireland* (Oak Tree Press, 1996), at Chapter 10.
2 This Act extended the Competition Act 1991 and the Mergers, Takeovers and Monopolies (Control) Act 1978 (as amended).
3 Or buy out. A 'buy out' is the expression used to indicate the purchase of a controlling interest in a company.

The Collins Report and merger regulation

48.32 The Competition and Mergers Review Group published its final report in May 2000.[1] The group was chaired by Mr Michael Collins, SC.

In the context of company mergers and acquisitions, Part 6 of the Report focused on such matters[2] as:

(1) mandatory notification;
(2) thresholds;
(3) the appropriate structure for control of mergers;
(4) the criteria to be applied in assessing mergers; and
(5) the application of the Competition Acts to mergers.

A summary of all the Review Group's recommendations on merger and acquisition control, is set out in pp 346 to 358 of the Report. Among the recommendations are the points listed below.

(1) The current system of mandatory notification should continue to exist where defined financial thresholds are exceeded.
(2) (a) the thresholds for notification based on a turnover test and the abolition of the gross assets test should be retained;
   (b) thresholds should be set in respect of two or more enterprises involved in the merger, being the acquirer and the target enterprise, to the exclusion of the vendor;
   (c) a new, additional turnover test should be introduced which would have the effect of excluding mergers where the turnover in the State of the parties involved is not significant. The test proposed is therefore that the merger should be notifiable only if:
      (i) the worldwide turnover of each of two or more of the enterprises involved (being the merging entities rather than the vendor) exceeds the threshold; and
      (ii) the turnover in the State of each of any one of the those enterprises also exceeds the threshold. In each case, the threshold should be increased to 38 million Euros.
   (d) the Minister should retain the power to dis-apply the thresholds in respect of particular categories of merger (so as to bring mergers in specified sectors, such as the media, within the scope of the Act even if the thresholds are not exceeded);
   (e) banking institutions should be subject to the merger legislation;
   (f) the methods of calculating turnover of financial institutions provided for in the EC Merger Regulation (see **48.35**) should be adopted at the national level; and
   (g) inter-group mergers should be exempted from the application of the Act.
(3) There were several majority Review Group recommendations which included:

---

1 The Stationery Office.
2 See pp 206–244 of the Report.

(a) that notifiable transactions should be notified to the Competition Authority and that a two-tier system be introduced allowing for a fast track procedure for mergers which give rise to no competition concerns and a second in-depth investigation phase for those which do give rise to such concerns;

(b) that the Competition Authority's decision that a proposed merger gives rise to no competition concern at the first stage would be final, subject only to the Minister's review on public policy grounds; and

(c) that the Minister would be entitled to take only non-competition public policy factors into account when departing from the view of the Authority; and that her decision should be fully reasoned and published.

(4) The Review Group recommended that the Competition Authority should apply pure competition criteria based on the test set out in the Merger Regulation. This would permit a merger to proceed provided that it 'did not create or strengthen a dominant position as a result of which effective competition would be significantly impeded in the State or in a substantial part of it'. This test should be written into the merger legislation or any consolidated legislation. As regards the criteria to be taken into account by the Minister, these should relate only to public policy matters.

These criteria should be specified in a non-exhaustive way in the Act and should include industrial policy, employment, regional development, environmental policy and the suitability of the proposed purchasers in the light of public policy considerations.

(5) The Group also recommended that s 4 of the Competition Act 1991 (see **48.29**) should no longer apply to mergers per se nor to any directly related restrictions which are notified as an integral part of the merger. The majority of the Group also recommended that s 5 of the 1991 Act should no longer be applicable to mergers which exceed the thresholds provided for under the merger legislation. Such mergers would fall to be assessed under the mergers criteria and, if approved by the Minister, could not then be attacked under s 5. Section 5 should, however, continue to apply to mergers falling below the thresholds, subject to two qualifications.[1]

Review of the Minister's decisions

48.33 The Review Group saw the decision-making role of the Minister continue (eg see particularly (3) and (4) above) and made several recommendations to control this use of executive power, among which were that:

(1) the decision of the Minister should be reviewable in judicial review proceedings on the grounds, inter alia, that the recommendation from the Competition Authority was irrational or in breach of natural justice. Judicial review proceedings should be instituted within one month from the making of the Minister's decision;

---

1 These two qualifications are detailed in the Recommendation. See p 349 of the Report.

(2) no appeal to the courts or to an independent body on the merits should be provided for. The general principles regulating leave to apply for judicial review should apply. The court should have power to vary the conditions imposed in the contested decision. Appeals to the Supreme Court should be excluded save for points of law of exceptional public importance or challenges to the constitutionality of the provisions of the merger legislation. The Competition Authority's or the Minister's file ought to be made available from the date of the relevant decision; and

(3) the question as to who should be considered to have standing to bring judicial review proceedings should be left to the courts to determine in accordance with the general rules on this issue.

Consolidation of competition legislation

48.34 The Review Group also stipulated that if their recommendations were to be acted upon in respect of mergers, then it would be appropriate for the Competition Acts 1991 to 1996 to be amended in order to bring the regulation of mergers within the scope of a consolidated Competition and Merger Act.

EU MERGER CONTROL

48.35 If a takeover or merger in any Member State could result in an anti-competitive situation arising within the EU, as a trading area, rather than in Ireland alone, the EU Commission (or any interested party) could take action under art 86 of the Treaty of Rome to prevent this 'abuse of a dominant position'.

In the *Continental Can* case,[1] the European Court of Justice held that mergers came within the provisions of art 86 of the Rome Treaty. However, at an EU level, arts 85 and 86 have been superseded by special legislation dealing with multi-State mergers. This legislation is the EU Merger Control Regulation[2] which came into force on 21 September 1990. It applied only to mergers where the aggregate world wide turnover of all the parties involved exceeded 5,000 million ECUs, and the aggregate Community-wide turnover of each of at least two of the undertakings involved exceeded 250 million ECUs. These thresholds were reduced to 2,500 million and 100 million ECUs respectively by EC Regulation No 1310/97,[3] thus reinforcing merger control at EU level.

---

1 *Europemballage and Continental Can Co v EC Commission* [1973] ECR 215.
2 4064/89. It is based on arts 87 and 235 of the Treaty of Rome. Article 235 allows the Council 'to take action . . . where . . . necessary to attain the objectives of the Treaty, including the maintenance of effective competition in the Common Market'.
3 Amending Regulation No 4064/89 on Control of Concentrations between Undertakings published in OJ No L 180 of 9 July 1997, p 1.

The EU Merger Control Regulation[1] excludes the jurisdiction of (national) Irish law for any merger coming within its scope. Thus, the specially created Merger Task Force in DG IV of the Commission has exclusive jurisdiction for large intra-EU mergers.

EU REFORMS

48.36   A parallel jurisdiction of Irish national and EU rules, compounded by a lack of clear demarcation of jurisdiction (other than in relation to mergers), has led to much complexity in interactions between both systems. In order to alleviate this complexity, the EU Commission published a White Paper in 1999. This White Paper proposed radical changes in the implementation of EU competition rules. Basically, the White Paper proposes a more decentralised (national) control system which would allow the Community to focus on these cases with a wider Community interest.[2] These reforms are likely to be more significant in the general competition area, rather than the narrow field of mergers, because there is already clearer demarcation of jurisdiction between national and EU merger control. In any event, the Collins Report took the White Paper proposals into account before making its recommendations, stating:[3]

> 'The proposals in the White Paper have been the subject of considerable comment, much of it since the Review Group published its Discussion Document. A consultation process is currently under way and the final form of the proposals will no doubt be both amended and elaborated upon before any change is made. It seems unlikely that any such change will be implemented before 2003 at the earliest. For these reasons, the draft proposals made by the Group were made in the first instance in the context of the present regime but the Group pointed out that it would nonetheless be foolish to ignore the clear wishes of the Commission as stated in the White Paper.'

---

1 See D. Cahill 'The EC Merger Regulation – A Review of Recent Developments' (1999) 6 CLP 272, at pp 272–277, and R. Bechtold 'Legal Problems involved in Cross-Border Mergers' (2000/01) *The European Legal Forum Journal* 19, at pp 19–22.
2 See I. Maher *Competition Law Alignment Reform* (Round Hall, Sweet & Maxwell, 1999).
3 At p 20.

PART X B

THE WINDING-UP OF COMPANIES

CHAPTER R

THE WINDING UP OF COMPANIES

Chapter 49

INITIATION OF WINDING-UP PROCEDURE BY CREDITORS, MEMBERS AND OTHERS

LIMITED LIABILITY COMPANIES

49.1 Limited liability companies are legal entities created under the law by following a registration procedure. The 'lives' of such companies can also be brought to an end by the occurrence of certain events or procedures leading to their dissolution.

DISSOLUTION

49.2 The most usual procedure for systematically dissolving a company is to wind it up or liquidate it. Three months after registration of the liquidators' final return,[1] the liquidated company will be dissolved. The majority of companies dissolved are never formally wound up. Instead, they come to an end when the registrar strikes them off the register – see Chapter 53.

Until a company is dissolved, it continues its existence as a corporate entity.

A liquidated company may be restored to the register – see **53.14**.

METHODS OF WINDING-UP

49.3 There are two methods of winding-up. These are compulsory winding-up by the court and voluntary winding-up. A voluntary winding up may be initiated either by investors or by creditors of the company.

Winding-up by the court

49.4 The Companies Acts give the court certain powers to intervene in the running of a company, and to order that it should be wound up in certain circumstances.

Grounds for compulsory winding-up

49.5 The court may order the winding-up of a company in the following circumstances, set out in s 213:[2]

---

1 See ss 263 and 273 of the 1963 Act.
2 Of the 1963 Act.

(1) if the company has, by special resolution, resolved that it be wound up by the court. In *Re Galway and Salthill Tramway Co*,[1] it was held that the directors of a company cannot present a winding up petition in the name of the company without the authority of a general meeting. It is the company, and not the directors, who must resolve that it be wound up by the court.

The members can, in general meeting, however, ratify the directors' actions:

(2) where a newly formed company does not commence its business within a year from incorporation, or a company suspends its business activities for a whole year;

(3) where the number of investors is reduced below the statutory minimum of two for private[2] and seven for public companies.

The circumstances set out in (1) to (3) above can be classified as *procedural* grounds for winding-up a company. Section 213(e) to (g) contains the following *substantive* grounds for winding-up:

(4) if the company is *unable to pay its debts*;

(5) if the court is of the opinion that it is *just and equitable* that the company should be wound up; and

(6) if the court is satisfied that the *company's affairs are being conducted in a manner oppressive* to any member or his interests.

Inability to pay its debts

49.6 Section 214[3] explains the circumstances in which a company will be deemed to be unable to pays its debts. There are three situations envisaged:

(1) if a creditor is owed a sum[4] exceeding £1,000 by the company, and has served on the company, by leaving it at the registered office of the company, a demand in writing requiring the company to pay the sum due, and the company has for three weeks thereafter neglected to pay the sum or to secure or compound for it to the reasonable satisfaction of the creditor.

In *Re Shannon Transport Systems Ltd*,[5] the High Court held that a petition to wind up a company on grounds of inability to pay its debts may be dismissed if the court decides that a genuine dispute is in existence between the parties as to the amount owed. Again, in *Re Pageboy Couriers Ltd*,[6] the court dismissed a petitioner's claim to wind up the company,

---

1 [1918] 1 IR 62 (HC). See also *Re Cannock Ltd* (Unreported) 8 September 1989 (HC).
2 Other than single-member companies.
3 As amended by s 123 of the 1990 Act.
4 A company not in a position to pay the sum due, or to secure or compound it to the reasonable satisfaction of the petitioner, was ordered by Finnegan J to be wound up in *Re Millhouse Taverns Ltd*, *Bar Review*, Vol 6, Issue 4, January 2001.
5 (Unreported) 3 February 1975 (HC).
6 [1983] ILRM 510. See also *Re J McLaughlin & Co Ltd* (1996) 3 CLP 215.

because his claim (for £5,000 director's fees) had at all times been disputed by the company on substantial grounds.

The Supreme Court will restrain the presentation of a winding-up petition for the duration of an earlier High Court injunction – see *Meridian Communications & Anor v Eircell Ltd, Irish Times Law Report*, 18 June 2001.

Keane J considered the factors which a court should consider in deciding whether or not to refuse a petition to wind up the company in *Truck and Machinery Sales Ltd v Marubeni Kumatsu Ltd*.[1] His view was that even if the debt was disputed on substantial grounds by the company, if the latter is insolvent, the court may refuse to restrain the petition to wind it up, thereby protecting the interests of the legitimate creditors.

If the company is insolvent and no genuine dispute over the debt exists, the court is likely to grant the petition. As Costello J stated in *Re Dubned Exports Ltd*:[2]

'I have come to the conclusion that the dispute ... is not a bona fide one and that Dubned Exports Ltd is now insolvent. It would be wrong, in these circumstances, not to grant the petitioner the relief ... to which he is entitled.'

Opposition by the company's creditors to the winding-up will be considered by the court but will not be the deciding factor. In *Re Irish Tourist Promotions Ltd*,[3] the company was wound up despite the creditors' objections. However, Costello J granted a petition to wind up the company in *Re Bula Ltd*,[4] saying:

'the petitioner's prima facie right to an order has not been displaced in any of the evidence. I take into account the fact that the majority of creditors in value and in number, favour this course to be adopted ...'

While McCarthy J in the Supreme Court[5] reversed Costello J's decision it has been suggested that this Supreme Court judgment is simply authority for the principle that the court has discretion in this matter.[6]

(2) where a creditor obtains a judgment or court order against the company in satisfaction of a debt, but is unable to obtain payment from the company because of its lack of assets; or

(3) if the creditor proves to the satisfaction of the court that the company is unable to pay its debts. The creditor may be able to do this by proving that:

---

1 [1996] 1 IR 13. See article by MacCann 'Restraining a petition to wind up a company' *Bar Review*, Vol 1, Issue 2, August 1996, pp 6 and 9.
2 (Unreported) 9 May 1986 (HC). See also *Re Milhouse Taverns Ltd* (2001) 8(3) CLP 74, (2001) 8(5) CLP 124.
3 (Unreported) 22 April 1974 (HC). As regards the position of creditors in subsidiary companies, see *Re Southard & Co* [1979] 1 WLR 1198.
4 (Unreported) 18 July 1986 (HC).
5 (Unreported) 13 May 1988 (SC).
6 See Lynch, Marshall and O'Ferrall *Corporate Insolvency & Rescue* (Butterworths, 1996), at pp 20–23.

(a) the company is not able to pay its debts as they fall due. This is known as the 'commercial insolvency' test; or

(b) the company's assets are less than its liabilities – the 'balance sheet' test.

In utilising both these tests, the company's contingent and prospective liabilities must be taken into account.

Just and equitable grounds

49.7 Winding-up for just and equitable reasons is treated as a separate ground for granting a petition under s 213(f). The court will not make the order winding-up the company, unless there is a special reason for so doing.

Examples of instances where the court has granted petitions on just and equitable grounds include:

(1) where the substratum (or main objects) of the company are gone, eg inability to obtain a patent which it was the main object of the company to work.[1] However, if there are two or more main objects, inability to achieve one of them does not necessarily justify winding-up the company;[2]

(2) where there is deadlock, ie perpetual disagreement, between two members, each of whom controls 50 per cent of the company's voting power.[3] The court's reasoning here transposes the mutual trust and confidence necessary for the working of a partnership to the working of a small private company. Under the Partnership Act 1890, the court has the power to dissolve a partnership if the partners are deadlocked.

In *Re Irish Tourist Promotions Ltd*,[4] there was deadlock in the management of the company. Notwithstanding, the creditors believed that they had a better chance of being paid if the company was not wound up. Despite the creditors' wishes, Kenny J ordered the winding-up of the company because its management was deadlocked.

(3) where the circumstances disclose some underlying obligation in good faith and confidence that the petitioner should participate in the management of the company as long as it continues in business.[5]

In *Re Murph's Restaurant Ltd*,[6] one director was effectively excluded from participation in management of the company by two other directors who were brothers. The court held this was grounds for winding-up under s 213. It would not make an order under s 205 because of the fundamental breakdown in the relationship;

---

1 *Re German Date Coffee Co* (1882) 20 Ch D 169.
2 *Re Kitson & Co Ltd* [1946] 1 All ER 435.
3 *Re Yenidje Tobacco Co Ltd* [1916] 2 Ch 426.
4 (Unreported) 22 April 1974 (HC).
5 See *Ebrahimi v Westbourne Galleries Ltd* [1973] AC 360.
6 [1979] ILRM 149.

(4) misapplication of company funds, eg where the directors withhold information from the shareholders in circumstances giving rise to suspicion.

   In *Re Newbridge Sanitary Laundry Ltd*,[1] the managing director, who was a large shareholder, refused to account for monies received by him for the company. Two shareholders presented a petition to wind up the company.

   Sir Ignatius O'Brien LC stated that the 'just and equitable' ground was to be viewed as a completely separate heading in the context of the substantive grounds set out in (the equivalent of) s 213. He then ordered that the company be wound up, despite the ratification of the managing director's actions by the members in general meeting;

(5) where the objects of the company are essentially illegal[2] or fraudulent.[3] However, the whole object of the company must be fraudulent: mere fraud in carrying on aspects of the company's business will not, of itself, justify a winding up;[4]

(6) where the business is being carried on for the benefit of the debenture-holders only.[5]

In *Re Vehicle Buildings and Insulations Ltd*,[6] Murphy J confirmed that a petitioner under s 213(f) 'must come to the court with clean hands'.

Section 93 of the 2001 Act makes an addition to s 213(f) to provide for the winding-up of an investment company on just and equitable grounds.

Oppression of a member

49.8   Section 213(g) provides that a company may be wound up by the court if it is satisfied that the company's affairs are being conducted, or the powers of the directors are being exercised, in a manner oppressive to any member or in disregard of his interests as a member and that, despite the existence of an alternative remedy, winding-up would be justified in the general circumstances of the case.

The court may, however, dismiss a petition to wind up under s 213(g) if it is of the opinion that proceedings under s 205 would be more appropriate. Section 205 gives the court a wide range of remedies (see **16.19**).

---

1 [1917] 1 IR 237.
2 *R v Registrar of Joint Stock Companies ex parte More* [1931] 2 KB 197 – a case involving the sale of tickets for the Irish Hospital Sweepstake.
3 *Re Thomas Edward Brinsmead & Sons, Tomlin's Case* [1897] 1 Ch 45.
4 *Re Medical Battery Co* [1894] 1 Ch 444.
5 *Re Chic Ltd* [1905] 2 Ch 345.
6 [1986] ILRM 239.

Who may petition the court to wind up the company?

49.9 Section 215, as amended by s 94 of the 2001 Act, provides that an application to the court for the compulsory winding-up of the company may be initiated either by:

(1) any creditor;
(2) any contributory;[1]
(3) in the case of oppression, any person entitled to apply for an order under s 205. This will generally be members;
(4) the company itself; and
(5) the trustee of an investment company.

A company will rarely present a petition itself. The majority of petitions to wind up a company compulsorily will be presented by the creditors.

Any creditor seeking to wind up the company must provide security for the costs of the petition and also satisfy the court that there is a prima facie case for winding up.

Petitions by contributories, by the Minister and by members

49.10 Section 215(a), (d) and (e) sets out the restricted circumstances in which contributories, the Minister and members may petition the court to wind up the company. The Minister will usually petition on foot of an inspector's report.

The court may also order a winding-up on foot of an examiner's report – see **46.16**.

Effect of winding-up order on creditors

49.11 Irrespective of who initiates a winding-up petition, once an order is made to wind up a company, s 223 makes it clear that it will operate in favour of all creditors and all contributories, as if made on their joint petition.

In *Re Pat Ruth Ltd*,[2] Costello J applied the principle that all pre-liquidation secured creditors should be treated equally, and held that lodgements to a company's bank account after the date of presentation of the petition were dispositions within the meaning of s 218, and therefore void (see also **49.15**).

Effect of winding-up order on directors and a receiver

49.12 The liquidation of a company renders the board of directors defunct,[3] although individual directors are not discharged from office. Such directors may in fact, be asked by the liquidator to supply him with information or assistance.

---

1 Ie any person liable to contribute to the assets of the company in the event of it being wound up – see **50.24**.
2 [1981] ILRM 51. But see A. Moore 'Payments received by cheque drawn on bank account of company following presentation of winding-up petition ...' (2001) 8 CLP 10, at pp 10–12.
3 Section 231 of the 1963 Act effectively transfers its powers to a liquidator.

The shareholders, on a liquidation, retain their voting powers for general meetings, and of course, retain a proprietorial interest in the liquidation of their company. The effect of liquidation on a receiver was explained in **43.24**.

Effect of winding-up order on an examiner

49.13 When a company is under the protection of the court, a liquidator cannot be appointed – see **45.19**.

Effect of winding-up order on company contracts and employees

49.14 Where the liquidator decides that the company cannot fulfil its contractual obligations on a pre-liquidation contract, the other party must make a claim for damages for breach of contract and prove his debt as an ordinary creditor in the liquidation process.

Section 290 of the 1963 Act also empowers the liquidator to disclaim land, shares or other unprofitable company contracts, with leave of the court – see **50.44**.

The rights of a party damaged by the operation of a disclaimer are set out in s 290(9). A disclaimer order under s 290 is only intended to affect the rights and liabilities of third parties to the extent necessary to preserve the company and its assets from incurring further liability on the disclaimed contract. As a result, Keane J held in *Tempany v Royal Liver Co*[1] that disclaimer under s 290 did not affect the right of a landlord of property to recover outstanding rent from a guarantor.

In *Re Forster & Co Ltd*,[2] Chatterton VC confirmed that the resolution or order for winding up a company operates in law as notice of dismissal to its employees.

Thus, on the appointment of a liquidator, the company's employees are automatically dismissed.[3] However, this may not be the case where a provisional liquidator is appointed, who is ordered to carry on the company's business.[4]

Dismissed employees enjoy some statutory protection as preferential creditors in respect of at least part of their arrears of salaries, wages and redundancy payment entitlements – see **50.52**.

The appointment of a provisional liquidator (see **49.16**) may terminate automatically the authority of company agents appointed by the directors.[5]

---

1 [1984] ILRM 273. See also *Re GWI Ltd* (Unreported) 16 November 1988 (HC).
2 (1887–1888) 19 LR IR 240.
3 Although the liquidator may waive this notice – see *Re Evanhenry Ltd* (Unreported) 15 May 1986 (HC).
4 See *Donnelly v Gleeson* (Unreported) 11 July 1978 (HC).
5 See *Pacific and General Insurance Co Ltd v Hazell* [1997] BCC 400, (1997) 4 CLP 236.

Effects of application to wind up

49.15   Any creditor or contributory (or the company itself) may apply to the court under s 217 to stop or restrain legal proceedings against the company whilst the petition is being considered by the court. The court may admit such a stay in legal proceedings on such terms and for such time as it thinks fit.

Any transfer of shares or disposition of company property after the commencement of the winding up, will be void under s 218, unless validated by the court. As the purpose of s 218 is to ensure, as far as possible, that the insolvent company's assets are all available for distribution amongst its creditors, the court will exercise the power of making a validation order sparingly. Generally, it will only do so in favour of persons dealing with the company in good faith and without notice, and when the transaction benefits the general body of creditors.[1]

In *Re Industrial Services Co (Dublin) Ltd (in liquidation)*,[2] Kearns J emphasised the obligation on institutional creditors such as banks to control the operation of company accounts after it had become clear that a company was in financial difficulty.

Commencement of winding-up by the court

49.16   A winding-up by the court will be deemed to have commenced at the time of the presentation of the petition for winding-up, unless a resolution has previously been passed for a voluntary winding-up. In this event, the winding-up will have commenced at the time of the passing of the resolution.[3]

Prior to the winding-up order, a petitioner can request the court to appoint a *provisional liquidator* at any time after presenting the petition – see s 226(1) and (2).

Members' voluntary winding-up

49.17   Section 251 sets out the circumstances in which the members can initiate the voluntary winding-up of the company.

---

1 See *In re John Daly & Co Ltd* (1887–88) 19 LR Ir 83, and *Re Ashmark Ltd (No 2)* (Unreported) 8 December 1989 (HC). In the latter case, the court clarified that the disposition of a cheque only takes place when it is honoured: the writing of the cheque is not a disposition.
2 (2001) 8(5) CLP 123 (HC), [2001] 7 ICLMD.
3 Section 220.

Circumstances in which company may be wound up voluntarily

49.18 A company may be wound up voluntarily:

(1) when the period, if any, fixed for the duration of the company, has expired or an event which the articles prescribes for the dissolution of the company has happened and the resolution[1] has been passed at a general meeting that the company be wound up voluntarily; or

(2) if the company has passed a special resolution that it be wound up voluntarily; or

(3) if the company resolves in general meeting that it cannot, by reason of its liabilities, continue in business and that it be wound up voluntarily.

Publication of resolution

49.19 When a company resolves to be wound up, it must give notice, within 14 days, in *Iris Oifigiúil.*[2]

Commencement of winding-up

49.20 A voluntary winding-up is deemed to commence at the time of the passing of the resolution.[3]

Consequences of voluntary winding-up

49.21 From the commencement of a voluntary liquidation, the company ceases to carry on business but the corporate state and corporate powers of the company continue until it is dissolved. In certain circumstances where it would be beneficial to the winding-up, the company may continue in business. Any alteration in the status of members or transfer of shares must, from the commencement of the winding-up, be authorised by the liquidator.[4]

Statutory declaration of solvency

49.22 Where it is proposed to wind up a company voluntarily, the directors of the company, or a majority of them, must make a statutory declaration to the effect that they have enquired in full into the affairs of the company and have formed the opinion that the company will be able to pay its debts in full within a period not exceeding 12 months from the commencement of the winding up. This declaration must be made within 28 days immediately preceding the date of the resolution for winding-up and be delivered to the registrar of companies by the date of the passing of the resolution. It must embody a statement of the company's assets and liabilities at the last practical date[5] before the making of the declaration.

---

1 This may be an ordinary resolution unless the articles prescribe otherwise.
2 Section 252.
3 Section 253.
4 Sections 254 and 255.
5 Which must, in any event, be not more than three months.

Independent verification

49.23   Section 256 was amended by s 128 of the 1990 Act to make provision for independent verification of the directors' declaration. Section 256(3) and (4) stipulates that verification must be by a person 'qualified at the time of the report to be appointed, or to continue to be, auditor of the company.' The independent auditor's report will have to confirm that the directors' opinion on solvency is a reasonable one.

Objections by creditors

49.24   If, within 28 days of the passing of the resolution for winding-up being advertised in *Iris Oifigiúil*, a creditor applies to the court and the court is satisfied that the creditor, together with any creditors supporting him, represents one-fifth at least in number or value of the creditors of the company, and the court is of the opinion that the company is unlikely to be able to pay its debts within the specified period, then it may order that the provisions of the Act relating to a creditors' voluntary winding-up[1] shall apply instead of the provisions relating to a members' voluntary winding up. If such an order is given by the court, then the company must, within 28 days, deliver a copy of the order to the registrar of companies. If no objections are made by creditors, then the liquidation will be known as 'a members' voluntary winding-up' and the provisions of the Act in relation to a members' voluntary winding-up shall apply.[2]

Liability of directors for declaration of solvency

49.25   Where, despite the directors' statutory declaration of solvency, the company is subsequently unable to pay its debts, the directors will be liable. Section 256(8) and (9) gives the liquidator, or any creditor or contributory of the company, the right to apply to the court. The court may then declare that a director who was a party to the declaration, without having reasonable grounds for his opinion, shall be personally liable without limitation for the debts of the company.

Failure to file the statutory declaration

49.26   If the directors of a solvent company whose members resolve to wind up voluntarily fail to file the statutory declarations of solvency, the proper course of action is to apply to the court to have the company wound up.[3]

Appointment of liquidator

49.27   The members control the appointment of the liquidator in a members' voluntary winding-up. The role of a liquidator appointed by the members is detailed in Chapter 51.

---

1 See Chapter 52.
2 Sections 257–264 – see Chapter 51.
3 *Re Oakthorpe Holdings Ltd* [1988] ILRM 62.

Creditors' voluntary winding-up

49.28 If no declaration of solvency is made, or if the creditors object successfully to a declaration of solvency, a voluntary liquidation will proceed as a creditors', rather than a members' winding-up. Again, if during a members' voluntary winding-up, the liquidator is of the opinion that the company will be unable to pay its debts, the winding up will convert to a creditors' liquidation.[1]

Initiation of a creditors' voluntary winding-up

49.29 To initiate a creditors' voluntary winding-up, the directors must convene a general meeting of members and pass a resolution to wind up the company.

Under s 266 of the 1963 Act, the company must call a meeting of creditors on the day that the resolution to wind up is passed, or on the following day. The notice of the meeting must be advertised in at least two daily newspapers circulating in the district where the registered office or principal place of business of the company is situated. Notice of the meeting must have been sent to creditors at least 10 days before the date of the meeting. A statement of affairs and a list of creditors' with the estimated amounts due to them, must be laid before the meeting of creditors by the directors. One director must preside over the meeting.

Appointment of liquidator

49.30 At both the company members' meetings and creditors' meeting mentioned above (see **49.29**), a person may be nominated as liquidator. If both meetings nominate a different person, then the person nominated at the creditors' meeting will be the liquidator. If no one is nominated at the creditors' meeting, the person nominated at the company meeting will be the liquidator. Where different people are nominated at both meetings and any director, member or creditor wishes, he may apply to the court for an order that the person nominated as liquidator by the company be made liquidator, instead of, or jointly with, the person nominated by the creditors.[2]

The role of the liquidator in a creditors' voluntary winding-up is outlined in Chapter 52.

---

1 Section 261 – see Chapter 51.
2 Or, indeed, that some person, other than the creditors' nominee, be appointed liquidator – s 267(2).

CONTROLLING ASSETS OF INSOLVENT COMPANIES NOT BEING LIQUIDATED

49.31   Section 251 of the 1990 Act applies certain winding-up provisions[1] to companies not in liquidation. It was amended by s 54 of the 2001 Act. Its purpose is to ensure that provisions that may be applied to companies in liquidation (concerning the rights of creditors, etc) cannot be avoided by the device of failing to wind up the company.

The amendments to s 251 have three effects. First, the sections to which s 251 applies are extended to include s 149 of the 1990 Act relating to the restriction of directors of insolvent companies in liquidation. The inclusion of this section allows applications for restriction of directors to be taken, notwithstanding the fact that a company has not been wound up.

Secondly, the Director of Corporate Enforcement has standing to apply to the court for an order or judgment pursuant to s 251 of the 1990 Act. Such an order may be used to summon officers to make payments in respect of the debts of a company; to require the delivery of property wrongly transferred from the company by its officers; to find that an officer of a company has committed fraud; or to find that an officer of a company has failed to keep proper books of account, thus contributing to the company's inability to pay all of its debts.

Thirdly, where a court makes an order for payment or delivery of property against a person pursuant to an application of the Director under the section, then, because the Director is not a general creditor of the company for goods and services, the court will not make that order in favour of the Director, except as to the Director's costs and expenses.

---

1 Section 251 of the 1990 Act, as amended, applies the following provisions to insolvent (but not being wound up) companies: (a) ss 243, 245, 245A, 247, 295, 297, 297A and 298 of the 1963 Act; and (b) ss 139, 140, 149, 209 and 204 of the 1990 Act.

Chapter 50

THE OFFICIAL LIQUIDATOR'S ROLE

WINDING-UP ORDERS

50.1 The overwhelming majority of compulsory winding-up orders are initiated by creditors.

Once the winding-up order has been made by the court, a copy must be sent[1] immediately to the registrar of companies for registration.

CONDUCTING THE WINDING-UP PROCEEDINGS

50.2 The court appoints a liquidator[2] to conduct the proceedings of the winding-up. In fact, the court may appoint a provisional[3] liquidator at any time after the presentation of a winding-up petition and before the appointment of the official liquidator.

Actions stayed

50.3 Once the winding-up order has been made, or a provisional liquidator appointed, all actions or legal proceedings against the company can only proceed with the leave of the court.[4]

The statement of affairs

50.4 Within 21 days of the making of the winding-up order or appointment of a provisional liquidator,[5] a statement of affairs must[6] be submitted by the company to the liquidator giving particulars of:

(1) the assets;
(2) the debts and liabilities;
(3) the names, residences and occupations of the creditors;
(4) the securities held by the respective creditors;
(5) the dates on which the various securities were given;
(6) such other information as may be prescribed by the court.

---

1 By the company – see s 221.
2 Or liquidators.
3 Whose powers may be restricted or limited by the court – see s 226(2).
4 Section 222.
5 Or within such extended period as the court may permit – s 224(3).
6 Unless the court thinks fit to order otherwise – s 224(1).

The statement of affairs must be filed and verified[1] by one or more directors and by the secretary or by any of the following persons whom the court may require:

(1) any officer or past officer of the company;
(2) anyone who has taken part in the formation of the company within a year before the date of the winding-up order;
(3) anyone employed by the company within the past year who is, in the opinion of the court, capable of giving the information required;
(4) anyone employed within the past year as an officer in another company which itself was an officer[2] of the main company.

Any person who is a creditor or contributory of the company may, at all reasonable times, inspect the statement of affairs and take a copy or extract therefrom.

The contents of the statement of affairs may be used in evidence against those responsible for filing it – see s 18 of the 1990 Act, as amended by s 28 of the 2001 Act.

Appointment of official liquidator

50.5 Section 300 of the 1963 Act disqualifies any body corporate from appointment as liquidator to a company. Nor can a disqualified director under s 160 of the 1990 Act, as amended by the Schedule, Part 2, of the 2001 Act, be appointed a liquidator. Statutory reforms were also enacted during 1990 to ensure the impartiality of individuals appointed to be liquidators.

Impartiality

50.6 Section 146 of the 1990 Act inserted a new s 300A in the 1963 Act. Section 300A disqualifies the following 'connected' persons from being eligible for appointment as liquidator. Connected persons include:

(1) a person who is, or who has been within 12 months of the commencement of the winding-up, an officer or servant (including auditor) of the company;
(2) except with the leave of the court, a parent, spouse, brother, sister or child of an officer of the company;
(3) a person who is a partner or in the employment of an officer or servant of the company;
(4) a person who is similarly connected with any other body corporate which is that company's subsidiary or holding company or a subsidiary of that company's holding company.

Again, s 301 makes it a criminal offence to bribe any member or creditor of the company to secure an appointment as its liquidator. Furthermore, under

---

1 By affidavit.
2 Acting through its own directors and officers and influencing the management of the main company.

s 301A, any creditor (or other person) who has a connection with the proposed liquidator, must disclose it to the meeting before voting on a resolution to appoint a liquidator.

Subject to the statutory disqualification and disclosure requirements relating to liquidators, the court may make any order it thinks fit to give effect to the wishes of the creditors and contributories on the appointment of a liquidator.

Publicity

50.7 Within 21 days after his appointment, the liquidator must publish notice of it in *Iris Oifigiúil*. He must also deliver a copy of the court order appointing him, to the registrar of companies.[1]

Section 303 of the 1963 Act also provides that every invoice, order for goods or business letter issued by or on behalf of the company, must contain a statement that it is being wound up. Section 303 applies to voluntary as well as compulsory liquidations.

Title

50.8 The liquidator should be described by the title of, for example, 'Official Liquidator of Delta Ltd', rather than by his personal name.

Terms of appointment

50.9 The court may determine whether the liquidator should give any security on his appointment. His remuneration will be fixed by the court.

Any acts done by the liquidator will be valid even if it is discovered afterwards that there was some defect in his appointment.

Position

50.10 The liquidator is appointed to act as an agent of the company. However, as Kenny J stated in *Re Belfast Empire Theatre of Varieties Ltd*:[2]

> 'While a liquidator may be a trustee for the company ... he is not ... a trustee in any sense of the word for its members and creditors. The true position is that he is an agent with fiduciary obligations arising from his office and with statutory duties imposed on him [by the Companies Acts 1963–2001]. If the company has not been dissolved he may be ordered to pay damages or compensation [under s 298] and if the company has been dissolved he may be sued for breach of these statutory duties.'

Resignation and removal of liquidator

50.11 Section 228(c) provides that a liquidator appointed by the court may resign or, on cause shown, be removed by the court.

---

1 Section 227.
2 [1963] IR 41 (HC).

When the court makes an order to pool the assets of related companies which are being wound up compulsorily (see **50.38**) it may, under s 141(3) of the 1990 Act, remove any liquidator of any of the companies and appoint any person to act as liquidator of any one or more of the companies.

Any vacancy which occurs in the office of liquidator will be filled by the court.

Procedures to be followed by liquidators

50.12   Section 312 of the 1963 Act extends the rule making authority of the courts to apply to the winding-up of companies, whether compulsorily or voluntarily. Accordingly, a number of Rules of the Supreme Court apply to the liquidation procedure, the most important of which are the 1986 Rules, SI 1986/115.[1]

Under these Rules, the liquidator must lodge all monies received by him into a special account within seven days from their receipt. Failure to do this will render him liable to pay compensation.

The Rules also provide for the signing of cheques, and the selling of company property by the liquidator. They also set out procedures for summoning meetings of creditors and contributories.

Procedure for calling meetings

50.13   Where the court so directs, the liquidator must summon a meeting of creditors or separate meetings of creditors and contributories, for the purpose of deciding whether a committee of inspection should be appointed to act with the liquidator and, if so, who is to be appointed to that committee. Where the creditors and contributories cannot agree on this question, the court may decide the matter as it thinks fit.

Committees of inspection

50.14   If the decision is taken to appoint a committee of inspection under the Act, it will be composed of creditors in such proportions as directed by all of the creditors and contributories and, in the event of disagreement, as determined by the court. This committee will meet at the times set out by it, and any member of the committee or the liquidator may call a meeting at any time.

The committee will act on a decision of the majority of the members present provided there is a majority of the full committee at the meeting. Any member of the committee may resign by giving signed notice in writing to the liquidator. If a member becomes bankrupt or absents himself from five consecutive meetings, his place becomes vacant. Also, a member may be removed by an ordinary resolution at a meeting of creditors if he represents creditors, or contributories if he represents contributories, of which seven days' notice has been given.

---

1 As amended by SI 1991/147 and SI 1991/278.

On a vacancy occurring, the liquidator will call a meeting of the creditors or contributories to appoint, by resolution, a person to fill the vacancy.[1]

General powers of the court

50.15   The Companies Act 1963 bestows considerable general powers on the court in respect of a court winding-up. These general powers are contained in ss 234 to 250 of the Act and include:

(1)   the power to order delivery of the company property to the liquidator – s 236;

(2)   the power to exclude creditors not proving in time – s 241;

(3)   the power to order the costs of winding up to be paid out of company assets – s 244;

(4)   the power to compel the attendance of company officers at meetings – s 246;

(5)   the power, on proof of probable cause, to order the arrest of an absconding contributory – s 247. Section 247 was amended by s 46 of the 2001 Act. Under the amended s 247, the power of arresting absconding contributors is enlarged to encompass other persons such as directors, shadow directors and other officers of the company. In addition, the Director of Corporate Enforcement (the Director), a creditor or any other interested party, is given the right to apply for an order under s 247;

(6)   the power to summon any person before it for examination under s 245.

Section 245 examination and order

50.16   Under s 245 of the 1963 Act, as amended by s 126 of the 1990 Act and s 44 of the 2001 Act, the court may, of its own motion or on the application of the Director, at any time after the appointment of a provisional liquidator or the making of a winding-up order, summon before it any officer of the company or person known or suspected to have in his possession any property of the company or supposed to be indebted to the company, or any person whom the court deems capable of giving information relating to the promotion, formation, trade, dealings, affairs or property of the company.

Such a person is not entitled to refuse to answer any question put to him on grounds of self-incrimination – see new s 245(6) substituted by the 2001 Act.

In *Re Comet Food Machinery Co Ltd (In Voluntary Liquidation)*,[2] the court reviewed the criteria to be used before deciding to examine a person under s 245 (and s 280).

The court held that this power to examine was discretionary, and an applicant creditor would have to demonstrate that, if granted, the examination would probably result in some benefit accruing to him. Furthermore, in reaching its

---

1   Section 233.

2   [1999] 1 1R 485 (SC), [1999] 1 ILRM 475.

decision, the court would attach considerable weight to the views of the liquidator on whether the examination was necessary.

In this particular case, the Supreme Court dismissed an appeal against the granting of an examination order by the High Court.

The court may examine such a person under oath, and require him to produce any accounting records or other documents relating to the company, that are in his custody or control.

A person being examined under s 245 cannot refuse to answer a question on the ground that his answer might incriminate him. However, O'Hanlon J, in *Re Aluminium Fabricators Ltd*, confirmed that a person's answers to a s 245 examination are not admissible against him in any civil or criminal proceedings, other than the winding-up proceedings in question.[1]

Whilst the person examined may enjoy this immunity in respect of his answers to a s 245 examination, Costello J in *Irish Commercial Society Ltd v Plunkett*[2] suggested that such answers could be used in evidence against other persons.

Section 127 of the 1990 Act added a new s 245A to the 1963 Act. Under s 245A, if, in the course of an examination under s 245 it appears to the court that any person being examined:

(1) is indebted to the company; or
(2) has in his possession or control any money, property or books and papers of the company,

the court may, of its own motion or on the application of the Director, order such person:

(a) to pay to the liquidator the amount of the debt or any part thereof; or
(b) to pay, deliver, convey, surrender or transfer to the liquidator such money, property or books and papers or any part thereof,

as the case may be, at such time and in such manner and on such terms as the court may direct. Section 245A was amended[3] by s 45 of the 2001 Act. The 2001 Act amendment provides that the Director of Corporate Enforcement may apply to have an order made against a person under s 245A, and also, where the court makes such an order, it may make a further order permitting the Director or the liquidator to enter premises and seize any money, property, books or papers of the company.

Inspection of books

50.16A   Under s 243(1) the court, at any time after the making of the winding up order, may also make an order for inspection of the books and papers of the company by creditors and contributors.

---

1 And also in respect of criminal proceedings for perjury arising out of these answers.
2 [1986] ILRM 624.
3 Adding subsections 245A(2)–(6).

An additional s 243(1A) was inserted by s 43 of the Company Law Enforcement Act 2001. Section 243(1A) provides that the court may similarly order the inspection and examination of company books and documents, by the Director of Corporate Enforcement.

Power of the court to order the return of assets which have been improperly transferred

50.17   Section 139 of the 1990 Act empowers the court, on the application of a liquidator, creditor or contributory, to order the return of certain property or assets which were fraudulently transferred.

In deciding whether or not it is just and equitable to make such an order, the court shall have regard to the rights of persons who have, bona fide and for value, acquired an interest in the property which is the subject of the application.

Specific powers of the liquidator

50.18   The statutory powers of a liquidator are contained in s 231[1] of the 1963 Act. Basically, the liquidator's powers are divided into the categories of those exercisable without the approval of the court or the committee of inspection, and those exercisable with prior court or committee approval.

Without prior approval

50.19   Without the prior sanction of the court or the committee of inspection, the liquidator has power:

(1)   to sell real and personal property by public auction or by private contract. However, the liquidator cannot sell by private contract a non-cash asset worth at least £1,000[2] to an officer of the company, unless he has given at least 14 days' notice of his intention to all creditors of the company;[3]
(2)   to do all acts and execute deeds, receipts, etc, and use the seal of the company where necessary;
(3)   to prove for calls when a contributory has been adjudged bankrupt;
(4)   to draw, endorse and accept bills of exchange;
(5)   to raise money on the security of the assets of the company;
(6)   to give security for costs in any proceedings commenced by the company;
(7)   to appoint an agent to do any business which the liquidator is unable to do himself; and
(8)   to do all such things as are necessary for the winding up of the company and distributing the assets. This may include ratifying a pre-incorporation contract – see **9.16**.

---

1   As amended by s 124 of the 1990 Act.
2   See s 29(2) of the 1990 Act.
3   See s 124 of the 1990 Act and s 231(2)(a) of the 1963 Act.

If the liquidator is in doubt about any of these matters he may apply to the court for directions. For example, in *Van Hool McArdle v Rohan Industrial Estates Ltd*,[1] the liquidator (optionally) sought the sanction of the court in relation to a sale of company property (see also **50.22**).

With prior approval

50.20   With the sanction of the court or the committee of inspection, the liquidator has the power:

(1) to bring or defend any action or proceeding on behalf of the company;
(2) to carry on the business so far as may be necessary for the beneficial winding-up of the company;
(3) to appoint a solicitor to assist him;
(4) to pay any classes of creditors in full;
(5) to make any compromise or arrangement with creditors;
(6) to compromise all calls and liabilities to calls and debts and liabilities between the company and contributories (see **50.23**).

Duties of the liquidator

50.21   The principal duty of the liquidator is to collect or get in the company property and pay its debts. His specific tasks include the following:

(1) to take the property of the company into his custody;
(2) to settle the list of contributories;
(3) to admit or reject proof of debts;
(4) to realise the company assets;
(5) to pay the debts of the company in the order prescribed by ss 284 and 285;
(6) to distribute the surplus (if any) amongst the contributories;
(7) to co-operate with the court in ensuring that irregularities he uncovers in the conduct of the company's affairs are brought to the attention of the appropriate authorities; and
(8) to co-operate with the Director of Corporate Enforcement.

We shall now consider these specific tasks in more detail.

Duty to take company's property into his custody

50.22   Section 229 makes it incumbent upon the liquidator, when appointed, to take into his custody or control all the 'property and things in action to which the company is, or appears to be, entitled'.

If, at any stage, there is no liquidator, the property will be deemed to be in the custody of the court.

In order that the liquidator may bring or defend, in his official name, any action or proceedings relating to the company's property, the court may, on

---

1 [1980] IR 137.

the application of the liquidator, direct that all or any of the property be vested in his name.[1]

Thus, although the company property does not automatically vest in the liquidator on his appointment, the court may make an order vesting all or any of the company's property in him.

Where the liquidator sells company property, he is under a duty to obtain the maximum price for it. This duty also devolves upon the court if the matter is referred to it – see *Van Hool McArdle* case in **50.19**.

Duty to settle list of contributories

50.23 One of the first duties of a liquidator is to settle the list of contributories. However, where it appears to the court that it will not be necessary to make calls on or adjust the rights of contributories, the court may dispense with the settlement of a list of contributories. Subject to this, the court shall, 'as soon as may be after a winding-up order', settle a list of contributories.

In settling the list of contributories, the court will distinguish between persons who are contributories in their own right and persons who are contributories as being representatives of or liable for the debts of others.

Meaning of contributory

50.24 The term 'contributory' means every person[2] who is liable to contribute to the assets of the company in the event of it being wound up. The main categories of contributory are likely to be present and past members.

Present members' liability

50.25 A present member is liable as a contributory up to:

(1) the amount (if any) *unpaid on his shares* in the case of a limited liability company;
(2) the amount undertaken to be contributed by him to the assets of the company in the case of a company *limited by guarantee,* plus any sums unpaid on shares held by him;
(3) the full amount needed to pay off the debts and liabilities of the company in the case of an unlimited company.

Past members' liability

50.26 A past member is liable on a similar basis to a present member where:

(1) it appears to the court that existing members are unable to make the payments required of them; and
(2) they ceased to be members within 12 months before the commencement of winding up; and

---

1 Section 230.
2 See ss 208–211 of the 1963 Act.

(3) the debts and liabilities were contracted while the past members were members.

Lists of contributories[1]

50.27   There are, generally, two lists of contributories. Present members are put on the 'A' list, whilst past members are placed on the 'B' list.

Rectification

50.28   Any person who has been wrongly placed on the list of contributories may apply to the court to rectify the list.

Liability of contributories

50.29   A contributory's liability does not cease on his death; it passes to his personal representatives.

Directors as contributories

50.30   Where the liability of a company's directors has been made unlimited under the provisions of ss 197 and 198 of the 1963 Act, then, in addition to his liability to contribute as an ordinary member, a director may be liable to make a further contribution if:

(1) he has been a director within one year of the commencement of the winding-up;
(2) the debts and liabilities were incurred before he ceased to be a director; and
(3) the court deems it necessary that he contribute in order to satisfy the debts and liabilities of the company.[2]

Duty to admit or reject proof of debts

50.31   Debts which must be proved by creditors include 'all debts payable on a contingency, and all claims against the company, present or future, certain or contingent, ascertained or sounding in damages'.[3]

The Act requires a just estimate to be made, so far as possible, of the value of debts which do not bear a certain value.

Bankruptcy rules and set off

50.32   Section 284 applies the same rules as bankruptcy to a winding-up situation with regard to:

(1) the respective rights of secured and unsecured creditors;

---

1 The rules on contributories outlined in this chapter apply, generally, to both compulsory and voluntary winding-up procedures.
2 Section 207(2).
3 Section 283(1).

(2) debts provable; and

(3) the valuation of annuities and future and contingent liabilities.

The application of the bankruptcy rules also means that set off provisions also apply in a winding-up. 'Set off' means the use of a debt owed by a creditor to the company to reduce a debt owed to him by the company.

Where there have been mutual dealings between a creditor and the company, the debt due from one can be set off against the debt due from the other, and the creditor need only prove for the balance.

Time-limits

50.33 Debts which are 'stale' and statute barred[1] under the Statute of Limitations 1957 will be rejected by the liquidator.

Procedure for ascertaining creditors

50.34 The court will direct the publishing of an advertisement fixing a time within which the creditors are to furnish the liquidator with particulars of their claims.[2]

The liquidator then decides which debts are allowable without further evidence, and which require to be proved.

The Rules of the Supreme Court provide a procedure for adjudicating on disputes concerning these 'provable' debts. Under this procedure, the decision of the court examiner (an office under the direction of the Chief Registrar – in 2001, the examiner was Ms Alacoque Condon) will put the liquidator in a position of being able to assess the total amount owing by the company to all creditors.

Duty to realise the company assets

50.35 The primary task of the liquidator is to 'liquidate' the assets of the company and use them to pay the proved debts of its creditors.

In realising the company assets, the liquidator will be assisted by the court. For example, the court has the power to order contributories (and others) to pay their debts to the company[3] by lodging money into a bank to the account of the liquidator.

When the liquidator suspects that a director is likely to remove company assets from the State, or to dissipate those assets, he can apply to the court for a *Mareva* injunction to prevent him from doing so. The court may also order the director to disclose the location of assets which are the subject of a *Mareva* injunction.

---

1 See also s 283(2) regarding dividends declared more than six years previously.

2 Section 241 gives the court the power to exclude creditors not proving in time.

3 See **50.15** et seq.

Section 55 of the Company Law Enforcement Act 2001 provides for the making of a *Mareva* injunction against directors and officers where the court applicant has a civil cause of action against them.

Maximising company assets

50.36 It could be argued that the liquidator also has a duty to maximise the company's assets. He is given statutory assistance in doing this by provisions relating to him obtaining contributions from:

(1) directors and others under their personal liability for:
    (a) failure to keep proper books of account;[1]
    (b) fraudulent and reckless trading;[2]
    (c) misfeasance or other breach of duty or trust in relation to the company;[3] and
(2) related companies.

Related companies

50.37 Section 140 of the 1990 Act empowers the liquidator or any creditor or contributory of any company that is being wound up, to apply to the court for an order that:

> 'any company that is or has been related to the company being wound up shall pay to the liquidator ... an amount equivalent to the whole or ... any of the debts provable in that winding-up.'

This is, potentially, one of the most significant provisions in the 1990 Act. On receipt of an application under it, the court may, if satisfied that it is just and equitable to do so, order the related company to pay the liquidator an amount equivalent to the whole or part of the liabilities of the company being wound up.

Section 140(2) sets out the criteria to be used by the court in deciding whether it is just and equitable to make an order. These tests are:

(1) the extent to which the related company took part in the management of the company being wound up;
(2) the conduct of the related company towards the creditors of the company being wound up;
(3) the effects such an order would be likely to have on the creditors of the related company concerned.

It is not sufficient for the person seeking the order simply to prove that the companies are related or that the creditors of the company being wound up have relied on the fact that the other company is or has been related to the

---

1 See Chapters 27–29.
2 Ibid.
3 See s 298, as amended by s 142 of the 1990 Act. Directors of subsidiary companies may also be liable under s 148 of the 1990 Act.

first-mentioned company. There must be clear evidence that the circumstances that gave rise to the winding-up are attributable to the actions or omissions of the related company.

For the purpose of the Act, a company is related on a number of tests including the normal subsidiary/holding company tests and tests which could apply to a consortium joint venture or common ownership relationship. In addition, a test in relation to the manner in which the separate businesses of the company are or are not identifiable can also be applied.[1] A company can be related if there is another company to which it and the company being wound up are related.

Pooling of assets of related companies

50.38 Section 141 of the 1990 Act provides for the pooling of the assets of related companies where both are being wound up. On the application of the liquidator of any of the companies, the court may make an order, on just and equitable grounds, that the companies be wound up together as if they were one company.

The criteria used by the court in deciding whether or not to make such an order include:

(1) the extent to which the circumstances that gave rise to the winding-up of any of the companies are attributable to the actions or omissions of any of the other companies; and
(2) the extent to which the businesses of the companies have been intermingled.[2]

In deciding the terms and conditions of an order under s 141, the court will have particular regard to the interests of those persons who are members of some, but not all, of the related companies.

Minimising the company's liabilities

50.39 In addition to increasing the number of sources from which a liquidator can seek contributories to boost the company's assets, he is also given statutory assistance in minimising the company's liabilities in respect of 'antecedent and other transactions'.[3] For example, certain floating charges may be automatically rendered void, transactions which fraudulently prefer one creditor to another may be avoided, and onerous property or unprofitable contracts may be 'disclaimed'. Any transfer of company assets after the commencement of the winding-up may also be rendered void by the court (see **49.15**).

---

1 See s 140(5)(a)–(f).
2 See s 141(3)–(6).
3 See ss 286–292 of the 1963 Act.

Avoidance of floating charges

50.40   Under s 288 of the 1963 Act, as amended by s 136 of the 1990 Act, certain floating charges created within the 12 months prior to the commencement of the winding-up shall be invalid unless it is proved that the company was solvent immediately after the charge was created.

The onus is on the holder of the charge to prove that the company was solvent at the time (see **40.14**).

If the company was not solvent, the floating charge may still be valid to the extent of any money advanced or paid or the actual price or value of goods (or services) sold to the company in consideration for the charge (interest may also be payable at the annual rate of five per cent). However, to be valid, such a transaction must take place at the time of, or subsequently to the creation of the charge. In *Re Daniel Murphy Ltd*,[1] Kenny J cited, with approval, the principle that any cash paid to a company 'at the time of the creation of the charge' cannot mean on the stroke of the clock or even within the same 24 hours. It is not a question of the clock; it is a question of what are the circumstances of each particular case and what is the real substance of the transaction. Judges are not prepared to 'strain' the words of a provision like this to invalidate bona fide transactions carried out honestly in accordance with the usual course of business – see **40.13** et seq.

Floating charges and connected persons

50.41   Where a floating charge has been granted in favour of a connected person, the period for invalidity is extended to two years. Generally, the term 'connected person' includes directors, shadow directors, directors' spouses and family members, related companies, etc.[2]

Floating charges and officers

50.42   Section 289 renders certain floating charges in favour of an officer invalid unless the company was solvent immediately after the charge was created, if the company is wound up within 12 months of the transaction.

Fraudulent preferences

50.43   Under s 286 of the 1963 Act, as amended by s 135 of the 1990 Act, any act disposing of company property or assets within six months of its winding-up will be deemed a 'fraudulent preference' and, thus, invalid. The six months period is extended to two years where the transaction is in favour of a 'connected' person. The onus of proof is on a connected person to prove that the preference was not fraudulent. In other cases, the onus of proof is on the liquidator. To discharge this burden of proof, the liquidator will have to prove that the transaction had, as its dominant intention, the giving of a preference to

---

1   [1964] IR 1 (HC).
2   See s 288(4).

one creditor over other creditors. The liquidator failed to discharge this burden of proof in *Corran Construction Co Ltd v Bank of Ireland Finance Ltd*,[1] but succeeded in *Kelleher v Continental Irish Meat Ltd*,[2] where there were irregularities surrounding the formalities of the transaction – see **40.6**.

In some cases, the liquidator was able to have transactions held as invalid by the court where the directors intended to prefer themselves over other creditors of the company.[3]

Disclaimer of onerous property and contracts

50.44 Section 290[4] of the 1963 Act empowers the liquidator to disclaim, with leave of the court, any property burdened with onerous covenants, unprofitable contracts or shares in companies. This power enables a liquidator to take effective action in stopping the financial haemorrhaging of the company's assets as a result of its existing contractual obligations. In these circumstances, the liquidator would be under a duty to act to minimise the company's liabilities (see also **49.14**).

Getting in the company's assets

50.45 Clearly, in getting in the company's assets, the liquidator must not only collect outstanding monies owed to the company by its creditors and contributories, he must also maximise the pool of assets by seeking other sources of funds from directors, related companies, etc. He must also minimise the company's liabilities by disclaiming onerous or unprofitable company contracts and avoiding any fraudulent preferences and certain floating charges.

Once the company's assets have been collected, the next task of the liquidator is to pay the company's creditors.

Duty to pay the company's debts

50.46 Whether the debts of the company can be paid in full or not, obviously depends on whether the company was solvent on winding up.

Where the company is solvent

50.47 The liquidator's duty in this situation is to pay all creditors' debts in full, and then distribute the surplus assets amongst the contributories/members in accordance with their rights.

---

1 (Unreported) 8 September 1976 (HC).
2 (Unreported) 9 May 1978 (HC).
3 See **40.6** and **40.7**.
4 *In the matter of Ranks (Ireland) Ltd* [1988] ILRM 751 – Murphy J held that the essence of s 290 is that the company is released from continuing onerous obligations, but only on terms that the other party to the contract has the right to prove the loss it sustained.

Where the company is insolvent

50.48   Where there are insufficient assets available to the liquidator to pay all creditors, his duty is to pay secured creditors with fixed charges first, then apply the remaining assets to pay other creditors in the order laid down by s 285.

Secured creditors with fixed charges

50.49   In Chapter 39, the various types of charges or security are explained.

A secured creditor with a fixed charge has several courses of action available to him. He may realise his security and prove for the balance (if any) of his debt. He may also surrender his security and prove for the whole amount or value and retain his security and prove for the balance.

Costs of the liquidation

50.50   The liquidator must retain a sum to meet the costs of the liquidation,[1] before paying any of the remaining debts. Section 244 gives the court the power to order the costs of winding-up to be paid out of company assets, where the company is insolvent.

Section 281 provides that in a voluntary liquidation, all costs, charges and expenses properly incurred in the winding-up, including the remuneration of the liquidator, shall be payable out of the assets of the company in priority to all other claims. Charges may include tax for interest on money placed on deposit by the liquidator – see *Burns v Hearne*.[2]

However, if the liquidator initiates legal proceedings against the former directors or controllers of the company, and fails in them, the costs of the successful defendant(s) may take priority even over the liquidator's own legal costs and remuneration in the liquidation: the Supreme Court deciding[3] that where an action is brought by a company after liquidation, the costs of the successful defendant (whether they fall within s 281 or s 285 of the 1963 Act) rank in priority to all other claims.

Section 285 ranking of debts

50.51   After the costs of the liquidation have been paid or provided for, the liquidator must pay the debts of the company in the following order:

(1)   preferred creditors;
(2)   floating chargees;
(3)   unsecured creditors;
(4)   members and contributories of the company.

---

1   Which would include his own remuneration.
2   (Unreported) 25 July 1988 (SC).
3   In *Comhlucht Páipéar Riomhaireachta Teo v Udarás Na Gaeltachta* [1990] 1 IR 320; applied in *Re CHA Ltd* [1999] 2 ILRM 76 (HC), [1999] 1 IR 437, where it was held that taxed costs within the meaning of s 244 of the 1963 Act should be paid in priority to all other claims in the liquidation.

Preferential creditors

50.52 The creditors whose claims are preferred under s 285(2)[1] include claims for:

(1) 12 months' rates levied by local authorities;
(2) 12 months' income and corporation tax levied by the Revenue Commissioners;
(3) four months' wages and salaries of employees, subject to a maximum of £2,500;[2]
(4) accrued holiday pay owed to employees;
(5) 12 months' social welfare contributions;
(6) compensation and damages for uninsured accidents to employees;[3]
(7) sickness or pensions payments due to employees;
(8) redundancy payments, claims for minimum notice and for unfair dismissal.[4]

In *Re Coombe Imports Ltd*,[5] the court held that the State is a preferential creditor for PRSI contributions which have been deducted by the employer but not paid to the State. Preferential status does not, however, apply to PRSI contributions which, although due, were never deducted.

50.53 Section 285(14) provides that the priority accorded to these preferential debts will only apply if they have been notified to the liquidator or become known to him within six months after the advertisements inviting claims have been published in at least two local daily newspapers. In *In the Matter of H. Williams (Tallaght) Ltd (in Receivership and Liquidation)*,[6] Geoghegan J stated that s 285(14) could not be extended to include constructive knowledge. What was required was actual notification or actual knowledge by the liquidator. The court had no implied power to extend the time limit imposed by statute.

If these preferred debts have been notified to him in time and cannot be paid in full, the liquidator will pay them pari passu. All preferential creditors rank equally amongst themselves – s 285(7)(a).

Floating chargees

50.54 Although floating chargees are secured creditors, their rights have been ranked below those of preferential creditors by s 285(7)(b). Accordingly, it is only if the liquidator still has funds after paying all the preferential creditors in full, that he will be able to make payments to the floating chargees.

---

1 As amended.
2 See s 285(3), (4) and (5).
3 A director was held to be an employee in *Re Dairy Lee Ltd* [1976] IR 314.
4 Under the Redundancy Payments Acts 1967–1979, the Minimum Notice and Terms of Employment Act 1973 and the Unfair Dismissals Act 1977, respectively.
5 [1999] 1 IR 492 (HC).
6 *The Irish Times Law Reports*, 27 January 1997.

Where there are insufficient assets to pay all the floating chargees, their priority will be based on the date of creation of their charges – the earliest created floating chargees being paid first.

Unsecured creditors

50.55   It is only if there are funds remaining after paying the floating chargees in full that the claims of unsecured creditors will be met.

Unsecured creditors' claims rank pari passu amongst themselves.

In an insolvent liquidation, the unsecured creditors are very vulnerable and unlikely to be paid their debts.

Members and contributories of the company

50.56   In a solvent liquidation, any surplus remaining after paying all the company's creditors must be distributed amongst the members according to their rights and interests.[1]

In a compulsory winding-up, it is the court which would adjust the rights of members amongst themselves and order the distribution of the surplus amongst them.[2] However, this task would be undertaken by the liquidator himself in a members'[3] or creditors'[4] voluntary winding-up.

Duty to co-operate with the court and the DPP

50.57   Section 299 of the 1963 Act, as amended by s 51 of the 2001 Act, provides for the prosecution of criminal offences committed by officers and members of a company.

In a winding-up by the court, the court may direct the liquidator to refer possible offences to the Director of Public Prosecutions (DPP). In doing so, the liquidator is under a duty to give the DPP all the information and assistance he deems necessary.

The court must also direct the liquidator to refer the matter to the Director of Corporate Enforcement – see **50.58**.

In a voluntary winding-up, the onus is on the liquidator himself to report any possible criminal offences to the DPP. Again, he must co-operate fully with the DPP in prosecuting these offences. If the liquidator fails to report an irregularity to the DPP, the court may direct him to do so on the application of any person interested in the winding-up.[5]

---

1 Section 275 of the 1963 Act.
2 Section 242.
3 See Chapter 51.
4 See Chapter 52.
5 See s 299(3)–(5).

Duty to co-operate with the Director of Corporate Enforcement

50.58 Sections 56 and 57 of the Company Law Enforcement Act 2001 provide for liquidators to make reports to the Director, and to produce their books and answer any question in relation to the conduct of a particular liquidation.

A liquidator must apply to the courts (within three to five months of providing such a report) for a restriction order against each director of the insolvent company, unless the Director relieves him of that obligation.

Section 58 of the 2001 Act requires a disciplinary committee or tribunal of a prescribed professional body[1] whose members conduct liquidation or receiverships to notify the Director of Corporate Enforcement where it finds that the member has not maintained proper records or where it suspects that the member may have committed an indictable offence under the Companies Acts.

TERMINATION OF LIQUIDATION AND DISSOLUTION OF THE COMPANY

50.59 When the liquidator has completely wound up the affairs of the company, he applies to the court, who will make an order that the company be dissolved.[2]

An office copy of the court order must be sent to the registrar within 21 days.

---

1 Such as an accountancy body recognised by the Minister under s 187 of the Companies Act 1990, whose members may qualify as auditors.
2 Section 249(1).

Chapter 51

MEMBERS' VOLUNTARY LIQUIDATION PROCEDURES

MEMBERS' VOLUNTARY WINDING-UP

51.1 A members' voluntary winding-up is not hostile to the company because the liquidation procedure is controlled by the members.

Section 258 of the 1963 Act empowers the company in general meeting to appoint one or more liquidators.[1] It may also fix their remuneration.

General powers of the court in all voluntary liquidations

51.2 The general powers of the court under ss 234 to 250 of the 1963 Act are restricted to companies in official liquidation.

Section 49 of the 2001 Act provides for the insertion of four new sections, 282A to 282D, into the 1963 Act. These new sections mirror ss 243, 245, 245A, and 247 respectively; in effect, extending the court's powers under these sections to companies in voluntary, as well as compulsory, liquidation (see **50.15** et seq).

Effect of liquidator's appointment

51.3 On the appointment of the liquidator(s), all the powers of the directors cease, unless the general meeting or the liquidator sanctions their continuance.

Duties and powers of liquidator

51.4 The function of the liquidator appointed by the members is to realise all the company's assets, pay all its creditors, and, as the company was solvent, to distribute the surplus assets amongst its members and contributories (if any) according to their class rights. As a result, many of the official liquidator's specific duties, detailed in Chapter 50, will also be applicable to the members' liquidator. For example, ss 283 to 313 of the 1963 Act apply to every mode of winding up and deal with such matters as:

(1) proof and ranking of claims;
(2) effect of winding-up on antecedent and other transactions; and
(3) methods of dissolution.

51.5 Sections 275 to 282 apply to all voluntary liquidations, whether controlled by members or creditors. Section 278, as amended by s 48 of the 2001 Act, requires the liquidator to notify the registrar of his appointment

---

1 It may fill any vacancies which arise in the office of liquidator in a similar manner – s 259.

within 14 days, and the registrar must send a copy of this notification to the Director of Corporate Enforcement.

Under s 276, the liquidator may:

(1) in the case of a members' voluntary winding-up, with the sanction of a special resolution of the company, and, in the case of a creditors' voluntary winding-up,[1] with the sanction of the court or the committee of inspection or (if there is no such committee) a meeting of the creditors, exercise any of the powers given to a liquidator in a winding up by the court to:
    (a) pay any classes of creditors in full;
    (b) make any compromise or arrangement with creditors or persons claiming to be creditors; or
    (c) compromise[2] all calls and liabilities to calls, debts and liabilities capable of resulting in debts, and all claims, present or future, certain or contingent, ascertained or sounding only in damages, and all questions in any way relating to or affecting the assets or winding up of the company, on such terms as may be agreed, and take any security for the discharge of any such call, debt, liability or claim, and give a complete discharge in respect thereof;

(2) without sanction, exercise any of the other powers given to the liquidator in a winding-up by the court;

(3) exercise the power of the court of settling a list of contributories, and the list of contributories shall be prima facie evidence of the liability of the persons named therein to be contributories;

(4) exercise the power of the court of making calls;

(5) summon general meetings of the company for the purpose of obtaining the sanction of the company by resolution or for any other purpose he may think fit;

(6) pay the debts of the company and adjust the rights of the contributories amongst themselves.[3]

The liquidator or any contributory or creditor may apply to the court to determine any question arising in the winding-up of a company, or to exercise all or any of the powers which the court might exercise if the company were being wound up by the court.[4]

Duty to call meetings

51.6 Sections 262 and 263 make provision for annual meetings and a final meeting.

---

1 See next chapter.
2 See s 279 regarding the binding of creditors by arrangements.
3 See s 275 on rules for distribution of company assets.
4 Section 280.

Annual meetings

51.7 The liquidator is under a duty to summon a general meeting of the company each year. He must lay before that meeting an account of his acts and dealings and of the conduct of the winding up during the preceding year. A copy of this report must be sent to the registrar within seven days of the holding of the annual meeting.

Final meeting

51.8 When the affairs of the company are fully wound up and all the creditors paid as forecast in the declaration of solvency, the liquidator must make up a final account, call a general meeting of the company and lay the final accounts before that meeting.

Within one week after the final meeting, the liquidator must send a copy of his final account to the registrar of companies, together with a formal return of the holding of that meeting.

Dissolution of the company

51.9 Three months after the registrar receives the liquidator's final account and return of the holding of the final meeting, the company is deemed to be dissolved.[1]

Powers of the liquidator in a reconstruction

51.10 Section 260 gives the liquidator specific powers to facilitate a reconstruction of the company. Where the whole or part of the business (or property) of the company being wound up is proposed to be transferred to another company (the transferee company), the liquidator may accept shares or other like interests in the transferee company as consideration for the sale of any property of the company being liquidated, provided sanction has been given by that company in the form of a special resolution. Dissenting shareholders, if any, may request the liquidator to purchase that part of their interest which their shares represent, providing they express their dissent in writing addressed to the liquidator within seven days after the passing of the resolution. In such circumstances, the price payable for their shares is to be determined by agreement or by arbitration.

If the liquidator elects to purchase the members' interests, the purchase money must be paid before the company is dissolved. Unless specifically provided to the contrary, the purchase money will be deemed to be part of the costs and expenses of winding up.

---

1 Section 263(4).

If company is insolvent

51.11 The whole basis underlying allowing members to control the winding-up of their company is the fact that the directors have certified that the company is solvent and in a position to pay all its creditors.

If, therefore, the liquidator is at any time of the opinion that the company will not be able to pay its debts in full within the period stated in the declaration of solvency, he must:

(1) summon a meeting of creditors for a day not later than 14 days after the day on which he formed that opinion;

(2) send notices of the creditors' meeting to the creditors by post not less than seven days before the day on which that meeting is to be held;

(3) cause notice of the creditors' meeting to be advertised, at least ten days before the date of the meeting, once in *Iris Oifigiúil* and once at least in two daily newspapers circulating in the locality in which the company's principal place of business was situated during the relevant period; and

(4) during the period before the day on which the creditors' meeting is to be held, furnish creditors free of charge with such information concerning the affairs of the company as they may reasonably require.

Section 261(2) makes it necessary for the liquidator also:

(1) to make out a statement as to the affairs of the company, including a statement of the company's assets and liabilities, a list of the outstanding creditors and the estimated amount of their claims;

(2) to lay that statement before the creditors' meeting; and

(3) to attend and preside at that meeting.

Consequence for the winding-up procedure

51.12 As from the day on which the creditors' meeting is held under s 261, the winding-up becomes a creditors' winding-up.[1]

Appointment of new liquidator by creditors

51.13 The creditors may appoint a liquidator at their meeting to replace the members' appointee. However, such a replacement will not affect the validity of any action previously taken by the members' appointee as liquidator.

Annual and final meetings

51.14 Section 264 makes provision for alternative arrangements relating to the calling of annual and final meetings, when the liquidator is of the opinion that the company is unable to pay its debts.

---

1 See next chapter.

Chapter 52

CREDITORS' VOLUNTARY WINDING-UP PROCEDURES

INTRODUCTION

52.1   A creditors' voluntary winding-up may appear to be a 'hostile' liquidation, but this may not really be the case.

The main difference between a 'member's' and a 'creditor's' voluntary liquidation is that, in the former, the members are allowed to control the winding up process because the directors have made a 'statutory declaration of solvency'. In effect, the directors are certifying that the company is solvent and will be able to pay the debts of all its creditors.

If, however, the directors cannot make this declaration, then any voluntary liquidation will be a creditors' winding-up.

Sections 266 to 273 of the 1963 Act are special provisions applicable to a creditors' voluntary winding up.

A creditors' voluntary winding-up was converted to a compulsory winding-up by the court because immediately before its liquidation, the company had entered into a three-year contract with one of its directors at £80,000 pa – see *Re Magnus Consultants Ltd.*[1]

MEETING OF CREDITORS

52.2   On the day the company members pass the resolution to wind up the company, a meeting of creditors must also take place, under s 266.[2]

Appointment of liquidator

52.3   If there is a difference of opinion between the creditors and the members as to who is to be appointed liquidator, it is the creditors' wishes that will prevail.[3] Thus, whilst it is the members who control the appointment of a liquidator in a members' voluntary winding-up, it is the creditors who do so when the company is not solvent.

Section 267 of the 1963 Act was amended by s 47 of the 2001 Act.

Under the amended s 267(3), the creditor's nominee for liquidator must be selected on a majority in value only of the creditors, as opposed to a majority in

---

1   [1995] 1 BCLC 203, (1995) 2 CLP 188.
2   See **49.29**.
3   Ibid, and s 267.

number and value as had been stipulated in r 63 of Rules of the Supreme Court (No 1) 1966.[1]

In both a members' and creditors' winding-up, the chairman of any meeting at which a liquidator is appointed must, within seven days of the meeting, notify the liquidator in writing of his appointment, unless the liquidator or his duly authorised representative is present at the meeting where the appointment is made.[2]

The appointment of a liquidator in a voluntary winding-up will be of no effect unless the person nominated has, prior to his appointment, given his written consent to the appointment.[3] He must also, within 14 days of his appointment, give the registrar of companies notice of his appointment.

52.4 The remuneration[4] of the liquidator is fixed by the committee of inspection or, if there is no committee, by the creditors. If any creditor or contributory feels that the remuneration is excessive, he may apply to the court to amend the remuneration. Such an application must be made within 28 days of the fixing of the remuneration by the creditors or the committee of inspection (see **52.6** below).

Any vacancy[5] in the office of liquidator may be filled by the creditors.

The court may, on cause shown, remove a liquidator and appoint another in his place.[6]

Effect of appointment of liquidator

52.5 When the liquidator is appointed, all powers of the directors cease, except so far as the committee of inspection or creditors sanction their continuance.

Committee of inspection

52.6 No committee of inspection is necessary in a members' voluntary winding up. However, in a creditors' voluntary winding-up,[7] a committee of inspection may be appointed to assist the liquidator.

Composition

52.7 The creditors, at their s 266 meeting, may appoint a committee of inspection comprising not more than five persons nominated by the creditors' meeting and three persons nominated by the company.[8]

---

1 SI 1996/28.
2 Section 276A.
3 Section 276A.
4 Section 269. All costs of voluntary winding-up, including the liquidator's remuneration, have priority over all other claims – see s 281.
5 Section 270.
6 Section 277.
7 As in a winding-up by the court.
8 Section 268(1).

The creditors can object to any of the persons appointed by the company and, if so, those persons cannot act unless the court so directs.[1]

Procedures

52.8 Generally, a committee of inspection in a creditors' voluntary winding-up will operate under the same s 233 procedures as a committee of inspection appointed to assist an official liquidator.[2]

DUTIES OF THE LIQUIDATOR

52.9 The basic duties of a liquidator appointed by the creditors will be similar to those imposed on other voluntary liquidators.[3] However, s 271 provides that the powers of the liquidator to accept shares as consideration for the sale of company property in a reconstruction will only apply in a creditors' winding-up provided sanction is obtained from either the court or the committee of inspection.[4]

Annual meetings

52.10 After the first year of the liquidation and each subsequent year, the liquidator must hold a general meeting of the company and a meeting of the creditors[5]. He must present an account of his acts and dealings during the preceding year to both meetings. He must also send a copy of the account to the registrar within seven days of the later of the two meetings.[6]

Final meetings

52.11 When the affairs of the company are fully wound up, the liquidator must present an account[7] of the winding-up, showing how the winding-up has been conducted and how the assets of the company have been disposed of, to a general meeting of the company and a meeting of the creditors. Each meeting must be called by advertising in two daily newspapers circulating in the district where the registered office of the company is situated, setting out the time, place and objects of the meeting. Such advertisements must be published at least 28 days before each meeting. The liquidator must send the account to the registrar within one week of the later of the two meetings. If a quorum is not present at either meeting, the liquidator must notify the registrar that a meeting was summoned and that a quorum was not present.

---

1 Section 268(2).
2 See **50.14**.
3 See Chapter 50.
4 Under s 260 – see **51.10**.
5 Within three months of the end of each year.
6 Section 272.
7 He must also send this account to the registrar – see s 273.

Dissolution of the company

52.12 Three months after the registrar has received the liquidator's final account and notification of the holding of the final meetings, the company is deemed to be dissolved,[1] unless the court, on the application of the liquidator or any interested party, makes an order deferring the date at which the dissolution of the company is to take effect.

---

1 Section 273(4) and (5).

PART XI

IMPROVING COMPANY LAW COMPLIANCE AND ENFORCEMENT

Chapter 53

STRIKING OFF, DISSOLUTION AND RESTORATION OF COMPANIES

53.1 As mentioned in **49.2**, the most usual procedure for systematically dissolving a company is to wind it up. Three months after registration of the liquidator's final return, the liquidated company is dissolved.[1]

A company which is transferring assets to another company under a scheme for reconstruction or amalgamation may, under s 203(1) (a), be dissolved without winding up, if the court so orders.[2] Where a company is actually being wound up and the registrar has reasonable cause to believe either that no liquidator is acting, or that the affairs of the company are fully wound up and the returns required to be made by the liquidator have been outstanding for a period of six months, the registrar can strike off the company using the same procedure as is used for defunct companies.

DEFUNCT COMPANIES

53.2 Section 311(1)[3] and (2) provides that where the registrar has reasonable cause to believe that a company is not carrying on business, he may send to the company, by post, a registered letter enquiring whether the company is carrying on business and stating that, if an answer is not received within one month from the date of that letter, a notice will be published in *Iris Oifigiúil* with a view to striking the name of the company off the register.

If the registrar either receives an answer to the effect that the company is not carrying on business or does not within one month after sending the letter receive any answer, he may publish[4] in *Iris Oifigiúil* a notice that at the expiration of one month from the date of that notice, the name of the company mentioned will, unless cause is shown to the contrary, be struck off the register, and the company will be dissolved.

At the expiration of the time mentioned in the notice, the registrar may, unless cause to the contrary is previously shown by the company, strike its name off the register. He must publish notice in *Iris Oifigiúil* and on the publication of this notice, the company is dissolved.

---

1 See **52.12**.
2 See **47.10**.
3 Of the 1963 Act, as amended.
4 Sending the company notice by registered post.

Effect of s 311 striking-off on directors' liability

53.3   Section 311(6) makes it clear[1] that, notwithstanding the company ceasing to exist as a legal entity, the liability, if any, of every director, officer and member is to continue, and may be enforced against them as if the company had not been dissolved.

Appeal against s 311 striking-off

53.4   The company, or any member or creditor can appeal under s 311(8), seeking to have the company name restored to the register – see **53.15**.

The court order

53.5   The court may, by a striking-off order, give such directions and make such provisions as seem just for placing the company and all other persons in the same position as nearly as may be as if the name of the company had not been struck off, or may make such other order as seems just.

An alternative order may, if the court considers it appropriate, include a provision that, as respects a debt or liability incurred by, or on behalf of, the company during the period when it stood struck off the register, the officers of the company or such one or more of them as is specified in the order shall be liable for the whole or part (as the court thinks just) of the debt or liability.

Notice by the Revenue Commissioners

53.6   Section 46 of the Companies (Amendment) (No 2) Act 1999 makes provision for notification to the registrar by the Revenue Commissioners. Section 46 inserts ss 12A, 12B, 12C and 12D in s 12 of the Companies (Amendment) Act 1982.

Generally under the amended 1982 Act, the registrar can also now have a company struck off if the Revenue Commissioners give notice that the company has failed to deliver a statement (under the Taxes Acts) to them confirming various particulars of the company, for example, details of a company's business address, or date of commencement to trade.[2]

STRIKING OFF FOR FAILURE TO SUBMIT ANNUAL RETURNS

53.7   During the late 1990s, the Companies Registration Office (CRO) initiated a compliance campaign to achieve an improvement in the filing of the annual returns by companies.

---

1 Section 311(7) also provides that dissolution under the s 311(1) and (2) procedure does not affect the power of the court to wind up a company, the name of which has been struck off the register.

2 In the case of a non-resident company, the details must include the territory in which the company is resident and either: (a) the name of the company trading in the State; (b) the controlling quoted company; or (c) the ultimate beneficial owners.

The first phase of the campaign led to over 40,000 company strike-offs from the register within 1½ years. Notwithstanding this, compliance rates only rose from 35 per cent to 60 per cent during that period. The second phase in the CRO's compliance campaign was to invoke criminal sanctions against company directors.

During the first phase the CRO had concentrated on striking off companies rather than pursuing the defaulting companies' directors.

The second phase was assisted by s 41 of the Companies (Amendment) (No 2) Act 1999. Section 41 amends s 240 of the Companies Act 1990 by allowing summary proceedings to be brought within three years of the discovery of, rather than the commission of, the offence. The CRO's intention was to initiate criminal sanctions against offending directors through the Chief State Solicitor's Office. Errant directors would face a variety of penalties including fines not exceeding £1,000; up to six months' imprisonment; or, for repeated offenders, disqualification from holding company directorships. These penalties were increased by the 2001 Act – see **55.10**.

Time limits for striking off

53.8   Section 127 of the 1963 Act, as amended, stipulates that the annual return must be completed within 60 days of the AGM and a copy, signed by a director and the company secretary, immediately sent to the registrar – see **33.13** et seq. An amendment of s 12(1) of the Companies (Amendment) Act 1982 by s 46 of the 1999 (No 2) Act effectively reduced the time allowed for companies to file outstanding returns to one year. Consequently, unless any annual returns which were outstanding for more than one year are delivered to the registrar, he can initiate the reminder and publications procedure to strike the company's name off the register, which in turn will result in the company's dissolution.[1]

MEASURES TO IMPROVE COMPLIANCE WITH FILING OBLIGATIONS

53.9   Sections 59 to 66 of the Company Law Enforcement Act 2001 contain a series of measures to improve compliance with filing obligations, particularly annual returns, and to provide more effective remedies where there is non-compliance, by giving the registrar power to levy fines. These sections constitute Part 6 of the 2001 Act, and those dealing with compliance were noted in **33.13** et seq. The McDowell Report had recommended that the registrar[2] should retain an enforcement role in respect of registration-type offences.

Registrar's power to impose fines

53.10   Section 66 of the 2001 Act contains a procedure whereby the registrar may levy fines in respect of a failure to file returns, without the institution of

---

1   See ss 12(1), (2) and (3) of the 1982 Act, and **53.2**.
2   The registrar has the power to reject documents sent to him in illegible form – see s 249A of the 1990 Act, inserted by s 107 of the 2001 Act.

court proceedings. This section provides that the registrar may give to a person who has failed to file a return, a notice to the effect that the offence is alleged against him and that, unless a fine is paid within 21 days and the return is filed, proceedings will be instituted. This gives the accused the option of paying the fine and avoiding a court case and possible conviction.

The responsibility for proving that a fine imposed under this section has been paid is placed on the defendant in any subsequent proceedings. This ensures that a defendant cannot simply rely on the defence that he remitted the relevant amount and that it is up to the registrar to prove the contrary.

Section 62 of the 2001 Act also seeks to avoid the registrar having to be represented in court by an officer, to give oral evidence of fact.

Section 62 amended s 370 of the 1963 Act so that a certificate in writing made by the registrar of, for example, the most recent date on which a requirement under the Companies Acts was complied with, is admissible as prima facie evidence, subject to rebuttal.

OTHER GROUNDS FOR STRIKING OFF

53.11 The Companies (Amendment) (No 2) Act 1999 also gives the registrar the power to have a company struck off where:

(1) the company is in breach of the Irish resident director/bond require-ment;[1] or

(2) the registrar believes that the company has no directors.[2]

CONSEQUENCES FOR THE COMPANY OF BEING STRUCK OFF

53.12 When the registrar removes a company's name from the register, the company's legal life ends. It is dissolved. Dissolution of a company brings its separate legal personality to an end: it also terminates the contractual relationships between the company and its members.

The assets of a dissolved company are vested in the Minister for Finance.[3] In the case of company assets consisting of real property, the interest of a mortgagee or fixed chargee are recognised and protected. However, there is no express statutory protection for creditors secured by charges over personal property, eg a floating chargee. Such a creditor would have to petition the court to have the company restored to the register, and if successful, to obtain additionally, an order from the court restoring his rights in the personal property charged.

While a court has express statutory power[4] to wind up a company struck off the register, because its assets are vested in the State, it is a practical necessity to have the company restored to the register, so that its assets revert back to it.

---

1 See s 43(15) of the 1999 (No 2) Act, and **8.14**.
2 See ss 47 and 48 of the 1999 (No 2) Act, and **33.8**.
3 Under s 28 of the State Property Act 1954.
4 See **53.3**.

The following notice published by the Companies Registration Office[1] illustrates the position concisely:

'*Time is running out for companies to avoid being struck off*

Each Friday for the last three weeks, the Registrar has published lists of companies in *Iris Oifigúil* whose names will be struck off the register unless they file all outstanding annual returns within one month of the date of the publication of their names.

Over 12,000 names have now been published. It is intended to continue publishing further lists every Friday.

Directors should make themselves fully aware of the legal and financial consequences of the strike-off process which could have implication for the assets of the company and their own personal liabilities.

While it is possible to have a company restored to the register, it is expensive to do so and may involve proceedings having to be taken in the High Court.'

RESTORATION TO THE REGISTER[2]

53.13   There are two general categories of dissolved companies to consider in the light of restoration to the register. These are companies which have been (a) wound up, and (b) struck off.

Restoring a liquidated company

53.14   It might be discovered after a liquidated company had been removed from the register that the company had owned unidentified property, or owed other debts. To deal with this situation, s 310(1) of the 1963 Act provides:

'where a company has been dissolved, the court may at any time within 2 years of the date of the dissolution, on any application being made for the purpose by the liquidator of the company or by any other person who appears to the court to be interested, make an order, upon such terms as the court thinks fit, declaring the dissolution to have been void, and thereupon such proceedings may be taken as might have been taken if the company had not been dissolved.'

Once the two-year period has expired, there seems to be little else to be done by a creditor whose debt has just come to light.[3]

The effect of dissolution actions brought by and against the company was considered in *Re Philip Powis Ltd.*[4] Sir John Knox found that the UK's equivalent[5] of s 310 did not give the court a discretion to validate legal proceedings in being at the time the company was dissolved. He held that

---

1 In *The Irish Times*, 17 May 2000.
2 See P. Leonard, 'Restoring Companies to the Register' *Bar Review*, Vol 6, Issue 3, December 2000. During 1999, 36,295 companies were dissolved; an increase of 260 per cent on 1998.
3 In *Pulsford v Devenish* [1903] 2 Ch 625, such a creditor was able to proceed where he proved that the liquidator negligently failed to notify him that the company liquidation was taking place.
4 [1997] 2 BCLC 481, (1997) 4 CLP 230.
5 Section 651 of the UK's Companies Act 1985.

where a company was dissolved, all legal proceedings in relation to it came to a end permanently and were not simply in abeyance.

Restoring a company dissolved after being struck off

53.15 Where a company is struck off without being wound up, the court, on an application within 20 years by the company, or a member or creditor, if it is satisfied that it is just that the company be restored, can order the name to be restored to the register. On this happening, the company is deemed to have continued in existence as if its name had not been struck off – see s 311(8) of the 1963 Act.

As a consequence, pre-dissolution contracts are validated and any post-dissolution contracts ratified – see s 311A(3).

Company property which had vested in the State will also re-vest in the company.

The High Court, in *Re Amantiss Enterprises, Framus Ltd v CRH plc*,[1] had to consider whether an order made under s 311(8) had the effect of automatically validating retrospectively all acts of the company between strike-off and restoration or whether specific orders were required to validate particular acts done when, in effect, the company no longer existed.

The court held that the words 'the company shall be deemed to have continued in existence as if its name had not been struck off' have the effect of automatically validating retrospectively all acts done in the name or on behalf of the company during the period that its name was struck off the register.

The court took into account the fact that often a strike-off is unknown to the company, its officers or third parties dealing with it. Strike-off notices can go astray or may not be passed on to the company, with the business continuing on the basis that the company is legally in existence. To remove legal validity from all of these transactions, the court considered, could result in injustice in a great many instances and 'would provide the unscrupulous with much opportunity for mischief'.

COMPLIANCE CAMPAIGN – THIRD PHASE

53.16 The third phase in the CRO's compliance campaign involved the creation by the Government of a new directorate of corporate enforcement with wide ranging powers of company law investigation and enforcement – see Chapter 55. Before focusing on these new statutory developments, we review the extent of non-statutory regulation by the Stock Exchange of listed companies. Such 'self' regulation is usually viewed in the context of corporate governance.

---

1 [2000] 2 ILRM 177.

Chapter 54

CORPORATE GOVERNANCE AND THE COMPANY LAW REVIEW GROUP

54.1 The concept of corporate governance originated in American law journals during the 1970s. It is now assuming importance in the context of non-statutory regulation of companies.

As shown in Chapters 3 and 4, a consequence of incorporation (and limited liability) is the divergence between company ownership and management. Companies are owned by shareholders and managed by directors. This separation of ownership and day-to-day control is the reason for corporate governance.

Plcs will often have directors and managers with agendas different to their owners' aspirations. Corporate governance is concerned with the prevention (and resolution) of such conflicts.

The Cadbury Report defines corporate governance as the system by which companies are directed and controlled. To cite the report:

> 'Boards of directors are responsible for the governance of their companies. The shareholders' role in governance is to appoint the directors and the auditors and to satisfy themselves that an appropriate governance structure is in place. The responsibilities of the board include setting the company's strategic aims, providing the leadership to put them into effect, supervising the management of the business and reporting to shareholders on their stewardship. The board's actions are subject to laws, regulation and the shareholders in general meeting.'

In recent years, corporate governance has been viewed as consisting of two equally important dimensions which both complement and restrict each other. These are:

(1) stewardship and accountability. This dimension involves additional monitoring of management performance to ensure more transparency and accountability by management to shareholders; and

(2) enhancing enterprise. This dimension is concerned with motivation of management behaviour to increase the profits/wealth of the business enterprise.

The shareholders' role in corporate governance[1] has already been summarised in **15.4**. During the last decade, public disquiet over directors' use of their powers in the UK led to four reports on aspects of corporate governance. These were the Cadbury, Greenbury, Hampel and Turnbull Reports – the latter being published during 1999.[2]

---

1 See also Chapters 15, 16 and 17, and J. H. Farrar *Corporate Governance in Australia and New Zealand* (OUP, 2001). Part I of this book includes a short history of corporate governance.

2 Final report, *Internal controls – guidance for directors on the Combined Code* (chaired by N. Turnbull) (Institute of Chartered Accountants, 1999) – see also **34.39**.

The Cadbury Report in 1992 recommended a Code of Best Practice for the boards of directors of all listed companies in the UK.

In suggesting 'Principles' to underpin a Code of Best Practice, the Cadbury Report considered that these should include accountability, ie:

> 'boards of directors are accountable to their shareholders and both have to play their part in making that accountability effective. Boards of directors need to do so through the quality of the information which they provide to shareholders, and shareholders through their willingness to exercise their responsibilities as owners.'

Essentially, the Code emphasised the important independent role of non-executive directors; called for audit committees to be set up; and suggested that directors should report on the effectivness of internal financial controls.

In Ireland, the Review Group on Auditing recommended in 2000 that all plcs should be required by statute to establish audit committees – see **34.41**.

Cadbury was followed by the Greenbury report which dealt largely with the question of executives' pay and bonuses.

The Hampel Committee on corporate governance was established in 1995. It reviewed both the Cadbury Code of Practice and the Greenbury reports comments on good practice in determining directors' remuneration. Having carried out this review, Hampel produced a set of principles and a code of good corporate governance embracing Cadbury, Greenbury and its own work.[1] The fruits of the Hampel Committee's labours became known as the Combined Code.

THE COMBINED CODE

54.2   The Combined Code, consisting of the principles of good governance and best practice prepared by the Hampel Committee, was adopted by the London Stock Exchange[2] in 1998.

The Combined Code is divided into two parts. Part 1 of the Combined Code consists of a set of principles dealing with companies and the following areas:

A   Directors;
B   Directors' remuneration;
C   Relations with shareholders;
D   Accountability and Audit; and
E   The role of institutional shareholders.

Part 2 then sets out detailed code provisions showing how the principles in Part 1 can best be implemented in practice. For example, Principle A1 (in Part 1) is that, 'every listed company should be headed by an effective board which should lead and control the company'.

---

1 See B. Clarke 'The Hampel Committee Report on corporate governance and the new "super" code' (1998) 5 CLP 93, at pp 93–95.
2 See R. Smeardon *A Practical Guide to Corporate Governance* (Sweet & Maxwell, 1998).

The board of directors[1]

54.3 Part 2 of the Combined Code contains the following supplemental provisions in order to implement Principle A1.

'A.1.1   The board should meet regularly.

A.1.2   The board should have a formal schedule of matters specifically reserved to it for decision.

A.1.3   There should be an agreed procedure for directors, in the furtherance of their duties, to take professional advice, if necessary, at the company's expense.

A.1.4   All directors should have access to the advice and services of the company secretary, who is responsible to the board for ensuring that board procedures are followed and that applicable rules and regulations are complied with. Any question of the removal of the company secretary should be a matter for the board as a whole.

A.1.5   All directors should bring an independent judgment to bear on issues of strategy, performance, resources "including key appointments" and standards of conduct.

A.1.6   Every director should receive appropriate training on the first occasion that he or she is appointed to the board of a listed company, and subsequently as necessary.'

The supplying of information to the board

54.4   Principle A4 in Part 1 of the Combined Code is that, 'the board should be supplied in a timely manner with information in a form and of a quality appropriate to enable it to discharge its duties'.

The relevant implementing provision in Part 2 (A.4.1) is that:

'Management has an obligation to provide the board with appropriate and timely information, but information volunteered by management is unlikely to be enough in all circumstances, and directors should make further enquires where necessary. The chairman should ensure that all directors are properly briefed on issues arising at board meetings.'

The role[2] of the company secretary

54.5   The Cadbury Code, recognising the important role of the company secretary, provided that all directors should:

(1)   have access to the advice and services of the company secretary; and

(2)   recognise that the chairman is entitled to the utmost support of the company secretary in ensuring the effective functioning of the board.

Following the Hampel Report, the Combined Code provides that the company secretary is responsible to the board for ensuring that applicable rules and regulations are complied with – see Principle A.1.4 in **54.3**.

---

1 See J. P. Parkinson, G. Kelly and A. Gamble (eds) *The Political Economy of the Company* (Hart Publishing, 2001). This book discusses, inter alia, the rise of the non-executive director.
2 See T. O'Dwyer 'The role of the company secretary' (1999) 6 CLP 249.

In Ireland, recommendations of the McDowell Report included:

(1) secretaries (and directors) should, on signing the existing consent to act form, acknowledge their obligations under companies legislation, and undertake to comply with these obligations; and

(2) the CRO should introduce guidance notes for secretaries (and directors).

Institutional shareholders[1]

54.6   Principle EI in the Combined Code provides that institutional investors should have a responsibility to make considered use of their votes, whilst principle E2 states that institutional shareholders should be ready, where practicable, to enter into a dialogue with companies based on the mutual understanding of objectives.

Implementing provision E.1.1 states that, 'institutional investors should endeavour to eliminate unnecessary variations in the criteria which each applies to the corporate governance arrangements and performance of the companies in which they invest'.

Code provision E.1.2 places a further responsibility on institutional shareholders to respond to any requests from their clients for information on their voting record in a listed company.

The role of institutional investors became a matter of public debate in Ireland as a result of the first AGM of Eircom plc – see **54.12**.

IMPLEMENTING THE COMBINED CODE IN THE UK

54.7   The London Stock Exchange during 1998 required companies listed on the Exchange to disclose whether they were complying with the Combined Code, which for this purpose was composed[2] of a set of Principles of good governance and a 'Code of Best Practice'. Listed companies were also expected to justify significant variations in the manner in which they applied the Combined Code in their annual returns and annual accounts.

During 1998, the Department of Trade and Industry (DTI) also announced that legislative reform concerning corporate governance could be expected to take place where experience shows that some legal underpinning is needed.[3]

---

1 See also G. P. Stapleton *Institutional Shareholders and Corporate Governance* (Clarendon Press, 1996).

2 See the *Stock Exchange Listing Rules*, para 12.43A and Appendix 'The Combined Code'.

3 DTI *Modern Company Law for a Competitive Economy* (DTI, 1998).

THE TURNBULL REPORT

54.8   The Turnbull Report was published in 1999. It seeks to provide internal company control guidance to the Combined Code for directors of listed companies. Turnbull considers that, 'the board should maintain a sound system of internal control to safeguard shareholders investment and the company's assets'.

Having stated that internal control is one of the principal elements in the management of risk used by a board to achieve a company's objectives, Turnbull gives a number of practical guidelines, including:

> 'The directors should, at least annually, conduct a review of the effectiveness of the group's system of internal controls and should report to the shareholders that they have done so. This review should cover all controls, including financial, operational and compliance controls and risk management.'

The Report also added that companies which did not have an internal audit function should from time to time review the need for one.

Significance of Turnbull Report

54.9   Principle D2 of the Code requires that the board of a listed company should adopt and maintain a system of internal control to monitor the risks which a company may face and to safeguard shareholders' investments and the company's assets. It is this aspect of internal control in the Combined Code on which the Turnbull Report provides guidance in the form of best practice.

The Turnbull guidance has been endorsed by the London Stock Exchange as the accepted interpretation of those aspects of the Combined Code relating to 'internal control'. As a result, non-compliance with Turnbull is likely to be viewed as a non-compliance with the Code itself.

A company's directors are required to review and report to shareholders, at least annually, on the effectiveness of all internal controls[1] and to meet the annual report disclosure requirement as to compliance with the Combined Code.[2]

Corporate governance and Irish listed companies

54.10   In the United Kingdom, a listed company must comment on compliance with the Combined Code in its annual report and accounts. In particular, para 12.43A of the London Stock Exchange Listing Rules states that:

> 'in the case of a company incorporated in the United Kingdom, the following additional items must be included in its annual report and accounts:

---

1   Principle D2.
2   Paragraph 12.43A, *Stock Exchange Listing Rules* – see **54.7** and **54.10**.

(a) a narrative statement of how it has applied the principles set out in Section 1 of the Combined Code, providing explanation which enables its shareholders to evaluate how the principles have been applied;

(b) a statement as to whether or not it has complied throughout the accounting period with the code provisions set out in section 2 of the Combined Code. A company that has not complied with the code provisions, or complied with only some of the code provisions or (in the case of provisions whose requirements are of a continuing nature) complied for only part of an accounting period, must specify the code provisions with which it has not complied, and (where relevant) for what part of the period such non-compliance continued, and give reasons for any non-compliance.'

The board of the Irish Stock Exchange had adapted and applied[1] the Combined Code and para 12.43A to Irish listed companies, with the exception of the rule requiring disclosure of directors' remuneration. This exception was withdrawn with effect from accounting periods on or after 1 January 2000.

The Irish Stock Exchange also concurs with the London Stock Exchange's response to the Turnbull Report guidance and is implementing its requirements in the same way. As a result, there now exists a similar approach to corporate governance in both the UK and Ireland.

Responsibilities of auditors

54.11 In both the UK and Ireland, a listed company's statement under para 12.43A(b) must be reviewed by the auditors before publication, only insofar as it relates to seven specific code provisions.

The auditors must then state in their report if, in their opinion, the company has not complied with specific requirements[2] of the *Listing Rules*.

THE EIRCOM PLC AGM

54.12 An estimated 4,000 disgruntled shareholders attended the first AGM of Eircom plc on 13 September 2000. The meeting was conducted in the glare of massive publicity, with wide radio and television coverage.

Essentially, the shareholders were unhappy because they had seen the market value of their investments drop significantly; while at the same time, very large bonus payments had been made to two directors and there was a resolution placed before the meeting to approve a generous share option scheme for 400 company executives. It appeared to the private (small) shareholders that while they, as part owners, were losing money; company directors, as managers, were making excessively large amounts of remuneration.

---

1 By issuing its 'Notes on the Listing Rules'. These Notes adopted and applied the Combined Code to Irish listed companies and were issued by authority of the board of the Irish Stock Exchange.
2 In para 12.43A(c)(ii), (iii), (iv), (ix) and (x) which deal mainly with details of directors' remuneration.

Virtually all the small private investors who attend the AGM voted against the share option scheme (and also against the re-election of several directors). However, the Chairman, Mr Ray McSharry, then called for a poll and used 1.15 billion votes in favour of the scheme; massively outvoting the private investors, a trust that held shares for employees and the Minister for Public Enterprise, Ms Mary O'Rourke.

The reason why the chairman won each poll was largely because institutional investors supported the board, rather than the small private investors making up the majority of the attendance at the meeting. These poll results gave rise to a call by Senator Shane Ross for more accountability by persons such as pension fund managers when exercising voting power on behalf of investing institutions. The differences of opinion between a large number of small shareholders and the board of Eircom plc was obvious to all. The publicity attending the meeting, allied to the dissatisfaction expressed by the government shareholder and the multitude of small private investors, has greatly politicised the whole concept of corporate governance in Ireland. Perhaps the best way to develop this form of self-regulation is via the Company Law Review Group.

This group was set up on a statutory basis by s 67 of the Company Law Enforcement Act 2001, and its statutory functions include advising the Minister for Enterprise, Trade and Employment on enhancing corporate governance[1] and encouraging commercial probity.

The concept of corporate governance affords an opportunity for the Stock Exchange to self-regulate listed companies by non-statutory means. Whether or not such self-regulation can be effective in Ireland[2] remains to be seen. Initiatives taken by the Company Law Review Group in advising the Minister on enhancing corporate governance could be significant in the future.

THE COMPANY LAW REVIEW GROUP (CLRG)

54.13   Section 68(1) of the 2001 Act identifies the specific functions which are to be carried out by the CLRG. Under s 68(1), the Review Group must monitor, review and advise the Minister on matters concerning:

(1) the implementation of the Companies Acts;
(2) the amendment of the Companies Acts;
(3) the consolidation of the Companies Acts;
(4) the introduction of new legislation relating to the operation of companies and commercial practices in Ireland;
(5) the Rules of the Superior Courts and case-law judgments insofar as they relate to the Companies Acts;

---

1 See 2001 Act, s 68(2).
2 And in the UK – see **53.7**.

(6) the approach to issues arising from the State's membership of the European Union, insofar as they affect the operation of the Companies Acts;

(7) international developments in company law, insofar as they may provide lessons for improved State practice; and

(8) other related matters or issues, including issues submitted by the Minister to the Review Group for consideration.

Section 68(2) clarifies the general aims underlying the establishment of the CLRG by providing that in advising the Minister, the Review Group must seek to promote enterprise, facilitate commerce, simplify the operation of the Companies Acts, enhance corporate governance and encourage commercial probity.

Other matters relating to the Review Group

54.14 Sections 69 to 71 of the 2001 Act deal with membership, remuneration, meetings and business of the Review Group. It is required to make an annual report to the Minister on its activities. Copies of this annual report must be laid before each House of the *Oireachtas.*

FUTURE COMPLIANCE AND ENFORCEMENT

54.15 Supervision of compliance with the Combined Code in Ireland is the responsibility of the Irish Stock Exchange. Because of Government concern over non-compliance with company law generally, a new office of Director of Corporate Enforcement was created by the 2001 Act.

Chapter 55

THE DIRECTOR OF CORPORATE ENFORCEMENT

55.1 A Working Group[1] on Company Law Compliance and Enforcement, chaired by Mr Michael McDowell, SC, reported in March 1999.

The Working Group found that Irish company law had been characterised by a culture of non-compliance[2] and by a failure by companies and their officers to meet their obligations under the Companies Acts. For example, there are about 280 criminal offences contained in the Companies Acts and the Working Group discovered that there had been very few prosecutions in respect of most of these offences.

The Group concluded that if the more complex provisions of the Companies Acts were to be enforced and if serious breaches of company law were to be remedied, the enforcement role envisaged under company law for the Minister for Enterprise, Trade and Employment would need to be transferred to a specialist unit with the necessary resources and skills to enforce the law on a consistent and independent basis.

The primary recommendation of the Working Group, therefore, was the establishment of an independent statutory officer – to be known as the Director of Corporate Enforcement – who would have general responsibility for the enforcement of company law.

The Government agreed to the implementation of the detailed recommendations made by the Working Group and decided further that the new statutory officer – the Director of Corporate Enforcement – should also take over the functions of the Minister for Enterprise, Trade and Employment in regard to the investigation of potential company law offences under Part II of the Companies Act 1990. It was judged to be more cost-effective, more efficient and less political if the decision on whether to initiate a company law investigation or a criminal investigation in any particular case was centralised with the Director.

The office of Director of Corporate Enforcement is now, therefore, the primary mechanism within the State to address corporate malpractice. It was established by the Company Law Enforcement Act 2001. The Working Group made a wide-ranging series of recommendations in regard to improving the enforcement of company law and achieving greater compliance with the requirements of company law, which were also implemented by the 2001 Act.

---

1 Comprising both independent members and representatives of a number of government departments and agencies.
2 See Chapter 53.

These recommendations included setting up the Company Law Review Group[1] on a statutory basis.

THE DIRECTOR OF CORPORATE ENFORCEMENT (DCE)

55.2   Section 7 of the 2001 Act provides for the establishment of the office of DCE, the incumbent of which is to be appointed by the Minister.

The DCE will be assisted in the performance of his statutory functions by his officers.

An officer of the DCE means:

(1) an officer of the Minister assigned to the Director;[2]
(2) a member of the Gardaí seconded to the Director, a seconded Garda remaining under the general direction of the Garda Commissioner; or
(3) a person employed by the Minister or the Director under a contract of service, or otherwise, to assist the Director.

Appointment of Director and acting Director

55.3   The terms and conditions of appointment for the Director are contained in ss 8 and 9. The circumstances under which an Acting Director may be appointed are stipulated in s 11. These include any period when the Director is absent from duty or outside the State.

Immunity

55.4   The Director and his officers are provided with immunity[3] from any civil action, brought against them personally, in respect of anything done in good faith by them in the performance of their duties.

Removal, disqualification or cessation of Director

55.5   The Director is ultimately responsible to the Minister for Trade, Enterprise and Employment, and can be removed by the Minister for stated reasons,[4] eg dereliction of duty or misconduct.

The Director will also cease to hold office in the event of him being elected to one of the Houses of the *Oireachtas* or the European Parliament, or becoming a member of a local authority.[5]

---

1 See **54.12**.
2 Director means the person appointed under s 7(2), and includes an acting Director – see ss 3 and 11 of the 2001 Act.
3 By s 15 of the 2001 Act.
4 Ibid, s 10.
5 See s 10(3) and (4).

FUNCTIONS OF THE DIRECTOR

55.6   Section 12(1) specifies the functions of the Director thus:

(1) to enforce the Companies Acts, including by the prosecution of offences by way of summary proceedings;

(2) to encourage compliance with the Companies Acts;

(3) to investigate instances of suspected offences under the Companies Acts. Section 113 of the 2001 Act gives him rights of access to bank records;

(4) at his discretion, to refer cases to the Director of Public Prosecutions where he has reasonable grounds for believing that an indictable offence under the Companies Acts has been committed;

(5) to exercise, insofar as he feels it necessary or appropriate, a supervisory role over the activity of liquidators and receivers in the discharge of their functions under the Companies Acts;

(6) for the purpose of ensuring the effective application and enforcement of obligations, standards and procedures to which companies and their officers are subject, to perform such other functions in respect of any matters to which the Companies Acts relate as the Minister considers appropriate and may by order confer on him; and

(7) to perform such other functions as may be assigned to him by or under the Companies Acts or any other Act.

The Director's functions include his powers and duties. The Director is to be independent in the performance of his functions, and can delegate them to one of his officers, who will remain subject to the directions of the Director only.[1] A delegation of the Director's powers must be exercised in accordance with s 13 of the Act, which provides, inter alia, that such delegation is revocable at will.

As recommended by the Working Group, s 14 transfers a number of the Minister's functions to the Director. The specific functions transferred are set out in Parts 1 and 2 of the Schedule to the Act.

The Minister's functions transferred to the Director

55.7   Part 1 of the Schedule lists two functions under the 1963 Act which are transferred, while Part 2 sets out thirteen functions under the 1990 Act which are also to be transferred to the Director.

Under the 1963 Act

55.8   The power of the Minister[2] to direct the calling of an AGM and her power to apply to the court[3] for the production and inspection of books when

---

1 See s 12(2)–(6).

2 Under s 131(3), (4), and (6) – see **15.46**.

3 Under s 384.

she believes an offence[1] has been committed are transferred to the Director by Part 1 of the Schedule.

Under the Companies Act 1990

55.9 The functions and powers[2] of the Minister in relation to company inspections, the appointment of inspectors, their powers and reports, etc are transferred, as is the Minister's power[3] to appoint inspectors to investigate irregular share dealings.

The report of an inspector appointed by the DCE[4] can now be used by a court, under s 160(2) of the 1990 Act, as grounds for the making of a disqualification order[5] against a director.

Other ministerial functions under ss 85, 94, 116, 117, and 118 are also transferred.[6]

The power to initiate criminal prosecutions under s 240

55.10 Section 240 of the 1990 Act makes provision for criminal prosecutions under the Companies Acts where no particular punishment had been specified. The Minister's power to bring and prosecute summary proceedings under s 240 has also been transferred to the Director in Part 2 of the Schedule.

Section 104 of the 2001 Act amended s 240[7] by increasing the maximum fines and prison sentences which may be imposed by the courts for summary and indictable offences under the Companies Acts.

Section 105 of the 2001 Act inserts a new s 240A, which makes provision for the court area in which summary proceedings may be brought. Essentially, s 240A provides that an offence in which a company and its officers are jointly charged, may be taken together in the court area in which the company's registered office is situated.

Director's power to levy fines directly

55.11 Where the Director has reasonable grounds for believing that a person has committed an offence, he may, without the institution of court proceedings, levy fines[8] in respect of summary offences under the Companies Acts.

---

1 In connection with the management of a company's affairs.
2 Under ss 11, 12, 14, 15 and 16 of the 1990 Act – see Chapter 35.
3 Under s 66 – see **27.27**.
4 Rather than the Minister.
5 See **30.20** and **50.5**.
6 These transfers are noted in **22.6**, **22.9**, **27.39** and **27.37** respectively.
7 See also **53.7**.
8 See s 109 of the 2001 Act.

PREVIOUS LITIGATION

55.12 Where the Minister is a defendant in legal proceedings which relate to a function transferred to the DCE, the Director will not be substituted for the Minister. This provision in s 14(5) effectively relieves the DCE from having to become involved in defending actions or decisions taken by the Minister before the office of DCE was established.

ACCOUNTABILITY AND DISCLOSURE OF INFORMATION

55.13 Section 16 of the 2001 Act provides a mechanism for formal reporting and accountability by the Director to the Minister and to the *Oireachtas*.

An obligation of confidentiality with regard to information which they may acquire in the course of their official duties is imposed upon the Director and his officials by s 17. However, s 17(2) and (3) provide for exemptions from this general confidentiality provision for the purpose of the performance by the Director of his investigative and enforcement functions.

Section 18 empowers any Garda, who considers he has information which may relate to the commission of an offence under the Companies Acts, to disclose it to the Director or one his officers.

Finally, the Freedom of Information Act 1997 is amended by s 112 of the 2001 Act so as to exempt from its provisions any records held or created[1] by the Director and his staff.

SCOPE OF THE DIRECTOR'S POWERS

55.14 The 2001 Act provides powers, not only in Part 2 which deals specifically with the DCE, but in other parts as well. The range of powers given to the Director under the Act can be classified into five main areas:

(1) investigative;
(2) powers to prosecute;
(3) injunctive;
(4) preventative; and
(5) supervisory.

Investigative powers

55.15 The Director has the general function of investigating[2] suspected offences under the Companies Acts. Part 3[3] of the Act transfers many of the Minister's former powers in this regard under Part II of the 1990 Act. As a

---

1 Under the Companies Acts.
2 In doing so, he enjoys the general investigative powers of a Garda Síochána.
3 Sections 19–39.

result, the Director may now, for example, seek to have the High Court investigate companies pursuant to s 8 of the Companies Act 1990 or enquire directly himself into company ownership under s 14 of that Act. The Director may also, exercise the power to examine books and documents of companies under s 19 of the 1990 Act: a power formerly used by the Minister to direct the examination of books, and documents in a number of high profile cases.

Section 30 of the Act gives the Director the right to seek a search warrant from the District Court where he considers that information, books or documents relating to offences under the Companies Acts may be held on any premises.

Section 33 provides for the exercise by the Director of any of his powers on behalf of company law enforcement agencies from other jurisdictions. In view of the international nature of modern business, this allows the Director to facilitate the enquires of such agencies where those enquiries require to be pursued in Ireland. In addition, it gives the Director a firm basis for seeking reciprocal assistance with his own enquiries from agencies outside the State.

Many of the changes in law brought about by Part 3 of the 2001 Act have been noted in the appropriate chapters.[1]

Powers to prosecute

55.16   The Director has the power to prosecute[2] offences under the Companies Acts by summary proceedings and, where appropriate, to refer cases for prosecution on indictment to the Director of Public Prosecutions.

Power to obtain injunctions

55.17   The Director has the power under s 96 (amending s 371 of the 1963 Act) to apply to the High Court for injunctions restraining companies or their officers from continuing to breach the Companies Acts. Section 99 also redefines the term 'officer in default'. These provisions allow the Director to take immediate action to prevent ongoing breaches of company law and, by so doing, to protect the interests of creditors and others whose rights may be affected.

Preventative powers

55.18   The Director has the power to apply to the High Court for orders to restrict or disqualify company directors and other officers where the conduct of those concerned in the management of the company's affairs warrants such action. This power is intended to prevent, or restrict the ability of, unscrupulous persons from continuing to use the vehicle of limited liability

---

1 In particular, chapters 15, 19, 22, 23, 27 and 35.
2 See **55.10** and **55.11**.

companies for reckless or illegal purposes to the detriment of their creditors and others.

Part 4[1] of the Act relates to the power of the court to order the restriction or disqualification of persons from acting as company directors or other officers or being involved in any way in the promotion, formation or management of companies.

The powers to restrict and disqualify persons are deemed central to maintaining the integrity of the system of company regulation.

The power granted to the Director[2] to examine a person's solvency status is mentioned in **30.26**. Sections 41 and 42[3] empower the Director to seek to have such persons restricted and disqualified by the High Court. In addition, the restrictions imposed by s 150 of the Companies Act 1990 and the grounds for disqualification under s 160 of that Act are both extended by these sections.

Part 5[4] of the Act contains provisions relating to the winding-up of companies and, in particular, those companies that are wound up insolvent.

The provisions of this Part are aimed at addressing the so-called Phoenix Syndrome, whereby companies go out of business leaving debts unpaid and their members or directors immediately start up new companies without having to account for their previous failures and debts. They also provide for action against companies and their officers where the resources of the company have been so depleted that there are insufficient assets for the company to be wound up.

The Director is given a range of powers in this Part of the Act to intervene in company liquidations; or, where the company is not liquidated because of the insufficiency of its assets, to ensure that persons responsible through recklessness or otherwise for company failures are brought before the courts to account for their actions. The Director may seek to have such persons made liable for the debts of their companies or ordered to return assets wrongly transferred from those companies.

Supervisory powers

55.19 Sections 53, 57 and 58 give the Director powers to perform the function assigned to him under s 12[5] of exercising a supervisory role over liquidators and receivers. These persons play a key role in ensuring that the provisions of the Companies Acts are properly applied in company liquidations and receiverships and the Director is responsible for ensuring that they meet their statutory obligations in this regard.

---

1 Comprising ss 40–42.
2 Under s 40, which added a new s 183A to the 1963 Act.
3 See **30.4**, **30.20** and **30.21**.
4 Comprising ss 43–58. The changes in law introduced by these sections are noted in Chapters 29, 30, 42, 49, 50, 51 and 52.
5 Of the 2001 Act.

Section 56 provides for reporting by liquidators to the DCE on the conduct of directors of insolvent companies in relation to the management of those companies. This will be a vital source of information and will provide the basis for decisions by the Director as to whether the High Court should be asked to apply restriction orders to such directors under s 150 of the Companies Act 1990.

THE REGISTRAR'S ENFORCEMENT ROLE

55.20   The Working Group had also recommended that the registrar retain an enforcement role in respect of registration-type offences.

Part 6[1] introduces new measures to improve compliance with filing obligations. For example, s 60 provides for the introduction of the concept of an annual return date which will be used to calculate the exact date in each year on which a company is due to file its annual return. This should greatly facilitate the enforcement by the registrar of the annual return filing requirement.

Part 6 also confers increased sanctions on the registrar. For example, s 66 provides for the imposition of on-the-spot fines[2] by the registrar in respect of failure to file returns within the time allowed. This forms part of a suite of measures available to the registrar, including late filing penalties, on-the-spot fines and prosecutions, to assist him in his attempts to improve filing rate compliance.

---

1 Comprising ss 59–66; their effects being noted in Chapters 33 and 53.
2 See **53.10**.

INDEX

References are to paragraph numbers.